Language and Literacy Disorders

Infancy through Adolescence

Nickola Wolf Nelson

Western Michigan University

Allyn & Bacon

Boston   New York   San Francisco
Mexico City   Montreal   Toronto   London   Madrid   Munich   Paris
Hong Kong   Singapore   Tokyo   Cape Town   Sydney

Executive Editor and Publisher: Stephen D. Dragin
Series Editorial Assistant: Anne Whittaker
Marketing Manager: Amanda Stedke
Production Editor: Joe Sweeney
Editorial Production Service: Omegatype Typography, Inc.
Composition Buyer: Linda Cox
Manufacturing Manager: Megan Cochran
Electronic Composition: Omegatype Typography, Inc.
Interior Design: Omegatype Typography, Inc.
Cover Designer: Linda Knowles

For related titles and support materials, visit our online catalog at www.pearsonhighered.com.

Between the time website information is gathered and then published, it is not unusual for some sites to have closed. Also, the transcription of URLs can result in typographical errors. The publisher would appreciate notification where these errors occur so that they may be corrected in subsequent editions.

Library of Congress Cataloging-in-Publication Data

Nelson, Nickola.
    Language and literacy disorders / Nickola Wolf Nelson.
            p.   cm.
    Includes bibliographical references and index.
    ISBN-13: 978-0-205-50178-6 (pbk.)
    ISBN-10: 0-205-50178-8 (pbk.)
    1. Language disorders in children.   2. Language disorders in adolescence.   I. Title.
    RJ496.L35N46   2010
    618.92'855—dc22   2008050910

Printed in the United States of America

10 9 8 7 6 5 4 3 2 1   HAM   13 12 11 10 09

Credits appear on page 582, which constitutes an extension of the copyright page.

Allyn & Bacon
is an imprint of

www.pearsonhighered.com

ISBN-10: 0-205-50178-8
ISBN-13: 978-0-205-50178-6

To my family across generations
And our shared stories of language, literacy, and education
And to all families who have provided the motivation and hope for this book

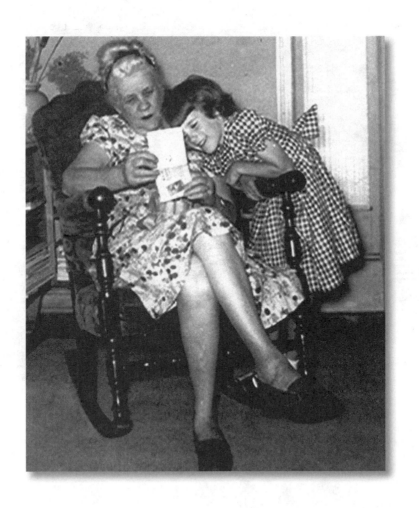

Brief Contents

Contents

CHAPTER 3

Language/Literacy and Related Systems   55

Part II   Policies, Practices, and Populations   85

CHAPTER 4

Policies and Practices   87

CHAPTER *5*

Primary Disorders of Speech, Language, and Literacy   122

CHAPTER *6*

Motor and Sensory Impairments   151

CHAPTER *7*

Cognitive–Communicative Impairments   177

Part III Assessment and Intervention   213

CHAPTER *8*

Infant and Toddler Policies and Practices   215

CHAPTER *9*

Infant and Toddler Intervention   239

CHAPTER *10*

Preschool Policies and Practices   268

CHAPTER *14*

Interventions for Special Populations   442

Preface

Language and Literacy Disorders is for children and adolescents affected by language and literacy disorders and the people who care about them—parents, teachers, clinicians, and researchers. It offers a contextualized framework and many practical recommendations for working with infants, toddlers, children, and adolescents (referred to collectively as *children*) who face challenges in acquiring language and literacy skills and related social communication and self-regulation abilities.

Central Focus and Audience

This book places a primary emphasis on the importance of *context* in understanding and treating language/literacy disorders. This means that parents, teachers, and peers appear as dominant players in every chapter. A related theme is that language development is nurtured best in contexts in which communicative partners seek to understand a child's intentions and meanings. Consistent with this theme, many of the recommended assessment and intervention activities focus on identifying where a particular child is currently functioning on a developmental continuum, so that authentic communicative interactions can be engineered and intervention scaffolding can be implemented to help the child reach the next level of development or complexity.

Within this framework, children with special needs are viewed as active participants in constructing more elaborate cognitive–linguistic systems and strategies. They also are viewed as individuals, made up of complex internal psycho–neural–biological systems and interacting with external familial, cultural–linguistic, and educational systems. Categorical diagnoses are introduced, and conditions such as hearing loss, dyslexia, and autism spectrum disorders play a prominent role in some discussions. More often, however, categorical diagnoses serve as background information, so that greater emphasis is placed on constructing individual profiles of children's developmental strengths and needs than on whether they meet the criteria for a particular label at a particular time.

By presenting techniques for assessing the language demands of key contexts and working toward them, the book also aims to avoid historical fallacies of special education and speech–language treatment programs that encouraged small steps for students with special needs while same-age peers were taking giant strides in development and education. The goal is for all students to participate in the natural contexts of home and schooling that will prepare them for employment and independent adult lives. Unless context is kept in focus, it is too easy to become myopic when setting therapeutic goals and selecting methods and materials for intervention. This book is about helping all children and adolescents develop the communication skills (spoken, written, and nonverbal) needed to participate actively and effectively in social and academic settings.

This book has dual purposes—to serve as a textbook for upper-level undergraduate and graduate students in speech–language pathology and special education and to serve as a resource for parents and practitioners in the many disciplines who work with children with language/literacy and communication disorders (hopefully, in collaboration with one another). My intention is for the book not only to help professionals in training and practice organize and construct new knowledge about language/literacy development and disorders, but also to facilitate new ways of thinking and problem solving that will help them implement effective interventions for children struggling with language/literacy, communication, and self-regulation.

To address these purposes, organization and clarity of content take precedence over completeness of literature review. Although the book is written in a scholarly tone and with an eye toward evidence-based practice, sources are cited sparingly to increase readability. Where available, the highest-quality research sources are reviewed for addressing particular needs. I have selected intervention studies not to be comprehensive but to provide examples of intervention approaches that are supported by some evidence. The evidence base for most aspects of language intervention is as yet insufficient for offering strong recommendations and thus should be viewed with caution. I have also tried to illuminate the theoretical underpinnings that drive clinicians and researchers to choose one approach over another. Action research is encouraged for monitoring and documenting whether programs are effective and progress is occurring for particular children. Literature searches and critical evaluations of newly published research are essential tools for students and practitioners to stay current about the most effective approaches as evidence continues to mount.

This book builds on a previous book, *Childhood Language Disorders in Context: Infancy through Adolescence* (Nelson, 1993, 1998). This is a new book, rather than a third edition. It includes all new content (with few exceptions), and it has a much stronger influence of encouraging literacy development along with spoken language and, in some cases, even as a scaffold for spoken language. By focusing on literacy development and disorders more directly and extensively, this book is designed to fill the need for a combined emphasis on speech–language–communication and literacy developmental needs for children from birth through adolescence.

To address the dual purposes of the book, a companion website (www.pearsonhigher ed.com/nelson) provides additional practice materials for students to review their growing understanding. The site also includes clinical observation tools that can be downloaded by instructors and practitioners to guide clinical practicum and praxis. Both within the print chapters and in the online resources, activities are suggested for enhancing the active learning experience and using this book to promote preprofessional and professional growth.

Part I: Frameworks for Clinical Practice

The first part of the book introduces frameworks for clinical practice. Chapter 1 discusses the importance of asking good questions, and Chapter 2 reviews the systems of spoken and written language and their relationships to one another and the other elements of typical development. Chapter 3 summarizes chief theoretical accounts of how language and literacy develop. It also describes the systems that support language development, including neuropsychological and genetic factors that have been investigated in recent years using new technologies to illuminate the nature of language and reading disorders.

Part II: Policies, Practices, and Populations

Part II comprises four chapters. Chapter 4 provides an overview of key policies that influence service delivery to children and adolescents with communication and language/literacy disorders. Chapters 5, 6, and 7 describe three segments of the population of children who may have difficulty with language and literacy development. Chapter 5 describes children with primary disorders of speech, language, and literacy development. Chapter 6 describes special challenges associated with primary motor and sensory system disorders. Chapter 7 describes diagnostic traits that are associated with cognitive–communicative disorders, including developmental disability, intellectual disability, autism spectrum disorders, acquired brain injury (including traumatic brain injury), child abuse and neglect, and interactive disorders of attention, emotion, and behavior.

The chapters in Part II are intended to provide information about distinctions in system involvement and how they influence individualized adjustments in assessment and intervention practices. Although one developmental blueprint can provide a template for all, even allowing for individual variation, one-size intervention does not fit all. Thus, information about differential diagnosis and treatment is introduced here and explored in greater depth in Part III.

Part III: Assessment and Intervention

The first six chapters of Part III minimize the distinctions across causally related conditions. In contrast, they promote the usefulness of normal development as a template for selecting intervention targets when language, reading, and writing skills are lagging behind. They also emphasize a needs-oriented framework by targeting communicative abilities that are *needed* for a child to function well and to participate successfully in age-appropriate contexts. Such an approach emphasizes similarities over differences and ability over impairment.

Chapters 8 and 9 describe policies and assessment and intervention practices for children in their infant–toddler years. Chapters 10 and 11 address the same topics for children in their preschool years. Chapters 12 and 13 do the same for children and adolescents throughout their school-age years and into young adulthood. This is a different breakdown in age categories than in the book's predecessors, and it aligns more with transitions governed by policy for preschool and school-age children. Chapter 14 addresses intervention for students in special populations, including children who are deaf or hard of hearing or who have visual impairments, children with intellectual disabilities or cognitive–communicative disorders, and children with autism spectrum disorders.

Acknowledgments

It is always difficult to adequately thank the many people who make a book like this possible. Steve Dragin's editorial influence can be seen in the concept for the book and its coverage. He did his best to contain my tendency to want to reference every key source on each subtopic, representing the voice and needs of students for clear material that can help them grasp the essential elements of complex topics. I have also benefited from the input of a number of expert consultants in areas with which I was less familiar, particularly Ann Tyler for phonology, Teresa Crumpton for audiology, and David Beukelman and Janet Sturm for children with complex communication needs. Robert Wall Emerson also introduced me to some of the latest concepts in literacy development by children with visual impairments, and Patricia Prelock expanded my knowledge of autism spectrum disorders.

My doctoral students in the Interdisciplinary Health Sciences Ph.D. program have stimulated the interdisciplinary flavor of this book as well as assisted with mundane tasks and provided cogent feedback. In particular, Michele Anderson, Dawn Anderson, Patricia

Tattersall, Heather Koole, and Kathleen Kroll have played major roles in making this book and related online tools possible. My graduate assistant in speech–language pathology, Andrea Quast, also was amazing in her attention to detail and ability to make well-reasoned suggestions to her professor about things to consider. Other graduate students read the book, provided feedback, developed minilessons, and supported the writing effort. I cannot name all of them, but they will recognize their influence on the stories in these pages.

I am fortunate to be in a wonderful setting, where my university and community colleagues include Ann Tyler, Jan Bedrosian, Teresa Crumpton, Yvette Hyter, Adelia Van Meter, and Candis Warner. When collaborations are successful, it is not always possible to differentiate whose ideas are whose, and their ideas have been a particular influence on me. I have also benefited from many conversations with professional colleagues around the country (too numerous to name but cited within), who have influenced the content of this book. Many of the good ideas in this book came directly from them.

Some of the work described in this book was supported by grants from the U.S. Department of Education, Office of Special Education Programs (grant nos. HO29B10245, H180G20005, HO29B40183, H324R980120, and H325H010023) and from the National Institute on Deafness and Communication Disorders (grant no. R15 DC01941-01). However, none of the opinions or positions in the book are meant to represent the official opinions of these agencies. I also benefited during the writing of this book from a named professorship, the Charles Van Riper Professorship, awarded to me by the president of Western Michigan University after nomination by my dean, Janet Pisaneschi, and chair, John M. (Mick) Hanley. I am very grateful for these tangible forms of support that made this scholarly work possible.

I would like to thank the reviewers for this edition: Kathleen R. Fahey, University of Northern Colorado; Carol M. McGregor, Brenau University; and Joyce L. Simpson, East Stroudsburg University.

Finally, I want to acknowledge my family, including my grandmothers, Pauline Keimig Wolf and Marjorie Waggoner Anderson, who had a major influence on my development as a person and an author. My parents, Lawrence and Betty Wolf, encouraged my sisters and me in all that we tried to do—particularly, a love of reading, writing, and creating. My sister Chris Wolf Edmonds, who I always viewed as my role model, played a central role in this book. She is its illustrator. The many original drawings and photocompositions are the result of her creative talent. It was wonderful working with her. My younger sister, Teresa Wolf Baumgartner, the English teacher, taught me in prior editing experiences to be sensitive to unneeded words and to stay alert to other opportunities to tighten up the message. My immediate family, including my three children (David, Nicky, and Clayton), their spouses and significant others, my seven grandchildren (Jessica, Justin, Jess Jr., Jonathon, Clayton, Jamie, and Julie), and many nieces and nephews also have influenced the stories in this book and appear in its illustrations. It is my husband, Larry, who deserves my deepest thanks for putting up with the messes, enduring my divided attention, and making all the wonderful meals. The book is dedicated to all of you.

PART one

Frameworks for Clinical Practice

Frameworks for Guiding Practice

Speech, Language/Literacy, and Communication

Language/Literacy and Related Systems

CHAPTER one

Frameworks for Guiding Practice

LEARNING *objectives*

After studying this chapter, you should be able to do the following:

1. Discuss the importance of questions to scientists, clinicians, and language learners.

2. Formulate evidence-based practice (EBP) questions using the PICO framework.

3. Apply the four questions of context-based language assessment and intervention.

4. Differentiate among models describing communication processes, needs, and opportunities.

Importance of Asking Good Questions

A goal of this chapter is to stimulate readers to ask insightful questions about infants and toddlers, children, and adolescents who are having difficulty learning language—both spoken and written. A questioning attitude supports information seeking and decision making. Questions focus the search for meaning and connections among ideas and concepts.

Questions and Evidence-Based Practice

A commonly cited definition of *evidence-based practice (EBP)** is "the integration of best research evidence with clinical expertise and patient values" (Sackett, Straus, Richardson, Rosenberg, & Haynes, 2000, p. 1). This triad of components is represented in the policy of the American Speech-Language-Hearing Association (ASHA, 2005b) and illustrated in Figure 1.1.

Good questions are at the root of EBP (ASHA, 2005b; Sackett et al., 2000). This is true both for clinicians and researchers. Worthwhile clinical questions emerge in everyday contexts that are relevant to the values and needs of people in diverse cultural–linguistic communities. Scientists also must formulate questions that are both possible to answer and worth answering.

ASC-AE Five-Step Approach to EBP

Evidence-based practice involves a five-step process represented by the acronym *ASC-AE* (Ask, Search, Critique—Apply, Evaluate):

1. Ask a question that is relevant to meeting a particular client's or group's needs.
2. Search for available evidence.
3. Critique the quality of the evidence.
4. Apply the evidence to one's own practice.
5. Evaluate effectiveness in terms of outcomes for a particular client or group.

Five-step frameworks like this one emphasize that EBP is a dynamic process practiced by individual clinicians addressing particular purposes. EBP should not be perceived as implementing only treatment approaches that have received the "EBP blessing" of some higher body. That ignores the other two elements of the EBP triad—clinical expertise and client and family values.

Ask a PICO Question

The first step of EBP is to ask a good question. A widely used framework for guiding the development of EBP questions uses the acronym *PICO.*

figure *1.1*

Triad of Components That Constitute Evidence-Based Practice

*In this book, bold italic type signals a word that appears in the online glossary at www.pearsonhighered.com/nelson.

The PICO framework has four components that can be tailored to be contextualized and person centered:

- *Person, Population, Problem, and Perspective:* This *P* component is referred to in medical circles as *patient/population.* In person-centered treatment approaches, it has four parts:
  - What do I know about my client as a whole **person** with a unique set of cultural–linguistic–familial experiences and perspectives?
  - What do I know about the **population** of children and adolescents who have the same or a similar diagnosis as this child?
  - What language and literacy **problems** are of greatest current concern to my client and those who know him or her best?
  - What can I learn through the **perspectives** of client, family, and teachers about cultural and curricular contexts and values?
- *Intervention:* What **intervention** procedures are most likely to achieve desired outcomes for this particular client?
- *Comparison or Contrast:* What alternative assessment, prevention, or intervention approaches should I **compare** or **contrast** with the one I am leaning toward as best?
- *Outcomes:* What functional **outcomes** can be defined that are observable and measurable and can provide evidence for how the intervention works?

A well-formulated question will incorporate all four of these components. For example, a PICO question for seeking evidence about intervention for a child who is showing a specific delay in spoken expression might be as follows:

> For a toddler who is producing fewer than five words at 22 months (i.e., a "late talker") [*P*], how effective is it to enroll the child in a direct service intervention program targeting expressive language development [*I*] compared with taking a "watch and wait" approach [*C*], as indicated by outcomes in terms of word production and numbers of words per utterance [*O*]?

Search for Evidence

After formulating a good question, the next step is to search for the best evidence available in the scientific literature. A textbook is not the best resource for finding the latest evidence regarding a particular foreground clinical question, but it can serve as a source for background questions about the nature of disorders (Sackett et al., 2000; Strauss, Richardson, Glasziou, & Haynes, 2005). Searches for empirical evidence involve the use of appropriate search engines and online resources, such as the Cochrane Collaboration (www.cochrane .org/reviews), or the What Works Clearinghouse (www.whatworks.ed.gov). Professional associations, such as the American Speech-Language-Hearing Association, also provide search tools for seeking the highest quality evidence to answer PICO questions.

Critique the Evidence

When sources are found that may help to address the PICO question, clinicians must then appraise the quality of the research. The step of critical appraisal demands some sophistication about research designs and scientific evidence. Schwartz and Wilson (2006) suggested that clinicians should consider the characteristics of participants, nature of treatments, type of study design (e.g., randomized control trial or single-subject study design), and results, including effect sizes. **Effect size** is an estimate of how much pre–post change can be attributed to the treatment. For example, the pre–post treatment change in a study may be significantly larger for the experimental group (who received the experimental treatment) than the control group (who received the comparison treatment), but the effect may still be too small to be clinically significant. One commonly used approach for measuring effect sizes, called *Cohen's d,* is reported in standard deviation units (Cohen, 1988). A general rule of thumb is to define a small effect as 0.2, a medium effect as 0.5, and a large effect as 0.8 and above.

Figure 1.2 illustrates an *evidence pyramid,* which places types of research study designs in a hierarchy of quality from lower (at the bottom) to higher (at the top) (ASHA, 2005b). Like many hierarchies, this pyramid places **randomized controlled trials (RCTs)** close to the top. Only a **meta-analysis,** which is a statistical reanalysis and comparison of results from several high-quality RCTs, is placed higher. A primary reason for valuing the RCT is that random assignment of participants to treatments reduces bias. Including a control group and giving equal time and attention to control participants also makes it possible to rule out Hawthorne or placebo effects, in which experimental group members get better by virtue of attention or expectation alone.

Large RCTs are costly, however, and it is not always possible to randomize participants to treatment and control groups. In addition, **treatment fidelity** can be a challenge when multiple sites and clinicians are involved. Individual differences and natural learning contexts are particularly difficult to control, so if a treatment approach is based on a principle of a high degree of individualization and natural responsiveness, it may not lend itself to an RCT. For all these reasons, the current state of research evidence for interventions for children with language and communication disorders remains quite limited, and caution

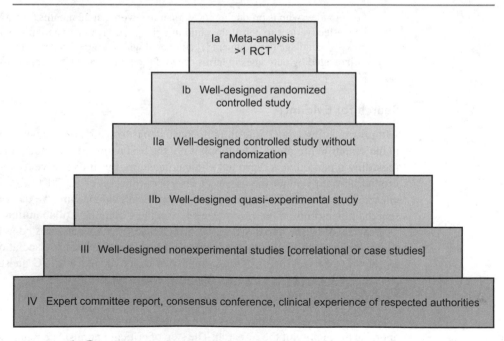

figure *1.2*

Evidence Pyramid Showing Typical Quality Rankings

Source: Adapted from outlines of quality ranking in online tutorials from the American Speech-Language-Hearing Association and Scottish Intercollegiate Guidelines Network.

should be exercised in basing treatment choices only on the available literature. Regardless of study type, if cultural–linguistic diversity is not evident in the samples used in investigations, then the ability to generalize results to broader populations is limited.

One meta-analysis of language intervention results was conducted by Law, Garrett, and Nye (2004). The analysis was based on a systematic review of research articles that met selection criteria as RCTs of speech–language interventions for children with primary speech–language delay or disorder. The search revealed 36 articles reporting 33 different trials, but only 25 studies met the selection criteria, and only 13 were suitable for a meta-analysis to compare results across studies. Law and colleagues concluded that intervention was effective for children with expressive phonological and expressive vocabulary difficulties, but evidence for intervention effectiveness for expressive syntax was mixed, and no evidence was found to support intervention effectiveness for receptive language difficulties. The meta-analysis also showed differential effects for children with mixed receptive and expressive language problems, who tended to benefit less from interventions than those with expressive problems only. Law and colleagues noted that children with receptive difficulties tend to be excluded from intervention studies, possibly obscuring relationships.

Given the current state of research, the choice of best methods may rely more on clinical expertise and patient values than on solid scientific evidence. As the evidence pyramid shows, other sources may guide practice, including case reports and quasi-experimental studies, which lack randomization but offer some degree of control. Because the state of knowledge is limited, clinicians are left with many questions and often rely on other sources, including textbooks such as this one.

Apply the Evidence

The fourth step of EBP is to apply the selected approach. The choice should be based on the evaluation of published evidence but also consistent with client and family values and the clinician's expertise. In communication intervention, it is rare to find a prepackaged approach that can be implemented as a series of steps without variation. Individualization requires clinicians to address each child's specific needs using input from those most involved (e.g., parent, teacher, and child).

Evaluate Outcomes

The fifth step of EBP is to evaluate the effectiveness of a particular intervention when it is applied with a given client. Clinicians might use several approaches to evaluate their interventions. At a minimum, they should gather baseline data and take periodic probes to monitor change. When two competing approaches are equally appropriate, it may be possible to compare them directly. The following is an example of a PICO question that could be used to set up such a comparison:

> For students with autism in grades four through six [P], what is the effect on the number of communication initiations with typically developing peers during five-minute probes as students arrive in the classroom [O] when peer volunteers are present who have been participating in a lunchtime social group (with the clinician present to scaffold interaction) [I], compared with probes taken at times when the specially trained peers are not present [C]?

Outcome measurements imply comparison to *baseline* probes taken prior to initiating the intervention. *Probes* are quick assessment samples taken to measure communication behaviors in specified but relatively naturalistic contexts. Probe conditions might be relatively more or less structured, but they should provide evidence of the degree to which the child or adolescent can demonstrate the targeted ability with minimal assistance or scaffolding. For example, baseline probes for a toddler might be taken in three different five-minute play samples, documenting the number of different words and multiword utterances used by the toddler. A narrative probe might involve a request to retell a story to a puppet using the pictures of a wordless picture book. Outcomes could include narrative components and language productivity. Written language probes for school-age students might be gathered in a whole-class session planned in collaboration with a teacher.

Outcome probes measure contextualized evidence that a client can demonstrate targeted knowledge, skills, or strategies in relevant everyday contexts. Continuing with the example for evaluating intervention for a child with autism, turn initiations could be measured in the lunch period social group. Generalization probes also could be gathered during arrival in the classroom. If no increases are noted in the number of times a child with autism says or gestures something to a peer, the clinician could step in and enlist the help of volunteer peers to encourage turn taking. Then the outcomes of the added intervention could be measured in terms of independent initiations on other days. If desired outcomes are documented, other schools might be encouraged to initiate social group lunch peer volunteer programs.

Outcomes for individual clients can be measured with techniques from single-subject research designs, starting with ***baseline measurements.*** Baseline probes are taken with minimal or no scaffolding over several sessions. In ongoing clinical programs, baseline data might consist of outcome data gathered in probes taken at the end of a previous intervention period. Clinical baselines often involve fewer data points than researchers would consider optimal, but they are not expendable. They provide a starting point for measuring progress.

In single-subject research designs, two methods—alternating treatment designs and multiple baseline designs—are commonly used to control for growth due to factors other than the intervention (e.g., development alone or mere attention). *Alternating treatment designs* compare a selected intervention [I] with a comparison [C] in terms of outcomes [O]. The design starts with documentation of a relatively stable baseline for the targeted communication ability prior to intervention. Then one condition is alternated with the other, creating what is sometimes called an *ABAB design*. The *B* condition may be no treatment (e.g., withdrawal of contingent reinforcement in a behaviorist intervention paradigm), and the expectation is that the new behavior will return to baseline levels if it is not being treated and reinforced. If the treatment is effective, the behavior should return to the higher level when the *A* treatment is reintroduced, confirming that it is the treatment that is responsible for the new behavior.

Multiple baseline designs start with the investigator/clinician gathering baseline data for several sessions on two (or more) similar but distinct communication targets, confirming that both skills are equally low prior to intervention. Then intervention begins, focused on one target but not the other. If the intervention can be credited with changing behavior, each skill should begin to show improvement only when it is targeted directly in intervention. If an untreated skill remains at baseline levels while the treated skill changes, the investigator can have confidence that the intervention is responsible for the change and not just general development.

Contributing to the Evidence Base

If EBP is to advance, practitioners must collaborate with researchers to generate questions and seek answers; similarly, researchers must relate their questions to clinical concerns and collaborate with clinicians to gather evidence (Apel, 2001). Best practice begins with insightful questions about the knowledge, skills, and strategies that children and adolescents with language and literacy disorders need to function effectively in the important contexts of their lives.

Questions, Attention, and Collaboration

Questions can focus attention on key elements of a problem. Smith (1975) defined **attention** as "questions being asked by the brain" and noted that "perceptions are what the brain decides must be the answers" (p. 28). This definition suggests that perceptions of phenomena, whether at the sensory level or conceptual level, are guided by implicit or explicit questions about meaning.

"Forests" and "Trees"

Clinical questions focus clinicians on macro- and microlevels, wholes and parts. Oversimplification can cause clinicians to **miss the forest for the trees.** This metaphor represents losing the big picture of a child's contextualized needs by focusing on small irrelevant details. The opposite is when clinicians or administrators lose sight of children's individualized needs and thus **miss the trees for the forest.**

Case Example 1.1 describes a case when a clinician's tight focus on details made him lose sight of the bigger picture. Damico (1988) described clinical choices that did *not* work for a student he called Debbie, as he discovered years later. Based on then-current best practice, Damico used drill-like activities to teach language rules as discrete entities (separate knowledge units that could be learned one at a time), which were largely decontextualized from the language expectations of the classroom. Debbie made progress applying syntactic rules in controlled contexts and was dismissed from therapy. As Damico later discovered, however, this decontextualized, discrete skills approach overlooked Debbie's language–literacy and social–communication needs. By the time Damico encountered Debbie in middle school several years later, he found those other problems had grown and were now overwhelming.

CASE example *1.1*

Learning from Mistakes Made with Debbie

Debbie was first seen by Damico (1988) during her first-grade year. She was a sociable child who made frequent eye contact and was curious and engaged in assessment tasks. Her scores on standardized tests were below age level, and her language sample showed a high grammatical error rate of more than 40 percent. Further analysis of the language sample showed 34 instances of semantic confusion, in which Debbie used generic terms (*stuff* or *thing*) or misused deictic terms of space (*here/there*), time (*tomorrow/today*), or person (*I/you*). For the remainder of her first-grade year, Debbie received language intervention targeting grammatical forms (but not semantic confusion). Her grammatical errors dropped, although her mean length of utterance (MLU) remained at 5.0 morphemes. She was dismissed from therapy, and the next year, she transferred to a different school.

Damico did not see Debbie again until seven years later, when he was asked to evaluate a seventh-grade girl with a severe communication problem. At first, he did not recognize her. Now Debbie was reading four grades below grade level. She claimed to have only three friends and was described as shy, quiet, and with poor social skills. Although Debbie could produce fairly long (MLU = 8.4 morphemes) and complex sentences with few grammatical errors, she had difficulties with pragmatics in discourse interactions for judging the amount of information, answering questions, maintaining topics, and conversing fluently. She had severe language difficulties and academic and social problems as well.

Source: Based on Damico, 1988.

Damico (1988) attributed this failure to fragmentation exacerbated by policies and procedures that did not ask what Debbie needed most but were biased by therapeutic fashions of the day. Damico also identified as problematic limited communication with Debbie's teachers and lack of follow-up regarding literacy development and social interaction. He observed that asking different assessment and intervention questions would have directed his attention to more relevant concerns, such as whether Debbie's language skill deficits would put her at risk for difficulty learning to read and write or for social dysfunction.

Lack of attention to spoken–written language connections was not uncommon in interventions in the early 1980s. It was not until the 1990s that connections between spoken and written language drew the attention of language researchers. Even then, scientists were asking questions mostly about phonological awareness (e.g., Blachman, 1994; Torgesen, Wagner, Rashotte, Burgess, & Hecht, 1997), and thus, they often missed connections to broader language skills. Only later did researchers direct attention beyond phonemic awareness to nonphonological sources of language/literacy difficulty (e.g., Catts & Kamhi, 2005b; Scarborough, 2005) and the importance of written expression (Graham & Harris, 2002).

The other side of this problem—missing the trees for the forest—can be found when widespread policies make it difficult to attend to individual children. For example, according to the No Child Left Behind Act of 2001 (NCLB; PL 107-110), the test scores of students in a given school must meet adequate yearly progress (AYP) standards or the school will be designated "in need of improvement." Unintended effects on individuals (metaphoric "trees") from widespread policy implementation (metaphoric "forests") can make it difficult to individualize instruction to meet each child's needs.

Questions and Collaboration

Shared questions and mutual goals are essential tools of collaboration. A classical definition of ***collaborative consultation*** is that it is

> an interactive process that enables teams of people with diverse expertise to generate creative solutions to mutually defined problems. The outcome is enhanced, altered, and produces solutions that are different from those that the individual team members would produce independently. (Idol, Paolucci-Witcomb, & Nevin, 1986, p. 1)

This definition specifies key elements of collaborative problem solving using several key terms: *interactive process, diverse expertise,* and *mutually defined problems.* All relate closely to questions that collaborative partners must use to collaborate effectively.

First, the collaborative model involves an ***interactive process,*** not a unidirectional one. In expert models of consultation, a clinician's goal is to get others to follow his or her advice; in interactive collaborative sessions, clinicians enter with more questions than answers. When clinicians experience difficulty in collaborative interactions, they may have approached the situation with more answers than questions. If the only real question is How can I get others to agree with me? then a clinician's ability for listening openly and collaborating authentically is compromised. On the other hand, if a clinician enters collaborative meetings with a questioning attitude, prepared for *interaction* rather than persuasion, then the collaborative process has a better chance of success. Case Example 1.2 illustrates this sort of problem solving.

Second, through collaboration, teams of people with diverse expertise pool their knowledge. Accepting that one need not have all the answers does not mean that expertise plays *no* role in the collaborative process. Rather, ***diverse expertise*** implies that professionals, parents, and students all bring expertise to the collaborative problem-solving process, completing the components of the EBP triad. Professionals who ask about the perspectives of others are open to new insights.

The third and perhaps most critical component of the definition of collaboration relates to the ***mutual definition of problems.*** When collaborative relationships become problematic so that teams are enmeshed in win–lose battles over competitive goals, questions can lead to mutual definitions of problems that can be addressed better through cooperative than competitive goals.

Becoming aware of questions that underlie varied goal-setting models can assist in this process. As Johnson and Johnson (1999) described, the essential elements of three prominent goal-setting models are as follow:

1. ***Competitive goal setting*** implies the question How can I get my way? It involves ***negative interdependence*** in that team members can achieve their goals only if others fail to achieve theirs. This characterized Case Example 1.2 regarding the initial discussions of Mindy's needs.

2. ***Individualistic goal setting*** implies independent questions across professionals, each asking What can I do for this child? It involves ***no interdependence*** in that team members set goals independently of one another and then staple them together to create an *interdisciplinary team report.* Individualistic goal setting often becomes the

┌─CASE **example** *1.2*

Collaborating to Make Decisions for Mindy

Ms. K, a speech–language pathologist (SLP), called for consultation regarding Mindy, a child on her caseload with autism spectrum disorder. Mindy had become the subject of competitive goal-setting discussions between school personnel and Mindy's parents. The special education teacher, in particular, believed that Mindy should be retained in second grade and spend more time in special education. In contrast, Mindy's parents wanted her to be promoted to third grade and spend more time in general education. Ms. K saw the situation as heading toward a due process hearing. She worried that the conflict was affecting her ability to work with Mindy and thought the parents might not fully understand the magnitude of Mindy's language problems and how they would likely affect her ability to learn in third grade.

The consultant observed Mindy in the speech–language therapy room, special education room, and general education classroom and worked with the team to plan an unofficial meeting that would *not* serve as Mindy's individualized education program (IEP) meeting. This would free the planning group to talk about mutual goals for Mindy without committing to any of the competing placement options. The meeting was held in a room with a blank whiteboard to signify that

the team was taking a fresh look at establishing mutually agreeable goals and using a process of cooperative goal setting that would recognize the contributions of all team members.

At the meeting, team members agreed that they all shared a primary goal for Mindy to function as independently as possible, and in general education as much as possible, while still making optimal progress in academic and social development. Where team members differed was in their views on the best placement choices for achieving the twin goals of independence and progress. Therefore, the blank whiteboard was set up as shown in Figure 1.3, with three columns across the top: one for independent functioning similar to that of peers, one for functioning that could be managed with special supports but in the general education classroom, and one for functioning that required the full support of special education or speech–language services. The rows were then used to outline the activities of the general education curriculum, with the input of Mindy's current second-grade teacher.

As Figure 1.3 illustrates, the team decided that Mindy was able to handle the reading and writing demands of the second-grade classroom with only minimal special supports. In particular, she could decode written texts at least as accurately

(continued)

as her peers, and she could function similarly to her peers in writing stories. Her problems lay in comprehension when reading (especially drawing inferences beyond literal meanings) and in describing characters' goals and feelings when writing, but these abilities were similar to those of her second-grade peers.

Social transitions associated with routines, such as arriving in the classroom in the morning and returning after lunch, were difficult, but Mindy was handling them with only moderate support. On the playground, she showed interest in playing with other children, but she had difficulty grasping the rules associated with games such as tag. Although she understood that the game involved running and trying to tag others, observation suggested that she did not understand the rule about one child being "it" but only until tagging another child.

The team agreed that math was the most difficult curricular area for Mindy—and one for which she required a completely different and special curriculum. The school's general education curriculum in math used language-laden, highly abstract instructional methods, which made it particularly difficult for Mindy to learn. Everyone

(parents, both general and special education teachers, administrators, and the SLP) agreed that Mindy's special education teacher was best suited for helping her acquire mathematical concepts using a special curriculum, but the teacher agreed to target vocabulary and concepts that would prepare Mindy to transition to the general education mathematics curriculum.

The meeting ended congenially, with Mindy's parents commenting that they felt as if they had been true members of the planning process for the first time. Later, when the true IEP meeting was held, Mindy's parents maintained their insistence that she be promoted to third grade; the special education teacher continued to work with Mindy; and after several more years of specialized instruction, Mindy was able to make progress in the general education math curriculum. She continued to participate in general education classroom activities with her grade-level peers.

Note: Case studies in this book from the author's experience are all based on actual events, although real names and certain details have been altered to protect the identities of participants.

default problem-solving model due to constraints of time and place. To some extent, this mode of problem solving was illustrated in how the team first tried to address Mindy's needs in Case Example 1.2.

3. *Cooperative goal setting* implies mutually defined questions, such as What are our mutual goals for this child? It involves ***positive interdependence*** in that members perceive they can only achieve their goals if others also achieve theirs. This is the ideal toward which teams aspire if they wish to function in fully collaborative modes. As shown in Figure 1.3, this type of problem solving was achieved for Mindy when the group began to collaborate in identifying curricular areas where she could function independently or needed greater support.

SUMMARY

This section has introduced a framework for using questions to guide thinking and learning about clinical problems. A questioning attitude can focus attention and facilitate learning and remembering. Questions can keep both the "forests" and the "trees" (wholes and parts) in focus. The three components of EBP also were introduced, along with a process guided by the ASC-AE acronym and the PICO system for questions about a particular clinical problem.

The section ended with questions to enhance the process of collaboration, starting with questions about mutual goals. Three modes of problem solving—competitive, inde-

figure *1.3*

Information Constructed in a Collaborative Discussion of Mindy's Special Education Needs

Activity	Level of Independence		
	Independent	Partially Supported (classroom-based services)	Special Education / Speech–Language Services
Arrival in classroom	Mindy handles arrival with minimal support as long as routine is not disrupted.		

Reading
  Language arts
  Social studies
	Her decoding is completely independent.	Mindy's reading comprehension requires partial support, but she can manage texts at grade level.	This is a goal of language intervention services.

Writing	Mindy can write stories that are at a similar level in length and word and sentence skills as that of peers.	She needs support to write about characters' goals and feelings.	This is a goal of language intervention services.
Mathematics		She cannot handle the general ed math curriculum, even with extra support.	Mindy needs full support for learning mathematical concepts in special education.
Social skills			Social skills are a goal of language intervention that are targeted jointly by the SLP and special ed teacher.

pendent, and collaborative—were distinguished. Collaborative models were contrasted with expert ones, and a recommendation was made to enter collaborative interactions with more questions than answers.

Contextualized Assessment and Intervention

Ethnographic Approaches

Ethnography is used by anthropologists and educators to understand a cultural milieu through the eyes of its participants. In clinical practice, insights are gained into the problem (i.e., the first element of the PICO framework) by listening carefully to people who live with it every day. This leads to a ***thick description,*** which is rich in terms of its depth of detail.

The best way learn about a family's personal and cultural values is to ask good questions, observe, and listen. Four tools of ethnographic anthropology have been borrowed by clinicians (Stone-Goldman & Olswang, 2003):

- ***Ethnographic interviewing*** involves using strategic questions to gain perspectives of others.
- ***Participant observation*** involves watching and interacting to interpret social–cultural rules for participation and interaction.
- ***Studying artifacts*** involves analysis of products for evidence of strengths and needs.

- *Interpreting multiple sources of data* involves looking for deeper meanings and points of agreement and then asking informants whether interpretations match perceptions, a process ethnographers call *triangulation.*

Understanding Parental and Child Preferences and Values

Parents are the primary information sources for young children. A challenge of parenting is to balance acceptance with expectation. Mastergeorge (2007) interviewed parents of children with developmental disabilities who were working to calibrate their expectations for their children. One mother described this challenge as follows:

> But just being like every other parent, you're trying to encourage them and when you have a child that is developmentally delayed, sometimes you find yourself kind of wanting them to do something and almost encouraging them. Trying over and over to get them to be like normal kids, and get them to try and try and try. And sometimes you just have to realize that that's not where they're at, at that point in time and they're gonna do something else now. From her being slow, I just had to learn patience, and that she had to do things at her own pace and at her own interest [level], and that some things she just wasn't interested in. For a while there, I'd see other little kids her age writing and coloring, and I thought she should be doing this, and I'd constantly push crayons at her. Well, she wasn't into that. I learned that I have to provide her with the options, but then let her pick up on whichever of those she wants, and then let her do it. (p. 68)

Another mother (Mastergeorge, 2007) explained the challenges of working with her son as he attempted difficult tasks:

> Somebody gave him a puzzle for his birthday, and it's real difficult. It's even hard for me to do. It's a very difficult puzzle. And it has small pieces, and they have odd shapes, and they don't really fit together—they sort of slide apart. And, I finally just put it away, because he would get it out, and dump it out, and then he couldn't do it. I've put it away on the shelf and in a few months when he eventually gets to the point that he can do it, it will be like a new puzzle. (p. 69)

Interestingly, the second mother was talking about adjusting the task difficulty for her child who did *not* have a developmental disability. Families of children with and without special needs are not all that different. School-age children can describe their own priorities along with their parents and teachers. Employers or prospective employers also can contribute information about the needs of adolescents and young adults.

Ethnographic Interviewing

Gathering input from multiple sources relies on ethnographic interviewing techniques (Spradley, 1979; Westby, Burda, & Mehta, 2003). *Ethnographic interviewing* incorporates elements of other speech events, such as friendly conversations and traditional case history taking, but differs from them as well (see Table 1.1). The clinician listens carefully to responses to ethnographic questions and pays attention to the words and other cues to deeper meanings. "The goal in interviewing is to have participants talk about things of interest to them and to cover matters of importance to the researcher [or clinician] in a way that allows participants to use their own concepts and terms" (Stainback & Stainback, 1988, p. 52). Clinicians pose follow-up questions contingent on information and terminology used by parents, teachers, or students.

Questions for ethnographic interviews are summarized in Table 1.2. They often begin with "grand tour" requests to describe a typical day or summarize a child's strengths and

table *1.1* Comparison of Communicative Features of Three Discourse Events

Friendly Conversation	Ethnographic Interview	Traditional Case History
Begins with greetings.	Begins with greetings.	Begins with greetings.
Explanation of purpose is optional.	Purpose is explained.	Purpose is explained.
Purpose is often just to socialize, although more specific purposes may be addressed as well.	Purpose is to gather information to learn about the interviewee's perspectives on a topic.	Purpose is to gather information that the interviewer can use to make health care decisions.
Topics vary, as negotiated through contributions by both partners.	Topics relate to the purpose of gaining perspectives on the problem, but the direction of the interview is contingent on comments made by the interviewee.	Topics relate to the purpose of gathering information about the problem and often are guided by a set of specific questions or checklists.
Turn taking is roughly balanced between participants, with each asking questions to show interest in the other.	Turn taking is unbalanced in that the interviewer asks relatively short, open-ended questions, which require longer responses by the interviewee.	Turn taking is roughly balanced in that the interviewer asks a prepared set of relatively closed questions and the interviewee provides brief answers that are to the point.
The partners send and receive verbal and nonverbal signals when they need to end the conversation.	The interviewer controls the flow of discourse and decides when it will end based on a pre-established schedule.	The interviewer controls the flow of discourse in the interview and typically decides when it will end based on a pre-established schedule.

needs. Questions about strengths place a value on abilities as well as disabilities. Grand tour questions are followed by mini-tour questions to learn more about the person's perceptions. When participants use specific terminology to refer to a student's abilities or disabilities, so-called native language questions can be used to ask them to describe an experience or example that illustrates what they mean by a particular phrase.

For example, when fourth grader DeAngelo told his clinician that he thought school was "boring," at first she asked him what he meant by *boring*. His response was that school was "just boring." Expressing further interest in DeAngelo's experience, the clinician asked him to tell about a time recently when he felt bored in school. He responded that it was "when the teacher explained the math lesson, and I didn't know what to do." Now the clinician had uncovered an area that could be probed further in curriculum-based language assessment and intervention. Her choice was supported when problems with the language of math were identified also by DeAngelo's mother and teacher as an area of particular difficulty for him.

Case Example 1.3 presents the results of ethnographic interviews regarding a fifth-grade student who was referred because he was struggling in school. Matt had scored at the first percentile on standardized achievement tests but had not been identified as having a disability. It was possible that an undiagnosed receptive language problem could help explain his academic difficulties. The illustrations in Table 1.2 correspond to this case example.

Sometimes clinicians only *appear* to listen to parents; their minds are made up about what to target in intervention before consulting parents. An example is the mother

table *1.2* Outline of Ethnographic Questions

	Ethnographic Question	**Illustration**
Descriptive Questions	**Grand Tour:** Seek information about broad experiences and viewpoints.	Tell me about a typical schoolday for Matt (you).
	Mini-Tour: Describe a specific activity or event.	What about the playground seems to be problematic for Matt (you)?
	Example: Take an experience and ask for an example.	The last time you thought Matt was rushing through just to finish his work, what kind of assignment was it?
	Experience: Ask about experience in a particular setting.	The last time you had a problem with another student on the playground, how did you handle it?
	Native Language: Seek an understanding of how a person uses labels, terms, and phrases.	When you say that Matt rushes through his work, what does it look like?
Structural Questions	**Inclusion:** X is a kind of Y.	What would you see as Matt's (your) particular strengths? What are your greatest areas of concern for Matt (yourself)?
	Spatial: X is a part of Y.	You say that Matt has social problems in some settings but not others. Can you tell me more about where the problems occur?
	Cause–Effect: X is a cause of Y; X is a result of Y.	What are some of the reasons that you don't like this school as much as your old one?
	Rationale: X is a reason for doing Y.	You say that Matt does not like to read. Do you have any ideas about reasons why?
	Location for Action: X is a place for doing Y.	Where do the students in your class turn in their work?
	Function: X is used for Y.	What do you (your students) use the planning book for in this class?
	Means–End: X is a way to do Y.	What have you tried to stop Desmond from teasing you?
	Sequence: X is a step (or stage) in Y.	Tell me about what happens after you tell the playground monitor about the problem.
	Attribution: X is attribute of Y.	What does Desmond do that makes him seem like a bully?

Source: Based on Spradley, 1979; Westby, Burda, & Mehta, 2003.

in Personal Reflection 1.1 whose 6-year-old son had physical and cognitive disabilities. At individualized education program (IEP) meetings, professionals kept insisting that literacy targets should wait until earlier developing skills of self-help and dressing were mastered.

CASE example *1.3*

Ethnographic Interviews and Prioritizing Goals for Matt

Matt was 10 years, 5 months old, and in fifth grade when his parents brought him to the university clinic for assessment of his language abilities. He recently had scored below the first percentile on a statewide achievement test and was having academic difficulties that seemed to reflect poor language skills.

Matt's language development problems had not been obvious. He began talking on schedule, and his parents were surprised when Matt's kindergarten teacher told them that Matt was struggling with language concepts in the early childhood curriculum. Matt had learned to read words accurately with little difficulty when he started school, but he did not like to read. His middle class, college-educated parents had taken him to libraries and bookstores to select books, but nothing seemed to stimulate his interest.

Ethnographic interviews were conducted with Matt, his mother, and his teacher. A classroom observation also was conducted, in which artifacts of Matt's work were gathered for later analysis.

Matt's Input

Matt's response to a general question about what it was like to be in fifth grade was "It's pretty hard." In response to a structural inclusion question, Matt indicated that the worst part of school was "recess." When asked to say more about what he did not like about recess (an attribution question), Matt said that he sometimes got in trouble for fighting. A contingent experience question was used to ask about a recent time when recess had been a problem. He proceeded to narrate an incident that had happened that day, in which another boy, Desmond, had called him "four eyes" and "window-pane eyes" and taunted him in other ways. When asked what happened next (a structured sequence question), Matt indicated that he cried and told the playground monitor, who in his view did noth-

ing. When asked about classroom activities, Matt indicated that his primary goal was "not to rush through work."

Matt's Mother's Input

When asked a mini-tour question about what had triggered her concerns about Matt's language, his mother referred to her first conference with Matt's kindergarten teacher, when she learned he "was a little behind." Matt's mother noted that he received psychometric testing then that showed that his verbal scale intelligence score was 25 points below his performance scale score; however, he was not placed in special education. Both Matt's parents were educators, and they did not want him to be labeled as having a disability. When Matt's mother was asked what she thought might account for his current academic and test score difficulty (a structured cause–effect question), she indicated, "It is probably a combination of low receptive language as well as inattentiveness." She added that she thought one of Matt's biggest problems at school was that he "tends to rush to complete things, disregarding accuracy."

Matt's Teacher's Input

Matt's teacher, Mr. G, said, "I think Matt's biggest problem is that he tries to get everything done first. He flies through everything." When asked to provide an example, Mr. G indicated that Matt claimed to check his work but that his finished products often had errors. When asked if he had any thoughts about cause, Mr. G indicated that he was not certain whether Matt missed a lot because of rushing or due to an underlying skill deficit. When asked about social skills, Mr. G described Matt as a "good kid" in class but noted that he had gotten into fights recently on the playground.

PERSONAL reflection *1.1*

"We'll buy him Velcro!"

Mother of a child with multiple disabilities, trying to get her child's IEP team to target academic abilities rather than dressing skills, who then continued, "Unless we start focusing now on learning to read as well as to talk and dress himself, he won't be able to handle all of the other demands that will face him in life."

⋯⋯⋯⋯⋯⋯⋯⋯⋯⋯⋯⋯⋯⋯⋯⋯⋯⋯⋯⋯⋯⋯⋯⋯⋯⋯⋯⋯⋯⋯⋯⋯⋯⋯⋯⋯

Another mother of an early elementary child with multiple disabilities expressed a similar value for literacy (see Personal Reflection 1.2) and frustration that her input was not fully respected. Professionals often prepare their reports and written recommendations in advance of the meetings; parents, on the other hand, may be viewed as recipients of information about their children, often couched as what their children *cannot* do rather than what they *can*. When parents offer conflicting views of what their children can do at home or differ with the planning team regarding priorities for intervention, they may be inappropriately considered to have unrealistic expectations.

PERSONAL reflection *1.2*

"You listen to me politely, but you never write it down!"

Mother of a child with multiple disabilities conveying her sense that her input to the IEP process was not being taken seriously.

⋯⋯⋯⋯⋯⋯⋯⋯⋯⋯⋯⋯⋯⋯⋯⋯⋯⋯⋯⋯⋯⋯⋯⋯⋯⋯⋯⋯⋯⋯⋯⋯⋯⋯⋯⋯

After this mother noted her concerns, the clinician listened to the underlying message and asked her to bring her own written remarks to the next IEP meeting. This is what the mother's written notes indicated:

> I'd really like to see beginning reading included in J's IEP this year. Hopefully by the end of the year, he'll be able to do some sight reading—his own full name, family names— *bathroom*—*drink*—miscellaneous needs. Plus sentence structure, and how to group sentences to tell a story or have a conversation by choosing his words. I'd like to see some math. If only 1–50 and the awareness of three digits and up. This is a secondary desire—reading is my biggest concern. I know this is a major request, but it's really time for academics to start showing up on his IEP as a *real* goal. Maybe he won't be able to grasp it, and at the year's end it will be continued or declined, but either way, I'd like his records to show that the effort was made. Thanks for asking for my input. I'll get with you soon to work out our game plan.

This mother provided a cogent and hopeful, but also realistic, picture of language/literacy goals for her child with multiple special needs. Similar to the mother who commented "We'll buy him Velcro!" she articulated clearly the value her family placed on literacy. An intervention plan that incorporates parental concerns and priorities is more likely to generate parental engagement in implementation.

Four Questions of Context-Based Language/ Literacy Assessment and Intervention

After important contexts and activities have been identified by those who know a child best (parents, teachers, child), clinicians can conduct context-based language assessment and intervention. This process is guided by the four questions that appear in Figure 1.4.

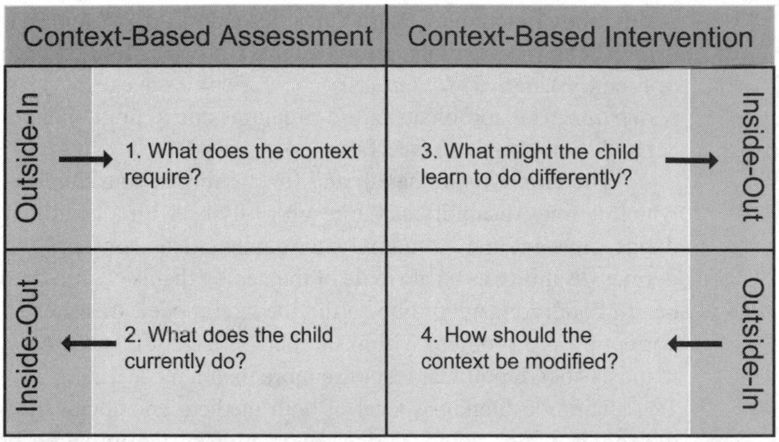

Context-Based Assessment	Context-Based Intervention
Outside-In → 1. What does the context require?	3. What might the child learn to do differently? → **Inside-Out**
Inside-Out ← 2. What does the child currently do?	4. How should the context be modified? ← **Outside-In**

figure *1.4*

Four Questions That Guide Context-Based Language Assessment and Intervention

By applying these four questions in systematic and recursive order (i.e., cycling through them deliberately and continuously), clinicians can update interventions regularly to be relevant to a student's current needs and abilities. How these questions are addressed depends on what a clinician knows about language, literacy, and communication. Background knowledge can be used to analyze complex communication activities, such as reading, talking, comprehending, following directions, solving math story problems, interacting with peers, regulating one's attention, and so forth. Any of these skills could be targeted in contextualized language and literacy assessment and intervention.

SUMMARY

This section has introduced essential elements of context-based language assessment and intervention. Context-based approaches start by identifying the contexts (including places, activities, and materials) that are most important to those most involved. Techniques of ethnography include interviews with those who know the child best, as well as participant observation and triangulation to identify common themes across multiple informants and contexts. For children and adolescents in the school-age years, this approach is known as *curriculum-based language assessment and intervention.*

Four critical questions are (1) What does the context require? (2) What does the child currently do? (3) What might the child learn to do differently? (4) How should the context be modified to enhance function? The four questions are just as applicable for family-centered approaches with infants, toddlers, and preschoolers in natural environments as for school-age children and adolescents.

World Health Organization Definitions

International Classification of Functioning, Disability and Health (ICF)

Questions of context-based assessment are compatible with World Health Organization (WHO) definitions of disability. The *International Classification of Functioning, Disability and Health* (ICF; WHO, 2001) describes living with conditions that affect the three domains: body functions and structures, activities, and participation. According to this system, *disability* is viewed as an umbrella term for *impairments* (i.e., problems in body structure or function); *activity limitations* (i.e., difficulties in executing activities); and *participation restrictions* (i.e., problems in life situations due to limited opportunities imposed by physical and social barriers) (see Table 1.3).

The emphasis on health and functioning is considered a *social model* of disability, which defines disability as the result of living with a health condition in an unaccommodating physical and attitudinal environment. This contrasts with a *medical model,* which defines disability as an attribute of the person that is caused by disease, trauma, or a related health condition. According to the medical model, treatment for disability should aim at correcting the problem within the person. According to the social model, treatment demands a social–political response more than a medical one.

The ICF blends aspects of both medical and social models into a *biopsychosocial approach,* which acknowledges interaction of the impaired body structure and function with personal factors and environmental/contextual factors. Personal factors include gender, age, coping styles, social background, education, profession, experience, overall behavior patterns, and cultural–linguistic heritage. Environmental factors include products and technology; natural environments and human influences; supports and relationships with family and strangers; attitudes, values, and beliefs; services; and systems and policies. The ICF describes how people with disabilities live, function, and participate. Impairments and limitations may be difficult to modify, but disabilities may be reduced by improving functioning, and that requires a focus on health and contextual factors as well as impaired structures and functions.

table *1.3* Framework of the *International Classification of Functioning, Disability and Health* (*ICF*) of the World Health Organization (WHO)

Body	
Function:	**Structure:**
Mental functions	Structure of the nervous system
Sensory functions and pain	The eyes, ears, and related structures
Voice and speech functions	Structures involved in voice and speech production
Activities and Participation	
Capacity:	**Performance:**
What the person can do without personal assistance or assistive devices	What the person can do in the current environment with assistive devices or personal assistance
Environmental (Contextual) Factors	
Physical factors:	**Social factors:**
Products and technology	Attitudes, relationships, and policies

Source: WHO, 2001.

Application of ICF Categories to Language Disorders

The three ICF domains of body functions and structures, activities, and participation correspond to three models of assessment—communication processes, needs, and opportunities (Beukelman & Mirenda, 1992). Each suggests a different question and perspective on the clinical process.

The *communication processes model* asks about the nature of a child's language impairment, viewing it as a specific problem of body function or structure. Clinical questions that emerge from the communication processes model ask What processes are impaired (*or not*) within the individual? This is an important element of language assessment and planning, but not the only one.

The *communication needs model* asks about the nature of a child's activity limitations in important academic and social communication contexts. Clinical questions that emerge from the communication needs model ask What does the individual need to be able to do to function well in important life contexts? This is a critical element for conducting context-based assessments, such as play-based language assessment or curriculum-based language assessment.

Finally, the *communication participation model* (also called the *communication opportunities model*) asks about opportunities a person has to participate in important life contexts. Such questions aim at reducing disability by increasing communication opportunity. Clinical questions that emerge from the communication participation model ask What opportunities does this individual have to participate in the important contexts of children's lives? This is a critical element for collaborating with family members, clients, teachers, policy makers, and system administrators to reduce disability and improve functioning by working to increase environmental access to typical learning contexts, as well as to specialized services and supports.

A child with cerebral palsy, for example, can be expected to have motor difficulties throughout his or her lifespan. Given the current state of knowledge about this chronic neuromotor condition, it is unrealistic to think that the basic impairment that affects body structures and functions can be repaired. The functional limitations, although also significant, may respond better to intervention, reducing the level of disability and yielding outcomes associated with better quality of life. By acquiring advanced language abilities and literacy skills and having access to individualized technological supports for talking and writing, children, adolescents, and adults with severe speech–motor impairments may be able to function as well as their peers in many activities, especially if they are given opportunities to participate with peers in social and educational contexts (Beukelman & Mirenda, 2005).

When barriers prevent participation, policies may support choices, decisions, and opportunities that increase access to therapeutic and educational supports and technologies. The comprehensive nature of a multifaceted, integrated approach is essential to minimize disability and maximize function and participation.

SUMMARY

This section has introduced the *International Classification of Functioning* (ICF) that was developed by the World Health Organization (WHO) to describe three domains that influence how people live with chronic health conditions and disabilities: body functions and structures, activities, and participation. The ICF is both a medical and social classification system for understanding disability, which contributes to comprehensive assessment and intervention focused on communication processes, needs, and opportunities for participation.

CHAPTER SUMMARY

Chapter 1 has introduced a framework for the rest of the book. The importance of asking good questions has been emphasized as underpinning such diverse phenomena as attention, language and cognitive development, clinical intervention, scientific inquiry, and interdisciplinary collaboration. Principles of evidence-based practice were introduced as encompassing these three components: best scientific evidence; clinician expertise; and child, family, and societal values. The acronym ASC-AE was offered as an aid to remember the five steps of EBP, and the acronym PICO was used to describe the four critical components of clinical questions.

Collaborative consultation was contrasted with expert consultation, and three models of problem solving were introduced: competitive, independent, and collaborative. Collaborative problem solving identifies mutual goals on which all participants can agree. Contextualized assessment and intervention techniques also were described. Ethnographic interviewing and related techniques are used for gathering client- and family-centered, contextualized views of the client's strengths and needs. Four questions were introduced for guiding context-based assessment and intervention practices.

Finally, the WHO/ICF framework was described for classifying disability and health. Assessment questions related to the framework ask about communication processes, needs, and participation opportunities. The frameworks introduced in this chapter can guide a comprehensive, contextualized approach to clinical problem solving that extends across age ranges, settings, and populations. These frameworks are consistent with a major theme of this book: *Problems are not just within children, and neither are the solutions.*

EXERCISES *and* STUDY QUESTIONS

1. Using the PICO framework, formulate a question that is of particular importance to you.

2. Conduct ethnographic interviews with a parent and child about the child's special needs.

3. How would the four questions of context-based language assessment and intervention apply to a hypothetical high school student whose reading decoding and comprehension difficulties are interfering with his ability to work independently in the history curriculum?

4. Define and describe the World Health Organization categories of impairment, functional limitation, and disability. Then relate them to three questions for guiding assessment about communication processes, needs, and opportunities for a child in your experience.

CHAPTER TWO

Speech, Language/ Literacy, and Communication

LEARNING *objectives*

After studying this chapter, you should be able to do the following:

1. Differentiate among speech, language (including literacy), and communication.

2. Discuss five language parameters—phonology, morphology, syntax, semantics, and pragmatics—and relate them to the three systems—content, form, and use.

3. Describe sound, word, sentence, and discourse levels in listening, speaking, reading, and writing modalities.

4. Discuss language/literacy socialization and cultural–linguistic variation.

Speech, Language (Including Literacy), and Communication

Assessment often begins by observing whether the three systems—speech, language, and communication—are affected equally or whether any of them might be relatively *spared* or *impaired* (see Figure 2.1). By asking about strengths and weaknesses across these three systems, clinicians can gain insights about what to do next.

Speech

Speech is a physiological function that uses structures that also support the life-sustaining functions of respiration and alimentation (eating); thus, it has been called an **overlaid function.** Speech production is controlled and coordinated by cognitive–linguistic processes in the central nervous system (CNS), which comprises the brain, spinal cord, and cranial nerves.

Impairment of any physiological structure or function can cause speech production to be relatively impaired, as when children with severe motor speech impairments have relatively intact language and communication abilities. For other children, speech is essentially spared while language and communication abilities are markedly impaired, as when children with autism spectrum disorders can produce formulaic or echolalic speech but cannot formulate generative language or communicate in socially appropriate ways.

As a motor act, speech production involves intricate coordination among several physiological systems—**respiration, phonation, articulation,** and **resonation.** Accurate speech production also requires sensory input and dynamic feedback from **auditory** (hearing), **proprioceptive** (position in space), **kinesic** (movement), and **tactile** (touch) systems so that speakers can use feedback to control articulators, with reference to central concepts of speech–sounds (phonemes) and sound patterns (hierarchical phonological and suprasegmental qualities). Central nervous system components (illustrated in Figure 2.2) send neural directions to the speech end organs for carrying out linguistically programmed orders.

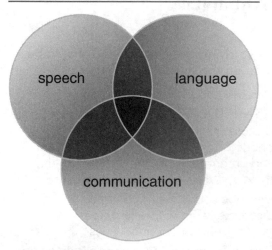

figure *2.1*

Speech, Language, and Communication Are Independent but Integrally Related Systems

Language and Literacy

Language is not a physical act and no verb exists, as in *to language.* Rather, language is a knowledge system. It constitutes a system of abstract symbols (i.e., a **lexicon**) and a **grammar** for incorporating the symbols into sentences. Grammar is not just about sentence structure. The broader concept of grammar includes pragmatic competence for using language functionally and appropriately to construct discourse in a manner consistent with expected social conventions. Stein and Glenn (1982) applied the term *story grammar* to a common macrostructure—narrative. Social conversation, arguing or convincing, storytelling, and reporting are a few discourse subtypes that fall within the three major categories—conversation, narration, and exposition. According to the American Speech-Language-Hearing Association (ASHA, 1982):

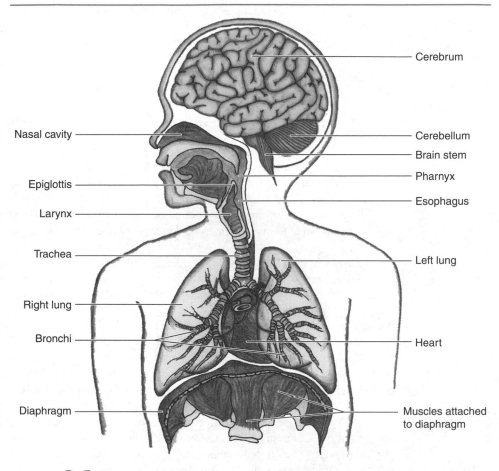

figure 2.2

Components of a Child's Speech Production System

Language is a complex and dynamic system of conventional symbols that is used in various modes for thought and communication. Contemporary views of human language hold that:

- Language evolves within specific historical, social, and cultural contexts;
- Language, as rule governed behavior, is described by at least five parameters— phonologic, morphologic, syntactic, semantic, and pragmatic;
- Language learning and use are determined by the interaction of biological, cognitive, psychosocial, and environmental factors.

Effective use of language for communication requires a broad understanding of human interaction including such associated factors as nonverbal cues, motivation, and sociocultural roles. (p. 44)

Language formulation and comprehension are inner processes that are not directly observable by any conventional means. Language becomes observable only when it is expressed through physical performance, such as speech, writing, and sign language. Strictly speaking, language and literacy are not separate entities. Literacy should be seen as a form of language, not separate from it, but the terms *language* and *literacy* are not synonymous.

Some forms of spoken language are highly literate, and some written language forms are less literate.

Basic levels of competence in reading and writing, although a step toward literacy, are generally not thought to represent its attainment. The achievement of literacy presumes higher-level competence with complex forms and abstract constructs. Gee (1990) described a "socially and culturally situated view" of literacy that takes it beyond simple definitions. He wrote:

> The 'normal' meaning of the word 'literacy' ('the ability to read and write') seems to be 'innocent' and 'obvious.' But, I will argue, it is no such thing. Literacy as 'the ability to write and read' situates literacy in the individual person, rather than in the society of which that person is a member. As such, it obscures the multiple ways in which reading, writing and language interrelate with the workings of power and desire in social life. (p. 27)

To arrive at a more appropriate definition of literacy, Gee (1990) recommended couching the definition in terms of primary and secondary discourse. He defined *literacy* as

> *mastery of,* or *fluent control over,* a *secondary Discourse* [italics and capitals in the original]. Therefore, literacy is always plural: *literacies* (there are many of them, since there are many secondary Discourses, and we all have some and fail to have others). (p. 153)

Among the multiple literacies, Gee included film, visual arts, and other forms of secondary discourse. Computer literacy is another familiar example.

Spoken language can occur on a continuum from less literate and informal to more literate and formal. Language used in conversation for functional purposes, for example, is not generally considered literate communication. On the other hand, formal discourse is exemplified by such literate oral forms as debate, formal discussion, and storytelling.

Literate discourse places different demands on language learners than social interaction discourse. Cummins (1992) used the term **basic interpersonal communication skills (BICS)** to refer to functional spoken language competence, which is the first step in acquiring basic competence with any new language. Cummins contrasted BICS with **cognitive academic language proficiency (CALP),** which characterizes higher-level forms of reading and writing and literate forms of spoken discourse. CALP differs from BICS in several ways. It is acquired after more years, based on more experience, and used in contexts that are academic as well as social.

Cummins (1992) studied language acquisition among immigrant children in Toronto and found that children could acquire BICS within the first two years, but CALP required five to seven years. Failure to distinguish BICS and CALP, he noted, could result in misinterpretation of results of psychometric testing (e.g., concluding delays when the results really represented incomplete second-language proficiency) or premature removal from second-language learning support services (e.g., concluding CALP had been reached when only BICS had been achieved).

The achievement of literate discourse is viewed as a primary function of schooling, but such a view tends to take for granted that the discourse of the dominant culture sets the standard for what should be considered literate. Authors who are concerned about issues of social justice have argued for a more inclusive concept of *multiple literacies* (e.g., Baugh, 2000). Gallego and Hollingsworth (2000) looked critically at how issues of power might contribute to achievement gaps for children from diverse backgrounds in school:

> As we tried to put the cognitive theories into practice, we found obstacle after obstacle in watching the populations of children we wanted to reach (and their teachers) struggle and

fail in school, even as such practices were intended to facilitate all children's literacy. We soon had researched enough patterns to know that those children had difficulty attaining the standard literacy because of a combination of social, political, and instructional factors rather than cognitive factors alone. Only through the praxis of our work as professionals did it become clear that the lack of success was due to the political gatekeeping functions of school literacy which often limits success in standard English (and therefore schooling and subsequent citizenship) to those already fluent in it through family and community discourse practices. (p. 4)

Gallego and Hollingsworth (2000) hypothesized that adding literacies traditionally excluded from the value structure of schooling could allow other children to bring their language fluencies to school. A system of multiple literacies would include not only *school literacies* but also *community literacies* and *personal literacies.*

Communication

Communication comprises at least four components—sender, receiver, medium, and message. A ***sender*** assumes an active role in formulating ideas into a ***message*** (linguistically encoded and nonverbal) for transmission to another. The ***medium*** for transmission might be speech, writing, gesture, or some combination of the three. Communication also requires a ***receiver*** who is able to make sense of the message.

Co-Construction Models of Communication

In older views, communication theory was based on what are now called ***tube theories of communication.*** A sender took the active role in constructing a message and sending it to the receiver, as if through a tube with no surrounding context. The receiver's role was essentially passive, as illustrated in Figure 2.3.

Newer views characterize communication as an interactive process that requires the active participation of a listener and a consideration of context. According to this view, communication partners co-construct meaning with shared reference and with context playing a major role in the process. In ***co-construction models of communication,*** communicative partners actively process both linguistic symbols and nonlinguistic signs to construct a closely matched message, open to elaboration and extension. Such co-constructive models

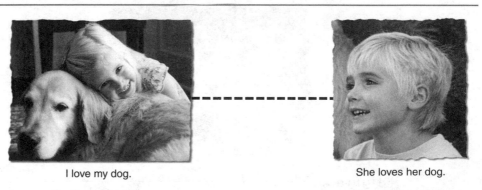

I love my dog.   She loves her dog.

figure *2.3*

Tube Theory of Communication as a Form of Information Transfer can be envisioned as triangles within circles (see Figure 2.4). A triangle is formed by the two communicative partners focusing visually or cognitively (in their "mind's eye," so to speak) on the content of the message as their shared reference (Bruner, 1975). The encompassing circle is formed when a receiving partner completes a communicative circle by responding contingently.

The term ***communication circles*** is used by Greenspan and colleagues to heighten awareness of the special needs of children with social communication disorders, including autism spectrum disorders. Greenspan, Wieder, and Simmons (1998) described a method called "Floortime" for teaching children with difficulties involving social interaction and other neurodevelopmental challenges. In Floortime exchanges, parents get down on their children's level both physically and metaphorically—observing them, interacting with them, responding to their signals, and helping them elaborate and expand their play—so that children learn to close communication circles and open new ones.

Grice's Maxims

Across the age span, communication exchanges are governed by implicit social conventions shared by members of a culture. These are called ***implicature*** or ***presupposition*** because

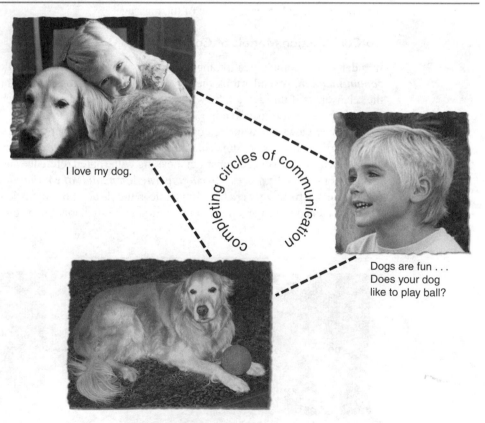

I love my dog.

completing circles of communication

Dogs are fun . . .
Does your dog
like to play ball?

figure *2.4*

Co-Constructive and Co-Referential Joint Focus Theory of Interactive Communication
The result is circles of communication that can be opened or closed by either participant.

they are based on implied shared assumptions (presuppositions) about what a communication partner (i.e., *interlocutor*) already knows and needs to know. Grice (1975) described four *conversational maxims* (i.e., general rules or principles):

- *Maxim of quantity*—Provide no more or less information than is needed by your partner to understand your message.
- *Maxim of quality*—Be truthful and say only what you have reason to believe to be true.
- *Maxim of relation*—Say only things that are relevant to the topic at hand.
- *Maxim of manner*—Be organized and avoid vagueness, wordiness, and ambiguity.

Children learn communication appropriateness while acquiring other aspects of speech and language ability. By adolescence, individuals are expected to have mastered implicature. Adolescents who do not follow the conventions of the conversational contract may appear strange or annoying and thus risk social isolation.

Communication can occur without language, as when shared understanding is achieved through nonverbal gestures and facial expressions. Communication does, however, require social sensitivity to the initiations, needs, and responses of communication partners. Communication signs and symbols vary in complexity, clarity, and intentionality. In some communication events, receivers assign intentional meanings to autonomic behaviors that are not intentional (e.g., facial expression, postural shifting, nervous gestures), and it is sometimes possible to misinterpret those signals. Several cognitive–communicative diagnoses are associated with high risks for misreading nonverbal social signals, including autism spectrum disorders, the after effects of child abuse and neglect, and emotional and behavioral disorders.

Speech Act Theory

Communication in the infant–toddler years develops in three stages—perlocutionary, illocutionary, and locutionary. These are additive stages, in that a child maintains earlier learned acts while adding new ones. Assessment of development within the three stages is appropriate for children or adolescents of any age functioning at early levels of communication (Bates, Camaioni, & Volterra, 1975; Prizant, 1984). Aspects of all three *speech acts* remain present as well in communicative exchanges across the lifespan (Austin, 1962; Bates, 1976).

Perlocutionary communication refers to the message that is constructed in the mind of the receiver. A *perlocutionary speech act* is a receiver's interpretation of a sender's intention. When Austin (1962) introduced the notion of speech acts, he was referring to the effects of a spoken utterance on the actions, thoughts, or beliefs of the one who heard it, as represented by verbs such as *convinced, scared, inspired,* and *enlightened.*

The *perlocutionary stage* of communication development extends from birth to about 8 to 10 months of age. During the perlocutionary stage, babies do not have intentional communication, but they certainly signal internal states and current needs for feeding, changing, comforting, and playing that are interpreted as communicative by others. Figure 2.5 provides an example of perlocutionary discourse produced by a mother interacting with her typically developing infant daughter. As the transcript of both verbal and nonverbal communication shows, this mother is attending closely to her daughter's communication signals and interpreting them as having meaning.

Infants who do not have such attentive parents can experience long-term detrimental effects. When parental neglect or depression leaves an infant without attachment to

figure 2.5 ———————————————————

Transcript of Mother Interacting with Infant Daughter

This exchange shows the mother's perlocutionary act of assigning communicative intention to her daughter's nonverbal signals.

```
$  Child, Mother
+  Gender: F
+  CA: 0;5
+  Context: Mother-infant interaction

=  M lifts C into the air.
=  C looks at the camera.
M  Hey you.
M  You just don't want to look at Mommy?
M  You just don't want to look at Mommy?
=  C looks back at M with a neutral face.
M  Say, I see you every day all day {exaggerated intonation and high pitch}.
M  I see you all the time.
=  C looks at M with eye gaze and a neutral face.
C  ek.
M  uhhh.
C  eh.
M  uh boo {M starts making the C fly by moving C close to her face}!
=  C smiles at the M and maintains eye contact.
=  M puts C on her hips.
=  M raises the C back into the air.
M  uh boo!
M  uh boo!
=  M smiles at C and maintains eye contact.
=  C smiles back at M.
M  yeah.
```

Source: Formatted for Systematic Analysis of Language Transcripts (SALT); Miller & Chapman, 2008.

a responsive communicative partner, neurodevelopmental effects can impair the child's social–emotional development long after social services have been put in place to satisfy his or her needs for physical care (Henry, Sloane, & Black-Pond, 2007; Hyter, 2007b).

Sensory and motor impairments may present barriers that make it difficult for parents and infants to read each others' communicative signals. Awareness of barriers can help lower them. Fraiberg (1979) observed that parents of blind babies (or sighted babies of blind parents) learned to make connections despite the absence of vision. Children who are born deaf or hard of hearing have a much better prognosis when their parents become aware of the hearing loss within the first six months (Yoshinaga-Itano, Sedey, Coulter, & Mehl, 1998). One possible explanation is that parents learn to attend more deliberately to their infants' communicative signals and work more intentionally to open and close circles of communication.

Illocutionary communication refers to intention in the mind of the sender. For example, a speaker's intention might be to ask a question to gain information or to make a comment to bring an idea to another person's attention. An ***illocutionary speech act*** is the sender's communicative intent for how the message should function. Speech acts are effective when a sender communicates intentionally and the receiver understands and responds to the sender's true intention.

The ***illocutionary stage*** emerges when a baby signals true communicative intention by looking between a communication partner and a desired object and gesturing communicatively. This ability emerges at around 8 months and is characterized soon thereafter by the index finger point. The full illocutionary stage generally emerges around 10 months in typical development and remains primary until around 18 months. By 18 months, many toddlers use words to serve functions previously communicated solely through gestures. Babies sometimes point to objects, people, and animals to request and sometimes to comment. Preverbal commenting involves drawing a caregiver's attention to an object of shared interest. It is a particularly important sign that social cognition is emerging, and its absence constitutes a danger sign for autism spectrum disorders (Wetherby, Prizant, & Schuler, 2000).

Locutionary communication refers to the formulation of communicative messages using actual words. A ***locutionary speech act*** is the sender's linguistically encoded message—that is, the actual utterance. An important element of the pragmatic parameter of language use is that locutionary speech acts and illocutionary speech acts do not always match exactly. Mismatches between locutionary and illocutionary speech acts are termed ***indirect communication*** (e.g., *Who cut your hair?*). This is in contrast to ***direct communication***, which occurs when a speaker's intentions and words match exactly (e.g., *I don't like your new haircut*). Indirect communication acts often are considered more polite, but they present expressive and receptive challenges to communicators who have pragmatic language difficulties. They also may vary across social–cultural boundaries. For example, in one culture, direct eye contact of a child while speaking with an adult may be interpreted as a sign of respect, whereas it may signal disrespect in another culture.

The ***locutionary stage*** emerges around 12 months, when children learn to produce real words. It is in full force when a child can use words effectively to communicate most of his or her intentions during the second or third year of life. It becomes refined into mature communication as children learn to soften intentions with polite ***locutionary acts.***

Nonverbal Communication

Because of its prior emergence, communication is the first target of intervention when biological or environmental factors place babies at high risk for developmental difficulties. Communication intervention can begin with the tiniest neonate and his or her caregivers. Even in cases of severe language impairment, ***nonlinguistic*** communicative signals (intentional or not), such as smiles and excitement gestures or fussing and crying, may be relatively spared. In spite of severe levels of physical or cognitive impairment, if a person can use gestures and other nonverbal means to trigger an intended idea or concept in the mind of another, communication is possible. Perlocutionary communication always is a possibility, even in the presumed absence of intention on the part of a child or adolescent with a severe disability.

Perlocutionary and illocutionary communication acts both may be achieved through nonverbal rather than verbal means. ***Nonverbal,*** another term for *nonlinguistic,* means technically "without words," spoken or written. It does not always carry that meaning for people in the lay public, however, or for some professionals. It is common to find examples of the term *nonverbal* being used to mean "without *spoken* words." This can lead to confusion.

An example is the diagnosis of *nonverbal learning disability.* This diagnosis may be made for children whose spoken language is basically intact and possibly precocious—as observed by early talking and early reading—but whose other communication abilities are moderately to severely impaired. A major concern about applying the term *nonverbal* in such a case is that it may cause interdisciplinary teams to overlook difficulties in language comprehension and abstract linguistic concepts, which are decidedly *verbal* skills in the sense that they involve words. Children with severe oral–motor control problems with strengths in language and nonverbal communication, compared with their impaired ability to speak, could be called *nonspeaking,* but they are not *nonverbal.* (However, the term *complex communication needs* is currently preferred.)

Three prominent mechanisms of nonverbal communication are proxemic, kinesic, and paralinguistic. ***Proxemic*** mechanisms constitute a form of nonlinguistic communication signaled by spatial relationships. Cultural conventions govern how close one partner can come to another during communication events without feeling uncomfortable. Most Western cultures have implicit proxemic norms similar to those illustrated in Figure 2.6.

Personal: 1.5–4 feet

Intimate: 0 to 1.5 feet

Public: 12 feet or more (to visible limit)

Social-consultative: 4–12 feet

figure *2.6*

Common Proxemic Conventions

Note that the distances vary for different communication events and are based on interpersonal relationships.

Children and adolescents who violate proxemic norms with their peers risk social rejection, but they can respond to explicit scaffolding. This is what occurred for Spencer (see Case Example 2.1), who received language and communication intervention as part of a writing lab approach (Nelson, Bahr, & Van Meter, 2004).

Kinesic mechanisms are another form of nonverbal communication based on movements and gestures. They may occur alone or in conjunction with verbal communication. Ekman and Friesen (1969) described five types of kinesic mechanisms:

CASE example *2.1*

Teaching Spencer about Proxemics

The case example for Spencer is based on a communication transcript (Nelson, Bahr, & Van Meter, 2004, p. 337) that illustrates scaffolding focused on social pragmatics, nonverbal communication, and proxemics. The episode occurred in a third-grade classroom in which a writing lab approach was being implemented for language instruction and intervention. Spencer was a student with multiple special needs, affecting pragmatics and social communication as well as other basic language skills. He spent the majority of his schoolday in a special education classroom but was included in the general education classroom for writing lab activities.

Spencer's pragmatic problems frequently led to conflicts with peers, particularly Tom. In this episode, a tussle erupted between the two boys in the back of the classroom. "What's going on?" the clinician asked. "He's messing with me," Tom said. Spencer indicated his intention: "I just want to see his story."

The clinician helped the two boys perceive the verbal and nonverbal elements of the interaction: "Tom, you said Spencer is messing with you. What is making you uncomfortable?" Tom explained, "He didn't ask. He's on my back, and he's touching me."

The clinician then reframed the cues: "You want him to ask," [Tom said "yes"] "and you don't like him touching you?" [Tom answered "no"]. "You think he is too close?" [Tom answered "yes"]. Then the clinician asked Tom, "How can you let Spencer know he is too close?" Tom replied, "I'll push him out of my face." The clinician asked, "That's one way, but what might happen?" Tom answered, "I'll get in trouble, but I don't care, if he's messing with me."

The clinician suggested a verbal alternative that would serve the function but without getting Tom in trouble: "What could you say to Spencer so he knows what you want him to do?" To this, Tom responded, "Back off." The clinician affirmed this response but recast it slightly: "Yes, you could say, 'You're too close. Step back.'"

The clinician then framed nonverbal affective cues: "Spencer, look at Tom. What does it look like when he's uncomfortable?" To this, Spencer responded, "Mad." The clinician affirmed this response and emphasized the importance of responding appropriately to facial expression cues: "Yes, he's making a mad face. What can you do when you see that?" Spencer said, "Stop." The clinician expanded, "Yes, you can stop. You can take a step back. You can ask, 'Why are you mad?'"

Then the clinician led the boys to experiment to identify personal distances that felt comfortable versus too close. After the boys agreed that an arm's length felt about right, the clinician suggested, "OK, Spencer and Tom. Let's practice. Spencer, how can you get Tom's attention without silly faces or touching?" Spencer responded appropriately, "Tom?" Tom responded, "Yea?" to which Spencer asked appropriately, "Can I see your paper?" This particular interaction ended when Tom responded, "Maybe later," which was a choice everyone respected. The relationship had changed, however. As the schoolyear progressed, Tom became one of Spencer's defenders against taunting by others.

1. *Emblems* are meaningful gestures, such as headshakes for yes/no and the OK hand sign. An emblematic gesture can be neutral in one culture but insulting in another.
2. *Illustrators* accompany a verbal message, such as holding spread hands apart to illustrate the size of a fish.
3. *Affective displays* are body and facial gestures that represent emotional states, such as anger, happiness, and skepticism. Although affective displays are universal, they vary in frequency and intensity across cultures, leading to potential misunderstandings.
4. *Regulators* are nonverbal signs that regulate, modulate, and maintain conversational turns. Hands are used as regulators more in some cultures than others, and direct eye contact may signal willingness to relinquish a turn in some cultures, whereas looking down has the same meaning in others.
5. *Adaptors* are self-oriented devices that are used with low awareness, such as postural changes, hair twisting, and other movements that serve to relieve tension and reduce anxiety.

Paralinguistic devices incorporate both verbal and nonverbal elements and thus do not fit perfectly in either category. They are closely aligned with the pragmatic system of language. Examples include speaking rate, loudness, intonation patterns, and enunciation of linguistically encoded messages to modify meaning (e.g., conveying irony or sarcasm) or highlight new information in an utterance. These are called *suprasegmental* components of speech production, contrasting with phonemes, which are considered the *segments.* Paralinguistic features convey meanings about a speaker's feelings that underlie a literal account of events. Children discover this when acquiring language, and adolescents perfect it as they become proficient in using language to make social connections or distance themselves from parents through sarcasm or irony.

Difficulties with gestural communication, eye gaze, and paralinguistic devices signal risks of pragmatic language impairment and autism spectrum disorders. Children with cognitive–communicative disorders have difficulty acquiring language and communication abilities and social relationships that depend on them. Young children who use gestures, eye gaze, and intonation to communicate nonverbally are less likely to have ongoing communication problems even if their early expressive language milestones are delayed, and children with limited nonverbal communication skills are at higher risk for ongoing difficulties (Wetherby, Yonclas, & Bryan, 1989).

SUMMARY

Definitions of speech, language, and communication abilities provide critical information that communication and language/literacy specialists can use for assessment and intervention. Speech is a motor act, which relies on CNS contributions and physiological systems of respiration, phonation, articulation, and resonation. Language involves knowledge of a conventional lexicon and grammar, is shared with others, and is used for communicative purposes. It evolves through the influence of geographical, historical, and sociocultural factors.

Communication, the third component introduced in this section, is characterized by interaction with partners, who co-construct meaning. The four rules of conversational implicature (Grice's maxims) relate to quantity, quality, relation, and manner. Speech act theory, which has three components—perlocutionary, illocutionary, and locutionary—was discussed in relation to early development, direct and indirect communication, and insights for people with disabilities.

Five Language Parameters

Language can be described as a unified system with five parameters—phonology, morphology, syntax, semantics, and pragmatics. Speech–language pathologists (SLPs) frequently use this five-parameter taxonomy to guide assessment and describe profiles of a child's language strengths and needs.

Phonology

Phonology is the sound system of language. A ***phoneme*** is the basic linguistic unit, or segment. It is defined as a sound category perceived by speakers as the smallest unit that can change the meaning of a word. A phoneme only *changes* meaning; it does not *carry* meaning (as a morpheme does). For example, the word *at* assumes a different meaning when the phoneme /h/ or /k/ is added to its beginning. Any word pair involving combinations of such words as *hat* and *cat* or *fat* and *mat* that differ by a single phoneme are called ***minimal pairs.***

By definition, a phoneme is a speech sound category. Phonemic recognition occurs regardless of physiological and acoustic variations in production of individual ***phones.*** Phones are single productions of speech sounds, or tokens. Tables 2.1 and 2.2 outline phonemes of English using symbols of the International Phonetic Alphabet (IPA).

The human ability to perceive diverse tokens (i.e., actual productions or phones) of a speech sound as members of the same phoneme class is particularly amazing considering the wide physical variations from one word context to another (e.g., Nittrouer, 2002). For example, /l/ is perceived categorically as the same phoneme by speakers of English, even though it varies motorically and acoustically in such word contexts as *light* and *metal.* In some cases, identifiable subphoneme variations are called ***allophones,*** as in the case of the syllabic *l* in words such as *needle.* The sound spectrum of a phone varies with word position partly because it is influenced by ***coarticulation*** with neighboring phonemes that occur before and after it in running speech. For example, speech sound spectrograms show evidence that speech mechanisms already are adjusting for the ends of words as their initial sounds are being uttered.

Phonetic influences also cross word boundaries. For example, low final sounds of prior words influence initial sounds of subsequent words to be produced with lower tongue placements, whereas high final sounds influence initial sounds of subsequent words to be produced with higher tongue placements. This suggests not only a physical influence but also a role for central speech mechanisms in the brain in forming a plan for suprasegmental influences across words. This linguistic influence is more than a string of individual phonemes produced one after the other. Hence, it is sometime referred to as ***nonlinear phonology*** (e.g., Bernhardt & Stemberger, 2000).

Central planning of smooth speech production in coordination with linguistic encoding (e.g., vocabulary choices, sentence structures, and discourse choices) allows mature speakers to generate spoken language that is fluent, intelligible, and usually transparent. ***Transparency*** refers to the fact that most listeners focus directly on the speaker's message and pay little attention to speech sounds unless something goes wrong.

Beyond *implicit* phonological knowledge, which speakers and listeners employ without awareness, a growing body of research has highlighted the importance of *explicit* phonological knowledge, which is employed with varying degrees of awareness. The term ***phonological processing*** is a broad term that applies to the use of phonological information to process spoken or written language (Hodson & Edwards, 1997). The term ***phonological awareness (PA)*** also has a relatively broad meaning that applies to a child's

table *2.1*   English Phonology and Symbols of the International Phonetic Alphabet: Consonants

	Speech Sound Production Features	Voiceless	Example Words	Voiced	Example Words
OBSTRUENTS[1]	Bilabial stop	p	**p**ie, **pupp**y, to**p**	b	**b**oy, **b**a**b**y, **b**i**b**
	Lingua-alveolar stop	t	**t**ime, mis**t**ake, ba**t**	d	**d**ime, **d**a**dd**y, be**d**
	Velar stop	k	**c**at, ti**ck**ing, boo**k**	g	**g**ood, bi**gg**er, tu**g**
	Glottal stop	ʔ	Ba**t**man, uh**o**h	—	—
	Labiodental fricative	f	**f**ig, a**f**ter, wi**f**e	v	**v**ine, e**v**ery, o**f**
	Lingua-dental fricative	/θ/ "theta"	**th**in, e**th**er, bo**th**	/ð/ "eth"	**th**is, ei**th**er, ba**th**e
	Lingua-alveolar fricative	s	**S**am, ma**s**ter, loo**s**e	z	**z**oo, ea**s**y, bee**s**
	Lingua-palatal fricative	ʃ	**sh**oe, pu**sh**ing, wi**sh**	ʒ	plea**s**ure, fu**s**ion, bei**g**e
	Glottal fricative	h	**wh**o, **H**o**h**o**h**o	—	—
	Lingua-palatal affricative	tʃ	**ch**in, i**tch**ing, wa**tch**	ʤ	**j**oy, **j**u**dg**ing, e**dg**e
SONORANTS[2]	**Nasal**				
	Bilabial	—	—	m	**m**an, **m**a**m**a, To**m**
	Lingua-alveolar	—	—	n	**n**ice, a**n**y, soo**n**
	Velar	—	—	ŋ "angma"	si**ng**, ri**ng**ing
	Liquid				
	Lateral	—	—	l	**l**ook, fo**ll**ow, ba**ll**
	Rhotic	—	—	r	**r**ed, bo**rr**ow, fa**r**
	Glide				
	Bilabial	—	—	w	**w**hen, q**u**een
	Alveolar	—	—	y	**y**ou, be**y**ond

[1] This section shows all consonants that can be both voiceless and voiced.

[2] This section shows sonorant consonants, which are only voiced and continuant.

explicit ability to detect and manipulate sounds and syllables in words. PA requires a degree of ***metalinguistic*** capability, in that the child must be capable of focusing on language units as an opaque object of thought (Gillon, 2004) and not just as a transparent means of communication.

table *2.2* English Phonology and Symbols of the International Phonetic Alphabet: Vowels

	Front		Central		Back	
	Vowel Symbol	*Example Words*	*Vowel Symbol*	*Example Words*	*Vowel Symbol*	*Example Words*
High	i	eat, beet, see	—	—	u	food, new
High–Mid	ɪ	it, bit, pin	—	—	ʊ	book, put, could
Mid	e	April, made	ɝ	bird, **fur**	o	know, boat
			ɚ	**mother**		
Low–Mid	ɛ	egg, pen	ʌ "caret"	bug, none	ɔ "open o"	bought, caught
			ə "schwa"	about, loosen		
Low	æ "ash"	cat, man	a	not	ɑ	father
	Diphthongs:	aʊ (cow, about)	aɪ (bite, **buy, fly**)	ɔɪ (boy, join)	eɪ (say)	oʊ (no)

Note: This table displays vowels that are only voiced and continuant.

Varied degrees of PA can be described on a continuum from **shallow** to **deep** (Justice & Scheule, 2004). An example of shallow PA is spontaneous creation of rhyming words in play. Deeper awareness occurs when children analyze words into component phonemes to generate spellings representing phonetic structures of spoken words. This continuum signals recognition of words as basic units of language, which can be further subdivided into component sounds—both important steps toward literacy.

Phonemic awareness is a subcategory of PA that refers to the ability to detect and manipulate individual phonemes within words (Catts & Kamhi, 2005; Gillon, 2004). Examples are tasks for grouping words that begin with a particular sound or detecting one that does not belong (**odd one out** tasks); taking off the final sound of a word (called **elision** tasks); and switching the order of initial and final consonants (called **transposition**). When children have not yet developed phonemic awareness, they are unable to switch focus from the meanings of words to their sound structures. An example of this occurred when one 6-year-old child was asked what word is left when the word *hair* is taken away from the word *haircut*. He replied, quite seriously, "Bald."

Phonics tasks involve the association of speech sounds with print symbols (i.e., letters). The ability to associate letters, called **graphemes,** with phonemes requires additional understanding. To learn phonics, children must first grasp the **alphabetic principle** that written words (in an alphabetic language such as English) comprise letters that represent sounds. This prepares them to grasp somewhat later the **orthographic principle** that patterns of letters represent syllabic and morphemic structures.

Morphology

Morphology is the system of meaningful units of language. A **morpheme** is the smallest meaningful unit of language, and each word consists of at least one morpheme. *Free* **morphemes** can stand alone (e.g., *walk*). **Bound morphemes** must be attached to other word roots (e.g., *walk/ing*). Bound morphemes are further subdivided into **derivational**

morphemes, which are prefixes or suffixes that derive new word forms (e.g., *speak, speaker, unspeakable*), and ***inflectional morphemes,*** which inflect word forms to fit grammatical slots in sentences.

Derivational morphemes serve a semantic role more than a syntactic one. They are used to derive new word forms with related, but slightly different meanings. Table 2.3 provides examples of derivational morphemes, many of which can be traced to Latin or Greek origins of English words.

Inflectional morphemes serve primarily syntactic functions. All inflectional morphemes in English are suffixes (i.e., they come at the ends of words), although not all languages work this way. Regular inflectional morphemes are added to nouns to make them plural or possessive (e.g., *He pulled off the bed's sheets*). Some plural forms are irregular (e.g., *mice, feet*), as are pronouns, which are inflected for case, as well as number or possession (e.g., *It was his turn to do the wash; She asked him to take her turn too*). English pronoun morphology is outlined in Table 2.4.

Verb forms also take on regular inflectional endings or have irregular inflections. Verbs are inflected for tense and number, as in the verb forms *is walking, walked, walks, has walked, have walked.* Inflectional morphemes appear on ***finite*** verbs in main clauses. Finite morphemes inflect main verbs (or auxiliaries) to fill particular grammatical roles in sentences. A simple sentence has only one clause structured with one finite main verb, which

table 2.3   Derivational Morphology (not an exhaustive list)

Prefix	Root Word	Suffix
pre-arrange ar-range de-ranged	range	arrange-ment arrange-er
un-kind	kind	kind-ness
re-think	think	think-er
tele-phone	phone	phon-ology
un-friendly	friend	friend-ship friend-ly friend-li-ness
in-decision	decide	deci-sion
ir-rational	rate	ra-tion ration-al ration-ale ration-al-ize ration-al-iz-ation
super-man sub-hu-man wo-man	man	man-ly man-li-ness woman-ly woman-ize-er
hyper-tone hypo-tone	tone	ton-al ton-er

table 2.4   Inflected Pronouns

Person	Singular			Plural		
	*Subjective**	*Possessive*	*Objective*	*Subjective*	*Possessive*	*Objective*
First	I am (I'm) I was	my, mine	me	We are (we're) We were	our, ours	us
Second	You are (you're) You were	your, yours	you	You (Y'all) are You were	your, yours	you
Third	He is (he's) She is (she's) It is (It's) He/she/it was	his, his her, hers its	him her it	They are They were	their, theirs	them

*Inflected forms of the copula *be* (present and past; contracted and uncontracted) appear in this column as well.

consists of a main verb and any auxiliaries (e.g., *He walked to my house; She walks every day; They were both walking yesterday; Come here*). A complex sentence is structured with more than one verb appearing either in two clauses (e.g., *She arrived at my house while I was washing my hair; I saw that he was eating his breakfast*) or in a complex clause with one primary verb (i.e., *finite form*, underlined in the following examples with a single line) and one secondary verb phrase (i.e., nonfinite form, underlined in the following examples with a double line) (e.g., *She saw me washing my hair;* or *He asked me to eat breakfast with him*). Some finite verb inflections are regular (e.g., *-s, -ed, -ing*), following a consistent pattern; others are irregular (e.g., *was, were; see, saw*). Table 2.5 outlines English inflectional morphemes.

Three forms of nonfinite (secondary) verbs are used in English: (1) **infinitives** take the classic uninflected form, *to verb*, and remain in that form in infinitival complements as the objects of main verbs (e.g., *I wanted him to eat his breakfast; She knew to start the test*); (2) **gerunds** are verbs used as nouns, usually by adding the morpheme *-ing* (e.g., *Drawing is my favorite hobby; He started drawing*); and (3) **participles** are verbs used as modifiers of nouns, either in present-participle form with *–ing* (e.g., *She saw him swimming in the lake*) or past-participle form with an *–ed* or *–en* ending (e.g., *She found the package, opened; The storm left the tree limb fallen on the ground*).

Morphological analysis plays a major role in many explanations of *specific language impairment* (*SLI*) (e.g., Leonard, 1989; Rice & Wexler, 1996). Children with SLI often omit bound morphemes in spontaneous and elicited spoken language samples in their preschool years (Rice, Wexler, & Hershberger, 1998), and morphosyntactic difficulties continue to characterize both spoken and written language disorders in their school-age years (Windsor, Scott, & Street, 2000). Not all dialects obligate the inclusion of inflectional morphemes in all contexts. African American English (AAE) allows the optional use of the third-person singular inflection in sentences such as *He drive a bus*. Thus, finite morpheme deletion is not an appropriate marker for diagnosing SLI in children learning AAE. Yet Oetting and MacDonald (2001) reported that grammatical difficulty with finite morphemes is evident even among children who speak less marked dialects of English, such as AAE. Oetting and Newkirk (2008) reported that other elements of syntactic complexity (e.g., subject relative clauses) have promise for identifying language disorder in dialectal speakers.

table 2.5 Inflectional Morphology (complete list of regular inflection morphemes in English)

Morpheme Type	Example Words	Allomorphs (Phonological Variations)
Plural	kites, boys, houses	-s, -z, - əz (*irregular:* mice, feet)
Possessive	Pete's, man's, juice's	-s, -z, - əz
Third-person singular	fights, wades, fixes	-s, -z, - əz
Past	walked, begged, waded	-t, -d, -əd (*irregular:* ate, saw, fought, hid, said, came)
Progressive	walking	-ing
Present participle	walking, hiding	-ing
Past participle	walked, hidden	-ed, -en (*irregular:* has seen, has come)
Comparative	bigger, prettier, higher	-er (*irregular:* better, more fun)
Superlative	biggest, prettiest, highest	-est (*irregular:* best, most fun)

Syntax

Syntax is the system of grammatical sentence structure. Fine points (*parameters*) of syntactic construction vary across languages, but syntactic universals (*principles*) can be detected as well. Linguists, such as Noam Chomsky (1957, 1965) and Steven Pinker (1994), use terms such as *argument, head,* and *IP* (for *inflected phrase*) and X-bar theory to describe universal grammar. In this book, traditional English grammar categories (*noun, verb, auxiliary verb,* etc.) are used to characterize syntactic roles. Across languages, verbs play a central role in developing and describing syntactic structure, dictating how a sentence conveys who did what to whom (Pinker, 1994).

One or more ***propositions*** constitute a sentence, each of which incorporates a ***predicate,*** which is the *event* or *state* indicated by the verb, and an ***argument,*** which names ***referents*** (i.e., *subjects* or *objects*) associated with the verb's event or state. The following proposition uses the predicate *eat* and the arguments *Java* (our dog) and her favorite thing, *cookies.* These sentences convey the same basic proposition (*Java + eat + cookie*), although illocutionary function (i.e., declarative, interrogative, imperative) and voice (i.e., active, passive) are altered:

> *Java ate the cookie.* [active, declarative]
>
> *The cookie was eaten by Java.* [passive, declarative]
>
> *Java, eat the cookie.* [imperative]
>
> *Java eats cookies.* [active, declarative]
>
> *Did Java eat the cookie?* [active, interrogative]
>
> *Was the cookie eaten by Java?* [passive, interrogative]

Active and passive forms can be ***paraphrases*** and have ***syntactic synonymy*** if they mean essentially the same thing. The ability to paraphrase is an important indicator of

syntactic proficiency and also of language comprehension, because
maintain a sentence's deep meaning while altering its surface form.
rogative) and comment forms (declarative) share a proposition, but th
locutionary speech acts (requesting information versus making a com
different intentions. The interrogative utterance *Does Java eat cookies*
from the meaning of the declarative form *Java eats cookies,* in that one
and the other does not. Thus, they are not paraphrases. On the other hand,   ⌣ok-
ies is a paraphrase of *Java eats cookies* because *Java = my dog.*

Interpropositional syntactic devices signal meaning connections among multiple
components of a sentence. Examples include attributive phrases (*Our chubby dog Java is a
glutton for cookies*), each of which could be a proposition of its own (*our dog is chubby, our
dog likes cookies, our dog is a glutton*). Other examples involve clausal relationships that
are temporal (*When I turned my head, Java ate the cookie*), causal (*Someone left the bag of
cookies on the floor, so Java ate them*), or disjunctive (*I would give you a cookie, Java, but
you're too chubby*). Some syntactic structures keep the finite structure of both clauses (*She
always eats cookies, which is making her fat*), whereas others combine a finite verb clause
with a nonfinite verb phrase (*I saw her licking up the crumbs*), as in this illustration of a
participial phrase with double underlining.

Clauses include a noun and a verb in a subject–predicate relationship. In a clause,
the predicate conveys the event or state of the proposition and dictates roles for the other
referents (arguments) in it. The sentence *I left the bag of cookies on the floor, and I went to
start the car* shows the coordination of two ***independent clauses*** joined by the coordinating conjunction *and.* It also includes an embedded nonfinite verb phrase elaboration (*to
start*). Because the subject of the two coordinated clauses is ***co-referential,*** a compound
verb phrase could be used to convey the same meaning (i.e., *I left the bag of cookies on the
floor and went to start the car*). This sentence also could be made more complex by relating events in a dependent clause to the main clause (e.g., *When I went to start the car and
left the cookies on the floor, Java started eating them*). The more structures incorporated
at deeper levels, the more complex a child's syntactic abilities can be presumed to be. It is
likely that a child who produces more complex sentences also can comprehend more complex sentences in the discourse of others.

From a developmental standpoint, coordinated independent clauses are easier to master than sentences with compound verb phrases, subordination, or multiple phrasal and
clausal embedding. For children in their preschool years, a straightforward method for
quantifying syntactic complexity is ***mean length of utterance (MLU).*** Such counts and
averages are made using base words and any inflectional morphemes for a corpus (i.e., body
or sample) of 50 to 100 spontaneous utterances.

Length-based measures continue to be useful for measuring spoken or written syntax
in the school-age years, but adjustments must be made so that run-on sentences do not
inflate the MLU. A *run-on sentence* includes three or more independent clauses strung
together in a series. Although run-ons are longer, they are not necessarily more mature.
Thus, simple counts of sentence length would inflate MLU and suggest higher syntactic
competence than a child actually possesses. Most typically developing children become
proficient at conjoining main clauses at a relatively early point, before they can handle
many other forms of complex syntax. For example, the following sentence is constructed
entirely of independent clauses:

> *The children ran across the room, and then they stopped, but they didn't see the
> books, and the books were sitting on the edge of the rug, so they tripped on them,
> and they fell, and they laughed, and they rolled on the floor.* [1 sentence; 44 words]

Although this sentence includes no grammatical errors, neither does it include any examples of later developing syntactic subordination or embedding. By contrast, the following sentence incorporates the same propositions but has 10 fewer words:

> *After running across the room, the children stopped, but they didn't see the books sitting on the edge of the rug, so they tripped on them and fell, laughing and rolling on the floor.* [1 sentence; 34 words]

An early language researcher, Kellogg W. Hunt (1965), recommended dividing utterances into T-units to capture growing syntactic ability to say more in fewer words. The label ***T-unit*** stands for *minimal terminable unit* (in contrast with run-on *interminable* units). A T-unit is a main clause and all other structures embedded in it or subordinated to it. Loban (1963) applied the term ***minimal communication unit*** (abbreviated ***C-unit***) to less formal spoken communication structures, including elliptical responses to questions and other incomplete but stand-alone forms.

Mean length of T-unit* or *C-unit (MLTU* or *MLCU) is a measure of syntactic complexity that is appropriate for school-age children. Unlike MLU, *MLTU* is computed as the average number of *words per T-unit* (rather than morphemes per utterance) in a sample. Division of sentences into T-units is illustrated in Table 2.6. In this case, results for the second sample (although too small on which to base a judgment) more accurately reflect its higher MLTU of 11.3 words, compared to the MLTU of 5.5 words for the multiple simple T-units of the first sample.

Syntactic ability involves forming and comprehending ***sentence structures*** that are sufficiently ***correct*** and ***complex***. An incorrect production might include glitches in verb agreement, pronoun inflection, or word order (e.g., *Us dog loves eat;* or *Java belong*). Sentences that are overly simple might not represent all the relationships among the propositions (e.g., *Java is a dog. She eats cookies. She is our dog.*).

table *2.6* Illustration Showing Paraphrases of the Same Content to Indicate How Mean Length of T-Unit (MLTU) Can Capture Evidence of Higher-Level Syntactic Structure

Example 1: Shorter T-units indicate less complexity.	**Example 2:** Longer T-units with the same propositional content indicate greater complexity.
$ Child	$ Child
C The children ran across the room, [6 words]	C After running across the room, the children stopped, [8 words]
C and then they stopped, [4 words]	
C but they didn't see the books, [6 words]	C but they didn't see the books sitting on the edge of the rug, [13 words]
C and the books were sitting on the edge of the rug, [11 words]	
C so they tripped on them, [5 words]	C so they tripped on them and fell, laughing and rolling on the floor. [13 words]
C and they fell, [3 words]	
C and they laughed, [3 words]	
C and they rolled on the floor. [6 words]	
[44 words / 8 T-units = 5.5 words MLTU]	[34 words / 3 T-units = 11.3 words MLTU]

Semantics

Semantics is the meaning system of language. The science of meaning, called ***semiotics,*** is the study of signs and symbols and their ability to represent meaning. It is meaning (not just vocabulary) that enables speakers and listeners to make mutual sense of messages, but a person's vocabulary (called a ***lexicon***) plays an important role in semantics.

Most linguistic symbols are considered arbitrary because they bear no physical resemblance to the things they represent (i.e., their ***referents***). The word *cat* is associated with feline creatures only because people who speak English have learned it that way. Literate language users also learn to associate more abstract terms, such as *feline,* with *cat,* forming these and hundreds of thousands of other associations of word with world knowledge across their lifespan.

Only ***onomatopoetic*** words, such as *meow* (the French say/spell this word *miaule;* Italians *miao;* Greeks *niaou;* and Chinese *miao*), represent phenomena directly, bearing a surface sound relationship to the concepts they represent. Similarly, in sign language, although most signs formed with the hands appear somewhat arbitrary, some are ***iconic*** and bear a surface visual relationship to the object to which they refer, such as the sign for *butterfly.* Other signs have an iconic link to the past, such as the sign for *girl,* which involves sliding the thumb along the cheek to allude to the bonnet ties of historical times. Many words carry multiple meanings. Regardless of origins, meanings can be understood only in context. For example, a person might hear a telephone *ring,* wear a *ring* around a finger, or clean a *ring* around a bathtub. Some meanings are literal references to actual events, and others have figurative meanings in some contexts but literal meanings in others (e.g., to *scratch the surface;* getting your *bell rung*).

An important question, and still much of a mystery, is what combination of nature and nurture allows young children to learn so many words so quickly in the early stages of development. The human brain can soak up tens of new words per day, hundreds per week, and thousands per year (Anglin, 1993). Differences have been found in the vocabulary input children receive based on sociocultural experiences within their families. Hart and Risley (1995) reported that preschoolers in the average professional family hear 2,100 words per hour, compared to 1,200 words per hour in the average working-class family and 600 words per hour in the average low-income family. These are what Hart and Risley called "meaningful differences," which may account, at least partially, for achievement gaps across socioeconomic groups of school-age children.

Although most children (particularly in middle-class homes) are bathed in rich word-learning experiences all day long, little formal word instruction occurs. Miller and Gildea (1987) estimated that teachers actively teach only about 200 new curricular words per year; yet students learn about 3,000 new words per year. Most of this vocabulary acquisition occurs seemingly automatically through spoken and written language interactions with people and books. By high school graduation, adolescents know 40,000 words if word roots alone are counted, two times that number if proper nouns and idiomatic phrases are added, and three to four times that number if the count includes all morphological variants of word roots, such as *write, wrote, written, writing, writer, rewrite, unwritten* (Miller & Gildea, 1987).

Although mechanisms of vocabulary acquisition are not fully understood, the human brain has evolved a high-level ability to learn words. The metaphor of a sponge captures the seeming ease of this process. Just as a damp sponge can absorb more than a dry one, a child who knows some verbal concepts finds it easier to learn more. This process of rapid association of words and their meanings is sometimes termed ***fast mapping*** or ***quick incidental learning (QUIL).*** Experiments using nonsense words or rare words have shown that children can learn new words with a single exposure, as one experiment showed when preschoolers learned to differentiate the new word *chromium* from other colors of luncheon trays (Carey & Bartlett, 1978). Importantly, the children did not confuse the color name with the label for the tray itself, the act of stacking it, or any of a number of actions, objects, and other concepts that were associated with the same experience. They grasped seemingly automatically that the reference was to the object's color, perhaps due to syntactic cues about the word's role in the sentence, a feature of cohesion called *lexical collocation.*

Semantics and syntax are closely integrated systems. Comprehension requires figuring out which semantic roles are played by which words and phrases. As discussed related to syntax, semantic roles are influenced by a sentence's verb. Fillmore (1968) recommended **case grammar** for describing language structure in terms of semantic roles (e.g., *agent, action, patient, instrument, location, object*), rather than syntactic ones (e.g., *subject, verb, indirect object, object*).

It is difficult to disentangle the semantic and syntactic features of verbs. Verbs can be categorized semantically as **action verbs** (e.g., *run, hit, push*) or **state verbs** (e.g., *is, seem, like*). Verbs also can be categorized as **concrete** or **abstract,** but concrete verbs (i.e., representing observable events) can be easily co-opted to figurative roles as abstract mental state verbs (e.g., *He <u>hit</u> on an idea* or *She <u>ran</u> into trouble*). Flexible and inventive use of symbols is a defining feature of human language use, and it is an important goal for children with language disorders.

Syntactic categories of verbs focus on whether they can take an object. **Transitive** verbs require an argument in the object as well as in the subject slot (e.g., *She hit the ball; He saw _____*). **Intransitive** verbs cannot take an object (e.g., *He was successful; She seemed unhappy*). **Ditransitive** (e.g., *give, put*) verbs obligate two subsequent arguments (e.g., *He gave her the book* [but not *He gave her*]; *He put the book on the table* [but not *He put the book*]). Some verbs have both transitive and intransitive meanings (e.g., *He felt the nubby book cover* and *He felt sick; She smelled the flower* and *The flower smelled good*).

Table 2.7 indicates other ways that words can relate based on lexical meaning within or across sentences. It also illustrates superordinate and subordinate hierarchical relationships.

table *2.7*   Lexical Relationships

Type	Definition	Examples
Synonym	A word with a highly similar or identical meaning of another with which it is interchangeable	*sick* is a synonym for *ill* *dog* is a synonym for *canine*
Antonym	A word with an opposite or nearly opposite meaning of another	*tall* is an antonym for *short* *dead* is an antonym for *alive*
Hypernym	A word that is more generic or broad than another given word whose meaning it fully entails (a superordinate relationship)	*vehicle* is a hypernym of *car, bus, train* *money* is a hypernym of *coin, dollar, quarter*
Hyponym	A word that entails part of the meaning of another given word but not all of it (a subordinate relationship)	*bus* is a hyponym of *vehicle* *dollar* is a hyponym of *money*
Homonym	A word that sounds alike or is spelled like another but means something different	*too* and *two* *there* and *their* *fluke* (of luck) and *fluke* (of a whale)

Pragmatics

Pragmatics is the system of appropriate language use in social contexts (Bates, 1976). It involves knowledge about how to vary verbal and nonverbal forms to communicate appropriately in varied social events. Language researchers have characterized pragmatics as "everything they used to throw out" when they analyzed language (Prutting, 1982).

Proficiency with pragmatics requires the integration of a wide range of cues for accomplishing varied communicative functions in a socially appropriate, contextually sound manner. Pragmatic competence is linked directly to social competence (Prutting, 1982) (see Personal Reflection 2.1), social cognition, and a *theory of mind* (Baron-Cohen, 1995). It incorporates knowledge about how to make one's intentions known and how to understand the intentions of others. Pragmatics plays a key role in constructing and comprehending connected discourse, making it possible to participate in conversation, tell or understand a story, or convey information in a manner that makes sense to others. Each of these aspects—intentionality, theory of mind, and discourse—is central to understanding pragmatics.

PERSONAL reflection *2.1*

"There is no way to interpret social competence unless communicative behavior and context are treated simultaneously."

Carold Prutting (1982, p. 132), a speech–language pathologist and language scientist, had an important influence on the field's appreciation of the importance of pragmatics.

Communicative functions are critical features of pragmatics. Intentional acts or functions are what speakers intend to *do* with an act of communication (i.e., its illocutionary force). When communication is successful, illocutionary and perlocutionary speech acts are consistent. Communicative functions include greeting, attention getting, requesting, commenting, responding, protesting, disagreeing, negating, persuading, entertaining, illustrating, emoting, chastising, and many more. Children who can express or comprehend only a limited range of communicative functions are likely to have difficulty communicating and getting along with others.

Theory of mind (ToM) refers to the human capacity to infer what another person knows or might be thinking and to intuit his or her intentions. In introducing the term, Premack and Woodruff (1978) noted, "A system of inferences of this kind is properly viewed as a theory, first, because such states are not directly observable, and secondly, because the system can be used to make predictions, specifically about the behavior of other organisms" (p. 515). ToM guides choices about what one should say based on assumptions about what one's communication partners already know (a requirement for implicature or presupposition, described previously in this chapter). Difficulty in forming ToM may explain pragmatic problems experienced by children with cognitive–communicative disorders, including children with autism spectrum disorders (Baron-Cohen, 1995), cognitive impairments (Abbeduto & Murphy, 2004), histories of abuse and neglect (Timler, Olswang, & Coggins, 2005), and even specific language impairment (Farrant, Fletcher, & Maybery, 2006).

A common approach to assessing ToM involves setting up a so-called false-belief scenario. For example, a child might observe a scene in which a girl doll hides a coin under a pillow while a boy doll watches. After the boy doll leaves the scene, the girl doll takes the coin from under the pillow and places it in a box instead. Then the boy doll is brought back into the scene, and the child is asked to predict where he will look first to find the coin. A child who has developed ToM will say that the doll will look first under the pillow, because that is where the doll saw it last and could not know that it has been moved. A child who has not developed ToM will expect the boy doll to look in the box where the *child* knows the object was moved (i.e., the box), even though the doll could not possibly have known that.

Discourse involves the organization of sentences into larger cohesive communication units. Discourse macrostructures (exceptions include poetry and self-talk) can be categorized into three basic types: *conversation, narration,* and *exposition.* Each can be further subcategorized into subtypes (see Table 2.8). Britton (1984) used the term *participant* to describe conversation as collaborative discourse. He contrasted it with *spectator* forms of discourse, such as narration and exposition, which tend to be preplanned and controlled by one partner, with others serving primarily as spectator, or audience.

Conversation draws on knowledge of pragmatic conventions. Prutting and Kirchner (1987) developed a 30-item list of them divided into three categories—verbal aspects, paralinguistic aspects, and nonverbal aspects. *Verbal aspects* comprise speech acts (both variety and whether they match); topic control (including selection, introduction, maintenance, and change); turn taking (including initiation, response, repair/revision, pause time, interruption/overlap, feedback to speakers, adjacency, contingency, and quantity/conciseness); lexical selection (both specificity/accuracy and cohesion); and variations of communicative style based on partner characteristics. *Paralinguistic aspects* comprise intelligibility, vocal intensity, vocal quality, prosody, and fluency. *Nonverbal aspects* include both kinesic and proxemic elements (physical proximity, physical contacts, body posture, foot/leg and hand/arm movements, gestures, facial expression, and eye gaze).

Narrative discourse can be embedded in a conversational context or occur as a primary communication event, such as reading a story, watching a movie, or recounting a personal narrative. Competence with stories is particularly critical for the acquisition of literacy (Wells, 1986). Stories also have strong implications for cognitive–emotional development, leading to understanding of how humans cope with problems, set goals, act on intentions, cope with disappointment, and persist in pursuits. Bruner (1985) described fully developed narratives as having not only a *landscape of action* but also a *landscape of consciousness* (requiring a ToM). Thus, stories have potential for addressing ToM difficulties in intervention, starting with dramatic play and later in written expression activities (see Part III of this book).

Expository texts may use a variety of macrostructures (see Table 2.8) to convey information. Exposition often takes literate forms, which are prominent in science and social studies textbooks, lectures, outlines, and instructions. Some expository texts are organized into descriptive hierarchies, with superordinate and subordinate categories, exemplars, and definitions. Others are organized with serial or procedural sequences. Still others present information as explanations of cause and effect, comparison and contrast, persuasion, opinion, and editorial.

Cohesive devices are used within multiple forms of connected discourse to relate concepts across sentence boundaries. Halliday and Hasan (1976) outlined four cohesive devices—reference, substitution, ellipsis, and conjunction.

Reference may be either *exophoric,* with reference to immediately observable components of the situation (e.g., *that book* [while pointing to the actual object]), or *endophoric,* with reference to other words in the text (e.g., *that book you read* ["pointing" with words to concepts represented by other words]). Personal pronouns (e.g., *he, she, it, they we*); demonstrative pronouns (*this, that, these, those, here, there, now, then*); and articles (e.g., *He bought a book. It was the one by Mark Twain*) all are tools of endophoric meaning. Paralinguistic intonation cues also can signal information that is given or new

table *2.8* Common Discourse Types and Structures

Conversation	Narration	Exposition
Social discourse	Narrative discourse	Expository discourse
Varied purposes	Varied purposes	Varied purposes
Social closeness	Entertaining	Instructing
Information exchange	Teaching moral lessons	Informing
Participant discourse	Spectator discourse	Persuading
Equal turn-taking	Author or one partner	Displaying knowledge
Negotiation of topic	controls topic	Spectator discourse
Presupposition	Signaled by opening	Author or one partner
May require repair	"Remember when . . ."	controls topic
Register varies with age and context	"Once upon a time . . ."	Presupposition of audience
Predictable structure	High point or problem	or partner knowledge
Greeting	Conclusion	Structure varies with purpose
Introducing topic	"It was quite a day"	Topic introduction
Maintaining topic	"The end"	Organized information
Contingent on prior turn	Story grammar	Closure
Topic shading	Setting	Description
Topic shifting	Problem or conflict	Definition
Termination	Intentional goal setting	Hierarchical categories
Leave taking	Plan	Compare and contrast
May be spoken or written	Action	Illustration
Email	Outcome	Analogy
Text messaging	Ending	Example
Instructional	Subtypes	Procedural
Teachers control	Personal narrative	Process
Convey procedure	Biography	Cause and effect
Convey content	Novel	Temporal sequence
Invite discussion	Mystery	Argument/persuasion
Students take fewer and shorter turns	Adventure	Statement of position
Predictable structure	Science fiction	Attempt to influence others'
Initiate	Short story	opinions or actions
Respond	Fable	Logical arguments
Evaluate	Parable	Inductive
Interview		Deductive
Interviewer		Conclusions
Controls topics		
Asks questions		
Interviewee takes longer turns		

Source: Adapted from Nelson, 1992; includes information based on Britton, 1984; Cazden, 1988; and Stein and Glenn, 1982.

(e.g., *I wanted a little <u>dog</u>* [not a cat] versus *I wanted a <u>little</u> dog* [not a big one]). Endophoric reference may be ***anaphoric*** (i.e., referring backward to an earlier item in the text) or ***cataphoric*** (i.e., referring forward to something coming up). An example of anaphoric cohesive reference is the pronoun *he,* referring to Marco Polo in the text:

> <u>Marco Polo</u> wanted to find another way to India, China, and Japan. <u>He</u> knew that those Asian countries could be the source of many wonderful things.

In this same passage, the cataphoric reference to *many wonderful things* prepares the reader for a later description of gold and beautiful colored silks.

Substitution is a cohesive device that involves introducing a common word once the specific referent has been established. Lexical substitution also can take advantage of ***lexical collocation*** (same placement or role within sentences) to convey cohesion. In the prior example, *those Asian countries,* was substituted for the three exemplars—*India, China, and Japan.* The phrase *the source* also refers to the same entities. Children who can take advantage of such cues have access to important tools for comprehending complex texts and expanding their vocabularies.

Ellipsis is a cohesive device that involves leaving out a word or phrase that would be redundant, making discourse more concise. Ellipsis can be used either in the case of co-referential nouns (*John played and John sang* becomes *John played and sang*) or verbs (*John sang ballads and Donna sang the blues* becomes *John sang ballads and Donna the blues*).

Conjunction was Halliday and Hasan's (1976) fourth category. As discussed in the section on syntax, conjunctions convey relationships among propositions, such as temporal (*while, since*), causal (*because, so that*), additive (*and*), disjunctive (*but*), alternative (*either . . . or*), or logical (*if . . . then*). Cohesion through conjunction also refers to transition words and phrases for conveying relationships across sentences or larger units of discourse (e.g., *however, therefore, on the other hand, additionally, also*). Children who do not make use of such elements may have difficulty comprehending what they hear or read and formulating cohesive discourse expressively.

SUMMARY

This section has described the phonological, morphemic, syntactic, semantic, and pragmatic parameters of language. Phonology is the sound system of language. Morphology is the system of smallest meaningful units. Morphemes play both semantic and syntactic roles. Syntax is the system of grammatical rules for forming (and comprehending) sentences. Semantics is the system of meaning. It incorporates vocabulary, but the creation of meaning involves much broader skills than word meaning alone.

Finally, pragmatics is the system for using language appropriately within social contexts. Pragmatics incorporates components of communicative intention; presupposition based on a theory of mind, and varied forms of discourse—conversation, narration, and exposition. Four devices were described for building cohesion across sentence boundaries—reference, substitution, ellipsis, and conjunction.

Content, Form, and Use

An alternative to the five parameters taxonomy is one that describes language as three intersecting systems—***content, form,*** and ***use.*** A Venn diagram showing overlap among three circles representing content, form, and use was popularized by Bloom and Lahey (1978) in their classic textbook on language development and disorders (see Personal Reflection 2.2). Figure 2.7 shows an adaptation of that figure overlaid with the five parameters discussed in the previous section.

PERSONAL reflection 2.2

"For individuals using language and for children learning language, the components of content, form, and use come together in understanding and saying messages."

Lois Bloom, a language scientist, and **Margaret Lahey,** a speech–language pathologist (Bloom & Lahey, 1978, p. 21), promoted a transformational view of language intervention based on normal language development and a model of language that remains highly influential.

Describing language as intersecting systems of content, form, and use requires less jargon (than *phonology, morphology, syntax, semantics, pragmatics*), making it a useful taxonomy for communicating with a wider audience of teachers and parents. The categories of language—content, form, and use—apply across the lifespan but are particularly helpful in describing emergent language development.

Content refers to the topics and concepts of communication, as well as semantic roles, such as *agent, action, object,* and *patient.* In simple terms, content is what language is about. In Figure 2.7, the portion of the circle labeled "Content" aligns with parameters of "Morphology" and "Semantics." Children who have difficulty learning the content of language may communicate primarily about concrete topics using simple, unelaborated forms and vocabulary that may not fit the context.

Form refers to language structure and its physical representation. Form relates to syntax but also involves the phonological and morphological shape of words, including inflections for fitting them into grammatical roles. Children who have difficulty with the form of language are likely to produce unelaborated sentences with grammatical errors and may struggle with reading decoding and strategies for spelling unfamiliar words (Catts & Kamhi, 2005). Children with specific language impairment (SLI) have particular difficulty acquiring morphosyntactic forms (Leonard, 1998). It is now also recognized that children with nonspecific language impairment (i.e., without a discrepancy between their nonverbal IQ scores and language test scores) have similar (but more severe) characteristics to those with SLI (Rice, 2004; Tomblin, Zhang, Weiss, Catts, & Ellis Weismer, 2004).

Use refers to functions of language for achieving communicative purposes in socially acceptable ways. Thus, language *use* aligns with *pragmatics.* Children who have difficulty with the use of language to achieve communicative intentions (and to recognize the intentions and suppositions of others)

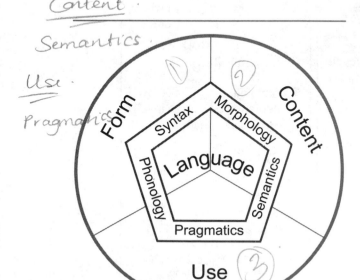

figure 2.7

The Domains of Content, Form, and Use Aligned with the Five Parameters of Language

are at risk for difficulty with social interaction. They may not be perceived as desirable communication partners, which may lead to additional difficulties as they move through school and prepare for independent living.

Language Levels and Modalities

A taxonomy with promise, but used less traditionally, is a levels-by-modality model. It can be described as having two to four levels—*sound/word* and *sentence/discourse*—across four modalities—*listening, speaking, reading,* and *writing.* This model is particularly useful for characterizing language abilities and disabilities during the school-age years, when reading and writing become a primary focus of language learning. The approach makes use of common terminology. Thus, it has advantages for facilitating communication among clinicians, teachers, parents, and students and captures the importance of helping children bridge their knowledge across language levels and modalities.

Collapsing the four levels of language into two is consistent with a simple view of reading (Gough & Tunmer, 1986) as encompassing reading decoding and comprehension. Beginning readers must apply sound- and word-level knowledge (e.g., phonemic awareness, the alphabetic principle, and vocabulary) to develop *word decoding* and *word recognition.* Simultaneously, they must apply sentence/discourse knowledge to achieve *reading comprehension.* Children with learning disabilities, attention deficits, and other cognitive–communicative disabilities have particular difficulty with such abilities, as do children with specific and nonspecific language impairment. Beginning writers must be able to draw on higher-level knowledge of sentence/discourse structures to organize their words into sentences and ideas into paragraphs to achieve a communicative purpose. These reciprocal functions are illustrated in Figure 2.8. To produce written language, children must think

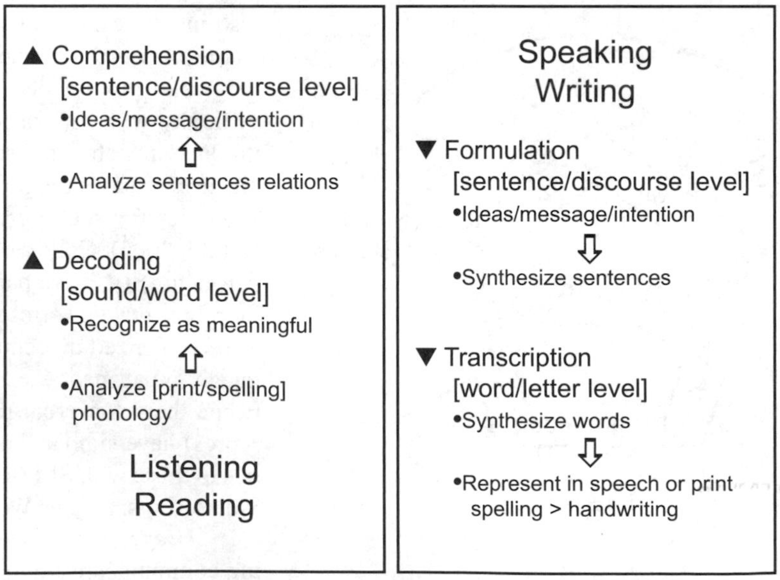

▲ Comprehension
[sentence/discourse level]
•Ideas/message/intention
⇧
•Analyze sentences relations

▲ Decoding
[sound/word level]
•Recognize as meaningful
⇧
•Analyze [print/spelling]
phonology

Listening
Reading

Speaking
Writing

▼ Formulation
[sentence/discourse level]
•Ideas/message/intention
⇩
•Synthesize sentences

▼ Transcription
[word/letter level]
•Synthesize words
⇩
•Represent in speech or print
spelling > handwriting

figure *2.8*

Reciprocal-Processing Components in the Levels-by-Modality Model of Spoken and Written Language

about what they want to say and be able to transcribe that inner language to words on a page, spelling words so that others can recognize them, even if they are not correct according to dictionary spellings.

SUMMARY

Two taxonomies were discussed in the prior section and this one. Both offer alternatives to the traditional five-category system of phonology, morphology, syntax, semantics, and pragmatics discussed previously. Although the technically more sophisticated five-category system is helpful for guiding assessment processes and intervention planning, its jargon makes it less than ideal for communicating with parents and teachers about what is right or wrong with a child's language systems. The three-category system of content, form, and use works well for guiding questions of assessment with young children. A levels-by-modalities model works well for describing the strengths and needs of school-age children and adolescents. A deep understanding of a particular child's strengths and needs can be constructed best by using the multiple taxonomies to view a child's language and literacy abilities from more than one angle.

Cultural–Linguistic Variation

Cultural–linguistic diversity within individuals, families, and larger systems must be considered when designing language and literacy assessment and intervention. Data on racial and ethnic diversity in the United States showed 74.7 percent of Americans reporting themselves as White; 21.1 percent Black or African American; 4.3 percent Asian; 0.8 percent American Indian or Alaska Native; 0.1 percent Native Hawaiian or Other Pacific Islander; 1.9 percent two or more races; and 6 percent other. Data on ethnicity showed 14.5 percent of the American population to be Hispanic or Latino. A fact sheet based on the 2005 American Community Survey showed that almost 52 million people in the United States (19.4 percent of the population over age 5) speak a language other than English at home (U.S. Census Bureau, 2006).

Differences in cultural–linguistic experience influence language acquisition in complex ways. Language learning is a dynamic process, and language systems are dynamic as well (see Personal Reflection 2.3). Cultural competence and family-centered interventions require sensitivity to the cultural–linguistic milieu in which each child develops and a sincere desire to understand cultures different from one's own. Cross, Bazron, Dennis, and Isaacs (1989) described *cultural competence* for health professionals as evolving over an extended period, and comprising at least five steps: (1) valuing diversity, (2) conducting self-assessment, (3) managing the dynamics of difference, (4) acquiring and institutionalizing cultural knowledge, and (5) adapting to diversity and the cultural contexts of particular communities they serve.

PERSONAL reflection 2.3

"Language and literacy acquisition are forms of socialization, in this case socialization into mainstream ways of using language in speech and print, mainstream ways of taking meaning, and of making sense of experience. . . . The student is acquiring a new identity, one that at various points may conflict with her initial enculturation and socialization, and with the identities connected to other social practices in which she engages."

James Gee (1990, p. 67), a sociolinguist, has illuminated the role of language diversity and conflicts faced by children and adolescents in the formation of social identity.

....

Language variation is a broad term for describing the pluralistic nature of speaking communities across United States. Wolfram, Adger, and Christian (1999) wrote:

> We use the term *language variation* to refer to the fact that a language is not uniform. Instead, it varies, corresponding to sociocultural characteristics of groups of people, such as their cultural background, geographical location, social class, gender, or age. *Language variation* may also refer to differences in the way that language is used in different situations such as in the home, the community, and the school, and on different occasions such as telling a friend about a trip or planning a trip with a travel agent. (p. 1)

Two primary categories of language variation are *bilingualism* (or *multilingualism*) and *dialect difference*. Such categories blur, however, in real life. Spanish-influenced English cannot be easily categorized as either Spanish or English. Rather, it involves a mixture of two languages by people participating in diverse language communities. Sociolinguists disagree about whether African American English should be considered a language or a dialect. As part of the national debate when Ebonics was recognized officially by the school board of Oakland, California, as the primary language of the majority of students in the district, the Linguistic Society of America passed a resolution (passed in 1997; reprinted in Baugh, 2000), which included the following statement:

> The distinction between "languages" and "dialects" is usually made more on social and political grounds than on purely linguistic ones. For example, different varieties of Chinese are popularly regarded as "dialects," though their speakers cannot understand each other, but speakers of Swedish and Norwegian, which are regarded as separate "languages," generally understand each other. What is important from a linguistic and educational point of view is not whether AAVE [African American Vernacular English] is called "language" or a "dialect" but rather that its systematicity be recognized. (pp. 117–118)

Dual Language Learning

The United States is a nation of immigrants. Other than American Indians and other indigenous peoples, the ancestors of all Americans either immigrated by choice or were brought to the country against their will by the slave trade. Immigration continues to add to the cultural–linguistic diversity (CLD) of U.S. children. McCardle and Leung (2006) reported that nearly one in five Americans speaks a language other than English, the most common being Spanish.

Influences of dual language learning are not based on any one factor. Roseberry-McKibbin (2007) listed multiple factors that affect language and literacy development for children learning more than one language:

> (a) languages spoken in the home, (b) parents' educational level, (c) country of birth of the student and parents, (d) length of residence in the United States, (e) socioeconomic status, (f) student's age and gender, (g) generational membership (first, second, third generation in the United States), (h) neighborhood and peer group, (i) degree of acculturation into American life. (p. 104)

Around the world, it is the norm for children to be engaged in learning more than one language at a time. Genesee, Paradis, and Crago (2004) recommended the term *dual language learners* to describe children who are either *simultaneous bilingual* or *second-language learners.* **Simultaneous bilingual children** "learn two or more languages from birth or at least starting within the first year after birth" (p. 4) through parents, grandparents, and other caregivers, so they have two first languages. **Second-language learners** begin to learn a second language after their first language is largely established (by approximately 3 years of age).

Second-language learners in U.S. schools often are referred to as *English language learners* (ELLs; McCardle & Leung, 2006). Such children face special challenges in acquiring English literacy along with English language, but research is revealing a complex picture of influences (see Personal Reflection 2.4). Language-influenced variations in pronunciation are often described as speaking with an **accent.** The influence of the first-language (L1) phonology on the second-language (L2) speaking patterns may be detected in adult learners, long after they gain grammatical competence in the second language.

PERSONAL reflection 2.4

"[An] example is Henry Kissinger, who retained his thick German accent although he is an otherwise successful second-language learner. The linguist Roman Jakoson, his followers fondly recall, had the ability to lecture in more than two dozen different languages, all of which came out sounding like Russian."

Ellen Bialystok and **Kenji Hakuta** (Bialystok & Hakuta, 1994, pp. 75–76), both linguists, named their book *In Other Words: The Science and Psychology of Second-Language Acquisition.*

Dialect Differences

Everyone who speaks a language speaks a dialect of it (Pinker, 1994). Wolfram et al., (1999) defined the term *dialect* as referring to "a variety of a language associated with a regionally or socially defined group of people" (p. 1). They also noted that the term *dialect,* when used as it is by sociolinguists, is neutral, in that "no evaluation is implied, either positive or negative" (p. 1). Popular uses of the term *dialect,* however, often carry connotations of social value, with some dialects carrying higher status than others. Wolfram and his colleagues emphasized that such preferences are matters of social influence, not linguistic superiority, and that "correctness involves decisions based on social, not linguistic, acceptability" (p. 8).

Most language tests and informal language sample analysis techniques in the United States and United Kingdom are built around standard English norms. The standard language of a country, such as *standard American English (SAE),* is defined politically by the form of spoken and written language used for a country's official business. Wolfram et al. (1999) pointed out that there is "really no single dialect that corresponds to a standard English" (p. 14). Rather, there is the formal version that includes the norms prescribed in grammar books and a number of informal versions in different speech communities in different regions of the country.

SUMMARY

Every person in the world looks through cultural blinders, at least to some extent. Each person's cultural and language experiences seem to him or her to be the normal, natural way that things should be. It takes conscious awareness to step back and consider whether other ways of doing things might be more normal and natural to other people, including clients and families.

Although clinicians cannot be expected to be familiar with every culture and language in a pluralistic society, they should be aware of the factors associated with language diversity, the processes of second-language learning, the nature of comparative linguistic analyses of key features, and the influence of bilingualism or second-language acquisition on learning to read and write. Clinicians also should be skilled at using cultural informants and interpreters to assist them in providing appropriate services to children whose families are culturally and linguistically diverse.

CHAPTER SUMMARY

Classification systems for language components and related components of speech and communication have implications for clinicians assessing a child's current strengths and weaknesses across language subsystems. Although spoken and written language abilities depend on the language user's *implicit* knowledge of the parameters of language, language clinicians require *explicit* knowledge of these parameters to diagnose and treat disorders of language and communication.

Classification systems organize approaches to observation and description so that all domains are covered and clinicians can convey a fully developed picture of a child's or adolescent's abilities. Assessment often starts with consideration of the relative involvement of speech, language, and communication systems, regardless of the choice of formal test. When describing language parameters, clinicians refer to phonology, morphology, syntax, semantics, and pragmatics. Alternatively, they may describe language as involving content, form, and use. The final system that was described in this chapter was a language-levels-by-modalities model, which is particularly useful for describing spoken and written language during the school-age years.

The chapter ended with a discussion of cultural linguistic diversity. The process of developing cultural competence is viewed as an extended one and one that requires an awareness of one's own cultural bias. Cultural competence also requires that one appreciate the rich experiences associated with cultural and linguistic diversity. In addition, individual clinicians must draw on multiple resources to understand a particular child's language-learning experiences. No language or dialect is viewed as being linguistically superior to another. Clinicians are advised to appreciate that a child and family may have multiple literacies, including a rich awareness of a diverse experiential or world view.

EXERCISES *and* STUDY QUESTIONS

1. For each of the five systems of language (phonology, morphology, syntax, semantics, and pragmatics), provide a basic description. Then name the primary symptoms of disorder associated with each system.

2. Practice with a partner. Take turns having a conversation in which one of you selects one of Grice's (1975) maxims to violate. The other should indicate which principle of implicature was being violated. Then observe others engaged in natural conversations.

3. Look for examples of each of the rules of implicature in operation and the kinesic mechanisms described by Ekman and Friesen (1969). Describe examples and compare them with those observed by peers, perhaps on a communication discussion board.

4. Describe the differences between a dialect and a language. What dialect do you speak?

5. What are some of the differences between simultaneous bilingualism and sequential second-language learning?

CHAPTER three

Language/Literacy and Related Systems

LEARNING *objectives*

After studying this chapter, you should be able to do the following:

1. Discuss seven theoretical perspectives represented by the acronym BLB-CCCS: biological, linguistic, behavioral, cognitive connectionist, cognitive constructivist, cognitive–emotional, and social interactionist.

2. Discuss the six principles of system theory.

3. Describe cognitive–linguistic, sensory–motor, social–emotional, and familial–cultural–educational systems.

4. Fill in components of a "pinball wizardry" model of language processing.

Understanding language development and disorders requires the consideration of more than language. Typical development involves synergistic advances in *internal* neuro–cognitive– linguistic, sensory–motor, and social–emotional systems. These advances are influenced by other systems that are *external* to the child. External systems include cultural systems conveyed primarily through the family and societal systems conveyed primarily through schooling. Internal and external systems interact dynamically, with bidirectional influences. Understanding these systems contributes to the ability to answer questions introduced in Chapter 1 about communication processes that might be relatively impaired or spared (the communication *processes* model), what the child needs to be able to do to function in important everyday activities (the communication *needs* model), and opportunities the child has to participate (the *participation* model).

Stages within developmental domains serve as heuristics to organize concepts about advances in development. Although theorists generally describe starting and ending points, stages are not as discrete as these descriptions imply. Stages represent qualitatively distinguishable characteristics arranged along a temporal continuum more like a ramp (i.e., without clear boundaries) than a set of stairs. Developmental stage theories guide assessment and help clinicians know what to target next in language intervention, but they also can be confusing. For example, how does Brown's (1973) Stage IV relate to Piaget's (1926/1969) Stage IV?

Figure 3.1 provides an overview of how these and other stages align in time. Although patterns of ebb and flow are linked across systems, individual differences exist in typical development; at any point, advances in one domain may eclipse those in another. If a strand of coordinated development gets too far out of synchrony, however, either ahead or behind, the atypical pattern of development may be symptomatic of disorder.

Theoretical Accounts

Explanations for language and literacy development are plentiful, resulting in discrepant accounts across disciplines and theorists. Interventionists who are unaware of the theoretical roots and rationale for their clinical choices may function more like technicians than clinicians. Technicians follow technical procedures step by step and without question; clinicians have a rationale for their assessment and intervention choices and use questions strategically. Moreover, clinicians think below the surface about what might be happening in the brains of the children whose language and literacy systems they are attempting to influence.

A Key Debate

Scientists and philosophers have argued for centuries about **nature** versus **nurture** (also called **nativism** versus **empiricism**). Around 300 BCE, Plato took the position (in *Phaedo*) that children are born with knowledge, so that development is merely the recollection of what one already knows. Seventeenth-century French philosopher René Descartes, also a nativist, attributed only a small role to the nurturing influences of experience. John Locke, an English contemporary of Descartes, took the opposite (empiricist) view that no ideas are innate. Locke presaged modern debates by arguing that human beings are innately equipped with minds capable of higher-level operations that set them apart from other species but not with pre-established bodies of knowledge. In his "Essay Concerning Human Understanding," he asked, "How comes [the mind] to be furnished? . . . Whence has it all the materials of reason and knowledge? To this I answer, in one word, from *experience*."

figure 3.1

Alignment of Development Milestones from Birth to Age 5

	1 mo.	4 mo.	8 mo.	12 mo.	18 mo.	24 mo.	30 mo.	36 mo.	3.5 yr.	4 yr.	5 yr.

Bates's Stages of Intentional Communication Development

Preintentional Perlocutionary	Intentional Illocutionary	Locutionary

Piaget's Stages of Cognitive Development (First Two Only)

Sensorimotor
Preoperational

SM I Reflexive	SM II Control of reflexive	SM III Repeats actions of others	SM IV Goal-directed and intentional	SM V New means to old ends	SM VI New means through mental combinations	Early Preoperational			Late Preoperational

Greenspan's Stages of Cognitive Emotional Development

I Shared attention and regulation	II Engagement and relating	III Purposeful emotional interaction	IV Social problem solving	V Creating ideas	VI Connecting ideas and thinking logically

Brown's Stages of Morphosyntactic Development

Pre Stage I	Early Stage I 1.0–1.5 Basic semantic relations	Late Stage I 1.5–2.0 Modulation of meaning	Stage II 2.0–2.5 Modalities of sentences	Stage III 2.5–3.25	Stage IV 3.25–3.75	Stage V 3.75–4.25 Embedding and coordination	Post Stage V 4.25+

Context-determined comprehension strategies

Source: Based on theoretical descriptions by Elizabeth Bates (Bates, Camaioni, & Volterra, 1975), Roger Brown (1973), Stanley Greenspan (1997; Greenspan & Wieder, 2005), and Jean Piaget (1926/1969).

The debate today centers around two similar questions relevant for clinicians: What is in the "black box" of the human brain and mind, and how much does it matter? What is outside the black box, and what role does it play? Nativists argue that the black box is filled with innately determined linguistic knowledge as part of a specialized language acquisition *module.* They say that the slate of the newborn human mind is far from blank. Linguist Noam Chomsky (1980), in *Rules and Representations,* argued, "We do not really learn language; rather, grammar grows in the mind" (p. 134). Stephen Pinker pursued a similar theme in two of his books, *The Language Instinct* (1994) and *The Blank Slate: The Modern Denial of Human Nature* (2002).

The empiricist view has been argued by psychologist and behaviorist B. F. Skinner (1957). In his book *Verbal Behavior* (published, incidentally, the same year that Chomsky published *Syntactic Structures*), Skinner argued that speech and communication are simply forms of behavior that can be explained entirely by the structure and history of environmental influence. He argued that any reference to mental structure is unnecessary and unscientific; it is only what is outside the black box that matters.

A third position, currently the most prominent, is that the content of the black box does matter but only in the sense proposed by Locke. According to this view, people are born knowing nothing but capable of learning anything (Sampson, 2005). The brain uses generic information-processing mechanisms to learn language, which is accorded no unique status, and the brain includes no modules set aside exclusively for language learning. This position, which was argued passionately by Elizabeth Bates, is summarized in a compendium of essays published posthumously in her honor, *Beyond Nature–Nurture* [emphasis added] (Tomasello & Slobin, 2005).

A final perspective on the nature versus nurture debate is that it is a false dichotomy. In the book *Nature Via Nurture* [emphasis added], Ridley (2003) argued that the debate should be put to rest. A bio-maturational perspective attributes critical roles to both nature *and* nurture in switching on the 30,000 or so human genes that determine how the human brain is structured. Nurture is required if nature is to unfold as it should.

Seven Theoretical Accounts

This section summarizes seven theoretical positions that influence clinical decisions regarding language assessment and intervention (summarized in Table 3.1). They are represented with the acronym BLB-CCCS—biological, linguistic, behavioral, cognitive connectionist, cognitive constructivist, cognitive–emotional, and social interactionist.

Biological Maturation Theory

Biological theorists are less concerned about the nature of language than the genetic and neurological systems that support it. Biological explanations might appear to be essentially nativist, but they are neutral, allowing for interactions among genetic and environmental influences (e.g., Ridley, 2003).

Norman Geschwind (1984), a neurologist, noted neuropsychological similarities between children with developmental language disorders, including dyslexia, and adults with aphasia. Howard Gardner, a psychologist, worked with Geschwind in Boston, studying adults with aphasia and also children. Out of this work, Gardner (1983) developed his theory of *multiple intelligences,* including a specialized linguistic intelligence associated with dedicated brain modules, such as Broca's area, Wernicke's area, the arcuate fasciculus, the angular gyrus, and the occipitotemporal region. Other neuroscientists have added evidence that the cerebellum and thalamus play special roles in language and literacy learning.

Almost all current theorists incorporate biological explanations into their theories. Theoretical accounts differ, however, with regard to brain specialization. Those that lean toward linguistic theory see the brain as having specialized language-learning *modules,* with certain regions of the brain playing specialized roles in language and literacy learning. Those that lean toward cognitive connectionist theory see the brain as being specialized only to a point, with much more plasticity than might have been previously imagined. Integrated accounts allow that neural networks and systems may be activated (linguistic theorists) or constructed (cognitive connectionists) as they process input that comes through exposure to linguistically encoded information from the environment. Biological maturationists recognize genetic predisposition, development, and experience as working together to form more efficient neural networks as development proceeds. These theorists cite evidence based on neuropathology (e.g., symptoms associated with focal lesions in adult aphasia) but also from static and dynamic neuroimaging techniques. *Static* imaging techniques include measures of brain size proportions from computerized tomography (CT) or magnetic resonance imaging (MRI) scans. *Dynamic* imaging techniques include functional magnetic resonance imaging (fMRI), evoked response potentials (ERPs), magnetoencephalography (MEG), and other techniques for sensing metabolic or electrical activity in the brain.

Linguistic Innateness Theory

Linguistic theorists view language as a uniquely human talent, not a cultural invention. Linguistic innateness theory is the classical nativist position. Its major proponents are Noam Chomsky (1957, 1980) and Stephen Pinker (1994, 2002). Linguistic theorists emphasize the role of phylogenetic development of human language capability through evolution of the species, regardless of culture. Linguistic innateness theorists minimize the role of language input and social interaction during development.

According to linguistic theorists, *universal grammar (UG)* is an innate human faculty, consisting of a finite set of rules that can generate an infinite variety of sentences. The regular aspects of language are generated by these rules. Irregular aspects are idiomatic and must be learned as part of the lexicon, not syntax. Formal grammar is the end product of language acquisition, following a series of intermediate grammars constructed by the dedicated (and genetically determined) *language acquisition device (LAD)* (as illustrated in Figure 3.2). This process is presumed to require only minimal exposure to the language of the environment. Linguistic theory assigns a primary role for language acquisition to modules in the brain but without explanation. Linguistic theorists argue that direct teaching cannot explain normal development, and efforts to teach language are likely to have little success, which could be discouraging to clinicians.

Evidence cited by linguistic theorists includes observation of the universal development of spoken language across all cultures with minimal input (e.g., as in the fast mapping of new vocabulary) and no formal instruction. Logical arguments of these theorists point to the paucity of input required for most children to induce highly mature language rules by age 5, at a time when they do not yet demonstrate the cognitive skills needed for inductive and analogical reasoning for more general purposes. The conclusion of such reasoning is that the language faculty or talent must be unique to humans and largely innate.

Behaviorist Theory

Behaviorists take the position that language is just another behavior to be learned. This is the classical empiricist position. Behaviorists view language as *verbal behavior,* which is essentially under the control of consequences mediated by others. B. F. Skinner (1957) described four verbal operants (*echoic, mand, tact,* and *intraverbal*) that are particularly

table 3.1 Summary of Seven Theoretical Perspectives

	Biological Maturation	Linguistic	Behaviorism
Nature of Language	Language is a product of brain structures and functions (affected by genetic and environmental influences), which play a primary role in supporting language acquisition.	Language is a specifically human talent (not a cultural invention). Language input and social interaction have minimal influence on development; an innate language acquisition device plays the major role in helping children acquire adult grammar.	Language is verbal behavior that is learned through shaping by antecedent and consequent events, which increase or decrease the frequency of specific behaviors.
Key Assumptions	Some macrostructures are more critical than others for language and literacy (Broca's and Wernicke's areas, arcuate fasciculus, angular gyrus, temporo–occipital lobe, cerebellum, thalamus) Microstructures (neurons, axons and dendrites, genes and metabolism) contribute to language acquisition. Tuning and pruning of neural networks is guided by genetic predisposition, development, and experience working together.	Universal grammar is an innate human faculty. Formal grammar is the end product of a series of intermediate grammars guided by a genetically determined language acquisition device (LAD). Through the LAD, the parameters of a particular language are learned within the framework of the principles of a universal grammar. Direct teaching cannot explain normal language acquisition.	The units of acquisition are not linguistic rules but functional acts, defined by how they control and are reinforced by the environment. Key functional acts are echoic, mand, tact, and intraverbal. Operant conditioning shapes the development of language through the influence of antecedent and consequent events on behavior involving three contingences: (1) discriminative stimulus, (2) response, and (3) consequence. Positive and negative reinforcement are consequences that increase behavior; punishment and extinction are consequences that decrease behavior.
Major Proponents	Norman Geschwind Albert M. Galaburda Sally Shaywitz & Bernard Shaywitz Virginia Berninger Bruce Pennington	Noam Chomsky Steven Pinker	B. F. Skinner Donald M. Baer O. Ivar Lovaas

Cognitive Connectionism	Cognitive Constructivism	Cognitive–Emotional	Social Interactionism
Language is learned, not innate. It relies on generic cognitive information-processing (attention, memory, etc.) and pattern-recognition mechanisms. Language input leads some neural connections to be strengthened by repeated activation, while others are weakened.	Language is a symbol system for representing concepts. Language is not innate, but cognitive precursors are. Evolution of thought and language both start with disequilibrium between current cognitive schemas and new evidence, followed by adaptation and elaboration.	Language is a means for connecting with others and expressing one's sense of identity. Development depends on intact biological systems and nurturing relationships with caregivers. Emotional security is the foundation on which other cognitive and language abilities are built.	Language is a tool of social interaction and cognitive development, although language and cognition are separate. Sociocultural experiences influence language development and thinking. Adult mediation plays a role in helping children construct knowledge of language and the world.
Language is defined in terms of patterns of a particular language, rather than an intrinsic universal grammar. Major roles are assigned to general cognitive information-processing abilities, including attention, perception, working memory, and retrieval. As information is attended to and perceived, neural networks (PDP mechanisms) are strengthened by multiple exposures to patterns, which are learned. Other competing connections are weakened and eventually disappear. The learning of forms is cued by their functions, with those that regularly serve the same functions learned first.	Conceptual schemas are key units. Adaptation processes include assimilation of new information into a current schema and accommodation of a schema to fit new data. Higher representational schemas evolve out of lower sensorimotor ones. Language symbols represent cognitive schemas; nonverbal symbols also may represent concepts. Language is neither innate nor learned but emerges as a result of the child's constructivist activity. Development consists of a series of three qualitatively different stages: sensorimotor, representational, and formal operations.	Language develops when children feel emotionally secure and attached. Units are communication circles that become increasingly elaborated. Either dysfunctional biological systems or caregiver problems can be at the root of interaction difficulties. Development proceeds through six stages or levels with emotional development paving the path to symbol development.	Language develops because of humans' propensity to interact socially. Important units are social interactions with intentional and symbolic communication. Thought and language are related, but there is a prelinguistic period in the development of thought and a preintellectual period in the development of language. Scaffolding in dyadic interactions with a more mature mediator is the main mechanism of development. Parents play important role in supporting language development by adjusting their linguistic input and responding contingently on child's output.
Elizabeth Bates Brian MacWhinney Michael Tomasello	Jean Piaget John H. Flavell	Erik Erickson Anna Freud Selma Fraiberg T. Berry Brazelton Stanley Greenspan Serena Wieder	Lev Vygotsky Jerome Bruner Betty Hart & Todd Risley Gordon Wells

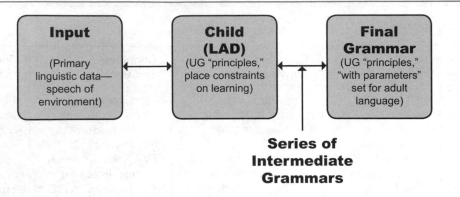

Series of Intermediate Grammars

figure 3.2

Model of Chomsky's Language Acquisition Device (LAD)

Source: Adapted from Cairns, 1996; Crain, 1991/1994.

relevant to the development of verbal communication skills. Strict behaviorists oppose the use of mentalistic terms such as *idea, plan,* and *concept.*

Explanations offered by behaviorists rely on principles of **operant conditioning,** which posit antecedent and consequent events that influence the shaping of behavior. In its simple form, this process involves three contingencies: a discriminative stimulus, a response, and a consequence. Four types of consequences are described: Two increase behavior (positive and negative reinforcement), and two decrease it (punishment and extinction). **Positive reinforcement** is a pleasurable consequence that increases the frequency of target responses in association with a discriminative stimulus that precedes it. **Negative reinforcement** is a noxious consequence that also increases the frequency of a target behavior but, in this case, by being removed contingent on the target behavior being emitted (e.g., the time-out ends when the child stops throwing a tantrum; the seatbelt buzzer in the car quits when the driver buckles up). Thus, negative reinforcement increases the likelihood that behavior will recur. **Punishment** is a noxious consequence that reduces a behavior's frequency because the organism seeks to avoid it in the future. **Extinction** reduces the frequency of a behavior by reinforcement being withheld (e.g., the child's tantrum ceases after garnering no attention).

According to behaviorists, the units of language acquisition are not linguistic rules but functional acts (defined by how they control and are reinforced by the environment). Key functional acts are outlined in Table 3.2.

Evidence cited by behaviorists comes from charting behavior that shows changes consistent with operant principles. Critics who accept some behaviorist principles but not all argue that they are inadequate for explaining higher-level language functions, such as the ability to generate novel utterances, use abstract reasoning, or respond to social–emotional cues that reflect another person's feelings. A practical concern is that communication behaviors trained in highly structured operant paradigms often show limited generalization to more natural contexts.

Connectionist (Information-Processing) Theory

Connectionists take the empiricist position that language is learned using the same set of information processes (attention, short term memory, etc.) that support other forms of learning. Connectionists describe each child as employing cognitive abilities and receiving input from

table *3.2*   Operant Terminology for Verbal Behaviors

Term	Definition	Example
Echoic	Exact repetition in which a response is controlled by prior verbal stimulus and maintained by a social reinforcer and possibly a tangible reinforcer	*Adult:* Say ball. *Child:* Ball. *Adult:* Good talking.
Mand	Request; reinforced by getting the thing being requested	*Child:* Want cookie. *Adult:* Here you go [giving cookie].
Tact	Labeling or commenting; reinforced by attention	*Adult:* What's that? *Child:* A book. *Adult:* You're right. That's a book.
Intraverbal	Verbal response that relates to an item, action, or property that is not present; reinforced by praise	*Adult:* What was the book about? *Child:* A dog. *Adult:* Good job. You remembered.

the social environment to construct language competence using old parts (information processes) and new input (language) (Bates & MacWhinney, 1989; see Personal Reflection 3.1).

PERSONAL reflection *3.1*

"The human capacity for language could be both innate and species-specific, and yet involve no mechanisms that evolved specifically and uniquely for language itself. Language could be viewed as a new machine constructed entirely out of old parts."

Elizabeth Bates (Bates & MacWhinney, 1987, p. 10), a cognitive psycholinguist, had a profound influence on thinking about children's language.

Connectionists view language as "actual patterns of particular people using particular languages" (Tomasello, 2003, p. 2). This differs from the linguistic view of language as an abstract, intrinsic universal grammar. Cognitive connectionists are interested in how children learn traditional language units that are part of English, including phonemes, morphemes, and syntactic components. These theorists also seek to understand other usage-based forms found in non-European languages, such as tonality (Asian) and clicks (African).

Explanations offered by cognitive connectionists assign major roles to general cognitive *information-processing* abilities, such as attention, perception, working memory, and retrieval. Neural networks perform parallel distributed processing (PDP) functions in the same manner that sophisticated computer programs do. Such mechanisms operate by detecting general patterns from a mixture of complex input. Neural networks not only process input; they are also modified as a result of it. Competing connections are weakened and eventually disappear, so that this theoretical model also is considered a *competition model* of language learning (Bates & MacWhinney, 1987). As explained by Plaut (2003):

In connectionist models, cognitive processes take the form of cooperative and competitive interactions among large numbers of simple, neuronlike processing units. Unit interactions are governed by weighted connections that encode the long-term knowledge of the system and are learned gradually through experience. The activity of some of the units encodes the input to the system; the resulting activity of other units encodes the system's response to that input. (p. 143)

Evidence for connectionist views comes from studies of neural systems, brain plasticity in disordered populations, and logical argument. Proponents claim that evidence of neural proliferation and pruning occurs in response to external input throughout the lifespan (in some periods more than others), accounting for language learning and other maturation. They cite studies that show that computer systems can learn grammatical patterns through repeated input. This supports their claim that language learning does not require a specialized language-learning module. Critics point out that computer learning cannot account for all of the sophistication and flexibility demonstrated by human beings using language in contexts they have never experienced before and with relatively limited exposure.

Constructivist Theory

Cognitive constructivist theorists view language as neither innate nor learned but as emerging through a child's constructivist activity, which is a feature of general conceptual development. Constructivists tend to agree with connectionists that language is not innate, although its cognitive precursors are. Constructivists describe those precursors differently, however—more as higher-level cognitive schemas than as lower-level information processes. They emphasize symbolic properties of language for representing conceptual knowledge about the world.

Explanations of cognitive constructivist learning have grown from the work of Swiss psychologist Jean Piaget (1926/1959). Piaget described the evolution of thought as starting with a disequilibrium between current cognitive schemas and new evidence in the environment. He observed that higher-level representational schemas evolve out of lower-level sensorimotor ones. Language symbols represent cognitive schemas and serve intelligent thought, but they are not the only symbols or the only means for representing reality.

Piaget (1926/1959) described a prelanguage stage in the development of thought and a preconceptual stage in the development of language. He noted, however, that the two systems (thought and language) become quickly intertwined in the developing child. Symbolic expression, language comprehension, and logical abstract reasoning support cognitive development and are supported by it. Piaget suggested that development occurs in three major stages (see Table 3.3).

Cognitive constructivist theorists describe *adaptation* processes as underlying the evolution of cognitive thought at points of disequilibrium. Adaptation processes include both *assimilation,* in which new experience is assimilated into existing schemas (e.g., when a baby places a toy telephone in his or her mouth, applying a schema used with other toys), and *accommodation,* in which schemas are modified to accommodate new experience (e.g., when the baby begins to hold the toy telephone to the ear in a symbolic gesture). Accommodation represents qualitative adjustments in cognitive schemas that result in (and reflect) higher-level understanding and transition into new developmental stages.

Evidence cited by cognitivists is based mostly on observation of children engaged in problem-solving activities (many involving perceptual–motor elements). *Object permanence,* which is observed when an infant looks for an object that has been removed from sight, is an early example. Object permanence transitions into concepts of causality as the child engages in *means–end behaviors.* Children first discover nonverbal means to achieve desired ends (e.g., pulling on a string to obtain a toy) and later use words to achieve similar ends (e.g., drawing attention by using a greeting or comment). Still later, children shift from undifferentiated use of words for the here-and-now present (preoperational stage) to the ability to use words to *represent* (or re-present) events from the there-and-then past.

table 3.3 Piaget's Development Stages

Stage or Substage	Approximate Age	Primary Features
Sensorimotor		
Substage I	0–1 month	Reflexive
Substage II	1–4 months	Control of reflexes
Substage III	4–8 months	Repeats actions of others in repertoire
Substage IV	8–12 months	Shows goal-directed and intentional communication by looking and pointing and shows object permanence by looking where object was last seen
Substage V	12–18 months	Shows new means to old ends by imitating novel behaviors, including first words
Substage VI	18–24 months	Shows new means through mental combinations using deferred imitation and using symbols to name things not currently present
Representational Thought		
Preoperational Thought	2–7 years	Communicates with language symbols and represents absent objects through drawing and gesture, but cannot yet conserve concepts that differ in two dimensions
Concrete Operations	7–11 years	Can conserve number, mass, or volume when one dimension is changed but not the original number, mass, or volume
Formal Operations	11 + years	Can demonstrate abstract reasoning and think hypothetically

Transitions occur from the ability to focus on only one dimension at a time (in the period of preoperational thought) to the ability to use mental actions and *reversible thought* to conserve a concept of one dimension while another dimension changes (in the period of concrete operations). Cognitivists use children's metacognitive explanations as evidence of qualitative shifts in problem solving abilities. Piaget's classic observational evidence came from demonstrations of reversible thought in three types of conservation problems (see Figure 3.3).

Piaget (1926/1959) also described cognitive development in terms of a child's growing ability to take the perspective of another person, first perceptually and then conceptually. Children cannot perform the "three mountains" task (see Figure 3.3) until around age 12, when the development of mature (formal) thought allows them to move beyond the stage of cognitive egocentrism. To leave their egocentric viewpoint, children must learn to *decenter,* or shift cognitively to the perception of another. Piaget credited language with a causal role in making this development of intelligent thought possible.

Stage theories, such as Piaget's, seem problematic if they are viewed as rigid and discrete. Critics have pointed out flaws in Piaget's stages, such as placing some abilities too late in development (e.g., infants can perform some imitative acts at birth, such as tongue protrusion, but Piaget placed imitation ability later in infancy), and grouping concepts into a single schema (e.g., conservation) when they appear at different times in different forms (e.g., number conservation develops before volume). Although such criticisms deserve

figure 3.3 ─────────────────────────────────────

Tasks Used by Piaget to Demonstrate Children's Cognitive Operations

Task	Description	Illustration
Mass	Child observes as one of two identical balls of clay is reshaped; a preoperational child will report that the longer "snake" is now "bigger," whereas a child with operational thought can reverse the action mentally and report that they are still the same.	
Number	Child observes as one of two strings of coins or poker chips is separated; a preoperational child will report that the separated string of chips now has "more," whereas a child with operational thought can report that they are still the same.	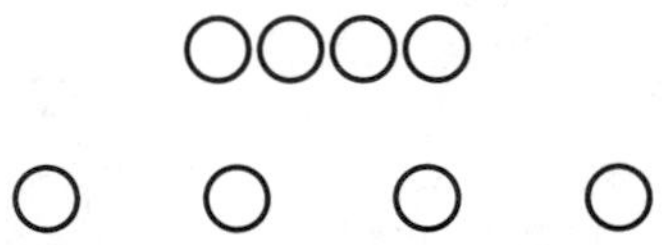
Volume	Child observes as liquid in one of two glasses of equal volume is poured from one of the glasses into a taller, thinner glass; a preoperational child will report that the new glass now has "more," whereas a child with operational thought can report that the volumes remain the same.	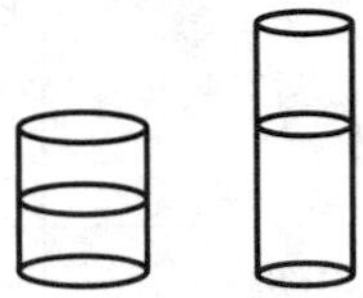
Three Mountains	Child views a physical arrangement of three model mountains of different heights. The child's task is to remain in one position and select a photograph that reflects how the scene would look from another person's perspective at a different point in the room.	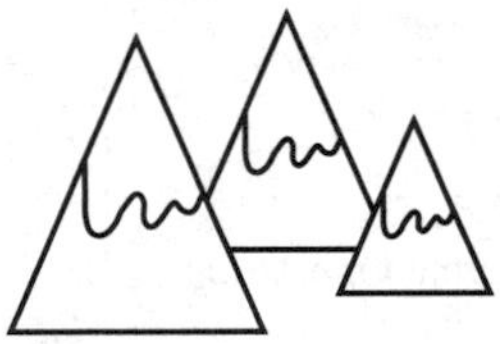

attention, Piaget's theories continue to have implications for clinical decision making, including perspective taking and formation of theory of mind (Flavell, 1999).

Cognitive–Emotional Theory

Cognitive–emotional theorists acknowledge interacting roles for nature and nurture. They emphasize the importance of emotional health and attachment to caregivers as essential to language development. Emotional well-being requires both an intact neurosensory system and a nurturing environment. Even when there are challenges that are related primarily to biological factors, the nurturing possibilities of parenting can make a difference (see Personal Reflection 3.2).

PERSONAL reflection 3.2 ────────────────────────

"Such extreme views polarized 'nurture' (it's mostly the parents' doing) and 'nature' (it's mostly biological). Not only are such views unable to account for all behavior, they are of little use to parents."

Stanley Greenspan (1997, p. 3), a pediatric psychiatrist, works with families affected by neurodevelopmental disorders of childhood, including autism spectrum disorders.

Studies of relationships between emotional and cognitive development can be traced to psychotherapists Erik Erikson (1940), Anna Freud (1965), and Selma Fraiberg (1980). All emphasized the importance of nurturing in infancy to the development of personal identity. The ability to form attachments also depends on the child's genetically tuned neurosensory systems. In pointing out these bidirectional influences on early attachment, pediatrician T. Berry Brazelton and colleagues (1974) emphasized the effects infants can have on their caregivers and vice versa.

The current major proponent for the cognitive–emotional perspective is child psychiatrist Stanley Greenspan. He and frequent collaborator psychologist Serena Wieder (Greenspan & Wieder, 2006) work closely with families with children with autism spectrum disorders and other developmental disabilities. Greenspan and Wieder described a comprehensive developmental approach to assessment and intervention based on *development, individual differences, and relationships (DIR)*. Greenspan and Shanker (2004) explained language development as building on the uniquely human "capacity to transform basic emotions into a series of successively more complex interactive emotional signals" (p. 1). Cognitive–emotional developments are described as occurring in a series of six overlapping stages, which begin at birth and pave the path to symbol development and early language development (see Table 3.4) (Greenspan, 1997; Greenspan & Wieder, 2006).

Evidence cited for the cognitive–emotional theory of development is drawn mostly from clinical experience, case studies, personalized accounts, and observational data. Greenspan and Wieder (2006) also reviewed literature supporting their proposed milestones. Critics of such theories might point out that feelings are inner responses that are difficult to observe and that additional mechanisms must be at work to explain language development as a special ability. Clinicians working in family-centered contexts can benefit from the DIR model that integrates development, individual differences, and relationships.

Social Interactionist Theory

Social interactionists view language primarily as a tool for making social connections and communicating ideas. They assign a primary role in language development to the nurturing effects of social mediation. Russian psychologist Lev Vygotsky was an early proponent of this theory. Vygotsky's (1934/1978) book *Thought and Language* was published in Russian after his early death. It was published in English in 1978 and has influenced modern theorists. Vygotsky viewed intelligence as the ability to benefit from instruction, measured by the *zone of proximal development (ZPD)* (illustrated in Figure 3.4), with internalization

table *3.4* Greenspan's Stages of Cognitive–Emotional Development

Stage	Approximate Age	Primary Features
I	0–3 months	Shared attention and regulation
II	2–7 months	Engagement and relating
III	3–10 months	Purposeful emotional interaction
IV	9–18 months	Social problem solving
V	18–30 months	Creating ideas
VI	30–48 months	Connecting ideas and thinking logically

of social dialogues serving as a support for higher-level thinking. Like his contemporary, Piaget, Vygotsky described a prelinguistic period in the development of thought and a pre-intellectual period in the development of language. Later, he saw thought and language as developing in tandem and influencing each other across the agespan.

Social interactionists assign critical language roles to parents, who treat infants' actions as communicative from birth, adjust their linguistic input to their children's developmental level, and show interest in their children's ideas across childhood. *Scaffolding* is a term for social mediation that is generally credited to psychologist Jerome Bruner (1975). It has been used by many educators (e.g., Hogan & Pressley, 1997) to describe adult mediation to help children achieve higher levels of competence than they could demonstrate on their own.

Like literal scaffolds, metaphoric scaffolds are designed to support learning until children can function at higher levels on their own (without the scaffold). Not all mediational discourse is scaffolding, however. In a classic study, Allington (1980) found that teachers talk differently to readers at different ability levels. Teachers used social constructive scaffolding more with better readers and interruption and correction more with poorer readers. They interrupted successful readers less often, waited longer for them to figure out words, and produced scaffolding comments related to sense making ("Does that sound right?" "Does it make sense?") (see Personal Reflection 3.3).

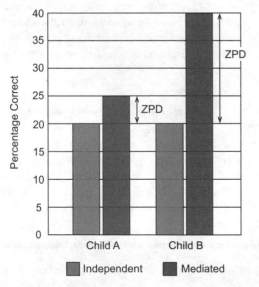

figure 3.4

Zone of Proximal Development

Vygotsky described the zone of proximal development (ZPD) as the difference between what a learner can do independently versus with appropriate mediation. In this hypothetical example, Child B, who is showing a larger ZPD, may have just lacked the appropriate prior experience to perform this task but was able to learn quickly with appropriate individualized mediation. Child A may be at higher risk of disorder and may require further, more intensive mediation.

PERSONAL reflection 3.3

"If we have learned anything from Vygotsky (1978), it is that 'children grow into the intellectual life around them' (p. 88). That intellectual life is fundamentally social, and language has a special place in it. Because the intellectual life is social, it is also relational and emotional. To me the most humbling part of observing accomplished teachers is seeing the subtle ways in which they build emotionally and relationally healthy learning communities—intellectual environments that produce not mere technical competence, but caring, secure, actively literate human beings. Observing these teachers accomplish both goals convinced me that the two achievements are not completely at odds."

Peter H. Johnston (2004, p. 2), an educational researcher, was reporting the results of his qualitative research, which formed the basis for his book on scaffolding, *Choice Words: How Our Language Affects Children's Learning*.

Evidence cited for social interactionist accounts of language acquisition include longitudinal studies of parent–child interactions gathered by recording interactions in natural contexts (Hart & Risley, 1995; Wells, 1986). Hart and Risley (1999) described this as a "social dance" of American family life that changes with the child's growing competence:

> Before their children say words, parents hold the floor and model the behaviors the family as a social group expects its members to learn, and the children contribute smiles, frowns, cooing, and babbling as their part. Then children begin to say utterances with words in them, which promotes longer interactions of prompting and responding until the children are talking as much as their parents. Then the children hold the floor and elaborate more often while their parents begin listening more, elaborating less and initiating fewer of the now more lengthy conversations. (p. 286)

Hart and Risley (1995) contributed essential evidence about social class influences on the language environments of young children. They studied the frequency of language interactions within families categorized as professional (*n* = 13), working class (*n* = 23), and low-income (*n* = 6), who allowed them to record words spoken at home between parent and child one day per month for 2.5 years. They found that the average child heard about 1,500 words per hour. However, children in professional families heard about 2,100 words, and children in low-income families heard only about 600 words per hour. Over the course of a year, this means that a child in a professional family hears around 11 million words while a child in a low-income family hears just 3 million. That is a big difference, which Hart and Risley noted in the title of their 1995 book, *Meaningful Differences in the Everyday Experience of Young American Children*. Following up on this study, Hart and Risley (1999) reported, "No matter what the family SES [socioeconomic status], the more time parents spent talking with their child from day to day, the more rapidly the child's vocabulary was likely to be growing and the higher the child's score on an IQ test was likely to be at age 3" (p. 3).

The quality of the discourse experience provided in homes (not just the volume of words) also makes a difference. Wells (1986) also compared families based on relative income levels and found that a key difference in predicting later school success was the frequency with which children heard narrative stories. In fact, this predictor was more powerful than any other, including the presence of books or drawing materials in the home. Hart and Risley (1999) reported that families in different socioeconomic groups "devoted similar amounts of talk to socializing their children, getting them properly fed and dressed, and keeping them safe and appropriately engaged" (p. 3), but they differed in the amount of discourse devoted to extra or optional talk, and it was this type of talk that correlated positively with verbal/cognitive competence at age 3. When optional discourse occurred, other things were happening beyond functional communication.

> When parents and children were staying to talk together with no need beyond social interaction, much more was happening than children hearing and saying words and sentences or learning reference and the names of things. Most of the optional talk occurred when parents and children were partners in mutual or parallel activities in which accomplishing something was rewarding but not imperative, doing a puzzle, for instance, or the child picking out socks to try on as the parent folded laundry. As partners in play, the children tended to be more cooperative, the parents more approving, and both of them less demanding and more likely to comment on nuances and elaborate what was said. The prohibitions required to manage the children's behavior were diluted by the amount of talk about a shared activity, and the vocabulary and concepts embedded in the talk were, without planning or effort, contributing to the accumulation of language and cognitive accomplishments that later tests would measure. (pp. 3–4)

Social interactionist theory holds particular promise for clinicians and teachers who envision an active role for themselves and others in fostering children's language development but who also see children as having inner resources that they bring to the process. Critics of social interactionist theory point to problems associated with the variable structure and highly individualized nature of child-centered social interactionist approaches. This, along with the dependence on scaffolding proficiency of mediators common to these approaches, makes it difficult to study them in randomized controlled trials.

SUMMARY

This section provided an overview of seven theories, grouped under the acronym BLB-CCCS. The primary tenets of each—developmental stages, evidence, and points of criticism—were reviewed. A legitimate question is whether the collective evidence points to one of approaches as best. Rather than try to select one to the exclusion of all others, aspects of several theoretical perspectives can be integrated to inform coherent approaches to language assessment and intervention. Clinicians cannot afford to adopt one theoretical position to the exclusion of all others. This does not mean that clinical practice should be atheoretical. Student clinicians should learn to recognize indicators of key theoretical viewpoints behind any research study or clinical practice and be deliberate in making clinical choices aimed at achieving relevant functional outcomes.

System Theory

System theory is a **metatheory** for integrating elements of multiple other theories. System theory is often credited to German biologist Ludwig von Bertalanffy (1968). It consists of six basic principles that can be applied across disciplines to explain both natural phenomena and therapeutic interventions. These six basic principles are described here in three balanced pairs to make them easier to remember and understand.

Systems Incorporate Both Wholes and Parts

The principle of **holism** emphasizes the whole as greater than the sum of its parts. A child is a whole system, as is a family, a school, a local educational unit, and a state or national government. This principle is balanced by the principle that any system can be described in terms of its **subsystems.** Child systems, family systems, and school systems all have parts or divisions.

These paired principles tie therapeutic choices directly to the involvement of families, policies, and school systems in fostering change. At the same time, clinicians must focus explicit attention on subsystems within the child or within broader systems that are causing difficulty or presenting barriers to language and literacy learning (see Personal Reflection 3.4).

PERSONAL reflection *3.4*

"Go as whole as you can and as part as you have to."

Barbara J. Ehren (2007), a speech–language pathologist and literacy and learning disability specialist, was speaking about the need to balance attention to parts and wholes in intervention.

Systems Are Stable but Changing

The principle of **homeostasis** represents the stability of systems and their resistance to change. The balancing principle of **morphogenesis** represents the fact that systems do change.

Change is a goal of any therapeutic process. According to the homeostasis principle, change does not come easy. Even (and sometimes especially) maladaptive systems are resistant to change. Speech, language/literacy, and communication systems have a degree of inertia. Saying a sound a certain way, using a particular grammatical form, reading without attention to meaning, and standing uncomfortably close to conversational partners might all be problematic aspects of communicative systems that are resistant to change.

On the other hand, systems are always changing. Clinicians who understand the principles of system theory see themselves as joining broader systems in collaborative roles with schools, families, and other key participants. They view their role as helping others in the system shed maladaptive beliefs and actions and adopt new, more facilitative ones.

An example comes from a third-grade teacher we worked with (Nelson, Bahr, & Van Meter, 2004) who viewed a special-needs child as a visitor in her room. The teacher was not sure this student with disabilities belonged there, commenting, "He can't even read." In fostering systemic change in this classroom, clinicians spent time in the room using a writing lab approach to demonstrate how to scaffold reading and writing for children with special needs and to help the teacher observe evidence of the student's good ideas so she could begin to appreciate his ability to learn and her ability to teach him. As the child's language system began to change, the classroom social support systems also began to change. This teacher no longer viewed the child as a visitor in her room and shared positive experiences involving the student. The student, in turn, was drawing his teacher's attention to his special word choices and telling her, "You're going to love this!"

Subsystems Have Boundaries and Interconnect with Circular Causal Patterns

The third set of balancing principles addresses interactions among subsystems. Subsystems have **boundaries,** which separate them to a degree. This principle is balanced by the principle that systems and subsystems influence each other through complex causative patterns that are **circular rather than linear.**

Awareness of boundaries between systems (e.g., schools and classrooms) and the explicit or implicit rules that govern them can keep a clinician from creating conflict when attempting to collaborate with others. Ignoring boundaries by failing to take into account a teacher's expertise, a family's cultural–linguistic diversity, or a child's personal preferences can jeopardize a collaborative relationship. Clinicians who seek to understand the situation through the eyes of the parents, teacher, or child may find their partners more accepting of collaborative consultation (see Personal Reflection 3.5).

PERSONAL reflection 3.5

"Sharing your classroom is like sharing your bathroom."

General education teacher who took part in a summer institute on collaborative approaches to language and literacy learning.

Understanding interactions across subsystems requires appreciation of circular causative patterns. Linear causative patterns imply a simple relationship in which *A* causes *B*.

System theory, however, reflects the more complex causal relationships that are involved when children struggle with language and literacy development. In particular, intersystemic causative patterns allow for circular causative effects, in which A^1 triggers change B^1, but that influences change A^2, which causes change B^2, and so on. Thus, clinical interventions become part of an ongoing cyclical pattern of bidirectional, intersystemic causation.

SUMMARY

System theory offers a way to organize the multiple internal and external systems involved in normal development. By taking a systemic view, clinicians can balance their attention on parts and wholes, stability and change, and boundaries and causative patterns that influence interactions among subsystems. System theory accommodates both intrinsic (nature) and extrinsic (nurture) systems, making it possible to integrate other theoretical explanations for development.

Systems Supporting Language Development

This section describes four interacting systems that are critical for language learning—neuro–cognitive–linguistic, sensory–motor, social–emotional, and familial–cultural. Each plays a central role in at least one of the seven (BLB-CCCS) theoretical perspectives described previously in this chapter. All can also play a role in language/literacy assessment and intervention (see Personal Reflection 3.6).

PERSONAL reflection 3.6

"The process [of language development] is a multifaceted one, requiring just about all of the child's perceptual, cognitive, social–communicative, and learning skills—applied over several years of nearly continuous interaction with mature language users."

Michael Tomasello and **Elizabeth Bates** (2001, p. 10), both cognitive psycholinguists, were advocating for a connectionist view of language acquisition.

Neuro–Cognitive–Linguistic Systems

A healthy brain plays an essential role in language learning, reading, and writing. Recent investigations have shed light on *prenatal* (before birth) and *postnatal* (after birth) development of the brain. Evidence also has been gathered regarding roles of brain *macrostructures* (e.g., cerebral lobes and hemispheres, cerebellum, thalamus) and *microstructures* (e.g., axons and dendrites). Within microstructures, scientists are studying *intracellular* (i.e., within cells) and *intercellular* (i.e., between cells) development and how it is influenced by a combination of genetic and environmental factors.

In typical development, both genetics and external activation of neural networks are responsible for strengthening some dendritic connections and pruning others. (See Figure 3.5 for a schematic representation of this process.) Finley (2005) noted that "synapses are both added and subtracted during learning" (p. 209). The presence of neural networks is presumed to support the automatic and rapid (i.e., fluent) processing of spoken and written words and their constituent units. When lower-level functions occur automatically, greater attentional and cognitive resources are available for performing higher-level cognitive–linguistic functions.

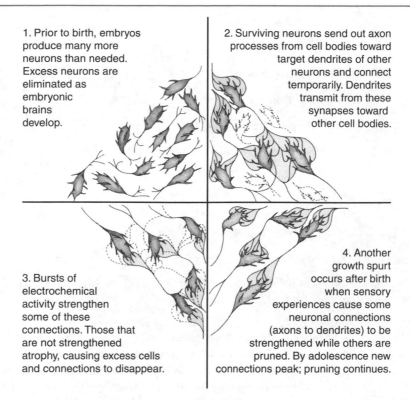

1. Prior to birth, embryos produce many more neurons than needed. Excess neurons are eliminated as embryonic brains develop.

2. Surviving neurons send out axon processes from cell bodies toward target dendrites of other neurons and connect temporarily. Dendrites transmit from these synapses toward other cell bodies.

3. Bursts of electrochemical activity strengthen some of these connections. Those that are not strengthened atrophy, causing excess cells and connections to disappear.

4. Another growth spurt occurs after birth when sensory experiences cause some neuronal connections (axons to dendrites) to be strengthened while others are pruned. By adolescence new connections peak; pruning continues.

figure 3.5

Neural Proliferation and Pruning Processes

Frame 1 represents neurons early in development with limited interconnectivity. Frame 2 represents some pruning of neural cells, along with proliferation of axonal and dendritic connections. Frame 3 represents additional pruning. Frame 4 represents a portion of a mature neural network.

Higher-level functions include sentence-level and discourse-level comprehension, formulation, and critical analysis. Areas of the brain are recruited in a connected and coordinated fashion when a person is involved actively in processing language and constructing meaning.

Macrostructures

As noted previously, theorists dispute the degree to which specific brain organization and macrostructural components (i.e., modules) play specialized roles in normal and disordered language and literacy development. While maintaining healthy skepticism, clinicians should be able to recognize and label traditional landmarks of the brain's macrostructures, such as lobes of the cerebral hemispheres and the key white-matter pathways that connect them, as illustrated in Figure 3.6.

Broca's and Wernicke's areas, in the left perisylvian region, seem to play specialized, dedicated roles in language processing, but it is important to recognize that traditional views are highly prone to oversimplistic explanations. The left hemisphere is credited as playing the major role in language acquisition for most people, with about 70 percent of speech–language functions residing in the left hemisphere for left-handed people and about 95 percent for right-handed people (Springer & Deutsch, 1989). The left hemisphere's predisposition to

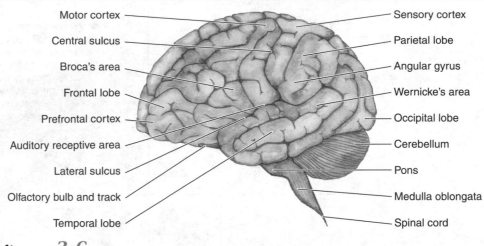

Motor cortex
Central sulcus
Broca's area
Frontal lobe
Prefrontal cortex
Auditory receptive area
Lateral sulcus
Olfactory bulb and track
Temporal lobe

Sensory cortex
Parietal lobe
Angular gyrus
Wernicke's area
Occipital lobe
Cerebellum
Pons
Medulla oblongata
Spinal cord

figure 3.6

Left Hemisphere of Adult Brain Showing the Major Lobes and the Primary Sensory and Motor Cortical Areas

learn language is supported by evidence allocating more processing space, even at birth, to the superior surface of the left temporal lobe next to Heschl's gyrus, which is the primary auditory reception area (illustrated in Figure 3.7). Functional neuroimaging studies with infants also have revealed a strong bias for speech processing to occur in the left perisylvian region, similar to that found for adults (Dehaene-Lambertz, Hertz-Pannier, & Dubois, 2006).

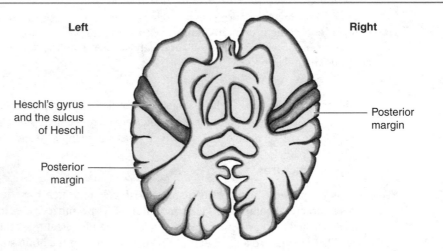

Left

Right

Heschl's gyrus and the sulcus of Heschl

Posterior margin

Posterior margin

figure 3.7

Transverse Section of the Brain Showing Left–Right Brain Asymmetry

This asymmetrical pattern is found in the majority of newborns at birth, suggesting a biological basis for most language learning to take place in the left hemisphere. The posterior margin of the planum temporale slopes back more sharply and the anterior margin of the sulcus of Heschl slopes forward more sharply on the left than on the right.

Source: Adapted from Geschwind & Levitsky, 1968.

As important as the left hemisphere is to language learning, the right hemisphere contributes to successful communication as well, particularly for interpreting paralinguistic, gestural information and figurative meanings (Ratey, 2001). The right hemisphere also plays a role in producing prosodic cues to meaning (Shah, Baum, & Dwivedi, 2006). The corpus callosum, which is illustrated in the transverse section of the brain shown in Figure 3.7, is an essential white-matter pathway that connects the two hemispheres, making transfer of information possible.

Auditory input to one ear crosses to the contralateral ear through decussating pathways in the brainstem and also across the corpus calossum. These pathways are represented in Figure 3.8. Another critical white-matter pathway is the arcuate fasciculus, which connects Wernicke's and Broca's areas, making it possible to convey perceptual information from the posterior to anterior regions of the left hemisphere. This means that speech received auditorially can be held in working memory, rehearsed internally, and repeated accurately.

Evidence for left hemisphere contributions to spoken language processing are inferred from functions that are lost when focal lesions are caused by a cerebrovascular accident (CVA; also called *stroke*). According to the Boston classification system (Helm-Estabrooks & Albert, 2004), lesions in Broca's area are associated with *nonfluent aphasia* in adults, characterized by retained content words, loss of fluent grammatical speech production and function words (e.g., *to, the, is, and*), and production difficulties at the phonetic level, associated with variable speech sound inaccuracies and sound sequencing struggles. Lesions in Wernicke's area are associated with *fluent aphasia* in adults, which is characterized by retained function words and fluent but empty-sounding speech with loss of content words. Speech production in Wernicke's aphasia often includes *paraphasias* (mispronounced or substituted words) that are produced fluently but with phonemic-level changes (involving whole phonemes), which make spoken language sound like jargon. Wernicke's aphasia also is associated with word recognition and language comprehension difficulty. In contrast,

Following the path of receptive processing: ear ⟶ cortex

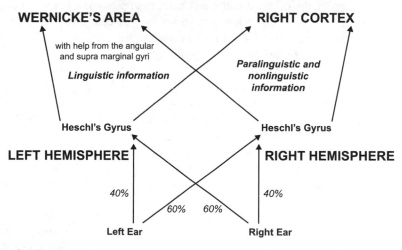

figure *3.8*

Graphic Representation of Ipsilateral (same-side) and Contralateral (opposite-side) Neural Pathways from the Ears to the Language Association Areas of the Cerebral Cortex

when Broca's and Wernicke's areas are spared by a lesion involving only the arcuate fasciculus, symptoms of *conduction aphasia* can be noted as specific impairment of the ability to repeat spoken stimuli in the presence of relatively intact language comprehension and production.

Some theorists (particularly cognitive connectionists) criticize the importance of brain localization evidence as presenting an oversimplified view of how the brain works. They point out that when one looks more closely at the wide range of evidence from people with aphasia learning different languages, it appears that the "lesion correlates of 'specific' linguistic deficits in adult aphasic patients are much more variable and complicated than was previously thought, supporting the contention that higher-level language skills are dynamic and distributed throughout the brain" (Dick et al., 2005, p. 242).

Brain Areas and Genes in Spoken Language Development

Genetic research based on familial studies has identified the FOX-P2 gene on chromosome 18 as essential for *synaptogenesis* (i.e., the development of intercellular synaptic connections) in Brodmann's Area 41b. This area is an auditory association area that appears to be essential for learning the past-tense markers on verbs. Cognitive connectionists caution against interpreting this as evidence for a grammar module but note that "the same ability requires virtually all the cortical areas, most of the genes, and highly elaborated language experience" (Finley, 2005, p. 212). Fisher (2006) also cautioned that "genes do not specify behaviours or cognitive processes; they make regulatory factors, signaling molecules, receptors, enzymes, and so on, that interact in highly complex networks, modulated by environmental influences, in order to build and maintain the brain" (p. 270).

Brain Areas and Genes Involved in Reading

A growing body of evidence highlights neurobiological differences in brains of people with language and literacy disabilities (e.g., Paulesu et al., 1996). Converging evidence supports a neurobiological basis of *dyslexia,* based on cerebellar anatomical differences in familial studies (Eckert et al., 2003). Anomalies in the cerebellar–frontal circuit are associated with problems of rapid automatic naming and reading but without primary spoken language impairment. Other research shows that the cerebellum, known for its role in coordinating motor activity, plays a role in integrating perceptual and cognitive processes, including reading (Fulbright et al., 1999).

A gene known as DCDC2 also has been isolated that may affect neuronal migration in some individuals with reading disability (Meng et al., 2005). Perhaps this or another gene could explain some of the structural evidence of cellular migration anomalies reported by Galaburda (1989) in earlier postmortem studies of the cerebral cortex in brains of individuals with dyslexia, as shown in Figure 3.9.

Evidence for a biological basis of dyslexia also comes from studies of cerebral hemisphere functioning (Shaywitz, Lyon, & Shaywitz, 2006). These studies have indicated overactivation in the left anterior hemisphere, specifically the inferior frontal gyrus, including Broca's area (associated with the production of spoken words). At the same time, underactivation occurs in posterior brain regions, including Wernicke's area (associated with the recognition of spoken words) and in the angular gyrus connecting the parietal and occipito-temporal regions (associated with integration of auditory, visual, and tactile information). Evidence that some areas of the brain work in isolation of others in dyslexia suggests that it is a disconnection syndrome (Paulesu et al., 1996).

Studies that point to a biological basis for dyslexia (Lyon et al., 2003; Shaywitz et al., 2006) also point to three areas critical to word recognition when reading. As illustrated

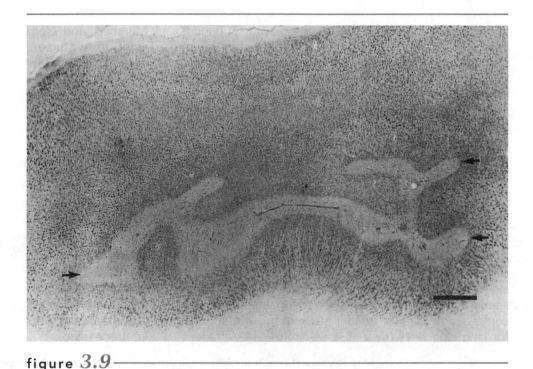

figure *3.9*

Brain of an Individual with Dyslexia

Arrows point to the distorted lamination of the cerebral cortex.

in Figure 3.10, these areas are activated when typically developing children attempt word analysis tasks that require integration of phonological, semantic, and orthographic information. The three areas include a left inferior frontal system (Broca's area) for analyzing words into phonologic segments for rhyming, reading, speaking, or spelling; a parieto-temporal system for analyzing the auditory components of words and connecting them to their meanings; and an occipitotemporal system that predominates "when a reader has become skilled, and has bound together as a unit the orthographic, phonologic, and semantic features of the word" (Lyon et al., 2003, p. 5).

A key question for clinicians is whether anomalous brain-processing patterns can be normalized with therapeutic interventions. Richards et al. (2006) documented changes in brain functioning after treatment for boys and girls from 9 to 12 years of age with dyslexia compared with a matched control group. Children with dyslexia showed the pretreatment pattern of abnormally active frontal lobe involvement, but after receiving treatment targeting morphological units, the abnormal pattern was replaced with findings of no difference between groups. Aylward and colleagues (2003) showed that reading intervention changed activation patterns for 10 children with dyslexia, bringing them closer to patterns for 10 normal readers. Shaywitz and colleagues (2004) also showed that phonological-based treatment resulted in heightened activation in the left posterior occipitotemporal region, related to improvement in fluent reading.

Studies such as these support interventions to help students form neurolinguistic connections between anterior (word pronunciation) and posterior (word meaning, pattern recognition) processing and to make connections across hemispheres to discourse and pragmatic abilities. Interventions should target the development of automatic, fluent processes

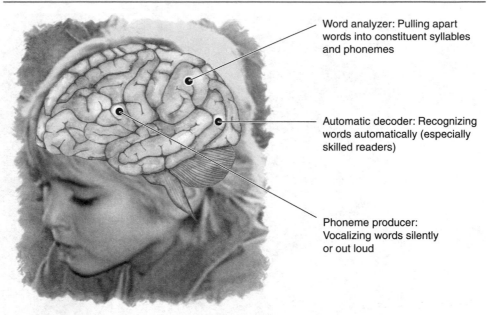

Word analyzer: Pulling apart words into constituent syllables and phonemes

Automatic decoder: Recognizing words automatically (especially skilled readers)

Phoneme producer: Vocalizing words silently or out loud

figure *3.10*

Three Major Areas of the Brain Activated When Young Readers Attempt Word Analysis Tasks

The phoneme-producing function in the left inferior frontal lobe is involved in early learning but remains overactivated for children with dyslexia. The word analyzer in the dorsal parietal–temporal region and automatic decoder in the ventral occipital–temporal regions are associated with fluent reading, and the automatic decoder in particular may represent the direct route that can be activated by skilled readers who no longer have to sound out words to recognize them.

Source: Shaywitz et al., 1998; Shaywitz, Lyon, & Shaywitz, 2006.

that move away from effortful productions involving overactivation of any one system, such as that involved in sounding out words with little attention to meaning.

The "Pinball Wizardry" Model

A schematic model of spoken and written language processing in the brain can help clinicians conceptualize language and communication systems required for processing a task successfully and isolating sources of difficulty. The "pinball wizardry" model (see Figure 3.11) can guide decisions about what to do next for school-age children with difficulty. The metaphor of pinball wizardry (Nelson, 1998) focuses on integration of multiple systems involved in meaningful communication (see Personal Reflection 3.7).

PERSONAL reflection *3.7*

"Without discarding the idea that people may differ in the brain structures that they have to work with, it is now known that for complex functions the brain must call on circuits which link several quite different parts of the brain and that such

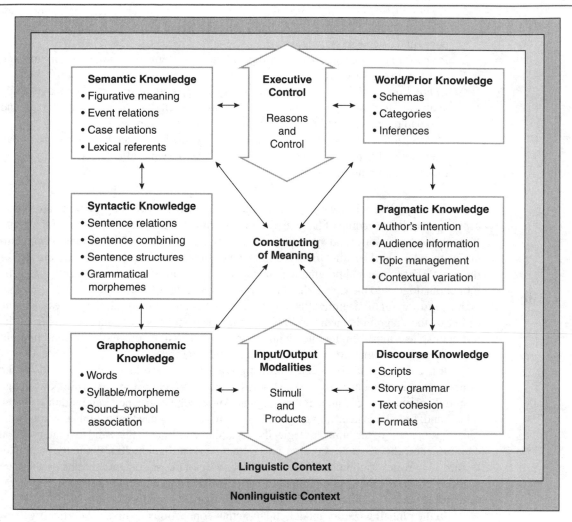

figure *3.11*

The "Pinball Wizardry" Model of Spoken and Written Language Processing

Source: © 1996 N. W. Nelson.

circuits only become functional for those persons who learn to do those things. We create many of the necessary links in the brain as we learn to engage in particular activities. If we do not learn we do not have the linked pathways."

Marie Clay (1979, p. 8), from the University of Auckland in New Zealand, led research efforts to understand how children transition from prereading to early reading proficiency.

Collectively, the model represents complex neural mechanisms that are used selectively and with strategic coordination (hence, the pinball wizardry metaphor) when competent language users engage in spoken and written language tasks. The full model is set in nonlinguistic and linguistic contexts and represents contributions from integrated systems of four types:

1. *Six cognitive–linguistic knowledge systems*—three linguistic systems (graphophonemic, syntactic, and semantic), accompanied by world knowledge, pragmatic knowledge, and discourse knowledge
2. *Peripheral processing skills*—sensory and motor systems for bringing information in and sending it back out
3. *Central-processing skills*—working memory for keeping information active while analyzing it, decoding or encoding it, forming associations, conducting storage and retrieval operations, and relating it to multiple levels of meaning
4. *Metacognitive strategies*—conscious (and less conscious) executive decisions to pay attention and to regulate other processes so they will work effectively and efficiently to achieve communicative purposes

In the pinball wizardry model, interactive language-processing systems are represented as parallel encoding of language and world knowledge across both sides of the brain. Phonological, semantic, and syntactic knowledge systems (maintained in long-term memory as they develop) are shown on the left side of the model (analogous to the left side of the brain). Discourse and pragmatic knowledge systems are shown on the right side of the model (analogous to the right side of the brain). The center of the model (and the process) is the construction of meaning. Placing this abstract culmination of all the processes in the center of the diagram is meant to imply that linguistic-processing contributions from the left hemisphere must be integrated with pragmatic-processing contributions from the right hemisphere if meanings are to be fully grasped and interpreted.

It is overly simplistic to consider that processes occur exclusively on one side of the brain or the other, that meaning is constructed in the corpus callosum, that world knowledge is stored only on the right side, or that language knowledge is grouped into modules. On the other hand, functional neuroimaging studies do provide evidence that neural networks draw on different areas of the brain strategically (e.g., Shaywitz et al., 1998) and that intervention can influence allocation of neural resources (e.g., Aylward et al., 2003), much as a pinball wizard would do. If clinicians can form a mental picture of students' brains as they are working currently, they may be more effective in fostering integrated processing systems rather than teaching splintered bits of knowledge that are soon lost.

In the pinball wizardry model, input–output connections involve subcortical systems and external sensory and motor pathways to and from cortical centers and end organs (such as fingers, mouths, and ears). These are illustrated with the arrow at the base of the model (see Figure 3.11). This bottom-up arrow represents connections to and from the child's brain, which is represented as being situated in the surrounding context of all the linguistic and nonlinguistic information available to human beings at any time. If every stimulus available in the environment elicited a response, a person would be completely disorganized and nonfunctional. Neuroimaging studies have shown that the executive control and self-regulatory functions required for inhibition, planning and organizing, and managing affect are largely the domain of prefrontal regions of the brain (Bashir & Singer, 2006). These top-down processes are represented in the model by the arrow at the top, which also connects to the context beyond the child, who is viewed as an active constructor of meaning. (Recall the definition of *attention* as "questions asked by the brain" from Chapter 1.) Smaller arrows represent white-matter pathways that form neural networks for supporting working memory and active processing (both for receptive and expressive language) that draw on stored knowledge across the brain. Higher-level strategic executive skills (top arrow) interact with, benefit from, and guide lower-level automatic recognition of symbols—hence, the pinball wizard metaphor.

Sensory–Motor Development and Systems

Language learning proceeds best when a child's sensory and perceptual processing systems are intact and integrated, making it possible to associate auditory and visual information with information from other senses as well (e.g., tactile information and proprioception of movement and position in space). Auditory–brain connections, represented schematically in Figure 3.8, are particularly crucial to learning spoken language.

Theoretical disputes about the nature of language learning assign differing roles to sensory input and information-processing capabilities such as attention and perception, which are used to make information available for higher levels of conceptual processing. Language processing may be viewed as a *bottom-up activity,* with upper-level comprehension and cognitive processes awaiting the arrival of perceptually processed input, or as a *top-down activity,* with perception, and even reception, benefiting from cognitive guidance. A third possibility is that language processing is bidirectional and interactive. This is what system theory would predict.

Attempts to understand bottom-up aspects of the process have led to perception-driven models of language learning. For example, three successive stages might be required to map sensory information into word-level representations: (1) reception of acoustic or visual input that leads to activation of a set of lexical possibilities, (2) selection of the best candidate for a match from among these (while competitors are suppressed), and (3) integration of the new lexical information with the ongoing sentence context (Marslen-Wilson & Warren, 1994).

Newer parallel distributed processing (PDP) models reduce the emphasis on steps occurring in a sequence. After reviewing evidence on normal behavior, neuropsychology, and electrophysiology, Aydelott, Kutas, and Federmeier (2005) concluded:

> The data support an interactive model of language comprehension, in which there is no clear division or unidirectional flow of information between perceptual and conceptual processes. Instead, the evidence reveals that there is transparent information transfer between these levels of analysis, such that variations in the perceptual input directly influence the activation of conceptual information, and that active conceptual information in turn directly influences perceptual analysis. Further, both the perceptual properties of the input and the availability of attentional resources play a crucial role in language comprehension. (pp. 309–310)

Kutas and Schmitt (2003) cited evidence from studies using evoked response potentials (ERPs) to conclude that language comprehension and production employ different processing patterns. They measured ERPs in response to word and picture stimuli that gave conflicting information and observed interactions and temporal sequencing among systems involved in comprehending and responding. Whereas language comprehension processes involved significant temporal overlaps and interactions, language production processes followed a more predictable serial order.

At least one clinical implication of this work is that children need intersystemic intervention approaches that focus both inward on language systems and outward on input to systems. An example would be to provide explicit instruction to help children with auditory-processing disorders fill any gaps in their language knowledge across systems and also to use sound–field amplification systems in classrooms to enhance input. The goal would be to help children apply both parallel and serial processes strategically for language comprehension and expression. Sensory and motor systems are best viewed not just as conduits of information in and out of a central processor but also as integral parts of a comprehensive system that yields meaning (Aydelott et al., 2005).

Social–Emotional Development and Sensory–Motor Systems

Language concepts and nonlinguistic conceptual structures are shaped by how a child experiences the world using his or her sensory and motor systems. Jackendoff (1992) offered an architectural model for conceptual structures, in which he proposed major roles not only for auditory–linguistic information but also for emotion, smell, and action. Jackendoff saw spatial representation, in particular, as being influenced by, as well as influencing, visual representation, haptic (i.e., tactile) representation, and proprioception (i.e., sensation of position in space).

As noted previously, Greenspan and Wieder (2006) emphasized the dual influences of nature and nurture. They noted the innate tendency of infants to attend to human faces, particularly eyes, and the role of synchronous movements in forming emotional attachments between mother and infant even prior to birth. Individual differences also play a role, influencing the nurturing of sensation and motor development through experience:

> What is pleasant for one infant, however, may be aversive to another. Each infant has her own ways of responding to sights, sounds, smells, touch, and movement. Some babies are highly sensitive and require gentle soothing. Others are underreactive and require more energetic wooing. Some babies discern sights and sounds quickly, others more slowly. Some will immediately turn toward a new sound or sight, whereas others take longer to notice. The infant therefore depends on her caregiver's ability to fit gaze, voice, and way of moving to her unique way of taking in and responding to the world. (Greenspan & Wieder, 2006, p. 15)

Children coping with systems that are either hyper- or hyposensitive to external sensation face extra challenges coping with confusing or overwhelming sensation. A sensory system that is **hyperarousable** overreacts to normal levels of sound, touch, or brightness; a system that is **hypoarousable** shows limited response to sensory input even though the infant or child has intact hearing or visual sensitivity. Not only are sensations experienced differently by many infants, but "each of an infant's sensory experiences occurs in the context of a relationship that gives it additional emotional meaning" (Greenspan & Wieder, 2006, p. 17).

The dual coding of experience (sensory and emotional) is maximized in adaptive parent–child relationships. Sensory–motor dysfunction may contribute to maladaptive patterns of interactions, however, requiring direct attention by interdisciplinary teams. Impaired sensory perception presents barriers to using the full range of sensory–emotional responses for learning. As a result, children "may be unable to organize purposeful, goal-directed movement and socially adaptive behavior" (Greenspan & Wieder, 2006, p. 17).

Familial, Cultural, and Educational Systems

The degree to which cultures and language influence thought has long been a matter of debate. Bennardo (2003) summarized evidence from ethnolinguistic investigations that speakers of some languages categorize information differently, suggesting that their cognitive schemas must differ as well. For example, Australian aboriginal speakers describe spatial relations of two objects with reference to cardinal points (*north, south, east,* or *west*) rather than *right, left,* or *front.* In fact, experiences within cultures may affect word choices and even thoughts. For example, English speakers say *The watch is running,* whereas Spanish speakers say *El reloj esta caminando* (The watch is walking), perhaps reflecting different perceptions of time.

Each person's world view may appear to him or her to be the only normal way to function. In fact, it is difficult to step outside and see one's world view as others see it, which may not seem normal at all. Such ability is necessary, however, for developing the sensitivity required for full cultural competence. Attempting to view one's professional efforts as others might see them (strange and foreign, perhaps) is a step toward developing sensitivity to other cultural systems and responsivity to the needs of families whose cultural experiences are different from one's own. This is a two-way street. Clinicians who can begin to sense the strangeness in what feels totally familiar to them may become more aware and respectful of what feels comfortable or strange to others. Clinicians who see themselves as consultants to whole family systems will work to understand a family's perspectives and values. As a result, they may have a better chance of being accepted by the family as an agent of change. This may be especially true if change is conceptualized in terms that make sense to family members who have helped to define goals based on priorities that fit their views of what is important (Hyter, 2007a).

Other systems that are external to the child include broader social systems and cultural groups of which the child is a member. The educational system, which also holds the responsibility to prepare children academically and socially, has an influence on priorities and choices as well. Within school systems and special service delivery programs, curricular, instructional, and attitudinal factors all can present opportunities or barriers to the optimal development and participation of a child, depending on how they evolve. Miscommunication across professional discipline boundaries also reflects differences in cultural upbringing. If one accepts the informal definition of *culture* as "the way we do things around here," it should not be surprising that clinicians, teachers, and parents all have diverse perspectives. Sometimes they must ask each other for clarification of how particular terms are being used and the deeper cultural meanings and values assigned to certain actions and choices.

Policies both influence sociopolitical systems, such as schools, and are influenced by them. Over the past 30 years, policies and procedures in the United States have resulted in two largely separate systems of education—general and special education. A problem with such separation is that children with disabilities have had limited access to the general education curriculum, and children with academic risks (for a variety of reasons, including possibly undiagnosed disability) have had limited access to specialized instruction. Changes in policy with the Individuals with Disabilities Education Improvement Act (IDEA '04) have made it possible to blur some boundaries between special and general education and to allow a portion of special education funds to be paid for services to general education students (discussed further in Chapter 4). One result is that children who are struggling with the language of schooling might gain earlier access to specialized instruction without having to undergo full diagnostic testing and labeling to qualify for special assistance.

Barriers or supports within school systems may vary across circumstances and times in a child's development. It is a goal of this book to provide information that will help teams of professionals, parents, and students to reduce the influence of the limiting factors in external systems and to enhance the positive ones. By doing so, interdisciplinary teams can establish policies and design general and special education programs and services to promote development, prevent failure, and increase children's self-efficacy in making positive choices about how they want to spend their lives, with or without language/literacy disorders.

SUMMARY

This section has described four interacting systems that play critical roles in language/literacy development—neuro–cognitive–linguistic, sensory–motor, social–emotional, and familial–cultural. Each reflects combined effects of nature and nurture to some degree, and each has special relevance to one or more of the theoretical perspectives discussed previously in this chapter.

Brain macrostructures were reviewed and mechanisms of intercellular synaptic proliferation and pruning were described. Adult aphasia syndromes were reviewed, including anterior syndromes with nonfluent symptoms (i.e., Broca's aphasia) and posterior syndromes with fluent symptoms (i.e., Wernicke's aphasia). Different mechanisms are at work in the etiology of language disorders in children (reviewed in Part II). The FOX-2P and DCDC2 genes have been associated with developmental spoken language and literacy disorders respectively. Sensory–motor mechanisms also may be related to hypoarousal or hyperarousal, presenting barriers to concept development and social emotional maturity. Finally, social–cultural systems were described, with an emphasis on culturally sensitive perspective taking.

CHAPTER SUMMARY

Chapter 3 sets the context for clinical decision making by introducing information about multiple subsystems and how they interact. The chapter began with a description of the ongoing controversy between theorists who view grammar as an essentially hardwired feature of human brains in contrast with those who view language learning as a process of connecting features of neural networks through exposure to the regularities of language. Seven theoretical perspectives on language development were presented, as represented by the acronym BLB-CCCS—biological, linguistic, behaviorist, cognitive connectionist, cognitive constructivist, cognitive–emotional, and social interactionist.

No matter what theoretical view one prefers, language development is worthy of awe. It transpires in a relatively predictable manner when supported by facilitative internal neurolinguistic networks and external social ones. The majority of spoken language development occurs without formal instruction. On the other hand, learning to read and write occurs mostly within the formal instructional contexts of schooling. Not all children arrive at school equally prepared to learn to read and write. Experiences at home play an important role in preparing children to read and write, interact socially, and regulate learning and emotions. System theory offers a means for integrating information about both internal and external systems that influence outcomes for children.

EXERCISES *and* STUDY QUESTIONS

1. Describe the key arguments in the debate about nature versus nurture and the essence of language. What is meant by the "black box"?

2. Name the seven theoretical perspectives represented by the acronym BLB-CCCS. Then list two of the major proponents of each and describe its key explanations, including any developmental stages.

3. Describe the six principles of system theory, and tell how the three pairs balance each other using the framework presented in this chapter.

4. What subsystems are required to support the normal development of language and literacy? Which are internal and which are external to the child?

5. Identify the macrostructures on a diagram of the left cerebral hemisphere. What regions have been shown to be overactive and underactive in children with dyslexia, at least until intervention has been provided? How are functions of the brain represented in the "pinball wizardry" model?

6. After thinking about the material presented in this chapter, what theoretical perspective is most persuasive to you and why? Is there one that you find difficult to understand? Is there one that you have trouble accepting? If so, what about it does not fit your personal framework and why?

PART two

Policies, Practices, and Populations

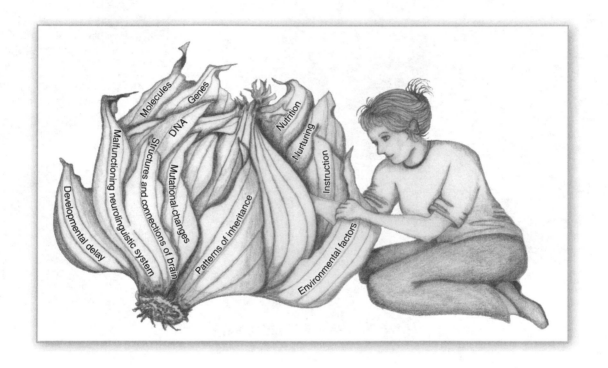

Policies and Practices

Primary Disorders of Speech, Language, and Literacy

Motor and Sensory Impairments

Cognitive–Communicative Impairments

CHAPTER *four*

Policies and Practices

LEARNING *objectives*

After studying this chapter, you should be able to do the following:

1. Describe the main features of three key pieces of legislation (Section 504, IDEA, NCLB).

2. Differentiate among team models as multidisciplinary, interdisciplinary, and transdisciplinary.

3. Describe recursive steps in providing services guided by current policy.

4. Discuss the pros and cons of categorization and provide examples of layered causal factors.

5. Define *prevalence* and *incidence*, *prevention*, and *prognosis* and provide examples of each.

Clinical practices and special education services are guided by evidence about the nature of disorders and how best to treat them and also by policy. Master clinicians understand policy, what motivated it, and how to comply with it. They also know how to focus on the needs of children as the true center of service delivery decisions and to keep policy dictates in perspective so services are not controlled by paperwork that serves no clear purpose. This is one example of the balance between "seeing the forest and the trees" that was encouraged in Chapter 1.

This chapter begins with a discussion of three key policy influences set in a brief history of the sociopolitical context through which they emerged. Then a flowchart is used to outline questions about what to do next at important decision points. Also discussed are questions about categorization and diagnosis and about causal factors and noncausal factors, such as cultural–linguistic diversity, which need to be differentiated from disorder. The chapter ends with a section on prevention and prognosis.

Policies

The U.S. educational policy that has the greatest impact on the provision of special education and related services to children from birth through age 21 years is the Individuals with Disabilities Education Improvement Act of 2004 (IDEA '04). The 2004 reauthorization was based on a law passed in 1975 as Public Law 94-142 (abbreviated PL 94-142, indicating passage by the 94th Congress of the United States). That law, which is now referred to as IDEA, was originally called the Education for All Handicapped Children Act (EAHCA). It was not the first law to address the needs of people with disabilities, but it was the most comprehensive, and it continues to have a profound influence on service delivery.

This section introduces the key provisions of IDEA (in its various iterations), as well as Section 504 of the Rehabilitation Act of 1973, which preceded it, and the No Child Left Behind Act of 2001 (NCLB; PL 107-110), which followed it. The timeline for these three key pieces of federal legislation, including major revisions of IDEA, is shown in Table 4.1. (In Part III of this text, specific requirements of the laws are discussed further as they apply to different ages of children.) Like all policies, these laws continue to evolve; thus, readers are encouraged to consult the relevant Internet sites for emergent versions of laws and regulations (www.ed.gov).

Federal policies are not just a matter of **laws** passed by Congress but also administrative **regulations.** Regulations are finalized following opportunities for input from parents, professional organizations, and other individuals via mail and public hearings. **Case law** also influences policy when outcomes of disputes are settled in court. Other policy influences at the state and local levels include state-level regulations and local guidelines, as well as organization-specific and funding-source policies, both public and private.

Case law set the stage for the key pieces of legislation that are described here. An early influence came from the case *Brown v. Board of Education* (1954), which challenged discriminative education practices based on race and thus raised issues regarding all children's rights to a free appropriate public education (Foorman & Nixon, 2006). The civil rights era that began in the 1950s continued into the early 1970s, when two important court cases challenged discrimination on the basis of disability. *Pennsylvania Association for Retarded Children v. Commonwealth of Pennsylvania* (PARC, 1971) resulted in a ruling that the state of Pennsylvania was obligated to "provide free public education to all children six to twenty-one years of age" (Sec. 2). Another case, *Mills v. Board of Education* (1972), was brought on behalf of children with behavior disturbance, hyperactivity, mental retardation, and physical impairment. The ruling in that case extended PARC to other disabilities and required that

table *4.1* Timeline for Passage of Key Pieces of Federal Legislation

Years	Congress	Law (or Reauthorization) and Key Features
1973–74	93rd	PL 93-112 The Rehabilitation Act of 1973 (Section 504) prohibited discrimination based on disability.
1975–76	94th	PL 94-142 The Education for All Handicapped Children Act (EAHCA) (Part B) established the right for all children to have access to a free, appropriate public education (FAPE) in a least-restrictive environment (LRE) based on an individualized education plan (IEP).
1985–86	99th	PL 99-457 The Education of the Handicapped Act Amendments of 1986 (Part H, which later became Part C) established options for states to offer programs for infants and toddlers based on an individualized family service plan (IFSP) and with a case manager.
1987–88	100th	PL 100-407 The Technology Related Assistance for Individuals with Disabilities Act defined *assistive technology* (AT) to include both services and devices.
1989–90	101st	PL 101-476 The Education of the Handicapped Act Amendments of 1990 renamed the law the Individuals with Disabilities Education Act (IDEA) and added categories for autism and traumatic brain injury.
1991–92	102nd	PL 102-119 The Individuals with Disabilities Education Act Amendments of 1991 added assistive technology to Part H, indicated that 3- to 5-year-old children could have either IEPs or IFSPs, and changed *case management* to *service coordination.*
1997–98	105th	PL 105-17 The Individuals with Disabilities Education Act Amendments of 1997 reauthorized IDEA with an emphasis in Part B on keeping students in the general education curriculum and changed Part H to Part C.
2001–02	107th	PL 107-110 The No Child Left Behind Act of 2001 (NCLB) was enacted as part of the reauthorization of the Elementary and Secondary Education Act (ESEA), which was originally passed in 1965.
2003–04	108th	PL 108-446 The Individuals with Disabilities Education Improvement Act of 2004 (IDEA '04) introduced a number of changes detailed in this chapter.

Note: The first number of a federal law indicates the number of the two-year congressional session in which it was passed (e.g., PL 93-112 was passed by the 93rd Congress).

alternative education services, including special education, be provided appropriate to each child's needs, along with due process protections for children expelled or suspended.

Section 504 of the Rehabilitation Act of 1973

The Rehabilitation Act of 1973 (PL 93-112) is civil rights legislation. It guarantees equal protections and rights for individuals with disabilities in any program receiving federal funds—including public elementary, secondary, and postsecondary schools. To qualify for accommodations under Section 504 of the Rehabilitation Act, an individual must have a physical or mental condition that substantially limits major life activities.

Section 504 does not provide funding for services, but students may qualify for Section 504 plans that specify reasonable accommodations to help them participate actively in general education, including physical access to school buildings for students who use wheelchairs. Every part of a school does not have to be accessible, as long as its programs as a whole are accessible. At the postsecondary level, students with disabilities must have access to housing comparable to housing for students without disabilities. Other educational accommodations under a Section 504 plan include assistive listening devices and sound field amplification systems, extra time to take tests, and being excused from a required school activity on the basis of a health condition. Section 504 applies particularly to students whose identified condition does not fall into one of the 12 special education diagnostic categories under IDEA 2004 (summarized in Figure 4.1). If a student has one of the 12 qualifying diagnoses, he or she would be eligible to have an individualized education program (IEP) and hence would not need a Section 504 plan.

Individuals with Disabilities Education Act (IDEA)

IDEA is considered the access law because it ensures access to education for children with disabilities. IDEA grew out of the civil rights movement. It has roots in the Elementary and Secondary Education Act of 1965 (ESEA, 1965; PL 89-10), which provided resources for instruction, particularly reading instruction under Title I, aimed at improving education for children living in poverty. Related laws authorized federal programs to train teachers to work with children with disabilities and to provide bilingual education. In the early 1970s, the previous laws and amendments of the ESEA were united into PL 91-230, which became Part B of the Education of the Handicapped Act (EHA). The EHA was the immediate antecedent to the Education for All Handicapped Children Act of 1975 (EAHCA; PL 94-142). The EAHCA first became known as IDEA when it was revised in 1997 (PL 105-17).

In 2004, IDEA was reauthorized as the Individuals with Disabilities Education Improvement Act (PL 108-446), although it still was abbreviated as IDEA (IDEA '04 in this book). President George W. Bush signed the reauthorized law in 2004, but the final code of federal regulations (CFR) for Part B of the revised act (for children ages 3 to 21 years) was not published in the *Federal Register* until August 14, 2006. The proposed regulations for Part C (for infants and toddlers) did not appear in the *Federal Register* until May 9, 2007, and the final regulations for Part C were not approved until 2008.

From the time it was originally passed as PL 94-142 until it became known as IDEA '04, the purpose of IDEA has been to ensure that all children with disabilities have access

figure *4.1*

Twelve Diagnostic Categories Recognized in IDEA '04

These categories are used to identify a child with a disability who needs special education and related services.

- Mental retardation
- Hearing impairment (including deafness)
- Speech or language impairment
- Visual impairment (including blindness)
- Serious emotional disturbance (referred to as *emotional disturbance*)
- Orthopedic impairment
- Autism
- Traumatic brain injury (TBI)
- Other health impairment
- Specific learning disability
- Deaf–blindness
- Multiple disabilities

to a free, appropriate public education (FAPE) in the least restrictive environment (LRE) based on an individualized education plan (IEP). Part B is one of four parts of IDEA '04:

- Part A includes definitions and general provisions.
- Part B specifies how services are to be provided to preschool and school-age students (ages 3 to 21 years) using IEPs.
- Part C specifies requirements for service provision to infants and toddlers (ages birth through 2 years) and their families, using individualized family service plans (IFSPs).
- Part D includes provisions for supporting research, personnel preparation, technical assistance support, and dissemination of information.

The LRE requirements of Part B include the notion that, whenever appropriate, children with disabilities must be educated with children without disabilities. Similarly, requirements of Part C indicate that services to infants and toddlers should be provided as much as possible in natural environments. IDEA '04 introduced several further specifications. One is that identification of students with disabilities under Part B must include consideration of whether the child has had appropriate instruction in reading. In addition to the initial evaluation or reevaluation of the student, an IEP team must consider the strengths of the student; the concerns of the parents for enhancing their child's education; and the academic, developmental, and functional needs of the student, as indicated by statewide and district testing.

With the implementation of IDEA '04, IEP teams may use alternative procedures to determine whether a child has a specific learning disability (LD). Previously, identification of LD was based on discrepancy between achievement and intellectual ability. Under the revised law, IEP teams may use a process that involves observation of children's response to scientifically based interventions. These *early intervening services* are not to be confused with *early intervention services,* which are designed for young children. Another distinction between the early intervening services (EIS) of Part B and the early intervention services of Part C is that EIS are general education activities, whereas early intervention services are special education services, so they must be a component of a child's IFSP or IEP. Although EIS are offered through general education, IDEA '04 allows the use of some Part B special education funds (no more than 15 percent) to support them. For example, a speech–language pathologist (SLP) or teacher consultant for students with LD (paid with special education dollars) could consult regarding programmatic needs of students receiving EIS. Such professionals might provide direct services to groups of general education students who are struggling with reading or oral language skills to determine their response to intervention (RTI).

No Child Left Behind Act

Whereas IDEA '04 is known as the access law, the No Child Left Behind Act (NCLB; PL 107-110) is known as the accountability law. It is designed to hold public school districts accountable for ensuring that all children, including those affected by poverty or disability, achieve academic success (Moore-Brown & Montgomery, 2005). The long-term goal of NCLB is for every child to read at or above grade level by the schoolyear 2013–2014. NCLB was signed into law on January 8, 2002, by President George W. Bush as a reauthorization of the ESEA (originally passed in 1965). It incorporated the following components:

- Information must be gathered annually to determine whether a school district has made its goals for *adequate yearly progress (AYP),* including results on district- and statewide academic and achievement tests, school attendance, and graduation rates.

- School districts may spend up to 15 percent of their special education funds to support general education activities, such as EIS and RTI initiatives.
- Methods for teaching reading (based on systematic reviews of studies by the National Research Council [1998] and the National Institute of Child Health and Human Development [2000]) should incorporate the *five essential components*—phonemic awareness, phonics instruction, reading fluency, vocabulary, and text comprehension.
- Schools that fail to reach their AYP goals are targeted for corrective action and labeled "schools in need of improvement." This means that they must provide supplemental services and that parents can move their children at the schools' expense.

NCLB also made funding available for a variety of special programs—Reading First, Early Reading First, Even Start Family Literacy, and Even Start Migrant Education Program—which are dispersed through a competitive federal and state grant application process. AYP testing results must be based on improved test scores for all children in a school district. At least 95 percent of students in each high-risk group must take the district- and statewide tests, and scores must be reported in disaggregated groups: economically disadvantaged, major racial/ethnic groups, students with disabilities, and students with limited English proficiency. Only 3 percent of children (i.e., those with the most profound disabilities) can take alternative assessments to determine whether they meet educational standards without the district losing its potential to achieve AYP (U.S. Department of Education, 2005). English language learners (ELLs) and children with limited English proficiency (LEP) may be tested in their native language for up to three years. After that, reading and math must be tested in English, although content knowledge still may be tested in ELLs' native language for up to two more years.

SUMMARY

Three key pieces of legislation were reviewed, along with the court decisions and laws that preceded them—the Rehabilitation Act of 1973, the Individuals with Disabilities Education Improvement Act of 2004 (IDEA '04), and the No Child Left Behind Act of 2001. These federal policies were characterized respectively as civil rights legislation, access to education for children with disabilities, and accountability for education of all children. Key provisions were described for each.

Clinical Practices

A context-based approach to language/literacy assessment and intervention is based on two primary assumptions. First, intervention is more likely to be successful when it is comprehensive, intersystemic, and contextualized; and second, the more intervention teams know about language and literacy, the better prepared they are to make a difference. The proper aim of clinical intervention is to foster language/literacy development for children who are struggling so that they can function successfully and experience satisfaction in important life contexts (see Personal Reflection 4.1).

PERSONAL reflection *4.1*

"They're always trying to 'fix' Marti—as if they can't accept the fact that she's handicapped. They spend all their time working on things she can't do without giving her a chance to enjoy the things she can."

Carol Knibbs (in Simons, 1987, p. 48) is a mother who described her priorities for her 14-year-old daughter with developmental disabilities affecting cognition.

In designing individualized programs, clinicians make use of three complementary but distinct sources of information:

- *Diagnostic information* can guide choices about best educational settings and accommodations for addressing specific challenges and providing participation opportunities. This information is gathered using a combination of formal tests validated for diagnostic purposes, guided observations, and sets of diagnostic criteria.
- *Developmental information* is used to identify gaps between functional levels and expected levels in relevant domains. This information is gathered through a combination of standardized and nonstandardized assessment methods, including criterion-referenced tools.
- *Contextualized performance information* is based on probes designed to identify gaps between observed abilities and demands of selected social, academic, and vocational contexts. This information is gathered through context-based assessment activities, which are guided by ethnographic interviews and the four questions introduced in Chapter 1.

Assessment and intervention processes should be reciprocal, ongoing, and recursive. They are designed to identify, understand, and narrow gaps between what children can do currently and the demands of contexts that are important to them and others. This information can then guide choices about intervention targets and methods that are evidence based (as much as possible), followed by ongoing assessment probes of the child's progress and evaluation of the program and methods. If progress is limited, modifications should be made and further probes should be taken to evaluate whether outcomes are improving.

Service Delivery as a Collaborative Process

Whether services are implemented in medical settings, homes, community centers, or schools, a team effort is needed to mobilize systemic factors to foster a child's development. Assessment and intervention teams include parents and professionals. Children and adolescents are part of the process as well. As noted in Chapter 1, collaboration begins with mutual goal setting. Cooperative goal setting differs from individualistic or competitive goal setting (see Personal Reflection 4.2).

PERSONAL reflection *4.2*

"What had once been a team quickly divided into 'sides,' with the school district on one and our family and some of the professionals who worked with Abigail on the other."

Nicole Underwood (2006, p. 40) described her family's journey through due process regarding conflict over the family's wish to have Underwood's daughter, Abigail, provided with a cochlear implant and taught in general education classrooms with related services offered for optimizing (mapping) her cochlear implant.

Policies govern IEP and IFSP planning and intervention teams. Planning decisions must be made by *multidisciplinary teams,* which are defined as "the involvement of two or more individuals from separate disciplines or professions, or one individual who is qualified in more than one discipline or profession" (Section 303.17 of Part C). Three basic models of team structure and functioning—multidisciplinary, interdisciplinary, and transdisciplinary—are illustrated in Figure 4.2. These team models vary along a continuum of direct collaboration and information and role sharing.

figure *4.2*

Three Models of Team Structure and Function

Type of Team	Team Structure	Team Function
Multidisciplinary	• Representatives come together periodically to share information but otherwise work independently. • Leadership is often based on hierarchical authority.	• Each profession works from a discipline-specific perspective. • Even though team members share their findings with one another, each member provides the services in his or her assessment and plan separately. • Relationships are limited and transitory.
Interdisciplinary	• Individuals trained in various disciplines coordinate their services deliberately but maintain clearly separate identities. • Members may be employed by different organizations but work actively to collaborate. • Team leadership may be based on hierarchical authority or rotate among team members.	• Clients may be assessed separately or with other professionals. • An integrated plan is formulated, but each professional retains the responsibility of providing the services he or she recommended. • Unlike a multidisciplinary model, members of an interdisciplinary team interact with each other before and after their individual interventions with the client. • On some occasions, members may cotreat a client while working on a number of goals concurrently.
Transdisciplinary	• Individuals trained in various disciplines take on aspects of each others' roles. • Members are usually employed by a single organization. • All duties are shared, including data keeping and team leadership, although they may be assigned to specific team members. • Relatively high time demands are placed on members.	• Professional lines blur more often than in the other two models. • Assessments, treatment plans, and interventions are often carried out jointly, perhaps using an *arena approach,* in which several professionals look on and discuss observations and conclusions as one individual interacts with the client. • Role exchange or role release may occur during the intervention stage, where a different professional may carry out a program recommended by another. • Extreme role blurring is seen as a serious disadvantage of this model.

A Flowchart of Clinical Questions

Clinical services begin with screening or referral, or as a step beyond EIS (i.e., RTI) services. Any of these entry portals could identify a child as needing evaluation to determine eligibility and need for special education services (including speech–language intervention). When services are justified, they are implemented with recursive stages of planning, implementing, and evaluating progress. A particular child may enter or reenter this cycle of activities at multiple points from infancy through adolescence. Numbers in the descriptive paragraphs that follow correspond to numbered decision points in Figure 4.3.

1. *Does the child have a problem that might signify a language disorder?* Entry into the formalized language assessment and intervention system is triggered by screening or referral. Screening does not result in diagnosis but in the identification of children with risks who need formal evaluation. Screening may be conducted by members of a transdisciplinary team or trained assistants. Referrals also may be triggered when a child is diagnosed with a related condition that presents known risks to language and literacy development (e.g., Down syndrome, profound hearing impairment, fetal alcohol spectrum disorder). Formal assessment and intervention also may come after failure to respond to tiers of preventive activities in RTI programs.

2. *Does language difference explain all or part of perceived gaps in a child's current abilities?* The selection of valid assessment procedures requires consideration of cultural–linguistic diversity. If a child is learning English as a dual or second language, alternative assessment methods and tools may be required. Cultural diversity questions apply to every child. If language difference is a major factor, a period of dynamic instruction and assessment could help a team decide whether to initiate a formal diagnostic process for a particular child. All assessment activities must be sensitive to familial–cultural differences.

3. *Does the child have a language disorder (possibly related to some comorbid condition)?* Information from parents, teachers, and children with suspected disorders is critical to making a valid diagnosis. General education teachers, educational psychologists, neuropsychologists, teacher consultants, school social workers, and physicians with various subspecialties also contribute. Diagnosis is never a completely unilateral decision. Considerations for diagnosing language disorder as a primary or secondary condition are discussed later in this chapter and in the remaining chapters of Part II. A child must be reevaluated every three years to determine if he or she continues to have a disability, but districts may "dispense with the triennial evaluation when the child's parents and the public agency agree that a reevaluation is unnecessary" (Section 300.303[b][2]). Under IDEA '04, identification of school-age students with disabilities must include consideration of whether the student has had appropriate instruction in reading and must take into account how he or she performed on statewide and school district testing.

4a. *Does the child qualify for special services?* Eligibility for an IEP is based on whether a child meets the diagnostic criteria for one of the named categories of disability (see Figure 4.1), "who, by reason thereof, needs special education and related services" (IDEA '04, Sec. 300.8).

4b. *Does the child need special services?* Questions about *need* are different from questions about *eligibility,* which are based on diagnosis of disability. Decisions about need are based on evidence that a child needs special services to benefit from education. For infants, toddlers, and young children, need is determined by an individualized family service plan (IFSP) team; for school-age children or adolescents, it is determined by an individualized education plan (IEP)

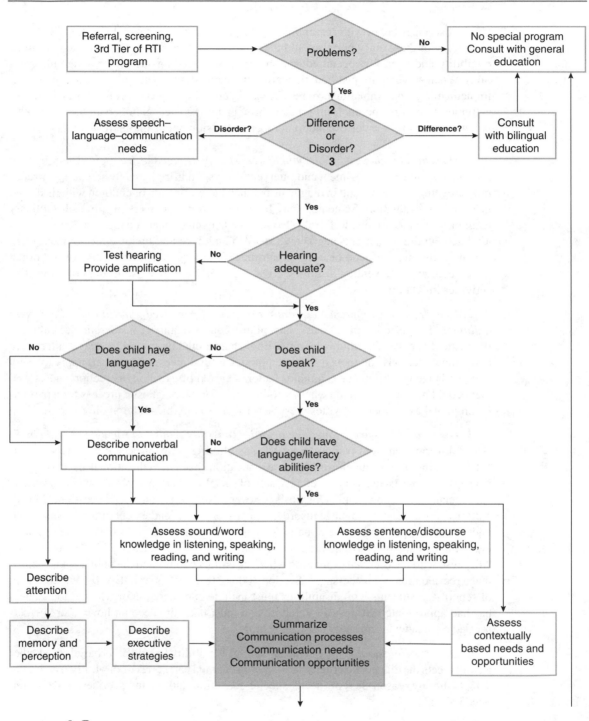

figure *4.3*

Decision-Making Flowchart for the Primary Steps of the Language Assessment and Intervention Process for a School-Age Child Under Part B of IDEA '04

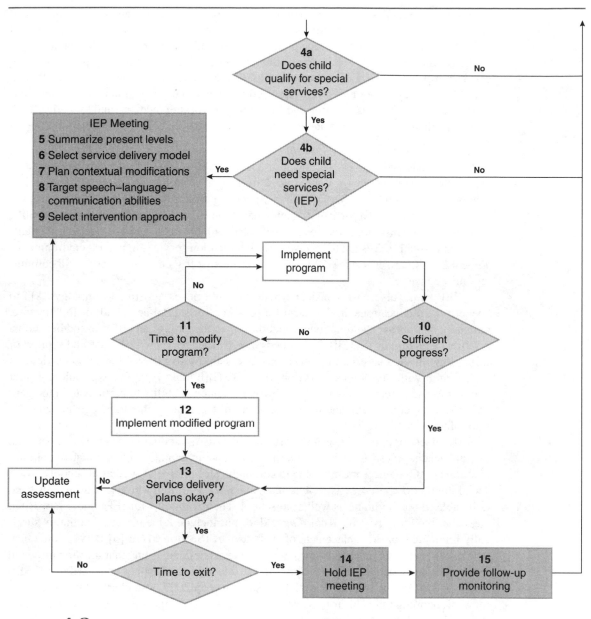

figure *4.3*

Continued

team. The need for transition services also must be considered at key points in a child's move-ment through the educational system and beyond. Children can receive related services on top of their primary special education (under IEPs) or early intervention services (under IFSPs). A child with an intellectual disability (cognitive impairment or mental retardation), for example, can receive language intervention services as a related service.

5. *What are the child's present levels of performance?* Regardless of the basis for eligibility, a child who needs language intervention services should have comprehensive assessment to identify his or her communication processes, needs, and opportunities. Descriptions of communication processes should address communication (including social interaction and pragmatics), speech production, and language abilities at the sound, word, sentence, and discourse levels across all four modalities (listening, speaking, reading, and writing). For preschool-age children, assessment also should include play skills and emergent literacy. Other areas to be assessed include speech perception and information-processing skills, such as attention and short-term or working memory, and executive functions for self-regulation and strategic compensation.

6. *What services (including assistive technology) does the child need?* Planning teams make decisions about goals, settings, providers, services, scheduling needs, and assistive technology based on what a student needs to benefit from education, rather than what a school system has to offer. Service delivery planning is based on team decisions about LRE for a particular child at a particular point in development. To the maximum extent possible, school-age students with IEPs are to be educated with typically learning peers, and infants and toddlers with IFSPs are to receive early intervention services in natural environments. Table 4.2 summarizes service delivery components that IEP committees and IFSP committees may consider.

IEP teams also must consider whether a child needs assistive technology (AT) to "benefit from education," in the case of a preschool or school-age child, or to "increase, maintain, or improve the functional capabilities," in the case of an infant or toddler with a disability (Section 614[d][3][B][v]). Funds may be used to improve the use and support of technology in the classroom to "maximize accessibility to general education curriculum for children with disabilities" (Section 611[e][2][C][iv] and [v]). Teams should consider whether assistive technology would improve the student's ability to participate in the general education curriculum, and if so, what types of technology should be considered (Marino, Marino, & Shaw, 2006).

Devices for personal use are not funded by IDEA, but distinctions between personal use and academic use are fuzzy. Children who need augmentative and alternative communication (AAC) devices must be able to communicate at home as well as at school and for social interaction purposes as well as academic ones. Children who use hearing aids need to be able to hear at home as well as at school. The regulations for IEPs under Part B are clear that the term *assistive technology* "does not include a medical device that is surgically implanted, or the replacement of such device" (Section 614[d][3][B][v]). A medical device or service, as interpreted through case law, is defined as one that must be provided by a physician. Cochlear implantation is thus excluded from funding under IEPs or IFSPs. The proposed regulations for Part C, published in May 2007, also clarified that programming or mapping of cochlear implant sound-processing components, termed *optimization* (typically done by audiologists), also would not be covered under IFSPs. Until public policies are adequately funded, many children will continue to lack access to appropriate assistive technology (including high-quality hearing aids and other listening devices) that can help them function like their peers in educational and other interactive settings. It is a problem that deserves greater attention and advocacy and one that was not resolved under IDEA '04.

7. *Should specific contexts be changed or introduced?* The four questions of context-based assessment and intervention (introduced in Chapter 1) start and end with outside-in questions about the demands of critical curricular (including social) contexts and whether they should be modified in the intervention process. Interdisciplinary and transdisciplinary collaboration processes can be used to modify contexts to support children's development and provide increased opportunities for participation.

table *4.2*　Variables Involved in Selecting Service Delivery Options

Variable	Common Types	Description
Settings	Home and family contexts	Families with young children may have service delivery in their homes or meet with families with similar needs in a center; families who live in remote settings may receive some services through distance technologies.
	Classroom based contexts —General education —Resource rooms —Self-contained	Children may receive services in either general or special education classrooms. Services in general education classrooms often are called *inclusive*. Services delivered in special education classrooms may be housed in general education buildings or in *center programs* designed for students with complex needs.
	Pull-out contexts —Small group —Individual	Children may leave their classrooms and travel to a separate therapy room to receive specialized services in a small group of peers or individually, either in a therapy room or other setting outside the classroom.
	Social contexts	Services may be delivered in playground activities, lunchtime social groups, or other nonacademic settings.
	Employment contexts	Adolescents or young adults with complex needs may receive context-based assessment and intervention services in employment settings.
People and Roles	Collaborative–consultative	Clinicians may assume collaborative roles with family members, teachers, peers, or employers as an adjunct to another service or as the primary mode of service delivery, also called *indirect*.
	Direct	Clinicians often interact directly with a child in pull-out setting, but direct services can be delivered in classroom settings as well.
	Parent or teacher implemented	Parents, teachers, or assistive personnel may serve as primary intervention agents or as incidental agents, actively seeking opportunities to work on targeted abilities in support of a primary intervention agent.
	Team taught	Clinicians may work with classroom teachers to plan lessons and implement intervention in conjunction with general or special education instruction. This would still be categorized as direct service.
Schedules	Length of sessions	Sessions vary in length from a few minutes of intensive daily drill on a particular targeted phoneme or speech skill to sessions of an hour or more in length in collaborative team teaching.
	Times per week	Twice-weekly sessions often are used with elementary school children, but scheduling every child in the same way violates policies that require individualized service delivery. Sessions may be scheduled once per week, three or four times per week, or daily, particularly in a language classroom program or using intensive block scheduling.
	Longer intervals	At some points in a child's program, weekly sessions may not be needed, and a plan may specify biweekly, monthly, or even longer intervals between direct contact for consulting or monitoring purposes.
	Block schedules	Block schedules schedule services for blocks of time, interspersed with blocks in which no direct services are provided but with the clinician available for consultation. For example, a 3:1 schedule might involve three weeks of three-day-per-week service delivery followed by one week of consultation and inclass service delivery.
	Variable schedules	To the extent that policies allow, it is helpful to build flexibility into schedules of IEPs and IFSPs so that adjustments can be made as indicated by a child's progress (or lack thereof) based on prior criteria established by the team.

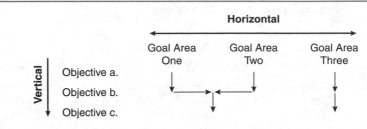

figure *4.4*

Combined Horizontal and Vertical Organization of Goals and Objectives

8. *Which speech, language/literacy, and communication abilities should be targeted in intervention?* Along with outside-in questions, context-based assessment and intervention are guided by inside-out questions to identify abilities to be targeted for an individual child. Goals are selected that are most likely to narrow gaps between a child's abilities and what he or she needs to be able to do. The answers require consideration of multiple input sources (e.g., ethnographic interviews, formal test results, informal assessment data, and dynamic assessment data). Although multiple developmental domains may need to be targeted, having too many goals can lead to fragmentation and lack of focus, so plans require coordination. Figure 4.4 illustrates a system for conceptualizing several horizontal goal areas, each with a vertical sequence of short-term objectives that can lead from baseline levels of functioning to the IEP goal. Short-term objectives specify what the child will do (defined in observable terms regarding what the *child* will do, not the clinician); under what conditions (such as the degree of scaffolding); and how well (criteria for knowing when the objective has been achieved).

IDEA '04 does not require short-term objectives to appear on a student's IEP unless the student is part of the 3 percent of students approved to be tested with alternative assessment methods. For students qualifying for alternative assessment, IEPs must include both long-term goals and short-term objectives, with relevance to standards of the general education curriculum. Although no longer required on all IEPs, short-term objectives can serve as benchmarks for monitoring progress and thus may be advisable.

9. *What intervention approach and activities should be used?* Intervention approaches and objectives are not matched one to one. Multiple activities may be used to target single objectives, or single activities may be used to target multiple objectives. Choices of approaches and related activities should be guided by the evidence-based practice (EBP) triad—scientific evidence, clinician expertise, and participant/client values. Figure 4.5 lists variables that may exist on a continuum from adult directed and highly controlled to child centered and more naturalistic. Choices about which method is best should be intentional and individualized. For example, a child may need a more structured approach to learn sound–symbol associations at the word level but a more naturalistic approach to acquire language skills at the sentence and discourse levels.

10. *Is progress occurring?* EBP involves gathering evidence on the effectiveness of an intervention for a particular child. In addition to keeping data within intervention activities, periodic probes should evaluate generalization within naturalistic contexts. For example, play samples, oral and written language samples, and read-aloud and paraphrasing samples may be coded for targeted abilities and compared against baseline levels.

11. *Has enough change occurred that it is time to add complexity or to target a higher developmental level?* Optimal plans start at a child's developing edge of competence and

figure *4.5*

Contrasting Intervention Variables from More Adult Directed and Structured to More Child Centered and Naturalistic

Adult directed	⟷	Child centered
Structured	⟷	Naturalistic
Prescribed sequence	⟷	Context-driven
Direct instruction	⟷	Constructive learning
Discrete skills	⟷	Integrated components

introduce challenging activities with intervention to stretch a child's zone of proximal development (ZPD; Vygotsky, 1934/1962, 1978). Vertical objective sequences (as illustrated in Figure 4.4) anticipate the need for regular adjustment in difficulty level. Figure 4.6 shows a range of variables that can be adjusted to make a task more demanding. Intervention teams also need to step back and reassess a plan more globally. An IFSP for an infant or toddler must be reconsidered every 6 months and an IEP, every 12 months. For school-age students, interim reports on progress should occur in conjunction with report cards.

12. *If not enough change is occurring, what modifications are needed?* If no change or very little change is occurring, modifications may be needed in program goals or intervention methods. Parent input is critical. Major changes require reconvening the IFSP or IEP team.

13. *Does the current service delivery model remain best for meeting the child's needs?* It may be necessary to modify service delivery and placement variables (outlined in Table 4.2) as well as other components of a child's program.

14. *Is it time for the child to exit formal intervention services?* At some point, a child may be ready to exit formal services. Changes in placement should be based on formal

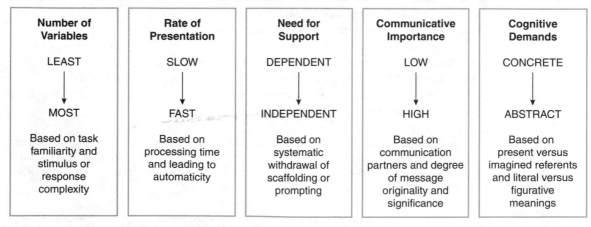

Number of Variables	Rate of Presentation	Need for Support	Communicative Importance	Cognitive Demands
LEAST	SLOW	DEPENDENT	LOW	CONCRETE
↓	↓	↓	↓	↓
MOST	FAST	INDEPENDENT	HIGH	ABSTRACT
Based on task familiarity and stimulus or response complexity	Based on processing time and leading to automaticity	Based on systematic withdrawal of scaffolding or prompting	Based on communication partners and degree of message originality and significance	Based on present versus imagined referents and literal versus figurative meanings

figure *4.6*

Intervention Variables That Can Be Adjusted to Control Task Complexity and Degree of Difficulty

reevaluation and require convening the IFSP or IEP team, which includes the parents and child or adolescent whenever appropriate.

15. *Does follow-up monitoring indicate a need for additional services?* Follow-up monitoring should occur after students leave special education. In systems in which a continuum of services becomes a reality, services may be viewed not as all-or-none choices but as flexible plans that can be adjusted with less demanding processes and paperwork, while still protecting children's right to a free, appropriate public education.

SUMMARY

Clinicians and intervention-planning teams follow a flow of recursive practices to provide specialized assessment and intervention services. Decision points are guided both by policy and best-practice concerns. Cultural sensitivity, personal sensitivity to a particular child's and family's needs, and collaborative practices are all essential components of clinical practice.

Categorization, Diagnosis, and Causation

Is it a good idea to test children for disability and assign a diagnostic label when a disorder is found? Questions about labeling have been hotly debated for decades, and no consensus has been reached.

Pros and Cons of Categorization

In hypothetical discussions, categories of disability have central, idealized prototypes—the proverbial textbook examples. In real life, disabilities have fuzzy, overlapping boundaries, making it difficult to fit real children with disabilities into neat diagnostic groups. A concern with diagnostic labeling is that labels may negatively influence how people view a child and interact with him or her, thus increasing the levels of disability rather than decreasing them. Even if exact diagnosis were possible, categorization might lead to stereotyping, with too much focus on the features of disorder and limited awareness of a child's positive traits and individual identity. On the other hand, categorical systems could be helpful to intervention planning precisely because they do narrow the focus to the most relevant areas of concern and suggest a means for organizing assessment questions and intervention approaches.

An international group of scholars (Florian et al., 2006) addressed questions of traditional classification systems that sort children into discrete disability categories and pointed to three main problems: (1) lack of recognition of complexity of human differences, (2) unnecessary stigmatization, and (3) not enough benefits to overshadow the limitations. They identified two sides of an international debate characterized

> on one hand, by positions that see disability and special needs as caused by individual limitations and deficits, and on the other hand, by positions that see disability and special needs as caused by the limitations and deficits of the educational systems in accommodating the diversity of children they serve. (p. 44)

This book acknowledges distinctions among diagnostic categories but emphasizes the potential for both positive and negative influences from the systems in which children interact. A primary goal of contextualized intervention is to modify systems in which children interact to reduce functional limitations and increase opportunities to participate, thus reducing disability, consistent with the WHO/ICF (2001) framework (introduced in Chapter 1; see also following section).

Categorization is not likely to disappear. It provides access to tangible benefits, such as special education services, assistive technology, and even supplemental Social Security payments to assist with the costs of raising a child with a disability. Policy requirements make it necessary to categorize children to find them eligible for special services and related funding. Classification also occurs because pattern recognition is a feature of human cognition. Classifying phenomena into groups with similar attributes is a natural act that contributes to learning. Categories are human inventions influenced by individual perceptions, cultural schemas, and political power structures (Hyter, 2007a). Categorization is the basis of reference to classes of concepts in language. Every common noun actually refers to a category of entities that share key features, including concrete nouns such as *cat* and abstract nouns such as *language impairment.*

It is important to be mindful of potential for misuse of classification, however, to prevent overcategorization and reduce stereotyping. The communication processes, needs, and opportunities model facilitates planning to reduce disability regardless of other factors associated with a particular diagnosis.

Sources Defining Disorders

Diagnostic criteria are established through a lengthy sociopolitical consensus-building process. Two primary sources of diagnostic classification criteria are the World Health Organization *International Classification of Functioning* (WHO/ICF; 2001) and *The Diagnostic and Statistical Manual of Mental Disorders* (4th edition; *DSM-IV;* APA, 1994). The *DSM-IV* (APA, 1994) was republished in a "text revised" version (*DSM-IV-TR*) in 2000; a fully revised *DSM-V* is expected in 2011. The *DSM-IV-TR* constituted a minor revision with changes in the descriptive text but not the diagnostic criteria. Other sources of diagnostic criteria are professional associations, such as the American Speech-Language-Hearing Association (ASHA), Autism Society of America (ASA), and International Dyslexia Association (IDA). Joint committees also are formed across agencies to develop definitions of disorders of mutual interest. Examples are the National Joint Committee on Learning Disabilities (NJCLD) and National Joint Committee for the Communication Needs of Persons with Severe Disabilities.

Some groups work within national, state, and local boundaries to identify children with disabilities and related conditions and to set policies and criteria for finding children eligible for special education services. Advocacy groups may work to inform policy and also may take positions that constitute a form of policy for group members. Some classification systems are international. Science has no national boundaries, so the evidence supporting diagnostic categories also may come from anywhere in the world.

On an individual level, clinicians often are responsible for diagnosing disorders, possibly as a prerequisite for determining eligibility for service. It is important to remember that categories are human inventions—and only hypotheses at that. Categorical decisions and classification are fallible and subject to prejudgment and cultural bias. Categories often are encoded in policies, but any policy can be changed. Clinicians have a responsibility to be reflective, person-centered, evidence-consulting professionals. To the extent categories improve communication and shorten the pathway to knowing what to do next, they may be a good thing. To the extent they narrow focus, impede understanding, or lead one down a wrong pathway, they may act as barriers to understanding rather than facilitators (see Personal Reflection 4.3).

PERSONAL
reflection *4.3*

"When you have a hammer, everything looks like a nail."

David R. Beukelman (1987, p. 94), a speech–language pathologist and clinical researcher, works with children and adults with complex communication needs and emphasizes the danger of starting with a preconceived notion of what one expects to see.

Questions about Causation

Consideration of *etiology* (causal factors) requires caution. Causes may be difficult to discern, disentangle, or change. Causative factors are layered, interactive, and circular. Scientists, clinicians, and parents all are interested in causal factors. Scientists seek etiological evidence for conditions of concern on a global level, practitioners on a local level, and parents on a personal level, but knowing etiology rarely indicates what to do next. Any dietary, pharmacological, or genetic counseling implications need to be understood as soon as possible. In most cases, however, causative factors must be inferred, rarely can be confirmed, and have minimal implications about what to do next in language assessment and intervention.

Causes Are Layered

As illustrated in the opening to Part II, uncovering causal factors for any aspect of disordered development can be compared to peeling an onion. It is possible to uncover one causal factor, only to find another layer beneath that one, and another, and another. For example, seeking the cause for a child's developmental delay might uncover a particular diagnosis, for which malfunction of the neurolinguistic system could be responsible—but what is the cause of the neurolinguistic system malfunction? Perhaps anomalies can be found in structures and connections of the brain, but those in turn could be attributed to a particular protein, gene, and DNA. At what point is the true cause located?

Beyond internal etiologies, causal questions should address external factors. Outer layers may include environmental toxins and other factors that could lead to mutational changes or other influences on genetic expression. Environmental social factors also may be associated with caregiving (nutrition, nurturing and safety, or drug or alcohol use during pregnancy) or participation barriers. For school-age children, the nature of academic instruction should be considered as well. External factors are recognized in the WHO-ICF (2001) model and by the mandate in IDEA '04 to consider a child's prior instruction in reading when diagnosing disability and identifying a need for special education.

Causes Are Circular

A system theory view of disability (introduced in Chapter 3) emphasizes that causes are circular. Consider head injury. Children with attention deficits, hyperactivity, and behavioral disorders are more likely to take risks that lead to accidents that cause traumatic brain injury (TBI) (Semrud-Clikeman, 2001); thus, sequelae (symptoms of damage) may be both a result of the damage and also a factor in causing the injury. Findings from longitudinal research also have shown language and literacy disorders to appear more or less severe at different developmental points (Bishop & Edmundson, 1987; Scarborough & Dobrich, 1990) or to fit one or another subtype category better at a different developmental point (Conti-Ramsden & Botting, 1999). Such findings are attributed to circular cause-and-effect patterns, in which timing of internal patterns of neurological growth move in and out of synchrony with advances in external demands, such as changing academic language expectations. As adolescents become more aware of their disabilities, they may adopt an "I don't care" attitude as a defense mechanism, which must be addressed directly in intervention if the vicious cycle is to be reversed. Circular patterns of causation highlight the need for intervention goals to address changing demands of external contexts while working to improve the internal functional capabilities of children and their sense of self-efficacy.

Causes are Multifactorial

Rutter (2007) (see Personal Reflection 4.4) emphasized the need to consider multiple factors in the causation of developmental disorders, noting that "several different causal pathways may all lead to the same endpoint"; thus, "there is no point in seeking to identify the single cause of any outcome, because there is no such thing" (p. 378). This does not absolve clinicians from asking whether risk or protective factors might be at work that should be considered in intervention planning. It does, however, lead to caution when trying to understand what might have caused a particular disorder of child development.

PERSONAL reflection *4.4*

"A causal effect is usually composed of a constellation of components acting in concert. The study of causation, therefore, will necessarily be informative on only one or more subsets of such components. There is no such thing as a single basic necessary and sufficient cause."

Sir Michael Rutter (2007, p. 377), from the United Kingdom, has been called the father of modern child psychiatry. He conducted early Isle of Wight studies of reading disorders and learning disability and has contributed to the understanding of the epidemiology of a wide range of disorders, including autism spectrum disorders and disorders related to deprivation of experience and attachment.

SUMMARY

This section has presented arguments in the debate on labeling and diagnostic classification. It has emphasized the wisdom of viewing classification as a set of hypothetical groupings that are formed by committees considering the current best research evidence. Several key sources were introduced that have played a major role in diagnosing disorder.

Questions of causation were considered as well, including issues related to layering of causes and the reciprocal nature of complex causal factors. When asked about causation by parents, clinicians should help them understand that causes are often layered, circular, and complex. As noted throughout this book, causes are not just within children, and neither are solutions.

Testing and Exclusionary Factors in Diagnosis

Standardized language and literacy testing often is used to assess a child's performance relative to peers in a normative sample. To interpret test scores, clinicians must understand how standardized tests are designed and how scores are derived. Test interpretation also requires consideration of factors besides disorder that might cause a child to score low on a standardized test. Cultural–linguistic mismatch is a prime example. No test can be completely free of cultural bias, and no one test score should be used to make a diagnostic decision. If a test is standardized on a group of children who differ systematically from the child being tested in some way other than disorder, standardized scores from that test should not be applied to make diagnostic decisions about the child.

Using Standardized Tests to Diagnose Disorders

Although cautions are warranted, standardized test scores provide a critical piece of evidence for diagnosing language disorders in children and adolescents. Test scores document discrepancies between what a particular child can demonstrate when attempting structured and controlled age-appropriate communication activities and what a typically developing child can demonstrate when attempting the same tasks.

Standardized tests work well for this purpose if they are culturally and linguistically appropriate. When they are not, one option is to rely on alternative forms of assessment. For example, developmental evidence can be provided by cultural informants in the child's milieu (see Case Example 4.1), or contextualized evidence may be used to assess whether the child shows functional limitations that seem resistant to change even when culturally appropriate instruction is intensified, as in RTI models. Alternative tools for children with cultural linguistic diversity are considered in the chapters of Part III.

Selecting an instrument to use for diagnostic purposes requires clinicians to be knowledgeable about test design and interpretation. At a minimum, clinicians need to understand how standardized tests are constructed, how they relate to the normal distribution, and how criteria are developed for diagnosing disorder based on a particular test. A tool that can be used for judging how well a test meets criteria for being a well-researched test based on scientific evidence appears as Figure 4.7.

Selecting a Test with Validity for the Intended Purpose

Evaluation of test validity requires asking the question Valid for what purpose? If the test is intended to diagnose language disorder, it should reflect the construct of language and sample enough content to constitute a valid assessment of the construct. Manuals for tests that have been developed using classical test theory generally provide evidence of both construct and content validity based on expert opinion and relationship to the literature. Construct validity is theoretical and judged by the degree to which the test reflects expert opinion and current evidence on the nature of language and language disorder. *Content validity* is judged by the evidence of how well the content of the test matches its stated purpose.

Newer tests may have been developed using evaluation methods that are based more on data than opinion. For example, *item response theory* (IRT) techniques test the validity of individual items based on pilot studies. IRT analyses measure the degree to which lower-level items are passed by children with relatively low general ability (and not missed by children with higher ability) but higher-level items are passed by children with higher levels of general ability (but not lower ability). Items that do not fit the desired profile are discarded or may be revised and reevaluated. Similarly, items that are biased for children with particular characteristics, such as a race or ethnicity identification, can be eliminated based on IRT results. This approach is better than using expert opinion or census-based percentages of children from representative racial/ethnic groups in a test's standardization sample (see Personal Reflection 4.5).

PERSONAL reflection *4.5*

"How do scores from a 75% white, 3.6% Asian, 12% African American, 0.9% Native American sample apply to my 100% Cambodian child?"

Elena Plante (Nelson, Plante, Brennan, Anderson, & Johnson, 2005), a speech–language pathologist and language scientist, was speaking about the problems of using a classical test theory to control for test bias for children from different racial and ethnic groups and her recommendation to use an IRT approach instead.

─CASE **example** *4.1*─

Adam and His Parents from Iceland

A pediatrician called one day to notify the speech–language pathologist (SLP) consulting in a regional school district about a baby who had just been born to Icelandic parents who were international graduate students at a nearby university. The physician wanted to be sure the family received appropriate support services as soon as possible. The couple's baby, a boy named Adam, had been born with a cleft lip and palate, and the family needed consultation. The consulting SLP visited the family in the hospital and arranged for a community transition meeting between the district's early intervention team and members of the hospital neonatal services team. She also accompanied the family on their first visit to an interdisciplinary cleft palate team in a city a few hours away.

Although the hospital-based cleft palate team assumed a primary role in addressing the child's physical impairment and related needs, the local SLP continued regular home visits. She consulted with the parents to make sure they understood the team's medical recommendations and to monitor and support Adam's development through his first 2.5 years. During this time, the family coped with early feeding challenges and surgical interventions. They actively sought information about the best ways to support the development of speech, language, and emergent literacy for their son.

Early in the process, the parents had decided that speaking Icelandic almost exclusively at home would be in the best interests of their child. They intended to return to their home country after completing their doctoral degrees and thought that hearing a single language consistently would be one less challenge for their son. As he neared his third birthday, however, Adam was producing only one- and two-word utterances, supplemented by gestures, and the parents became concerned about their son's limited vocabulary. They also

were concerned about his frequent ear infections and were beginning to see communicative frustration, temper tantrums, and fewer attempts at interaction. They requested a formal assessment of his language skills to see if he might need language intervention and/or placement in a parent–toddler intervention program that met weekly.

This presented a dilemma, however, for the SLP, who did not speak Icelandic and who knew that administering a formal test in English would be inappropriate. The IFSP team, including the parents, then developed an assessment plan that included the parents' gathering a language sample in Icelandic and translating it into English for the SLP, who then would compare it to broad developmental expectations that apply across cultures in the first few years of life. The clinician also located an authorized adaptation of the MacArthur–Bates Communicative Development Inventories (CDIs) (Fenson, Marchman, Thal, Dale, Reznick, & Bates, 2004) for Icelandic through the test's advisory board website. This allowed the parents to provide additional information about their child's words, gestures, and emerging sentences.

Considering all the evidence—including that exposure to more than one language has not been found to be a risk factor for language delay and might even have positive benefits—the family decided to begin to use English for interaction in selected activities. For example, they used English during play dates with neighborhood parents and children, when interacting with Adam using books in English, and on family outings into the community. The IFSP also was modified so that Adam could attend a nursery school program with other toddlers with and without disabilities, and he and his father began to attend the district's weekly parent–infant interaction sessions while his mother was teaching.

A number of formal tests are described in the developmental and special population chapters and listed in the Part III Appendix. Some tests are designed as comprehensive measures for assessing language using a set of varied subtests. Others are designed to provide in-depth information in selected areas of concern, such as early communication acts,

figure *4.7*

Reviewer Checklist

This checklist can be used to seek information in a test's technical and/or examiner manual indicating that it is supported by scientific evidence.

Background Information			
Test name _____		**Date of Review** _____	
Publisher _____		**Reviewer** _____	
Year of original publication _____		**Ages and purpose for which test may be used**	
Current edition _____ **Year** _____		_____	
Ages for which test is appropriate _____		_____	

Test Validity	Yes	No	Reviewer comments:
Is there information to indicate that the test is built on a valid construct?			
Is there information to indicate that the test covers the content adequately?			
Is there information about sensitivity and specificity that support the test's validity for diagnostic purposes?			
Has bias been addressed by using item response theory (IRT) techniques and not just adding proportions of children in different cultural–linguistic groups to the standardization sample?			
Test Reliability	Yes	No	Reviewer comments:
Is there evidence of stability within the test's subtests (reported as Cronbach's alpha of 0.80 or higher)?			
Is there evidence of test–retest reliability?			
Is there evidence of interscorer reliability?			
Child/Clinician Friendliness	Yes	No	Reviewer comments:
Are children likely to be willing to take this test?			
Is this test interesting to give?			
Is this test easy to score?			
Does this test provide useful information?			

language comprehension, or phonemic awareness. Still others are designed to be sensitive to particular diagnostic symptoms, such as features of autism spectrum disorders, hearing impairment, or phonological-processing capabilities. Some tests are designed for children from particular racial/ethnic groups or linguistic or dialectal communities.

An important indicator of a test's validity for diagnosing language disorder is research evidence about its sensitivity and specificity. *Sensitivity* is the degree to which a test is good at identifying *all* cases of the disorder, reflected as a high rate of identifying children with confirmed disorders as having the disorder, and a corresponding low rate of *false negatives,* in which children known to have the disorder are not identified by the new test. *Specificity* is measured as the degree to which a test is good at identifying *only* cases of the disorder, reflected as a high rate of identifying children with confirmed typical language (TL) as having no disorder, along with a corresponding low rate of *false positives,* in which children known to have TL are identified by the test as having a language disorder. Figure 4.8 illustrates specificity and sensitivity data for a hypothetical new test based on comparison with so-called gold standard procedures. A *gold standard procedure* provides trusted classification of children as having a disorder or not. In many cases, a gold standard is an existing standardized test with known psychometric properties, augmented by clinician judgment.

When selecting a formal test, clinicians should check to make sure that the test's technical manual provides information about how well the test meets sensitivity and specificity criteria and the scientific rigor of procedures used to document that evidence. Sensitivity and specificity can be optimized by adjusting the cut score at which disorder is indicated. This argues against using rigid threshold criteria (e.g., 1.33 standard deviations [SDs] below the mean) to decide whether a child is scoring outside normal limits. A better alternative is to use cut scores that are designed to maximize sensitivity and specificity results for a particular test, as described in the test's manual (Spaulding, Plante, & Farinella, 2006). These values can be maximized, and the risk of false-positive or false-negative results can be reduced, by adjusting threshold scores signaling disorder. For example, Tomblin, Records, and Zhang (1996), in their epidemiological study of specific language impairment (Epi-SLI), reported that a cutoff score of –1.14 SDs resulted in 86 percent sensitivity and

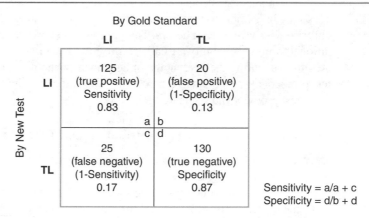

figure *4.8*

Hypothetical Results from Evaluating the Sensitivity and Specificity of a New Test Compared to an Existing Gold Standard

These results are based on a set of hypothetical data for 300 children, with 150 identified as having the disorder (LI = language impairment) based on the gold standard methods and 150 identified as not having the disorder (TL = typical language). This shows the new test meeting acceptable (> 80 percent) sensitivity by correctly identifying 83 percent of children who had the disorder as having it and acceptable specificity by correctly identifying 87 percent of children who did not have the disorder as not having it.

99 percent specificity in their sample. On this basis of data from this Epi-SLI study, Tomblin et al. (1997) established the prevalence rate for SLI at 7.4 percent (see Chapter 5).

Teams may be willing to risk a certain type of error to achieve a broader purpose. For example, a team involved in an early identification screening program could set a cut score relatively high to be sure to capture all children who may potentially have difficulty. They may be aware that casting a broad net will increase the rate of false positives (reducing a test's specificity) but may decide to do so because of a value to reduce false negatives so as to increase sensitivity to children with learning risks, perhaps so they can receive early intervening RTI services that do not require labeling.

A test's sensitivity and specificity may vary across sociocultural groups. Thus, evidence of both properties should be evaluated across groups to make sure the test does not falsely identify or miss children with particular racial/ethnic characteristics.

Selecting a Test with High Reliability

Reliability is a measure of the stability of the results of a particular instrument. A test can only be valid for a particular purpose if it is reliable first. According to classical test theory, reliability is measured in terms of its **internal consistency,** typically computed with a statistical test called *Cronbach's alpha.* This method of assessing reliability reflects the degree to which an individual's score is a good estimate of his or her true score, with a low level of measurement error. Based on convention, an acceptable Cronbach's alpha value would be 0.80 or above. Values over 0.90 are considered good, values below 0.70 are considered poor, and values between 0.60 and 0.70 are considered mediocre. If test designers find a low level of internal consistency, classical test theory would dictate adding items to improve the test's reliability. Doing so can yield improvements in the reliability statistic but it has a corresponding negative effect of lengthening the test. When IRT approaches to item evaluation are used, greater reliability is achieved by trimming items rather than adding them.

A reliable test is consistent in producing similar results each time it is administered. This may be demonstrated by readministering the test after an appropriate time period to children who have taken it before. This approach is known as *test–retest reliability.* Two additional forms of reliability are called *intrascorer* and *interscorer* reliability. They are evaluated by computing the percentage of agreement when the same clinician scores the same test protocol at two points in time or when two different clinicians independently score the same test protocol and compare their scores.

Understanding the Normal Distribution and Test Interpretation

Once a test has been thoroughly evaluated and standardized, it can contribute critical information for diagnosing disorder. No one test or procedure should ever be used as the sole basis for a particular diagnostic decision. Multiple sources of input from more than one instrument and person are essential to arrive at a valid diagnosis of primary or secondary language and literacy disorders, as discussed in the other chapters of Part II.

It also is important to know how to interpret standardized scores. *Raw scores,* which are generally based on counting correct or incorrect responses, cannot be interpreted unless they are normalized. To do this, they need to be transformed to *standardized scores* (usually by consulting tables in test manuals or by using a software scoring tool that accompanies a test). Transformed scores may be reported as standard scores, percentile scores, or age-equivalent or grade-equivalent scores.

Standard scores are based on data from a sample with a normal distribution, as illustrated in Figure 4.9. They may be expressed as *z*-scores (numbers of standard deviations from the mean, when the mean is set at 0), IQ-type scores (using a mean of 100 and standard deviation [SD] of 15), or other scoring methods. For example, suppose a child earns a raw score of 36 on a test and the mean score for children of the same age is 48; with a standard deviation of 6, the child scored exactly 2 SDs below the mean (computed as (36 − 48) / 6 = −2), which may be reported as a *z*-score of −2.0. By consulting Figure 4.9, one could see that only 2.27 percent of the normally distributed population would be expected to fall below that level. Thus, the child earning such a score would be considered to be very low functioning compared to same-age peers in the standardization sample.

Percentile scores indicate a child's ranking among comparable children taking a particular test (also represented in Figure 4.9). A percentile score indicates the percentage of others in the same age group in the standardization sample who scored lower than the child in question. For example, when a child scores at the 50th percentile, that means that half of children in the standardization sample scored lower and almost half scored higher. No one can score higher than the 99.9th percentile because it is impossible to score higher than 100 percent of people taking a test. Thus, the 50th percentile is an average score, comparable to a standard score of 100 in a perfectly normal distribution.

Equivalent scores are expressed relative to average scores that were earned by children in the standardization sample at a comparable age or grade. Age-equivalent and grade-equivalent scores may seem easy to understand, but they are not well suited to making

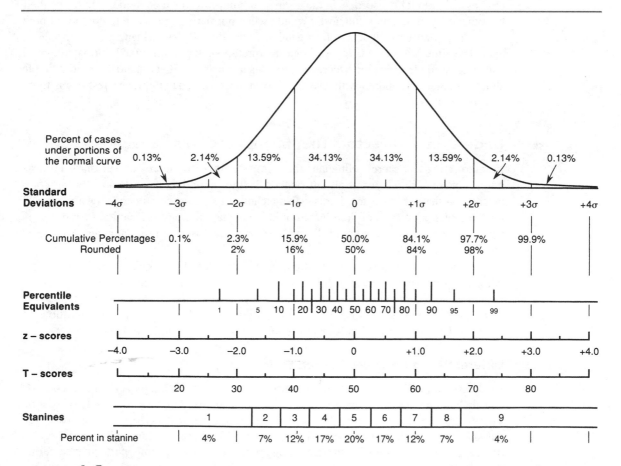

figure *4.9*

Normal Distribution Illustrating Relationships among Varied Methods for Computing Standard Scores

diagnostic decisions about disorders. Lahey (1988) pointed out many psychometric flaws with equivalency scores and recommended that "when there is a choice between both types of reporting for an instrument, standard scores should be utilized" (p. 162).

Confidence intervals may be reported as well, generally using tables provided in the test manual that reflect measurement error, which is always present but varies in magnitude. A higher degree of confidence (more than 95 percent, for example) would require the clinician to indicate a wider range of scores within which a child's true score would be certain to fall. Clinicians cannot be very confident that a single value (as compared with a confidence interval range) represents a child's true score, because it does not take measurement error into account.

How Should the Standardization Group Be Composed?

Language researchers debate whether children with language disorders should be included in normative standardization samples. Proponents of including children with disorders (e.g., Ukrainetz McFadden, 1996) have warned that not to do so would cut off the lower tip of the normal distribution and thus artificially skew it, increasing false positives and lowering specificity.

Peña, Spaulding, and Plante (2006) took the opposing position. They argued that including children with disorders in the normative group was not a good idea and tested their hypothesis by simulating diagnostic results when normative groups were composed both ways—with and without scores from students with disabilities influencing the normative data. The simulation results showed that interpretations based on mixed normative group data decreased identification accuracy, justifying a conclusion that a standardization sample should *not* include children with disorders if designers wanted to improve a test's sensitivity and specificity.

Understanding Factors That Might Lead to Misdiagnosis

In interpreting test scores, clinicians must consider that low scores on standardized tests might not reflect disorder at all but rather a lack of experience for demonstrating competence on the particular test items. Mismatches in experience can occur for a variety of reasons, such as when children have not had adequate literacy instruction or when they have been raised in poverty with limited exposure to books and the language associated with formal education.

Other risks can arise when children come from culturally–linguistically diverse populations or when they are English language learners. Although such children might need temporary instructional supports, they should not be identified as having a disorder. On the other hand, it is possible for a child to have a disorder in conjunction with conditions of diversity. Underidentification is just as problematic as overidentification.

Differentiating Problems Related to Poverty

As described in Chapter 3, extreme poverty is associated with language-learning contexts that do not adequately prepare children for the academic language demands of school. These contents also may not adequately prepare children to take formal tests. Research has shown that early communication experiences differ based on family income to such a degree that socioeconomic status (SES) can predict a child's academic performance during the school-age years.

Poverty is associated with less exposure to a wide range of vocabulary. Researchers also have described discourse level differences based on SES (Hart & Risley, 1995, 1999;

Wells, 1986). Children from low-income families are engaged more in talk about immediate daily-living concerns (e.g., what the child should do or not do, eat, or wear) than interactions around stories or discussions that extend beyond practical concerns. Large gaps in academic achievement between children being raised in low-income and middle-income families were a major motivator for passage of the NCLB legislation discussed previously in this chapter.

Poverty does not cause language disorders, but it does introduce a risk factor affecting acquisition of higher-level language and literacy skills in school. Poverty and related family stressors also can exacerbate the effects of childhood language disorders, complicating the assessment and intervention process for clinicians. Stereotyping children in poverty is just as problematic as other forms of stereotyping, however; it is important to respect family boundaries and to recognize that low-income and single-parent families, grandparent guardians, and foster parents all are capable of providing loving and nurturing home environments. Dynamic assessment activities and RTI initiatives can be helpful to sort out influences of poverty from disorder when children are struggling with language and literacy in educational settings.

Differentiating Problems Related to Cultural–Linguistic Diversity

Clinicians should avoid equating cultural–linguistic diversity with low SES. On the other hand, long-standing power structures make it difficult for people in particular racial/ethnic groups to share in socioeconomic rewards, which are distributed unequally (Hyter, 2007a).

As Boyd and Brock (2004) pointed out, the number of children with limited English proficiency in U.S. schools increased from around 1 million in 1986 to around 2.5 million in 1992, with an increase to 6 million expected by the year 2020. In contrast, the teaching force in U.S. schools is made up largely of homogeneous European American women who tend to come from working- to middle-class backgrounds and whose only language is English. Boyd and Brock argued that such mismatches matter because teachers from mainstream monolingual backgrounds are often "under-prepared to teach effectively students whose backgrounds are different from their own" (p. 3).

Similar statistics were reported in a 2007 survey of speech–language pathologists (SLPs) who are members of the American Speech-Language-Hearing Association (ASHA). Of the 66,992 SLPs who reported their racial group (46,980 did not specify race), results showed 92.9 percent White, 2.5 percent multiracial, 2.7 percent Black or African American, 1.6 percent Asian, 0.3 percent Native American or Alaskan Native, and 0.1 percent Native Hawaiian or Pacific Islander. Only 3.2 percent reported their ethnicity as Hispanic or Latino.

One can develop cultural competence for appreciating differences beyond one's own cultural experiences, but it requires a conscious effort by a reflective human being who recognizes the difficulty of overcoming bias. As described in Chapter 2, developing cultural–linguistic competence starts with acknowledging the limitations of one's narrowly focused cultural–linguistic lens, followed by conscious efforts to bring into view other perspectives and to keep extending one's views with each new encounter. Given the wide range of diverse cultures and languages in the world, multicultural competence is a lifelong quest.

Avoiding bias is not the same as denying differences. In standardized testing, controlled presentation of stimuli does not mean that every child experiences a particular test in the same way. Difficulty in test taking is relative to a child's experience with the content of the test. Assessment methods must be adjusted when a child's experiences do not match the assumptions of a standardized test so that language differences are not be confused with disorders. Over-identification of children from diverse cultures as having disorders not only is bad practice, but it also violates policy. The regulations for IDEA '04 indicate that states must have in effect, consistent with the purposes of 34 CFR Part 300 and with section 618(d) of the Act, policies and procedures designed to prevent the inappropriate overidentification or disproportionate representation by race and ethnicity of children as children with disabilities, including children with disabilities with a particular impairment described in 34 CFR 300.8 of the IDEA regulations. (34 CFR 300.173) (20 U.S.C. 1412[a][24])

Disproportionality suggests that bias may have played a role in assessment and eligibility determination. Establishing quotas for children in certain racial/ethnic groups, however, is not an appropriate solution. Children who demonstrate a disorder based on culturally linguistically appropriate procedures and who need special services should be eligible for services whether or not a proportional level has been reached.

Underidentification of children from groups with diverse cultural–linguistic experiences is equally problematic. Children from minority cultural groups are just as likely as children from majority cultures to have a primary language/literacy disorder (see Chapter 5) or a disorder secondary to any of the conditions described in Chapters 6 and 7. When symptoms of disorder do occur, it is important to identify them as early as possible to provide appropriate services. Reduced access to assessment and intervention services should not become the default approach to avoiding test bias and disproportionality. Educational teams must continue to educate themselves about language and literacy learning, both within and across cultures. Thus, they may be more effective in ensuring that all children have opportunities to participate in and to benefit from educational experiences tailored to their needs.

Assessing Spoken Language in Children Who Are Dual Language Learners

Dual language learners may be learning two languages simultaneously or sequentially. Genesee, Paradis, and Crago (2004) noted that dual language learning is the norm across the world and that children only seem different when "monolingual children are treated as the reference point for understanding all children's language development" (p. 3). Children who begin learning English as a second language once they reach school are called *English language learners (ELLs).*

Genesee and colleagues (2004) also noted that parents and teachers who have experience with dual language learners may be in the best position to identify bilingual children who are having difficulty by noting when a child "does not learn verbal material in the classroom or at home as quickly or as well as others" (p. 194). Such observations may lead to referral for formal testing. The regulations of IDEA '04 address the language of formal testing by stating the following:

> Each public agency must ensure that assessments and other evaluation materials used to assess a child under Part 300 are provided and administered in the child's native language or other mode of communication and in the form most likely to yield accurate information on what the child knows and can do academically, developmentally, and functionally, unless it is clearly not feasible to so provide or administer. (Section 300.304[c][1][ii])

Goldstein (2006) recommended that SLPs use a variety of procedures to differentiate language *difference* from *disorder* in children who are dual language learners. Noting that language skills rarely are distributed equally across the child's two languages, Goldstein recommended that assessments should examine a child's skills in both languages. A dual language learner, for example, might know one set of words in one language and another set of words in the other language. Sociolinguistic factors (e.g., associations of vocabulary clusters with particular speakers and settings) also might account for differences in word learning and other aspects of spoken and written language knowledge.

Assessing Reading Ability in Children Who Are Dual Language Learners

Dual language learners in family environments that provide rich exposure to at least one language are at no greater risk for language- and literacy-learning difficulties than monolingual children. On the other hand, ELLs have some risks for learning to read a less familiar language more slowly than native speakers of that language (McCardle, Mele-McCarthy, & Leos, 2005; Vaughn, Mathes, Linan-Thompson, & Francis, 2005).

Response to intervention (RTI) approaches are appropriate for ELLs and children with other forms of cultural–linguistic diversity. For dual language learners, it may be helpful to provide early intervention services in both their languages. Hammer and Miccio (2006), for example, found that bilingual children's receptive language skills in both English and Spanish were associated positively with their letter–word identification skills at the end of kindergarten. They also found that typically developing bilingual children from low-income families tended to be behind at the start of kindergarten in phonological awareness and letter identification skills but acquired those skills quickly when given explicit instruction in early reading. Páez and Renaldi (2006) found that kindergarten measures of English vocabulary and phonological awareness, as well as Spanish word-reading skills, were significant predictors of English word-reading skills in first grade. Other researchers have found evidence that bilingual children can benefit from combined oral–written language instruction in either language (Pollard-Durodola, Mathes, Vaughn, Cardenas-Hagan, & Linan-Thompson, 2006) or both languages (August et al., 2006).

Literacy instruction in one language can have positive effects on the rate of learning to read in the other. First-language skills are associated with second-language skills, but only if children have a particular literacy skill in the first language (August et al., 2006). Furthermore, children may require explicit instruction to make connections across languages. Early intervening services for dual language learners may incorporate explicit instruction in English and attempts to form bridges to other cultural–linguistic experiences to assess response to intervention.

SUMMARY

Accurate diagnosis and effective intervention for language and literacy disorders require assessment of the various systems involved. Children must be viewed as individuals, and care must be taken not to confuse disorders with other factors that may cause a child to score lower on a particular measure, including lack of access to instruction, poverty, cultural–linguistic mismatch to a test, dual language learning, or the presence of a comorbid disorder (e.g., hearing loss) that makes it difficult to measure language ability accurately.

Differential diagnosis is made more difficult when several complicating factors (e.g., low socioeconomic status and second-language learning) are at play, but skilled clinicians may apply multiple techniques, including dynamic assessment and parental and teacher report, to sort out differences from disorders. An extended period of observation and multiple sources of input can help clinicians avoid mistakes associated with either over- or underidentification of children with diverse cultural–linguistic experiences and socioeconomic challenges.

Prevalence, Prevention, and Prognosis

Prevalence and Incidence

Prevalence refers to the total number of cases with a particular disorder within a specified population at any point in time—such as the proportion of all school-age children with an existing diagnosis based on epidemiological figures reported for a particular year. *Incidence* refers to the number of newly identified cases of a disorder or condition within a particular timeframe, often one year, but sometimes per day, or even per minute.

Information about prevalence and incidence sometimes is difficult to interpret, as definitions and diagnostic procedures change or differ across epidemiological investigations. Categorical frequency counts are dictated by policy. Federal special education data use *nonduplicated* frequency counts, which can lead to misconceptions. For example, Table 4.3 shows 330,043 children with a primary speech or language impairment and only 12,065 with a primary specific learning disability in the age range 3 to 5 years, but these proportions flip to 5,570 for speech or language impairment and 146,649 for LD in the years 18 to 21. It is likely that at least some of these children switched from a diagnosis of language impairment to LD as they moved through school.

table 4.3   Students Served under IDEA Part B by Disability Category (Fall 2005)

| Disability Category | Age Range (in years) | | | | |
| | Preschool | School Age | | | |
	3 to 5	6 to 11	12 to 17	18 to 21	6 to 21
Developmental delay (applicable ages 3 through 9)	260,692	79,070	N/A	N/A	79,070
Primary Disorders					
Speech or language impairment	330,043	994,098	157,547	5,570	1,157,215
Specific learning disability	12,065	920,888	1,712,681	146,649	2,780,218
Sensory–Motor Disorders					
Orthopedic impairment	8,201	30,321	28,075	4,731	63,127
Multiple disabilities	8,515	51,045	54,443	18,426	133,914
Hearing impairment	7,846	32,305	35,364	4,718	72,387
Visual impairment	3,424	11,742	12,309	1,945	25,996
Deaf–blindness	236	611	730	251	1,592
Cognitive–Communicative Disorders					
Mental retardation	22,759	172,214	301,674	71,604	545,492
Traumatic brain injury	1,077	7,898	13,329	2,282	23,509
Autism	30,305	110,529	72,136	10,792	193,637
Emotional disturbance	5,789	131,768	311,339	29,277	472,384
Other health impairment	13,135	231,785	308,606	20,637	561,028

Source: Based on tables provided by the U.S. Department of Education, Office of Special Education Programs, Data Analysis System (DANS). Tables were current as of July 17, 2006.

Prevention

Prevention is important both for the general population and for individual children. Prevention activities may address primary, secondary, or tertiary concerns.

Primary Prevention

Primary prevention activities aim at reducing new occurrences of a disease or disorder. If genetic and rehabilitation scientists can learn more about the primary causes of a condition, etiological factors may be removed, or at least mitigated, and new cases can be prevented. For example, researchers are seeking factors that might explain the apparent upswing in autism spectrum disorders (discussed further in Chapter 6) with the goal of prevention. Primary prevention efforts also are involved when prospective mothers are warned of the dangers of drinking during pregnancy and when families receive genetic counseling. Concerns about primary prevention are important but beyond the scope of this book.

Secondary Prevention

Secondary prevention involves early identification of disorder, with the aim of providing early intervention to minimize long-term functional limitations or disability. Clinicians, teachers, and parents all play active roles in secondary prevention. For example, early diagnosis of hearing impairment is critical to providing technological and developmental supports that can lower the risks of language and literacy difficulties later in a child's development (Yoshinaga-Itano, Sedey, Coulter, & Mehl, 1998). Similarly, families of children with autism spectrum disorders need early access to strategies for engaging their children in communicative interactions and social participation to reduce isolating effects of the disorders (National Research Council, 2001). Another example is when children with severe neuromotor dysfunction receive technological supports and instruction so they can participate optimally in literacy learning events in school and home (Erickson, Koppenhaver, & Cunningham, 2006). Such services can prevent the long-term outcomes of undereducation and limited literacy skills. Secondary prevention activities are important elements of contextualized approaches to assessment and intervention.

Tertiary Prevention

Tertiary prevention activities aim at remediating current problems after they have appeared. Assessment and intervention services address a general goal of tertiary prevention. When children face developmental challenges, the three WHO-ICF framework questions about communication processes, needs, and opportunities are intended to foster normal development and prevent disability.

Prognosis

A ***prognosis*** is a prediction about the effect a condition may have on a particular child's developmental outcome. Prognostic statements are informed by evidence from large epidemiological studies and other published literature about the longitudinal effects of the condition in question. They also are informed by an individual clinician's prior experience.

Establishing a prognosis can be a daunting proposition, even for experienced clinicians. A negative prognosis can have discouraging effects, but an unrealistically positive prognosis also can create problems. According to the interactive systems view promoted in this book, therapeutic change occurs as a result of collaborative interactions involving inner systems of children and external supports from clinicians, parents, teachers, and others.

Many unknowns surround predictions for how these factors will come together for a particular child, and there is a degree of uncertainty in any prognosis.

Change requires dedicated energy by all involved, accompanied by the expectation that change is possible. A negative prognostic statement can become a self-fulfilling prophesy. A prognosis always should be honest, yet it is honest to indicate that there are many unknowns and that many factors can influence change. Some characteristics tend to act as protective factors. This section considers both self-fulfilling prophecy and protective factors. An overriding principle is never to damage a family's ability to hope.

Self-Fulfilling Prophecy

Self-fulfilling prophecy occurs when expectation for change influences the degree and direction of change. It is also called the *Pygmalion effect* (based on Greek mythology) and the *Rosenthal effect* (based on a study by Rosenthal and Jacobson [1968/1992]). Rosenthal and Jacobson's classic study showed that when teachers believed that some of their students had higher abilities than others (even though they did not), the presumably better students made twice the academic gains as the students the teachers believed were lower functioning.

A similar phenomenon, the *Hawthorne effect,* is named after an experiment done at the Hawthorne electrical plant in Illinois. Although researchers first attributed increased worker productivity to the experimental treatment of better lighting, they found the increases actually were associated with any positive attention to the workers' well-being. Social science researchers control for the Hawthorne effect by providing equal time and attention to control groups, withholding the treatment of interest only. Medical science researchers use similar controls for the *placebo effect* in pharmaceutical trials to ensure that improvement can be attributed to the treatment being investigated and not simply the patient's expectation of improvement.

Although these varied terms for the effect of positive expectation, or self-fulfilling prophecy, are related, they are not identical. The Rosenthal effect comes from beliefs of the external change agent, which may be transferred to the student. The placebo effect comes from beliefs of the patient or person experiencing change and perhaps those supporting him or her, such as parents and clinicians. The Hawthorne effect comes from interactions of external and internal factors. All relate to the purpose of this book, which is to promote language and literacy development by working collaboratively to optimize interactions between internal and external systems. Master clinicians and educators seek to take advantage of positive expectation and to encourage it (see Personal Reflection 4.6). Any gains that result from a partnership fueled by the belief that change is possible are not false if they can be sustained. Such gains also can provide the foundation for further gains.

PERSONAL reflection *4.6*

"No pessimist ever discovered the secret of the stars or sailed an uncharted land, or opened a new doorway for the human spirit."

Helen Keller (1880–1968) was an educator and philosopher who acquired blindness and deafness in early childhood.

Protective Factors

Children with disordered language development are found in families with a variety of resources, both material and psychosocial. Spoken language disorders present risks for difficulties of literacy learning and social interaction. Some factors, however, seem to protect a child from having a full-blown expression of a disorder or from having the long-term repercussions sometimes associated with that disorder. These include variations in the diagnostic conditions, personal traits and familial supports, and educational and intervention resources:

1. *Protective factors associated with disorder type.* Disability categories are associated with varied risks for negative effects on quality of life. Children with language impairment uncomplicated by comorbid conditions are relatively resilient in terms of broadly defined life success. Records, Tomblin, and Freese (1992) compared young adults (matched for age, nonverbal intelligence, and socioeconomic status) with and without history of language impairment and found that, although the adults with impairment continued to show evidence of disorder across most language measures, there were no differences between the two groups on measures of quality of life and life satisfaction. Research also has shown that higher cognitive abilities act as a protective factor for children with language impairment, affecting their learning curve (Rice, 2004). Generally speaking, the more specific a disorder is to a particular subsystem (so that other language subsystems or related cognitive, sensory, or motor systems remain unaffected), the better the prognosis for the child.

2. *Protective factors associated with personal resilience.* Individuals respond differently to adversity. Some people simply are more resilient than others. *Resilience* is a "dynamic process wherein individuals display positive adaptation despite experiences of significant adversity or trauma" (Luthar & Cicchetti, 2000, p. 858). It is tempered by the psychological principle that plasticity and change are possible in most circumstances but more difficult the longer an individual remains on a maladaptive developmental pathway (Sroufe, 1997). This argues for early identification and intervention for possible disorders so that an intervention team and family can initiate secondary and tertiary prevention efforts as soon as possible.

3. *Protective factors associated with educational and intervention resources.* Early identification and collaborative services aim at secondary prevention goals. Collaborative consultation can help parents, teachers, and other staff develop confidence in their ability to contribute to children's development. DesJardin (2006) found evidence for this effect in mothers of children who were deaf or hard of hearing. Those who reported feeling involved and confident demonstrated more facilitative communication recasts and open-ended questions when interacting with their children than those with lower confidence.

The more families, children, and support systems can use a proactive, optimistic approach to face each new developmental challenge, the more team members will be able to call on multiple resources to support the process. Even if an impairment cannot be "fixed" (as noted by the mother in Personal Reflection 4.1), communication needs can be addressed and a child's participation opportunities can be enhanced (consistent with the framework of Chapter 1).

Sharing Prognostic Information with Parents

The expectation to share prognostic information is part of the ethical responsibility of clinicians conducting diagnostic assessment activities. Advice to keep open "windows of hope" does not mean that clinicians should present a false prognosis or sugarcoat one that is more negative than positive. Rather, it means presenting the most accurate prognostic information available with compassion and making the honest admission that much is unknown.

Many factors can influence a child's development, and clinicians always can encourage hope as a positive force to be nurtured. For example, one might say the following:

> The research indicates that the prognosis for children with this condition is not so good, but there are many unknowns. Children are individuals with many abilities and unique qualities. We will use hope to our advantage and expect positive change as a real possibility. At the same time, we need to be realistic about the challenges ahead. We will measure change and look for the best methods to make growth possible. Meanwhile, your child is the same special person today as before you had this diagnosis—a person who will benefit from your love, attention, and enjoyment, no matter what else may come.

At times, parents may suggest a goal or approach that other members of a team consider unrealistic. Teams who function well can discuss such differences of opinion openly and avoid competitive goal setting. Members of a team may agree to disagree about components of a plan. They also might decide to use the IEP or IFSP process to experiment with a period of trial therapy focused on higher-level expectations, with plans to evaluate effectiveness after a specified period of time. In cases of disagreement, professionals must beware of the potential for subconscious sabotage and adopt the premise that more change may be possible than they anticipated.

When families face an adverse prognosis, it may be especially tempting to grasp onto any new so-called miracle cure, but the evidence for such claims may be purely anecdotal or testimonial. Over recent decades, treatment fads have included approaches that promised the following: dramatic normalization of motor skills if a group of volunteers patterned the child's limbs through crawling and other bilateral movements for many hours per day; surprising expression of highly complex ideas using facilitated communication if an adult provided contrary pressure while supporting the child's hand as he or she typed out messages on a keyboard; normalized cognitive development if a child took megadoses of vitamins; and improved attention and language learning if the child received specially filtered or time-altered music or speech through headphones or other forms of altered sensory input. Each of these approaches has had strong believers and has been supported by testimonials. Case studies and other evidence have encouraged hope that the approach might have dramatic results.

Over time, however, hope usually fades when widespread miraculous results cannot be verified. If parents insist on trying such approaches with their child, clinicians can help them search the literature and may suggest objective individual trials and documentation. They also can help parents avoid feeling guilty about not pursuing every new miracle cure that comes along.

SUMMARY

Concepts of prevalence (proportion per unit of a population affected by a disorder) and incidence (new cases per year) were introduced in this section. Prevention efforts address primary, secondary, and tertiary goals, depending on whether they are aimed at avoiding the condition in the first place, ameliorating potential long-term consequences through early intervention, or reducing the effects of problems after they are identified. Concerns were raised about self-fulfilling prophesies and prognosis. Concepts associated with this phenomenon are termed the Pygmalion or Rosenthal effect, the Hawthorne effect, and the placebo effect. Protective factors (characteristics of the disorder, personal and familial characteristics of resilience, and educational and intervention supports) can influence the expression of a particular disorder or its long-term prognosis.

CHAPTER SUMMARY

This chapter presented three key pieces of federal legislation that influence clinical practice—Section 504 of the Rehabilitation Act, IDEA, and NCLB. Clinical practices were summarized as a set of recursive steps and questions represented with a flowchart. Diagnostic labeling has both pros and cons, and the process of classification is both hypothetical and political. Questions of causation are controversial. Seeking the causes of disorders was compared to peeling away the layers of an onion. Causes also may be circular, making it difficult to separate causes and effects. Conditions that may depress test scores without representing a disorder include low socioeconomic status, cultural–linguistic diversity, and dual language learning. Factors that may serve a protective function even when a disorder is present include characteristics associated with some disorder types, personal and family traits, and educational and intervention resources.

EXERCISES *and* STUDY QUESTIONS

1. Make up a hypothetical case and use the flowchart to describe each step of the practice process with that child, from identifying him or her as needing assessment to deciding that intervention services are no longer needed.

2. Name the three key pieces of legislation that were described in this chapter. Compare and contrast their major features.

3. Describe at least three differences between an IEP and an IFSP.

4. Interview practicing clinicians working in two different settings, and find out which policies have the greatest influence on their everyday practice.

CHAPTER five

Primary Disorders of Speech, Language, and Literacy

LEARNING *objectives*

After studying this chapter, you should be able to do the following:

1. Describe criteria diagnosing primary disorders of speech sound disorder (SSD), language impairment (LI), and learning disability (LD).

2. Discuss findings of research on specific and nonspecific LI or LD and why ability–achievement discrepancy and cognitive-referencing policies are problematic.

3. Discuss relationships of spoken and written language abilities and disorders using a simple model of phonological (sound-/word-level) and nonphonological (sentence-/discourse-level) language skills.

Disorders of language/literacy development are considered ***primary*** when they "cannot be accounted for by any known etiology" (Law, Garrett, & Nye, 2004, p. 924). They are ***secondary*** when they "can be accounted for by another primary condition such as autism, hearing impairment, general developmental difficulties, behavioral or emotional difficulties, or neurological impairment" (p. 924).

The term *comorbid* is sometimes used when an individual fits the criteria for more than one diagnosis. Thus, language impairment (LI) could be comorbid with a speech sound disorder (SSD), learning disability (LD), hearing impairment, emotional impairment, or any other condition. As discussed in this chapter, some forms of SSD appear to stand alone, but SSD also may be an integral feature of some forms of LI. Similarly, LD may leave language systems seemingly intact (e.g., a learning disability for mathematics only); however, diagnoses of LI and LD often constitute different labels for the same underlying condition applied at different times by different professionals.

Speech Sound Disorders

Speech sound disorder (SSD) is diagnosed as a primary condition when a child lags significantly behind peers in producing words with age-appropriate phonetic representation of phonemic segments but no structural or neurological cause is evident to explain the difficulty. Alternate terms are ***phonological disorder, articulation disorder,*** and ***functional articulation disorder,*** but these terms imply alternate concepts of the disorder as well. The term *speech sound disorder* is preferred because it is neutral with regard to cause.

Differential diagnosis of SSD requires assessment of the speech subsystem components outlined in Chapter 2—respiration, phonation, articulation, and resonation. Some impairments of speech sound production appear to involve primary neuromotor difficulty or dysfunction. Two such classifications, *dysarthria* and *apraxia,* are discussed further in Chapter 6 as forms of motor speech disorder. Apraxia, in particular, is a controversial diagnosis, and some would classify it as a more severe form of developmental SSD.

Diagnosis of SSD is based on administration of a standardized test for articulation/phonology, accompanied by analysis of a sample of a child's connected speech. Other components of a comprehensive evaluation for diagnosing SSD are case history, stimulability testing (of ability to produce problematic phonemes when supported by dynamic assessment techniques), hearing screening, oral–peripheral examination, language testing, and assessment of phonological awareness for children near school age (Tyler, 2005a). It is important to assess a child's language and speech because approximately 60 percent of children with phonological disorders have co-occurring language impairment (e.g., Bishop & Edmundson, 1987; Shriberg & Kwiatkowski, 1994). Haskill and Tyler (2007) documented that symptoms of SSD interact with morphosyntactic problems associated with specific language impairment (SLI) and may be an integral part of SLI.

As toddlers begin to talk, their speech production is understandably immature. It shows steady elaboration, however, as motor production capabilities and linguistic representations of the phonological structure of words develop rapidly in tandem. Children with SSD do not follow this typical pattern of continuous development and may need therapeutic intervention to elaborate and fine-tune their speech production systems.

In preschool-age children with SSD, speech production difficulties often interfere with intelligibility, making it difficult to sort out speech production issues from language production issues. By school age, children with SSD may be able to produce speech that is intelligible but demonstrate instability of word production (particularly multisyllabic words) inappropriate for the child's age. After age 9, when the developmental period should be complete (Shriberg, 1997), some children continue to produce certain speech sounds inaccurately. Such residual problems often are limited to substitutions or distortions of later developing liquid or sibilant sounds, such as producing /r/ and /l/ as /w/ (noted as $r \rightarrow w$; $l \rightarrow w$) and /s/ produced as /θ/ (noted as $s \rightarrow θ$). (The arrow is read as "goes to.") These may be referred to as *single-phoneme* or *residual* articulation disorders.

Articulation, Phonology, and Speech Perception

Disputes about whether to categorize disorders of speech sound production as articulation or phonological impairment are based on conflicting views on the nature of the difficulty. *Articulation impairment* implies a disorder of phonetic speech performance at a purely peripheral functional level. *Phonological impairment* implies that the difficulty stems from underdeveloped phonological concepts at a central linguistic level. A *perceptual impairment* is a third possibility for explaining the difficulties underlying SSD.

An alternative to such *either–or* questions would be to consider the relative involvement of multiple contributory systems, including the phonetic placement and motor control of articulatory performance, knowledge of the phonology of language at a conceptual level, and perceptual skills for processing phonetically encoded information. Multiple systems (at least these three) are required for typical development of speech sound production. Interactive effects also would be predicted by connectionist theories and circular causative patterns that are a principle of system theory (discussed in Chapter 3). Evidence of mutual dependencies between motor and language development based on neurophysiological and behavioral studies has led to "reconsideration of traditional models of speech-sound disorders in which language and motor domains are viewed as modular" (Goffman, 2005, p. 51). SSD is an appropriate diagnostic label for any condition that involves disordered speech sound production, reflecting varied involvement and interactions of speech perception, phonological conception, and motor speech production systems (Munson, Edwards, & Beckman, 2005).

Theoretical Approaches for Describing Developing Speech Systems

Some early developing speech production characteristics are not considered signs of disorder because they fall within the range of patterns expected for the child's age and can be attributed to typical development. It is remarkable (though often taken for granted) that young, typically developing children can segment a stream of speech into identifiable words and store them as separate lexical items. Most children can link sound patterns to word meanings long before they can reproduce all features of complex phonetic patterns with accuracy in their own speech. Although toddlers understand many words, when they attempt to say those same words, their productions are often simplified in predictable ways.

Linguistic phonologists and speech scientists have investigated several theories and applied different nomenclature to account for patterns of simplified phonetic structures produced by toddlers and young children. Following are four descriptions of developmental phenomena summarized by Ingram (1997) as having implications for assessment activities:

- *Traditional phonemic theory,* leading to an inventory of adult phonemes that are present, absent, or transposed in a child's speech (e.g., absence of the phoneme /s/ in any word position)
- *Phonological process theory,* leading to an inventory of simplification processes used by a child to make phonologically complex words more pronounceable (e.g.,

fronting, stopping, or final consonant deletion), which is based on natural phonology explanations suggested by Stampe (1979)
- ***Distinctive feature theory,*** leading to an inventory of distinctive features (e.g., [+ voicing] [+ velar]) in a child's repertoire, based on linear distinctive feature explanations suggested by Chomsky and Halle (1968) and Jakobson (1941/1968)
- ***Nonlinear phonology theory,*** leading to application of a hierarchical model of features, including prosodic features, that are specified and unspecified in a child's developing system (e.g., Bernhardt & Stoel-Gammon, 1994; Bernhardt & Stemberger, 2000) (see Figure 5.1)

Any of these developmental approaches involves analysis of a corpus of a child's actual words produced in running speech. The clinician then must decide whether the child is moving at an acceptable rate toward a mature model of spoken language production or if speech sound learning seems to have stalled or gone astray.

Speech Sound Disorder Subclassification

Shriberg (1997) suggested classifying ***childhood speech disorders*** as three types—speech delay, residual errors, and special populations. Each has implications for clinical decisions about what to do next.

Speech Delay

Speech delay is a diagnostic term for marked phonological production difficulties, which often are accompanied by symptoms of language delay (Shriberg, 1997). Speech delay

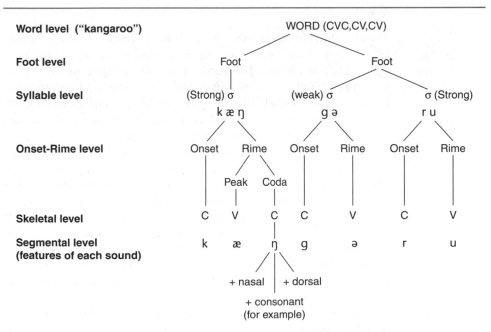

figure *5.1*

Analysis of the Nonlinear Structure of the Word *Kangaroo*

Source: Based on Bernhardt & Stemberger, 2000; Bernhardt & Stoel-Gammon, 1994; Gillon, 2004.

is diagnosed based on "persisting deletion and substitution errors not observed in typi-cally developing children of the same chronological age" (p. 108). Shriberg noted that "a significant percentage of children with speech delay appear to have associated cognitive–linguistic, learning, and other special education needs" (p. 108). This suggests that speech delay may be part of a larger problem, reflecting impairments affecting broader develop-mental systems that must be considered when planning assessment and intervention. Some children start with a diagnosis of speech delay but move to a different diagnostic category when they continue to demonstrate language and literacy difficulties after their speech is fully intelligible. Others are later diagnosed with a comorbid sensory–motor or cognitive–communicative condition (see Chapters 6 and 7).

What are the implications of early signs of speech delay for later risks when learning to read and spell? By school age, children with speech delay may be producing speech that seems close to same-age peers yet continue to exhibit difficulties in phonological repre-sentation on measures of phonological awareness. Such indicators should be monitored, as they constitute an ongoing risk for literacy/learning difficulty (e.g., National Research Council, 1998; Stanovich & Siegel, 1994; Torgeson, Wagner, Rashotte, Burgess, & Hecht, 1997). Intervention for speech delay also should incorporate activities aimed directly at building phonological awareness and emerging phonics (e.g., Gillon, 2004).

Articulation difficulty of the residual type (i.e., involving only a few later developing phonemes) seems not to indicate a greater risk for phonological awareness and other literacy-related difficulty (e.g., Catts, 1993), but speech perception difficulties do indicate literacy-learning risks (e.g., Rvachew, 2006). When other language systems (syntax, semantics, or pragmatics) are affected along with phonology, a higher risk for long-term literacy-learning difficulties can be predicted (Catts, 1993; Scarborough, 2005). Speech–language–literacy relationships are considered more fully in the last section of this chapter.

Residual Errors

The classification of ***residual errors*** applies to speech sound distortion errors that persist after 9 years of age, often involving one or more of the phonemes /r/, /l/, and /s/ (Shriberg, 1997). State and local policies and the opinions of speech–language pathologists (SLPs) vary regarding placement and intervention decisions for children with residual errors af-fecting only one or two speech sounds. In this form of articulation difficulty, phonemes generally are present in words and sequenced correctly but produced inaccurately according to adult expectations (e.g., /s/ → /θ/ or /r/ → /w/).

Regional and social dialects allow some variation in phoneme production (particu-larly involving vowels and word endings), and those clearly should not be viewed as articu-lation deficits. Some children with residual errors, however, are unable to produce target sounds even in imitation of a clinician or after brief instruction used for dynamic assess-ment. The clinician then concludes that the child is not ***stimulable*** for that phoneme and is at higher risk for failing to develop it without intervention. Such a child usually qualifies for special services under IDEA '04 as having speech–language impairment. Some school districts might consider this a form of response to intervention (RTI), but it differs from the forms of academic general education instruction that usually constitute early elementary school RTI programs.

Shriberg (1997) noted that residual speech disorders might receive low priority for treatment because they have limited implications for academic performance compared to other speech–language impairments. He commented:

> Unlike phoneme deletions and phoneme substitutions, phoneme distortions have not been associated with deficits in the phonological skills underlying reading, writing, and other ver-

bal skills. . . . Their consequences have not been associated with intelligibility deficits, and in the current pluralistic culture, they may not be associated with unfavorable stereotypes. (p. 107)

Under IDEA '04 (and previous versions), eligibility for special services is based on diagnosis of disability in one of the 12 categories (including speech or language impairment) when it has an effect on educational performance. Opinions differ on this issue, but those in favor of providing services point out that oral communication is a basic skill and hence automatically a part of educational performance. If a child needs speech–language services to complete the developmental process of learning to produce all phonemes, articulation intervention might be considered part of a child's right to a free, appropriate public education (FAPE).

An added consideration for keeping articulation intervention services accessible in school service delivery is that residual SSDs are relatively easy to correct with treatment, but by age 9, they are unlikely to change on their own. Children who still have residual speech sound production errors in third grade have the maturity to understand directions about tongue placement and airflow and may be more motivated to improve speech that may be drawing social penalties. These factors could support a decision by an individualized education program (IEP) team to provide articulation therapy in school if the parents and child want it and if the child's general education teacher agrees it is needed. In most cases, articulation intervention services should not be protracted. Brief but intensive pull-out sessions can be used to establish correct production so that the student misses as little general education time as possible (although controlled research is needed to support such a conclusion). Once correct production of the targeted speech sound(s) has been established and the phoneme can be produced automatically in rapid syllable drills, the program can transition to supports for self-monitoring and further carryover in the classroom. In the final phase, periodic classroom-based carryover probes might be used to monitor maintenance of newly acquired speech skills until generalization is confirmed. Engaging children in setting their own goals for correcting their speech can motivate them to complete their treatment sooner (see Case Example 5.1).

Special Populations

The term ***special populations*** refers to children with SSD whose primary needs are in other health or educational areas. Special populations with high risk for SSD along with other diagnoses can be grouped into three categories based on the primary affected systems—speech–hearing mechanisms, cognitive–linguistic processes, and psychosocial processes (Bernthal & Bankson, 2004; Shriberg, 1997). Children with speech–hearing mechanism diagnoses, such as hearing impairment, cerebral palsy, and craniofacial anomalies, are discussed in Chapter 6. Children with cognitive–communicative and psychosocial diagnoses are discussed in Chapter 7.

SUMMARY

Primary disorders of the speech production system may or may not involve language and literacy risks to any great degree. Primary disorders of speech sound production can be divided into the three categories—speech delay, residual errors, and special populations. Four options were introduced for describing developmental speech production—traditional phonemic theory, phonological process theory, distinctive feature theory, and nonlinear phonology. Controversies were discussed regarding eligibility for speech intervention services when residual errors constitute a student's only difficulty.

─CASE **example** *5.1*─────────────────────

| **Walter and the Articulation Challenge** |

Walter pronounced his name "Waltoo" and used a *w/r* distortion consistently in his spontaneous speech. He was a sixth-grader who was receiving speech services for this residual articulation error at school, where he also received LD resource room services with a focus on written composition. It was due to the written language needs that Walter became a participant in an interdisciplinary after-school writing lab.

Walter was a willing participant in writing lab activities, but it was not long before he shared that he really disliked being pulled out from his general education classes at school to work on articulation of /r/. Walter's description suggested that his clinician was using a traditional approach to correct his articulation and viewed the role of therapy as working on speech only. That should have been fine for the residual errors on /r/ but did not address Walter's literacy-learning issues, which were a greater concern for him and his teachers.

Further consultation with Walter revealed that his approach to controlling the situation with the clinician at school was to resist changing his speech. The writing lab clinician said to him, "Walter, don't you see how this works? All you have to do to get dismissed from speech therapy at school is to start using the /r/ correctly all the time. Then you will have more time to work on the things that you want to work on."

Walter grasped the concept quickly, took control of the change process, and, in six weeks, was ready to be dismissed from the school speech therapy program as corrected. Although it would have been nice to see the focus of the school-based SLP service switch to Walter's other language intervention needs, the IEP team's choice to limit his special placement to the LD resource room at that point was consistent with the goals and values expressed by Walter, his parents, and his general education teachers.

Language Impairment

The terms *language impairment (LI)* (e.g., Law et al., 2004) and *developmental language disorder* (e.g., Rice & Warren, 2004) are used to signal a primary diagnosis involving language. This diagnosis is used in contrast to a language disorder secondary to comorbid disabilities. LI is diagnosed when expectations for typical development of language are not met and children are delayed in achieving developmental milestones by a significant degree. The American Speech-Language-Hearing Association (1993) defined *language disorder* as follows:

> A language disorder is impaired comprehension and/or use of spoken, written and/or other symbol systems. The disorder may involve (1) the form of language (phonology, morphology, syntax), (2) the content of language (semantics), and/or (3) the function of language in communication (pragmatics) in any combination. (p. 40)

Prevalence estimates for LI based on epidemiological studies of the general population of Canadian and American children at the beginning of schooling have ranged from 3 to 13 percent (Beitchman, Nair, Clegg, & Patel, 1986). Tomblin et al. (1997) reported data from a comprehensive epidemiological study in Iowa and Illinois (known as the Epi-SLI study) that showed a prevalence rate of 7.4 percent (8 percent for boys and 6 percent for girls). They also found evidence that LI was underdiagnosed because 71 percent of kindergarten-age children who met criteria for a diagnosis of SLI had not been previously identified. Underdiagnosis also may occur in later childhood and adolescence when children shift to a different diagnostic category, such as learning disability, while continuing to demonstrate symptoms of LI that may by then be more subtle.

Diagnosis of LI is made on the basis of standardized test scores and nonstandardized but systematic methods. A diagnosis of LI may be made if the child's language development is significantly delayed or deficient in the areas of language content or form or if pragmatic–communicative issues suggest a disorder of language use. As described in the flowchart in Chapter 4 (Figure 4.3), determining the status of a child's hearing should be an early priority, and the results should be considered when interpreting language test results. Consideration also should be given to whether the child's prior cultural–linguistic experiences make it appropriate to use diagnostic tests that have been standardized on a mainstream population. As described in Chapter 4, the mere presence of a census-related proportion of children from a similar racial/ethnic category in a standardization sample does not make the test appropriate.

If standardized testing is appropriate, performance on well-chosen measures contribute to diagnosis of LI when a significant discrepancy is identified compared with typical developmental expectations. Significance is determined by using prescribed cut scores whose sensitivity and specificity has been demonstrated scientifically. Diagnosis should never be based on a single measure or procedure, no matter how well designed and researched the tool; rather, it should be supported by evidence from more than one type of measure, including input from parents and teachers.

Both theoretical and practical questions can be raised as to whether LI represents a categorical difference in the nature of children's language systems or just a dimensional one. Is language *delay* (i.e., slowness in maturing) different from *disorder* (i.e., unusual patterns of maturing)? Does delay lead to disorder? Is delay a mild form of disorder? Such questions are particularly salient in the early years from toddlerhood into preschool. Questions also can be raised about whether children with LI ever catch up with their peers and what happens when they begin to read and write. These questions are addressed in the sections that follow.

Late Talking

Developmental milestones can provide relevant criteria for deciding to evaluate a child's language. Developmental milestones indicate that first words should appear by close to 1 year of age (at least by 18 months), two-word combinations should appear by 2 years, and three-word combinations by 3 years—making these milestones relatively easy to remember. Delays in reaching such milestones often are recognized by parents and other health care providers and may constitute some of the earliest symptoms of developmental difficulty in other developmental domains beyond language.

When symptoms of language delay are noted, the causes should be investigated. Is hearing normal? Is a comorbid developmental disorder present? Are caregiving risks involved? Are other risk factors present (e.g., premature birth, low birthweight, familial patterns of LI or LD)? If so, early identification and intervention should be considered. But what about children who appear only to be late in producing speech and have no other risk factors? Are they likely to catch up?

When children are slow to talk yet achieve other developmental milestones on time, show no symptoms of other developmental disorders, use gestures and other nonverbal means to communicate with their family, have normal hearing, and can understand many words and sentences, they fit the diagnosis of **late talker** or **specific expressive language delay.** The terms are essentially synonymous and can be applied to the same child but imply somewhat different views of the situation. The term *late talker* implies a temporary condition that stretches normal limits but is likely to resolve on its own given enough time and parental support (i.e., without special intervention). The term *specific expressive language delay* (SELD) implies a greater need for concern and possible intervention.

Research has shown that the majority of children who produce few words as toddlers do eventually catch up with their peers—usually by the time they reach school age (e.g., Girolametto, Wiigs, Smyth, Weitzman, & Pearce, 2001; Paul, 1996; Rescorla, 2002)—but not all do. The problem is in predicting which late-talking children will develop into typical language and literacy learners and which will show persistent difficulty that should have been addressed with early intervention services.

Especially if multiple risk factors are present (e.g., family history of language problems, chronic otitis media, cognitive delay, social communication difficulties, environmental risks), a safe recommendation is for late-talking children to receive comprehensive assessment and ongoing family-centered consultation services. This would include monitoring for signs of more extensive difficulties and delays (e.g., Paul, 1996; Paul, 2007), not only in the preschool years but at each point the child encounters increased demands for more complex and literate language learning (e.g., kindergarten, third grade, middle school). RTI programs may provide an appropriate mechanism for doing so.

In some cases, language delays or disorders seem to resolve at one developmental point but reappear later (Rescorla, 2002; Scarborough & Dobrich, 1990). Regardless of diagnostic status, parents of late talkers, like all parents, should have access to information about how to optimize their child's communication, speech, and language development and to encourage their child's emergent literacy abilities as well (e.g., Apel & Masterson, 2001a).

Language Impairment Subclassification

Is LI one disorder or many? Is there a form of specific language impairment (SLI) that differs from all other forms? In other words, does SLI have a unique phenotype?

A *phenotype* is a cluster of traits representing expression of interactions between genetic and environmental factors and characterizing a group or subgroup of those having a common disorder of development (see Personal Reflection 5.1). Regarding a phenotype for SLI, Watkins (1994) wrote, "We have yet to establish a widely accepted profile of linguistic behavior associated with the disorder" (p. 1).

PERSONAL reflection *5.1*

"New insights about genetic effects bring increased recognition of the finely tuned interactions of neurocortical, genetic, and behavioral elements of inherited factors, and the role of environmental events such as intervention."

Mabel Rice and **Steven Warren** (2004, pp. 1–2) were introducing their book *Developmental Language Disorders: From Phenotypes to Etiologies.*

One reason for lack of a clear phenotype may be that LI actually comprises several phenotypes. Questions regarding the nature of a typical SLI profile and possible subtypes have been addressed over several decades. This section considers the nature of SLI first and then evidence for it and other subclassifications.

Specific Language Impairment

SLI is defined as "a significant impairment in spoken language ability when there is no obvious accompanying condition such as mental retardation, neurological damage, or hearing impairment" (Leonard, 1998, p. 1). Criteria for identifying SLI were developed by researchers Stark and Tallal (1981), who wanted to study children's language disorders in their purest form and therefore identified children who were low in language but at least average in other areas. Stark and Tallal's inclusion criteria required children to show a 12-month discrepancy between expressive language levels and nonlanguage cognitive developmental levels.

Age scores, however, have notorious psychometric problems. Many subsequent language researchers operationalized the diagnosis of SLI as a standard score of 75 or below (i.e., 1.67 standard deviations below the mean) for language ability in a child who demonstrated a standard score for nonverbal cognitive ability of 85 or above (i.e., no worse than 1 15-point standard deviation below the mean). Three theoretical explanations have been offered for the nature of SLI, implicating linguistic, information processing, or cognitive–communicative components.

Linguistic Explanations for SLI. Some researchers have hypothesized a specific deficit in morphosyntactic learning as the key to SLI. Rice (2004) is a primary proponent of this position. She described SLI as a specific delay in grammatical learning that can be observed in English-speaking children as an extended period of time to learn grammatical tense markings of finite (i.e., inflected) verb structures (including copula and auxiliary forms of *be*, auxiliary *do*, and third-person singular *-s*). Children with SLI, Rice observed, tend to demonstrate a period of *extended optional infinitive (EOI)* use. This means that children with SLI tend to use the uninflected infinitival form of verbs (e.g., *[to] walk*), rather than mark verbs accurately for finite (main verb) grammatical tense (e.g., *walks, walking, walked*). Based on this theoretical explanation, Rice and Wexler (2001) developed a formal test, the Rice/Wexler Test of Early Grammatical Impairment (TEGI), which is designed to be sensitive to symptoms of grammatical difficulty in expressive language production.

The use of verb-tense markings as a diagnostic indicator of SLI has problems for overidentifying speakers of dialects that are less marked for finite verb tense, such as African American English. Oetting and MacDonald (2001), however, found that grammatical difficulty could be identified even in children who are speakers of less marked dialects of English. To address concerns about test bias, Seymour, Roeper, and de Villiers (2003) developed a Diagnostic Evaluation of Language Variation (DELV) to be sensitive to grammatical-learning difficulties among dialectal speakers without penalizing variations in use of dialectal features. Owen and Leonard (2006) also found that children with SLI (ages 5 years, 1 month, to 8 years, 0 months) have difficulty with markers of grammatical complexity beyond finite verb-tense marking (e.g., in infinitival phrases such as *Ernie knew to wear a hat*).

Information-Processing Explanations for SLI. Other researchers have explained SLI as a disorder of information processing. They hypothesize short-term or working memory deficits as underlying and accounting for children's language deficits. For example, Baddeley, Gathercole, and Papagno (1998) proposed that children with short-term memory deficits would have difficulty learning new words because of difficulty forming phonological representations of brief and novel speech events. This, in turn, would make it difficult for them to create new phonological entries within their long-term lexicons.

Addressing questions about memory, Cowan (1996) differentiated ***short-term memory,*** which he defined as "rich, detailed, and temporarily held information about the surface properties of language," from ***working memory,*** which is "when information is needed temporarily in the services of current mental activity" (p. 2). Cowan also described the importance of memory in language processing:

Short-term memory is critical for thought. For example, it is impossible to comprehend a word within conversation or text without keeping in mind the necessary background information established by the prior words in the sentence, and often by preceding sentences. Similarly, it is impossible to speak or write a word of discourse without keeping in mind the intent of the sentence, what the listener or reader has been told thus far, and the goal for making the intended meaning clear. Thus, for language reception, short-term memory serves the role of accumulating information while comprehension occurs. For language production, it serves the role of maintaining information while planning happens. (pp. 1–2)

To investigate the role of memory and the information-processing hypothesis, Archibald and Gathercole (2006) administered a variety of short-term and working memory tasks to children with SLI (ages 7 to 11 years). Short-term memory tasks, such as memory span for digits and nonword repetition tasks, required brief storage and exact repetition of stimuli. Working memory tasks required deeper language processing and manipulation. In support of information-processing theory, Archibald and Gathercole found that the children with SLI had deficits of both short-term and working memory that were more marked than their deficits in language, implicating information-processing deficits as the root cause of the LI.

Leonard (1994) explained the information-processing hypothesis by noting that some features of language input, particularly morphological markers, might be less salient and more difficult to perceive and hence more difficult to process. This would account for children's "extraordinary difficulty in the area of morphology because many grammatical morphemes in English take the form of word-final nonsyllabic consonants and unstressed syllables that do not appear in positions (namely, clause-final position) in which significant lengthening occurs" (p. 92). Haskill and Tyler (2007) found support for this explanation when they studied links between phonological and morphological difficulties among 83 children classified into four groups: (1) language impairment only, (2) speech–language impairment with minimal or no final cluster reduction or consonant deletion, (3) speech–language impairment with frequent final cluster reduction or consonant deletion, and (4) a no-impairment control group. Haskill and Tyler compared the groups' performances for finite and nonfinite morpheme production and sentence structure and concluded that children with speech–language impairment generally had poorer morphosyntactic skills than peers with LI but no difficulty with phonology in speech production.

A related explanation to the perceptual saliency hypothesis is that children with SLI can process phonological information adequately when given enough time but experience difficulty when attempting to process rapidly changing phonological information (Tallal, Stark, & Mellits, 1985). Such an explanation might account for apparent capacity deficits (Ellis Weismer, 1996) among children with SLI who cannot process information quickly enough to remember it. That is a companion to the memory deficit hypothesis that language cannot be remembered long enough to be processed. Leonard and colleagues (2007) found evidence in profiles for 14 children with LI that speed of processing and verbal working memory are separable factors, both of which help to explain SLI.

Others (e.g., Montgomery, 1996) have suggested that beyond phonological loop (surface level) deficits, the memory deficits experienced by students with LI involve problems at the level of a central executor function, which accounts for children's difficulty with auditory sentence comprehension as well as for memory deficits tapped by digit span and other measures of retention alone. This hypothesis draws on a cognitive constructivist paradigm, as well as on information-processing theory, and suggests that problems arise because children with LI are less efficient at allocating memory and language-processing resources when they attempt complex tasks, such as processing complex sentences and language within the curriculum.

Cognitive Explanations for SLI. Cognitive constructivist explanations for SLI were summarized by Johnston (1994). She emphasized complex developmental relationships between language and thought and noted that unidirectional causal relations—in which one accounts fully for the other or in which their development is fully independent—are unlikely. By definition, children with SLI have language difficulty isolated from general cognition, which is considered completely intact. Indeed, children with SLI can perform many cognitive operations better than younger language-matched peers. On the other hand, research has revealed significant (although subtle) differences in the nonverbal cognitive abilities for children with SLI, as well as their language abilities, when compared with same-age typically developing peers (e.g., Kamhi, 1981).

Links between language and cognition are supported by recent studies using visual perceptual taking (VPT) and theory of mind (ToM) tasks. Farrant, Fletcher, and Maybery (2006) measured ToM with false-belief tasks that required 5-year-old children with SLI to engage in mental perspective taking. They measured VPT by asking children to perform mental perceptual operations of increasing difficulty, similar to Piaget's "Three Mountains" task (described in Chapter 3). In a level 1 VPT task, children were asked to interpret perceptually *what* another person could see; in a level 2 task, they were asked to interpret *how* the object would look to the other person. The results showed that children with SLI performed significantly poorer than typically developing peers on the false-belief tasks and also on the level 2 VPT tasks but not on the level 1 task.

Consistent with Piaget's (1926/1959) description of later development, in which language plays a causal role in the development of intelligent thought, children with SLI might lack access to this important bridge from perception to concept (Farrant et al., 2006). A child's language difficulties might be linked to difficulty moving beyond Piaget's stage of **cognitive egocentrism,** making it difficult to decenter or shift cognitively from the child's own perspective. These findings are consistent with similar findings for children with autism spectrum disorders (ASD) (Baron-Cohen, 1995) and may suggest a common thread connecting SLI to ASD, as hypothesized by some researchers (e.g., Bishop, 2000; Rapin & Allen, 1983).

Evidence for LI Subtypes

A number of researchers have sought evidence for subclassifying LI. Aram and Nation (1975) tested 47 children who were receiving clinical services. They administered tests of phonology, syntax, and semantics and applied factor analysis to identify six subgroups. Three factors accounted for most of the variance: (1) low to high ability to repeat spoken input, (2) phonological system deficits alone compared with added difficulties with non-phonological language skills; and (3) modality effects for comprehension or production. These categories foreshadowed evidence for a *simple model* of spoken and written language relationships, which is discussed later in this chapter.

Rapin and Allen (1983), working in New York, suggested a taxonomy of subtypes based on their clinical experiences and observations. Rapin and Allen's classification comprised four subtypes: (1) verbal auditory agnosia (i.e., inability to make sense of auditory language input despite adequate peripheral hearing); (2) semantic–pragmatic syndrome; (3) autism; and (4) syntactic–phonologic syndrome. Rapin (1998) later removed autism from the taxonomy but continued to identify language difficulty as a core component of autism. She then added (5) a lexical–syntactic subtype (characterized by difficulties of word retrieval and sentence comprehension) and (6) two subtypes involving difficulty within the sound system of language—dyspraxia and isolated phonological production deficit.

Bishop and Edmundson (1987), working in the United Kingdom, based their system on a study of 83 preschool children receiving LI services. It included (1) phonological impairment alone (often observed earliest in development); (2) phonological impairment in conjunction with semantic and syntactic difficulty; (3) expressive impairment; and (4) receptive impairment. Bishop and Edmundson also observed that symptoms sometimes changed over time as children moved through developmental stages.

Conti-Ramsden, Crutchly, and Botting (2003), also in the United Kingdom, used a combination of psychometric testing and teacher interviews to seek evidence of LI subtypes within a clinical population. They found evidence for a five-category system: (1) phonological alone; (2) phonological–syntactic; (3) lexical–syntactic; (4) semantic–pragmatic; and (5) verbal auditory agnosia.

Bishop's (2000) work extended Rapin and Allen's (1983) identification of similarities among children with autism and LI, especially involving semantic–pragmatic systems. Children with semantic–pragmatic problems had conversational interactions that were socially inappropriate but did not meet the definition of classical autism (Bishop & Norbury, 2002). They produced excessive speech but had difficulty understanding and formulating coherent connected discourse (Bishop & Adams, 1989), leading Bishop (2000) to describe a separate syndrome she called ***pragmatic language impairment (PLI).*** PLI is characterized by primary difficulties in the areas of social communication and discourse comprehension.

Tomblin and Zhang (1999) tested 1,929 kindergarten children in their Epi-SLI study. Their results added evidence for a group of children with articulation-only impairment who differed from the larger group of children with LI. They also found that language measures loaded on only one general factor—not separate factors for language expression and reception, as subtest names imply. After testing the same cohort at the second, fourth, and eighth grades, Tomblin and Zhang (2006) concluded that the children's difficulties were explained best by a model with two dimensions—vocabulary abilities and sentence abilities. Although a single-dimension model fit the data well in the lower grades, vocabulary and sentence abilities explained variation better than traditional categories of reception and expression.

Pragmatic difficulties seem to constitute a fundamentally different form of LI. Tomblin and colleagues (2004) tried to fit existing classification systems to profiles for 604 children they followed from kindergarten to second grade in the Epi-SLI study. Like Bishop (2000), they found that pragmatic difficulties dissociated from other phonological and semantic–syntactic language skills. Some children had relative strength in pragmatics and also weak abilities in phonology, syntax, and semantics; others seemed to fit Bishop's definition of PLI in terms of having weak pragmatic skills in the presence of basically intact phonology, syntax, and semantics.

Nonspecific Language Impairment

"Children with LI may be classified as having a nonspecific language impairment (NLI) if both verbal and nonverbal abilities are below normal limits" (Catts, Fey, Tomblin, & Zhang, 2002, p. 1143). Tomblin and colleagues (2004) compared children with SLI and NLI in their longitudinal sample and found that differences were minimal and more dimensional than categorical. Tomblin and Zhang (2006) assessed the same group at a later age and found no difference in profiles for the children with SLI and NLI as they matured.

Rice (2004) reported similar findings of dimensionality in her team's research on the morphosyntactic marker of the extended optional infinitive (EOI). Children with SLI and NLI both had difficulties acquiring verb-tense markers, but children with NLI exhibited difficulty of greater magnitude than children with SLI. When Rice's team tracked grammatical tense markers for 24 young children with SLI and NLI longitudinally from kindergarten through fourth grade, they found that the grammatical performance of children with NLI lagged behind those with SLI during grades two and three but reached their level by grade four. Further analysis showed that it was not just lower cognitive ability that accounted for

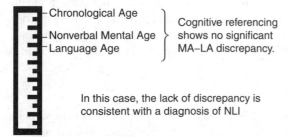

Frame A

- Chronological Age
- Nonverbal Mental Age
- Language Age

Cognitive referencing shows a signigicant MA–LA discrepancy.

In this case, a discrepancy is consistent with a diagnosis of SLI

Frame B

- Chronological Age
- Nonverbal Mental Age
- Language Age

Cognitive referencing shows no significant MA–LA discrepancy.

In this case, the lack of discrepancy is consistent with a diagnosis of NLI

figure 5.2

Diagnosis Using the Discrepancy Model

The result is a diagnosis of specific language impairment (SLI) in Frame A and nonspecific language impairment (NLI) in Frame B. It is now acknowledged that both profiles indicate a need for special services.

the delay. When grammatical performance of children with NLI was compared to that of children with lower cognitive ability but without LI, the children with LI performed differently, indicating that low cognitive ability alone could not account for their difficulties.

Problems with Cognitive-Referencing Policies in Practice

Cognitive-referencing requirements (similar to those used to diagnose SLI in research) have been criteria in many state and local policies in the past, but IDEA has never required a discrepancy between nonverbal cognition and language test scores to diagnosis a child as having LI. Casby (1992) studied state eligibility requirements and found that cognitive-referencing requirements were evident in 31 out of 50 state policies for determining special education eligibility. Cognitive-referencing policies base eligibility on finding children's language scores to be significantly lower than their nonverbal cognitive test scores, regardless of how discrepant their language scores are from those of normative age-peers. This situation is illustrated in Figure 5.2.

When no discrepancy is found, the assumption is that although the child's language skills might be low, those skills simply are commensurate with the child's overall cognitive development. Such an interpretation is based on an assumption that special education services (in this case, SLP services) are not justified, because a child with such a profile (i.e., no discrepancy between language and nonlanguage abilities) would be unlikely to benefit from them.

Clinical researchers have argued for some time (e.g., Lahey, 1990) that mental age and language age scores are problematic. Researchers have revealed fallacies with other arguments used to support cognitive referencing. Counter evidence includes the following:

- Tests of nonverbal intelligence are influenced by children's verbal abilities (Francis et al., 1996; Plante, 1998; Tomblin & Zhang, 1999).
- Tests of nonverbal intelligence measure visual–perceptual development more than conceptual development, particularly in lower-level items used at younger ages (Johnston, 1982a; Kamhi, Minor, & Mauer, 1990).
- Some combinations of language tests and cognitive tests show a discrepancy for individual children when others do not at some points in development but not others (Cole, Dale, & Miller, 1992; Cole, Mills, & Kelley, 1994).
- Formal tests often yield biased results for children from diverse cultural and linguistic communities (Lahey, 1992; Seymour, 1992).
- Formal tests fail to assess needs for language intervention in everyday contexts (Westby, StevensDominguez, & Detter, 1996).
- The use of arbitrary cut scores for judging language impairment based on formal language tests is flawed by the fact that only a few instruments provide evidence of

sensitivity and specificity for making evidence-based judgments of disorder (Spaulding, Plante, & Farinella, 2006).

- Children with NLI can benefit from language intervention in a comparable manner to children with SLI, although perhaps a little more slowly (Fey, Long, & Cleave, 1994; Rice, Tomblin, Hoffman, Richman, & Marquis, 2004).

It should be clear by now that theoretical assumptions underlying cognitive referencing are not supported by research. Yet as states have begun to abandon cognitive-referencing requirements for eligibility for LD services (as required by IDEA '04), clear alternatives are not in place (McDermott, Goldberg, Watkins, Stanley, & Glutting, 2006). Should any child who scores low on a language test be eligible for service? How should *low* be defined?

One possibility is that RTI programs may be used to probe and address symptoms of spoken language difficulty along with academic skills associated with reading, writing, and math (Ehren & Nelson, 2005). SLPs have unique opportunities to collaborate with others to develop innovative programs for interfacing language intervention with universally designed language instruction in general and special education contexts. Testing, diagnosing, and placing a child on a caseload to receive individualized services is not the only option.

SUMMARY

Language impairment, language disorder, and *developmental language disorder* are roughly synonymous labels for primary disorders of language learning in childhood. Primary LI generally becomes evident in early childhood, although more subtle LI and comprehension problems may not be diagnosed until the school-age years. Late talking does not always signal the presence of LI. Many late talkers do catch up, but monitoring is warranted.

Researchers have classified subtypes of primary language impairment. Grammatical morpheme-learning difficulty is a central feature of SLI. Other LI subtypes are differentiated based on involvement of phonological or nonphonological language systems. Cognitive-referencing policies are unsubstantiated by evidence. Differences between SLI and NLI are dimensional rather than categorical. Both groups of children need intervention. Converging evidence also supports a qualitatively different group of children with pragmatic language impairment (PLI). Children with PLI demonstrate relative strengths at the sound and word (phonological) levels and in basic sentence formulation but with social communication difficulties and problems comprehending deeper sentence- and discourse-level meanings.

Learning Disability

The term *learning disability (LD)* encompasses a heterogeneous group of disorders. The diagnosis of LD can be made in the preschool years (National Joint Committee on Learning Disabilities, 2006) but generally is made by educational assessment teams when children reach school age. Diagnosis of LD often occurs after children have struggled with academic learning. Approximately 80 percent of children who are identified with LD have a disability in reading (National Research Council, 1998).

Some children diagnosed with LD in school have a history of spoken language difficulty but not all. Language impairment involving reading or writing may not be associated with obvious symptoms in spoken language, but subtle spoken language symptoms may be overlooked in children who are struggling to learn to read and write. To emphasize the language basis underlying many forms of LD, some researchers, particularly in the field of speech–language pathology, identify children with both spoken and written language-learning difficulties as having ***language-learning disabilities (LLD)*** (Silliman, Butler, & Wallach, 2002; Wallach, 2005).

Prevalence rates for LD are difficult to pin down. They are associated with varied views on the identification and diagnosis of LD and are limited by the state of current scientific evidence. Kavale and Forness (2003) noted that "in place of epidemiological studies, LD prevalence is often established through policy statements issued by national organizations" (p. 83). Such processes are inherently political and may reflect advocacy to serve more students under the LD rubric. This may account for the fact that 52 percent of all children with disabilities in the United States (more than 2.5 to 2.8 million children) with special education needs are served under the classification of LD.

Defining Learning Disability

The use of the term *learning disability* is credited to Samuel Kirk (1962), an author of the Test of Psycholinguistic Abilities (Kirk, McCarthy, & Kirk, 1968). In the 1960s, Kirk's term replaced prior labels, such as *minimal brain damage* and *minimal brain dysfunction (MBD)*. This set the stage for viewing LD as a problem in acquiring basic academic skills, including speech, language, reading, and writing. Kirk described LD as

> a retardation, disorder, or delayed development in one or more of the processes of speech, language, reading, writing, arithmetic, or other school subject resulting from a psychological handicap caused by a possible cerebral dysfunction and/or emotional or behavioral disturbances. It is not the result of mental retardation, sensory deprivation, or cultural and instructional factors. (p. 263)

The first iteration of the federal access to education law now called IDEA included a definition for LD based on Kirk's (1962) original definition. By then, however, wording about cerebral dysfunction was removed, and emotional disturbance was included among conditions to be ruled out as possible causes of unexpected academic difficulties. Fletcher, Morris, and Lyon (2003) noted that dropping the broader category of minimal brain dysfunction at around this time reflected growing awareness that attention-deficit/hyperactivity disorder (ADHD) was a distinct disorder, with difficulties primarily in the behavioral domain, compared to LD, with difficulties primarily in the academic domain. The original federal definition of LD, which was published in 1977 as part of the regulations accompanying PL 94-142, read as follows:

> The term "specific learning disability" means a disorder in one or more of the psychological processes involved in understanding or in using language, spoken or written, which may manifest itself in an imperfect ability to listen, speak, read, write, spell, or do mathematical calculations. The term does not include children who have LDs which are primarily the result of visual, hearing, or motor handicaps, or mental retardation, or emotional disturbance, or of environmental, cultural, or economic disadvantage. (U.S. Office of Education, 1977, p. 65083)

When the U.S. Office of Education published this definition, it also proposed a discrepancy formula that states could use to operationalize the definition. Negative public response during the period of review resulted in the formula not being included in the regulations, but initial regulations "did retain the general idea of the need for a severe discrepancy between achievement and intellectual ability for identification as learning disabled" (Hallahan & Mock, 2003, p. 24).

Numerous modified definitions of LD have been proposed since then. The National Joint Committee on Learning Disabilities (1991), which is made up of representatives from a variety of professional associations interested in children and adults with learning disabilities (including the American Speech-Language-Hearing Association), specifically avoided referring to underlying psychological processes in its definition:

> Learning disabilities is a general term that refers to a heterogeneous group of disorders manifested by significant difficulties in the acquisition and use of listening, speaking, reading, writing, reasoning, or mathematical abilities. These disorders are intrinsic to the individual, presumed to be due to central nervous system dysfunction, and may occur across the lifespan. Problems in self-regulatory behaviors, social perception, and social interaction may exist with learning disabilities but do not by themselves constitute a learning disability. Although learning disabilities may occur concomitantly with other handicapping conditions (for example, sensory impairment, mental retardation, serious emotional disturbance) or with extrinsic influences (such as cultural differences, insufficient or inappropriate instruction), they are not the result of those conditions or influences. (p. 19)

One reason the NJCLD moved away from references to a processing disorder was to avoid basing interventions on prerequisite processes that were related only marginally to reading, such as finger tracing and digit-recall exercises (see Personal Reflection 5.2). This caution should not be lost on today's clinicians.

PERSONAL reflection 5.2

"If you want children to learn to read, you have to teach them reading."

Donald Hammill (personal communication, June 20, 2008), a leader in the field of learning disabilities and the author of many tests and materials, has been influential in focusing attention directly on reading rather than processes supposed to underly it.

Relatively minor modifications were made in the official definition of LD in federal legislation since 1977 until the reauthorization of IDEA in 2004. In the 2004 version, the requirement for cognitive referencing was specifically removed from federal policy, so that assessment teams no longer must diagnose LD based on a discrepancy between *ability* (usually operationalized as intelligence test scores) and *achievement* (e.g., test scores in reading or math). The revised wording indicates permission for identification of LD based on problem-solving methods, opening the door to response to intervention (RTI) approaches. Key excerpts from IDEA '04 related to diagnostic criteria and processes for LD indicated the following:

> In general, the term 'specific learning disability' means a disorder in one or more of the basic psychological processes involved in understanding or in using language, spoken or written, which disorder may manifest itself in the imperfect ability to listen, think, speak, read, write, spell, or do mathematical calculations. (Part A, Section 602, Definitions, Paragraph [30])

> A local educational agency shall not be required to take into consideration whether a child has a severe discrepancy between achievement and intellectual ability in oral expression, listening comprehension, written expression, basic reading skill, reading comprehension, mathematical calculation, or mathematical reasoning. (Section 614 [b][6][A])

> In determining whether a child has a specific learning disability, a local educational agency may use a process that determines if the child responds to scientific, research-based intervention as a part of the evaluation procedures. (Section 614 [b][2 &3])

Learning Disability Subclassification

A large body of research has been aimed at explaining the nature of LD. Efforts to identify subtypes or phenotypes of LD based on processing preferences (e.g., visual versus auditory learners, left-brain versus right-brain learners) have been largely unsuccessful. The lack of supportive research data for such subtypes has led many to abandon processing and profile models of LD "because the research could not identify interactions between interventions and information-processing modality, neuropsychological profiles, or learning styles and orientations" (Fletcher et al., 2003, p. 34). This was consistent with earlier arguments by the NJCLD to avoid placing too much emphasis on processing deficits as the root cause of LD.

Specific Learning Disability

Similar to SLI, definitions of *specific learning disability (SLD)* are based on the premise that difficulty achieving academic success in the area of spoken and written language and mathematics are unexpected compared to a child's essentially normal development in other domains. In discussing diagnosis on the basis of discrepancy, Fletcher and colleagues (2003) noted that *unexpectedness* could be defined in more than one way:

> Historically, LD has existed as a disorder that was difficult to define. Implicit classifications viewed LD as "unexpected" underachievement. The primary approach to identification involved a search for intraindividual variability as a marker for the "unexpectedness" of LD, along with an emphasis on the exclusion of other causes of underachievement that would be "expected" to produce underachievement. (p. 30)

Fletcher and colleagues (2003) pursued the topic of unexpectedness by reviewing two prominent methods that have been used to diagnose LD. The first, the *intraindividual differences model,* focuses on ability-to-ability discrepancies within the same child, including those required by an achievement–ability formula (i.e., cognitive referencing or discrepancy model). The second, the *problem-solving model,* known currently as the *RTI model,* also focuses on discrepancies within the same child, except that in this case, the intrachild comparison is from time 1 to time 2 rather than across domains. Addressing the question of LD specificity, Fletcher and colleagues (2003) noted, "Classification research over the past 10 to 15 years has provided little evidence that IQ discrepancy demarcates a specific type of LD that differs from other forms of underachievement" (p. 31). Research has shown that specific LD differences are dimensional, rather than categorical, and that SLD is not qualitatively different from other forms of underachievement. This should sound familiar, as it is parallel to research findings regarding SLI and NLI, which should not be surprising given that the two conditions (LD and LI) may represent different perspectives on a single phenomenon.

Dyslexia

Dyslexia is a type of SLD. The diagnosis of dyslexia applies when children have impaired skills for analyzing words into their phonological, syllabic, and morphemic components and for learning to read and spell (Catts & Kamhi, 2005a; Snowling, 2000). Due to historical and sociocultural factors, the term *dyslexia* is more likely to be used by medically trained personnel and those in private schools than by professionals in public schools, who use the term *learning disability* (Kamhi, 2004; Catts & Kamhi, 2005a). The term *specific reading impairment* also applies.

Research points to deficits in the phonological aspects of language as a root cause of reading difficulty in dyslexia (Snowling, 1995; Stanovich & Siegel, 1994). The definition used by the International Dyslexia Association (IDA; 2002) and the National Institute of

Child Health and Human Development (McCardle & Chhabra, 2004) emphasizes the word-level (phonological system) deficits. The definition on the IDA website is as follows:

> Dyslexia is a specific learning disability that is neurological in origin. It is characterized by difficulties with accurate and/or fluent word recognition and by poor spelling and decoding abilities. These difficulties typically result from a deficit in the phonological component of language that is often unexpected in relation to other cognitive abilities and the provision of effective classroom instruction. Secondary consequences may include problems in reading comprehension and reduced reading experience that can impede growth of vocabulary and background knowledge. (IDA, 2002)

Stanovich (1986) dubbed secondary vocabulary learning difficulties the "Matthew effect," because it is a phenomenon in which "the rich get richer and the poor get poorer."

Hyperlexia and Specific Comprehension Deficit

In contrast to dyslexia, some children demonstrate *hyperlexia,* which involves a pattern of precocious surface-level reading accompanied by problems with abstract language comprehension and pragmatic–social communication (Aram, 1997). Hyperlexia may be more a symptom than a syndrome. It can co-occur with a number of diagnoses, including autism spectrum disorders, mental retardation, and schizophrenia (Aram & Healy, 1988). By itself, precocious surface reading with limited comprehension is not diagnostic of any one syndrome.

Catts and Kamhi (2005a) specifically avoided using the term *hyperlexia* in the second edition of their text on language and reading disabilities, indicating a preference for *specific comprehension deficit.* Catts, Hogan, and Adlof (2005) indicated that doing so would avoid "the association with autism or the narrow connotation that hyperlexia sometimes denotes" (p. 27).

Nonverbal Learning Disability

The term *nonverbal learning disability (NLD)* has been used to describe children with relative strengths in the surface processing of spoken and written language but with deficits in language use for supporting social interaction and higher-level language comprehension (Foss, 1991; Rourke, 1995). Neither the term *hyperlexia* nor *specific comprehension deficit* is considered synonymous with the label *nonverbal learning disability,* yet similarities can be noted among the three classifications and with the syndrome Bishop (2000) named PLI.

Byron Rourke, a Canadian neuropsychologist, has been a proponent for recognizing nonverbal learning disability as a particular phenotype associated with certain genetic syndromes (e.g., Fragile X and Williams syndrome) and conditions (e.g., fetal alcohol spectrum disorder, agenesis of the corpus callosum). The primary symptoms of NLD are relative deficits in social pragmatics, tactile, and visual–spatial skills in someone with strengths in phonology and syntax, at least at a surface level. Rourke (1995) hypothesized that the common set of assets and difficulties observed in this phenotype might be traced to under-developed, damaged, or dysfunctional white-matter pathways (long axonal fibers covered with myelin sheaths), the largest of which is the corpus callosum, which connects the two cerebral hemispheres (Rourke, 1995; n.d.).

Rourke (1995) described a particular set of strengths and deficits that characterize NLD. Strengths include rote verbal memory and a high volume of speech output but with unusual prosody (rhythm and fluency). Academically, children with NLD may show excellent single-word decoding skills while reading and good verbatim memory for oral and written verbal material but difficulty with comprehension (described previously in this chapter as characteristics of hyperlexia). Other primary deficits include bilateral tactile–perceptual deficits and marked difficulty with visual–spatial–organizational skills and mathematics. Formal thought and general concept formation, problem solving, strategy generation, and hypothesis testing are impaired. Deficits also are noted in social perception, social judgment, and social interaction skills, and these increase with age. Psychosocial symptoms of anxiety and depression may be observed as well. Although some individuals with NLD appear to be hyperactive during early childhood, they may become normally active with advancing years and eventually may be described as hypoactive.

The diagnosis of NLD is not widely recognized or applied, although Telzrow and Koch (2003) noted that related forms of LD have been described by other labels. Denckla (1983) described a form of social–emotional LD, Grace and Malloy (1992) described right hemisphere developmental LD, and Cleaver and Whitman (1998) described white-matter LD.

The NLD classification is introduced in this chapter because of its relationship to other primary forms of LI and LD. NLD shares characteristics with specific comprehension deficit and pragmatic language impairment (PLI). Even though it does not fit cleanly as a primary disorder of language or literacy, the label *nonverbal* LD does not fit perfectly either. The use of *nonverbal* tends to obscure the higher-level language comprehension problems that children with NLD experience along with their difficulties with abstract reasoning. Care must be taken to ensure that children with such needs receive the social communication and language comprehension services they need.

SUMMARY

More school-age children are diagnosed with learning disabilities than any other special-needs diagnosis. The LD grouping is a heterogeneous one, comprising children with difficulty learning language in any of its modalities (listening, speaking, reading, or writing) and hence may be called *language-learning disability (LLD)*. The diagnosis of LD also applies to children who have difficulty learning quantitative concepts related to mathematics and who may not have symptoms of LI, although that should be ruled out.

Dyslexia is a form of LD that is characterized by prominent impairment in the phonological aspects of language. Resulting difficulties are observed in acquiring the alphabetic principle, sound–symbol associations, reading decoding, fluent word recognition, and spelling. The decoding problem is likely to interfere with reading comprehension, but listening comprehension is relatively intact. Due to the reading difficulties, secondary impact on vocabulary and academic learning have been hypothesized (called the "Matthew effect"), but the limited evidence for this hypothesis suggests a need for more research.

Precocious reading may appear in a fully healthy learner. Hyperlexia (also called *specific comprehension deficit*) is diagnosed when a child demonstrates early reading decoding but has difficulties in listening and reading comprehension. Neither hyperlexia nor specific comprehension deficit is a diagnostic category in IDEA '04, but these diagnoses may be subsumed under other categories, including LD, LI, or ASD, depending on the other symptoms. The term *nonverbal learning disability* does not appear as a category IDEA '04, nor is it listed in the *DSM-IV-TR* (APA, 2000). However, it has similarities with PLI and is associated with cognitive–communicative diagnoses such as Fragile X and Williams syndrome.

Spoken and Written Language Associations and Dissociations

Disorders involving language and communication across modalities are related, at least to some degree, by virtue of difficulty in acquiring and associating symbols with meaning for

table *5.1* Prognostic Factors Found in Research on Children Identified with Language Impairment (LI) Followed Longitudinally

Better Prognosis	Poorer Prognosis
Less severe and fewer language systems involved when identified[d,m,n]	More severe when first diagnosed and more language systems involved[d,m,n]
Problems limited to articulation[c,g,h,o,q]	Problems involve language systems other than articulation[c,g,h,o,q]
Higher nonverbal IQ[a,d,l,n]	Lower nonverbal IQ[a,d,l,n]
No comorbid deficits (e.g., hearing or cognitive impairment)[a,d,n]	More associated deficits[a,d,n]
No family history of language or reading disability[g,l,n,o]	Family history of language or reading disability[g,l,n,o]
Low-risk birth[l,n]	High-risk birth[l,n]
Younger when first identified (< 6;6 yrs.) and younger when still having difficulty[n,p]	Older when first identified (> 6;6 yrs.) and older when still having difficulty[n,p]
Communicative as an infant[n]	Noncommunicative as an infant[n]
Participates in groups with peers[n]	Prefers to play alone[n]
Parents say positive things about child[n]	Parents rely on physical discipline[n]
Able to retell story with pictures at age 5 yrs.[d]	Unable to retell story with pictures at 5 yrs.[d]

Potential Problems as Children Reach School Age and Adolescence

Persistent problems with language and speech: 40%,[b] 50%,[h] 56%,[d] 80%[p]

Difficulty learning to read: 30%,[e,f] 40%,[b] 75%,[l] 90%[p]

Predictors of reading difficulty from best to poorest include letter identification, concepts of print, phonological awareness, expressive vocabulary, sentence/story recall, full-scale or verbal IQ, rapid serial naming, receptive language, word/digit memory, receptive vocabulary, expressive language, visual memory, performance IQ, speech production/articulation, speech perception, visual and motor skills.

Children with speech-only difficulties in preschool are far less likely to have reading difficulties later; those who continue to have difficulty in school often have difficulty with phonemic awareness and related reading difficulty;[c,g,h,o,q] high nonphonological skills at age 6 are a protective factor for children with a family history of dyslexia.[o]

Reading difficulties in the area of word identification can emerge as late as fourth grade.[j]

Children with nonspecific LI are more likely to require classroom placement for mild mental retardation (20%), LD placement, or tutoring (69%,[a] 52%[i]).

Mild problems only with social interaction: only 8% reported to have significant social–emotional difficulties.[i]

Sources:

[a] Aram, Ekelman, & Nation, 1984—20 adolescents originally identified as preschoolers with LI, evaluated 10 years later.

[b] Aram & Nation, 1980—63 children identified at less than 5 yrs.; evaluated again at 9 yrs. (included children with nonspecific LI and comorbid disorders).

[c] Bishop & Adams, 1990—followed children with speech-only impairments from the Bishop & Edmundson study and tested them at age 8;6.

[d] Bishop & Edmundson, 1987—68 children with SLI; 19 more with low nonverbal IQ and general delay; evaluated at ages 4;0, 4;6, and 5;6 yrs. of age.

[e] Catts, Hogan, & Fey, 2003—604 children of the 7,000 kindergarten children identified in the Tomblin et al. (1997) epidemiological study were tested for language, reading, and cognitive abilities in second and fourth grades; the 183 children who met criteria as poor readers were classified by type.

[f] Catts, Hogan, & Adlof, 2005—the 183 children from Catts et al. (2003) were tested for language, reading, and cognitive abilities again in eighth grade.

[g] Gallagher, Frith, & Snowling, 2000—followed 63 children with a familial (genetic) risk of dyslexia and 34 children from families who showed no risk of dyslexia from preschool to age 6.

[h] Hall & Tomblin, 1978—18 adults with LI and 18 adults with articulation impairments only; 13- to 20-yr. follow-up interviews with mothers.

[i] King, Jones, & Lasky, 1982—50 adolescents (some with motor, hearing, or cognitive deficits); identified as preschoolers; +15 follow-up with mothers.

[j] Leach, Scarborough, & Rescorla, 2003—identified 66 children in fourth and fifth grades who met criteria for reading disability, more than one-third of whom had no prior history of reading problems at younger ages.

[k] Nathan, Stackhouse, Goulandris, & Snowling, 2004—followed 19 children with speech-only difficulties, 19 with speech and language difficulties, and 19 controls from ages 4 to 7 yrs.

[l] Scarborough & Dobrich, 1990—4 children evaluated at 2;6 yrs., 5 yrs., and end of grade two.

[m] Scarborough, 1998, 2005—61 research samples were subjected to meta-analysis to identify predictors of future reading scores by kindergarten measures of phonological and other cognitive and language skills.

[n] Schery, 1985—718 children originally identified at 3;1 to 16;4 yrs.; records were reviewed to identify correlates of improvement over past two to three yrs.

[o] Snowling, Gallagher, & Frith, 2003—56 children with familial risk of dyslexia were tested at ages 6 and 8 yrs. for phonological and nonphonological language abilities.

[p] Stark et al., 1984—29 children with SLI who were identified at 4;6 to 8;0 yrs. were evaluated at 8 to 12 yrs. of age.

[q] Stothard, Snowling, Bishop, Chipchase, & Kaplan, 1998—tested 10 children with speech-only impairments from the Bishop & Edmundson study when they were adolescents.

communicative purposes. The language-levels-by-modalities model introduced in Chapter 2 focuses on integration of sound, word, sentence, and discourse abilities to perceive, decode, and comprehend language input or to formulate, encode, and transmit language output as children develop competence across modalities.

Questions arise, however, as to which systems are involved, when in development, to what degree, and how predictably. If a child has difficulty learning to talk, for example, how predictable is it that he or she will have difficulty learning to read and write as well? Conversely, if a child struggles to read and write but has no history of spoken language impairment, might there be signs of language weakness that could have been uncovered if one had probed deeper? How much does speech impairment predict language impairment and literacy-learning difficulty? Table 5.1 summarizes a body of longitudinal research that indicates factors that are associated with better and poorer prognosis for long-term outcome when children identified with LI are followed for several years.

Speech Production, Phonological Awareness, and Reading Ability

Some fairly strong evidence points to a relationship between knowledge of speech sounds and early word decoding. The broad term ***phonological awareness (PA)*** refers to the metalinguistic skill involved in "understanding that spoken words can be broken down into smaller parts" (Gillon, 2004, p. 11). This includes the "explicit awareness of the abstract units that compose spoken words, including syllables, onset and rime units, and individual phonemes" (Rvachew, Ohberg, Grawburg, & Heyding, 2003, p. 463). Gillon (2004) applied the concepts of nonlinear phonology (introduced previously in this chapter) to break down a word's phonological structure hierarchically:

The word *basket* can be represented according to its stress pattern as having one foot (i.e., has one stressed element). The word can then be divided at the syllable level into a strong or stressed syllable *(bas)* and a weak or unstressed syllable *(ket)*. Each syllable, in turn, can be divided further into an onset (i.e., the consonant or consonant cluster that precedes the vowel) and a rime unit (i.e., the vowel and following consonants in the syllable). The onset-rime level can be further segmented into individual speech sounds or phonemes, and the features or characteristics of each phoneme (e.g., that /b/ is a voice sound made by the lips closing together and interrupting the airflow) are also represented in a hierarchically organized manner. (pp. 3–4)

Under the umbrella of phonological awareness, the more specific term ***phonemic awareness*** refers to explicit understanding that words are composed of individual speech sounds (Gillon, 2004). Difficulties of phonemic awareness and other phonological-processing skills bear uncertain relationships to speech production difficulties but relatively predictable relationships to the ability to learn to read and write.

Stackhouse (1997) observed that "successful speech and literacy development are both dependent on an intact underlying phonological processing system" (p. 188). That is, learning to read and to spell both rely on phonological-processing skills, which are used for "the segmentation of spoken and written material (i.e., phonological awareness)" (p. 188). Several studies have shown that children with speech sound disorders do have difficulty with PA relative to children who do not have a speech or language impairment (e.g., Larrivee & Catts, 1999; Rvachew et al., 2003; Webster & Plante, 1992).

Although this relationship is plausible, it is not as predictable as one would think (Scarborough, 2005). Catts (1993) followed groups of children with speech impairment only and with speech and language impairment from kindergarten into first and second grades. Children with articulation impairment only "generally performed at or above the level of the normal group in reading achievement" (p. 955), and only about half of the 56 children with speech and language impairment were not reading within normal limits in the first and second grades. Catts found that phonological awareness and rapid-naming tasks predicted word recognition but did not add anything unique to reading comprehension; however, measures of semantic–syntactic language did predict reading comprehension. These results are consistent with the application of a simple model of sound/word (phonological language skills) and sentence/discourse (nonphonological language skills) abilities across spoken and written language systems.

Also investigating relationships between SSD and phonemic awareness, Rvachew and colleagues (2003) compared the phonological abilities of 4-year-old children with and without phonological impairment. The children with expressive phonological delays (SSD) scored significantly lower than the control group on measures of phonological processing and awareness, even though their vocabulary skills were normal. Rvachew and her colleagues recommended assessing phonemic awareness skills for children with SSD even if they show few other signs of language development difficulty.

Sutherland and Gillon (2005) conducted a similar study with 26 children at ages 4 and 5 years, nine with severely impaired speech and seventeen with typically developing speech. Phonological representation and judgment, as well as nonword reading ability, were moderately correlated with phonological awareness, speech production, and letter knowledge measures. A majority of the speech-impaired children (six out of nine) scored 1 standard deviation below the mean on at least two of the tests of PA, whereas only three of the seventeen typically developing children scored low on the measures of PA. Sutherland and Gillon concluded that speech impairment is a risk factor for difficulty in PA, which in turn is a risk factor for difficulty with word-level decoding when learning to read.

Rvachew (2006) investigated causal relationships further by conducting a longitudinal study of children with SSD at two points in time. She studied the association among three potential predictor variables (vocabulary, speech perception, and articulation) on the outcome variable of phonological awareness. The children were assessed at the end of their prekindergarten year and again at the end of kindergarten with tests of receptive vocabulary, articulation, speech perception, and PA skills. The results showed that speech perception and vocabulary skills in 4-year-olds were associated with the development of PA abilities during the kindergarten year. After controlling for prekindergarten vocabulary size and speech perception skills, problems with articulation accuracy prior to kindergarten did not explain the unique variance in PA at the end of kindergarten. Rvachew interpreted these findings as suggesting that speech perception served as the common factor linking articulatory ability and phonological awareness, which may have accounted for correlations of articulation and PA abilities in this and other studies.

Nathan, Stackhouse, Goulandris, and Snowling (2004) investigated relationships between speech and reading among children with SSD from ages 4 to 7 years. Their sample included 19 children with SSD only, 19 children with speech and language impairments, and 19 typically developing children. In this study, preschool speech production skills and language abilities both predicted PA at an early stage of reading, which in turn predicted later literacy outcomes. The researchers concluded that literacy skills "depended on the severity and persistence of the speech problem and whether or not language problems were also involved" (Nathan et al., 2004, p. 388). Once the effects of PA were controlled, however, neither speech perception nor speech production predicted further variation in reading accuracy or spelling skills.

Carroll and Snowling (2004) compared children with isolated speech impairment to children from families in which dyslexia was common. Children in both groups had lower PA and word recognition abilities than those in a control group matched for age. The group with SSD only also had lower scores on letter knowledge. Bishop and Adams (1990) suggested a *critical age hypothesis* to explain how speech problems predict reading difficulties but only if they persist to the point when phonological skills are at high demand for learning to read. Related to this hypothesis, Snowling (2005) reviewed prior research and concluded, "It seems that children who have speech problems when phonological skills are required for learning to read are at high risk of reading problems if their speech difficulties are accompanied by poor phoneme awareness" (p. 64).

Epidemiological reports indicate that by 5 to 6 years of age, speech and language impairments co-occur in only 2 percent of children, and only 5 percent to 8 percent of children with SLI demonstrate SSD (Shriberg, Tomblin, & McSweeny, 1999). These figures are quite remarkable when compared with evidence that approximately 60 percent of children who exhibit phonological disorders as they are learning to talk have language symptoms as well (e.g., Bishop & Edmundson, 1987; Shriberg & Kwiatkowski, 1994). Speech production, phonological awareness, and language ability are related skills, but it is clear from these findings that they are not completely overlapping. Case Example 5.1, which appeared earlier in this chapter, provided an example of articulation difficulty co-occurring with literacy problems in a sixth-grade boy with written composition problems. This case illustrated overlaps and dissociations across speech and language systems. Even when Walter's articulation was corrected, his literacy difficulties remained, requiring further language intervention.

Broader Language Skills and Reading Ability, Including Comprehension

Spoken language and literacy abilities clearly are related but in complex ways. Some children with language impairment have relatively strong phonological skills and word decoding abilities but still have reading deficits in the area of comprehension.

Nation, Clarke, Marshall, and Durand (2004) assessed a variety of spoken language skills among a group of children with poor reading comprehension and compared them with the skills of a control group of children with typical reading. The researchers assessed phonology, semantics, morphosyntax, and broader language skills, including pragmatic sensitivity to context, nonliteral language, and ambiguity. A majority of the children with comprehension deficits (but not all) met the researchers' criteria for SLI, in spite of having relative strengths in the area of phonological processing and no prior diagnosis of LI. In fact, 30 percent met the criteria for moderate language deficits (lower than the 10th percentile on two measures), and 43 percent met the criteria for severe deficits (lower than the 3rd percentile on at least one measure).

Scarborough (1990b) analyzed factors that differentiated preschool children who later demonstrated reading disabilities (RD) from those who did not (all with similar IQs and socioeconomic status). Different abilities separated the two groups of children (with and without RD) at three points during their preschool years:

- At ages 2.5 and 3 years, the two groups were differentiated by syntactic and speech production abilities (but not vocabulary or speech discrimination skills).
- At ages 3.5 to 4 years, the groups were differentiated by syntactic, receptive vocabulary, and object-naming skills (but not speech).
- At age 5, they were differentiated by object-naming, phonemic awareness, and letter–sound knowledge (but not syntax).

Scarborough (2005) advocated for a multifactorial model to explain the differences in results not only for different children but for the same children at different ages. Such a model should incorporate nonphonological as well as phonological language skills.

Pursuing this approach, Nation and Snowling (2004) followed reading skill development in 72 children from age 8.5 to 13 years. They found that, in addition to phonological measures, nonphonological measures of oral language vocabulary and listening comprehension at age 8.5 predicted reading comprehension not only at that age but also at age 13. In adolescence, language variables beyond phonology still accounted for extra variance in reading comprehension, word recognition, and the ability to read words with irregular spellings.

Botting, Simkin, and Conti-Ramsden (2006) also followed 200 children with SLI from ages 7 to 11. They found support for single-word reading at age 7 as a predictor for reading accuracy and reading comprehension at age 11. They also found that sentence/discourse measures in expressive and receptive modalities administered at age 7 predicted the presence of word reading fluency as well as comprehension problems at age 11.

In earlier reports of disorders of spoken language development, Scarborough and Dobrich (1990) had noted that children could appear to have LI at some points but not others. During periods of developmental plateau, children with LI might appear to catch up but lag behind again later when their language weaknesses make it impossible to keep up with able students, who quickly learn to meet the challenges of higher-level academic language.

Considering these results, particularly from longitudinal studies, Scarborough (2005) argued against a phonological hypothesis as a single-system difficulty underlying both spoken and written language disorders. Summarizing her analysis, she concluded, "Speech articulation and even phonological awareness itself, when measured early, have not been markedly better predictors of subsequent awareness differences than have the nonphonological language skills" (p. 9).

Evidence for a Simple Model of Deficits in Spoken and Written Language

Although no single model can explain the various factors, a *simple model* of reading, with decoding and comprehension as two components (Gough & Tunmer, 1986; Hoover & Gough, 1990), has promise for clarifying complex relationships. Such a model can explain differences between disorders specific to reading and also those involving spoken language. It focuses on the relative involvement of phonological (sound-/word-level) skills needed for word decoding and spelling and nonphonological (sentence-/discourse-level) skills needed for reading comprehension and written language formulation. As illustrated in Figure 5.3, the horizontal trajectory in a simple model for differential diagnosis represents low-to-high phonological abilities for processing the structure of words and relating them to meaning. The vertical trajectory represents low-to-high abilities for processing the nonphonological aspects of language (particularly syntax and discourse level structures) and using them to comprehend spoken and written sentences and discourse.

Typical development is represented in this model in the upper-right quadrant as involving a high phonological–high nonphonological profile. Dyslexia is represented in the upper-left quadrant as involving low phonological–high nonphonological abilities associated with decoding deficits in reading but intact skills for listening comprehension. About 36 percent of the poor readers studied by Catts, Hogan, and Fey (2003) fell into this category. It contrasts with a low phonological–low nonphonological profile for children

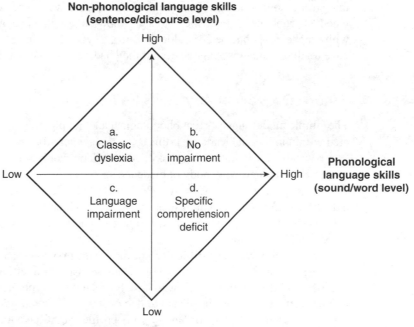

figure 5.3

A Simple Model Predicting Diagnostic Profiles Relating Phonological Language Skills at the Sound/Word Level with Nonphonological Language Skills at the Sentence/Discourse Level

Source: Based on Bishop & Snowling, 2004; Catts & Kamhi, 2005a.

with LI, who tend to have difficulty across all language levels and modalities. Consistent with the low–low profile, Catts and colleagues found that 36 percent of poor readers fell into a category of mixed RD, involving both decoding and comprehension deficits. Finally, a high phonological–low nonphonological profile appears in the lower-right quadrant. This is the pattern associated with specific comprehension deficit. Catts and colleagues found that 15 percent of poor readers demonstrated the pattern of relatively intact decoding abilities accompanied by deficits in reading comprehension.

Catts, Hogan, and Adlof (2005) continued to follow the poor readers from the Epi-SLI study into the eighth grade. The readers were tested at each grade with a battery of word recognition, listening comprehension, and reading comprehension tests. At any grade, 27 percent to 29 percent of the children met the criteria for poor readers (compared to 16 percent of the total population), but approximately 20 percent who met criteria in one grade did not qualify as poor readers in any other grade. The following weighted percentages of students with poor reading profiles were reported by grade level:

- *Second grade:* 32 percent with dyslexia; 36 percent with mixed RD; 16 percent with specific comprehension deficit; 15 percent with nonspecified RD
- *Fourth grade:* 22 percent with dyslexia; 33 percent with mixed RD; 31 percent with specific comprehension deficit; 14 percent with nonspecified RD
- *Eighth grade:* 13 percent with dyslexia; 33 percent with mixed RD; 30 percent with specific comprehension deficit; 24 percent with nonspecified RD

Based on their longitudinal data, Snowling, Gallagher, and Firth (2003) suggested that strong nonphonological language skills at age 6 were a protective factor for children who had problems in grapheme–phoneme knowledge at that age. A subgroup of 6-year-olds with grapheme–phoneme difficulties but strong syntactic–semantic skills were less likely to have reading problems at age 8, even if they had a familial risk for dyslexia.

Where Do Vocabulary Skills Fit?

The simple model suggests that phonological and nonphonological abilities can be dissociated within individual learners. If this is the case, where do vocabulary skills fit?

Vocabulary is a word-level skill. The lexicon can be described by its phonological properties, and a growing body of evidence shows phonetic effects on lexical learning and vice versa (e.g., Munson, Edwards, Beckman, 2005; Rvachew, 2006). Vocabulary also is a direct semantic component of meaning making, which plays a role in the nonphonological aspects of language essential for forming syntactic units and constructing cohesive ties across units of discourse.

Some children have difficulty not only with phonological awareness but also with other aspects of vocabulary processing that are seen as word retrieval and rapid-naming difficulties. Children with dyslexia who have both symptoms (phonemic awareness and rapid-naming difficulties) have been said to demonstrate a *double-deficit form* of dyslexia (e.g., Wolf & Bowers, 1999). Children with this profile might have a relatively well-developed receptive vocabulary but still have difficulty retrieving word forms for rapid-naming tasks or when reading or formulating language. Manis, Seidenberg, and Doi (1999) found that children with rapid automatic naming (RAN) difficulty in grade one were more likely to have difficulty with reading at grade two. RAN also explained variance beyond that explained by phoneme awareness.

Vocabulary development can be affected by language- and literacy-learning difficulties in other ways. As noted earlier, Stanovich (1986) introduced the term the "Matthew effect" to convey the expectation that lower decoding ability would be associated with lower desire to read, as well as reduced ability to read. This would perpetuate a vicious cycle of less reading and lower vocabulary. As a result of limited access to reading as a major source for vocabulary learning, older children and adolescents would show increasingly wide differences in reading comprehension and other language abilities as they grew older.

Stanovich (1991) called predictions based on associations among phonemic awareness, reading ability, and vocabulary knowledge a "beautiful hypothesis" (p. 78). Countering the phonological skills hypothesis, with related effects on vocabulary, Scarborough (2005) (see Personal Reflection 5.3) pointed to a number of "ugly facts" that are inconsistent with it. For example, when Catts, Hogan, and Fey (2003) followed students with reading disabilities into the fourth grade, they did not find the decline in reading comprehension scores that the Matthew effect would predict.

PERSONAL reflection 5.3

"I would argue that the phonological model does not fully explain the development of reading disabilities outside the primary grades. To account for the ugly facts that have been revealed by research with younger and older populations, the well-established causal chain that operates during the early grades needs to be incorporated into a broader model that postulates a second causal chain, a persisting underlying condition, or some other mechanism that can account for the phenomena in question. Without such expansion, the phonological model provides only part, albeit a very important part, of ongoing research efforts to reach a full understanding of how, when, and why the process of learning to read can go awry."

Hollis Scarborough (2005, p. 20), a cognitive psycholinguist, was drawing conclusions after reviewing the developmental relationships between language and reading in a chapter called "Reconciling a Beautiful Hypothesis with Some Ugly Facts."

Another prediction would be that late-emerging reading difficulties should involve comprehension deficits but not reading decoding difficulties. Some counterevidence has been found for that prediction as well. For example, Leach, Scarborough, and Rescorla (2003) showed that late-emerging reading decoding problems can occur. They identified four subgroups among fourth- and fifth-grade readers. The majority had no difficulty. The remaining three subgroups included 18 percent who showed reading comprehension deficits only, 42 percent who showed mixed word-level difficulties and reading comprehension deficits, and 39 percent who showed sound/word deficits in both speech production and accuracy of word recognition and spelling. Many of those in this last group with word-level difficulties had long-standing reading difficulties that had been identified earlier based on reading decoding problems, but some who later showed marked difficulty with reading decoding had been successful with early aspects of learning to read.

What had changed for these students? There could be several explanations, but one of them might be that later-occurring vocabulary items (e.g., words with Latin and Greek etymological roots) require different word-level analytical abilities than earlier learned words. The phonological skills that might work relatively better for making phoneme–grapheme (sound–letter) associations in early reading and spelling need to be augmented in later grades by knowledge of higher-level Greek- and Latin-influenced morpheme–orthographic patterns, such as *-ology, hyper-*, and *hypo-* (Henry, 1989; Carlisle & Stone, 2005). One hypothesis is that lower vocabulary knowledge and related deficits of phonotactic knowledge (i.e., how phonemes may be organized in words of a particular language) might account for some later-appearing word decoding difficulties, even though a child's language comprehension skills are basically intact.

SUMMARY

Although not all relationships are completely understood, evidence supports the need to consider spoken and written language abilities side by side in language assessment and intervention. Some speech, language, and reading skills are dissociated with each other, particularly in students with primary disorders. If so, therapeutic interventions can be designed to take advantage of relative strengths in one domain to support work in another. The goal is to help children build connections that will support more functionally effective integrated systems. This should be done not only for children with primary disorders of language and literacy but also for those with secondary disorders. A simple model was presented for understanding spoken and written language disorders as involving different combinations of sound-/word-level (phonological) and sentence-/discourse-level (nonphonological) abilities.

CHAPTER SUMMARY

This chapter introduced systems for classifying and diagnosing primary disorders of speech, language, and literacy. Secondary conditions, which are associated with other comorbid diagnoses, are the topic of the next two chapters. Readers have been reminded not to treat diagnostic categories too rigidly and to maintain a focus on children as individuals while seeking to understand the challenges they face and how best to help them.

Primary disorders were grouped into speech sound disorders (speech delay, residual errors, and special populations), language impairment (both specific and nonspecific), and learning disabilities (also specific and nonspecific), including dyslexia and nonverbal learning disability. Research was reviewed that showed differences between SLI and NLI to be more dimensional than categorical. No evidence was found to support cognitive-referencing policies that have been used in the past to determine eligibility for language intervention.

Finally, associations and dissociations of spoken and written language were discussed, and a simple model was presented for understanding spoken and written language disorders as involving different combinations of sound-/word-level (phonological) and sentence-/discourse-level (nonphonological) abilities.

EXERCISES *and* STUDY QUESTIONS

1. Create your own outline of the primary forms of language and literacy disorders that were reviewed in this chapter, noting the symptoms that characterize each.

2. Assume that you have been hired by a school district that says you may not find a child eligible for speech–language intervention services if he or she (a) has difficulty with articulation only or (b) does not show a discrepancy between language skills and nonverbal cognitive ability.

Prepare a rationale for why each of these restrictive policies may be inconsistent with IDEA '04 requirements for children to receive any special services they need to benefit from a FAPE.

3. You are asked to do an inservice presentation for the teachers in your school district about the relationships between spoken and written language development. List five main points that you would like the audience to take away from your presentation.

CHAPTER *six*

Motor and Sensory Impairments

LEARNING *objectives*

After studying this chapter, you should be able to do the following:

1. Describe criteria for diagnosing motor impairments involving dysarthria and childhood apraxia of speech (CAS), sensory impairments involving deafness or hard of hearing (D/HH) and blindness or low vision (B/LV), and central disorders affecting neuromotor and neurosensory control and regulation.

2. Discuss the implications for speech, language/literacy, and communication development for children with motor and sensory impairments.

Definitions of disability types under IDEA '04 (and prior versions) hinge on identifying functional limitations that indicate a need for special education and related services. IDEA '04 offers the following general definition of a *child with a disability:*

> Child with a disability means a child evaluated in accordance with Sec. 300.304 through 300.311 as having mental retardation, a hearing impairment (including deafness), a speech or language impairment, a visual impairment (including blindness), a serious emotional disturbance (referred to in this part as "emotional disturbance"), an orthopedic impairment, autism, traumatic brain injury, another health impairment, a specific learning disability, deaf-blindness, or multiple disabilities, and who, by reason thereof, needs special education and related services. (Section 300.8)

Difficulty with language and communication development may be primary (as discussed in Chapter 5) or a sign that other developmental systems are impaired. Language clinicians with knowledge of comorbid conditions refer children to other professionals as needed (in multidisciplinary models) or engage with them in diagnosis and treatment for the comprehensive set of symptoms (in interdisciplinary or transdisciplinary models).

From the perspective of language and literacy disorders, the co-occurring conditions are called *comorbid*. From the perspective of other diagnostic conditions, language and literacy symptoms are considered *secondary*. Children from special populations may need intensified language support whether or not they are diagnosed as having a language disorder as a secondary condition. Individualized education program (IEP) teams can add language intervention as a related service to the IEP of any child who qualifies for special education in any other category.

Motor System Impairment

Children with orthopedic impairment may have problems with oral–motor system control as well as difficulty with limb control, both of which have direct effects on the ability to produce intelligible speech or writing. Two classifications of speech disorders associated with neuromotor dysfunction are *dysarthria* and *apraxia*. Either diagnosis could be viewed as a primary disorder of communication and could qualify as speech or language impairment under IDEA or as "other health impairment." Language and literacy disorders may co-occur with neuromotor system disorders but, in such cases, would be considered secondary. Language and literacy difficulties are more predictably associated with apraxia than dysarthria.

Dysarthria

Dysarthria is the term for speech disorders that are secondary to neuromotor system impairment affecting speech–motor control and related reflexive functions. Dysarthria results from disorders of central nervous system (CNS) origin but with effects on peripheral nervous system (PNS) functions controlling both *reflexive* oral–motor functions (e.g., chewing, sucking, and swallowing) and *voluntary* oral–motor functions (e.g., imitative or generative speech and intentional oral gestures). Symptoms of reflexive dysfunction include drooling and difficulty eating and drinking. Symptoms of voluntary dysfunction include difficulty imitating speech sounds and facial gestures. Observation of impaired functions for eating and drinking, along with inexact and slurred speech patterns in both imitative and spontaneous productions, are essential criteria for a diagnosis of dysarthria.

Children who exhibit symptoms of dysarthria often are diagnosed as having cerebral palsy (CP) (Hardy, 1983; Pellegrino, 2002). CP is estimated to occur in between 2 and 2.5 children per 1,000 births (Cockerill & Carroll-Few, 2001). The immediate cause for a child's CP symptoms often cannot be confirmed. All babies are reflexive in their actions early in development. Thus, CP may not be diagnosed immediately, even though its causes are thought to be due to injuries to the motor control centers of the brain (cerebrum, cerebellum, and basal ganglia) when the brain is deprived of oxygen (called *anoxia*) during the prenatal, perinatal, or immediately postnatal periods. Anoxia is not the only cause. Too much bilirubin in the blood can cause hyperbilirubinemia and *kernicterus,* which is a form of brain damage associated with athetoid CP, and possible hearing loss, vision problems, and intellectual disability/mental retardation. Jaundice may be a signal of bilirubin build-up, but it occurs fairly commonly among newborns and generally is treated successfully in the neonatal unit.

Neuromotor disorders may result in paresis (partial paralysis) of the limbs as well as speech–motor control systems of the trunk, neck, and head. Symptoms include muscular *hypofunctioning* (i.e., muscular weakness), associated with the so-called floppy child syndrome, or muscular *hyperfunctioning* (i.e., excessive muscle contraction or uncontrolled motion), associated with spastic or athetoid CP. In CP, neuromuscular control problems occur at the level of the upper motor neuron (UMN) pathways in the brain, rather than in the lower motor neuron (LMN) pathways from the spinal cord to the peripheral muscles that carry out the action. UMN damage causes CP, whereas LMN causes paresis (muscular weakness) or paralysis (loss of ability to move). In UMN conditions, muscle control is impaired but motion still is possible. CP can affect primarily the lower limbs *(paraplegia),* the upper limbs *(diplegia),* the left side or right side *(hemiplegia),* or all four limbs *(quadriplegia).* Any of these patterns of limb involvement may affect arm and hand coordination for drawing, handwriting, or typing and may be associated with greater or lesser impairment of speech–motor coordination for speaking. About half of children with CP have feeding difficulties, with direct implications for speech production difficulties as well.

For some children with CP and other neuromotor control difficulties, speech–motor control is so difficult as to make intelligible speech production essentially impossible. The prefix *an-* in the term *anarthria* (Redmond & Johnston, 2001) indicates the absence of articulatory ability, whereas the prefix *dys-* (for dysfunction) in the term *dysarthria* suggests dysfunction but without complete loss. The term *dysarthria* is used here. Children with severe dysarthria may rely on augmentative and alternative communication (AAC) to support their oral and written communication. They can be characterized as having *complex communication needs (CCN)* (explained further later in this section).

Childhood Apraxia of Speech

In contrast to dysarthria, *apraxia* involves central motor-planning difficulties affecting voluntary oral–motor movements, including speech, but without affecting peripheral reflexive functions, leaving chewing and swallowing basically intact. Commonly used terms for apraxia in children are *childhood apraxia of speech (CAS)* (Lewis, Freebairn, Hansen, Iyengar, & Taylor, 2004; Peter & Stoel-Gammon, 2005), *developmental apraxia of speech (DAS)* (Betz & Stoel-Gammon, 2005), and *dyspraxia.* The acronym CAS is used here.

Apraxia affects both the accuracy and sequencing of phoneme production. Symptoms that differentiate CAS from the functional speech sound disorders described in Chapter 5 include a limited phonemic inventory accompanied by marked difficulty producing smooth transitions from one articulatory position to the next (Velleman, 2003). CAS has an estimated prevalence of about 1 to 10 children per 1,000 and may be the primary diagnosis for about 5 percent of children with speech sound disorders (Shriberg, Aram, & Kwiatkowski, 1997). CAS is a controversial diagnosis, and prevalence figures vary with the philosophies of diagnosticians. Although CAS has no accepted underlying cause and clear etiological factors have not been isolated, a central neurological deficit is presumed to interfere with motor planning in motor association areas of the brain.

Differential diagnosis of CAS from dysarthria depends on evidence that a child can use oral motor systems adequately for reflexive acts but not for speech. Most children with apraxia of speech also have difficulty performing intentional, voluntary imitation of non-speech oral gestures, such as extending the tongue tip or elevating it behind the top teeth, although they can produce such motions automatically for vegetative functions, such as retrieving food from the upper lip or behind the teeth. By contrast, children with dysarthria demonstrate difficulty performing both voluntary speech acts of oral–motor imitation or speech and reflexive motor acts. Peter and Stoel-Gammon (2005) summarized symptoms of CAS as including

> a limited phonemic inventory; omission errors; vowel errors; inconsistent articulation errors; altered suprasegmental characteristics such as disordered prosody, voice quality, and fluency; increased errors on longer units of speech output; difficulty imitating words and phrases; predominant use of simple syllable shapes; impaired volitional oral movements; reduced expressive vs. receptive language skills; and reduced diadochokinetic [syllable repetition] rates. (pp. 67–68)

Betz and Stoel-Gammon (2005) investigated the assumption that children with CAS would have inconsistent patterns of speech sound substitutions compared with children with other forms of phonological delay. Their analysis (based on three children) showed that children with CAS produced more errors than children with phonological delay but with similar consistency. This suggested a dimensional difference related to severity rather than categorical difference in the nature of the disorder. Such an interpretation would place CAS at the severe end of a continuum of developmental speech sound disorder (SSD).

By adolescence, most children with CAS can produce intelligible speech, but many have persisting language-processing problems that appear as phonological-sequencing difficulties and problems with nonword repetition. They may sound as if they learned English as a second language. Children with CAS also have higher risks for comorbid disorders of reading and spelling (Lewis et al., 2004).

Children with Complex Communication Needs

Children whose speech production capabilities are extremely limited, no matter what the cause, are said to have ***complex communication needs (CCN).*** The term is appropriate for any child or adult who may need to rely on ***augmentative and alternative communication (AAC)*** to interact (Beukelman & Mirenda, 2005). If a young child cannot speak intelligibly, it is difficult to know how much language he or she would be able to generate if intelligible speech were possible. It is also difficult to gauge a child's cognitive abilities when he or she has limited means of expression due to impaired motor control. Dynamic assessment activities might offer the best options for trying to gauge and support the developing cognitive abilities of children with CCN in conjunction with their language.

The terms *nonspeaking* and *nonverbal* are sometimes confused. ***Nonspeaking*** implies insufficient natural speech capability to support functional communication; ***nonverbal*** implies a lack of words. Children with severe speech–motor impairment may be called *nonspeaking* if they cannot articulate enough intelligible speech to rely on it for communication. If children use any words or other verbal symbols to communicate, they may be nonspeaking, but they are not *nonverbal.*

Even if the child's speech is so severely impaired that it is essentially nonfunctional for communicating with anyone who does not know him or her well, a child with CCN may demonstrate relatively spared language and communication abilities. Such occurrences provide evidence of dissociations between motor–speech control and language. Studies have shown receptive syntax abilities to be relatively spared among children with *severe speech and physical impairment* (*SSPI;* Redmond & Johnston, 2001). Vocabulary development may be delayed (Bishop, Byers Brown, & Robson, 1990) and difficulty with phonemic awareness and word reading is common (Iacono & Cupples, 2004), but cause–effect relationships are not clear.

Children whose cognitive-, language-, and social-learning systems are relatively intact can learn to use AAC to communicate sophisticated messages in spite of motor impairments. They need supportive communicative environments and a receptive audience, with access to both low- and high-technology supports to do so. They also need explicit instruction and computer supports to acquire the ability to read and write (Beukelman & Mirenda, 2005).

Children with CAS are at particularly high risk for language- and literacy-learning difficulties, suggesting influence on central concepts of speech sounds (i.e., phonology), as well as motor production difficulties. Lewis and her colleagues (2004) summarized research that showed as many as 75 percent of children with CAS have co-occurring language disorders and associated difficulties with reading and spelling.

Children with severe motor system impairments have higher risks for additional sensory and cognitive–linguistic system challenges in conjunction with their motor performance difficulties. Comorbid sensory disorders may stem from common underlying causative factors (e.g., anoxia or infection) that affect brain development in multiple areas, as suggested by the "peeling the onion" discussion of Chapter 4. In mixed or multiple system disorders, general intellectual disability (ID/MR) can co-occur with dysarthria or apraxia, as can other difficulties. CAS also is hypothesized to be a primary factor when some children with autism spectrum disorders are slow to produce speech (e.g., Freitag, Kleser, & von Gondartf, 2006).

Children with mixed disorders face particularly high developmental challenges and added complexity to their already complex communication needs. Intervention teams should work from the principle that there are no prerequisites for considering AAC (National Joint Committee for the Communication Needs of Persons with Severe Disabilities, 2003) or for focusing intervention efforts on communication, language, and literacy. The least dangerous assumption (Donnellan, 1984; see Personal Reflection 6.1) is that it is safer to assume that a child has more competence than may be immediately apparent, rather than less.

PERSONAL reflection *6.1*

"The criterion of least dangerous assumption holds that in the absence of conclusive data, educational decisions ought to be based on assumptions which, if incorrect, will have the least dangerous effect on the likelihood that students will be able to function independently as adults."

Anne Donnellan (1984, p. 141), researcher, special educator, and advocate for people with severe disabilities and complex communication needs, indicated that it is safer to "assume that poor performance is due to instructional inadequacy rather than to student deficits" (p. 150).

Children with ID/MR as part of their CCN may need augmented supports for receptive as well as expressive communication. Some individuals remain at presymbolic levels of communication throughout their lives. Nevertheless, they are not noncommunicative. Their perlocutionary communication acts, which include nonsymbolic expressions of pleasure and discomfort, can be interpreted by others as meaningful. Expressions of joy, discomfort, and distress may be assigned functional message values and responded to accordingly. AAC supports can be designed to support receptive and expressive communication represented with concrete objects as well as abstract symbols.

Access to written language read aloud by others is important for students with profound multiple disabilities that include cognition. Such input is aimed at providing rich experiences and supporting a child's intellectual development. Cultural and literacy experiences are important adjuncts to physical care and feeding that go beyond comfort and sustenance. At first, when being read to, children who have severe difficulty with communicative expression may respond primarily to spoken rhythms rather than to symbolic representation of meaning, but one can hope for growing comprehension and assume that benefits result from social closeness. Communication can be assessed through affective responses and perlocutionary signals and other forms of communicative interaction that differ from standardized tests. Failure to respond should not be taken as a signal to withdraw exposure to environmental enrichment.

Children with all degrees of ability and disability need access to concepts of print as well. Therefore, it is important to make sure that children with mixed needs can see print on the page while they are hearing written language read aloud. If their sensory systems are affected, additional technologies should be used to compensate. All spoken and literate language interactions should take place in a supportive, responsive, child-centered social milieu, which includes surroundings and peers that are chronologically age appropriate as much as possible.

SUMMARY

Neuromotor disorders may involve SSD as primary and language/literacy impairment as secondary. Children with dysarthria and apraxia are members of separate populations but share signs of speech delay and poor intelligibility. Both are forms of SSD that stem from dysfunction in the speech–motor control areas of the CNS. Dysarthria involves neuromotor signs affecting peripheral reflexive functions of chewing and swallowing as well as voluntary functions of speech. It often is associated with cerebral palsy and has unpredictable relationships to cognitive–linguistic difficulties. Childhood apraxia of speech (CAS) affects only voluntary movements, leaving reflexive movements essentially intact. CAS occurs on a continuum with other forms of SSD, and research suggests it represents a dimensional difference rather than a categorical one. CAS involves central phonological processing and carries a predictably higher risk for other language- and literacy-learning issues. Children with autism spectrum disorders have a heightened risk of CAS. Children with severe speech and physical impairments may have complex communication needs (CCN) and need augmentative and alternative communication (AAC) supports for both their spoken and written communication. The provision of technology supports can be combined with intervention targeting intelligible speech and instruction in academic language and literacy.

Auditory System Impairment

Children with impaired sensory systems experience special challenges to language and literacy learning secondary to those conditions. Children with primary disorders of language and literacy learning and/or cognition may also have sensory deficits, which then can be considered secondary. It is not always possible to tell which is primary and which is secondary when children face multiple developmental challenges. Under IDEA '04, prioritization of needs is a collaborative IEP team decision. The important thing is to view children as people first, with strengths and abilities as well as impairments, giving priority to input from parents, other caregivers, and the children themselves, whenever possible.

Deafness and Hard of Hearing (D/HH)

Hearing is critical for acquiring spoken language. Complete (or near complete) loss of hearing is called *deafness*. Lesser degrees of loss also can interfere with language acquisition. Access to ambient language is limited even when a child's loss is only in the mild to moderate range. When less language is overheard, access is reduced to important input for developing full language competence (e.g., Hart & Risley, 1999). Auditory language input remains an essential feature supporting language/literacy acquisition across the school-age years. If it is compromised in any way, even by a relatively mild or unilateral hearing loss (McKay, 2006), children are at risk for having difficulty learning auditory–oral language and to read and write (Yoshinaga-Itano & Downey, 1996).

Unfortunately, symptoms of hearing loss in infants and toddlers may be subtle, and parents may not be able to detect when their babies are not hearing until much valuable time has been lost. Martin and Clark (2006) reported the following:

> In the absence of hearing screening at birth, many children with abnormal hearing proceed into the third year of life or beyond before a hearing problem is suspected. A hearing disorder in a child is often not detected because parents believe that, if their own child had a hearing loss, they would somehow know it because he or she would be obviously different from other children. (p. 189)

Early Identification of Hearing Loss

Yoshinaga-Itano and colleagues (1998) found that babies fared much better if they were identified and intervention services were provided prior to 6 months of age. Early identification is so important that the U.S. Congress passed the Newborn Infant Hearing Screening and Intervention Act in 1999 to authorize grants to states to provide early hearing detection and intervention (EHDI) programs for newborns prior to leaving the hospital. Congress reauthorized the grants in 2000 through the Children's Health Act of 2000 (PL 106-310) and included provisions related to early hearing screening and evaluation of all newborns, coordinated intervention, rehabilitation services, and research. By 2007, 40 of the 50 United States had EHDI laws. Five had voluntary compliance programs to screen the hearing of 95 percent or more of newborns, compared with only about 40 percent of infants being screened in 2000.

One to three infants per 1,000 are born deaf or hard of hearing (D/HH) each day. That amounts to 33 babies per day when projected across the population of the United States. Estimated prevalence figures suggest that about 3 million U.S. children currently have D/HH diagnoses, and the number is even higher if high-frequency and conductive loss are included (Schow & Nerbonne, 2007).

Early identification is not enough by itself to support secondary and tertiary prevention efforts. Advocacy materials posted on the website of the American Speech-Language-Hearing Association (2007b) indicated that as many as one-third of babies who were identified in infant screening programs had not received complete diagnostic evaluations by 3 months of age, and less than half of infants who had been diagnosed were actually receiving early intervention services by the critical point of 6 months of age.

White (2006) recommended several steps to allow more young children who are deaf or hard of hearing (D/HH) to gain access to early amplification and intervention:

1. EHDI programs should be coordinated more closely with infant and toddler child-find efforts, referral systems, and intervention programs under Part C of the IDEA '04.
2. Professionals and parents should have access to training so they know how to promote normal conceptual and language development.
3. Advocacy must focus on better ways to fund high-quality digital hearing aids for infants and toddlers. Coverage for hearing aids is excluded from many private insurance plans, and Medicaid pays only for the least costly amplification, not for the amplification best suited to the child's needs. Thus, many children are fitted with less expensive analog aids rather than digital ones because digital aids are more expensive even though they might be preferable.

Classification of Hearing Loss

Hearing loss is a broad category. It may be *congenital* (i.e., present at birth or shortly after) or *acquired* (i.e., arising later in childhood, adolescence, or young adulthood). Hearing loss also may be differentiated as *prelingual* (i.e., onset before the acquisition of language and speech) or *postlingual* (i.e., onset after a first language is acquired). Timing can make considerable difference in the prognosis for a child's speech and language development. Even a short period of typical development can provide critical information about the phonology and prosody of speech that can help children form a mental model of spoken language.

Acquired hearing loss may be categorized further as *progressive* (i.e., becoming increasingly worse over time) or *sudden* (i.e., with acute or rapid onset). Sudden hearing loss requires immediate medical attention to determine its cause and treatment. Infectious diseases (e.g., meningitis), tumors, and ototoxic drugs (which may be required for life-saving cancer treatments or to fight dangerous infection) can cause sudden hearing loss in childhood that may be temporary or permanent. Hearing loss also may be designated as *fluctuating* (i.e., varying from day to day—more often conductive) or *stable* (more often sensorineural).

Figure 6.1 illustrates parts of the ear. The *outer ear* consists of the *pinna* (which collects sound and helps detect the direction of its source) and the *external ear canal,* extending to the eardrum, or *tympanic membrane.* The *middle ear* starts on the other side of the tympanic membrane, which is attached to the first in a series of three tiny *ossicles,* or bones—the *malleus* (hammer), *incus* (anvil), and *stapes* (stirrup). The *Eustachian tube* connects the middle ear to the posterior nasopharynx, making it possible to equalize air pressure with the outside atmosphere. The *inner ear* is made up of the cochlea and the vestibular system. The *vestibular system* uses the three semicircular canals (in three planes) to contribute to balance and equilibrium. The *cochlea* (a snail-shaped structure with hair cells connecting to the eighth nerve) has a pliable oval window (attached to the footplate of the stapes) and a round window that allows the fluid inside to move. The fluid in the cochlea moves with the physical sound waves to stimulate the hair cells on the basilar membrane, along which the hair cells are distributed, connecting to the eighth cranial nerve. In this manner, acoustic energy gathered by the outer ear changes to physical energy in the middle ear and neural energy in the inner ear, from whence it is transmitted to the brain.

Three basic *types of hearing loss* are identified—conductive, sensorineural, and mixed. *Conductive hearing loss* arises from problems in the conduction of sound through the outer or middle ear. *Sensorineural hearing loss* is associated with impairment in the *cochlea* and the *retrocochlear* neural pathways, which extend beyond the cochlea using the eighth cranial nerve (the auditory nerve); it synapses in the brainstem and ends in the temporal lobe of

figure *6.1*

Parts of the Ear

Parts of the ear include the (a) *outer ear,* from the pinna through the external auditory canal to the tympanic membrane; (b) *middle ear,* with the three small ossicles—malleus, incus, and stapes—that transmit sound mechanically to the oval window of the inner ear, and the Eustachian tube connecting the middle ear to the nasopharynx; and (c) *inner ear,* with the vestibular system of semicircular canals on three planes and the cochlea, with hair cells that convert sound waves to neural energy, for transmission to the brain.

the brain. After synapsing in the brainstem, some neural fibers cross to the ***contralateral*** (opposite) side of the brain; others remain ***ipsilateral*** (on the same side). ***Mixed hearing loss*** involves a combination of sensorineural and conductive hearing loss.

Audiologists use specialized test procedures and equipment to diagnose hearing loss in infants and toddlers. In the newborn period (birth to 6 months of age), audiologists must utilize objective measures, including auditory brainstem response (ABR) testing, transient evoked or distortion product otoacoustic emissions (TEOAE/DPOAE), and high-frequency tympanometry (T. Crumpton, personal communication, April 13, 2008). By 6 months of age, an infant can sit up sufficiently and orient clearly enough to use visual reinforcement audiometry (VRA). This involves conditioning the baby to turn in the direction of a sound source, reinforced by associated antics of a mechanized toy. From 2 to 5 years, children generally can be tested with conditioned play audiometry, in which they are reinforced for placing a peg in a board or ring on a stick in response to a sound. By age 5, most children can learn to raise their hand to indicate hearing a faint sound (Spivak, 2007).

When children can indicate reliably that they hear barely audible pure tones, ***air conduction*** and ***bone conduction audiometric testing*** are used to differentiate sensorineural, conductive, and mixed loss. In air conduction testing, a person listens to pure tones presented through earphones; thus, any physical obstruction between the sound source and the cochlea, plus any transmission difficulties introduced in retrocochlear neural pathways, can result in higher thresholds. Thresholds are plotted on an audiogram as the lowest decibel (dB) levels at which a person can detect sound at a particular frequency, which is measured in cycles per second called *Hertz (Hz)*. Pure tones are presented in frequencies ranging from low (250 Hz) to high (8,000 Hz, or 8 KHz) to measure hearing across the sound spectrum in which speech occurs.

To determine whether a loss is purely conductive, sensorineural, or mixed, bone conduction test results are compared with air conduction results. A bone conduction test is administered by placing a bone conduction oscillator (vibrating device) on the bone behind the ear. This circumvents the outer and middle ear and tests the sensorineural pathway directly, but it also transmits sound across the skull to the opposite ear, so masking noise must be presented to the opposite ear to ensure that responses are based on the test ear only. Sensorineural loss is diagnosed when thresholds are depressed and air conduction and bone conduction thresholds match. Conductive loss is diagnosed when an air–bone gap is found, so that air conduction thresholds are depressed but bone conduction is normal. A mixed loss is diagnosed when an air–bone gap appears, with bone conduction thresholds depressed but not as much as air conduction thresholds (Bess & Humes, 2003).

To assess middle ear function, audiologists use immittance techniques to probe physical responsiveness at the level of the tympanic membrane and middle ear. ***Static acoustic compliance*** is a measure of the mobility of the tympanic membrane. ***Tympanometry*** is a measure of middle ear function. Static admittance is a measure of middle ear compliance and is sensitive to many middle ear conditions, such as otitis media with effusion. Tympanometric peak pressure (TPP) is a measure of pressure in the middle ear. Tympanometric shape can be used to classify tympanograms according to the height and location of the tympanometric peak (Margolis & Hunter, 2000). ***Acoustic reflex*** measurements can determine whether the middle ear ossicular system stiffens as it should in response to intense sounds (Martin & Clark, 2006). Otoadmittance methods are considered *objective* because they require no behavioral response on the part of the child. Thus, they can be used with children who are young or have cognitive limitations.

A relatively new diagnosis, ***auditory neuropathy (AN),*** also called ***auditory dyssynchrony*** (Stredler-Brown, n.d.), involves impairment beyond the cochlea (possibly involving more than one site of lesion). This diagnosis has unique characteristics and perceptual consequences in children. Zeng and Liu (2006) described characteristics of AN as involving disrupted auditory nerve activity (indicated by highly distorted or absent auditory brainstem responses) concurrently with normal or nearly normal cochlear function (indicated by otoacoustic emission and/or cochlear microphonics). Particularly relevant to this book, AN/AD is associated with impaired capacity for temporal processing and difficulty in speech understanding, especially in noise, which is disproportionate to the degree of hearing loss measured by pure tone thresholds (Starr, Picton, Sininger, Hood, & Berlin, 1996).

A common method for quantifying the ***degree of hearing loss*** is to report the pure tone average (PTA) of thresholds at the three main speech range frequencies of 500, 1,000, and 2,000 Hz. A related but different method is to report the speech recognition threshold (SRT), which is the quietest sound level at which spoken words can be repeated. Table 6.1 summarizes classification of degrees of hearing loss and offers a description of the potential effects of each degree of loss on language and literacy learning. It also summarizes specialized instruction and language intervention needs.

The ***configuration*** of hearing loss refers to the profile of hearing across frequencies. For example, Figure 6.2 shows an example of a hearing profile in which good hearing in the low frequencies (closer to the ideal threshold of 0 dB) is accompanied by poor hearing in the high frequencies (with thresholds of 20 dB or louder before the person can barely hear the sound). Sloping loss with good hearing in the speech frequencies may be considered mild to moderate, but it might still have significant communicative, educational, and social implications. Other configurations reveal a greater loss at low frequencies (particularly with conductive problems) or a relatively flat loss. Hearing loss configurations may be classified as ***unilateral*** (occurring in just one ear) or ***bilateral*** (affecting both ears) and may be either ***symmetrical*** (with similar degree and configuration in both) or ***asymmetrical*** (with relatively greater loss in one ear). Sloping losses have implications for greater effects on speech perception.

Language Risks Associated with Sensorineural Hearing Loss

Sensorineural hearing loss (SNL) is a permanent hearing impairment that cannot be medically or surgically corrected. (Cochlear implants offer a different sort of option.) SNL can be caused by a number of factors in childhood, including birth injury, head trauma, disease,

table *6.1* Degrees of Childhood Hearing Impairment Based on Pure Tone Averages (PTA) and Possible Influence on Language Acquisition

Description	PTA*	Without Amplification	Special Needs
Normal range	0–15	Hears all speech sounds.	None
Mild loss	16–40	Hears vowel sounds normally; may miss some unvoiced consonants; has risks for learning plurals, contracted verb forms, phonemic awareness, reading, and learning vocabulary from overhearing.	Needs early amplification and explicit attention to communication development; in preschool and general education, needs preferential seating, special attention to phonemic awareness, and monitoring of vocabulary and literacy development, with intervention as needed.
Moderate loss	41–65	Misses most speech sounds at normal conversation levels; loses access to overhearing; has risks for difficulty with attention, language development, and literacy learning.	Needs amplification; early intervention; language preschool; specialized instruction and intervention focused on listening, speaking, reading, and writing during school age, with placement in the least-restrictive environment that can still support special learning needs.
Severe loss	66–90	Hears little or no speech or sound of normal conversation; has risks for difficulty with attention, language development, and literacy learning.	Needs early intervention focused on visual communication as well as making optimal use of residual (amplified) hearing; needs intervention to develop intelligible speech; explicit instruction in language and literacy with possible placement in a special classroom. May be a candidate for a cochlear implant if hearing is severe to profound in low frequencies and profound in mid to high frequencies.
Profound loss	91 plus	Hears no speech sounds or other sounds; has risks for difficulty with attention, language development, and literacy learning.	May be a candidate for a cochlear implant as early as 12 months of age. Needs early intensive intervention and supports across the school-age years for listening, speaking, reading, and writing.

*PTA is expressed in decibels (dB) as an average of pure tone thresholds at 500, 1,000 (1K), and 2,000 (2K) Hertz (Hz), which are cycles per second.

Source: Based on Culbertson, 2007; Holmes & Rodriguez, 2007; Northern & Downs, 1991.

tumor, ototoxic drugs, genetic syndromes, and noise exposure. SNL affects the ability to hear faint sounds but also distorts sounds, affecting speech perception. Rates of mild to moderate SNL and mixed losses tend to be relatively constant during the school-age years from kindergarten to grade twelve, but high-frequency, noise-induced losses become more prevalent during adolescence and in adulthood (Shepard, Davis, Gorga, & Stelmachowicz, 1981). Primary prevention efforts include protection from loud noise, including damage caused by listening with ear buds and personal stereo systems.

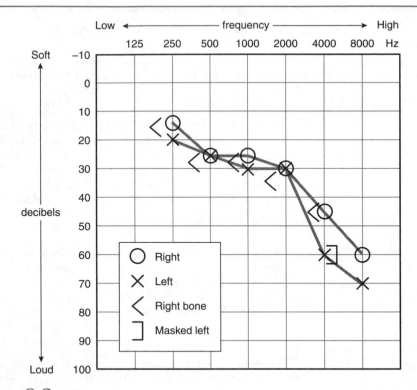

figure 6.2

Results of an Audiogram

This hearing loss profile shows air conduction thresholds in the range of normal limits for low-frequency sounds, sloping into the range of moderate impairment for the high-frequency range in both ears (Right ear = red O; Left ear = blue X). Bone conduction thresholds (<), in close agreement with air conduction thresholds, support a diagnosis of sensorineural loss.

A child with SNL may be further classified as being hard of hearing or deaf. A diagnosis of ***hard of hearing (HH)*** traditionally is made when a child's hearing is functional enough to make language acquisition possible and when the child's PTA and SRT are between 35 and 69 dB HL in the better-hearing ear (Northern & Downs, 1991). With improved amplification technology, the threshold for losses in the hard-of-hearing range has been extended to 80 or even 90 dB.

In comparison, ***deafness*** is diagnosed when a child cannot process linguistic information through hearing with or without amplification and when hearing loss is measured with a PTA or SRT worse than 80 to 90 dB. The audiometric profile indicates that the person is audiometrically deaf, although "deafness also can be described functionally as the inability to use hearing to any meaningful extent for the ordinary purposes of life, especially for verbal communication" (Schow & Nerbonne, 2007, pp. 5–6).

Many aspects of traditional binary classifications of deafness versus hard of hearing have become dated as modern amplification and surgical techniques have allowed children to move from one classification to another. The acronym D/HH is sometimes used to refer to conditions of either type. In the 1980s, Boothroyd (1982) wrote, "With amplification and appropriate intervention, children with severe losses (and some with profound losses) can become functionally hard-of-hearing, in the sense that they can understand what is said to them, using vision as a support" (p. 53). Even greater flexibility in prognosis may be observed in the twenty-first century, as detection in infancy has become common and as improved hearing aid technologies and earlier cochlear implants (as young as 12 months) have revolutionized the nature of aural habilitation and language and literacy instruction for children with hearing loss.

The effects of any hearing loss on speech and language development depend on multiple factors, including the type of loss, its degree and configuration, any knowledge of speech and language prior to the loss (*prelingual* versus *postlingual*), the quality of amplification, when it was fitted, how often it is worn, and familial–cultural and other child-specific variables. It is difficult to predict with any certainty from an audiogram alone a child's prognosis for acquiring spoken language and developing phonemic awareness and other linguistic knowledge critical for learning to read and write.

Speech acoustics can provide some hints as to which sounds will be heard or missed by a child with a particular configuration of loss. The diagram in Figure 6.3 shows how the acoustic energy of speech sounds, which is expressed in decibels and perceived as loudness, is distributed across the three frequencies that are used in computing the PTA. Intervention teams can consider how a particular child's SRT (e.g., a sloping loss, as in the

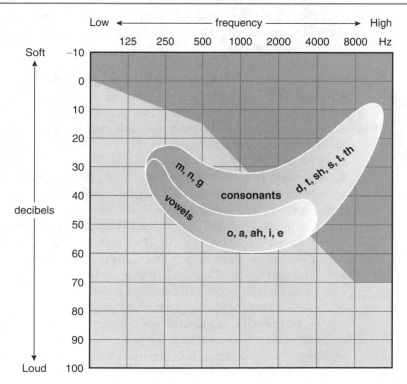

figure 6.3

The "Speech Banana"

This diagram illustrates how the frequency patterns of speech energy for particular phonemes map onto an audiogram, showing a common profile of high-frequency loss. Phonemes that overlap with the darkly shaded area are difficult for the person with this profile to hear.

illustration) might interact with such information, so that unamplified speech (particularly high-frequency sounds) are essentially impossible for some children to hear. Language cannot be learned auditorily if it cannot be heard. Therefore, high-quality amplification and attention to making the speech signal audible above any surrounding noise are both critical features of an interdisciplinary team's approach to intervention. Visual modes of language input also are a possibility.

Choices about communication modalities for use with children who are D/HH include auditory–verbal only, auditory–visual with speech reading, sign language only, or combined methods (often called ***total communication***). The choices are not trivial. They have significance for social interaction and formal and informal education. On the other hand, research has shown that early explicit focus on communication is more critical than which communication mode is selected (Yoshinaga-Itano et al., 1998).

Members of the Deaf community (the capital *D* signifies the culture of Deafness) do not consider children to have an impairment just because they are born deaf. They hold the cultural view that Deafness is a *difference,* not an *impairment,* and point out that children who learn American Sign Language (ASL) from birth have a first language that is completely functional for them. Children of Deaf parents acquire ASL as a natural part of growing up in a Deaf community. Language-learning difficulties arise, however, when children with severe to profound hearing loss are born to hearing parents who are not part of a community of Deaf people proficient in ASL. Hearing parents of deaf children trying to learn ASL may have difficulty providing a rich enough sign language environment to foster full ASL competence, but sign language can support the communicative interactions of parents and children.

Even when children are proficient in ASL, difficulties arise when they begin to learn to read and write in English, similar to learning to read in a second language (Paul, 1996). Although ASL is a fully functional language, it is not a direct translation of English and has no written form. Several approaches have been developed to bring the spoken English and sign language closer together, such as signed English, signing exact English, and total communication. Research has shown, however, that few children with severe hearing loss using traditional amplification have exceeded fourth-grade levels of literacy, regardless of the communication mode (Krose, Lotz, Puffer, & Osberger, 1986).

Members of the Deaf community have become more accepting of cochlear implants in recent years. With their 2000 Position Statement on Cochlear Implants, the National Association for the Deaf (NAD) recognized that cochlear implants can serve as a tool for use with some forms of communication (Holmes & Rodriguez, 2007).

Cochlear implants are revolutionizing access to auditory linguistic input for children with severe to profound losses, with implications for improving the prognosis for literacy as well. Children with profound losses may receive a cochlear implant as young as 12 months of age (see Table 6.1), resulting in dramatic effects on choices about modes of communication and educational placement. Young children can become quite skilled at using auditory input when they have a cochlear implant early (Ertmer, 2002), and prognosis for speech and language development is better with earlier implantation (Robbins, Koch, Osberger, Zimmerman-Phillips, & Kishon-Rabin, 2004).

Access to auditory information made possible by cochlear implants prepares children better for literacy learning as well. For example, Dillon and Pisoni (2006) found that children with cochlear implants demonstrated higher-level phonological knowledge in both nonword repetition and single-word reading tasks than children with other forms of auditory support and that the advantage could be found for sentence comprehension as well. This is consistent with prior research that showed that children in kindergarten through grade twelve with cochlear implants scored considerably above levels of reading found in prior studies with children who were prelingually deaf but had no cochlear implant (Spencer, Tomblin, & Gantz, 1997).

A cochlear implant differs fundamentally from a hearing aid. A hearing aid amplifies sound to make it loud enough for a faulty system to hear. A cochlear implant uses electrical signals to bypass impaired nerve endings, transmitting acoustic information directly to the auditory nerve. Thus, a cochlear implant cannot work if the auditory nerve itself is damaged or absent. Figure 6.4 illustrates the major components of a cochlear implant device. The external hardware components consist of three parts: (a) a microphone, which fits over the ear and connects with a cord; (b) an external speech processor (also called a *sound processor*), which receives sound from the microphone and converts it to digital signals; and (c) a transmitting coil, which attaches to the skull behind the ear with a magnet and transmits the digital signal from the speech processor to the internal device. Two internal implanted components complete the technology: (d) a receiver/stimulator that converts the digital signal to electrical energy and (e) a multiple-channel electrode array that bypasses damaged hair cells and stimulates the auditory nerve directly. High-frequency information is sent to electrodes in the basal end of the cochlea, and low frequency information is sent to electrodes in the apical (pointed) end of the cochlea. This corresponds to natural arrangements of high- and low-frequency receptors across the cochlea.

Research in this area is still relatively new. More results will be forthcoming as children who receive cochlear implants at younger ages are followed longitudinally through school. Cochlear implants are not a panacea, but they can have a dramatic impact on a child's prognosis for language and literacy learning (see Case Example 6.1). Comorbid

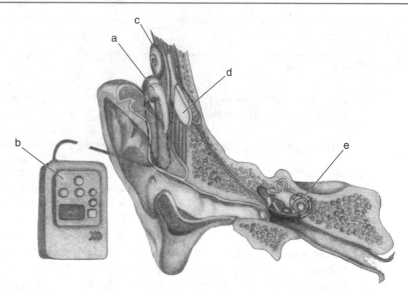

figure *6.4*

Cochlear Implant

A cochlear implant comprises both external hardware and an internal implanted device. The external hardware components are (a) a microphone, with a cord connecting it to the speech processor; (b) a speech processor, with a cord connecting it to the transmitting coil; and (c) a transmitting coil, held to the scalp with a magnet. The internal components are (d) a receiver/stimulator, including a magnet to which the external coil adheres; and (e) an intracochlear electrode array.

CASE example *6.1*

Michael's Adjustment to Living with Profound Hearing Loss

Michael developed typically and had normal hearing until almost age 5, when meningitis left him with a profound hearing loss in one ear. Unilateral hearing loss can make it difficult to localize sound and presents risks for learning in school, but Michael was a bright child and was doing well as he started kindergarten. Then one evening, his mother suddenly discovered that her son had lost the hearing in his other ear and now appeared completely deaf. Other than a recent ear infection, which had been treated with antibiotics, there had been no outward signs of illness. Yet when Michael was tested the next day, his hearing loss in both ears was indeed profound.

Michael's response for the first few months was to act out his anger at being suddenly deaf. Being angry was a perfectly rational response for a 5-year-old. His mother felt guilty, wondering if there were something she or anyone could have done to prevent the loss in his second ear. The after effects of meningitis can be unpredictable, however, and the etiological pathway is not always clear.

Michael was found eligible for a cochlear implant within a short time. He also received high-quality educational services from a program for hearing-impaired children. As Michael moved beyond the angry period, his prior knowledge of language enabled him to benefit quickly from the implant and to perceive speech in a new way.

After two years, Michael returned to his home school and became an honor student, who also participated in track in middle school. He did not use the external components of his implant device while running the high hurdles, his best event, but watched the other runners to know when to start. In one race, someone made a false start, but it was not until Michael cleared the last hurdle and turned around that he realized what had happened because he had not heard the second shot and he was accustomed to being ahead of the other runners. Michael handled what could have been an embarrassing moment with a smile and a shrug and then returned to the starting line and won the race again.

cognitive or other difficulties influence children's ability to benefit optimally from such technology, remarkable though it is.

Language Risks Associated with Conductive Hearing Loss

Conductive hearing loss usually is temporary and may be resolved without treatment. Although controversial, surgical treatment may be indicated, including the placement of *pressure equalization tubes (PE tubes;* also called *tympanostomy tubes)* in the tympanic membrane to create a temporary opening in order to relieve pressure in the middle ear and improve hearing. Conductive loss reduces the ability to hear faint sounds but has less effect on speech perception than SNL. The rate of temporary conductive hearing losses is high in the early elementary school years, fluctuating for some children from one day to the next, but it tends to decrease as children grow older (Shepard, Davis, Gorga, & Stelmachowicz, 1981).

Serous otitis media is a condition in which fluid and pressure build-up in the middle ear and interfere with the transmission of sound. It also may be called *otitis media with effusion (OME)* or *middle ear effusion (MEE).* Serous otitis media may begin in conjunction with a head cold or allergies. Although middle ear infections can be treated with antibiotics, overprescription has contributed to making some strains of bacteria antibiotic resistant, so physicians are reluctant to prescribe antibiotics unless infection is confirmed. If pressure associated with serous otitis media continues to build with no relief, a perforated eardrum may result, possibly causing permanent scarring of the tympanic membrane; the placement of tympanostomy tubes may prevent such an outcome. Other causes of conductive hearing loss may justify surgical interventions, including physical obstruction in the outer or middle ear from a foreign body, a benign tumor, or absence or malformation of the outer ear (called *congenital atresia*).

The relevant question for the current discussion is the degree to which middle ear effusion and accompanying fluctuating conductive hearing loss affect language learning and present risks for later literacy learning, particularly when middle ear problems occur frequently in the first three years of life. Comprehensive reviews of the literature suggest that the picture remains unclear (e.g., Feldman et al., 2003; Roberts, Wallace, & Henderson, 1997). Some studies have identified a small effect of middle ear effusion on depressed language development scores (often measured as vocabulary development), whereas others have identified no effect.

One large prospective longitudinal study (Paradise et al., 2007) enrolled more than 1,000 children near birth and followed them prospectively. At ages 9 to 11 years, 391 of the children were tested again with a battery of attention, social skills, language, literacy, and achievement tests. The immediate question was whether early tympanostomy tubes (immediately after middle ear effusion [MEE] was detected) would improve developmental outcomes over late insertion (after waiting several months to see if the condition would resolve on its own). When tested at ages 3, 4, and 6 years and again from 9 to 11 years, no statistically significant differences were found between the two groups on any of the measures. The research team concluded that prompt insertion of tubes did not improve developmental outcomes over later insertion that was provided only if the problem persisted.

Studies have compared language development for children with and without frequent middle ear problems. Some have shown that multiple factors, including frequency of MEE, influence the prognosis for language and literacy development. Risk is more predictable when hearing also is depressed (Shriberg, Friel-Patti, Flipsen, & Brown, 2000). Other factors found to increase risk are poverty and low maternal education (Feldman et al., 2003; Roberts et al., 1997). A conservative preventive approach is for parents of children with frequent middle ear problems to receive consultation about how to foster language and emergent literacy interactions deliberately.

(Central) Auditory-Processing Disorder

Some children demonstrate normal hearing on audiometric tests of the peripheral hearing mechanism but deficits in their attention to and central processing of detailed acoustic information received through audition. Such children may be diagnosed as having *auditory-processing disorder (APD)*. APD has been known as *central auditory-processing disorder (CAPD),* but a consensus group recommended using the term *APD* because all auditory processing takes place in the central auditory nervous system (CANS); hence, the words *central* and *processing* are redundant (Jerger & Musiek, 2000).

Reflecting this shift in terminology, a working group of the American Speech-Language-Hearing Association (2005) used the acronym (C)AP to describe normal *central auditory processes* as follows:

> Auditory Processing [(C)AP] refers to the efficiency and effectiveness by which the central nervous system (CNS) utilizes auditory information. Narrowly defined, (C)AP refers to the perceptual processing of auditory information in the CNS and the neurobiologic activity that underlies that processing and gives rise to electrophysiologic auditory potentials. (p. 2)

The group also defined (C)APD as "difficulties in the perceptual processing of auditory information in the CNS as demonstrated by poor performance in one or more of the [above] skills" (p. 2). Those skills included sound localization and lateralization; auditory discrimination; auditory pattern recognition; temporal aspects of audition, including temporal integration, temporal discrimination (e.g., temporal gap detection), temporal ordering, and temporal masking; auditory performance in competing acoustic signals (including dichotic listening); and auditory performance with degraded acoustic signals. (p. 2)

English (2007) condensed the list to three listening domains, which audiologists typically assess to diagnose APD among school-age children: (1) *temporal aspects of hearing* or *pattern recognition,* which is the ability to sequence auditory information when presented rapidly; (2) *monaural discrimination,* which is the ability to perceive words when the signal is degraded or presented with competing noise in the same ear; and (3) *binaural acoustic information processing,* which includes the ability to understand a signal presented to one ear while ignoring competing sound in the other and to use *dichotic* listening for identifying separate signals presented exactly simultaneously to opposite ears.

Immediate causes for perceptual-processing difficulties are difficult to isolate, but Moeller, Schow, and Whitatker (2007) noted that most authorities ascribe APD to one of three possible explanations: (1) delay in development, (2) disordered development, or (3) specific central lesion. Prevalence rates for APD are lacking, perhaps because the diagnosis remains controversial and depends on varied referral practices and individual diagnosticians. Diagnosis of APD requires testing of the central auditory system by an audiologist, with input from a speech–language pathologist (SLP) and other professionals to rule out higher-order language-processing difficulties or attention deficits as their primary cause (Musiek, Bellis, & Chermak, 2005). Although primary language disorders must be ruled out, APD can co-occur with other disorders. This presents a diagnostic dilemma. As stated in the ASHA (2005) technical report:

> (C)APD is a deficit in neural processing of auditory stimuli that is not due to higher order language, cognitive, or related factors. However, (C)APD may lead to or be associated with difficulties in higher order language, learning, and communication functions. Although (C)APD may coexist with other disorders (e.g., attention deficit hyperactivity disorder [ADHD], language impairment, and learning disability), it is *not the result of* these other disorders. For example, children with autism or ADHD often present with listening and/or spoken language comprehension difficulties; however, these difficulties are not due to a deficit in the CANS per se, but rather to their higher order, more global disorder. Thus, it would not be appropriate to apply the diagnostic label of (C)APD to the listening difficulties exhibited by these children unless a comorbid deficit in the CANS can be demonstrated. (p. 2)

The potential for circular causal patterns involving intersystemic factors (as discussed in Chapter 3) is high. When auditory-processing and phonemic awareness difficulties both are observed in a child having difficulty following classroom instructions or acquiring language/literacy, it is difficult to sort out causes and effects. During diagnostic tasks, it is essentially impossible to keep the brain's knowledge of language and its segments from influencing how a child responds to auditory-processing tasks. Any part of an interconnected sensory–cognitive–linguistic processing mechanism, including executive control functions, could cause difficulties or support compensation in any other (Musiek et al., 2005).

If children are referred for APD testing, it is likely because they are struggling in some way academically. Teams may use APD testing to inform interventions, but planning may benefit more from the four questions of contextual-based assessment (introduced in Chapter 1 and discussed in Part III). This involves assessment of inside-out areas of language weakness to identify targets that should be strengthened to close performance gaps, accompanied by outside-in efforts to optimize the child's hearing environment and improve signal-to-noise ratios.

SUMMARY

Parts of the ear were reviewed, along with tests and classification systems (type, degree, and configuration) for diagnosing and describing deafness and hard of hearing (D/HH) in children. The EHDI program is a classical example of secondary prevention. Better outcomes in later language and literacy learning have been documented for children identified prior to 6 months, regardless of modality of communication. Children with postlingual D/HH have a better prognosis for acquiring language and literacy skills. Educational, medical, and technological interventions, particularly cochlear implants, make it possible for children born with D/HH to learn spoken and written language. Conductive hearing loss associated with middle ear effusion (MEE) is an added risk factor for children experiencing other developmental (e.g., Down syndrome, SLI, learning disability) and environmental challenges. Evidence for a direct effect on language-learning difficulties is equivocal. Fluctuating hearing loss is common in childhood, and prospective longitudinal studies have not shown a direct causal link to language delay or disorder.

(Central) auditory-processing disorder (C)APD is a controversial diagnosis that requires interdisciplinary collaboration by audiologists and speech–language pathologists to exclude peripheral hearing loss and primary language impairment as causative factors. Intervention is similar, with explicit instruction in phonological and phonemic awareness, accompanied by improved auditory signal-to-noise ratios in the environment.

Visual System Impairment

Blindness and Low Vision (B/LV)

Children with congenital *blindness or low vision (B/LV)* have sensory input difficulties that may affect language acquisition. At first glance, visual impairment appears not to present much of a barrier to auditory–oral language acquisition; however, children with B/LV face unique challenges associated with acquiring concepts and vocabulary that depend on coordinating visual information with spoken language and for developing awareness of social interaction cues that are expressed nonverbally, such as in eye gaze and facial expression.

Classification of Visual Impairment

The term *visual impairment* is used when a person's eyesight cannot be corrected to a typical level, even with glasses, or when a person's visual field is extremely limited. The term does not apply to acuity problems that can be corrected to typical levels using glasses. *Low vision* criteria vary across sources and internationally, but in the United States, low vision is diagnosed when acuity (as measured with Snellen chart criteria) cannot be corrected to better than 20/70. This is similar to seeing at 20 feet what someone with unimpaired vision can see at 70 feet. *Legal blindness* is diagnosed when a person's visual acuity is 20/200 or worse (American Foundation for the Blind, 2007). Visual field deficits are diagnosed when a person's range of vision (without turning the head) is less than 20 degrees (compared to about 160 to 170 degrees typically). *Blindness* is defined as acuity of 20/400 or worse or a visual field of less than 10 degrees. In IDEA '04, the definition of *visual impairment* is "impairment in vision that, even with correction, adversely affects a child's educational performance. The term includes both partial sight and blindness" (20 U.S.C. 1401[3]; 1401[30]).

Congenital conditions (present at birth or within a month or so) that can cause B/LV include anoxia, hydrocephaly (excess pressure related to fluid build-up in the brain), and congenital cytomegalovirus (a prenatal viral infection) (Miller, Menacker, & Batshaw, 2002). Children born prematurely and at extremely low birthweight may experience *retinopathy of prematurity (ROP),* in which abnormal blood vessel growth and scarring of the retina of the eye affect vision. Although medical treatment is available for ROP, it is not always completely effective.

Other forms of visual impairment are *amblyopia,* which is a regressive developmental condition that occurs when an eye–brain connection is not working, and *strabismus,* which affects the ability to control eye movement for focusing and binocular vision. In amblyopia, information coming from an otherwise healthy eye is not processed by the brain, and the eye progressively ceases to function unless treated by inducing constraints in the strong eye so the weaker eye–brain connection begins to function better. In strabismus, binocular vision and depth perception introduce risks for learning to read and for other educational and social functions. Strabismus occurs in up to 40 percent of children with CP and in children who are farsighted (Miller et al., 2002).

Prevalence rates of blindness are under 1 percent, making it a low-incidence condition. That does not mean, however, that conditions of low vision or blindness are of low significance to the children affected. Using 1990 census data, Nelson and Dimitrova (1993) reported that 0.15 percent of the general population in the age range of birth to 17 years have a *visual impairment* (defined as "inability to see or read ordinary newspaper print even when wearing glasses or contact lenses" (p. 80). Wall and Corn (2004) confirmed this prevalence rate among schoolchildren in Texas and also determined that 24 perent of schoolchildren identified with visual impairment met criteria for blindness. Prevalence rates for visual acuity, visual field, and motor control problems affecting vision are higher among children with multiple developmental disabilities. For example, in one epidemiological study (Drews, Yeargin-Allsopp, Murphy, & Decouffle, 1992), two-thirds of 10-year-old children with B/LV also had another disability (e.g., intellectual disability, CP, epilepsy).

Language Risks Associated with Visual Impairment

Areas of language development at risk when visual input is disrupted include (1) lexical learning due to difficulty associating words with things or pictures not seen; (2) pronoun reference, presenting as *I/you* confusions or by children referring to themselves by their proper names or with the third-person pronouns *he/she;* and (3) social pragmatics, associated with limited access to nonverbal gestural and facial expression for social turn taking and partner responsiveness. Erin (1990) compared language characteristics for four children who were blind, four with low vision, and four who were sighted. The results showed contrasts in several areas (syntactic complexity, pronoun usage, and language functions), with symptoms more prominent for children who were blind compared to those with low vision.

To understand the potential effects of visual impairment on language learning, consider the role vision plays when it functions normally. Vision is a distance sense that helps children coordinate spoken language input with images of objects and events as they are experienced. Infants use finger pointing to perform speech acts that comment on or request toys, other objects, or food during the illocutionary phase of development. They do so because they can see objects and establish joint focus with an adult (see Figure 6.5).

Children with sight can acquire concepts incidentally through casual vision (Koenig & Farrenkopf, 1997), just as children who have hearing can acquire language incidentally through overhearing (Hart & Risley, 1995). Research has shown that children with congenital blindness and no comorbid cognitive impairment are not delayed in early word acquisition, although they may be delayed in the ability to demonstrate Piaget's (1952) concept of object permanence (Bigelow, 1990).

Semantic features represented in a child's mental lexicon may be acquired through touch and verbal description as well as vision. A child who is sighted may have a mental concept of an *apple* as a semiround, sweet-tasting, red thing, which also can be other col-

figure *6.5*

Developing Communication Skills

A child who learns to coordinate a finger point with directional eye gaze has a powerful communication tool for making protodeclarative comments and directing a parent's attention. Accommodations need to be made for distance referencing for children with blindness and low vision.

ors; a child who is congenitally blind may be able to state that an apple is red but would more likely have encoded the concept of *apple* as "a small, smooth-textured, semispherical, sweet-tasting object" and lack a corresponding stored visual image (Steinman, LeJeune, & Kimbrough, 2006, p. 37). A child who is congenitally blind also may need to be exposed to more variations of an object before being able to generalize the concept. For example, a young blind child might think that all dogs are exactly like his or her own family pet unless specifically exposed to a variety of other dogs and explicitly taught that all are dogs. This phenomenon of associating a semantic concept with a set of referents that is too limited may be called **underextension,** which contrasts with the **overextension** phenomenon when a toddler calls a *horse* a *dog,* apparently based on categorical criteria that are overly inclusive.

Sight influences the ability to acquire language concepts beyond nouns and communication functions beyond commenting or requesting. Vision plays an important role in helping children learn about the meanings of verbs, prepositions, and other relational terms,

┌───┐

─CASE **example** *6.2*──

Teaching Kenny Personal Reference Cues

Kenny was a 3-year-old participating in a language preschool program for children with special needs. Although many of the children in the program had primary speech–language impairments, Kenny's language development needs were secondary to his congenital blindness. Kenny consistently referred to himself in the third person (e.g., "Kenny wants to go outside. He wants to play.") These personal reference difficulties were much easier to interpret from Kenny's frame of reference. He was much more likely to hear people talk *about* him rather than talking *with* him. His IEP team decided to heighten the personal reference cues for Kenny, along with cues for opening and closing circles of communication. They instituted scaffolding discourse, saying, as naturally as possible, "Hi Kenny. *I*, Mrs. M, want to go outside. Do *you*, Kenny, want to go outside too? What do you think we should play?"

└───┘

including pronouns (*I, you, he/she/it*) and other forms of deixis (e.g., *here/there, this/that*). *Deixis* applies to references to person, place, or time that vary depending on one's communicative perspective. References to person and place are supported heavily by vision. The pronouns *I, you, he,* and *she* refer to different people, depending on who is talking. The term *near* (or *this* or *here*) is used by one communicative partner, while *far* (or *that* or *there*) may be used by a distant partner to refer to the same object. Because visual cues to deixis are missing, a preschool child with blindness may go through a stage of referring to himself or herself in the third person (see Case Example 6.2), even though syntax and other word choices seem typical. Even after basic pronouns are acquired, children with congenital blindness may continue to demonstrate a self-referential way of viewing the world. This can make it difficult to acquire and talk about spatial concepts and to use frames of reference other than the child's own, which has implications for social functioning.

As discussed in Chapter 3, underpinnings of later social interaction abilities are established in early infant–caregiver interactions that depend partially on vision. When vision is impaired, protective factors can help children with B/LV acquire fully functional communicative skills. Fraiberg (1979) (see Personal Reflection 6.2) observed that modifications in social interactions are natural when infants have limited sight, yet most blind children achieve the usual milestones of human attachment in the first two years of life. Preferences for their mothers are shown in differential smiling and vocalizing, manual tactile seeking, embracing, and spontaneous gestures of affection and comfort seeking. From 7 to 15 months of age, blind toddlers, like sighted ones, begin to avoid and manifest stress reactions to strangers and reject them as interaction partners. During the second year, blind children's anxiety at separation and comfort at reunion provide evidence that blind babies value their mothers as indispensable human partners in the same way sighted babies do.

PERSONAL reflection *6.2*──

"What we miss in the blind baby, apart from the eyes that do not see, is the vocabulary of signs and signals that provides the most elementary and vital sense of discourse long before words have meaning."

Selma Fraiberg (1979, p. 152), a pediatric psychotherapist, underscored the importance of vision in early communication.

....

Deafblindness

Deafblindness is a rare but challenging condition, in which sensory input is impaired in both auditory and visual modalities. The National Technical Assistance Consortium for Children and Young Adults Who Are Deaf-Blind (NTAC, 2004) reported a census count of over 10,000 children (ages birth to 22 years) in the United States who had been classified as having deafblindness. Because some genetic causes of deafblindness are progressive, prevalence rates rise in adulthood as new cases are added.

A diagnosis of deafblindness by itself says little about a person's capabilities or learning potential (see Personal Reflection 6.3). As noted by Gee (1995), "Persons with deafblindness are a highly diverse group of individuals with unique learning characteristics and a wide range of capabilities" (p. 371). The challenges of dual sensory loss are not just additive, as noted by McInnes & Treffry (1982):

> The deaf-blind child is not a deaf child who cannot see or a blind child who cannot hear. The problem is not an additive one of deafness plus blindness. Nor is it solely one of communication or perception. It encompasses all these things and more. (p. 2)

PERSONAL reflection 6.3

"Sometimes people can only see a person's disability, They are blinding themselves with their own prejudices, A person's true strength is within them."

James Gallagher (2007), a person who describes himself as "totally blind and almost profoundly deaf," was writing on the website he uses to inform others about the condition.

As is the case for either deafness or blindness by itself, loss of hearing or vision need not be complete for deafblindness to be diagnosed. Often, some residual sensory input from one sense or the other is available. According to IDEA '04:

> Deaf-blindness means concomitant hearing and visual impairments, the combination of which causes such severe communication and other developmental and educational needs that they cannot be accommodated in special education programs solely for children with deafness or children with blindness. (Sec. 300.8 [c][2])

Deafblindness can result from prenatal maternal infection or disease, such as herpes or syphilis. Maternal rubella was a frequent cause of deafblindness before widespread vaccination acted as a primary prevention. Deafblindness also can result from maternal substance abuse or from postnatal diseases (e.g., meningitis, encephalitis) or trauma (Wolff Heller & Kennedy, 1994). Children with congenital deafblindness are at higher risk for related cognitive-processing disorders, motor system impairments, and other learning challenges.

Many cases of deafblindness are caused by Usher syndrome, which is a genetic condition transmitted by an autosomal recessive gene (McInnes & Treffry, 1982). Usher syndrome accounts for 3 percent to 6 percent of all children born deaf and a similar percentage of children who are hard of hearing. Hearing loss occurs first, with blindness appearing later and developing progressively (due to retinitis pigmentosa). Three patterns are described: Type 1 (USH1) involves profound deafness and severe balance problems at birth, with vision problems appearing by early childhood; Type 2 (USH2) involves moderate to severe hearing loss at birth but with normal balance and slower loss of vision; and Type 3 (USH3) involves postlingual progressive hearing loss beginning in the teen years, with blindness occurring in midadulthood (Scarola, 2007).

In conditions of deafblindness, any inner language that has been developed prior to loss of hearing function can make a difference, regardless of its completeness. Literacy skills open many communication options that otherwise would be unavailable, adding to the imperative to help children facing loss of both vision and hearing to learn to read (finger-spelling in their hands as well as print or braille on the page) and write. Assistive technologies and specialized forms of communication are particularly critical for the wide range of people with deafblindness.

SUMMARY

B/LV can affect the acquisition of spoken and written language. Parents of blind babies can heighten experiential and communicative input to facilitate emotional attachment and foundations for acquiring language concepts and pragmatic–social aspects of language use. Braille and other technological supports can support literacy learning. Deafblindness can result from a variety of congenital factors, genetic and infectious, which may or may not leave a child's cognitive system basically intact. Although the challenges of dual sensory loss are substantial, depending on the timing of loss of each sense and access to assistive technology and other supports (e.g., fingerspelling in the hand), children or adolescents with deafblindness but no other cognitive–linguistic limitations may be able to function and communicate with a reasonable degree of independence.

Other Sensory System Problems

Some children have difficulty processing near sensation, including (a) internal ***proprioceptive*** feedback regarding the body's position in space; (b) ***somatosensory*** (tactual) feedback from touching objects with different textures, including food in the mouth; and (c) ***kinesthetic*** feedback regarding the weight and positioning of the body in motion. Some children experience hypersensitive distance sensation, causing unusual responses to visual input, or ***hyperacusis,*** with adverse reaction to sound at normal loudness levels.

Variable response to sensation is a risk factor for negative effects on normal development (see Chapter 3). Problems associated with interpreting any form of sensory input and responding appropriately can lead to a diagnosis of ***sensory integration disorder (SID).*** Hyperarousal and hypoarousal to normal sensory stimuli can be observed readily among some infants and young children but may be overlooked when other issues of self-regulation and social interaction seem primary. Interdisciplinary teams are more likely to consider such potential explanations for a child's irritability, social avoidance or withdrawal, or picky food choices if the team includes an occupational therapist who knows how to work with SID (Ayres, 1989; Mauer, 1999). Sensory-processing problems in the school-age years include the inability to ignore background sensations while attending to other types of activities.

Noting possible influences of sensory system difficulties on widespread aspects of social and communication development, Greenspan and Wieder (2006) suggested the diagnostic term ***neurodevelopmental disorder of relating and communicating (NDRC)*** for children with developmental difficulties that involve multiple systems, including sensory disregulation, a condition formerly called ***multisystem developmental disorders (MDD)*** in the *Diagnostic Classification: 0–3* (Diagnostic Classification Task Force, 1994). Both terms encompass disorders referred to in the *Diagnostic and Statistical Manual of Mental*

Disorders (*DSM-IV-TR*) (APA, 2000) as *pervasive developmental disorders,* which are on the autism spectrum. Such disorders affect "social relationships, language, cognitive functioning, and sensory and motor processing" (p. 231).

Two important questions are whether and to what degree such conditions relate directly to language and literacy disorders. It might be enticing to think that improved sensory integration could lead directly to improved language ability, but that is unlikely (Kamhi, 2004). On the other hand, distorted sensation can influence children's interactions with objects and people, thus influencing language acquisition indirectly and making it an appropriate intervention target for an interdisciplinary intervention team.

Some infants and toddlers with developmental delays have sensory-processing difficulties involving social–emotional eye gaze, shared attention, and joint actions routines of early childhood that suggest autism spectrum disorder (Woods & Wetherby, 2003). Such children may fit the diagnostic classification of NDRC in their early years but later be diagnosed as having *pragmatic language impairment* (*PLI*). Other hypersensitive children may represent the extreme end of typical development. Children's needs and responses to sensory stimulation may change across the course of development as they gain higher-level insights and the ability to use language to understand their unusually powerful, limited, or variable sensations.

Interdisciplinary diagnostic teams can consider multiple factors that might influence how a young child interacts. Teams should give at least as much consideration to multiple systems that might benefit from therapeutic attention as to assigning a particular diagnostic label. Such consideration should include observation of difficulties associated with the near senses of touch and proprioception, as well as the distant senses of vision and hearing.

There are clearly much larger questions to be answered, but they involve the contributions of multiple disciplines that are beyond the scope of this book. The point here is that for children to benefit optimally from opportunities to learn spoken and written language, they need to feel safe and comfortable and not be distracted by unusual sensitivities that interfere with communication, social closeness, and sense making.

SUMMARY

Distorted or exaggerated responses to sensory input can influence a child's development, including input from both the near senses (proprioception, somatosensory, kinesthetic) and the distant senses (vision and hearing). Diagnostic terms introduced in this section include sensory integration disorder (SID), multisystem developmental disorder (MDD), and neurodevelopmental disorder of relating and communicating (NDRC). Some children with these early diagnoses may later meet criteria for diagnosis with a form of autism spectrum disorder or pervasive development disorder, not otherwise specified (PDD-NOS), which is discussed in Chapter 7.

CHAPTER SUMMARY

Motor and sensory system impairments include neuromotor conditions of dysarthria and apraxia that affect speech (and to a less predictable degree, language). Some children with motor impairments have complex communication needs (CCN) and rely on augmentative and alternative communication (AAC). Hearing impairment includes deafness and hard of hearing classifications (D/HH). (Central) auditory-processing disorder (APD) also may be diagnosed. Blindness and low vision (B/LV) has minimal influence on language and literacy learning when it occurs by itself but often co-occurs with other conditions. Deafblindness presents extreme challenges but varies based on the time of onset and completeness of sensory loss. Other sensory impairments, such as sensory integration disorder (SID), can influence self-regulation and social interaction.

EXERCISES *and* STUDY QUESTIONS

1. Describe your "dream team" in terms of the disciplines you would like to have involved when diagnosing young children with complex sensory, motor, cognitive, and language/literacy learning needs, and indicate the contribution you would expect each to make to the diagnosis.

2. Create your own outline of the motor and sensory system disorders that have been described in this chapter. Which of these disorders might justify reevaluation under IDEA '04 at three-year intervals, and which might be less likely to need formal reevaluation to see if the child still qualifies as having a disability under IDEA.

3. Name at least two diagnoses introduced in this chapter that are considered controversial, and discuss the nature of the controversy for each.

CHAPTER *seven*

Cognitive–Communicative Impairments

LEARNING *objectives*

After studying this chapter, you should be able to do the following:

1. Describe criteria for diagnosing intellectual disabilities (ID/MR) and key congenital syndromes; autism spectrum disorders (ASD), including Asperger's syndrome; traumatic brain injury (TBI) and other forms of acquired brain injury (ABI); fetal alcohol spectrum disorder (FASD) and other forms of environmental trauma in childhood; and disorders of attention, emotion, and behavior.

2. Discuss the implications for speech, language/literacy, and communication development for children with cognitive–communicative impairments.

Depending on one's theoretical perspective, language may be viewed as being more or less intertwined with general cognitive ability. This chapter addresses diagnostic concerns for children with a range of cognitive–communicative impairments. Cognitive–communicative and social–emotional impairments can affect not only concept development, social communication, and self regulation but also language systems, particularly semantics and pragmatics. Children with cognitive–communicative disorders share symptoms marked by difficulty using integrated thought–language processes to support the ability to learn and remember new information and skills, comprehend how the world works and how other people think, interact socially with peers and adults, and regulate their emotions and behavior.

Developmental Disability

The term *developmental disability (DD)* fits all the conditions discussed in this chapter and some discussed in Chapter 6. Contrary to common misunderstandings, the term *developmental disability* has broader meaning than intellectual disability (ID/MR) alone. DD applies to a wide range of conditions, including autism spectrum disorders and cerebral palsy, regardless of whether intellectual disability is involved. According to the U.S. Department of Health and Human Services (n.d.):

> Developmental Disabilities are physical or mental impairments that begin before age 22, and alter or substantially inhibit a person's capacity to do at least three of the following:
>
> **1.** Take care of themselves (dress, bathe, eat, and other daily tasks)
> **2.** Speak and be understood clearly
> **3.** Learn
> **4.** Walk/Move around
> **5.** Make decisions
> **6.** Live on their own
> **7.** Earn and manage an income

In early childhood, medical and educational personnel use terms such as *developmental delay* or *early childhood developmental delay* as a temporary diagnosis for children at risk for developmental disability. They apply when a child is not meeting developmental milestones but a specific diagnosis is not yet clear. Symptoms of delay may change across the first few years of life. In infancy, problems may be noticed first as inadequate sucking reflex, floppy muscle tone (hypofunctioning), or spasticicity (hyperfunctioning) and unusual responses to auditory, visual, or tactual stimuli. Later in the first year, problems may be observed in delays of the motor skills of sitting, crawling, and walking and in the communication skills of eye gaze, babbling, and first words. As the child progresses, other patterns may emerge. "When a child continues to show significant delays in all developmental spheres, mental retardation is the likely diagnosis" (Batshaw & Shapiro, 2002, p. 291).

IDEA '04 gives state education agencies and state health agencies the option to define criteria for diagnosing developmental delay in early childhood. If a state decides to diagnose developmental delay, it can define the age range to which the temporary diagnosis may apply. The allowable age range is 3 through 9 years or some subset thereof. Section 300.8(b) indicates the following, including the specified five areas of delay:

> *Child with a disability* for children aged three through nine (or any subset of that age range, including ages three through five), may, subject to the conditions described in § 300.111(b), include a child—

(1) Who is experiencing developmental delays, as defined by the State and as measured by appropriate diagnostic instruments and procedures, in one or more of the following areas: Physical development, cognitive development, communication development, social or emotional development, or adaptive development; and

(2) Who, by reason thereof, needs special education and related services. (Section 300.8[b])

The alternative to adopting a general definition of developmental delay is for state and local educational systems to find children eligible for special education and related services as having one of the twelve disabilities named in IDEA '04 (see Table 4.3 in Chapter 4). This chapter describes the IDEA '04 classifications of *mental retardation, autism, traumatic brain injury,* and *emotional disturbance.* It also includes conditions used to qualify a child as having *other health impairment* or *multiple disabilities.*

Intellectual Disability (Mental Retardation)

Disorders that involve dual symptoms of low IQ and problems with adaptive behavior previously have been called **mental retardation,** but professional and parental organizations have promoted changes in terminology. The American Association on Mental Retardation (AAMR) has advocated for people with developmental disabilities since 1876. It recently changed its name to the American Association on Intellectual and Developmental Disabilities (AAIDD) and stated, "While it is widely perceived that mental retardation (MR) is a condition that exists, it was also recognized that the term is prone to abuse, misinterpretation, and has devolved into an insult, especially for people with disabilities and family members" (p. 1) (see Personal Reflection 7.1).

PERSONAL reflection *7.1*

"Mom, I know I'm retarded, but I'm not stupid."

Nicole Kaufman, a young adult with intellectual disability, was quoted by her mother, Sandra Kaufman (1988, p. 103) in her account of her daughter's growth toward independence.

Federal regulators considered changing the label *mental retardation* in the regulations for IDEA '04, but found no compelling reasons for a change and observed that the term *mental retardation* was used in the statute. Mental retardation in IDEA '04 is defined as "significantly subaverage general intellectual functioning, existing concurrently with deficits in adaptive behavior and manifested during the developmental period, that adversely affects a child's educational performance" (34 Code of Federal Regulations §300.7[c][6]).

Diagnosis of intellectual disability/mental retardation (ID/MR) requires identification of limitations in two areas: (1) intellectual functioning, generally measured with an IQ test, although that is becoming controversial; and (2) adaptive behavior, expressed as limitation of conceptual, social, and practical adaptive skills. Diagnostic criteria also require that ID/MR appears before the age of 18, which is earlier than the age of 22 years specified as the cutoff for diagnosing developmental disabilities. The AAIDD definition indicates that ID/MR should be considered neither a medical nor a mental disorder; moreover, it is not something a person *has,* but rather a state of functioning.

Assessment of adaptive behavior must accompany measurement of IQ when diagnosing ID/MR. The Vineland Adaptive Behavior Scale-II (Sparrow, Cicchetti, & Balla, 2005) assesses communication skills (receptive, expressive, and written); daily living skills (personal, domestic, and community); socialization skills (interpersonal, play and leisure, and coping); and motor skills (fine and gross). The use of adaptive behavior as a diagnostic criterion reduces the likelihood that environmental factors or the cultural linguistic bias of IQ tests will lead to inaccurate diagnosis. If an individual can demonstrate adequate adaptive life skills in his or her natural environments, then he or she does not fit the classification of ID/MR, even with a low IQ.

The prevalence of ID/MR between ages 5 and 65 years has been estimated to be approximately 1.5 million people and the overall rate was 7.6 cases per 1,000 population (Centers for Disease Control and Prevention, 1996), but prevalence estimates vary with the definition of ID/MR. When prevalence estimates are based on statistical projections using the *Diagnostic and Statistical Manual of Mental Disorders* (*DSM-IV-TR*) (APA, 2000) criteria relative to the normal curve, approximately 2.5 percent of the population should have IQ scores meeting criteria for ID/MR, whereas at the other end of the normal curve, 2.5 percent of the population should have superior intelligence (Batshaw & Shapiro, 2002). Due to sex-linked genetic syndromes, approximately twice as many males have ID/MR as females (2:1 ratio).

ID/MR Classification

Traditional terminology and diagnostic subcategories (mild, moderate, severe, profound) have been maintained in the *DSM-IV-TR* (APA, 2000). They are based on a combination of IQ scores and adaptive behavior criteria and have implications for treatment and prognosis.

Mild Functional Limitations

Mild ID/MR is diagnosed when an individual scores in the IQ range of 50–55 to 70–75 and has adaptive behaviors that enable him or her to function close to age-level peers in preschool, achieve sixth-grade-level academic skills, and achieve a fairly high degree of literate language use and understanding by late adolescence. Adults with mild ID/MR often hold jobs and live with minimal supervision and support. Approximately 85 percent of individuals with intellectual disabilities fall into this category (APA, 2000).

Moderate Functional Limitations

Moderate ID/MR is diagnosed when an individual scores in the IQ range of 35–40 to 50–55 and has moderately affected adaptive behaviors. Individuals at this level acquire social communication skills and academic skills at approximately second-grade level. Acquisition of literacy skills is possible and should be targeted through deliberate instruction. In late adolescence and adulthood, individuals with moderate ID/MR can perform semiskilled work in general society or sheltered workshops. They may live with a fair degree of independence given moderate supervision and assistance. Approximately 10 percent of individuals with intellectual disabilities fall into the category of moderate functional limitation (APA, 2000).

Severe Functional Limitations

Severe mental retardation is diagnosed when an individual scores in the IQ range of 20–25 to 35–40. Individuals at this level have adaptive behaviors that are severely affected, making it difficult to function with any degree of independence. Both language and academic skills remain limited throughout the school-age years, with limited literacy abilities (e.g., recognition of common environmental symbols and print). Such individuals often have comorbid motor and sensory difficulties but, with appropriate special education, can learn self-care routines in home-living contexts and perform tasks with close supervision in employment. This low-incidence condition affects approximately 3 percent to 4 percent of individuals with ID/MR (APA, 2000).

Profound Functional Limitations

Profound mental retardation is diagnosed when an individual scores in the IQ range below 20–25 and his or her adaptive behaviors are profoundly affected. It is challenging to discover what individuals with this level of impairment actually know or think due to comorbid sensory–motor limitations. Comprehensive supervision and assistance often are required. Approximately 1 percent to 2 percent of individuals with intellectual disabilities fall into this category (APA, 2000). It is important to remember, however, that even when symbolic language skills are extremely limited, communication is possible. As Donnellan (1984) suggested, the least dangerous assumption is that a person with extreme limitations is capable of understanding and learning more than first appears possible.

Expected Revisions in the *DSM-V* and Focus on Strengths

When the fifth edition of the *Diagnostics and Statistical Manual of Mental Disorders* (*DSM-V*) is published by the American Psychiatric Association (expected in 2010), the four functional categories—mild, moderate, severe, profound—are likely to be replaced by descriptions that depend less on intelligence test scores. Functional limitations and related needs may be the defining traits in the *DSM-V,* but the classification of ID/MR is particularly heterogeneous. It encompasses a wide range of ability levels and profile variations, not to mention individual and personal strengths. Strength-based approaches capitalize on what children *can* do, rather than what they *cannot* do—an emphasis that must not get lost when considering diagnostic criteria.

Causal Factors Associated with ID/MR

It is frequently impossible to pinpoint a specific cause for nongenetic ID/MR. Some children with ID/MR experience seizure disorders indicating central nervous system impairment but with no clear etiology. Others have a medical history that includes high-risk pregnancy, premature birth, or low birthweight. Children with such risk factors can develop typically, however, and perinatal risk factors are not enough alone to cause cognitive limitations. Some forms of developmental disability can be diagnosed on the basis of physiological evidence. One preventable form of ID/MR, *phenylketonuria (PKU),* is one of several "inborn errors of metabolism," for which newborn screening is routine (Batshaw & Tuchman, 2002).

PKU can be successfully treated, but other inborn errors of metabolism are less well understood. Other syndromes that involve ID/MR have confirmed genetic or chromosomal etiology. Six relatively common syndromes are summarized in the subsections that follow: Down syndrome, Fragile X syndrome, Prader-Willi syndrome, Angelman syndrome, Williams syndrome, and cri-du-chat syndrome.

Down Syndrome

Down syndrome (DS) was described in 1866 by Dr. John Langdon Down (Roizen, 2002). Children with DS have identifiable facial and body features, including short fingers and unusual palm creases, wide-spaced first toes, epicanthal folds around the eyes, colored speckles in the iris of the eye (called *Brushfield spots*), and small ears, nose, and chin. DS also brings an "increased risk of abnormalities in almost every organ system" (Roizen, 2002, p. 309) and risks for speech and language difficulties beyond those explained by the child's cognition (Abbeduto & Murphy, 2004). Every child with Down syndrome, however, is a unique individual with personal traits and strengths (see Personal Reflection 7.2).

PERSONAL reflection 7.2

"I am introducing you to my son, Joshua. Josh is 7 years old. He's diligent to the task, a unique kid, a hard worker and, yes, Josh has Down syndrome. I mention the Down syndrome last because Josh is a person first. Josh is not a 'Down's'; he's not a 'Down syndrome child'; but rather, he's an individual who happens to have Down syndrome. He's not a category or a diagnosis. He is a person before he is anything else."

Thomas J. O'Neill (1987, p. xviii), president of the National Down Syndrome Congress, was expressing his pride in his son and making an important point.

DS is considered to be one of the most common genetic causes of mental retardation (Abbeduto & Murphy, 2004). It results from a chromosomal deficit involving an extra chromosome 21 (of 23 pairs; 46 total) called *trisomy 21,* so that a child has a total of 47 chromosomes rather than 46. Trisomy 21 is associated with increased maternal age. One in 2,000 women has a chance of having a baby with trisomy 21 at age 20, but the risk rises to 1 in 20 for mothers at age 45. Advances in technology allow DS to be diagnosed prenatally on the basis of a chromosomal test. This may be responsible for the decline in prevalence of DS since the 1970s from 1.33 per 1,000 to 0.92 per 1,000, presumably due to "termination of a significant number of affected pregnancies" (Roizen, 2002, p. 308).

The immediate cause of trisomy 21 at the cellular level is nondisjunction during meiosis (division) of the nuclear material in the egg. Although trisomy 21 accounts for 95 percent of DS births, two other chromosomal events are *translocation Down syndrome,* which involves the attachment of a long arm of an extra chromosome 21 to chromosome 14, 21, or 22, and *mosaic Down syndrome* or *mosaic trisomy,* which indicates that some but not all cells are affected. Rather than maternal age, inheritance patterns are implicated for translocation forms of DS. No clear etiology has been found for mosaic conditions. Slightly more males (59 percent) than females (41 percent) have trisomy DS, but the reverse is true for translocation forms, with females (74 percent) having the condition more frequently than males (26 percent). Children with trisomy and translocation DS are similar in ability levels and other characteristics, but children with mosaic DS tend to score higher on IQ tests and have fewer medical complications. Many children with DS score in the IQ range for mild to moderate mental retardation (Roizen, 2002).

Both speech and language development may be affected beyond levels expected based on general cognitive delays. Articulation difficulties and conductive hearing loss are associated with structural differences in craniofacial morphology associated with DS. These include short front-to-back head dimensions (called *brachycephaly*), associated shortened oral and pharyngeal structures, and a high vaulted palate. Children with DS have difficulty manipulating their tongues, which appear large relative to their oral cavities, and so their tongues protrude at rest and contribute to articulation difficulties. Articulation and intelligibility concerns often are noted as priorities for parents (Kumin, 1994).

Language development for children and adolescents with DS (ages 5 to 20 years) has been compared to that of younger children (ages 2 to 6 years) matched for nonverbal mental age and mother's years of education. In language comprehension, Chapman, Schwartz, and Kay-Raining Bird (1991) found that children with DS scored significantly better on a test of receptive vocabulary than syntax, and the gap increased with age. In a companion study of language production, Chapman, Seung, Schwartz, and Kay-Raining Bird (1998) found that children and adolescents with DS showed more severe expressive deficits than predicted by their receptive abilities or nonverbal cognitive abilities. Results showed that adolescents with DS could produce utterances with greater complexity than expected (mean length of utterance, or MLU, > 3.0) but omitted more grammatical function words than peers of the same mental age with similar MLUs, thus supporting the hypothesis of a specific deficit of syntactic expression. Chapman and colleagues concluded, "Continuing speech–language intervention to increase communicative skill in expressive language vocabulary, syntax, grammatical morphology, and intelligibility appear warranted throughout adolescence for individuals with Down syndrome" (p. 872).

Spoken language difficulties of auditory–sequential memory, syntax comprehension, and expressive language have an impact on reading and writing. Difficulties with phonological awareness (PA) is a significant problem for children with DS (Cossu, Rossini, & Marshall, 1993; Cupples & Iacono, 2000; Fletcher & Buckley, 2002; Verucci, Menghini, & Vicari, 2006). It can be expected to have a particularly strong impact on word-level reading decoding and spelling, but it is difficult to sort out historical lack of instruction from characteristics of the syndrome that might limit the ability to learn to read and write. Cossu and colleagues (1993) described children with DS who could not master PA tasks but learned to read nevertheless. They concluded "that reading should be taught by teaching reading skills (including letter–sound correspondences), not phonological awareness skills" (p. 129).

Cupples and Iacono (2000) found associations among PA, other language skills, and oral reading for 22 children with DS between the ages of 6 years, 7 months and 10 years, 3 months. They tested participants again nine months later and found PA associated with early oral reading ability. Cupples and Iacono also found that early PA ability predicted later nonword reading but not the reverse, suggesting causal links. Similarly, Fletcher and Buckley (2002) found that PA varied among a group of 17 children with DS between the ages of 9 years, 2 months and 14 years, 5 months, with PA correlating positively with measures of reading and spelling, including the ability to spell nonwords. This suggests that children with DS might benefit from the same type of instructional activities that all children do. Their literacy education should focus on PA and phonics, along with other word-level analysis skills and sentence/discourse skills for comprehending and expressing meanings through written language (as illustrated in the opening photo to this chapter).

Social interaction and cognition also are an area of concern for children and adolescents with DS. Abbeduto and Murphy (2004) argued for a broad social interactionist view of children and adolescents with ID/MR (DS and fragile X syndrome, specifically). Their research focused on interpersonal and social–cognition skills for theory of mind false-belief tasks. Results showed that adolescents and young adults with DS had delays in false-belief reasoning relative to other abilities. Abbeduto and Murphy argued for direct attention on social–cognitive competence, noting that "although previous work in this area has often led to the conclusion that social cognition is a strength for individuals with Down syndrome, such conclusions have often failed to distinguish sociability from social–cognitive competence" (p. 93).

Fragile X Syndrome

Fragile X syndrome (FXS) is the most frequent *inherited* cause of mental retardation (Meyer & Batshaw, 2003), and after DS the second-most-frequent *genetic* cause of mental retardation (Bailey et al., 2004). In 1943, Martin and Bell described FXS in two generations of a family who shared clinical symptoms (Meyer & Batshaw, 2002). Almost 50 years later, the inheritance pattern was attributed to a single gene (FMR1) (Verkerk et al., 1991) required to produce a protein necessary for brain function (*fragile X mental retardation protein;* abbreviated FMRP). FMRP is critical for early brain development, particularly proliferation and pruning of dendrites (illustrated in Chapter 3), with associated "activity-dependent synaptic function, maturation, and plasticity" (Bailey et al., 2004, p. 123). Physical features observed in FXS syndrome, particularly males (e.g., elongated head, arched palate, large ears and hands), may not be recognized until later childhood and adolescence.

Because the missing gene is on the X chromosome, FXS affects more males (1 per 4,000, due to their XY chromosome combination), than females (1 per 8,000 births, due to their XX chromosome combination) (Bailey et al., 2004). Females tend to carry the trait, with one of their two X chromosomes demonstrating the fragile characteristic (named because the long arm of the X chromosome appears constricted and threadlike). When affected, females demonstrate milder forms of MR accompanied by difficulties with math and sequential processing, as well as shyness, social anxiety, and impaired social skills (Meyer & Batshaw, 2002, p. 322).

FXS bears similarity to autism spectrum disorders. The National Fragile X Foundation (n.d.) reported, "Fragile X syndrome can cause a child to have autism or an Autism Spectrum Disorder (ASD) though not all children with fragile X syndrome have autism or an ASD." Bailey and colleagues (2004) summarized prior research documenting overlap between the two conditions, noting that 20 percent to 25 percent of individuals with FXS meet the diagnostic criteria for autism, and 4 percent to 5 percent of cases of autism spectrum disorder are attributable to FXS.

Communication symptoms associated with FXS that also are observed in autism include echolalia; jargon; perseveration on words, phrases, or topics of conversation; and comments that are tangential or irrelevant. Speech and language impairments observed in FXS include impaired articulation, sound repetition, telegraphic speech, and missing morphology. Social interaction difficulties are common and may include difficulties with eye gaze and gestural communication. Behavioral symptoms include difficulties with transition, social anxiety, sensory defensiveness, and temper tantrums. It has been hypothesized that all such symptoms might be secondary to a central problem of hyperarousal to sensory stimuli, which contrasts with the central problem in autism, which is failure to orient to social stimuli and appearance of aloofness. It is hypothesized that individuals with FXS are more interested in social interactions and sensitive to the facial cues of others than children with autism, but their hyperarousal may cause anxiety in social situations, making them withdraw (Bailey et al., 2004).

Abbeduto and Murphy (2004) investigated the language skills and social behaviors of adolescents and young adults with fragile X syndrome compared to DS. They found individuals in both special populations to "have especially serious problems in using language for social interaction" (p. 93). The main differences were associated with the broader behavioral phenotype of each syndrome. Whereas expressive language limitations played an especially important role in DS, limitations of attention and theory of mind played a larger role in fragile X. At this point, the literature offers few insights into the literacy abilities or limitations of individuals with FXS.

Prader-Willi Syndrome

Prader-Willi syndrome (PWS) also results from a chromosomal disorder, involving either deletion of chromosome 15 from the father or duplication from the mother. PWS affects males and females equally, with an incidence of about 1 in 10,000 to 15,000 births. Infants with PWS have **hypotonia** (low muscle tone) and feeding problems, although children with PWS tend to become obese later in development. PWS is characterized by **micrognathia** (small lower jaw), narrow palatal vault, and related hypo- and hypernasality. Speech, language, and communication problems include articulation difficulty, short MLU, limited vocabulary, difficulty with narrative and conversational discourse, and impaired social skills (Lewis, Freebairn, Heeger, & Cassidy, 2002).

Angelman Syndrome

Angelman syndrome (AS) was first described by an English physician, Dr. Harry Angelman, in 1965 (Angelman Syndrome Foundation, n.d.). Angelman noted common characteristics of children as including no speech; a stiff, jerky gait; frequent laughter; and (often) seizures. Initially, the disorder was presumed to be rare, but the AS Foundation (n.d.) has indicated problems with underdiagnosis and frequent misdiagnosis as cerebral palsy or autism. AS occurs when chromosome 15 is deleted from the mother or duplicated from the father. Current estimates of incidence range from 1 in 12,000 to 1 in 30,000 new births, with occurrence in all racial/ethnic groups. Symptoms of autism in AS may be associated with neural irregularities in the hippocampus and cerebellum, which are also implicated in autism (Towbin, Mauk, & Batshaw, 2002).

Children with AS typically have normal prenatal and birth history, normal head circumference, and no obvious birth defects. Developmental delay may be evident by 6 to 12 months of age, but the most common age of diagnosis is 3 to 7 years, when characteristic behaviors and features become evident. Although children with AS often have epilepsy, many show structurally normal brains on MRI and CT scans. Some have mild **cortical atrophy** (brain shrinkage) or **dysmyelination** (lack of myelin sheaths on the white matter axons of the brain). Development is delayed but does not show regression. Intellectual disability results in severe functional limitations, with movement or balance disorders, ataxia of gait, and tremulous movement of limbs (hence, the confusion with CP). Other unique characteristics include laughter/smiling; apparent happy demeanor; easily excitable personality, often with hand-flapping movements; hypermotoric behavior; and short attention span. Children with AS may have few or no words, but verbal reception and nonverbal communication skills are higher than verbal expression skills.

Williams Syndrome

Williams syndrome (WS) is a relatively rare genetic condition that occurs when a number of genes are missing due to deletion of the long arm of chromosome 7 (Gordon, 2006; Mervis, 2004). It was first recognized in 1961 (Williams Syndrome Assocation, n.d.). WS occurs in approximately 1 per 20,000 births (Gordon, 2006; Zukowski, 2004) and equally in all racial/ethnic groups and both sexes. WS involves a characteristic facial appearance, including a small upturned nose, long **philtrum** (channel from nose to upper lip), wide mouth, full lips, small chin, and puffiness around the eyes, leading people with WS to be described as elfinlike in appearance.

Although present at birth, WS may be misdiagnosed in the early stages as low birthweight or failure to thrive. Children with WS often have feeding difficulties with colic-like symptoms, linked to **hypercalcemia** (elevated blood calcium levels), low muscle tone, severe gag reflex, poor suck–swallow, and tactile defensiveness. Hyperthyroidism and cardiovascular problems are common (Gordon, 2006).

Young children with WS may demonstrate **hyperacusis** (overly sensitive hearing), experiencing sounds as painful or startling. Nevertheless, many individuals with WS have an affinity to music and special talents for learning it. Most people with WS have some degree of intellectual impairment, with particular difficulty learning numbers and visuospatial concepts. Distractibility is common in mid-childhood but lessens by adulthood (Gordon, 2006).

WS interests language researchers because unique strength in sentence-level language production skills tend to mask language comprehension difficulties. Karmiloff and Karmiloff-Smith (2001) hypothesized, based on cognitive–information processing and linguistic theory, that "the superficially impressive language skills of individuals with WS may be due to good auditory memory rather than an intact grammar module" (p. 110). Zukowski (2004) found that individuals with WS could generate complex structures (e.g., relative clauses) in elicited tasks, even though they had difficulty comprehending similar structures in the language of others. For example, one boy with WS, age 10 years, 5 months, was able to generate the complex sentence "Bill is looking at the, the horse that the other kid is sitting on" (p. 106). Yet errors of mapping meaning onto structure were common, such as moving the relative clause from the object to subject position. When the experimental elicitation task required object relatives, such as "The truck *that the girl is jumping over* turned red" (italics added) participants with WS tended to change them to subject relatives, such as "The girl *who's jumping over the truck* turned red" (p. 107). Although such sentences were well formed syntactically, they changed the meaning of the communication. Zukowski concluded that lack of grammatical competence could not explain comprehension difficulties in WS. The dissociation of comprehension and production is intriguing. It reminds clinicians about the need for comprehensive assessments across systems that might be disconnected but perhaps could be used to support each other, given appropriate intervention.

Adolescents and adults with WS show an uneven pattern of strengths in speech, vocabulary knowledge, long-term memory, and some social skills, accompanied by deficits in fine motor, visual–spatial, and pragmatic language–communication skills (Gordon, 2006; Mervis, 2004). They are known for relatively strong social skills, including politeness and willingness to interact with strangers, particularly adults. Rourke (1995) viewed WS as a form of nonverbal learning disability (see Chapter 6), but the language comprehension difficulties experienced by individuals with WS suggest that nonverbal is a misnomer.

Howlin, Davies, and Udwin (1998) documented literacy abilities for 67 adults with WS, with IQ scores ranging from 50 to 69. They found that 47 (70 percent) of the participants scored above the basal level on tests of both single-word recognition and reading comprehension, and 46 (69 percent) scored above the basal level on spelling. Reading comprehension scores were significantly below word recognition scores. This pattern is consistent across studies and fits the oral language profile and simple model discussed in Chapter 5.

Laing, Hulme, Grant, and Karmiloff-Smith (2001) questioned reports of relative strength in reading ability and recommended examining the process by which children with WS learn to read. They noted that "children with WS come to the task of learning to read with a different and uneven pattern of language skills compared to those of typically developing children" (p. 730). Among those differences are high vocabulary (relative to IQ scores), unusual semantic processing, and overdependence on phonological encoding (including high ability for nonword repetition). Laing and colleagues found reading to be more limited than first apparent, particularly in ability to use semantic information and reading comprehension relative to reading decoding.

Cri-du-chat Syndrome

Cri-du-chat syndrome is named for the French phrase *cry of the cat* because of a characteristic high-pitched birth cry, which sounds like the mewing of a cat. This syndrome is associated with the deletion of the short arm of chromosome 5. It occurs in an estimated 1 in 20,000 to 50,000 births (Genetics Home Reference, n.d.). The syndrome often involves low birthweight and slow growth, ***microcephaly*** (small head circumference), ***hyperteleorism*** (wide-set eyes), cleft lip and palate, low-set ears, and conductive hearing loss. Hypersensitive hearing (hyperacusis) also may occur. Children with cri-du-chat syndrome learn to communicate at a basic level but have limited language skills. They may show obsessive attachment to objects, repetitive movements, and self-injurious behaviors (SIB).

SUMMARY

The broad category of individuals with ID/MR is far from homogeneous. It encompasses a wide range of cognitive–communicative and related development issues diagnosed based on the dual symptoms of low scores on an intelligence test (generally defined as IQ scores of 70–75 or below) and difficulties in adaptive behavior across multiple settings. This section has summarized the characteristics and etiologies for Down syndrome, fragile X syndrome, Angelman syndrome, Prader-Willi syndrome, Williams syndrome, and cri-du-chat syndrome. Children and adolescents can be diagnosed with ID/MR even if there is no identifiable syndrome or etiological factor.

In the past, many children with ID/MR and clear difficulty with language and literacy learning were denied services because of misguided cognitive referencing policies. Erroneous assumptions also have been made about whether it was possible for school-age students with ID/MR to learn to read and write or comprehend content from the general education curriculum. Thus, many students with ID/MR who might have benefited from services targeting their speech, language, and literacy have been underserved and undereducated.

Autism Spectrum Disorders

Autism is currently viewed as part of a spectrum of disorders termed ***pervasive developmental disorders (PDD)*** in the *DSM-IV-TR* (APA, 2000). This classification group has in common severe and pervasive impairments in several areas of development. PDD is not a diagnosis by itself but comprises five diagnoses: autistic disorder, Asperger disorder, childhood disintegrative disorder (CDD), Rett's disorder, and PDD not otherwise specified (PDD-NOS). The term ***autism spectrum disorders (ASD)*** may be used synonymously with PDD to refer to disorders that share a triad of symptoms affecting (1) social interaction, (2) verbal and nonverbal communication, and (3) restricted and repetitive patterns of behavior (APA, 2000; Wetherby & Prizant, 2000). Wing (1988) called this the triad of social interaction, communication, and "imagination."

Autism

The diagnosis of autism originated with Kanner's (1943) case descriptions of social aloofness and repetitive behavior. According to the *DSM-IV-TR* (APA, 2000), the diagnosis of ***autistic disorder*** is made based on four inclusionary criteria and one exclusionary criterion. The exclusionary criterion is that the disorder cannot be explained better by any other PDD diagnosis. Inclusionary criteria specify that symptoms must appear prior to 3 years of age and involve the following triad of social interaction, communication, and repetitive behaviors:

- *Social interaction:* Impairment in reciprocal social interaction must be documented by at least two of the following four symptoms: (1) impairment in use of nonverbal behaviors for interaction (interpersonal eye gaze, facial expression, and body posture or gestures); (2) failure to develop age-appropriate peer relationships; (3) absence of showing, bringing, or pointing to objects of interest to share enjoyment, interests, or achievements with other people; and (4) lack of social or emotional reciprocity.

- *Communication:* Impairment in the quality of verbal and nonverbal communication must be documented by at least one of the following four symptoms: (1) delay or lack of spoken language, with no attempt to use gesture or other nonverbal communication to compensate; (2) impaired ability to initiate or sustain a conversation with others; (3) idiosyncractic or stereotyped and repetitive use of language; and (4) absence of spontaneous make-believe or social imitative play appropriate to developmental level.
- *Repetitive behaviors:* Impairment in the form of restricted, repetitive, and stereotyped patterns of behavior, interests, and activities must be documented by at least one of the following four symptoms: (1) preoccupation (abnormal in intensity or focus) with stereotyped and restricted patterns of interest; (2) inflexible adherence to specific, nonfunctional routines or rituals; (3) stereotyped and repetitive motor mannerisms, such as hand flapping or complex whole-body rocking or other movements; and (4) preoccupation with parts of objects.

Autism is the most common diagnosis in the PDD grouping, with a prevalence rate of 2 to 5 cases per 10,000 (*DSM-IV-TR*; APA, 2000). Fombonne (2007) conducted a careful analysis of the international literature on epidemiology, which suggested a higher prevalence rate of 60 per 10,000 (or 0.6 percent) for all forms of PDD combined. In the United States, a large ASD surveillance project conducted by the Centers for Disease Control and Prevention (CDC) showed an average of 6.7 children out of 1,000 with an ASD, which translates to 67 cases per 10,000 (CDC, 2007). Results from Fombonne's systematic review and the CDC study suggest an increase in prevalence of alarming magnitude, indicating that one 1 out of every 150 children born may have a risk of ASD and that approximately 1.5 million Americans and their families now are affected (Autism Society of America, 2007). Autism is found in all countries and all racial, ethnic, and socioeconomic groups. It is at least four times more prevalent in boys than in girls (Fombonne, 2007).

The apparent rise in the incidence (i.e., new cases) of ASD has been of great interest across international boundaries and in the popular press as well as in the scientific literature. Wing and Potter (2002) noted that apparent rises in incidence might be authentic but also might be an artifact of changes in diagnostic criteria, variations in research methods, increasing awareness of the disorder, increasing awareness of co-occurrence with other cognitive or psychiatric conditions, development of specialist services for the condition, and greater understanding of age of onset.

The causes for ASD are not yet fully understood, but the neurobiological core hypothesis is now widely accepted (compared to earlier hypotheses about psychodynamical causes), and evidence is mounting for genetic causes based on sibling and twin studies (Towbin et al., 2002). Bailey and colleagues (2004) also reviewed the evidence from neuro-imaging studies that linked impaired psychological processes (e.g., executive function and social cognition) to regions of the brain known to support such functions, including the prefrontal cortex, superior temporal gyrus, amygdala, and cerebellum. Other hypotheses currently prominent in the lay literature are that autism is associated with birth complications or the administration of vaccinations in early childhood, but essentially no support from the scientific literature supports either of these hypotheses (Towbin et al., 2002).

Questions about the nature of autism ask about a cognitive profile unique to the spectrum versus a general form of cognitive impairment. Autism can co-occur with ID/MR and often does. That is, beyond the pure symptoms of ASD, children with autism appear to have cognitive limitations that interfere with their learning. The essence of autism includes difficulty integrating details into a coherent schema in any domain and difficulty forming a theory of mind (ToM), in particular, with limited ability to intuit the mental states of others, including their false beliefs, intentions, desires, and feelings (Baron-Cohen, 1995; Frith, 1989). These social–cognitive problems make it difficult for a child with autism to coordinate attention with others and to benefit from cultural structuring of social roles.

Descriptions of communication and language impairments in autism go beyond the features itemized in the diagnostic criteria. Wetherby, Prizant, and Schuler (2000) summarized research on communication, providing indicators for early diagnosis of autism. One critical indicator that is evident in preverbal communicative interactions is limited joint attention. Wetherby and colleagues summarized a body of literature that has supported its diagnostic importance:

> It is not that children with autism do not communicate, but, rather, that they do not readily communicate for social goals and purposes. That is, they communicate predominantly or exclusively to regulate the behavior of others to get them to do something (request) or to stop doing something (protest). What is lacking is the use of communication to draw another's attention to an object or event (comment or label). (p. 110)

Greenspan and Wieder (1997) conducted a retrospective chart analysis for 200 children diagnosed with autism between 22 months and 4 years of age. The results showed that 96 percent had significant receptive language problems, 55 percent had no evidence of receptive language comprehension, and 41 percent had only intermittent ability to understand single words and follow simple directions. On the positive side, 95 percent demonstrated some capacity for emotional relating, 30 percent showed engagement based on need fulfillment, and 40 percent showed reciprocal gestures and imitation. The remaining 24 percent engaged in reciprocal relating. Perhaps the most important diagnostic symptom was that 68 percent showed no complex gestures (e.g., taking a caregiver to the door and motioning to go outside).

This agrees with other evidence about delays in the use of conventional gestures for showing, waving, and pointing and for conveying symbolic meanings, such as agreement by head nodding. "Unlike children with language impairments or hearing impairments, children with autism do not compensate for their lack of speech by using other modalities, such as gestures" (Wetherby et al., 2000, p. 113). Limited capacity for symbol use can be observed in the lack of dramatic play. Children with autism may demonstrate unusual preoccupation with some objects and skilled sensorimotor manipulations (e.g., lining up cars or spinning circular toys or wheels), but they may lack the ability to engage in make-believe and dramatic play with peers.

Although children with autism may have good motor skills, objective observation suggests that motor difficulties are present as well. For many children with autism, difficulties in learning to speak and gesture are compounded by apraxia. Apraxia associated with autism may involve difficulty in planning, executing, and sequencing movements that involve the hands or whole body, not just the mouth (as in CAS) (Wetherby et al., 2000).

Children who can use fluent speech by age 5 have a better prognosis for continued academic and social development (Wetherby et al., 2000). This means that they engage in spontaneous use of multiword combinations for communicative purposes. Children with autism who do learn to talk often go through a period of *echolalia,* in which they repeat the speech of others either immediately or after some delay, termed *immediate echolalia* or *delayed echolalia* respectively. Wetherby and colleagues (2000) noted that echolalia may serve a productive language-learning function. They offered the following explanation:

> The way children who use echolalia learn to talk is by initially repeating phrases associated with situations or emotional states and subsequently learning the meanings of these

phrases by finding out how they work. Over time, many children learn to use these "gestalt forms" purposefully in communicative interactions and eventually are able to break down the echolalic chunks into smaller meaningful units as part of the process of transitioning to a rule-governed, generative language system. Pronoun reversals are a byproduct of echolalia because the child repeats the pronoun heard, making the pronoun used in reference to self and other reversed. For example, the child may use the echolalic utterance "Do you want a piece of candy?" as a way to request the candy, although it sounds as though the child is offering the candy. (pp. 113–114)

Children with autism may have greater interest in learning to read and write than to speak (see Case Example 7.1). Although *hyperlexia* (i.e., precocious ability to read words but with limited comprehension) may occur among children with a variety of special needs,

---

CASE example *7.1*

Mark and the Role of Literacy in Language Learning

Ann Hewetson (2005) described her experiences parenting Mark, who was diagnosed with autism. Hewetson (who lives in the United Kingdom) kept a journal of Mark's early development, highlighting factors that helped him move beyond repetitive behaviors and begin to communicate.

Around Mark's second birthday, the family discovered his special interest in printed words and used this discovery to help Mark recover some of the words he appeared to have lost around age 1:

> There are now printed words everywhere in the house. Every object has its coloured card—*table—chair—fridge—door*. Mark, while he ignores the object, is drawn almost with magnetic force to the coloured labels. He traces the letters, patting them with his fingers, investing each with a life force of its own. Almost automatically we repeat the words and even the letters. It has become a habit, a part of the daily routine. (p. 18)

In the weeks that followed, Hewetson added this note to her journal:

> Mark begins cautiously to use some single words. All are words he had learned from the labels. Going over to the fridge, he says "fridge"; touching the wall, he calls out "wall." The words are pronounced clearly and with faultless diction. (p. 25)

It was somewhat later that Hewetson figured out how to use Mark's interest in literacy (and chocolate) to help him transition to listening and other forms of interaction as she read larger units of text aloud. She made the following entry when he was around age 4, and still talking little:

> I sit on the soft grey chair in the hall, a picture book in my hand. From the top pocket of my pinafore a bar of chocolate sticks out. Mark runs up and down the hall engaged in his current ritual of turning the light switches, now within his reach, on and off. He has been doing this for almost an hour without stopping, seemingly oblivious to my presence.
>
> Taking the chocolate from my pocket, I rustle the paper. He listens. Having got his attention I begin to read aloud to him. He comes over and we share a square of chocolate. Continuing to read I show him the book. He is not interested—running back to the lights. Enough for today.
>
> A week later I begin the daily reading session with a different coloured pinafore, a different bar of chocolate, and the same book. He stays longer, long enough to share half the bar and for me to read him a page. The lights come on again. Tomorrow I will be obtuse and not open the chocolate bar. I will just read aloud. About to close the book, at my side I hear "choc." I point to my top pocket. He will have to climb up on my knee to get it. He hesitates—going back to the light switches. Closing the book, I begin to get up. He is back. Sitting down again I keep very still. Scrambling up on my knee he grasps my hand using it as a claw-grab to get the chocolate out of the pocket. Opening the bar, I offer him a square. We munch—I read. He flops on my knee—listening.
>
> The bar is finished.
>
> I read on.
>
> He listens. (pp. 28–29)

it is most common among children with autism. Mirenda and Erickson (2000) commented, "It is not surprising that some young children with autism are able to combine their strong visual skills with the phonological skills needed to read words prior to understanding their meaning" (p. 350).

There is also evidence of comprehension adequacy in reading. Research shows that adolescents with autism and no cognitive impairment are able to extract meaning at approximately the same level as children of similar cognitive ability but without autism (Snowling & Frith, 1986). Any deficits in reading comprehension appeared to be related to limitations in cognitive–linguistic abilities rather than autism per se.

Asperger Syndrome

Asperger syndrome is diagnosed based on two essential features from the autism triad—severe and sustained impairment in social interaction and restricted, repetitive patterns of behavior, interests, and activities. The third member of the triad—impaired development of spoken communication—must be specifically excluded. The operational definition for ruling out *clinically significant general delay in language* in the discussion of *Asperger Disorder* in the *DSM-IV-TR* (APA, 2000) is that single-word production must emerge by 2 years and communicative phrases by 3 years. If these milestones are not met but the other symptoms are observed, autism is the more appropriate diagnosis.

In addition to ruling out delay in language development, other exclusionary criteria are clinically significant delays in cognitive development, self-help skills, adaptive behavior (other than social interaction), and lack of curiosity about the environment. Individualized education program (IEP) teams also must rule out any evidence that would justify diagnosis of another form of PDD or schizophrenia. By definition, Asperger syndrome is not the appropriate diagnosis if a child also has ID/MR, although such a child might be diagnosed as having autism.

The requirement to rule out impaired development of spoken language for a diagnosis of Asperger syndrome may be confusing. On this basis, some educational agencies rule out provision of communication intervention for children with Asperger syndrome. Such blanket policies violate the individualized-planning provisions of IDEA '04 and overlook a major area of potential need among these children. Similar to the misnomer of *nonverbal learning disability* discussed in Chapter 5, it is misleading to say that children with Asperger syndrome do not have communication difficulties involving language. They may learn to say words and to use the grammar of language on schedule, but taking such a unidimensional view of language development overlooks semantic–pragmatic and discourse-level difficulties. Children and adolescents with AS characteristically have difficulty engaging in conversations with others about interests other than their own. Such problems may be determined by an IEP team to justify speech–language intervention services, even though other aspects of spoken language are adequate.

Problems of literacy learning may be overlooked because it is common for children with Asperger syndrome to read on schedule or even precociously. Reading may be at a surface level, however, with limited comprehension, justifying the label *hyperlexia*. Children with Asperger syndrome often continue to have difficulty interpreting abstract meanings and characters' intentions in narratives during their school-age years, reflecting similar social perception difficulties in life.

Childhood Disintegrative Disorder

Childhood disintegrative disorder (CDD) is identified in the *DSM-IV-TR* (APA, 2000) as PDD marked by regression in functioning following at least two years of apparently normal development. Thus, CDD must be diagnosed after age 2 but before age 10. Diagnosis is based on loss of skills in at least two of five developmental areas: receptive or expressive language, social skills or other adaptive behaviors, bowel or bladder control, play, or motor skills.

CDD is considered part of the autism spectrum because it involves abnormalities in at least two of the three cardinal symptom areas: social interaction, communication, and restricted, stereotyped, or repetitive patterns of behavior, interests, and motor mannerisms. The exclusionary criterion is that CDD cannot be explained by another specific PDD diagnosis or schizophrenia.

Rett Syndrome

Rett syndrome (RS), called *Rett's Disorder* in the *DSM-IV-TR* (APA, 2000), is listed as one of five forms of PDD. RS was first described in 1966 by Austrian physician Dr. Andreas Rett but was not widely recognized as a syndrome until 1983. RS appears only in females. The gene mutation that causes RS was first reported in 1999 as involving MECP2 (pronounced "meck-pea-two"), a single gene on the X chromosome. This gene controls the synthesis of a protein that acts as a biochemical switch for other genes and proteins. When the protein is unavailable or malformed, it causes RS, although the exact mechanisms are not yet fully understood. In some cases, EEG findings show abnormalities, and seizures may occur (APA, 2000).

The symptoms of RS appear in four stages (NINDS, 2007) following a period of normal functioning and growth. A unique diagnostic feature is stereotypic hand movements that resemble hand wringing or hand washing. The four stages are as follow:

- *Stage I* (beginning between 6 and 18 months of age), called the *early onset stage,* usually lasts for a few months. The child has relatively subtle signs of losing interest in the social environment, reduced eye contact, and less interest in toys, followed by deceleration of head growth and delays in gross motor skills such as sitting and crawling.
- *Stage II* (beginning between 1 and 4 years), called the *rapid destruction stage,* is when diagnosis is usually made based on slowing of head growth; rapid or gradual loss of spoken language, social interaction, and communication; and hand wringing, possibly accompanied by breathing irregularities, unsteady gait patterns, and difficulty initiating movements (apraxia).
- *Stage III* (beginning usually between ages 2 and 10 years), called the *plateau stage,* can last for most of a girl's life and involves improvement in behavior; less irritability, crying, or autisticlike characteristics; and more interest in environment, alertness, attention span, and communication skills. Apraxia, motor problems, and seizures remain prominent, however.
- *Stage IV* (beginning at variable times across adulthood), called the *late motor deterioration stage,* can last for years and is characterized by reduced mobility with accompanying muscle weakness, rigidity (stiffness), spasticity, dystonia (increased muscle tone with abnormal posturing of extremity or trunk), scoliosis (curvature of the spine), and potential loss of the ability to walk. Repetitive hand movements may decrease and eye gaze may improve, while cognition and communication remain stable.

Pervasive Development Disorder, Not Otherwise Specified

The diagnosis of *pervasive development disorder, not otherwise specified (PPD-NOS)* is made when individuals demonstrate symptoms of PDD but do not meet the criteria for any of the four other ASD classifications. PDD-NOS applies to children and adolescents with *atypical autism* (APA, 2000), who show late onset (past age 3 years), subthreshhold levels of impairment, or symptomatology that is atypical. Diagnosis of PDD-NOS also requires exclusion of other potentially confounded diagnoses, such as schizophrenia and avoidant personality disorder.

SUMMARY

Autism spectrum disorder (ASD, called *pervasive developmental disorder* in the *DSM-IV-TR* (APA, 2000), includes diagnoses of autism, Asperger syndrome, childhood disintegrative disorder, and Rett syndrome. Social–communicative impairment is a central feature of any autism spectrum disorder. Difficulty with spoken communication characterizes autism, RS, and CDD. The exception to this pattern is Asperger syndrome, in which spoken language milestones are achieved on schedule and ID/MR must be ruled out, whereas, it is a relatively common feature of other categories in the PDD classification. Although children with Asperger syndrome have adequate spoken language systems, they experience social communication difficulty. Some children with ASD show unusual strengths in processing written language, particularly on a surface level (based on intact phonological language skills), with variable comprehension.

Acquired Brain Injury

Acquired disorders of cognitive–communicative functioning appear as a consequence of external causal factors. When traumatic causal factors are known, diagnosis of the primary condition is based on history rather than diagnostic tests, although tests may be helpful to identify secondary conditions, such as cognitive–linguistic impairment. *Traumatic brain injury* (TBI) is listed as one of the twelve diagnostic categories in IDEA '04. Other forms of *acquired brain injury* (ABI) occur due to accidental anoxia or disease, justifying a label as *other health impairment*. A third classification of acquired disability is *acquired seizure disorder,* which appears after a period of normal development and without a clear cause (called *idiopathic*). If accompanied by symptoms of auditory agnosia, acquired seizure disorder may be diagnosed as Landau-Kleffner syndrome (LKS).

Symptoms of impaired cognitive–communicative processes subsequent to TBI and other forms of ABI (called *sequelae*) are assessed by professionals, including speech–language pathologists (SLPs) and neuropsychologists, who seek to identify patterns of spared and impaired functions. Although sequelae may vary in severity, they frequently involve cognitive information processing difficulty on two levels—lower-level information processes, such as attention and memory, and higher-level executive functions, such as planning, self-reflection, and abstract reasoning.

To fully understand the nature of an acquired disorder in a particular child, diagnostic teams must consider historical evidence of comorbid developmental conditions as well as the immediate history of the acquired condition. The existence of prior disorders of spoken or written language is not unusual and may be an important part of the diagnostic and prognostic picture. Children with developmental disabilities, such as learning disabilities and attention-deficit/hyperactivity disorder, may be prone to risky behavior and more likely to sustain TBI or other accidental injury to the brain (Shaffer, Bijur, Chadwick, & Rutter, 1980).

Traumatic Brain Injury

Traumatic brain injury (TBI) was first included as a separate category when IDEA was reauthorized as PL 101-476 in 1990. In IDEA '04, *TBI* is defined as an acquired injury to the brain caused by an external physical force, resulting in total or partial functional disability or psychosocial impairment, or both, that adversely affects a child's educational performance. Traumatic brain injury applies to open or closed head injuries resulting in impairments in one or more areas, such as cognition; language; memory; attention; reasoning; abstract thinking; judgment; problem-solving; sensory, perceptual, and motor abilities; psychosocial behavior; physical functions; information processing; and speech. Traumatic brain injury does not apply to brain injuries that are congenital or degenerative, or to brain injuries induced by birth trauma. (IDEA 2004, Sec.300.8[c][12])

Approximately 1 out of 25 children receives medical attention for a head injury each year (Michaud, Semel-Concepción, Duhaime, & Lazar, 2002). As many as 1 to 2 million children per year experience trauma to the central nervous system (CNS) (Blosser & De-Pompei, 1994). Any agent that can cause trauma to the head may be responsible, including vehicular or pedestrian accidents, falls, sports injuries, and gunshot wounds. Males are twice as likely to experience TBI as females, particularly in the age range 15 to 25 years.

TBI can be classified as an *open head injury (OHI)* or *closed head injury (CHI).* In OHI, the skull is fractured and the *meninges* (i.e., three levels of protective brain coverings called *dura mater, arachnoid,* and *pia mater*) may be punctured, adding danger of infection. In CHI, the brain may swell and have no place to expand, also causing further injury. CHI also can result from *shaken baby syndrome,* which is a criminal act of child abuse. Shaken baby syndrome causes rupturing and bleeding of blood vessels between the brain and skull. The bleeding and brain swelling can cause additional compression and further injury, leading to seizures, long-term disability, coma, or death.

TBI classification (Michaud et al., 2002) varies depending on whether injuries were caused by *impact* (moving) or *inertial* (stationary) forces:

- *Scalp and skull injury* may not be associated with brain damage. Scalp injuries alone rarely cause brain injury, but skull fractures may, particularly when they go beyond *linear fractures* (cracks in the skull) to yield *depressed factures* (in which bone presses against underlying brain tissue).
- *Brain contusion* is bruising of the brain. Impairment depends on extent of the bruise and associated hemorrhaging, as signaled by clinical symptoms involving speech, blurred vision, and unusual behavior.
- *Concussion* occurs when trauma causes brief loss of consciousness and possible amnesia for the moment of the event. It occurs most frequently from falls and contact sports and results in relatively mild injuries to the nerve fibers of the brain.
- *Epidural hematoma* is a blood clot that forms between the skull and the outer covering of the brain. It may originate either in an artery or vein, possibly due to a low-height fall in young children, and may be associated with few symptoms at first, but secondary swelling may result in symptoms of headache, vomiting, unilateral weakness, and confusion, requiring immediate attention.
- *Acute subdural hematoma* is a blood clot beneath the dura mater but above the surface of the brain. It often results from shearing forces rather than direct impact (as in epidural hematoma), making recovery similar to that for diffuse axonal injuries (see next item).
- *Diffuse axonal injury (DAI)* involves shearing of long fibers (white matter) in the cerebral cortex from violent rotation (often in motor vehicle accidents). It may be more severe in younger children, whose axons are only partially myelinated and more susceptible to injury.

Traumatic brain injuries disrupt a wide range of cognitive abilities, including problem solving and intellectual ability, as well as information-processing skills such as attention, working memory, and retrieval from long-term memory. Trauma may damage parts of the brain that control any other system, including motor or sensory systems. In the acute phase of brain injury, ***posttraumatic amnesia (PTA),*** or loss of recent and long-term memory, is common. A period of initial ***mutism*** (inability to speak) also is common in children. The end of PTA is marked by consistent orientation to place, date, and time and the ability to store long-term memories (Rosen & Gerring, 1986).

Brain damage in TBI is diffuse and often bilateral. It can cause acquired symptoms of aphasia (Lees, 2005), as well as motor, cognitive, and sensory deficits and possible seizure disorder. Language and literacy difficulties following head injury are common but not completely predictable. Levin and Eisenberg (1979) found that 31 percent of 64 children with CHI continued to demonstrate language deficits six months after the injury, with primary symptoms of ***dysnomia*** (i.e., naming difficulties) (13 percent of the sample) and impaired auditory comprehension (11 percent of the sample). Ewing-Cobbs, Fletcher, and Levin (1985) followed children and adolescents diagnosed with ***moderate to severe head injury,*** defined as coma that persisted for at least 15 minutes; brain damage was confirmed via computerized tomography (CT) scans, and neurological deficit was confirmed via medical examination. The language difficulties that remained after PTA included problems with confrontation naming, object description, verbal fluency, and writing to dictation. Older children also fared better than younger ones, suggesting that recovery of preonset functions may be easier than learning new skills after brain injury. ***Severe head injury*** is diagnosed when children or adolescents experience PTA for more than three weeks, placing them at greater risk for reading and other academic difficulties that may require placement in special classrooms (Chadwick, Rutter, Brown, Shaffer, & Traub, 1981).

Children and adolescents with TBI often have difficulty with social–emotional judgment, as well as difficulty with attention, memory, and learning, well into the recovery process. Such issues may have a significant impact on functioning when students with TBI return to school after a period of recovery in acute care and rehabilitation settings. Lees (2005) noted that the prognosis for recovery from TBI could be poor when initial language loss is severe and persists for more than six months and that acquisition of written language can be impaired when TBI occurs in young children.

Acquired Brain Injury

Diagnosis of *acquired brain injury (ABI)* is based on known etiology. Any sudden onset or ***progressive*** (i.e., worsening over time) pattern of childhood language disorder or cognitive–communicative symptoms justifies immediate medical referral. There is no time to wait and see. With early medical intervention, secondary prevention may limit the degree of impairment a child experiences, in addition to saving his or her life.

Encephalopathy (i.e., pathology of the brain) is the term used to describe a brain injured by disease or the late effects of treatment for a disease such as cancer. Infectious diseases, such as meningitis and encephalitis, can result in widespread brain damage, possibly resulting in sensory and motor system deficits as well as cognitive ones. Other systemic causes of ABI are accidents (e.g., smoke inhalation or drowning incidents) and any other causes of ***anoxia*** (i.e., deprivation of oxygen to the brain), with a wide range of effects on cognitive–communicative and motor functions.

Disease processes associated with ABI can be classified into three groups (Lees, 2005):

- ***Unilateral cerebrovascular lesions*** usually are focal, may involve visual field defects, and are associated with good prognosis for language recovery.

- *Cerebral infections* (e.g., meningitis and encephalitis) involve lesions that may be focal or diffuse; when purely cortical (i.e., confined to the outer layers of the brain), infections cause relatively moderate impairments.
- *Cerebral tumors* usually have focal effects but may influence wider aspects of cerebral function if tumors are extensive or if treatment with radiotherapy or chemotherapy results in late effects of damage to the brain.

Children with congenital heart conditions may be at particular risk for a *cerebrovascular accident* (*CVA,* commonly called a *stroke*), which generally causes focal (confined), unilateral lesions. Occlusive **embolisms** are blood clots that travel from blood vessels near the heart to arteries on one side of the brain, where they lodge and cut off the supply of blood (and oxygen) to the brain. CVA also may result from hemorrhage of an **arteriovenous malformation (AVM),** which is congenitally tangled configuration of arteries and veins. Hemorrhagic CVA tends to damage more brain tissue than occlusive stroke and can be life threatening, particularly if it affects the brainstem, which is associated with the vital autonomic functions of breathing and blood circulation.

Infection is more likely to cause diffuse damage than unilateral focal lesions associated with CVA. Infectious diseases can cause brain injury and functional limitations that range from mild to profound, depending on the etiology and response to treatment for the infection.

Tumors of the brain affect brain functioning directly by destroying or displacing tissue. Life-saving treatment for tumors and other forms of cancer, such as leukemia, also can cause ABI as an indirect effect. A standard treatment protocol for acute lymphocytic leukemia (ALL) is a combination of brain irradiation and chemotherapy. Brain irradiation can result in neuropsychological late effects on white-matter pathways, which may or may not show up on initial magnetic resonance imaging (MRI) (Kramer, Norman, Grant-Zawadzki, Albin, & Moore, 1988), with encephalopathy resulting in intelligence deficits and other neuropsychological deficits within months or years following cranial irradiation and chemotherapy (Hutter, 1986; McCalla, 1985). Children receiving irradiation before 5 years of age are more likely to experience cognitive difficulty, whereas children treated with chemotherapy alone show no global or specific neuropsychological impairment (Copeland et al., 1985). The dual treatment protocol does improve survival rates, however, with no significant evidence of increased late effects, so it remains the recommended treatment (Waber et al., 2004).

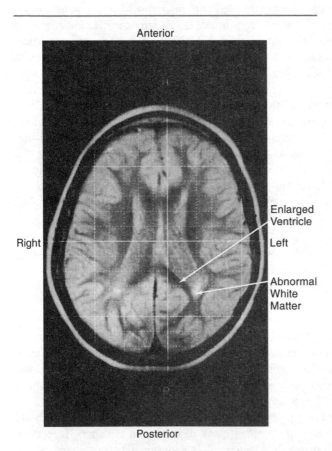

figure *7.1*

Magnetic Resonance Image (MRI) of the Brain of an 8-Year-Old Child

This child had undergone irradiation and chemotherapy (spinal column injection of methotrexate) from the age of 3 to about 5 years. The MRI shows reduced white matter (connecting areas of the brain) and enlarged cerebral ventricles (i.e., intracerebral spaces, suggesting shrinkage of brain tissues).

Nevertheless, some children do experience negative outcomes. Figure 7.1 shows an MRI scan with marked effects on the brain of an 8-year-old child who had marked neuro-psychological late effects after a combination of irradiation and chemotherapy (often spinal column injection of methotrexate) from age 3 to about 5 years to treat ALL. This scan shows enlarged **sulci** (*sulcus* is the term for a crease in cortical tissue) and **ventricles** (i.e., spaces within the hemispheres that are filled with cerebrospinal fluid), indicating shrinkage of healthy brain tissue, similar to what might be seen in an elderly adult with dementia. Language and related concerns for this child are discussed in Case Example 7.2.

CASE **example** 7.2

Sarah and Bravery in Meeting Cognitive–Linguistic Challenges after Leukemia

Sarah was 8 years old when her parents brought her to the university clinic for evaluation. Sarah's parents and school district were struggling to find the most appropriate placement for her. Her parents shared their story of how their wonderful baby had developed into a toddler who was advanced in all areas, particularly motor skills and language. Then, there came the awful day when they learned that Sarah had acute lymphocytic leukemia. Although dual treatments of brain irradiation and chemotherapy saved Sarah's life, she was left with significant cognitive–communicative functional limitations.

Children with developmental cognitive impairments typically exhibit better receptive than expressive language skills. Sarah's pattern of acquired disability was just the opposite. She had developed significant language abilities before the acquired brain injury, and she was able to draw on that knowledge but only sporadically. Her information-processing abilities were severely affected. Her hearing was normal, and in fact, she could perceive surface sound patterns well enough to imitate them, but she could not understand the message. Thus, when asked a direct question, she either failed to respond or responded with a perseverative response (e.g., repeatedly mentioning a hole in her tights) or *echolalic* remark (i.e., repeating the question without meaning). Sarah's lack of responsiveness, accompanied by relatively better verbal expression, made it appear that she was refusing to comply with requests rather than not understanding them. She also showed strengths of verbal expression when she could initiate and control the topic. Sarah liked to participate with peers in play, but the possibility of seizures, along with balance problems, made physical play a safety risk.

Diagnostic therapy showed that Sarah could respond better when requests were framed as comments followed by pauses, giving her the opportunity to respond but without obligation. Picture storybooks were used as primary therapy material. Sarah particularly liked a book about a bunny family. The clinician would read a page and then say, as if thinking aloud, "I wonder what those bunnies are going to do next." Sarah would fill in appropriately a prediction of events on the next page. Gradually, Sarah was able to engage in other topic-related turn-taking exchanges. Her school district and parents decided to move her out of the self-contained special education classroom, where she had begun imitating symptoms exhibited by the other children in the room, and into an inclusive classroom setting, which better suited her needs. Sarah continued to struggle academically and socially, but she also continued to learn and expand her circle of friends.

As she moved through school, Sarah's parents shared their feelings about their experiences at multiple points on her modified developmental path. They expressed pride in their daughter's accomplishments but also provided insights into the recursive grieving process. They explained how they experienced a new sense of loss each time Sarah's classmates or younger sister reached a new developmental milestone—starting school, transitioning to middle school, going to the first prom. This family taught everyone at the university clinic much about parents' and children's bravery.

Children with focal unilateral brain lesions tend to recover quickly and have few long-term deficits in their spoken language abilities (Aram, 1988). This brings up questions of brain plasticity. When brain tissue dies but recovery occurs, which areas have assumed the functions of the damaged tissue? In the case of children with focal left hemisphere lesions, studies have found that brain plasticity is ***intrahemispheric*** (i.e., within the same hemisphere) rather than ***interhemispheric*** (i.e., across the two hemispheres). The evidence comes from neuroimaging techniques that have revealed injured brains to show approximately the same patterns of activation as uninjured brains. That is, they involve predominantly left hemisphere engagement during language tasks and predominantly right hemisphere engagement during visuospatial tasks (Papanicolaou, DiScenna, Gillespie, & Aram, 1990).

In spite of good recovery of basic language abilities, many children with right or left hemisphere brain injuries experience residual effects on attention, impulse inhibition, memory, reasoning, and speech perception (Aram & Ekelman, 1988). Related academic effects include mild to severe difficulties learning to read and write, particularly when language and memory problems are present and when only limited reading and writing abilities have been developed prior to onset (Aram, Ekelman, & Gillespie, 1989).

Acquired Seizure Disorders, Including Landau-Kleffner Syndrome

Two forms of acquired seizure disorder are associated with language difficulties that Lees (2005) termed *acquired childhood aphasia:*

- ***Epileptic aphasia*** may occur as a result of repeated convulsions, either as a postictal (i.e., postseizure) disorder or a feature of minor epileptic status. In such cases, language involvement may be fleeting, but associated learning problems occur after long and repeated convulsive episodes.
- ***Landau-Kleffner syndrome (LKS)*** may be preceded or followed by epilepsy (although one-third of individuals never have epilepsy). The primary symptom is the inability to process phonetically encoded information receptively (auditory agnosia), although word-finding and expressive language problems also occur. Prognosis is poor when language comprehension deteriorates over a long period and shows little recovery during the first six months. The prognosis is better when the loss of language is acute and recovers in the first six months, and it is variable when seizures can be controlled by antiepileptic drugs but temporal lobe status fluctuates.

LKS is diagnosed when a child shows sudden onset of childhood aphasia characterized by loss of ability to comprehend spoken language, often with ***idiopathic epilepsy*** (i.e., from unknown causes). LKS usually is diagnosed in young children (ages 3 to 7 years) who previously were developing normally. The syndrome was first described in 1957 by William M. Landau (a neurologist) and Frank R. Kleffner (a speech–language pathologist), who described six cases of children with the disorder at the Central Institute for the Deaf in St. Louis. LKS is rare; from 1957 to 1990, only 160 cases were reported in the literature (NIDCD, 2007). Intelligence usually is spared, as is speech production, but the inability to understand speech eventually affects the reciprocal ability to produce speech. Older children, who have acquired more speech prior to onset, have a better prognosis (Bishop, 1985).

Campos and de Guevara (2007) reviewed evidence that showed that over 75 percent of cases of LKS appeared before age 7 but there were some reports of onset as early as 18 months and as late as 13 years of age. They summarized research indicating that seizures do not necessarily appear at the onset of the disorder but are experienced by 70 percent of children with LKS at some time. Clinical diagnosis is made on the basis of an abnormal EEG, in which abnormalities are centered in the temporal lobes (Towbin et al., 2002). Deterioration of previously existing speech and language skills in young children may lead LKS to be confused with childhood disintegrative disorder. The receptive language difficulties in LKS, however, represent symptoms of ***auditory agnosia*** (a central hearing impairment), rather than general comprehension deficit. Although children can hear what is being said, they cannot process its phonological structure (e.g., they cannot repeat it) and hence cannot understand it. Children who previously learned to read and write may continue to demonstrate literacy skills (including comprehension) and may use written language to communicate. Sign language is also an option. It is the auditory modality that is impaired in people with LKS, not their language comprehension per se.

The course of the disorder and prognosis for recovery are uncertain. Seizures may cease in adolescence. Some children recover receptive language skills, but the prognosis is not predictable (NIDCD, 2007). Onset may be associated with behavioral or psychological problems, which are a natural response to sudden loss of access to communication, and interdisciplinary team approaches are required for addressing the whole child and family. When sudden and severe communication disorders arise, one of the most important early services that communication specialists can provide is to ensure that some form of communication support is available immediately. For example, picture boards, gestures, and simple signs, as well as reading and writing (if appropriate), may be used to reduce a child's frightening feelings of isolation and provide a way to express feelings.

SUMMARY

Acquired disorders include traumatic brain injury and other forms of acquired encephalopathy. TBI and ABI may be comorbid with preexisting developmental language or learning disorders and with attention-deficit/hyperactivity disorder. They can involve damage to areas of the brain that result in motor speech impairment but not predictably so. Children and adolescents with TBI and ABI may retain typical ability to speak clearly and to read well if they have already acquired those skills before the onset of the brain injury. Literacy development is particularly at risk if not acquired before the trauma or disease. Executive functions and self-regulatory abilities are particularly at risk, as well, justifying comprehensive interdisciplinary treatment over an extended period of development.

Child Abuse and Neglect

Child abuse and neglect can damage a child's neurocognitive and psychological systems before birth (i.e., in the ***prenatal*** period), at any point after birth (i.e., in the ***perinatal*** and early ***postnatal*** periods), or into adolescence. The earlier, more protracted, and more severe the conditions of abuse or neglect, the greater the impact on a child's developing neuropsychological system. Even a single severe shaking by a temporary caregiver can lead to acquired brain injury that is life threatening and results in severe disabilities. Michaud and colleagues (2002) noted that ***inflicted head injury*** is the leading cause of traumatic death in infancy and accounts for almost 20 percent of hospital admissions for head injury in children younger than 7 years and for 33 percent of admissions in children younger than 3 years.

Hyter (2007b) defined *complex trauma* as "exposure to domestic violence or maltreatment—defined as neglect—as well as physical, sexual, and psychological or emotional abuse" (p. 93). In this section, *fetal alcohol spectrum disorder (FASD)* is described first, followed by complex trauma related to abuse and neglect and *failure-to-thrive syndrome,* which can be associated with more than one risk factor, including physiological problems that have nothing to do with maltreatment. It is common for one form of trauma to be associated with another. A pattern of neglect in which an infant or toddler's need for attachment and nurturing is not met can lead to changes in brain development (Perry, 1997). Failure-to-thrive often occurs among infants who are neglected. Children affected by prenatal alcohol exposure have two to three times more risk for later physical abuse than children without FASD (Hyter, 2007b). The dual effects of fetal alcohol exposure and subsequent maltreatment can exacerbate lifelong social and emotional challenges in forming relationships and managing self-regulation of emotions and behaviors (Henry, Sloane, & Black-Pond, 2007).

Many environmental factors confound language outcomes for children affected by child abuse and neglect (Fox, Long, & Langlois, 1988; McCauley & Swisher, 1987; Sparks, 1989a, 1989b). Confounding variables include socioeconomic status, parents with general cognitive delay, predisposition to difficulty related to prematurity or poor prenatal care, tendencies for children at risk for communication problems to be more difficult to care for initially, and lack of clarity in identifying varying degrees of abuse and neglect as separate or co-occurring conditions. Teen pregnancy also can be a risk factor (Osofsky, 1990).

Fetal Alcohol Spectrum Disorder

Fetal alcohol spectrum disorder (FASD) is an umbrella term for a preventable form of developmental disorder in which babies are born addicted to a substance consumed by their mothers during pregnancy. Maternal consumption of alcohol has by far the most devastating effects, even compared to powerful illegal drugs such as cocaine (see Table 7.1). The risk is

table *7.1* Risks for Language and Learning Difficulties among Children Whose Mothers Used Alcohol or Cocaine While Pregnant

Risks from Fetal Alcohol Exposure	Risks from Fetal Cocaine Exposure
Standardized receptive language scales may show low scores.	Irritable and stiff as newborns.
Marked discrepancy may be observed between high verbal skills accompanied by inability to communicate effectively.	More difficulty with verbal and nonverbal reasoning than nonexposed children during childhood.
Poor judgment and common sense include difficulty predicting the consequences of one's behavior.	Self-regulation difficulty, distractibility, increased activity, and difficulty with sound discrimination during childhood.
Academic achievement and adaptive skills are lower than expected based on intelligence and achievement test scores.	Most children exposed prenatally are unaffected.
Overlapping symptoms with ADHD (attention deficits) and ODD (oppositional defiant disorder) include frequent loss of temper and control.	Affected children do not appear to have mental retardation or learning disabilities.
Symptoms remain throughout life.	Early intervention tends to be effective.

Source: Based on Sparks, 1993.

particularly high when a mother's drinking is excessive and occurs in the first trimester of pregnancy, when a mother may not be aware she is pregnant. During the mid-1990s, it was estimated that 10 percent of pregnant women abused alcohol, 20 percent smoked cigarettes, 10 percent used marijuana, 1 percent used cocaine, and 0.5 percent used opiates such as heroin (Wunsch, Conlon, & Scheidt, 2002). Streissguth (1997) described alcohol as the most frequently ingested *teratogen* (i.e., chemical agent that alters the development of the fetus).

FASD is not a clinical diagnosis but a descriptive term that covers a spectrum of disorders with a range of symptoms. The Substance Abuse and Mental Health Services Administration (SAMHSA, 2007) reported that as many as 40,000 babies born each year have some form of FASD. Fully expressed *fetal alcohol syndrome (FAS)* includes a pattern of physical, developmental, and functional problems, with a prevalence estimated between 0.5 and 2 per 1,000 births. The term *fetal alcohol effect (FAE)* applies when the syndrome involves some of the behavioral characteristics of the disorder but not the full set of physical symptoms. Newer diagnostic terms for FAS without the full facial phenotype are *alcohol-related neurodevelopmental disorder (ARND),* which refers to effects on the central and peripheral nervous systems, and *alcohol-related birth defect (ARBD),* which refers to effects on the skeletal system and organs (SAMHSA, 2007). In some cases, children exhibit only the behavioral and emotional problems of FASD without signs of developmental delay or physical growth deficiency (Chamberlin & Narins, 2005). When cases of ARND or ARBD are combined with cases of FAS, the prevalence rate rises to 10 per 1,000 births, or 1 percent (SAMHSA, 2007).

Diagnosis of full FAS generally involves four diagnostic criteria: (1) evidence that the mother drank excessively or engaged in binge drinking during gestation; (2) growth retardation (less than the tenth percentile) for weight, height, or head circumference; (3) facial characteristics of absent or indistinct philtrum, thin upper lip, and small space between palpebral fissures (eye openings) (see illustration in Figure 7.2); and (4) evidence of damage to the central nervous system (e.g., in the form of developmental delay, ID/MR, seizures, poor coordination and fine motor skills, or behavioral problems). The diagnosis of FASD requires input of a collaborative, interdisciplinary team, including social service providers as well as health care professionals, special educators, and speech–language pathologists (Rogers-Adkinson & Stuart, 2007).

Many FASD symptoms are related to other forms of developmental delay, complicating the diagnosis. Cognitive–communicative difficulties include poor socialization skills and difficulty building and maintaining friendships. Cases of FASD and ARND are said to account for 10 percent to 20 percent of the cases of mild mental retardation (Wunsch et al., 2002). Even children with FASD who have IQs in the average range lack imagination or curiosity in their play and show learning difficulties, including poor memory and difficulty with concepts of time and money. Executive function difficulties often interfere with thoughtful planning and self-reflection, as well as performance on perspective taking and theory of mind (ToM) tasks (Timler, Olswang, & Coggins, 2005). Children with FASD are more likely to have difficulty modulating sensory input (tactile, kinesthetic, taste, smell, audition, and vision) (Atchison, 2007). Behavioral problems are common, including hyperactivity, inability to concentrate, social withdrawal, stubbornness, impulsiveness, anxiety, and oppositional defiant disorder (Henry et al., 2007).

Adolescents with FASD may show triple effects involving inherited psychological tendencies, attention difficulties, and higher risk for substance abuse themselves. Gelo and O'Malley (2003) described risk for a later triple diagnosis of developmental disability, psychiatric disorder, and addictive disorder. Adolescents may show personality change caused by a mixture of genetic predisposition and prenatal alcohol exposure, with a mixture of affective instability, intermittent explosive disorder, and substance abuse.

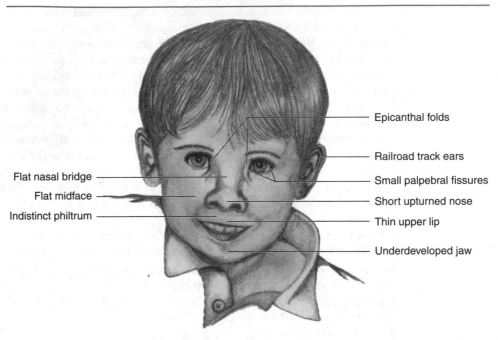

Epicanthal folds

Railroad track ears

Flat nasal bridge

Small palpebral fissures

Flat midface

Short upturned nose

Indistinct philtrum

Thin upper lip

Underdeveloped jaw

figure 7.2

The Facial Features of a Child with Fetal Alcohol Spectrum Disorder

The features of FASD include an absent or indistinct philtrum (i.e., creases from the upper lip to the nose), a thin upper lip, and a small space between the palpebral fissures (i.e., small eye openings).

Abuse and Neglect

Definitions of child abuse and neglect depend on whether they have been written for legal, medical, or social purposes. Sparks (1989a) summarized five types of abuse and neglect:

1. *Physical abuse* includes (a) shaking, beating, or burning resulting in bodily injury or death; and (b) physical acts that result in lasting or permanent neurological damage.
2. *Sexual abuse* includes (a) nonphysical forms of indecent exposure or verbal attack of a sexual nature; and (b) physical forms, including genital–oral stimulation, fondling, and sexual intercourse.
3. *Emotional abuse* includes (a) excessive yelling, belittling, teasing, which are considered forms of verbal attack, and (b) overt rejection of the child.
4. *Physical neglect* includes (a) abandonment with no arrangement made for care; (b) inadequate supervision for long periods, as well as disregard for potential hazards in the home; (c) failure to provide adequate nutrition, clothing, or personal hygiene; and (d) failure to seek needed or recommended medical care.
5. *Emotional neglect* includes (a) failure to provide warmth, attention, affection, normal living experience; and (b) refusal of treatment or services recommended by social or educational personnel. (p. 124)

The Administration on Children, Youth, and Families (ACYF, 2006) reported incidence statistics for 2005 in slightly different but related categories: physical or emotional neglect (62.8 percent), physical abuse (16.6 percent), sexual abuse (9.3 percent), psychological or emotional abuse (7.1 percent), and medical neglect (2 percent). By race/ethnicity, proportions of children maltreated were reported in the following categories: White (non-Hispanic) (50 percent); Black (non-Hispanic) (23 percent); Hispanic (9 percent); American Indian/Alaskan native (1 percent); Asian (1 percent); Pacific Islander (0 percent); multiple race (2 percent). In the total group, 47 percent abused or neglected children were male and 51 percent were female (with a few unknown). The report showed that a total of 899,454 children (12 per 1,000) in the United States were known victims of maltreatment in 2005, and 1,460 children died of abuse or neglect that year.

Failure-to-Thrive Syndrome

Failure-to-thrive (FTT) is diagnosed when a young child falls below the third percentile on growth charts. It is associated with a variety of underlying causes, including chronic disease or congenital anomaly (Batshaw, 2002), but it also may be a sign of child maltreatment. Wunsch and colleagues (2002) noted that approximately 70 percent of children with FAS have severe feeding problems that lead to FTT.

When laboratory and physical examination reveal no organic explanations for the child's FTT, emotional neglect may be suspected. Symptoms suggestive of physical or emotional neglect include weight below the third percentile with subsequent weight gain when normal nurturing is introduced, no evidence from physical examination or laboratory results that can explain growth failure, and significant psychosocial disruption in the child's environment (Barbero, 1982).

Language and Literacy Problems Associated with Child Maltreatment

Social communication difficulties are the most predictable feature of communication disorder associated with FASD (Timler et al., 2005) and other forms of abuse and neglect. Such difficulties are intertwined with lower-level cognitive–communicative difficulties of attention and memory, as well as with higher-order executive function problems with planning and self-reflection. Cause–effect and attempt–consequence components, key features of narratives and conversation, present particular difficulties for students with FASD. One hypothesis is that difficulties result directly from structural linguistic deficits that make it difficult to comprehend cause and effect and the consequences of one's actions (Thorne, Coggins, Olson, & Astley, 2007; Timler et al., 2005).

Another dominant feature is the apparent lack of ability to take the perspective of a conversational partner. This cognitive–social interaction hypothesis offers an alternate explanation to the linguistic hypothesis (Timler et al., 2005). As discussed in Chapter 2, a requirement for effective pragmatic communication is the ability to judge how much and what kind of information to convey in social interactions. This judgment is based, in turn, on assumptions about what communication partners already know. Such a hypothesis points to a potential deficiency in the children's development of theory of mind (ToM). Effective narration requires semantic elaboration and unambiguous referencing, keeping in mind the needs of communicative partners. Both ToM and ability to represent the "landscape of consciousness" in narration are difficult for children with FASD and may even constitute a diagnostic marker (Thorne et al., 2007).

An additional hypothesis is that children with risks from FASD and other forms of maltreatment lack the concepts and vocabulary of emotional and mental states. Such a disorder is called **alexithymia** (literally, absence of words for emotions), which involves "difficulty identifying, understanding, and expressing feelings" (Way, Yelsma, Van Meter, & Black-Pond, 2007, p. 128). Integration across systems is required for children to link emotions to the vocabulary of feelings. Children with well-integrated systems are better able to understand verbal and nonverbal cues to the feelings of others so they can respond appropriately and map vocabulary onto those experiences.

The research literature offers few specifics about literacy development among children affected by FASD and other forms of maltreatment. Cognitive limitations can be expected to present barriers to academic achievement and understanding higher-level abstract concepts. On top of direct problems affecting language and social pragmatics, limited self-awareness may interfere with students' metacognitive abilities and distort perceptions in the academic arena as well as social interactions. Duquette, Stodel, Fullarton, and Hagglund (2006) used a case study method to document the difficulties of a group of eight high school students with FASD. They found that although the students did not meet the usual academic standards and had acquaintances rather than friends, they perceived themselves to be academically and socially successful. The researchers concluded that the students were able to persist in high school despite academic limitations largely because of strong support provided by adoptive parents.

Preventing Future Cases

Child abuse and neglect occur when parents make horrible choices, sometimes traceable to bad choices made by their parents in a self-perpetuating cycle of maladaptive interactions (Fraiberg, Adelson, & Shapiro, 1987). It is a natural response for clinicians, teachers, social workers, and adoptive parents to feel outrage when encountering cognitive–linguistic, physical, emotional, and social challenges that are so substantial and ostensibly preventable. Breaking the cycle requires an intersystemic approach that applies social and educational resources to the root problems. Legal, health care, educational, and rehabilitation professionals can collaborate at multiple levels of prevention.

Many cases of abuse and neglect, both before and after birth, are associated with parental addiction. Addiction is a form of disease, with biological cravings causing all other concerns, including the care and safety of a child, to seem less important (Wunsch et al., 2002). Addiction treatment programs are forms of primary prevention. Social programs aimed at helping families gain access to essential resources and avoid hopelessness also serve primary prevention roles. Secondary and tertiary prevention programs can be aimed at reducing children's functional cognitive–communicative limitations, making it possible for them to participate effectively in age-appropriate social and academic contexts.

SUMMARY

In this section, fetal alcohol spectrum disorders and other forms of neurodevelopmental difficulty secondary to maltreatment (various forms of abuse and neglect) were described. Confounding factors (both internal and external) were noted. Disorders that result from the influence of complex trauma involve functional limitations in social interaction, self-regulation, and executive control. Cognitive–communicative difficulties involving social perception and executive functioning require comprehensive interdisciplinary treatment over an extended period of development.

Interactive Disorders of Attention, Emotion, and Behavior

Attentional, emotional, and behavioral disorders defined in the *DSM-IV-TR* (APA, 2000) are classified in IDEA '04 as *emotional disorder* or *other health impairment*. Interactive disorders may co-occur with languages and literacy-learning difficulties, particularly in the domains of social communication and pragmatics. All involve unusual or impaired patterns of communication between children and their caregivers, teachers, and peers. Interactive disorders also may involve impairment of intrapersonal messages serving self-regulatory and executive functions. Diagnoses of disorders affecting interaction and self-regulation require interdisciplinary contributions of clinical psychologists, social workers, and other mental health professionals, including psychiatrists. SLPs often serve as members of interdisciplinary teams, particularly regarding differential diagnosis related to the possible presence of language impairment as a causal or comorbid factor.

Attention-Deficit Disorders

Attention-deficit/hyperactivity disorder (ADHD) is a neurobehavioral syndrome that begins in early childhood (prior to age 7). No medical or psychological tests are currently available to make the diagnosis (Stein, Efron, Schiff, & Glanzman, 2002). Rather, ADHD is diagnosed based on observation, usually documented with checklists completed by multiple observers in multiple situations. The key diagnostic feature for ADHD is a persistent (i.e., more than six months) pattern of inattention and/or hyperactivity and impulsivity that is unusual (i.e., more frequent or severe) compared to other children at the same developmental level. The familial nature of ADHD suggests a genetic cause. Disorders of attention occur at higher rates in families with mood and anxiety disorders, learning disorders, substance-related disorders, and antisocial personality disorder (APA, 2000).

ADHD may be both under- and overdiagnosed, because the diagnostic process involves a degree of subjectivity and cultural differences exist in expectations for children's behavior. Stein and colleagues (2002) reported that cross-cultural worldwide prevalence rates continue to rise. Estimates based on application of the *DSM-IV-TR* criteria (APA, 2000) indicate an increase in prevalence rates from 2 percent to 9 percent. Stein and colleagues considered a number of possible reasons, including changes in diagnostic criteria and awareness of the disorder, as well as a possible true increase in prevalence.

ADHD has been called by different names and associated with a wide variety of syndromes. In the 1980 edition of the *DSM-III* (APA, 1980), the term *attention-deficit disorder with hyperactivity* replaced former terms of *hyperkinesis* and *minimal brain dysfunction.* With the introduction of the *DSM-IV* (APA, 1994), *attention deficit* was grouped with other forms of *disruptive behavior disorder,* which included conduct disorder and oppositional defiant disorder.

Using the criteria of the *DSM-IV-TR* (APA, 2000), diagnosis of ADHD is made based on problems in two categories—attention and hyperactivity–impulsivity. These data then help determine whether the condition is the predominantly *inattentive,* predominantly *hyperactive–impulsive,* or *combined* type of ADHD. A diagnosis of *ADHD, not otherwise specified,* may be made if diagnostic criteria are only partially met. A subtype is diagnosed if the child's profile for the past six months fits one set of criteria but not the other; a diagnosis of combined type is made if both sets of criteria have been met for the past six months. Additional requirements are clear evidence of clinically significant impairment in social, academic, or occupational function; indication that at least some of the symptoms were present before age 7; and indications of difficulty in two or more settings (e.g., school, work, play, home). The predominantly inattentive type has approximately equal distribution across genders; whereas the predominantly hyperactive–impulsive and combined types are more prevalent among boys, with estimates of the male-to-female ratio ranging from 9:1 to 3:1 (Stein et al., 2002).

The *predominantly inattentive* type of ADHD is diagnosed based on problems in six of nine areas: (1) close attention to details to avoid careless mistakes; (2) sustaining attention; (3) listening when spoken to directly; (4) following through on instructions and completing tasks; (5) organizing tasks and activities; (6) attempting tasks that require sustained mental effort; (7) keeping track of materials necessary for tasks and activities; (8) resisting distraction by extraneous stimuli; and (9) remembering what needs to be done in daily activities (APA, 2000).

The predominantly ***hyperactive–impulsive*** type of ADHD is diagnosed based on problems in six out of nine areas. Symptoms of ***hyperactivity*** are (1) fidgeting or squirming; (2) leaving one's seat when sitting is expected; (3) running or climbing when inappropriate; (4) difficulty playing quietly; (5) appearing "on the go" or "motor driven"; and (6) talking excessively. Symptoms of ***impulsivity*** are (1) blurting out answers before questions have been completed; (2) difficulty waiting for a turn; and (3) interrupting or intruding on others (APA, 2000).

Several neurobiological explanations have been hypothesized for ADHD. The frontal lobe, as the executive center of the brain, is implicated. The cerebellum and basal ganglia (corpus striatum and globus pallidus) also may be implicated because of their role in motor planning, behavioral inhibition, and motivation. Other explanations focus on neurotransmitters that facilitate connections across brain centers. Stein and colleagues (2002) noted that a currently plausible "working hypothesis is that ADHD is characterized by hypoactive frontal-striatal-cerebellar pathways that are functionally enhanced by increasing dopaminergic transmission with stimulant medication" (p. 394). Pharmacological treatment with stimulant medications is based on this hypothesis.

ADHD often occurs comorbidly with learning disabilities and academic problems. No pattern of linguistic deficits is specific to the syndrome, but children with language impairment are at increased risk for ADHD (Cantwell, Baker, & Mattison, 1979). Disorders of reading and writing also are more likely to be diagnosed among children with ADHD (Rutter, Tizard, & Whitmore, 1970). Snowling, Bishop, Stothard, Chipchase, and Kaplan (2006) followed a group of children with a preschool history of specific language impairment (SLI) to investigate whether they had a heightened risk of psychosocial difficulties and found that the general risk was relatively low but that varied early profiles were associated with different outcomes at ages 15 to 16 years. Children whose language delay had resolved by 5.5 years had a good outcome. Those whose language difficulties persisted beyond this point had heightened risk for attention and social skills deficits following three patterns: (1) students with attention deficits tended to have specific expressive language delay; (2) students with social difficulties tended to have both receptive and expressive difficulties; and (3) students with low IQ on top of attention and social skills difficulties tended to demonstrate global language difficulties.

Although ADHD is not a category of disability in IDEA '04, children with ADHD may qualify for special education services based on speech or language impairment, learning disability, emotional disturbance, or other health impairment. Children with ADHD may receive general education accommodations under a Section 504 plan, but they may need assessment for language and literacy disorders as well.

Emotional Disorders

Emotional disorders include elective mutism; anxiety disorders; mood dysregulation and bipolar patterns; prolonged grief reaction; depression; reactive attachment disorder; traumatic stress disorder; adjustment disorder; gender identity disorder; and sleep, eating, or elimination disorders (Greenspan & Wieder, 2006). A full description of psychiatric diagnosis and treatment is beyond the scope of this book.

The etiology of *serious emotional disturbance* (as it was called in earlier version of IDEA) may be psychogenic, possibly reflecting inadequate nurturing and other adverse early caregiving environments. Caution should be exercised, however, to avoid falling into an attitude of "blame the parents." This caution is meant for parents, as well as professionals, because conscientious parents tend to blame themselves and wonder if they could or should have done something to prevent their child's emotional distress (see Personal Reflection 7.3).

PERSONAL reflection 7.3

"You're not the cause, but you can be the solution."

Stanley Greenspan (1995, p. 1), a pediatric psychiatrist, used this chapter title in his book for parents on *The Challenging Child.*

Many difficulties are suspected to be due to biophysiological expressions of genetic differences that are not yet fully understood. When children's emotional systems are biologically predisposed to hyper- or hypoarousal or other unusual responses to the social–emotional cues from within or from others, the intersystemic circular causal patterns introduced in Chapter 3 are involved. Communicative difficulties (both interpersonal and intrapersonal) often accompany systems in turmoil. Complex conditions require comprehensive interdisciplinary assessment and intervention approaches involving parents, teachers, and health care professionals from psychiatry and psychology, as well as professionals from social work, special education, and speech–language pathology. The role of the SLP is to assess communication to identify primary disorders that may be triggering unusual or intense emotional responses so that interventions can target whole systems (both inside and outside the child) and help the child move in more functional directions.

This section focuses on two emotional disorders that involve communication directly—elective mutism and depression. Obsessive-compulsive disorder (OCD) and tic disorders, including Tourette's syndrome, are discussed briefly as well. Any disorder that involves emotional distress as a primary symptom carries a high risk of co-occurrence with any of the other cognitive–communicative challenges discussed in this chapter. Children with emotional disturbances or behavioral disorders (considered subsequently) can be particularly challenging to teach because their emotional needs make it difficult for them to learn and they demonstrate unusual responses to events and consequences.

Selective Mutism and Other Forms of Anxiety Disorder

A diagnosis of ***selective mutism*** (also called ***elective mutism***) (APA, 2000) requires documentation of adequate expressive and receptive language ability in at least some contexts, coupled with extended periods (i.e., for at least one month and not limited to the first month of school) of no talking in certain situations. Selective mutism is diagnosed based on consistent failure to speak in specific social situations that involve an expectation of speaking, such as school, despite speaking adequately in other situations (APA, 2000). SLPs play an important role by gathering information about the child's ability to use spoken language at an appropriate level in at least some selected contexts. This requires gaining access to other contexts either directly or through recorded communication samples gathered by parents.

Selective mutism occurs in less than 1 percent of children and more frequently in girls than boys. It may reflect a subjective state of overwhelming fear and vigilance (Attwood, 2007). It tends to co-occur with regulatory sensory-processing disorders and may reflect patterns of interaction in infancy that "do not optimally support the child's initiative and self-regulation" (Greenspan & Wieder, 2006, p. 157).

Theories of causation for mutism influence intervention choices. If mutism is perceived to be elective and hence a behavioral choice of the child, then interventions based on behaviorist principles (e.g., such as withholding privileges until a child speaks) may seem the most appropriate. Conversely, if mutism is perceived to be an emotional response to fear, then intervention approaches focus on developing nurturing, supportive, and confidence-building contexts, with the aim of increasing the child's comfort and ability to relax in the problematic situation (e.g., school). Alternative forms of expression (including reading and writing) can support verbal communication until the child feels ready to talk in the difficult situation. Still another possibility is that the mutism may be perceived to be a response to a physiological condition characterized by sensations of extreme anxiety, in which case a pharmacological treatment might be the primary intervention, supplemented by cognitive behavior therapy. See Case Example 7.3 for a discussion of how one interdisciplinary team pursued several of these options.

CASE example 7.3

Consuela and Attempts to Help Her Overcome Selective Mutism

Consuela was a kindergarten girl who had not yet spoken to her teacher or classmates in school more than halfway through the school year. The teacher's approach had been to give Consuela time to adjust, but this approach had not worked. Finally, Ms. K had referred Consuela to the multidisciplinary evaluation team. The speech–language consultant who had been called in for the assessment decided to use an indirect approach, visiting the school and casually approaching Consuela and other children waiting in the school lunchline. The SLP began interacting with the other children, making comments, and presenting opportunities for Consuela to respond nonverbally but not giving her direct attention or asking questions. It was not long, however, before Consuela's classmates volunteered, "She doesn't talk." The secret was out, and after that, there was no reason to avoid a more direct approach.

The multidisciplinary evaluation team decided that the next step must involve confirmation that Consuela actually could talk in other situations and that her mutism was selective to school and similar settings. Her parents audiorecorded a conversation at home, and she was observed interacting verbally with her sister on the playground. The diagnostic team concluded that criteria for a diagnosis of selective mutism were met and discussed what to do next.

The team began intervention with a behaviorist paradigm based on readings of the current literature and recommendations of the school psychologist. Expectations were established and privileges were withheld with the stipulation that Consuela must first utter a spoken request. That approach continued for a short while but with no effect. It was clearly the wrong approach. The apparent anxiety that prevented her from talking in school was stronger than any positive or negative reinforcement techniques the team tried. Besides, the intervention team worried about Consuela's low affect in school and the emotional impact the approach might be having. They decided to take a different approach that was motivated more by the cognitive–emotional and social interactionist perspectives. This approach would address Consuela's anxiety and fears by providing access to other forms of communication and offering several places where communication would seem safe.

The team made changes in the school environment to reduce the pressure on spoken communication, installing a portable bulletin board as a screen in a corner of the general education classroom where she could interact with the teacher and special service providers one-to-one during part of the day. Consuela grew increasingly verbal in this environment, starting by making nonverbal choices and responses using a simple communication board, then whispering, and later talking and reading softly to her teacher, who was able to observe that she was learning. It also was arranged for Consuela to have recess with her older sister, so they could talk on the playground.

The symptom of selective mutism (i.e., not talking) differentiates the disorder from other forms of anxiety disorder, such as ***separation anxiety disorder.*** Separation anxiety is diagnosed based on early onset (prior to 6 years) when a child experiences excessive anxiety about leaving home or people to whom he or she is attached. Symptoms may include social withdrawal, apathy, or sadness or unusually powerful fears about animals, monsters, plane travel, or other perceived situations (APA, 2000).

Selective mutism can appear in conjunction with other cognitive–communicative disorders. Fragile X syndrome, especially in females, can be associated with extreme forms of social anxiety and withdrawal. Selective mutism also has been described as a symptom of Asperger syndrome. Szatmari (1991) noted that, in some cases, overwhelming anxiety associated with Asperger syndrome can give rise to phobias about speaking in certain social situations or with selected people to such a degree that selective mutism results. Attwood (2007) described events that can elicit the feelings of anxiety, including unexpected changes in routine or anticipated change (e.g., a substitute teacher), public criticism or praise, or a sensory experience. He commented:

> Very sensitive sensory perception, especially for sounds, can cause the person with Asperger to worry about when the next painful sensory experience will occur. My sister-in-law has Asperger syndrome, and the sound of a dog barking is an excruciating experience for her. At times, this has caused her to be almost agoraphobic, fearing leaving her home as a journey to the local shops could include hearing a dog bark. (p. 136)

Depression in Childhood and Adolescence

Severe, ongoing depression is termed ***dysthymic disorder*** (also called ***dysthymia***) in the *DSM-IV-TR* (APA, 2000). The essential feature for diagnosis of dysthymia is a chronically depressed mood that appears for most of the day, essentially every day. *Chronicity* is defined as a period of two years in adults but only one year in children. Although women are two to three times more likely than men to be diagnosed with dysthymic disorder, it affects both sexes equally during childhood. Another difference in childhood forms of dysthymia is that the child's mood may appear more irritable than depressed. Other symptoms include difficulty sleeping or eating (under or over), low self-esteem, high self-criticism, poor concentration, pessimism, feelings of hopelessness, and difficulty making decisions. Difficulty with academic achievement and social interactions are common (APA, 2000).

One reason to raise concerns about childhood depression in this book on language and literacy disorders is that depression and other psychiatric disorders frequently co-occur with other forms of cognitive–communicative difficulty. They may occur with primary language and literacy disorders as well. Attwood (2007) described anxiety and depression as falling on a continuum and responding to the same medications and cognitive–behavioral therapy, but he differentiated the disorders based on messages people tell themselves. Anxiety is associated with worrying "What if *X* happens?" whereas depression leads to the assumption "The worst outcome is unavoidable" (p. 140).

Obsessive-Compulsive Disorder

Obsessive compulsive disorder (OCD) involves a compulsion to complete a routine that is excessive in terms of time (more than one hour per day) or its functional effects. Adults with the disorder tend to be aware that the obsessive-compulsive behavior is not normal (e.g., repeated hand washing or checking to see if the stove is turned off), but their anxiety about unforeseen negative consequences makes it difficult for them to control the behavior. Children are less likely to be aware that their OCD behaviors are unusual. In addition to being related to anxiety disorders, OCD has a high comorbidity with Tourette's disorder, with estimates ranging from 35 percent to 50 percent of co-occurrence and with 20 percent to 30 percent of people with OCD reporting current or past tics.

Tic Disorders, Including Tourette's Disorder

Several types of tic disorders are defined in the *DSM-IV-TR* (APA, 2000). A *tic* is a motor movement or vocalization that occurs many times per day in patterns that are sudden, stereotyped, rapid, and nonrhythmic (APA, 2000). Tic disorders may represent movement disorders rather than emotional ones, but they can have profound effects on social interactions, occupational opportunities, and other important areas of interactive functioning and self-esteem.

    Tourette's disorder is diagnosed based on the presence of vocal tics as well as motor tics that appear prior to 18 years of age (although not necessarily simultaneously) and last for at least one year, with no more than a three-month period free of tics. Vocal tics may be both nonverbal (e.g., sounds, sniffs, grunts, or coughs) and verbal (e.g., noncommunicative words or obscenities). The production of pejorative terms or obscenities as tics is known as *coprolalia.* Although coprolalia is a dramatic symptom and particularly well known, it actually occurs in less than 10 percent of cases of Tourette's disorder (APA, 2000).

Schizophrenia in Childhood

Schizophrenia is diagnosed based on psychotic symptoms of delusions and hallucinations and loosening of associations, in which spoken language may be so disorganized as to be called "word salad." Schizophrenia rarely emerges until the late teens to mid-30s, but early forms of schizophrenia and bipolar disorder have been noted in children, and it is an exclusionary factor for diagnosing other emotional disorders (APA, 2000).

Behavior Disorders

Children with *emotional disorders* are likely to communicate negative messages to themselves, but children with *behavioral disorders* tend to act out their unhappiness. Disruptive behavior disorders discussed in this section are termed *conduct disorder* and *oppositional defiant disorder* in the *DSM-IV-TR* (APA, 2000).

Conduct Disorder

Conduct disorder is diagnosed as either child onset or adolescent onset depending on whether it occurs before or after age 10. It requires observation of a repetitive and persistent pattern of behavior in which the rights of others or other major rules or age-appropriate societal norms are violated. The diagnostic behaviors fall into four areas: (1) aggressive conduct that threatens physical harm to people or animals (including bullying); (2) nonaggressive conduct that causes property damage; (3) deceitfulness or theft; and (4) serious violation of rules (APA, 2000).

    According to prevalence rates in the *DSM-IV-TR* (APA, 2000), conduct disorder is one of the most frequently diagnosed conditions in outpatient and inpatient mental health facilities. It occurs at rates as high as 6 percent to 16 percent among males under age 18 and as high as 2 percent to 9 percent among females. Males are more likely to have an early onset and to exhibit confrontational aggression and vandalism. Females are more likely to exhibit lying, truancy, substance abuse, and early sexual behavior. Twin and adoption studies suggest that the etiology has both genetic and environmental components. The first are indicated by such factors as a difficult infant temperament and a biological familial pattern. Environmental components may include parental rejection and neglect, overly harsh or inconsistent childrearing, frequent changes of caregivers, and institutionalization. Children and adolescents in this category have higher risks of substance abuse and antisocial behavior in adulthood (APA, 2000).

Diagnosis of conduct disorder is made by mental health professionals based on a pattern of behavior marked by clinically significant impairment in social, academic, or occupational functioning, usually in more than one type of setting (e.g., social, academic, work). Cultural factors are considered in making the diagnosis. That is, the diagnostician must determine that the conduct disorder reflects *inner dysfunction* rather than a rational response to living in a setting where aggressive behavior or stealing may serve a protective function. Such may be the case for children who have been adopted from a war-torn country or who are being raised in a severely impoverished, drug-infested, high-crime neighborhood.

One reason to include this diagnostic category in a book on language and literacy disorders is the indication that conduct disorder is associated frequently with problems of academic achievement, particularly in reading and other verbal skills, and language and literacy skills often are below the levels predicted by intelligence test scores (APA, 2000). Children and adolescents with behavior disorders also may have difficulty in perspective taking and understanding the intentions of others (ToM issues), low self-esteem (although perhaps masked by a tough exterior persona), and inadequate social communication skills to interact in a functional manner with peers and adults. Although children with conduct disorder convey problematic messages to others, they also need help to adjust the messages they convey to themselves. Suicide is a risk for children and adolescents with conduct disorder.

Oppositional Defiant Disorder

Oppositional defiant disorder (ODD) is diagnosed based on a recurrent pattern of negative, defiant, disobedient, and hostile behavior toward authority figures, which is unusual in its frequency and intensity and leads to significant impairment in social, academic, or occupational functioning. It must persist for at least six months and be characterized by at least four of the following seven behaviors: (1) losing temper; (2) actively refusing to comply with adults' requests and rules; (3) deliberately doing things that will annoy others; (4) blaming others; (5) being touchy or easily annoyed; (6) being angry and resentful; or (7) being spiteful or vindictive (APA, 2000).

ODD occurs in approximately 2 percent to 16 percent of children. It usually emerges before age 8 and not later than early adolescence. ODD occurs in a familial pattern in which cause–effect and nature–nurture issues are difficult to disentangle. On the nature side, it is more common among children who have at least one biological parent with depression, substance-related disorder, ADHD, conduct disorder, or oppositional defiant disorder. On the nurture side, it is more common among children who have been affected by neglectful, harsh, or inconsistent caregiving and by frequent changes in caregivers. Children with ODD have a high risk for comorbid ADHD, learning disorders, and communication disorders (APA, 2000).

SUMMARY

Disorders of attention, emotion, and behavior affect interactions in home, school, and social or work environments. The frequency with which language- and literacy-learning difficulties are experienced by these children means that comprehensive assessment should address those areas in addition to the symptoms of the primary disorder. Children with any of these impairments may have difficulty with both interpersonal and intrapersonal communication.

CHAPTER SUMMARY

A child's diagnosis should never obscure his or her identity as a person, with a personality, needs, and ideas that are unique to him or her as a human being. Using person-first language (e.g., *child* with Down syndrome; *person* with autism) is not just a matter of being politically correct; it signals recognition that children with disabilities are individuals. Their disorders may affect one or more of their developmental systems adversely, but their personalities and preferences can reflect many positive factors about them as well. Children's talents, likes, and dislikes are unique to them as individuals and reflect their membership in particular families and cultural–linguistic communities.

The need for language and literacy intervention is not always obvious when children can talk but have other major cognitive, emotional, or behavioral symptoms that seem primary to any communication and literacy-learning difficulties. Yet children who have any of the cognitive–communicative disorders discussed in this chapter are likely to need specialized or more intensive instruction to develop optimal language, literacy, and social communication skills.

As discussed throughout this chapter, cognitive–communicative disorders carry a high risk of impaired perspective taking. The ability to detect verbal and nonverbal signals of the inner states of others may be affected, so that others' intentions are misperceived or ignored. That makes it very difficult to make friends or to solicit social support for coping with any of life's demands. Understanding nonliteral and abstract meanings of language at the word, sentence, and discourse levels and grasping pragmatic conventions of language use are particularly vulnerable areas for children and adolescents in these diagnostic groups. In fact, children with the primary form of language impairment that has been labeled *semantic–pragmatic disorder* (Rapin, 1998) or *pragmatic language impairment (PLI)* (Bishop, 2000) may be difficult to distinguish from children with high-functioning autism or Asperger syndrome (Attwood, 2007). Additionally, children and adolescents with any of the cognitive–communicative disorders discussed in this chapter may have difficulty using verbal mediation skills to reason through theory of mind tasks or to perform executive functions associated with planful, goal-directed behavior.

Addressing the multiplicity of difficulties associated with cognitive–communicative impairments requires an interdisciplinary approach. Making an honest assessment of a child's strengths, as well as his or her impaired functions, is critical to knowing what to do next. That is a major theme of this book, along with the consistent reminder of a basic principle of contextualized system theory approaches: *Problems are not just within children—and neither are solutions.*

EXERCISES *and* STUDY QUESTIONS

1. Describe commonalities among the five groups of cognitive–communicative disorders discussed in this chapter.

2. What new insights have you gained from this chapter regarding the differences between sound/word and sentence/ discourse levels in acquiring abilities for reading decoding and comprehension?

3. Discuss what differential diagnosis suggests about relationships between general cognition and social cognition.

PART three

Assessment and Intervention

Infant and Toddler Policies and Practices

Infant and Toddler Intervention

Preschool Policies and Practices

Preschool Intervention

School-Age Policies and Practices

School-Age Intervention

Interventions for Special Populations

CHAPTER eight

Infant and Toddler Policies and Practices

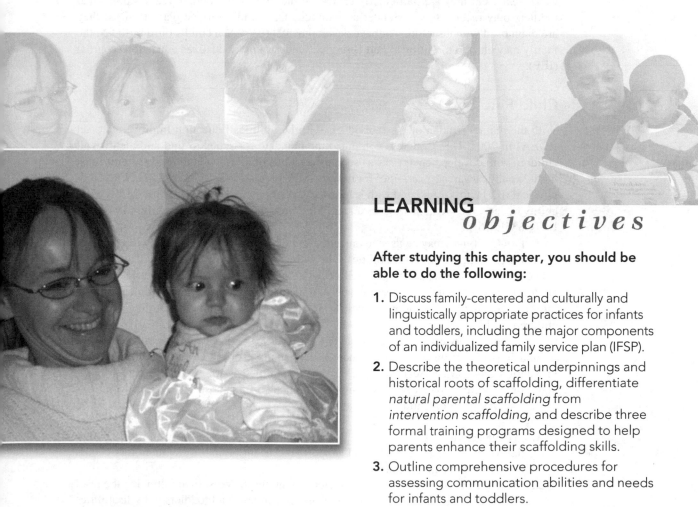

LEARNING *objectives*

After studying this chapter, you should be able to do the following:

1. Discuss family-centered and culturally and linguistically appropriate practices for infants and toddlers, including the major components of an individualized family service plan (IFSP).

2. Describe the theoretical underpinnings and historical roots of scaffolding, differentiate *natural parental scaffolding* from *intervention scaffolding,* and describe three formal training programs designed to help parents enhance their scaffolding skills.

3. Outline comprehensive procedures for assessing communication abilities and needs for infants and toddlers.

Chapter 8 introduces a developmentally appropriate template for organizing assessment and intervention for children in the prelinguistic and early stages of communication, language, and literacy functioning. Developmental expectations are outlined in Tables A and B in the Part III Appendix for children from birth to age 5 years across the five domains—cognition, receptive language, expressive language, social interaction and play, and literacy.

In planning intervention, chronological age appropriateness is important, along with a child's developmental level and contextualized needs. When achievement of prelinguistic and early symbolic functioning extend into the preschool and school-age years, early language targets must be addressed in a manner that is age and contextually appropriate. This chapter describes family-centered practices in natural environments for infants, toddlers, and older children up to the level of two-word utterances and outlines assessment procedures for children functioning at this level.

Policies and Practices for Infants and Toddlers

Child Find services are defined by IDEA '04 as extending across the age span from birth to 21 years, but they are particularly critical in the infant and toddler years. Infants and toddlers may receive services under an individualized family service plan (IFSP) if they are diagnosed with disabilities or have developmental risks. At a child's third birthday, the family may elect to transition to Part B services under an individualized education program (IEP).

Child Find Services

With the reauthorization of the Individuals with Disabilities Education Improvement Act (IDEA) in 2004, U.S. Congress continued the mandate for states to find and identify all children with developmental risks as soon as possible. Statewide Child Find systems must include public awareness activities for parents "with premature infants, or infants with other physical risk factors associated with learning or developmental complications, on the availability of early intervention services under Part C and of services under Section 619 of Part B" (§ 635[a][6]).

Part C services may be used to prevent disability as well as provide early intervention for children with identified disabilities. The introduction to Part C notes an "urgent and substantial need to enhance the capacity of state and local agencies and service providers to identify, evaluate, and meet the needs of all children." It also focuses on children in high-risk populations, including homeless or "minority, low-income, inner city, and rural children, and infants and toddlers in foster care" (§ 631[a][5]). Referral for early intervention assessment services is urgent whenever a child has experienced a "substantiated case of trauma due to exposure to family violence (as defined in Section 320 of the Family Violence Prevention and Services Act)" (§ 635[c][2]) or "is identified as affected by illegal substance abuse or withdrawal symptoms resulting from prenatal drug exposure" (§ 637[a][6]).

The five goals of Child Find are as follows:

1. to enhance the development of infants and toddlers with disabilities, minimize potential for developmental delay, and support significant brain development that occurs during a child's first 3 years of life
2. to reduce the educational costs to society, including schools, by minimizing the need for special education and related services after infants and toddlers with disabilities reach school age

3. to maximize the potential for individuals with disabilities to live independently in society
4. to enhance the capacity of families to meet the special needs of infants and toddlers with disabilities
5. to enhance the capacity of state and local agencies and service providers to identify, evaluate, and meet the needs of all children (paraphrased from § 631 of IDEA '04)

Part C of IDEA '04

Part C is the component of IDEA '04 that covers early intervention services for infants and toddlers from birth to 3 years. At age 3, under earlier forms of the law, children's services switched automatically for the remaining preschool years (from age 3 to 5 years) from Part C, which uses the IFSP process for providing early intervention services, to Part B, Section 619, which uses the IEP process for providing a free, appropriate public education (FAPE). The reauthorized IDEA '04 provided a new option to continue Part C services after a child's third birthday. Since 2005, parents have been able to opt to continue their young child's service delivery with an IFSP under Section 635(c)(1) of Part C rather than switch to IEP services for providing FAPE under Section 619 of Part B.

Eligibility for Part C Services, Including Risk for Disability

Part C services may be provided for any infant or toddler who has an identified disability or any infant or toddler who is at risk for disability. The term *infant or toddler with a disability* is defined in the law (§ 303.21) as "an individual under three years of age who needs early intervention services." Disability must be diagnosed with "appropriate diagnostic instruments and procedures" that show a developmental delay in

> one or more of the following areas: (i) Cognitive development; (ii) Physical development, including vision and hearing; (iii) Communication development; (iv) Social or emotional development; (v) Adaptive development. (§ 303.21)

Alternatively, a child may be eligible for Part C services who

> has a diagnosed physical or mental condition that—(i) Has a high probability of resulting in developmental delay; and (ii) Includes conditions such as chromosomal abnormalities; genetic or congenital disorders; severe sensory impairments; inborn errors of metabolism; disorders reflecting disturbance of the development of the nervous system; congenital infections; and disorders secondary to exposure to toxic substances, including fetal alcohol syndrome. (§ 303.21)

Infants and toddlers who have not been diagnosed with disability also may be eligible for Part C services because they are at risk for disability (according to IDEA '04, Section § 303.5), which states:

> At-risk infant or toddler means an individual under three years of age who would be at risk of experiencing a substantial developmental delay if early intervention services were not provided to the individual. At the State's discretion, at-risk infant or toddler may include an infant or toddler who is at risk of experiencing developmental delays because of biological and environmental factors that can be identified such as low birth weight, respiratory distress as a newborn, lack of oxygen, brain hemorrhage, infection, nutritional deprivation, and a history of abuse or neglect, being directly affected by illegal substance abuse or withdrawal symptoms resulting from prenatal drug exposure. (20 U.S.C. 1432[1] and 1437[a][6])

Risk factors during infancy often are differentiated into three categories:

1. *Established risk* occurs when an infant is born with an early identified condition (e.g., hearing impairment, identified through newborn infant hearing screening and follow-up testing; or Down syndrome, identified either prenatally or at birth) that is known to be associated with challenges to one or more domains of typical development.
2. *Environmental risk* occurs when the infant (who might otherwise be biologically sound) encounters life experiences (e.g., abuse or neglect) that place him or her at risk for developmental delay.
3. *Biological risk* occurs when a history or prenatal, perinatal, neonatal, or early post-natal events (e.g., low birthweight, prematurity, asphyxia, intracranial hemorrhage) suggests the possibility (as yet unconfirmed) that early insult to the child's central nervous system may contribute to developmental difficulty during childhood.

As discussed in Chapter 4, causal influences often are layered, interactive, and multi-factorial. Risk categories are not mutually exclusive; the same child may demonstrate more than one type of risk, or one risk factor may contribute to another. Established (e.g., hearing impairment) and environmental risk factors (e.g., maternal alcohol consumption) were discussed in Chapters 6 and 7. General biological risk factors related to prematurity and low birthweight are outlined in Table 8.1.

Predictions for later sensory–motor or cognitive development risks based on formal tests administered during infancy should be regarded with caution. Research has shown that assessment of cognition in infancy has only limited ability to predict later develop-

table *8.1* Biological Factors Associated with Risk for Developmental Difficulties

Risk Factor	Levels Associated with Risk (Incidence Data)	Potential Behavioral and Communication Difficulties
Prematurity	Premature: Born at less than 37 weeks gestation (7% to 8% of all newborns)	Risks from prematurity relate to birthweight and any additional risk factors (e.g., respiratory distress, metabolic disorder, intracranial hemorrhage).
	Very premature: Born at 24–28 weeks' gestation	Very premature infants may require a hospital stay of 3–4 months.
Birth weight	Low birthweight: less than 2500 g Very low birthweight: less than 1500 g Extremely low birthweight: less than 1,000 g or 750 g*	Survival rates for children with very low birthweight and extremely low birthweight have increased with technological advances, but risks of sensory–motor and intellectual deficits increase with smaller size at birth: • 1,500–2,499 g (6–8% sensory–motor deficits) • 1,000–1,499 g (14–17% sensory–motor deficits) • 750–999 g (20% sensory–motor deficits; 8–13% low IQ [70–84]) • less than 750 g (20% or more sensory–motor deficits; 20% low IQ)

*1,000 grams = 2 lb., 3 oz.; 750 g = 1 lb., 10 oz.

Source: Based on Aram, Hack, Hawkins, Weissman, & Borassi-Clark, 1991; Sparks, 1993.

mental outcomes. Some studies have shown that children with extremely low birthweight or preterm delivery do have risks for less optimal fine motor skills and lower cognitive abilities at 36 months (e.g., Lie, 1994). Others have shown that low birthweight does not predict cognitive development at age 5 years. In fact, Cohen and Parmelee (1983) found that infants' early visual attention and other social factors predicted later outcomes better than standardized measures of intelligence. Hack and colleagues (2005) also found that cognitive measures taken at 20 months, when accompanied by no signs of neurosensory impairment, tend to underestimate children's cognitive abilities at school age. The caution is to use assessment measures carefully and to bear in mind the discussions of Chapter 4 about prognosis and resilience and other protective factors when selecting formal assessment tools and interpreting their results, particularly for infants and toddlers.

Content of Individualized Family Service Plans (IFSPs)

The content of an IFSP outlined in Section 303.344 of Part C is paraphrased here. It establishes requirements for information in eight areas:

1. the child's status, including the child's present levels of physical development (vision, hearing, and health status), cognitive development, communication development, social or emotional development, and adaptive development
2. family information, including (with concurrence of the family) the family's resources, priorities, and concerns
3. measurable results or outcomes expected for the child (including preliteracy and language skills, as developmentally appropriate) and the family, criteria, procedures, and timelines used to determine progress and whether modifications are necessary
4. early intervention services, which are based on peer-reviewed research (to the extent practicable), to meet the unique needs of the child and the family and to achieve the results or outcomes identified, including length, duration (i.e., projecting when a given service will no longer be provided), frequency, intensity, and method of delivering the services (e.g., number of days or sessions; individual or group); natural environment setting (i.e., actual place) in which early intervention services will be provided, and justification for any service not to be provided in a natural environment (Once children reach 3 years of age, the IFSP must include an educational component that promotes school readiness and incorporates preliteracy, language, and numeracy skills.)
5. other services (as appropriate), including medical and other services that "the child or family needs or is receiving through other sources, but that are neither required nor funded under this part; and if not currently provided, a description of the steps the service coordinator may take to assist the child and family in securing those other services"
6. dates and duration, including the projected date for the initiation of each service (which should be "as soon as possible after the IFSP meeting"), and anticipated duration of each service
7. service coordinator, defined as a "person representing the profession most immediately relevant to the child's or family's needs," who is "qualified to be responsible for the implementation of the early intervention services," including transition services and coordination with other agencies and persons
8. transition from Part C services, including steps to support the transition of the child to preschool, early education, Head Start and Early Head Start, or child care programs (This area may include other appropriate services, such as preparation of the parents and child for changes in service delivery, transmission of Child Find information about the child to the local education agency or other relevant agency, and, with

parental consent, transmission of additional information to the appropriate agency to ensure continuity of services, including evaluation and assessment information and copies of students' IFSPs.)

The types of services provided to families of children at risk for disabilities must be individualized to the needs of each child and family. The requirement to conduct "assessment of the family under § 303.320(c)" could be easily misconstrued. It refers to planning *with* the family, not *about* the family. Figure 8.1 provides an example of the main components of an IFSP developed with familial input.

A variety of services are listed for potential coverage under IFSPs, including family training, counseling, and home visits; special instruction; speech–language pathology and audiology services and sign language and cued language services; occupational therapy; physical therapy; psychological services; service coordination services; medical services only for diagnostic or evaluation purposes; early identification, screening, and assessment services; health services necessary to enable the infant or toddler to benefit from the other early intervention services; social work services; vision services; assistive technology devices and services; and transportation and related costs to enable the infant's or toddler's family to receive "another service described" in the section. The law also specifies that IFSP services must be provided by qualified personnel, which includes special educators; speech–language pathologists and audiologists; occupational therapists; physical therapists; psychologists; social workers; nurses; registered dietitians; family therapists; vision specialists, including ophthalmologists and optometrists; orientation and mobility specialists; and pediatricians and other physicians.

A report by Data Analysis System (DANS) of the U.S. Department of Education, Office of Special Education Programs, based on data from the fall of 2004 (updated in 2006), showed the frequency of different forms of services that appeared on children's IFSPs across the U.S. and its territories (DANS, 2006). They included (from most to least frequently offered service) family training, counseling, and home visits (54,268); audiology (14,787); nursing services (9,292); assistive technology services and devices (8,907); health services (7,091); and medical services (6,354).

Transition from IFSP to IEP

At the child's third birthday, the parents may elect to have their child and family continue to receive services under an IFSP or transition to educational and related services through an IEP (under Section 619 of Part B). One key difference between an IFSP and an IEP is that an IFSP defines the service unit as the family, whereas an IEP defines the service unit as the child. Another is that the *periodic review* of the IFSP must be conducted every six months (or more frequently if the family requests a review or conditions warrant one), although actual revision of the IFSP is now required only once per year, as it is for an IEP. Requirements for IFSPs also indicate that intervention teams must ensure that services are provided in natural environments, which are defined as "settings that are natural or normal for an infant or toddler without a disability" (§ 303.26).

Family-Centered, Culturally Appropriate Services

Under Part C, family-centered services must be delivered in natural environments (unless justification is provided for modified environments). Family-centered practices include sensitivity to cultural–linguistic diversity in all its forms. Caregivers play a major role in establishing language- and literacy-learning contexts from birth to age 5, as do preschool

figure *8.1*

Example Showing Components of an Individualized Family Service Plan (IFSP)

Individualized Family Service Plan (IFSP)

Today's Date: 2-22-09   **Agency Initiating IFSP:** Public School

Child Information				
Child's Legal Name: Carlos Diaz		Nickname: Carlos	Date of Birth: 11-1-07	Sex: x M __ F
Address: 123 Main Street		Phone (home): 222-2222		Phone (daycare): 222-1111
Address: Hometown, USA		Medical Insurance No.: 123456789		

School District of Residence: Hometown Schools	County: Homestead	Ethnic Heritage: Mexican Amer. (3rd generation)	Native Language: Spanish and English

Name	Relationship to Child	Birth date (Optional)	Address	Phone (home)	Phone (cell)
Manuel Diaz	Father		Same as above	Same	222-1212
Carmen Diaz	Mother		Same as above	Same	222-1234
Maria Diaz	Sister		Same	Same	—

If parent/guardian needs an interpreter, give language: Parents are bilingual, fluent in both Spanish and English.

Agencies and Persons Working with the Family (Fill in anytime)

Start Date	Agency	Contact Person(s)/ Title	Phone	Type of Service	End Date	Send Copy of IFSP?
11-5-07	Hometown Hospital	Jane Jones, audiologist	222-5555	Hearing testing; hearing aids		X
2-5-08	Hometown Schools	Hector Ramirez, speech-language pathologist	222-3333	Service Coordinator, Communication development		

Child's Strengths and Needs

Child's Name: Carlos Diaz	Birth Weight: 6.14	Birth Date: 11-1-07	Number of Wks premature NA

Area	Present Level of Development		Date	Name/Type of Evaluation	Person Doing Evaluation	Agency
	Parent Input	Professional Input				
General	Easy baby. Seems fine except for hearing	Responsive child interested in his environment	1-15-08	Cognitive screening Bayley Scales	Developmental Psychologist	Hometown Schools Early Intervention
Hearing	Doesn't respond to sound but does to gestures	Profound bilateral hearing imp.	11-5-08	Neonatal screening ABR	Audiologist	Hometown Hospital
Communication	Watches everything	Responsive child, follows eyes, coos and makes sounds	2-15-09	Rossetti Infant-Toddler Scale	SLP	Hometown Schools

(continued)

figure *8.1*

Continued

<table>
<tr><td colspan="5">Child Eligibility</td></tr>
<tr><td>Part C of IDEA</td><td>☒Yes   ❑ No   ❑ Unknown</td><td>Based on: Established Condition: hearing imp.</td><td>Developmental Delay: NA</td></tr>
</table>

<table>
<tr><td colspan="7">Service Plan</td></tr>
<tr><td colspan="4">Service Coordinator: H. Ramirez</td><td colspan="3">Phone: 222-3333</td></tr>
<tr><td>Interim</td><td>✗ Initial</td><td>Review</td><td>Annual</td><td colspan="3">Transition (90 days before entry into new program or third birthday)</td></tr>
<tr>
<td>OUTCOMES
What would we like to have happen, by when, and how will we know when it happens.</td>
<td>WHO & WHAT
What service or activity is needed and who will do it.</td>
<td>WHERE, WHEN & HOW
When will the services occur, how often, how long each time, individual or group</td>
<td colspan="2">DATE SERVICE</td>
<td>PAYOR
Who will pay for it</td>
<td>REVIEW
Date/ Rating/ Comments</td>
</tr>
<tr>
<td></td><td></td><td></td><td>Begins</td><td>Ends</td><td></td><td></td>
</tr>
<tr>
<td>1) Will use hearing aids to learn language and communicate.

2) Vocalize and gesture to share attention.

3) Interact in preverbal communication and show intention by 10 months.

4) Understand and say words by 12 months.</td>
<td>Fitting & monitoring hearing aid use by audiologist.

Parent education by consultant for hearing impaired children.

Communication development support by speech-language pathologist.</td>
<td>Audiology services in university clinic until fitting as frequently and long as necessary.

Monthly home-based services— 2 hr each.

Group parent-infant training weekly for 10 weeks.

Group follow-up sessions weekly.</td>
<td>11-5-07

3-1-08

3-1-08

5-20-08</td>
<td>When complete

Ongoing

5-20-08

Ongoing</td>
<td>Private insurance + Parents

Public School

Public School

Public School</td>
<td></td>
</tr>
</table>

Source: © N. W. Nelson, 2007.

teachers and day care providers. Siblings and peers can be engaged as well to provide social supports for healthy social–emotional and communicative development.

When clinicians interact with family members using approaches that truly are family centered, they employ fewer questions and more active listening (Crais, 1995). They use the ethnographic techniques described in Chapter 1 for learning about families and their cultures, as well as about a particular family's unique values and needs. These techniques include direct interactions, perspective gathering using ethnographic interviews, joint observations, and discussions with parents about factors that facilitate or act as barriers to effective functioning and participation for their child. Culturally sensitive clinicians use a language parents can understand, an interpreter if necessary, and accessible vocabulary and a communication style that invites interaction.

Westby, StevensDominguez, and Oetter (1996) described how an ethnographic interviewer might encourage families to add detail when describing a typical day with their child: "You said that Ian doesn't talk, but he's good at letting you know what he wants. Tell me what he does to let you know what he wants" (p. 150). Such an ethnographic approach might then lead to a discussion about new ways to help Ian develop gestures and sounds that will move him toward talking. The clinician and parent also might discuss how to scaffold new communicative functions so that Ian can express his wants and desires and also comment nonverbally by drawing his parents' attention to things that interest him.

Involving family members directly in planning and intervention does not mean shifting full responsibility from clinicians to families for making all the decisions and doing all the work. In gauging a family's resources and coping skills, clinicians must remember that the family of an infant with newly identified risks is in the initial stages of coping with adverse news. A number of factors influence a family's resources at this critical point (Barber, Turnbull, Behr, & Kerns, 1988), including characteristics of the child's diagnostic condition and family, such as family size and form, cultural and religious factors, socioeconomic elements, and geographic region.

Some families face multiple risks, including caregiver risks associated with parental special needs, low socioeconomic status, absence of one or both parents, emotional or financial challenges, substance abuse issues, and other barriers to caregivers' ability to cope. Grandparents may serve as guardians, or children may be placed in foster homes or with adoptive parents, perhaps following previous adverse environmental experiences that are not fully known. Some parents lack organizational skills, trust, or motivation for seeking professional assistance.

Interdisciplinary teams need to be particularly patient, persistent, respectful, and sensitive when offering services to families with multiple needs. Even parents with stable marriages, good jobs, education, and support from extended family members and friends are likely to feel unprepared for the intense challenges of coping with an infant or toddler with developmental risks or a diagnosed disability.

Providing Culturally and Linguistically Appropriate Services

Views and attitudes about disability vary across cultures and also families within cultures. Clinicians must remain alert to mismatches between their own cultural views and those of the families with whom they are working. Cultural values and practices influence such events as when and whether children shift from bottle to cup, eat with a fork and spoon, say "Please" and "Thank-you," and name colors, letters, and numbers. Evaluation of children's developmental accomplishments must be considered in a culturally fair manner and with no communication of blame or judgment to parents who have not taught such skills.

Discourse expectations also differ across cultures. If a family's culture places differing value on how much children should talk in the company of adults (e.g., Crago, 1990; Heath, 1983), for example, that expectation should be factored into interpretation of assessment results (see Personal Reflection 8.1) and decisions about how to train parents as conversational partners. Van Kleeck (1994) noted that clinicians' cultural assumptions might diverge from families' expectations for adult–child conversations in areas such as social organization and interaction, the value of talk, how status is handled in interactions, beliefs about intentionality, and beliefs about parental roles in teaching language to children. Parents should not be expected to assume roles that conflict with their cultural values or individual patterns of interaction.

PERSONAL reflection *8.1*

"The researcher's perspective. One of the boys was particularly intriguing even from the beginning of taping. His language seemed advanced for his age, and he talked frequently. His tapes had more entries than any other child's tapes. From my perspective he was a very bright and very verbal little boy. As time went on I became curious as to why he seemed to talk more than the others. I asked an Inuk teacher for her reactions to this child.

The Inuk teacher's perspective. The teacher listened to my description of how much he talked and then said:

> Do you think he might have a learning problem? Some of these children who don't have such high intelligence have trouble stopping themselves. They don't know when to stop talking.

I was amazed by her response. It was as if my perspective had been stood on its head."

Martha Crago (1990, p. 80), an ethnographer and communication scientist, describing insights gained by using ethnographic techniques to analyze cultural differences in discourse expectations.

Cultures also differ in their views of disability and developmental difference. If members of a culture view disability as something to be denied or hidden, clinicians need to consider this in their early interactions with the family. On the other hand, terms such as *denied or hidden* represent ethnocentric views of another person's culture. Lack of interest in talking about a disorder may be more a sign of acceptance than denial. Most Native American languages, for example, do not have terms for *retardation* or *disability*. People who develop differently are integrated into the tribal culture and community. Native American families therefore may be distrustful of special education and choose to remove their children from school, rather than have them placed in special classes (Robinson-Zañartu, 1996).

Appropriate cultural and linguistic practices are required when assessing children and working with families whose primary language is not English. Interpreters must be trained and only engage in assessment activities with the clinician present (Langdon & Cheng, 2002). Using a simple translation of a test does not work, because simply changing the words ignores the meanings and prior experiences of the family and child in the context of their own culture. Interpreters need to understand the importance of conveying meaning as faithfully as possible, in both directions. When clinicians and interpreters work together over time, they can develop a synergy for facilitating communication. Interpreters with experience in the family's culture also may be able to serve as cultural informants, helping to interpret deeper meanings of certain expressions or general messages and alerting clinicians about concerns for how information may be received.

It takes time to earn trust and become familiar with the cultural expectations of families that differ from one's own. It may be tempting for clinicians to avoid cross-cultural and different language situations because of lack of confidence about reaching a valid decision about a child's need for services (Kritikos, 2003). On the other hand, it can be enriching to make the effort to gain deeper understanding into a particular family's world view and expectations and dreams for their child. Special services do not always involve formal testing and labeling. Using multiple methods may help illuminate a family's perspectives and needs.

Some evidence supports family-centered planning. Chao, Bryan, Burstein, and Ergul (2006) used a randomized controlled trial to study family-centered service delivery in an ethnically diverse community in the southwestern United States. Participants were parents of 41 children (ages 3 to 5 years) attending developmental preschools because of risks for language and behavior problems. Parents in the experimental group took part in weekly assessment and planning meetings that used "problem identification and clarification, problem analysis, goal setting, planning strategies and implementation, evaluation of outcome data, and consideration of need to modify plans" (p. 149). Results showed that children in the family-centered condition improved more on formal tests of early language and behavior than those in the traditional service delivery control group.

Natural Environments for Family-Centered Services

Consistent with IDEA '04, family-centered services must be provided in *natural environments,* or settings that are typical for infants and toddlers without disabilities or delays. The most natural environment for infants and toddlers is the family's home. Providing services in the home is not possible for all infants, however; some spend the first few weeks or even months in a neonatal intensive care unit (NICU) or require ongoing medical support services. Special considerations for providing services in these and other contexts are discussed in the sections that follow. In developing position papers regarding the role of SLPs with the infant and toddler population (Wilcox, 2008), the members of the committee emphasized a view of natural environments that are part of the "child and family's typical and valued activities and events, and include parents and caregivers as partners in the child's communication activities" (Woods, 2008, p. 15).

Hospital-Based Services

The NICU may be the initial natural environment for service delivery for families with neonates with high-risk conditions. Sick, premature, and other high-risk neonates receive treatment from interdisciplinary teams within the NICU. Other children may be born at full term and healthy but with clear evidence of a genetic or other condition that justifies special services (e.g., cleft lip and palate or hearing loss). These children also may be referred at birth to hospital-based intervention teams, who assist parents to understand their infants' special needs and how to cope with them. At some point, services transition to other settings, but hospital-based teams often are the first to help parents understand their children's needs and their families' eligibility for services under IDEA '04.

Increased survival rates of infants born prematurely or with life-threatening conditions may result in increased incidence of adverse neurodevelopmental sequelae (i.e., effects of disease). Such conditions require appropriate management of communication, cognition, feeding/swallowing problems, and self-regulation. SLPs on NICU teams provide evaluation and intervention for communication, feeding, and swallowing; conduct parent/caregiver education and counseling; and engage in team education and collaboration (ASHA, 2004).

Evidence suggests that parents of sick children become more engaged earlier when they are supported in taking an active role in their children's care. Als and Gilkerson (1995) recommended that nurses and other professionals should employ a novice-to-expert framework (i.e., a scaffolding approach) to facilitate parents' ability to care for their neonates with special needs. This involves helping parents develop confidence in their new roles. Ward (2005) reviewed research on preferences of parents facing difficult treatment decisions in the NICU. Regardless of geographic region or race/ethnicity, parents expressed a desire to receive complete and timely information about their children's medical and other health care needs and to be given time to assimilate it so they can participate actively in making informed decisions.

Home-Based Services

The home is clearly a natural environment for providing family-centered infant and toddler services, but that does not mean it is always the optimal service delivery site. Children's homes offer practical advantages as accessible and reasonably economical settings for service delivery, especially in rural settings and for families with limited transportation (Bailey & Simeonsson, 1988). Home settings also are associated with potential disadvantages for parents reluctant to take on primary roles in intervention (Crais, 1995) and for children who need wider access to professional specialists, peers, toys, and equipment (Bailey & Simeonsson, 1988).

Some IFSPs specify regular home visits by one or more team members. Examples of home-based services include helping infants transition from hospital settings to home or helping families meet feeding challenges for a child with oral–motor needs. Home visits also can be used for assessment and intervention activities focused on early communication and language development. Clinicians' specialized expertise about early communicative development can be complemented by parents' specialized expertise about their child. This can lead to a richer profile about what works best to facilitate a child's social–emotional development and cognitive–communication abilities.

Center-Based Services

Family members also may bring their young children to a center or clinic for family-centered services. For example, parents or other caregivers might participate in circle-time nursery games and play activities with their infants and toddlers and learn to support their development, often guided by a transdisciplinary team (e.g., occupational therapist, speech–language pathologist, and early childhood educator). This type of service delivery setting also offers opportunities for parents to interact with other parents facing similar challenges.

Day Care and Clinic Room Services

Day care providers can participate in individualized training sessions and contribute information based on their daily interactions with the child. Direct services also can be provided in day care and early Head Start settings or in clinic treatment rooms, which can be arranged with inviting play areas for young children. Combinations of service delivery approaches also may be used.

Roberts, Prizant, and McWilliam (1995) measured the effects of language intervention services in an inclusive day care setting for 15 children who ranged in age from 1 to 5 years. The children exhibited a variety of moderate cognitive and developmental delays (e.g., with established risks, such as Down syndrome, or biological risks due to prematurity or spina bifida). Roberts and colleagues analyzed discourse interactions during in-class intervention sessions and compared them with samples gathered out of class. Both settings included activity play areas (e.g., cooking, dress-up), in which clinicians used a child-initiated responsive language intervention approach. A teacher and other children were present in the inclass sessions, whereas no other teacher or children were involved in the individual treatment room sessions. The results revealed differences in discourse patterns. Clinicians took more turns during the out-of-class ($M = 104$) than the inclass ($M = 74$) sessions, but children complied with a higher percentage of requests in the out-of-class (76 percent) compared to the inclass (61 percent) sessions. Children made no response to a higher percentage of requests during the inclass (26 percent) than the out-of-class (12 percent) sessions. These data elucidated different discourse opportunities and patterns but did not lead to conclusions that one service delivery choice was uniformly better than another.

Scaffolding Language Development in Naturalistic Contexts

In the process of family-centered service delivery, a key intervention technique is scaffolding. Clinicians scaffold parents, parents scaffold children, and collaborative partners scaffold each other. Effective professionals invite parents' active participation and empower them to serve as full partners in the assessment and intervention process.

During a child's infancy, the parents often play the primary role for a child with a disability or developmental risks, generally with the support of consultation from communication specialists and other professionals. As the infant transitions into a toddler and then a preschooler, clinicians and other early childhood service providers often provide increasingly direct intervention in day care or preschool settings outside the immediate presence of the child's caregivers. In those settings, clinicians are likely to interact with other child care providers or preschool teachers along with parents. Consistent with the system theory approach described in Chapter 3, comprehensive services are aimed at involving broader family and societal systems in the intervention.

Historical Roots and Definitions of Scaffolding

The metaphor of scaffolding often is attributed to Jerome Bruner (1975; Wood, Bruner, & Ross, 1976). He used the term *scaffolding* to describe processes that educators, parents, and others use naturally to support learners to reach levels of functioning that are higher than they could achieve independently. Scaffolding is based on combined theoretical foundations of cognitive constructivism and social interactionism.

Early in the twentieth century, Lev Vygotsky (1934/1962) wrote, "With assistance, every child can do more than he can by himself—though only within the limits set by the state of his development" (p. 103). As introduced in Chapter 3, Vygotsky termed the developmental limits within which a child's ability can be stretched his or her *zone of proximal development* (*ZPD*). Children with disabilities are likely to have ZPDs that are more constricted and have lower thresholds. Important for children with disabilities, the ZPD framework also indicates that, with appropriate mediation, every child can learn. The general goal of intervention is to extend the child's developing edge of competence and to stretch the ZPD to make the child increasingly open to learning from varied experiences in unscaffolded contexts.

Intuitive Parental Scaffolding

The literature on parent–infant interaction indicates that most parents intuitively scaffold their infant's earliest communicative interactions. Research has shown that a parent or other caregiver "intuitively slows down, simplifies, exaggerates, repeats and varies facial expression, prosody of speech, and other behaviors in a way that complements the newborn's sensory, perceptual, integrative and motor constraints and capacities and facilitates perception of and familiarization with the parent's behavior" (Papoušek, 2007, p. 259). By framing critical cues, parents mediate their child's attempts to understand the world and participate in it.

Neurological underpinnings for reciprocal interactions of mammalian parents and children have been found in mirror-neurons networks in the premotor cortex of primates. The premotor cortex is an area of the frontal lobe related to goal directed behavior or intentional action (Rizzolatti, Fadiga, Gallese, & Fogassi, 1996). Related studies of human infants' brains using event-related potentials (ERPs) have shown prefrontal response to parental attention to infant behavior. Papoušek (2007) summarized research suggesting that brains of human infants are predisposed to mirror their parents' input and thus to engage in "human empathy, affective resonance, understanding attention and intentions, observational learning, and language acquisition" (p. 260). Mirror neurons also may "provide the neurobiological basis for the phenomenon of newborn imitation, of mutual facial and vocal mirroring, immediate coupling of perception and action, and of early intersubjective affective sharing" (p. 260).

Parental Scaffolding of Children with Disabilities or Risks for Disability

Questions have arisen about how parental scaffolding varies when children exhibit developmental risks. One research team (Forcada-Guex, Pierrehumbert, Borghini, Moessinger, & Muller-Nix, 2006) followed 47 preterm infants (born at less than 34 weeks of gestational age) and 25 full-term infants. They assessed patterns of mother–infant interactions at 6 months (corrected age) and 18 months, rating mother interactional patterns for sensitivity, control, and unresponsiveness and infants for cooperation, compliance, difficulty, and passivity. Infant outcomes at 18 months showed that preterm infants in controlling pattern dyads displayed more behavioral symptoms, feeding problems, and lower scores on measures of personal–social and hearing–speech development than full-term or preterm infants in cooperative pattern dyads.

Similar questions arise about toddlers who are late talkers. Although some evidence suggests that worried parents may use a more directive and less child-contingent style (e.g., Conti-Ramsden, Hutcheson, & Grove, 1995; Girolametto & Tannock, 1994), other evidence suggests that the overdirective pattern may not be all that common (Paul & Elwood, 1991; see Personal Reflection 8.2).

PERSONAL
reflection 8.2

"The great majority of parents are doing the best they can to get through to an often hard-to-reach child. They don't need to be made to feel that they are at fault if their child is not developing normally. They probably aren't at fault, and even if they are, feeling bad about themselves won't help. Rather than subjecting parents to an intimidating assessment of their own communication skills, we would be better off just to ask them what makes communicating with their child hard for them. We can then offer suggestions to address the concerns they raise."

Rhea Paul (2007, p. 279), a speech–language pathologist and children's language researcher, was commenting on assessing the communication skills of parents.

Transactional effects also seem to be involved. Paul and Elwood (1991) indicated that mothers of toddlers with slow language development are different only in their less frequent use of lexical contingency devices—grammatical expansion and semantic extension (both forms of conversational recast). Yet "the proportion of expansions and extensions relative to the number of child utterances is not different, indicating that when late talkers give their mothers something to expand, the mothers do so, but that the late talkers do not give their mothers as much speech to work with as do the normal toddlers" (p. 982). It follows that as children learn to talk more, their parents will have more to expand grammatically and extend by adding new content.

Rescorla and Fechnay (1996) found that mother–child synchrony and reciprocity were similar for mothers interacting with late-talking toddlers between 24 and 31 months of age compared to mother–child pairs matched for nonverbal and socioeconomic status. Individual differences also were observed. Maternal patterns of high control and low synchrony were associated with patterns of lower compliance and synchrony for children.

Promising early intervention strategies for infants and toddlers can be categorized into three groups (Wilcox, 2008). **Responsive interaction strategies** include recasting and other forms of scaffolding. ***Directed interaction strategies*** are based on behaviorist principles, such as prompting, shaping, reinforcement, and fading. ***Blended strategies*** make use of directive behavioral strategies but in natural environments to promote generalization.

Intervention Scaffolding

Intervention scaffolding is based on cognitive constructivist theory that learners play an active role in acquiring new concepts and skills. It also draws on social interactionist theory that others can mediate learning, making constructive learning possible (Feuerstein, 1979; Rogoff, 1990). Vygotsky (1934/1962) noted that each child's learning is constrained by his or her current level of development. Prominent forms of intervention scaffolding that are introduced in this section include social mediation, conversational recasts, and focused stimulation.

Social mediation is another term for scaffolding. When used as an intervention technique, social mediation is a process by which mediators frame cues and focus a less-skilled learner's attention on contextualized cues to enable him or her to construct a more mature cognitive–linguistic schema. A difference between instructional and naturalistic scaffolding is that instructional (or intervention) scaffolding is more goal directed and deliberate. Multiple partners may provide intervention scaffolding—clinicians, parents, siblings, and peers. Given their sensitivity to what their children already know, attentive parents often are particularly well situated to mediate their children's learning within their ZPDs. With consultation, parents may become even better at scaffolding their children's language development.

According to Feuerstein (1979), social mediation involves "framing, selecting, focusing, and feeding back environmental experiences" to produce in the child "appropriate learning sets and habits" (p. 179). This definition is particularly useful for language clinicians seeking to build scaffolding skills and to teach them to others. By strategically selecting and framing cues in the physical and social environment, mediators focus a child's attention on connections between concepts and associated language content, form, and use. This supports children to engage in constructivist mental activity facilitating elaborated and integrated neural systems and connecting them strategically across children's brains. Figure 8.2 adopts Feuerstein's terminology to provide scaffolding tips for clinicians.

figure *8.2*

Tips for Scaffolding Learners

Start with something the learner knows.

Comment on cues in the context that can help the learner form new connections.

Ask questions that serve as guides, not tests, and allow wait time for processing.

Frame cues the learner may be missing, and focus attention on key features of the event.

Feed back information to help the learner identify mismatches and fix inconsistencies.

Ownership means encouraging the learner to set goals, take the lead, and explore original ideas.

Listen to the learner's message, and respond contingently to the meaning.

Don't forget to take the scaffold down; learning is not complete until it can stand on its own.

Source: © N. W. Nelson, 2007.

Conversational recasts constitute a specialized form of scaffolding, combining both modeling and feedback. Table 8.2 summarizes a range of adult–child interaction patterns. Those at the top represent adult-directed teaching methods. They might be considered instructional prompting techniques, but most social interactionists would not categorize prompts as scaffolding. Conversational recasts—expansion and extension—are forms of scaffolding. Camarata and Nelson (2006) described a *conversational recast* intervention procedure as one in which a clinician responds contingently to a child's limited initiation by producing a slightly more mature model, reflecting the child's form but adding something.

Focused stimulation (Leonard, 1981) is a form of intervention scaffolding that varies from general stimulation by targeting specific linguistic forms (Ellis Weismer & Roberston, 2006). Another difference is that a recast follows a child's utterance, whereas focused stimulation involves provision of controlled language input. Children's productions are not

table *8.2* Continuum of Adult–Child Interaction Techniques

Directive	Adult Interaction Techniques	Discourse Illustrations
More ↑	Telling	Adult: *Do you know what this is?* Child: [no response] Adult: *It's a "dog."*
	Request for imitation, followed by modeling to shape correct word production.	Adult: *Can you say "dog"?* Child: *ba.* Adult: *No, "dog"!* [emphasizing the /d/ and saying the word slowly] Child: *ba!* [louder]
	Testing ("teacher talk") IRE: • Initiate • Respond • Evaluate Focus on eliciting correct response to known-answer questions.	Adult: *What's that?* Child: *ba.* Adult: *Good. You're right. That's a dog.*
	Syntactic expansions or structural recasts that frame cues about sentence structure and language form.	Adult: *What's happening here?* Child: /Da haI/ (*Dog hide*). Adult: *Yes, the doggie is hiding.* [spoken slowly with emphasis on *is*] Child: /Da haI-I/ (*Dog hiding*).
Less ↓	Semantic extensions with content recasts that extend the child's meaning, responding to the child's ideas and elaborating on them.	Child: /da/ (*Dog*) Adult: *Yes, the dog is hiding.* [pause] *Uh oh, look who's coming.* Child: /bI da/ (*Big dog.*) Him / kɛI / (*Him scary.*) Adult: *Yes, he's a big scary dog. See his big teeth.* Child: [turns page] /Da rʌnI/ (*Dog running.*) Adult: *Yep, that little dog is running. He's trying to get away.*

The techniques are illustrated for a 3-year-old engaged in shared book reading, with more adult-directed forms at the top and more child-centered forms at the bottom.

Source: Based on Camarata & Nelson, 2006; Cazden, 1988; Cole, Maddox, & Lim, 2006; Paul & Elwood, 1991.

directly requested, but neither are they discouraged. Using focused stimulation, adults (either parents or clinicians providing direct service) expose children to multiple examples (called *exemplars*) of a specific linguistic target within meaningful linguistic contexts. The target may be specific vocabulary, two-word utterances of a particular type, any other grammatical morpheme, or a pragmatic function.

Teaching Parents Scaffolding Techniques

Relatively more or less structured programs and materials are available to teach parents to scaffold their children's language development. Several are discussed in this section. The efficacy of family-centered social mediation approaches and their long-term effects are supported by a growing body of research, which is summarized here as well.

An early approach was the *ecological* (also called *ECO*) parent-training approach developed by James MacDonald (1989) and his colleagues at the Nisonger Center in Ohio. This ecological approach exemplifies features adopted by later parent-training approaches for facilitating early communicative interactions based on the following five principles:

1. The *partnership principle* involves teaching parents to engage in balanced turn taking.
2. The *matching principle* involves teaching parents to interact and communicate at a level the child can match.
3. The *sensitive responsiveness principle* involves teaching parents to notice and respond to subtle advances in the child's abilities.
4. The *child-based nondirectiveness principle* involves teaching parents to scaffold the child to construct new concepts using child-centered rather than adult-directed procedures.
5. The *emotional attachment principle* helps parents appreciate the importance of a stable base of emotional attachment for preparing the child to form relationships with others.

A similar parent-implemented but child-centered approach is referred to as DIR, for Development, Individualization, Responsiveness (Greenspan & Wieder, 2005). The DIR approach, also called *Floortime,* is described in a number of sources, including the *Floortime DVD Training Series,* which illustrates application of the model for children with special risks or needs, including autism spectrum disorders. The approach is founded on these concepts:

- *Developmental* understanding of the child's emotional development relative to six developmental milestones—shared attention and regulation, engagement and relating, purposeful emotional interaction, social problem solving, creating ideas, and connecting ideas together and thinking logically
- *Individual difference* understanding of the child's unique way of "taking in the world—sights, sounds, touch, etc.—and responding to it," and how the "child's individual differences can interfere with his or her ability to relate, communicate, and think" (p. 1)
- *Relationship-based* parental interactions that fit the child's state of development and individual differences

The Hanen program for parents, It Takes Two to Talk (Girolametto & Weitzman, 2006; Manolson, 1992), has been subjected to perhaps the most scientific investigation. Speech–language pathologists who wish to implement this program receive special training so they can work with parents in groups to teach them three sets of child-responsive interaction strategies:

- *Child-centered strategies* involve getting face-to-face with the child and following his or her lead, as promoted by the acronym mnemonic OWL (Observe–Wait–Listen).
- *Interaction-promoting strategies* involve balanced turn taking, with parents matching their turns to their child's, asking questions to keep conversations going, and waiting for their children's turns, using cues only when needed.
- *Language-modeling strategies* involve using contingency techniques to interpret experience, expand on what the child says, and extend the topic.

Intervention studies (reviewed by Girolametto & Weitzman, 2006) have provided evidence that parents who receive training interact more effectively with their children. This research also has shed some light on which parent interaction techniques are most effective. Results indicate an advantage when parents *extend* children's content and meaning over when they *expand* grammatical language structures.

McDade and McCartan (1998) investigated use of the Hanen program to teach parents of toddlers with expressive language delay to change their interactive behaviors. Children in the treatment group made greater gains on pre–post test measures and showed improved social conversation and language skills compared with children in a no-treatment control group. Law (1999) compared the Hanen program with traditional clinic-based treatment and a no-treatment control group. Law's participants were families with low socioeconomic status and children with mixed expressive/receptive language difficulties. All of the children made language gains, whether they were enrolled in either the treatment or no-treatment groups (i.e., delayed treatment), which made it impossible to attribute the children's language growth to the intervention.

Baxendale and Hesketh (2003) compared results for 19 toddlers (with mixed receptive/expressive language delays) and families enrolled in Hanen treatment programs with 18 similar children and families receiving traditional clinic-based intervention. A high proportion of children (71 percent) improved regardless of treatment method, but the Hanen parent groups required more clinician time than those receiving traditional service delivery. Different approaches appeared better suited for different child and family situations. For instance, children with receptive language difficulties appeared to benefit more from the Hanen approach (i.e., with parents following their focus of attention and matching their language level), whereas children with expressive language difficulties seemed to benefit more from traditional clinic therapy. Greater efficiency for treating expressive language difficulties may come with immediate targeting of problematic structures (rather than waiting for parent training). Baxendale and Hesketh also noted that some parents may not need training if they already use responsive strategies at baseline and that parents may differ in their learning styles and preferences. The Hanen program, in particular, might be better suited to middle-class families.

Some of the most impressive parent-training data were reported by Gibbard (1994), who randomly assigned mothers of 36 children—ages 2 years, 3 months to 3 years, 3 months—either to half-day parental language training sessions (i.e., experimental group) or a no-intervention control group ($n = 18$ per group). SLPs provided group parent-based intervention sessions every two weeks for a 6-month period. Using a variation on focused stimulation, clinicians developed linguistic objectives for each student and explained and clarified each objective to his or her parents through structured teaching demonstrations for each set of language objectives. Parents were taught to think about how they might target each language objective using the particular routines and interests of their child, following their child's lead at home in naturally occurring situations.

In a meta-analysis comparing several similar studies, Law, Garrett, and Nye (2004) showed that Gibbard's (1994) research resulted in particularly impressive effect sizes. That is, the expressive language skills of the experimental group children were more than 1.5 standard deviations (SDs) above the control group (no treatment) children on several dependent measures—overall expressive syntax development (2.33 SDs); number of utterances in the language sample (1.63 SDs); mean length of utterance (MLU) (1.54 SDs); and parent report of phrase complexity (2.10 SDs). In a second study (also in Gibbard, 1994), eight children received individual direct speech and language service delivery. They made similar gains to nine children whose mothers received the parental-language training sessions and superior gains to eight children whose mothers participated in a general learning parental-training control group. This research supports other findings that for toddlers with expressive language delay, focusing stimulation on particular linguistic targets, rather than more general language or learning stimulation, is more effective.

Research on other parent-training programs has provided evidence of long-term benefits for children. Fowler, Ogston, Roberts, and Swenson (2006) measured effects 20 years after providing early training for parents to promote reciprocal interactions with their infants. Fowler's home-based *language enrichment approach* was conducted with parents of typically developing infants in homes with a wide range of sociocultural and educational backgrounds. Participants included immigrant parents who were non-English speakers as well as highly educated members of mainstream cultural groups in Canada. Parent training was conducted in families' homes when children were between 3 and 12 months of age. Parents were taught to engage their infants in balanced and reciprocal turn-taking exchanges (both verbal and nonverbal) and encouraged to talk with children to develop their language comprehension prior to expecting them to talk. Interviews, testing, and record reviews conducted 20 years later showed positive outcomes in children's school performance, cognitive functioning, motivation, and self-esteem, exceeding predicted levels for similar populations.

Studies conducted in natural environments support parent intervention approaches as well. Both Wells (1986) and Hart and Risley (1995, 1999) showed that children developed more language and cognitive skills (regardless of the family's socioeconomic resources) when their parents engaged them frequently in optional/extra talk (e.g., storytelling) about topics beyond everyday demands and practical concerns (e.g., what to wear or finishing their meals).

SUMMARY

This section summarized the policy requirements of IDEA '04 for children with special needs or developmental risks in the infant and toddler years from birth through the third birthday. The child's third birthday is a transition point, at which time the parents may elect to have their child and family continue to receive services under an IFSP or may transition to having their child receive educational and related services through an IEP, with the option of having an existing IFSP become the child's IEP. The recipient of services under an IFSP is the whole family, not just the child.

This section also introduced family-centered practices, with emphasis on cultural sensitivity and attending to parents' verbal and nonverbal signals about what they find important and comfortable. A variety of contexts can serve as natural environments for service delivery with infants and toddlers. Scaffolding occurs intuitively for most parents but also can be fine-tuned for intervention contexts. Although children with language disorders may not be as quick to respond to scaffolding exchanges as their typically developing peers and siblings, their scaffolding needs are similar; the difference is that they may need heightened cues and more frequent experiences.

Indirect intervention approaches involve teaching parents new skills for interacting with their children. Three formalized parent-training approaches are the ECO program, DIR, and the Hanen program. A caution is that social interactionist and cognitive constructivist techniques of mediated learning tend to be more consistent with parenting practices of middle-class, mainstream families than families living in differing sociocultural circumstances. Scaffolding approaches are consistent with the context-based assessment and intervention philosophy of this book, but it is important to remember that family-centered and evidence-based practices require selecting approaches with reference to family preferences and values (Johnson, 2006) as well as the best scientific evidence.

Comprehensive Assessment for Infants and Toddlers

Developmental profiles can be constructed using a combination of formal assessment tools and contextualized and informal observation and communication sample analysis techniques. Both formal and informal methods play a role in assessing the strengths and needs of infants and toddlers and the resources of their families.

Selecting Formal Assessment Tools for Infants and Toddlers

Formal assessment tools provide structured materials and administration protocols, supporting diagnostic decisions. Results are interpreted using guidelines and data tables provided by the test's developers based on evidence. Some tools have a stronger research base than others. Formal tools include standardized tests and research-based criterion-referenced checklists and other protocols for gathering parental input. Table C in the Part III Appendix provides a listing of formal assessment tools and their descriptions for infants, toddlers, and preschool-age children from birth through age 5 years.

Vocabulary and communication checklists based on parent reports constitute an important component of comprehensive early language assessment. The MacArthur-Bates Communicative Developmental Inventories, Third Edition (CDIs; Fenson, Marchman, Thal, Dale, Reznick, & Bates, 2006), are well-researched tools that are used frequently as parent report measures. The CDIs also are available in Spanish. The Language Development Survey (Rescorla, 1989) is another parent checklist with research support.

Some formal tools (both standardized and criterion referenced) assess comprehensive language and communication development based on direct observation, sometimes accompanied by parent reports. Examples are the Rosetti Infant-Toddler Language Scale (Rosetti, 2005) and the Communication and Symbolic Behavior Scales (CSBS; Wetherby & Prizant, 2002). The CSBS also taps early communication skills that are particularly at risk in children with autism spectrum disorders. Other formal tools are designed specifically to detect early signs of special conditions, including autism. Examples reviewed in Table F in the Part III Appendix are the Autism Diagnostic Observation Schedule (ADOS) (Lord, Rutter, DiLavore, & Risi, 1999) and the Childhood Autism Rating Scale (CARS; Schopler, Reichler, & Renner, 2002). Others are tests designed to measure cognitive ability, including tests that yield an IQ, which must be administered by a credentialed psychologist. These include the Bayley Scales of Infant Development II (Bayley, 1993), the Stanford-Binet (Thorndike, Hagen, & Sattler, 1986), and the Wechsler Preschool and Primary Scale of Intelligence, Revised (WPPSI-R; Wechsler, 1989).

Conclusions about the validity of a particular assessment tool can be drawn only with reference to the specific purpose for which the test is intended (McCauley & Swisher, 1984; Plante & Vance, 1995; Spaulding, Plante, & Farinella, 2006). This requires a careful review of the test's research base and psychometric properties, as described in its technical manual. The review criteria for conducting such an evaluation (see Chapter 4) include seeking evidence that a test provides information about a specific cutoff score for maximizing the test's sensitivity (minimizing false-negative errors) and specificity (minimizing false-positive errors).

Using Less Formal Assessment Probes to Guide Intervention Choices

Systematic but less formal observations of an infant's or toddler's communication abilities tend to be more authentic and ecologically valid because they are fully individualized and situated in naturalistic contexts. They also yield a picture of communication processes as dynamic and malleable to change. Context-based assessments are consistent with the framework outlined in Chapter 1 for considering communication processes, needs, and opportunities. They go beyond measuring strengths and needs in internal communication processes to considering how the child is meeting communication needs currently and how others are optimizing his or her opportunities for communication within important life contexts. Although naturalistic samples typically do not yield standardized scores for the purpose of diagnosing disorder, they are well suited to other assessment purposes, such as informing intervention planning and monitoring progress.

Gathering and Analyzing Naturalistic Communication and Language Samples

Informal assessment activities for infants and toddlers may be guided by the four questions of contextualized assessment and intervention practices (from Chapter 1) to assess infants or toddlers in play or emergent literacy contexts. Initial probes provide baseline data. Periodic follow-up probes conducted under similar conditions can be used to document change. The goal in gathering language and communication samples is to elicit a sample of the child's most mature language and/or communication skills possible. As a general rule, the younger the child, the shorter the samples, and the more critical it is to involve parents in gathering them.

Naturalistic samples should be videorecorded when assessing the communicative abilities of prelinguistic infants and toddlers or any child who communicates primarily through nonverbal means. In such samples, coding mutual and coreferential eye gaze (i.e., looking at the same object, as illustrated in the opening photo for Chapter 8), for example, can signal the degree to which the child and caregiver are engaging in synchronous interactions and how the next developmental steps might be facilitated.

For infants and toddlers, short samples of parent–child interactions can be videotaped in multiple contexts. A clinician and parent might view the videos together, as in the Hanen parent program (Girolametto & Weitzman, 2006) and the Floortime approach (Greenspan & Wieder, 2005). Then, they can collaborate to identify what worked best (or not), noting circumstances in which children were more or less responsive and communicative.

Using Observational Charts to Construct Profiles across Domains

Informal developmental checklists and observational charts are helpful for structuring collaborative discussions by interdisciplinary teams of professionals and parents about a particular child's needs. Table 8.3 shows a summary chart (based on the developmental chart in Table A of the Part III Appendix), which was completed collaboratively by a parent and clinician for the child, Andrea, described in Case Example 8.1. By inviting the parents to help fill out a chart collaboratively, clinicians convey their willingness to listen actively to the

table *8.3*   Shaded Summary Chart Showing a Profile for Andrea (age 6 years, 3 months), Described in Case Example 8.1

Approx. Age	Cognition	Receptive Language
0–8 months	Preintentional (Sensorimotor I, II, & III): Transitions from reflexive to goal-oriented behavior.	Startles to noise. Orients to sound source. Quiets when spoken to.
8–12 months	Early Intentional (Sensorimotor Stage IV): Uses familiar means to achieve novel ends.	Laughs at familiar interaction sequences. Inhibits action in response to *no*.
12–18 months	Late Intentional (Sensorimotor Stage V): Uses novel means to achieve familiar ends.	Points to objects (e.g., body parts) in response to "Show me _____."
18–24 months	Representational Thought (Sensorimotor Stage VI): Internal problem solving using images, memories, and symbols.	Shows word recognition. Responds to two-word commands and questions about agent, action, object, and location.
25–48 months	Early Preoperational Thought: Indicates what another person can see but cannot perform false-belief tasks.	Answers *yes/no* questions. 2;6 yrs: answers *what, what-do, where* questions. 3;0 yrs: answers *whose, who, why, how many* questions.
48–72 months	Late Preoperational Thought: Systematic trial and error. Can respond appropriately to false belief theory of mind tasks by around 48 months.	Demonstrates verbal comprehension of prepositional instrument or manner relations. Responds to two-part action commands.

Source: © N. W. Nelson, 2007.

parents' descriptions of their child. As a result, the IFSP or IEP team has a more complete and optimistic but realistic developmental profile of the child's abilities and needs that can inform decisions about what to do next in assessment and intervention. In Andrea's case, her mother and clinician discussed abilities outlined in each cell and decided how to shade in the cells to reflect Andrea's current level of functioning in each domain.

SUMMARY

Comprehensive assessments for infants and toddlers involve the administration of a combination of formal tools, parent report measures, and informal observations in targeted areas,

Expressive Language	Social–Emotional & Play	Emergent Literacy
Has differentiated cry. Produces vocalizations. Produces syllabic babbling. Makes intentional gestures.	Shares attention and can self-regulate. Recovers from distress within 20 minutes.	Shares reference on pages of book when engaged by caregiver.
Takes vocal and gestural turns. Uses conventional gestures (*bye-bye, no*).	Cries when parent leaves. Plays nursery games. Recovers from distress within 10 minutes.	Looks at pictures in book with adult and listens to short segments of story. Imitates scribbling.
Uses first words in intentional acts. Uses word plus gesture to express a variety of functions.	Closes communication circles with words and gestures. Engages in solitary or onlooker pretend play.	Names pictures or makes sound effects in books. Scribbles spontaneously with crayon.
Has vocabulary spurt. Onset of two-word utterances (MLU = 1.5). Talks more frequently.	Engages in parallel play. Combines two ideas in pretend play; acts on doll. Begins to reason about feelings.	Imitates literacy events in play. Listens to short story read aloud. Attempts to make shapes with crayon. Pretends to write name.
Brown's Stages: I: MLU 1.75 (24 mos.) II: MLU 2.25 (28 mos.) III: MLU 2.75 (30 mos.) IV: MLU 3.50 (36 mos.)	Engages in parallel play, symbolic play, and associative group play (around 40 mos.). Uses pretend play to recover from distress.	Listens to longer stories. Demonstrates print awareness. Demonstrates phonological awareness in nursery rhymes. Makes letter shapes.
Brown's Stage V: MLU 3.75 (42 mos.). Elaborates phrases and combines and embeds clauses.	Shows increased dramatization and realism in play. Develops friendships. Plays games in groups with rules (by 72 mos.). Spends extended time at one activity.	Comprehends longer texts. Retells story. Acts out stories in play. Expands phonological awareness and learns phonics. Decodes and spells words phonetically.

sometimes guided by checklists. Because the family is the recipient of services under an IFSP, family members are integrally involved in the assessment process for infants and toddlers.

CHAPTER SUMMARY

This chapter describes policy influences on the delivery of services to infants and toddlers. The requirements for an individualized family service plan (IFSP) specify the family as

—CASE **example** *8.1*—

Using Andrea's Developmental Profile to Guide Intervention Planning

Andrea's development is profiled in Table 8.3. She is 3.5 years old and has cerebral palsy. She is functioning at levels similar to her chronological-age peers in three of five domains, including emergent literacy. Her cerebral palsy affects her whole body, including her speech–motor mechanism, which make her speech attempts unintelligible and her expressive language difficult to assess. Also due to motor control problems, Andrea cannot yet hold a pencil or scribble her name. She demonstrates "hi–bye" routines and other forms of gestural, nonverbal communication to make her intentions known, and she vocalizes and gestures while pointing to things in the environment and pictures on her communication board.

It is apparent that Andrea is communicating and filling expressive turns, but she is not yet combining symbols into two-word utterances, which suggests a delay in language expression. She conveys age-appropriate comprehension through her gestures, yes/no responses, and eye pointing, and she is beginning to answer *wh*-questions with her communication supports and whole-hand pointing to some of the pictures in her favorite books. Her eyes are lively, and she appreciates humor in the books her parents read to her.

This profile suggests that Andrea needs direct speech and language intervention services. She also needs upgraded access to augmentative and alternative communication (AAC) tools that can support her in the development of verbal (symbolic word) expression. She needs adapted toys and props along with opportunities to play with peers. The pictures and other symbols on her communication board should be accompanied by printed words to support emergent reading.

the recipient of services. The family can choose to have their child transition to an IEP at his or her third birthday (at which point the child becomes the recipient of services) or to continue receiving services under the IFSP. Scaffolding was described as a form of intuitive parent support. Three programs were introduced for educating parents about how to scaffold their children's early development—the Hanen, ECO, and DIR programs. This chapter also emphasized cultural–linguistic sensitivity as a critical characteristic of family-centered practices. An outline of a typical assessment for children in the earliest stages of language development was suggested, including a formal language test, parent report measure, and informal probes of parent–child interactions.

EXERCISES *and* STUDY QUESTIONS

1. Differentiate an IFSP from an IEP, and describe transition points and options for parents. Outline the components of an IFSP.

2. Contrast a family-centered approach with one that is not family centered. What features distinguish a family-centered approach?

3. Name and describe at least three approaches for educating parents to interact more effectively with their infants and toddlers for encouraging early nonverbal communication acts and verbalizations.

4. Outline the basic components of an assessment for an infant or toddler, and justify the need for each component.

CHAPTER nine

Infant and Toddler Intervention

LEARNING *objectives*

After studying this chapter, you should be able to do the following:

1. Describe family-centered assessment and intervention procedures set in natural environments.

2. Describe intervention techniques targeting prelinguistic organization to intentional communication; joint action routines and early play; first words to two-word utterances; and emergent narratives and literacy.

Chapter 9 describes family-centered practices for infants and toddlers, targeting four goal areas—prelinguistic organization to intentional communication; joint action routines and early play; first words to two-word utterances; and emergent narratives and literacy. Early communication, play, and early literacy contexts overlap and can be used to support each other. Integration across domains is an overarching goal of intervention.

Prelinguistic Organization to Intentional Communication

The earliest forms of communication have been termed *behavioral state communication* (Dunst & Lowe, 1986). Research has shown that early prelinguistic forms (e.g., gesture, eye gaze, visual attention) are good predictors of future communication and language skills (Wetherby, Yonclas, & Bryan, 1989; Woods & Wetherby, 2003). Difficulty with eye gaze and gestures signals a risk for autism spectrum disorders or other social interaction problems. Concerns are raised if children fail to engage in mutual eye gaze, to establish joint reference with adults through gestures and eye gaze (as illustrated in the photo in the opening of Chapter 8), or to "comment" on objects by looking back and forth between the adult's eyes and the object of focus. Thus, this section begins by discussing regulation of behavioral states and joint attention as steps toward intentional communication.

Emotional Stability and Early Social Communication

It may seem strange to discuss self-regulation (an inward-looking skill) in the same section as social interaction (an outward-looking skill). However, the relationship across these social–emotional domains is close and essential. Without social mediation from and interaction with an attentive and loving caregiver, any child, but especially an infant or toddler, will find it difficult to establish emotional health and a sense of self-efficacy. Similarly, without emotional health and self-regulation, it is difficult to establish healthy social interactions with others.

The interactive development of the social interaction and social–emotional systems is emphasized by professionals who promote cognitive–emotional views of development (e.g., Greenspan & Wieder, 2006). Such theorists suggest that, whether a child has risks for disability or not, an attentive caregiver plays a critical role in promoting a child's calm, attentive approach to learning and communication and his or her capacity to reorganize in distressing circumstances. Thus, the goals and related assessment and intervention approaches in this section aim at promoting healthy interactions during infancy as a critical base for later language and literacy development.

Assessing Emotional Stability and Mutual Attention

In typical development, the parents and neonate seek out each other's eyes from the moment of birth. *Intersubjective* eye gaze is an important mechanism for forming attachment, both for infants and parents (and siblings) (see Figure 9.1). Both environmental and biological risks can present barriers to the establishment of mutual attention and the ability to regain stability when distressed.

Figure 9.2 (page 242) is an observation tool for guiding assessment of an infant's ability to reorganize when he or she is distressed (based on Als et al., 1982; Sparks, 1989b). Clinicians may use the tool in collaboration with parents to assess an infant's emotional stability and facilitative parent–infant interactions. The goal is to identify the supports most likely to help the child reorganize and achieve homeostasis under stressful circumstances

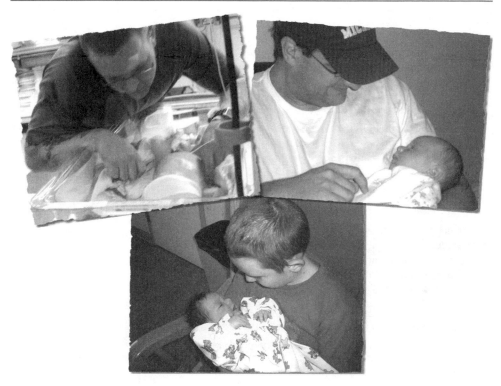

figure *9.1*

Intersubjective Eye Gaze of Parents and Infants

This behavior starts at birth and is an important means for forming attachment for siblings and fathers as well as mothers.

that occur naturally from internal or external sources. The assessment also should focus on what happens when parents attempt to achieve intersubjective eye gaze with their child. Joint completion of this observation chart by the parents and clinician can be used when planning services and monitoring expected individualized family service plan (IFSP) outcomes; updates can be added as new developments are observed.

Targeting Emotional Stability and Social Interactions

Goal 9.1. The child will engage in positive social interactions with caregiver support, signaled by mutual eye gaze, and will show the ability to regain stability when upset. This goal is appropriate for an infant (or child at any age) who demonstrates frequent loss and difficulty regaining behavioral and emotional stasis (stability). It aims at helping infants and those supporting them to develop improved regulation of behavioral state and emotions. Signs of disorganization can include inconsolable crying, angry reactions, or resistance to being cuddled or fed. Sustained mutual eye gaze is an important sign of positive interaction.

For infants and toddlers (and older children functioning at early developmental stages), intervention involves collaborative efforts to explore variations of timing, positioning, and comforting that help a child reorganize physiologically and emotionally at moments of distress. A speech–language pathologist (SLP) and occupational therapist (OT) might serve as critical members of an interdisciplinary service delivery team working with

figure *9.2*

Observation Tool for Emotional State Regulation and Mutual Attention

Observation of Emotional State Regulation and Related Factors	Observational Evidence

Describe baseline indicators:
❏ Frequency and duration of mutual engagement
❏ Frequency and duration of loss of control
❏ Time(s) of day or activities:
  ❏ When interactions are most positive
  ❏ When loss of control occurs most frequently
	Qualitative data:

What factors contribute to the child's homeostatic balance?
❏ Change in positioning
❏ Reduction in intensity of interactions
❏ Waiting before initiating further interaction
❏ Change in timing or type of feeding or other care routines
❏ Change in clothing or other tactile contact
❏ Desensitization techniques
 	
What factors seems to trigger loss of control or balance?
❏ Position or handling techniques associated with wanting to:
  ❏ Be held and cuddled
  ❏ Avoid being held or cuddled
❏ Frustrating circumstances (e.g., loss of bottle or pacifier, restrictive or too light or heavy clothing)
❏ Stressful sensory factors:
  ❏ Sound
  ❏ Touch
  ❏ Temperature
❏ Other:
	Qualitative analysis:

What goal might be set to target increased ability to regain homeostatic balance and organization? **What subgoals and methods would support the main goal?**	**Goals, criteria, and methods to try:**

Source: Based on Als et al., 1982; Sparks, 1989b.

parents and infants and toddlers with needs in this area. The team can use the observation tool in Figure 9.2 to establish objectives and guide intervention.

Interdisciplinary team members can watch for symptoms of hypersensitivity to tactile and other sensory stimuli (e.g., as demonstrated by an exaggerated startle reflex). If present, team members can explore desensitization techniques and other methods for supporting the child to demonstrate improved homeostasis and functioning. Desensitization techniques involve systematic, controlled exposure to lower doses of noxious stimuli (e.g., touch or noise) to reduce children's sensitivity over time. These techniques are used by OTs and pediatric nurses, who also can work with parents to identify positions and other soothing techniques, such as swaddling the infant tightly in a blanket, which seem to increase the baby's ability to regain homeostasis when upset.

For intervention to be well received by new parents, clinicians need to adopt a collaborative style that incorporates cultural sensitivity and a commitment to family-centered practice. They must keep in mind that it may be only days, weeks, or months since the parents have become responsible for the care of an infant with known developmental risks. Effective consulting requires a form of scaffolding for parents, in which mediators frame cues to assist parents to construct coping skills, rather than to tell them what to think or do. Clinicians also should take care not to usurp parents' roles with their infant in an attempt to show them how to do something better. For example, if a clinician picks up an infant to demonstrate a better way to hold or quiet him or her, new parents may experience this as a blow to their fragile confidence and become even less likely to explore alternate holding techniques in the future.

Clinicians can engender confidence in their expertise and ability to help while acknowledging that parenting is a challenge, especially when children have special needs, and that no one has all the answers. Every child is an individual, and together, they will explore what works best for this particular child. Clinicians can scaffold parents to gain confidence in their own ability to send positive signals of love and safety and to recognize cues of their infant's response to parental overtures. For example, a clinician might say, "Look how she seeks out your eyes" or "He really seems to quiet when he hears your soothing voice," adapting the message for children with sensory impairment, who can be fostered through holding and touch.

Gillette (1992) offered other dos and don'ts for helping new parents develop skills for interacting with high-risk infants. Among what not to do, Gillette warned clinicians not to make directive statements such as "Make eye contact with your child each time you feed him" and "Wait before you tell her to do that again," which family members might interpret as judgment that they are doing something wrong. A better approach would be to make simple comments that frame the cues that seem most helpful and represent positive aspects of the interactions, such as "The two of you seem to go after each other's attention with your eyes while he takes the bottle" and "I notice that the more you wait, the more she seems to do." Occasionally, a clinician might use a guiding scaffold, such as "I wonder what she'll do if you smile at her now" or "Some babies need a little more quiet time before they will engage actively; let's see what happens if you wait." Occasionally, the clinician might make a suggestion: "I have an idea; let's see how he responds when I try this." In general, however, it is best for clinicians to take a supporting role to the parents, who take the direct role with the infant.

Assessing Early Communicative Interactions

Wells (1986) commented, "By six months, then, a baby and his or her chief caregivers have established the basis for communication: a relationship of mutual attention" (p. 34). After stability and mutual intersubjective attention have been achieved, the target can shift to facilitating prelinguistic communication routines by engaging in mutual attention through facial expression and imitating sounds the child produces. In these exchanges, the infant and caregiver take turns making sounds and watching and matching each other's facial expressions and emotional states. Figure 9.3 offers a tool for observing early vocalizing that summarizes typical developmental expectations for vocalization, babbling, and intonation. It can be used for assessment, selection of intervention targets, and documenting progress.

As early exchanges develop into preverbal reciprocal dialogues, they are considered *protoconversations* (Bateson, 1975) (see Figure 9.4, page 245). Brazelton (1982) described the phases of reciprocal dialogues as involving initiation, orientation to the expected interaction, acceleration to a peak of excitement, deceleration (avoiding overstimulation), and disengagement (e.g., by turning away).

Targeting Reciprocal Dialogues and Imitation of Caregivers

Goal 9.2. The child will engage in synchronous reciprocal dialogues and show emerging imitation skills when supported by the caregiver. This goal aims at helping parents treat all

figure *9.3*————————————————————————————

Observation Tool for Early Preverbal Vocalization and Speech–Sound Production

Observation of Vocal Development and Speech Sound Production	Observational Evidence
Birth to 2 months ❑ More crying and discomfort sounds than noncrying sounds ❑ Noncrying sounds tend to be reflexive, neutral, and vowel-like (vocalic)	
2 to 4 months ❑ Marked decrease in crying (after 12 weeks) ❑ Vocalic sounds predominate, but consonantlike sounds emerge (especially glottal sounds: /g/, /h/, /ʔ/, /k/) ❑ Consonant–vowel (CV) combinations emerge (e.g., *coo* or *goo*)	
4 to 6 months ❑ Increase in consonant segments ❑ Variation in vowels ❑ Production of CV syllables ❑ Variation of intonational contours	
6 to 10 months ❑ Canonical reduplicative babbling (e.g., *bababa*) ❑ Variations of intonation contours ❑ Early nonreduplicative CV syllables ❑ Utterances produced with full stop	
10 to 12 months ❑ Variegated babbling (advanced reduplicative babbling) ❑ Varied CV and CVC combinations with sentencelike intonation ❑ Approximations of meaningful single words	
12 to 15 months ❑ CV combinations with labial and alveolar sounds	
15 to 18 months ❑ Varied CV combinations increase, but open syllables (with no final consonants) predominate	
18 to 24 months ❑ CVC combinations (closed syllables) become more frequent ❑ Production patterns include fricatives and dorsals as well as clusters and final consonants	

Source: Based on Davis, 2005; Proctor, 1989.

their child's behaviors as communicative and also to engage the child in exchanges of turn taking and imitation.

Reciprocal dialogues can be facilitated by helping parents imagine their child's emotional perspective. One technique for parents of young or severely involved children is to get them to put into words the messages they think are in their children's minds (e.g., "Mommy, I'm hungry" or "Daddy, play with me."). Encouraging parents to become aware of their own theory of mind capabilities (for what is in their infant's mind) can lead to increased perlocutionary responsiveness. Parents also can be encouraged to observe, comment, and then wait for a vocal or behavioral response from their child.

figure *9.4*

Observation Tool for Assessing Preverbal Communication Turn Taking (Protoconversations)

Observation of Reciprocal Interaction within Protoconversations	Observational Evidence
Baseline indicators: ❑ Frequency with which child initiates interactions ❑ How the child shows orientation to the partner ❑ Duration of stage of acceleration to peak of excitement ❑ Duration of stage of deceleration ❑ Length of time before child turns away or signals overstimulation	
Caregiver interaction techniques and their effects: ❑ Phasing (monitoring infant signals to time stimulating input to be most effective) ❑ Adapting (using predictable input sequences to assist infants to assimilate new information, e.g., new facial expression, sound, or baby game) ❑ Facilitating (structuring routines to support infant success) ❑ Elaborating (monitoring child's focus of attention and then using gestures, vocal, and verbal stimuli to respond contingently and elaborate the experience) ❑ Initiating (using gestures to draw child's attention to new information or stimuli) ❑ Directing (telling or showing infants what to do and then assisting them to comply, e.g., to remove cloth from head during peek-a-boo games)	

Source: Based on Bateson, 1975; Brazelton, 1982; Schaffer, 1977; Greenspan & Wieder, 1997.

The propensity for a child to imitate can be observed even in newborns. For example, if while holding the eye gaze of her infant the mother of a newborn slowly protrudes her tongue, the newborn infant often will imitate the motion. This is consistent with research on reciprocal mirror-neurons networks (Rizzolatti, Fadiga, Gallese, & Fogassi, 1996). It is a neuropsychological trait that can support further learning and is only beginning to be investigated.

One of the best ways to teach imitation is to start by imitating the child. Parents can imitate facial expressions and vocalizations and then introduce minor variations when their child reciprocates. The observe-and-match technique is consistent with MacDonald's ecological model (MacDonald, 1989; MacDonald & Carroll, 1992), which was described in Chapter 8. It involves helping parents learn to match their child's actions and interests as they become more facilitative partners for the child in communication and play. Helping parents develop a playful attitude and enjoyment of their children is part of this process (see Personal Reflection 9.1).

PERSONAL reflection *9.1*

"Children are not learning to talk in order to be able to behave like their parents for the sake of conformity, but rather to be able to communicate with them in collaborative activities in which the roles played are *reciprocal* rather than imitative."

Gordon Wells (1986, p. 42, italics in original), a sociolinguist, was commenting on the catalyst for early language in his book, *The Meaning Makers*, which presented the results of his longitudinal study of language acquisition.

It is important to judge the best times and durations for such exchanges. Infants may yawn or show other physiological signs when they become overstimulated. By engaging caregivers in assessing their infant's reciprocal turn-taking behaviors, clinicians can scaffold them to notice cues and become more sensitive to their infant's signals and needs for phasing of interactions so they can ramp up stimulation and excitement, as needed, or calm it down in response to those signals.

Early Intentional Communication

Preverbal intentional communication sets the stage for later social interaction and supports the pragmatic aspects of language development. It should be assessed for all children, but is particularly significant for children with autism spectrum disorders and other cognitive–communicative disabilities (Wetherby et al., 1989; Woods & Wetherby, 2003).

The preverbal communication act of commenting (also called making *protodeclaratives;* Bates et al., 1979) is a positive prognostic indicator for productive language if present and a negative indicator if absent (e.g., McCathren, Warren, & Yoder, 1996). Commenting is essentially social, soliciting another's attention to an object or self. Shifting eye gaze between the object and the communicative partner provides a clear sign of intentional communication. Bigelow, MacLean, and Proctor (2004) described joint attention episodes as "triadic exchanges that involve both the infant's and a partner's awareness of the other's mutual focus of attention on a third object or event" (p. 518). Such episodes emerge during the second half of the first year and mark the "development of secondary intersubjectivity or awareness that their experience with objects can be shared with others" (p. 518). This awareness is triggered when a parent focuses on the object of the infant's attention and comments (see Figure 9.5).

Communication acts that involve requesting are more resistant to communication risk than commenting, but the quality of requesting acts needs special attention in assessment.

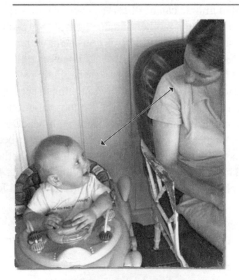 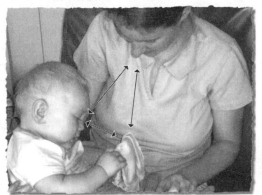

figure *9.5*

Mother–Child Interactions

These photos show an episode of mother–child intersubjective gaze (left: mutual attention, represented best by a reciprocal straight line), followed by shared attention (right: represented with a triangle), with joint reference to a washcloth that has drawn the infant's attention.

Without eye contact, requesting is not judged to be a fully intentional communication act. Children with social communication difficulties make requests for actions or objects with minimal focus on the social interaction aspects of the exchange. For example, a child with autism may place a parent's hand on a bag of candy or a wind-up toy as a sign of intention to gain the desired object or have the action executed. Other children with special needs also may be slow to use communicative gestures for pointing and showing. Thal and Tobias (1994) studied toddlers with specific expressive language delay (SELD) between 18 and 33 months and found them to be slow in producing commenting gestures as well as words. Mundy, Kasari, Sigman, and Ruskin (1995) documented slower gestural development, as well as later word emergence, among children with Down syndrome.

Assessing Preintentional to Intentional Communication

Prelinguistic (also called *preverbal*) communication gradually transitions from the pre-intentional (i.e., perlocutionary) stage of development to the intentional (i.e., illocution-ary) stage. This transition is a critical step on the pathway toward fully effective symbolic communication (the locutionary stage). Figure 9.6 summarizes characteristics of children's movement through these three stages of early communication development that should be assessed with informal observation techniques and in collaboration with parents.

Assessment and intervention planning for children who are not developing typi-cally must take into consideration how contextual variables interact with a child's current developmental status to influence the expression of communicative intentions. Coggins, Olswang, and Guthrie (1987) observed typically developing infants from 9 months to 24 months to describe the longitudinal emergence of comments (for directing attention) and requests (for directing actions). Two-thirds could demonstrate commenting by 12 months and requesting by 15 months. Less structured contexts worked better for eliciting com-ments; more structured contexts worked better for eliciting requests. Not until 21 months were structured contexts as effective as unstructured ones for eliciting comments.

Figure 9.7 (page 249) provides an observation tool for documenting and promoting preverbal intentional communication (based on Bruner, 1975; Coggins et al., 1987; Roth & Spekman, 1984). It includes assessment of attention seeking and commenting, requesting, and reciprocating and can be used to encourage development of illocutionary communication acts.

Targeting Intentional Communication

Goal 9.3. The child will transition from preintentional to intentional communication. After identifying gaps in functioning within a particular context (also called a *milieu*), clinicians can arrange to focus children's attention on cues for communication that they previously missed in that milieu.

Yoder, Warren, Kim, and Gazdag (1994) gathered evidence for a milieu approach tar-geting early communicative intentions. The goal was to establish a milieu that obligated the child to make a request that included all three components required for establishing clear intentionality—a look at the adult, a look at the object, and a discrete gesture or vocaliza-tion. Any component not present in a particular interaction was prompted. For example, if a child initiated a request by reaching and vocalizing but failed to look at the clinician's face, the adult would prompt it with a direct request, such as "Look at me." If no request was initiated, the adult then would ask, "What do you want?"

Recognizing that such an approach was highly adult directed, Yoder and colleagues (1994) set a goal to promote more natural parent–child communication. They hypothesized that when children began to use more frequent and clear nonverbal communication cues, their parents naturally would begin to map language onto those acts. To test the hypothesis,

figure *9.6*

Stages of Additive Intentional and Linguistic Communicative Development

Observation of Intentional Communication Development	Observational Evidence
Perlocutionary Stage (0–8 months) Intention inferred by adult ❑ Active environmental exploration ❑ Vocal and gestural signals not directed at others ❑ Contingent social outcomes not anticipated ❑ Linguistic comprehension not in evidence	
Illocutionary Stage (8–12 months) Intention conveyed nonverbally *Primitive Illocutionary* ❑ Signals directed at others expecting specific outcomes ❑ Signals may be subtle and only interpreted by caregivers ❑ Signals apparently goal directed, as indicated by persistence or frustration if goal not reached ❑ Early linguistic comprehension in context-bound routines *Conventional Illocutionary* ❑ Evidence of clear concept of communication ❑ Conventional use of gestures and vocalizations to achieve specific outcomes ❑ Prelinguistic symbols interpreted by wider range of people ❑ Greater persistence if communicative goals not met ❑ Evidence of linguistic comprehension in context; some multiword utterances and object labels understood out of context	
Locutionary Stage (12 months and older) Words used to express intention *Emerging Locutionary* ❑ Linguistic forms (words or signs) used consistently for communication (some idiosyncratic) ❑ Word use is decontextualized ❑ Forms are conventional and understood by many ❑ Nonverbal devices (gaze, gestures) remain in repertoire ❑ Increased comprehension, in and out of context *Locutionary* ❑ Language primary means of sending and receiving messages ❑ Language knowledge includes varied sentence types, grammatical morphemes, complex sentences ❑ Language used to talk about temporally and spatially displaced content ❑ Most language misunderstood, except abstract and nonliteral	

Source: Based on Bates, Camaioni, & Volterra, 1975; Prizant, 1984.

the researchers had mothers play with their toddlers in the same room with the same toys after each intervention session. As predicted, the mothers (who had not observed the sessions) used more linguistic mapping (e.g., saying "ball" or "bye-bye") as their children began to demonstrate intentional gestures more frequently. This study supported the transactional process of adults' influences on children's communication opportunities, and vice versa.

Warren and colleagues (2006) continued to develop this line of intervention, calling it *responsivity education/prelinguistic milieu teaching (RE/PMT)*. They described RE/PMT as an approach for children functioning developmentally between 9 and 15 months of age

figure *9.7*————————————————————————————

Observation Tool for Preverbal Intentional Communication

Observation of Preverbal Expression of Communicative Intention	Observational Evidence

Attention Seeking and Commenting Acts
❑ Spontaneously uses greeting actions (*hi* or *bye*)
❑ Intentionally seeks attention to self
  ❑ Vocalizes until adult looks and then smiles
  ❑ Tugs on parent to secure attention
❑ Demonstrates intentional commenting (seeking attention to objects) [by 12 months]
  ❑ Extends object in hand to show adult
  ❑ Picks up object to show adult
  ❑ Points to object or looks back and forth between object and adult
  ❑ Vocalizes with any of the above
  ❑ Verbalizes with any of the above
❑ Demonstrates intentional informing
  ❑ Pointing out a particular feature (e.g., broken wheel)
  ❑ Drawing attention to a particular component of an object or event	

Requesting Acts
❑ Demonstrates intentional requests for objects
  ❑ Stretches hand toward object while leaning; may whine or vocalize
  ❑ Stretches hand toward object with ritual gesture
❑ Demonstrates intentional requests for actions [by 15 months]
  ❑ Reaches to signal wish to be picked up
  ❑ Brings book or toy to adult and signals wish to interact
  ❑ Looks toward movable object (e.g., windup toy that has potential to move or has ceased moving) and makes a ritual requesting gesture for adult to reactivate it
  ❑ Looks at, touches, points to, or hands object to adult and vocalizes or verbalizes	

Reciprocating Communication Acts
❑ Spontaneously acknowledges or responds to adult request
  ❑ Moves to signal compliance with familiar routine
  ❑ Smiles when parent initiates familiar play routine
  ❑ Hands object back to adult when requested
❑ Spontaneously protests or rejects
  ❑ Cries or fusses when toy is taken away and reaches for it
  ❑ Cries or fusses when parent leaves interaction, puts child down, or performs some other undesired action
  ❑ Pushes away object or food to signal rejection	

Source: Based on Bruner, 1975; Coggins, Olswang, & Guthrie, 1987; Roth & Spekman, 1984.

but noted that children with developmental delays might not reach that point until they are 2 to 3 years of age. The PMT portion of the approach is delivered by a clinician interacting directly with a child, whereas the RE portion involves a clinician interacting with the parents. This approach is based on a *transactional model* of social communication development, which "presumes that early social and communication development are facilitated by bidirectional, reciprocal interactions between children and their environment" (Warren et al., 2006, p. 49). It is also an example of a *blended strategy,* as described by Wilcox (2008) and the ASHA committee on service delivery for infants and toddlers.

Yoder and Warren (2001) conducted longitudinal research with 58 children with developmental delays (from 17 to 32 months of age) who had been engaged with their mothers in two forms of intervention. The research began with pretesting, followed by treatment sessions for 20 minutes per day, three or four days per week, for six months. Half of the children received PMT, in which the mother learned to promote her child's responsiveness by (a) following the child's attentional lead; (b) engaging in turn taking, such as social play routines; (c) using prompts, such as time delays by holding a ball until the child indicates a request for the adult to roll the ball back; and (d) providing natural consequences, such as giving the ball when requested. The other half of the children received a responsive small group (RSG) treatment, in which an adult played with the child and responded with comments on his or her play but did not directly attempt to prompt any communicative form or function.

Children who received PMT made greater gains in both lexical diversity and on a standardized language test than those who received the RSG treatment, but results differed based on the mother's education and pretreatment interaction style. Children of less well educated mothers who were less responsive at the beginning of the study benefited more from the responsivity education (RE) within the RSG, whereas children of better educated mothers who were more highly responsive at the beginning benefited more from the prompting techniques of PMT. Yoder and Warren (2001) hypothesized that positive experiences with communicatively responsive parents may enable children to persist in attempting to communicate even when mothers introduce time delays and other directive techniques.

In a subsequent study, Yoder and Warren (2002) provided RE for all families to prime all children to respond positively to the PMT. Some children participating in the RE/PMT group—particularly children with Down syndrome and those with higher levels of commenting and vocalization at onset—made fewer gains than children in the control group. In discussing this body of research, Warren and colleagues (2006) noted that the RE/PMT intervention worked best with children who had lower skills initially.

Fey and colleagues (2006) investigated several modifications in RE/PMT (as recommended by Yoder & Warren, 2002). The responsiveness protocol was modified so as not to require all three components (gestures, vocalizations, and gaze shifts) to credit intentionality but to respond to gestures or gaze shift alone as intentional. SLPs provided the treatment (rather than paraprofessionals) and responded to the communicative intention of the act—for example, giving the child the juice and saying "juice" rather than imitating the utterance "didi" produced while the child reached for the juice. Because the best results had occurred in prior research for children with lower abilities, children were enrolled who had no more than 10 expressive words or signs. In total, 51 children (ages 24 to 33 months) were assigned randomly to receive either RE/PMT or standard services for six months. Each group included 13 children with Down syndrome. While the children were receiving the modified PMT, the parents received eight one-hour individual sessions of RE, modeled after the Hanen program. The parents were not taught to implement PMT in these sessions but "to recognize real or possible communicative attempts . . . and to respond to them meaningfully" (p. 530). Specifically, parents learned to demonstrate heightened awareness of their child's communication behaviors, to wait for their child to produce interpretable behaviors, to attend to their child's focus of attention and follow his or her lead, and to provide appropriate responses contingent to their child's communication acts. Parents learned to respond to nonverbal requests (e.g., giving the requested object) with contingent verbal responses, such as linguistic mapping of nonverbal acts and recasting of less mature verbal acts. The results showed that the children in the RE/PMT group made significantly greater gains than the children in the comparison group, who received no special treatment.

The results of these collective studies suggest that when parents learn to modify their responsiveness to their toddler's messages and treat them as intentional, communicative acts, the child is likely to benefit. More naturalistic responses to the child's communicative messages seem to have advantages over more structured and controlling responses.

SUMMARY

Supporting prelinguistic organization and the development of intentional communication requires attention to a child's emotional stability and social interaction with caregivers. The studies reviewed in this section show that when parents learn to modify their responsiveness to their toddler's messages and treat them as intentional communication acts, the child is likely to benefit. More naturalistic responses to the child's communicative messages seem to have advantages over more structured and controlling responses.

Joint Action Routines and Early Play

Techniques for expanding children's intentional communication acts involve teaching parents to observe and match their children's interests and actions within the context of familiar *joint action routines (JARs),* beginning with reciprocal imitation. As children gain in competence during prelinguistic turn taking, parents begin to introduce variations in routines and use time delays to provide opportunities for their children to signal intention to extend the game.

Joint Reference

Infants gradually transition from intersubjective (i.e., mutual) attention to shared (i.e., joint) attention focused on other people, animals, and things in the environment. As children transition from preintentional to intentional communicative interactions, reciprocal *dialogues* (i.e., protoconversations) between infants and caregivers become increasingly elaborate, and children move through phases of intentionality toward symbolic communication.

Assessing Joint Reference

Joint reference and play are key features in the progression from presymbolic to symbolic functioning, which in turn is critical to the development of language. Figure 9.8 provides an observation tool based on the process of joint referencing.

Parents engage their young children in familiar joint action routines (JARs) in contexts of daily care (e.g., mealtime, bathtime) and play. Figure 9.9 shows an example of an 11-month-old child engaging in a familiar routine of chase and peek-a-boo with his father. In the peek-a-boo exchange, the infant constructed a technique of lying flat on the floor to peek under the ottoman to gauge his father's position and direction of movement, turning and squealing when his father changed direction. Evidence of similar signs of engagement should be sought when assessing young children with development problems. The intervention process can involve typically developing siblings as well.

Targeting Interactive Routines and Sense Making

Goal 9.4. The child will engage in interactive routines (e.g., peek-a-boo, patty cake) with a caregiver. Bruner (1975) described parents' use of *joint attention* and *joint referencing*

figure *9.8*

Joint Reference and Early Word Production Observation Tool

Observation of Preverbal and Early Verbal Forms of Joint Referencing (with approximate age expected in typical development)	Observational Evidence (with date and age observed)
❏ Parent brings objects in closer, shakes them, and says "Oh look," eliciting gaze at object. (4–6 weeks)	

❏ Infant follows visually:
  ❏ Parent's bodily movement
  ❏ Parent's movement of object of focus (8 weeks)	

❏ Infant can distinguish vocalizations directed to him or her and seek the source. (3 months)	
❏ Infant can follow parent's line of regard (i.e., direction of looking) and soon infant's response quickens when adult says "Look!" (4 months)	
❏ Infant may respond to parent's use of object or event name and intonational pattern to establish joint reference. (6 months)	
❏ Intentional communication begins. Gradually, child shifts from "reach-for-real" when desiring a particular object to using "reach-for-signal" gesture, in which infant shifts gaze from object to parent and back again. (8 months)	
❏ Child gradually replaces full hand reach as requesting gesture with finger point. This coincides with emergence of preverbal comments, in which infant points to direct attention and not just to request objects. In response, parents begin to increase labeling of objects identified by child. (10–12 months)	
❏ When child begins to use true words to name things, balance shifts so that parents seek to get child to look, point, or verbalize within ongoing dialogues. Gradually, parental questioning decreases as child's discourse skills advance. (12–18 months and beyond)	

Source: Based on Bruner, 1975; Coggins et al., 1987.

figure *9.9*

Illustration of a Joint Action Routine (JAR) for Encouraging Early Communicative–Social and Conceptual Development to scaffold their infant's and toddler's attention to key features and patterns in experiences they share. Parents scaffold the development of joint attention and referencing by following their child's line of regard and commenting (e.g., by pointing to or manipulating objects of their child's attention and naming them).

The family-centered intervention process for this goal should begin by helping parents follow the child's line of regard and comment on objects of the child's attention. Extra cues may be used to heighten the exchange, such as picking up a stuffed toy and jiggling it, holding up a book and turning the pages, pointing and commenting at the family dog, bringing the child's bottle or toy up to the adult's face, establishing eye contact, and smiling. When the child shows signs of pleasure and attention, the adult can repeat the routine in similar circumstances on other days and introduce variations and elaborations (e.g., sound effects, more motions) to keep the child interested.

As the child gains improved ability to sustain attention on objects of joint reference, the parents can be encouraged to expand episodes into more elaborate nursery games and other JARs to support the development of language and thinking. Routines may be built into playtime (e.g., peek-a-boo, How big is baby? Creep mousey), bath time (e.g., "Where's baby's tummy?"), feeding ("Here comes the airplane!"), exploring new motor skills (e.g., climbing steps), and bedtime (e.g., reading *Goodnight Moon*). Keeping a parent journal can document the effectiveness of intervention while heightening parents' attention to their child's interests. If the parents are willing, it should be treated as a collaborative enterprise, with celebrations of new JARs and elaborations of old ones, and not as homework or an exercise for evaluating caregiving.

Early Play

Gradually, JARs and individual play with objects evolve into higher-level forms of play. As described by Piaget (1926/1959), babies in the sensorimotor stage of early cognitive development initially apply strategies for manipulating objects in a nonsymbolic but playful manner. As they develop further, they begin to use objects to imitate conventional functions (e.g., phone to ear; brush to hair). From that point, it is not long before they begin to play with objects as symbols of other things. Higher forms of symbolic play are characterized by three processes: (1) *symbolization,* or using one object to represent another, such as a block to represent a vehicle or a marker pen to represent a microphone; (2) *decontextualization,* or using actions in a playful manner separated from typical settings, such as pretending to eat when it is not snacktime; and (3) *decentration,* using actions in play that they are unable or not allowed to perform in real life, such as cooking, caring for a baby, shopping for groceries, serving fast food, and driving a car.

Assessing Early Play

The assessment of early play can be facilitated by observation tools that outline the primary features of an expected developmental sequence. Figure 9.10 provides a tool for observing four early phases of nonsymbolic play (based on Casby, 2003), showing how they transition into symbolic play (based on Nicholich, 1981; Westby, 1988). The observation tool can be used to document the presence of existing and emerging abilities and to guide dynamic assessment, scaffolding abilities just above the child's current level of functioning to explore the extent to which his or her ZPD can be stretched.

Exploratory play begins around 2 to 4 months and extends to around 10 months (Casby, 2003). Using exploratory play, infants assimilate objects into current sensorimotor schemas. Mouthing, shaking, banging, stacking, pouring, pushing, blowing, and other sensorimotor exploratory actions also help infants explore physical properties of the perceivable

figure 9.10

Observation Tool for Assessing Early Play

Stage (approx. age)	Thematic Content, Decontextualization, and Organization	Self/Other Relations	Language		
			Functions	**Forms and Meanings**	

Stage (approx. age)	Thematic Content, Decontextualization, and Organization	Self/Other Relations	Functions	Forms and Meanings
Exploratory play (2–10 months)	❑ Manipulates single objects by grasping, holding, or mouthing them	❑ Often solitary but may be embedded in joint action routines with caregiver	❑ Transitions from perlocutionary to illocutionary acts by end of this period	❑ Preverbal
Object manipulation (nonfunctional) play (5–12 months)	❑ Combines two objects in playful way by banging, stacking, pushing, or lining them up	❑ Often solitary but may be embedded in joint action routines with caregiver	❑ Illocutionary acts (e.g., pointing) are used to communicate true intentions by end of this period	❑ Early vocalizations include squeals and playful noises
Functional play (10–18 months)	❑ Pretends to use objects for typical functions, such as holding phone to ear, pushing truck while making motor noise, pretending to drink from empty cup, and pretending to brush own hair	❑ Acts are based on self as agent ❑ Joint action routines with caregiver become more varied (peek-a-boo, horsie rides, tickle games)	❑ Shows intentional commenting and requests	❑ Gestures and vocalizations are paired ❑ First words appear
Symbolic play (16–18 months) **Westby's Stage I** (17–19 months)	❑ Demonstrates tool use (e.g., pulling on yarn or using stick to retrieve toy) ❑ Uses lifelike props for pretending to participate in familiar, everyday activities (e.g., sleeping, eating, reading books) in short, isolated schemas ❑ Begins to use one object to represent another	❑ Acts are based on self as agent (called *autosymbolic play*), e.g., pretends to drink from cup or comb own hair ❑ Noninteractive parallel play	❑ Directing ❑ Requesting ❑ Commanding ❑ Interacting ❑ Self-maintaining ❑ Protesting ❑ Protecting self-interests ❑ Commenting ❑ Labeling object or action ❑ Indicating personal feelings	❑ True verbal communication begins (example semantic categories and words): ❑ Recurrence (*more*) ❑ Existence (*there*) ❑ Nonexistence (*all gone*) ❑ Rejection (*no*) ❑ Denial (*no*) ❑ Agent (*Daddy*) ❑ Object/entity (*book*) ❑ Action or state (*going; is*) ❑ Location (*outside*) ❑ Attribute (*hot*) ❑ Possession (*mine*)

Source: Based on Casby, 2003; Westby, 1988.

world and, in the process, to learn about solids, liquids, shapes, textures, sounds, tastes, and so forth. The exploratory phase overlaps with the phase of ***object manipulation play*** (termed *nonfunctional play* by Casby). Object manipulation play predominates in typical development from around 5 to 6 months until 10 to 12 months and is characterized by experimental manipulation of objects in nonfunctional ways, such as by stacking, inserting one in another, and lining them up. ***Functional play*** begins around 10 to 12 months when children pretend to use objects for their typical functions, such as holding a phone to the ear, pushing a truck and making a motor noise, and pretending to drink from an empty cup. ***Symbolic play*** emerges around 16 to 18 months when children use one object to symbolize another and begin to perform play actions on dolls (around 21 months) rather than themselves. Symbolic play later becomes elaborated into *dramatic play* as more complex scene setting and interactive schemas are developed throughout childhood.

Early language, vocal imitation, and symbolic play are correlated in typically developing children (Bates et al., 1979), but questions arise about the relationship of play and language for children with language impairment (LI). Some research has shown that play and language, though related, can develop separately. Terrell, Schwartz, Prelock, and Messick (1984) used the Symbolic Play Test (Lowe & Costello, 1976) to compare play and language development for 15 typically developing children (ages 16 to 22 months) and slightly older language-matched children with LI (ages 32 to 49 months), when both groups were at the one-word stage. Ratings were made for the level of the child's symbolic play behavior (e.g., number of schemas, such as plate on table or doll on chair) when toys were introduced in four semistructured situations: (1) large doll; then saucer, cup, and spoon; then brush and comb; (2) toy bed, pillow, blanket, and small girl doll; (3) toy chair, table, tablecloth, fork, knife, plate, and small boy doll; and (4) toy tractor, attachable trailer, small man doll, and logs. Children with LI achieved play scores significantly higher than language-matched (but younger) peers. Terrell et al. (1984) concluded that LI was separable because the children with LI were able to symbolize, act on, and combine symbolic elements in play even though their language was severely delayed. This suggested that they had the ideas but lacked the language.

Roth and Clark (1987), also using the Symbolic Play Test, found different results. They also compared play and social communication abilities for six children with LI to eight (younger) language-matched typically developing peers but found deficits both for symbolic play and social communication. For example, more than half of the children with LI failed to put the girl doll to bed or the man doll on the tractor. Other research has shown that when children begin to elaborate their play by combining objects and using one to act on another, they also are moving toward production of two-word utterances (Schwartz, Chapman, Terrell, Prelock, & Rowen, 1985).

These combined results support the recommendation to assess both verbal and nonverbal symbolic functioning. Children with LI as a primary or secondary condition constitute a heterogeneous group. Some have co-occurring play and social skill deficits, whereas others have strengths in play and social skills but deficits in expressive phonology, morphology, and syntax. The two types of profiles may justify different plans of intervention.

Targeting Symbolic Play

Goal 9.5. The child will transition from presymbolic to symbolic play. Children with cognitive–communicative impairments and other comorbid conditions, including pragmatic language impairment or autism spectrum disorders, often need direct modeling of symbolic play behaviors as well as language.

Repetitive play routines with adult modeling of play routines using toy objects in meaningful playful exchanges may be the best way to promote higher levels of play. An observation tool, such as the play scale outline in Figure 9.10, can guide clinicians, preschool teachers, and parents in collaborating to scaffold features of the next higher level beyond baseline functioning. By targeting play and language together, children with combined cognitive and linguistic deficits can access richer cues about meaning. Playful interactions also can reduce anxiety and remove the need to judge responses as correct or incorrect. Cues about meaning can be made explicit, and interventions can be incorporated into daily routines so that multiple repetitions occur in meaningful contexts.

SUMMARY

Joint action routines and early play are targeted best in the context of family-centered intervention. Parents, clinicians, and preschool teachers can provide the contexts that can support children in early intentions and symbolic functioning by building playful routines that can be reenacted many times and elaborated as the child gains skill. Play involves the development of symbolization, decontextualization, and decentration. A template of early play development includes the stages exploratory play, object manipulation (nonfunctional) play, functional play, and symbolic play (by 18 months or so). Following such a template can guide clinicians in knowing what to scaffold next.

First Words to Two-Word Utterances

Verbal communication (i.e., communication using real words) grows out of preverbal reciprocal communication and vocal turn-taking. Parents anxiously await their child's first real words, which appear typically around his or her first birthday, although the normal developmental period for first-word emergence extends to 18 months. Prior to first true words, **vocables** (also called *protowords*) may appear. These are wordlike forms with recognizable and consistent sound patterns, but they do not refer symbolically to consistent referents. For example, a child may produce the reduplicative consonant–vowel syllable /gaga/ to refer to *bottle, book, dog,* and a favorite toy *truck.* These preverbal vocal abilities were outlined in Figure 9.3.

Early Words

Only when productions are recognizable as being relatively consistent and the child uses them to refer to the same concept in more than one context are they considered true words. Many children go through a phase of mixing real words with vocables or jargon. *Jargon* is a form of variegated babbling, in which sentencelike variations in intonation make it sound as if a toddler is making comments, asking questions, making requests, or expressing opinions.

As typically developing children move through the preschool years, many experience a vocabulary spurt between one and two years of age. Vocabulary development is an individualized and lifelong process. The information processes that support vocabulary development are evident as children notice new words, perceive their sound structures, understand their meanings, articulate them well enough to be understood, and store them in personal lexicons for later retrieval in appropriate and novel contexts. The ability to segment connected speech into individual words and to fastmap sounds and meanings onto associated experiences is part of the amazing feat of normal language development.

Metalinguistic concepts of words as objects emerge during the preschool years, especially for typically developing children in supportive environments where literacy is valued. This goes beyond the ability to detect word boundaries to the ability to rhyme and manipulate words as objects in language play. Children engaged in emergent literacy experiences also come to understand that words and sounds can be represented by letters printed on a page. These connections are to be encouraged and are described as intervention targets in the section on emergent literacy later in this chapter.

Assessing Early Words

True word production is credited when children begin to produce words with recognizable forms to accomplish communicative functions that were accomplished previously through gestures and other nonverbal means. This usually occurs several weeks or months after children have begun to comprehend words in familiar contexts.

Nelson (1985) proposed that learning to talk is essentially a process of entering into a system of shared meanings. She observed that early words often are inseparable from the contexts in which they are experienced, noting that "the child's representational system is largely organized around events that are undifferentiated, unanalyzed schemas without separable elements or concepts" (p. 121). Thus, young children may only be able to understand or use words within familiar contexts, which is an important element to keep in mind during assessment. Even in contexts in which parents and children are engaged in joint reference focused on a common object, "the protolanguage form seems to be *part* of the activity rather than *referring* to the object of the activity" (p. 121). Gradually, words come to appear in multiple contexts, refer to varied content, and be used for varied functions.

In typical development, word learning starts fairly slowly but soon picks up speed. Assessment activities should be dynamic enough to identify evidence of the rate of learning. Crais (1990) estimated that typically developing children add approximately five word roots per day from 18 months to 6 years of age, at which point they can comprehend around 14,000 words. Goldfield and Reznick (1990) studied the transition from slow to rapid word learning by examining mothers' diary records for 18 toddlers followed longitudinally from 14 months to 22 months. They found individual differences among the children (as described by K. Nelson, 1973), with the majority (13 of the 18 toddlers) showing a vocabulary spurt as they approached 2 years that functioned as a "naming explosion." Goldfield and Reznick's data showed that almost three-quarters of the words learned during this period were nouns. Five of the toddlers, however, showed more gradual word learning and acquired a balance of nouns and other word classes. They encoded a range of experience with a more varied lexicon, and with more gradual growth.

When children are learning more than one language simultaneously, they may add different words in each language, which also has implications for assessment. Pearson, Fernandez, and Oller (1995) reported that bilingual toddlers use many words in one language but not the other. On the other hand, some words overlap between the two languages. If there are concerns about the language-learning abilities for a dual language learner, his or her vocabulary should be assessed in both languages (Goldstein, 2006).

Patterson (1998) described young bilingual children as having lexical knowledge "spread across two languages" (p. 47). She recommended using total vocabulary (i.e., in Language A + Language B) to provide the measure of expressive vocabulary knowledge for dual language learners. Patterson developed an adapted version of Rescorla's (1989) Language Development Survey to gather parent reports for 102 children between the ages of 21 and 27 months who were learning both Spanish and English in the southwestern United States. (The adapted survey appears in an appendix to Patterson's article.) The children ranged in word production from 7 to 525 total words at age 21 to 22 months (with a mean of 101 words and a median of 49). At 26 to 27 months, mothers reported the range of children's total vocabulary in both languages to be 59 to 431 words (with a mean of 208 words and a median of 214). Because of these wide ranges, Patterson was cautious about suggesting clinical guidelines for identifying risk for language disorder. She noted, however, that concern and follow-up assessment would be justified for children who had vocabularies below the tenth percentile for each of three age groups (with thresholds of 20 words at

21–22 months; 37 words at 23–25 months; 82 words at 26–27 months) and children who were not combining words by 26–27 months.

When assessing children's early language development, it is important to recognize that formulaic phrases sometimes serve as "giant words." Although such forms appear to represent multiword phrases, they actually may be learned as unanalyzed chunks (e.g., "Here-ya-go," "All-done," "All-gone"). Figure 9.11 provides an assessment and intervention chart that summarizes early words based on categories that appear frequently in research on typically developing children (e.g., Bloom & Lahey, 1978; K. Nelson, 1973; Roth & Spekman, 1984). It can be used in conjunction with more formal inventories of word development. In a classic study of 18 typically developing children, K. Nelson (1973) reported percentages (from highest to lowest) for types of words in the children's early expressive lexicons for general nominals (49 percent), specific nominals (14 percent), action

figure *9.11* ————————————————————————————

Observation Tool for Early Words

Observation of Categories of Words in Child's Early Lexicon (with expected age and examples)	Observational Evidence
Early Word Comprehension (10–18 months) ❑ Name of family member or pet ❑ Label for game or social ritual *(bye-bye, peek-a-boo)* ❑ Manipulable object or toy (blanket, phone) ❑ Body parts (nose, belly) ❑ Food related (cookie, bottle)	
Early Spoken (or Signed) Words, with Related Meanings and Function (10–18 months) ❑ Attention-seeking and personal–social words for engaging in rituals *(hi, yes, no, nite-nite, please, peek-a-boo)* ❑ Protesting words for rejecting or prohibiting action *(no, stop)* ❑ Negative words for commenting on nonexistence, cessation, or disappearance *(no, all gone)* ❑ Recurrence words for commenting on or requesting objects or actions *(more, again, another)* ❑ Function words for noting existence of objects, people, or animals or for requesting information about them *(it, this, that, there, what, where)* ❑ General nominals for naming categories of objects, people, or animals *(ball, doggie, sock)* ❑ Specific nominals for naming particular objects, people, or animals *(blankie, Mama, Daddy, Java)* ❑ Action words for making comments or requests: general *(give, gimme, do, make, get)* or specific *(throw, wash, eat, kiss, up, help)* ❑ Modifiers for commenting on attributes of objects, people, or animals *(big, hot, dirty, heavy)* ❑ Possessives for commenting on person or pet having ownership or association with object *(doggie* while pointing to dog's bed; *Mommy* while holding up mother's sock)	

Source: Based on Bloom & Lahey, 1978; K. Nelson, 1973; Roth & Spekman, 1984.

words (13 percent), modifiers (10 percent), personal–social words (8 percent), and function words (4 percent).

Formal tools may help parents become more aware of the words their children are using and help them recognize opportunities for scaffolding further word production. That is, an assessment process can inform intervention directly and help shape parental perspectives while also benefiting from them. Two commonly used early vocabulary assessment tools are the Language Development Survey (Rescorla, 1989) and the MacArthur-Bates Communicative Developmental Inventories, Third Edition (CDIs; Fenson et al., 2006) (see Table C in the Part III Appendix). In using these checklists, parents identify words (and other early developing gestures and structures) that they have heard their children use (or not). The intersystemic result may be that parents heighten their recognition of opportunities for mapping linguistic symbols onto concepts that arise in natural contexts, perhaps engineering environments to enhance opportunities for word learning.

Targeting First Words and Single-Word Utterances

Goal 9.6. The child will produce first words and single-word utterances representing varied communicative content used for multiple functions. First words are not just used for naming but for many other functions as well. Children need to hear words to learn them, and they need to hear them in JARs and other meaningful contexts.

Intervention for early word learning includes consulting with families about how to elaborate familiar routines and to map them onto an appropriate set of words that fit children's interests. K. Nelson (1973) differentiated two groups of typically developing children. She called children prone to naming things and using substantive words *referential* and children prone to using formulaic phrases and function words for social purposes *expressive*. Horgan (1980) used the terms *noun lovers* and *noun leavers* for these same patterns.

Parents are important agents of vocabulary intervention for toddlers, because they have many opportunities to engage with their young children in meaningful routines. Tomasello (1988) called joint attention episodes "hotspots" for learning, noting that mothers' speech to infants during joint attention episodes (but not otherwise) is associated with advances in infants' early vocabulary. Lederer (2001) investigated intervention for parents and late-talking toddlers (23 to 29 months old) in a program called TOTtalk. Toddlers and mothers participated in 11 weekly group sessions in which target vocabulary was preselected and mothers learned to engage in a "naturalistic, interactive approach to language stimulation" (p. 227). Results showed measurable gains in both targeted and overall vocabulary and in socialization skills. This finding adds to the previously reported positive results for other parent intervention studies when explicit goals and focused scaffolding techniques are employed.

To enhance contextualized meaning, vocabulary intervention for toddlers and preschool-age children is often embedded in activities targeting other goal areas (e.g., play, narration, or book sharing). This ensures richer contextual support. Child-centered approaches start with the focus of the child's interest and attention and scaffold from there, but as research on word learning suggests, completely naturalistic encounters may not be enough for children with LI. By focusing attention on a targeted set of words, adults facilitate children's ability to form more elaborate neurolinguistic connections between sound patterns of words and concepts of reference in comprehensible schemas (e.g., Leonard, 1981). To add lexical items to their vocabularies, children with language delays or disorders may need experiences with targeted words and their referents many times in meaningful contexts and with clarity of perceptual cues.

Evidence suggests that, whether implemented by parents or clinicians, focused stimulation approaches can assist young children with LI to acquire more words with more complex phonological structures. Girolametto, Pearce, and Weitzman (1996) combined parent training with focused stimulation to investigate whether targeting the production of words would have indirect secondary effects on children's phonological abilities. In their study, 25 mothers of toddlers (23 to 33 months of age) with expressive vocabulary delays were randomly assigned to intervention or control groups. Mothers in the experimental group learned to employ frequent, highly concentrated presentations of target words without requiring responses. Toddlers who received this intervention made significant gains in phonological diversity (i.e., complex syllable shape and consonant inventory, with more consonant sounds in both initial and final position) but not in accuracy of production (i.e., percent of consonants correct).

Consistent with research with dual language learning (e.g., Cole, Mills, & Kelley, 2006; Tabors, 1997), parents should be encouraged to support vocabulary development in the language with which they are most comfortable. Similarly, educators can encourage vocabulary development in the language with which they are most comfortable. It is appropriate for children to know different words in different languages, and benefits may accrue to both.

Two-Word Utterances

Between their first and second birthdays, most typically developing children transition from producing single-word *holophrases* (i.e., one-word utterances that function like sentences) to successive one-word utterances and then to two-word utterances. The onset of two-word utterances signals the transition from early development of language content and use to the added development of language *form*. Two-word utterances often are characterized as being formed by a combination of content–form processes based on semantic–grammatic rules. Most children are poised for an explosion of grammatical learning by the time they reach 3 years of age.

Cognitive constructivist processes are often credited for the striking cross-cultural similarities in semantic relationship acquisition patterns observed at the two-word level by children around the world. Brown (1973) attributed this commonality to toddlers' universal preoccupation with people, actions, and entities (as agents, actions, and objects) at the same time they begin to combine words. These cognitive developments also coincide with advances in intentionality, a social interactionist concept. The semantic–grammatic rules (a linguistic concept) emerge for moving from exclusively single-word to multiword utterances when children begin to encode successive single semantic components. What makes multiword utterances sentencelike is that they represent not just one semantic category, or *case*. Rather, they represent more than one case (e.g., nominative, agentive, objective, attributive, dative, or locative) arranged in meaningful sequential combinations, often with verbs representing varied actions or states. This sets the stage for two-word utterances.

Assessing One- and Two-Word Utterances

Assessment of early language production must consider both nonverbal and verbal evidence, including words that may be difficult to understand. It is not always possible to differentiate words and phrases from nonwords and vocables in the speech of toddlers, especially those with speech–language delays. At the one-word stage, a nonverbal gesture or contextual cue might symbolize an unspoken component of an utterance. Some early language learners combine a protoword (i.e., vocable) with a real word (e.g., "beda baby") or use formulaic phrases to function as giant words (e.g., "Here y'go"). Others produce successive one-word utterances before combining them syntactically (e.g., saying "Mommy, laugh," both with falling intonation).

As development continues, children gradually incorporate two semantic roles into true two-word constructions, representing simple *semantic–grammatic* relationships. Figure 9.12 provides a tool for observing common two-word relationships using categorization schemes based on Brown (1973) and Bloom and Lahey (1978). Clinicians might introduce play objects to serve varied semantic roles—agents (e.g., *cowboy, horse*), entities (e.g., *hay, bucket, rope*), locations (e.g., *barn, fence*), or contrastive attributes (e.g., a *big* horse and a *little* horse). As a child begins to demonstrate improved production of varied two-word forms, probes may be designed to measure his or her growing independent performance generalized to a new set of toys. The goal is for children to produce generative (i.e., not just imitative but spontaneous) two-word utterances independently to convey a variety of meanings. Productive use can be documented when the child is able to combine words to represent novel semantic–grammatic relationships, rather than just imitate adult models.

Targeting Two-Word Utterances

Goal 9.7. The child will use two-word utterances to convey a variety of semantic–grammatic relationships in functional contexts. Two-word combinations can be targeted in the same sessions as vocabulary and play, as can the goal of increased clarity of word intelligibility. Play sessions can present opportunities for dynamic assessment probes when it is not clear whether a child is using true words.

　　Along with production, it is important to assess and provide intervention for comprehension of varied two-word combinations. This can be accomplished within play contexts in which the child is encouraged to act out relationships, with the child as agent first (e.g., "Push chair" or "Get Mommy's purse") and then using doll figures to vary the agent (e.g., "Baby eat" or "Bear sleep") and recipient (e.g., "Feed baby and bear"; "Mommy make dinner for Daddy"). When gathering comprehension probes for assessment purposes, it is important not to convey nonverbal cues (e.g., gaze or gesture) that can cue a child to respond

figure *9.12*

Observation Tool for Two-Word Utterances

Two-Word Semantic–Syntactic Constructions (with examples)	Observational Evidence (examples, context, date observed)
❑ Agent + action *(Mommy come. Doggy sit.)* ❑ Action + object *(Drive car. Eat cereal.)* ❑ Agent + object *(Daddy sock. Baby book.)* ❑ Entity + Attribute *(Crayon dirty. Big doggy.)* ❑ Possessor + possession *(My bottle. Mommy purse.)* ❑ Recurrence *(More cookie.)* ❑ Nonexistence *(Allgone milk.)* ❑ Disappearance *(Bye-bye car.)* ❑ Rejection (of proposal) *(No eat.)* ❑ Denial (of statement) *(No poopy.)* ❑ Demonstrative + entity *(There potty.)* ❑ Noun + locative *(Baby bed.)* ❑ Agent + locative *(Mommy upstairs.)* ❑ Entity + locative *(Spoon floor.)* ❑ Verb + locative *(Go pool. Sit chair.)* ❑ Noticing + locative *(Me here.)*	

Source: Based on Bloom & Lahey, 1978; R. Brown, 1973.

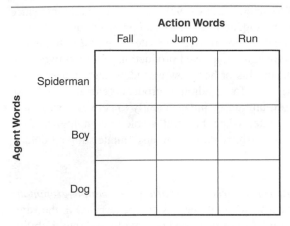

figure *9.13*

Agent-Plus-Action Matrix with Example Stimuli for Guiding Intervention Focused on Two-Word Combinations

Source: Adapted from Goldstein, 1985.

correctly without comprehending the words. Nonverbal cues do provide important scaffolds when working to promote language comprehension in intervention.

Parents should be engaged as partners in working on both comprehension and production of multiword utterances. The Hanen program (e.g., Girolametto & Weitzman, 2006; Manolson, 1992), Floortime DIR approach (Greenspan & Wieder, 2005), and other parent-training approaches introduced in Chapter 8 can be used to help parents improve skills for matching their attention and language to the interests and actions of their child.

Intervention can be guided by the observation tool in Figure 9.12 to establish targets and monitor progress in comprehending and producing unique two-word combinations. Figure 9.13 illustrates how a matrix might guide intervention for early two-word utterances. This particular matrix targets different agent-plus-action combinations, as suggested by Goldstein (1985). It can ensure that children receive multiple opportunities to combine a controlled set of words, and it also can be used to monitor children's knowledge of the flexible properties of language for putting words together in varied combinations. Focused stimulation and conversational recast techniques are appropriate for encouraging two-word combinations to fill a matrix such as this one.

Milieu language intervention also is designed to promote acquisition of early language structures. Milieu language intervention can be delivered as a hybrid technique blending adult-directed structure (originally motivated by behaviorist theory) with child-centered scaffolding (based on social interactionist theory). Warren and Bambara (1989) studied milieu intervention with three children (ranging from 42 to 75 months in age) diagnosed with borderline to moderate intellectual disabilities (ID/MR). They incorporated *mand-model* (e.g., *Tell me* [mand] *"dog bark"* [model]) and *incidental teaching* (e.g., eliciting responses and reinforcing them using natural activities and consequences) procedures based on behaviorist predecessors. They also introduced child-centered, *systematic commenting* techniques based on focused stimulation methods. When implementing the child-centered part of the treatment, adults observe and follow the child's lead and use more comments than directives. Systematic commenting involves these five elements:

(a) Attending to the child's activity and interests (Trainer: "Wow, look at your tower!").
(b) Responding/acknowledging child verbalizations (Child: "Look it fall." Trainer: "Crash, what a mess.").
(c) Maintaining child's topic (Child: "I do again." Trainer: "Make the tower very tall." Child: "Fall again").
(d) Asking open ended questions (as opposed to yes/no questions).
(e) Establishing clear expectations for child responding (e.g., waits for child's response after a question). (Warren & Bambara, 1989, p. 460)

Using systematic commenting, adults make frequent comments describing the child's and adult's activity (e.g., "I'm making cookies. Oh, look what John's doing. He's making a snake.") Target forms are emphasized by recasting the model into a two-word utterance the child might imitate (e.g., "I'm *making cookies,* see? *Make cookies.*"). Comments also serve as antecedents to direct prompts. For example, the adult shakes baby powder on a doll while saying "Let's *shake powder* on the baby" and then holds out the powder and prompts the child "What do you want to do?"

In Warren and Bambara's (1989) research, all three children with mild to moderate cognitive limitations learned to produce action–object combinations generatively. The word *generatively* is important. It means that the children could generate their own two-word semantic–syntactic action-plus-object combinations, generalize them to novel contexts and materials, and produce them in nonobligatory conversational situations as requests and comments. The children were not relying on imitation or adult models of a few overlearned combinations. Warren and Bambara concluded that the hybrid combination of mand-model, incidental teaching techniques, and systematic commenting helped the children acquire two-word constructions and generalize them to new contexts.

Focused stimulation (Leonard, 1981) also can be used to encourage the production of two-word utterances. Using this approach, adults (either parents or a clinician providing direct service) expose a child with language delay/disorder to multiple exemplars of two-word utterances within meaningful linguistic contexts but without requests for imitation. Robertson and Ellis Weismer (1999) used focused stimulation accompanied by parallel talk, expansions, and recasts to target linguistic and social skills for late-talking toddlers. Children in the treatment group received 12 weeks of clinician-implemented language intervention focused on vocabulary and two- and three-word utterances and made significant gains in lexical repertoire, total words produced, number of different words, and mean length of utterance (MLU) in morphemes. Robertson and Ellis Weismer also found unexpected improvement in the proportion of intelligible utterances, children's social skills, and reduction in parental stress.

Schwartz, Chapman, Terrell, Prelock, and Rowen (1985) also targeted early two-word productions by modifying adult–child discourse patterns. Participants were ten children with LI (ages 2 years, 8 months to 3 years, 4 months), who were producing only single-word utterances at baseline. Of the ten children, eight participated in ten intervention sessions and two served as controls (participating in an alternate activity). The intervention used scaffolding questions, modeling, and conversational recast techniques in a *vertical structure* pattern. This involved a separate elicitation of each semantic component, followed by a full-sentence recast combining the two components in a sentence (e.g., Adult: "Who's this?" Child: "Daddy." Adult: "What's Daddy throwing?" Child: "Ball." Adult: "Yeah, Daddy's throwing the ball."). Session data and pre–post test results both showed marked increases in the number of multi-word productions for most children in the experimental group but not in the control group.

Bain and Olswang (1995) found that children with LI required heightened cues and greater density of similar patterns to generate their own examples of two-word utterances. Additionally, children who already could produce two-word utterances produced a greater variety in free-play language sample contexts than in structured contexts, and children who could respond to the least intensive scaffolding met goals for independent productivity the fastest (representing their wider ZPD). Other studies also have shown that conversational recasts contingent on the meaning of what a young child says are more likely to elicit imitation of a portion of the expanded form (Scherer & Olswang, 1984). Conversational recast methods also have been shown to outperform requests for imitation in efficiency (i.e., fewer trials to criterion) and effectiveness (i.e., more mature language forms) (Camarata & Nelson, 2006; Saxton, 2005).

These collective findings support the recommendation to target integrated language abilities in naturalistic language intervention contexts as much as possible, with deliberate goal setting and careful monitoring for signs of change. This supports the general goal to promote integration across systems beyond the therapeutic milieu. At the same time, care must be taken to ensure that children are getting heightened language input and intervention scaffolding when providing completely naturalistic experiences is not enough.

SUMMARY

Intervention targeting one- and two-word utterances involves working with children in naturalistic contexts such as symbolic play, in which language can be mapped onto concepts of joint attention that are in the child's frame of reference. Based on communication samples and other assessment results, clinicians can set up language intervention contexts to provide focused stimulation of a targeted set of communicative functions (e.g., commenting as well as requesting and naming) and semantic roles (e.g., agents, actions, objects, locations, and attributes). Research supports recommendations to engage children with language development needs in communicative turn taking, with adults providing models of relevant vocabulary and semantic–grammatic forms contingent on a child's meaning, making direct requests for imitation only rarely. Research suggests that ongoing exposure to vocabulary in more than one language for dual language learners does not create added language-learning risks.

Emergent Narratives and Literacy

Infants and toddlers in middle-class families engage with their parents in frequent shared book reading interactions from a very young age (see Figure 9.14). In the process of being talked with and read to, young children gain experience in listening to a type of language that is literate. Literate language read aloud contains vocabulary that parents otherwise would be unlikely to use in the everyday routines of eating, bathing, and dressing. It also includes language formulated in sentences and discourse structures that otherwise would not likely be encountered by children so young.

Family literacy experiences give children who receive them a significant advantage in preparing for the decontextualized language of schooling. It is important to encourage such

figure *9.14*

Shared Book Reading

Book-reading interactions provide young children with experience with literate language.

experiences for children with disabilities and other language-learning risks as well, such as risks associated with low socioeconomic status. Children with the most severe and complex disabilities still can be read to with reference to corresponding pictures, even if the adults in their world are not sure whether the children are capable of understanding, providing opportunities to participate in literate language experiences.

Early Narration

Narratives begin to develop early. At around 20 to 24 months, typically developing children begin to talk about objects from the past and future (Lucariello, 1990). This freeing of talk from the here and now is called **temporally displaced** or **there-and-then** talk. Lucariello observed mothers interacting with their toddlers (ages 2 years to 2 years, 5 months) and found frequent examples of temporally displaced talk in highly scripted contexts about children's routines. Research has shown that narrative ability is one of the best predictors of school success for children with learning disabilities and language impairments (Bishop & Edmundson, 1987; Feagans & Appelbaum, 1986; Wells, 1986).

Assessing Early Narratives

Assessment of early narration is challenging because it occurs most readily in naturalistic contexts. Young children are likely to use narrative discourse to talk about events that are unusual or that trigger an emotional response, such as a hurt knee or scrape on an elbow. Sutton-Smith (1986) described attempts at fictional storytelling between ages 2 and 3 years for children learning African American English (AAE) or Standard American English (SAE). She noted that both groups interacted in stories that were verselike and contained sound and prosodic play, often about scary events that children face.

In the early stages, toddlers use a combination of verbal and nonverbal forms, including gestural reference to objects and events, to relay narrative information. For example, an 18-month-old child toppled a stool onto his foot while trying to pull up on it. After being comforted by his mother, he toddled around to his grandmother, pointed to his foot, and made nonverbal but vocal comments about what had happened. Another grandson, at approximately 30 months, told how his brother, who was not present, had gotten in trouble for punching him in the arm, saying "Dylan, bad boy" (while punching himself in the arm). A few weeks later, this toddler, who still was not quite 3, told a temporally displaced story about getting an X-ray for a lump on his jaw. It was an event at which his other grandmother, a nurse, was present. He narrated, "Nana say, 'Sit still.'"

Targeting Narratives about Events Not Present

Goal 9.8. The child will produce early narratives about events not present. Parents and clinicians can target the co-construction of stories (also called story *recounts*) about unusual events that occur within daily routines. Such scaffolding is appropriate both for toddlers and older children functioning at the level of one- and two-word utterances. It is important to serve as the authentic audience when an early functioning child has a story to tell. The support of familiar routines and shared storybook reading can make it possible for children with limited language skills to use temporally displaced talk that otherwise might be impossible. Early narratives may benefit from having an adult who was present scaffold the child immediately after a special event (or a scary one) has occurred to tell the story to another adult. Day care providers, both parents, and parent–clinician, parent–grandparent, and parent–sibling pairs can be engaged in supporting such language advances.

Emergent Literacy

The term *emergent literacy* (Clay, 1967, 1979; Sulzby & Teale, 1991) conveys that "children's use and understanding of literacy precedes their development of conventional reading and writing abilities" (Kaderavek & Justice, 2002, p. 396). An emergent literacy perspective acknowledges a reciprocal, dynamic interrelationship between children's oral and written language development, with each influencing the other in early childhood (Snow, 1983; Teale & Sulzby, 1986).

Emergent literacy abilities are predictive of later academic achievement (e.g., Catts et al., 2001; Stuart, 1995). Kaderavek and Sulzby (2000) compared the emerging production of narratives in oral and written language contexts (i.e., with and without books) by children with and without specific language impairment (SLI). Both groups used more characteristics of written language in emergent storybook readings than in oral narratives, although the children with SLI were less able to produce language features associated with written language. Experience with books can enhance children's knowledge about print conventions, alphabet knowledge, phonological awareness, grapheme–phoneme correspondence, and the components of stories (Justice & Ezell, 2000; Kaderavek & Justice, 2002). Intervention in this area targets both sound-/word-level and sentence-/discourse-level abilities.

Assessing Emergent Literacy

Assessment of emergent literacy at the infant–toddler level should be designed to observe two levels of functioning—word-level awareness and social interaction around books. Assessment of sound/word play at this level focuses mostly on whether the child attends to words and tries to imitate them. When adults manipulate words playfully and the child responds differentially, it can signal emerging awareness of words as objects. Signs of early print–symbol awareness also can be assessed based on the child's response to *logographic* symbols, such as the golden arches of McDonald's fast food restaurants.

Assessing emergent literacy at the sentence/discourse level should include observation of the interest and attention children show when adults try to engage them in interactions with books. It includes observations of children listening to books being read aloud and signs of their knowledge about how to hold a book, turn the pages, look at the pictures, point to objects named, point to words (in contrast with pictures), and close and put the book aside when finished. Book interaction at the sentence/discourse level establishes a firm foundation for literate language comprehension, which should be assessed along with signs of concepts about how to interact with books and print. Kaderavek and Sulzby (1998) described an observational protocol for parent–child joint book reading that could be used as a tool for consulting with parents about how to make shared book experiences more understandable and enjoyable. Chapter 11 includes an observational tool that has some components suitable for infants and toddlers as well.

Targeting Emergent Literacy

Goal 9.9. The child will participate in early play with the sounds of words and early graphic symbols. Sound and word play can prepare a child to tune into the sound structures of words. (An 18-month-old child responded to the words *gag* and *baloney* with hilarity when his mother produced them playfully in the context of a mealtime JAR.) Interactive babbling and simple rhyming play can be engaged in similar action routines. (A 6-month-old child laughed when her silly grandmother produced "blah" talk, saying "*Blah* blah blah *blah* blaah blaaah" with strong variation in intonation pattern.)

Early graphic symbols also can be brought into play activities, including logographic symbols such as empty fast food cups and fried chicken tubs. Literacy artifacts (e.g., maps, restaurant menus, writing pads and pencils) also can be introduced into symbolic play scenarios.

Goal 9.10. The child will participate actively in interactive storybook reading. Research has shown a positive significant relationship between parent–child shared book-reading activities and children's subsequent reading skills (Bus, van IJzendoorn, & Pellegrini, 1995; Scarborough & Dobrich, 1994). Interactive storybook reading can serve as a particularly rich context for targeting discrete elements of written language, including narratives.

In intervention and prevention activities, interactive book reading involves the use of scaffolding to promote more complex and diverse communicative acts (Kaderavek & Justice, 2002). For a child functioning at an early level of development, scaffolding may include comments on his or her focus of attention, cloze procedures, turn-taking cues, comprehension questions, responsive labeling, and recasts expanding and extending the child's utterances in the context of book interactions (Girolametto, Verbey, & Tannock, 1994; Norris & Hoffman, 1990).

SUMMARY

Early storytelling and emergent literacy activities provide complementary contexts for early language intervention. Opportunities and scaffolding can be provided in intervention to help children narrate experiences, often with an emotional component (e.g., a scary moment or hurt toe), to an interested audience who cares about the meaning. This can set the occasion for scaffolding children to use language to decenter cognitively, to talk about things and experiences not immediately present, and to comprehend the language of books. Emergent literacy shared-book experiences also can help children learn to listen to stories being read aloud, and to interact with books to learn the alphabetic principle, to understand narratives, and to learn new things.

CHAPTER SUMMARY

Goal areas in this chapter target several early developing transitions, from prelinguistic organization to intentional communication, presymbolic to symbolic play, first words to two-word utterances, and spoken interactions into emergent narratives and literacy. Early communication, play, and early literacy contexts overlap and can be used to support each other. Integration across domains is an overarching goal of intervention for encouraging development for children with developmental risks or known disabilities. Important foundations for literacy are established with infants, toddlers, and other children functioning at similar levels in conjunction with shared attention and joint action routines.

EXERCISES *and* STUDY QUESTIONS

1. List four goals that might be appropriate for infants and toddlers to achieve. Explain the difficulty underlying each goal.

2. What risk factors are particularly indicative of social–pragmatic difficulties?

3. Describe techniques for encouraging early word production.

4. Describe a comprehensive program for preparing infants and toddlers for emergent literacy.

CHAPTER *ten*

Preschool Policies and Practices

LEARNING *objectives*

After studying this chapter, you should be able to do the following:

1. Discuss the transition from Part C to Part B, Section 619, services under IDEA '04, and outline major components of individualized education programs (IEPs) and service delivery models appropriate for preschool-age children and older students functioning at preschool developmental levels.

2. Outline comprehensive identification and assessment procedures for preschool-age children and others functioning at early stages of language and literacy development.

Chapter 10 extends the developmentally appropriate template for assessment and intervention through the preschool years and into kindergarten. Developmental charts in Tables A and B in the Part III Appendix summarize information about coordinated developmental sequences during this age range across the five domains—cognition, receptive language, expressive language, social interaction and play, and emergent and early literacy.

In U.S educational policy, the period of early childhood extends to age 8 years. For children with developmental disabilities, even more time and intensified experiences may be required to achieve early milestones. In all intervention choices, chronological age appropriateness is important along with attention to an individual child's developmental level and contextualized needs. When achievement of early developmental milestone extends into the school-age years, targets must be addressed in both age-appropriate and contextually appropriate ways.

Policies and Practices in the Preschool Years

Child Find services, which begin in infancy, remain in place in the preschool years from ages 3 to 5 years (and extending up to age 21). States must establish procedures for finding all children who have disabilities or are at risk for disability, no matter what age. The states also must have policies and procedures in place to ensure a smooth transition to Part B, Section 619, preschool services for toddlers who have been receiving early intervention services under Part C.

Procedures for Transitioning from IFSP to IEP Services

Part B regulates services for children with disabilities from ages 6 through 21 years. When a child becomes eligible for preschool services, his or her school system must plan with the parents/caregivers to convene a conference "not less than 90 days (and at the discretion of all parties, not more than nine months) before the child is eligible for the preschool services" (§ 637[a][9][A][ii][II]).

At a child's third birthday, a family who has been receiving services under Part C (Services to Infants and Toddlers) may choose for their child to have an IEP under Part B, Section 619. As an alternative, if the parents and planning team members agree, the family may elect to continue receiving early intervention services from their Part C provider using an individualized family service plan (IFSP). To help parents decide whether their child's needs are best served under an IFSP from their Part C provider or an IEP from Part B, the public agency must provide a detailed explanation of the differences between an IFSP (including the natural environments statement) and an IEP (including preliteracy activities and other preparation for academic learning). In some states, both Part C and Part B services are coordinated through regional and local education agencies, making the transition from IFSP to IEP services relatively seamless.

When a child transitions from an IFSP to an IEP, the Part C service coordinator must be invited to the initial IEP meeting to assist with smooth transition of services. IDEA '04 requires IEPs for preschool-age children to incorporate an educational component addressing school readiness, preliteracy, language, and numeracy skills. Other provisions related to the development of IEPs for school-age children are described in Chapter 12.

Service Delivery Models for Preschool-Age Children

During the years from 3 to 5, clinicians often work directly with children in small groups or in one-on-one clinical interactions. Clinicians also continue to play important *indirect* service delivery roles with parents and preschool teachers. Indirect roles include helping preschool teachers maximize opportunities within preschool classroom environments to enhance children's language, play, and emerging literacy skills. Purposes of early intervention include preventing later functional limitations by facilitating typical language development.

Parents, teachers, and peers of preschool-age children can be engaged actively in scaffolding children's language development. As described in Chapter 8, scaffolding differs from more directive instructional approaches or prompting techniques, which are characterized by instructions to "Say this," "Do that," or "Tell me what this is." Scaffolding is more child centered and constructivist. It begins by providing the lowest level of support that can help a child function well, then introduces more intensive supportive techniques as needed, and finally reduces the support to evaluate the child's independence as a learner.

Teaching Parents to Scaffold Language in Shared Book Reading

Some approaches are designed specifically to teach parents to scaffold spoken language and emergent literacy. For example, Language Is the Key (LIK): Constructive Interactions around Books and Play is a parent-training approach that emphasizes the role of interactive book reading (Cole, Maddox, & Lim, 2006). The LIK approach encourages parental roles in language and literacy for children with disabilities and developmental risks and also for English language learners (ELLs). It involves teaching child-contingent communication patterns, including dialogic, shared book reading. Dialogic book reading is illustrated in Figure 10.1.

In adapting the LIK approach for dual language learners, Cole and colleagues (2006) advised parents of children learning multiple languages to communicate at home using the language they know best. These researchers emphasized a primary role for parents in helping their children use language to learn and become interested in books, noting that professionals at school can play a primary role in helping children learn English. Other interaction techniques are represented by the acronym CAR:

- *Comment* on your child's interests.
- *Ask* questions about those interests.
- *Respond* to your child's utterances by adding a little more information.

Research evidence supports approaches for training parents to support emergent literacy. Whitehurst and colleagues (1988), for example, trained parents of typically developing preschoolers to engage in interactive dialogic book reading, including following the child's interests, asking open-ended questions, repeating what the child says, praising it, expanding on it, and following up with related questions. Based on random assignment, parents received two half-hour, home-based training sessions or a control condition in which they were asked simply to read to their children. Parents in the intervention group used the interaction strategies more frequently than those in the control group, and children's grammatical complexity and expressive language increased after six weeks of dialogic reading, with differences maintained at nine-month follow up.

Parents play a particularly important role for preschool-age children in diverse populations. Children from diverse groups (including those with low socioeconomic status) progress better when their parents read to them, not just their preschool teachers (Lonigan & Whitehurst, 1998; Whitehurst et al., 1994), although teachers are important too.

Teaching Preschool Teachers to Scaffold Language and Literacy Development

Formal programs or informal collaborative consultation can help preschool teachers interact more effectively, scaffold higher-level language abilities, and plan language-rich envi-

figure *10.1*

Sample of Interactive Book Reading

Sample	Commentary
$ David, Mum + CA: 3;0	
D The Giant Sandwich (4 sec pause) M Who's this here on the first page? D The wasps. M The wasps are coming. [Turns the page.] Here's some more, look. Wow! [Reads] One hot summer in Itching Down Four million wasps flew into town.	D "Reads" book title showing knowledge of books, and this particular book. M Uses a teacher-talk question to introduce a key part of the setting and establish the problem.
D I don't like wasps . . . flying into town. M Why's that? D Because they sting me. M Do they? D Mm. I don't like them. M They only sting you if they get angry. If you leave them alone they won't sting you. But four million would be rather a lot, wouldn't it? They'd get rather in the way. [Reads] They drove the picknickers away . . . D Mm. M They chased the farmers from their hay They stung Lord Swell [chuckles] on his fat bald— D Pate. M D'you know what a pate is? D What? M What d'you think it is? D Hair. M Well—yes. It's where his hair should be. It's his head—look, his bald head. All his hair's gone. D Where is it? M Well, he's old, so it's dropped out. He's gone bald.	D Expresses feeling about a scary subject. M Requests elaboration; shows interest in D's perspective. D Expresses causal relationship. M Extends topic in reassuring manner and then returns to exaggerated number in story and frames cues about meaning. M Hesitates, to give D a chance to fill in partially rhyming word. D Completes phrase. M Questions knowledge of vocabulary meaning. M Encourages use of context to derive word meaning. D Offers plausible association. M Scaffolds by commenting with bridge to what D does know and then framing visual and verbal cues to help D construct more accurate meaning of *pate* while introducing word *bald*.

Note: In this sample, David (age 3) has asked his "Mum" to read a familiar book as they are sitting on the sofa. The sample has been reformatted using SALT transcription conventions; the commentary has been added.
Source: From Wells, 1986, pp. 152–153.

ronments to set the stage for literacy learning. Children benefit when preschool teachers provide examples of language forms and functions that are slightly advanced of their current abilities, stretching their zones of proximal development (ZPDs) (e.g., Bunce, 1995; Dickinson, 2006; Girolametto & Weitzman, 2002; McKeown & Beck, 2006). The goal for consultants is to help teachers maximize scaffolding techniques (e.g., open-ended questions, expansions, and recasts) in a variety of preschool classroom contexts, such as center time, storybook reading, and snacktime (Justice, Mashburn, Hamre, & Pianta, 2008).

Justice et al. (2008) pointed out differences between high-quality scaffolding discourse focused on spoken conversation and intervention discourse supporting emergent literacy, noting that both are important. Research indicates that intervention can help young children accelerate their emergent literacy development (e.g., Justice, Chow, Capellini, Flanigan, & Colton, 2003; van Kleeck, Gillam, & McFadden, 1998; Whitehurst et al., 1988), but programs must incorporate activities that introduce children systematically to "the logic of the alphabetic system" (Adams, 2002, p. 74). That may require adult-directed instruction that is more explicit as well as child-centered scaffolding that can be more implicit (Justice et al., 2003, 2008).

One approach for teaching early childhood teachers about spoken–written language connections is called the Literacy Environment Enrichment Program (LEEP; Dickinson & Caswell, 2007). LEEP draws on literature that relates the emergence of early reading and writing to experiences with spoken language in supportive environments (e.g., Sulzby & Teale, 1991; Whitehurst & Lonigan, 1998), including methods for developing awareness of the sound structure of language (e.g., Lonigan, Burgess, & Anthony, 2000). Dickinson and Caswell investigated teachers' implementation of LEEP following an intensive inservice training course aimed at encouraging advanced language, vocabulary, and purposeful uses of print. Head Start teachers participated in LEEP training that addressed how to facilitate emergent reading and writing, conduct supportive conversations, establish literacy-rich environments, use children's literature and play, transcribe conversations, and teach phonemic awareness. Results of pre–post testing showed that 30 intervention group teachers demonstrated more fall–spring changes in classroom support for literacy than 40 comparison group teachers, who had been randomly assigned to wait for training.

Justice and colleagues (2008) investigated a more traditional professional development activity in which early childhood teachers attended a two-day workshop about an emergent literacy curriculum but received "little explicit instruction in its quality implementation" (p. 55). The curriculum, called My Teaching Partner—Language and Literacy Curriculum (MTPLL), targets eight high-priority language and literacy goals in a 36-week program: phonological awareness, alphabet knowledge, print awareness, vocabulary, linguistic concepts, narrative discourse, pragmatics, and social language. The 135 preschool teachers in this study received only two days of training, which was supplemented with weekly lesson plans with specific objectives, sample lesson scripts, materials (e.g., vocabulary pictures), manipulatives (e.g., tapping sticks for phonemic awareness), access to videos on a website, and video equipment to make periodic recordings of their lessons to serve as research data. The teachers implemented the program in preschools for children with familial risks of poverty, homelessness, limited parental education, chronic illness, violence, crime, unemployment, instability, developmental problems, and limited English proficiency. Videotaped sessions were analyzed for quality indicators of language instruction, including conversation with students, student-initiated language, repetition and extension, self- and parallel talk, and advanced language. Indicators of quality literacy instruction were lessons that were explicit, purposeful, and systematic.

Although the videos showed faithful implementation of the curriculum, the quality indicators were disappointingly low (Justice et al., 2008). Specifically, few teachers used techniques associated with accelerated language development (e.g., asking open-ended questions, repeating and extending children's utterances, modeling advanced vocabulary), and few provided literacy instruction that was explicit, systematic, and purposeful. The implication is that preschool teachers need educational activities that are more specific, ongoing, and interactive than can be provided through a one- or two-day workshop format. These teachers also needed consultation regarding precise use of metalinguistic terms differentiating speech sounds, such as /s/, from letter names, such as *s*.

Teaching Peers to Scaffold Language, Literacy, and Play

Research has shown that more able and well-adjusted peers can be engaged to scaffold the language, literacy, and social abilities of peers with disabilities. For example, McGregor (2000) taught more able peers (with shared cultural–linguistic experiences) to help younger students and children with disabilities tell complete stories. Goldstein, Schneider, and Thieman (2007) taught typically developing peers to mediate social and communicative interactions of children with autism and other developmental disabilities. Girolametto and Weitzman (2007) taught teachers to scaffold peer interactions and arrange naturalistic environments to support them.

Figure 10.2 illustrates peer-to-peer discourse in play in comparison with clinician-scaffolded discourse. One is not necessarily better than the other. They are just different

figure *10.2*

Play Samples in Two Contexts: (A) with natural peer scaffolding following previous scaffolding of the interaction by clinician and (B) with direct intervention scaffolding by a clinician

Sample A[a]	Sample B[b]
$ Adam, Tamika	$ Josh, Clinician
= A grabs a set of play keys	= J and examiner are playing with a set of plastic bugs and lizards and a plastic tower.
A I gotta get to work real quick.	
A I'm gonna bring the kids back.	J What doing?
T Okay.	C What am I doing?
A I'll be safe.	C Making it so we can play.
T If you're gonna have my keys, you're gonna ride in my car and I gonna have your car.	C Now we can play {talking for bug}.
	C Yay!
A Oh okay.	C Look, I have a bug.
A (I'll call you) I'll call you.	C Flying.
= Adam moves toward closet, which he is using as a pretend car.	J Flying.
	J Climbing this tower (making lizard climb tower).
T Make sure you say hello.	C Climbing this tower and slide down.
= Adam picks up play telephone.	J Slide down.
A Hello, hello, hello.	C Climbing the tower, oh slippery.
= Adam looks over at Tamika.	C Fall down.
T What?	J I fall down.
A I'm stuck in the car.	C Fell down, you fell down.
A I just drivin.	= Clinician makes plastic bug fall.
A I going to the grocery.	C I fell down.
A I can't talk to you right now in the car.	C Help, I'm stuck.
A Bye.	J I'm stuck, help.
	C We're both stuck.
	= Child pulls figures out of crack.
	C Oh, thank you for the help.

[a]In Sample A, Adam is an African American child, age 4 years, 5 months, in a Head Start classroom. He is receiving services weekly for phonological delay and articulation (not represented in this transcription). Adam was playing in a dramatic play housekeeping area with another child, Tamika.

[b]In Sample B, Josh is a European American child, age 4 years, 4 months, who is receiving services for children with language development difficulties. His diagnosis indicates childhood apraxia of speech (although his articulation difficulties are not represented in this transcription) and sensory integration difficulties.

approaches for addressing different points in children's development. Both can be employed in inclusive service delivery models.

Providing Direct Services in Preschool Classrooms and Clinic Room Settings

Some studies have evaluated preschool service delivery models. Valdez and Montgomery (1997) randomly assigned 39 Head Start children with language impairment (LI) (but no comorbid neuromotor or cognitive disorders) to receive inclass or pull-out treatment. Children in the pull-out group showed greater pre–post gains in receptive language scores but no other clinically significant differences. The authors concluded, "The inclusion model is just as effective as a traditional pull-out model in conducting speech/language services for children with mild, moderate, and severe communication disorders" (p. 65). Wilcox, Kouri, and Caswell (1991) also studied service delivery models for preschoolers. They found that both classroom-based and pull-out approaches were effective but that children in the classroom-based instruction generalized target words better to home.

More intensive scheduling of intervention services also may be more effective. Barratt, Littlejohns, and Thompson (1992) compared dispersed scheduling one day per week to intensive scheduling in blocks of four days per week. Participants were children (ages 2 to 5 years; White and Nonwhite) diagnosed with LI but no physical or cognitive impairment. Clinicians worked with children in their preschool classrooms in inner-city London using play-based treatment focused on individualized goals targeting language form, content, and use. Both groups received 24 sessions delivered over six months, with the four-day intensive treatment schedule clustered into three-week blocks delivered in both halves of the six-month period. This design controlled both the length of the observation (six months) and the total number of sessions (24) received by each child. Language tests showed that, although there were individual differences, language expression scores improved more than comprehension scores for both groups. Expression scores also improved several times more for the group receiving intensive treatment than for the group in weekly treatment. The authors concluded that intensive scheduling was preferable for producing measurable gains in language expression.

SUMMARY

This section has summarized policy requirements of IDEA '04 that are specific to identifying and planning services for children with special needs or developmental risks in the preschool years from birth through age 5. The child's third birthday is a transition point, at which time parents may elect to have their child and family continue to receive services under an IFSP or transition to an IEP. A variety of contexts can serve as appropriate service delivery settings in the preschool years.

This section described programs for teaching parents, teachers, and peers to scaffold language and emerging literacy development. Both inclass and pull-out sessions are associated with improvements in children's language, although smaller group interventions may produce better results in comprehension and classroom-based instruction may produce better results for vocabulary learning. More intensive schedules also produce better expressive language results than sessions scheduled only one day per week.

Comprehensive Assessment in the Preschool Years

Combinations of a formal test, parent report measure, and language sample are recommended for assessing early language and communication abilities during the preschool years (e.g., Nelson & Warner, 2007; Paul, 2007). They serve the dual purposes of diagnosing disability and gaining a comprehensive picture of a child's strengths and needs to be used in intervention (and prevention) planning.

Formal Assessment Tools

Formal Tests for Diagnosing Disorder

Table D in the Part III Appendix summarizes formal tests appropriate for the preschool years, including norm-referenced and criterion-referenced tools for screening a child's present levels of development across multiple domains. Examples are the Hawaii Early Learning Profile (HELP; Furuno, O'Reilly, Hosaka, Inatsuka, & Zeisloft-Falbey, 1994) and Developmental Indicators for the Assessment of Learning (3rd ed.) (DIAL-3; Mardell-Czudnowski & Goldenberg, 1998). Such tests often are used to screen for language- and literacy-learning risks as children prepare to enter kindergarten as part of a Child Find plan.

As always, clinicians must confirm that an instrument is valid for its intended purpose by examining the test's technical manual (McCauley & Swisher, 1984). When Spaulding, Plante, and Farinella (2006) reviewed technical manuals for forty-three language tests, they found that only nine reported data on sensitivity and specificity, and only five of these indicated that the test had an identification accuracy of 80 percent or better. In interpreting diagnostic information, it is also important not to rely on a preset cut score (e.g., less than -1.25 standard deviations) to diagnose disorder but to consult the manual to identify the cut score that was found by the test developers to result in optimal sensitivity and specificity (Plante & Vance, 1995).

Two diagnostic tools for which adequate validity data have been reported are the Preschool Language Scale (4th ed.; PLS-4) (Zimmerman, Steiner, & Pond, 2002) and the Structured Photographic Expressive Language Test-Preschool (SPELT-P2; Dawson et al., 2005). Such tools can be used by speech–language pathologists (SLPs) to assess a child's communication and language strengths and needs and to make diagnostic decisions about whether he or she meets the criteria for diagnosing language disorder. Although diagnostic decisions should never be made on the basis of a single measure, at least one formal test (selected so as to be culturally and linguistically appropriate for a particular child) generally plays a significant role. The PLS-4 is one of the few preschool-level tests that meets the greater than 80 percent sensitivity and specificity criterion for diagnosing language disorder (Spaulding et al., 2006). It has a sensitivity of 0.80 and specificity of 0.88 when a cut score of -1.5 standard deviations (standard score of 85) is used. The SPELT-P2 has a reported sensitivity of 0.83 and specificity of 0.95 when a standardized cut score of greater than 79.2 is used. The Clinical Evaluation of Language Fundamentals-Preschool (2nd ed.) (CELF-P2; Wiig, Secord, & Semel, 1992) has reported sensitivity of 0.82 and specificity of 0.86 when a standardized cut score of 85 is used.

Some tests appropriate for preschool-age children are designed for specific purposes. For example, the Test of Early Grammatical Impairment (TEGI; Rice & Wexler, 2001) is designed to detect problems in morphosyntactic development that are characteristic of children with specific language impairment (SLI) and was reported by Spaulding et al. (2006) to have good sensitivity and specificity. The Diagnostic Evaluation of Language Variance (DELV; Seymour, Roeper, & de Villiers, 2003) is designed for assessing children learning African American English (AAE), but it may be used more appropriately as a criterion-referenced measure because it did not meet the 80 percent sensitivity and specificity criteria for norm-referenced tests.

Nonbiased Assessment Options

All formal tests are biased to some degree. Bias occurs when some children are likely to perform more poorly on the test not because of lesser ability but because of experiences that do not match those measured by the test. Sophisticated procedures may be used in test development to evaluate and remove biased items, but it is impossible to eliminate bias altogether. No test can be all things to all people. Simply adding children from representative groups to a standardization sample does not solve the problem. It is also not adequate simply to translate a particular test directly into the language spoken by a particular child's family.

Bias comes not only from lack of exposure to culture-specific themes and concepts but also from lack of experience with the unique forms of discourse and other expectations involved in test taking (Stockman, 1996; Washington & Craig, 1992). For example, some children are unfamiliar with structured assessment tasks that require pointing or naming for the purpose of testing. Therefore, children from diverse cultural–linguistic backgrounds might require more informal methods that extend over time and use dynamic assessment techniques.

Observation, interviews, questionnaires, and language samples offer alternatives to formal tests for children from diverse backgrounds (Kayser, 1989). Some tools are designed to assess particular language domains within particular cultural–linguistic groups. For example, the Minimal Competency Core (Stockman, 1996; Schraeder, Quinn, Stockman, & Miller, 1999; described subsequently) and Black English Sentence Scoring (BESS; Nelson & Hyter, 1990; described in Chapter 11) both offer assessment tools for children learning AAE. Parent report measures also have been adapted for children learning both Spanish and English (e.g., Patterson, 1998), including a Spanish version of the MacArthur-Bates CDIs, the MacArthur-Bates Inventario del Dessarrolo de Habilidades Comunicativas (Inventarios) (Jackson-Maldonado et al., 2003).

Some options also make it possible to compare language sample results for a particular child with information in developmental databases. For example, database options in the software program, Systematic Analysis of Language Transcripts (SALT; Miller et al., 2006) include English and Spanish scripts that can be used to prepare a child for retelling a story accompanying Mercer Mayer's (1969) book *Frog, Where Are You?* (Miller & Chapman, 2008; Miller et al., 2006). Results for dual language learners can be transcribed, analyzed, and compared with information in the database. Research on transcription and coding accuracy for such stories with modifications for Spanish morphology (Miller & Iglesias, 2007) also supports reliability of the measures (Heilmann et al., 2008).

Dynamic assessment is especially helpful with children from diverse linguistic and dialectal groups. Test–teach–retest procedures introduce known experiences, which may or may not have been part of the child's prior cultural–linguistic experience. Assessment is then based on the child's ability to learn new content within the supportive experiences. This is similar to a response to intervention (RTI) paradigm in that children can be engaged in non–special education interventions prior to diagnosing them as having a disorder. Lidz and Peña (1996) summarized studies that showed that Latino and African American children with and without LI can be differentiated based on disorder, rather than language or dialectal difference, by referring to pre–post test scores collected during dynamic assessment.

Stockman's (1996) Minimal Competency Core (MCC) (Figure 10.3) is a criterion-referenced protocol for identifying language impairment in African American preschool-age children (Schraeder, Quinn, Stockman, & Miller, 1999). Observation is guided by a research-based checklist of threshold skills expected by age 3 for African American children developing typically. This relatively informal assessment is based on a two-hour play sample with race cars and books. The criterion for judging productivity is a minimum of four exemplars with at least two variants to demonstrate flexibility. Children are considered not to have LI if they demonstrate the "set of linguistic features that the least competent normal child should demonstrate" (p. 359).

Another option, described in Chapter 11, is Black English Sentence Scoring (BESS). Children's use of AAE variants is penalized with scoring systems based on standard En-

figure *10.3*

Checklist Based on Stockman's Minimal Competency Core

This checklist specifies the minimal expectations for a typically developing 3-year-old African American child. The criterion for judging typical development for African American children between 33 and 36 months of age is for a child to produce a minimum of four exemplars of each feature (with at least two variants each) in a two-hour play sample using toys and books.

Phonological Features Core
- ❏ Nasals __ /m/ __ /n/
- ❏ Stops __ /p/ __ /b/ __ /t/ __ /d/ __ /k/ __ /g/
- ❏ Fricatives __ /f/ __ /s/ __ /h/
- ❏ Glides __ /w/ __ /y/
- ❏ Final consonants
- ❏ Initial blends

Pragmatic Functions Core
- ❏ Initiates interactions: __ (Says "Hi")
- ❏ Initiates language: __ Comments on objects and events, __ Asks questions, __ Requests objects and actions
- ❏ Responds to prior speech acts: __ Relates comment to prior speaker turn, __ Answers questions, __ Imitates spontaneously
- ❏ Manages interactions: __ Requests repetition ("Huh?"), __ Repeats words on request, __ Closes interactions (says "Bye")

Semantic Relations Core
- ❏ Major categories: __ Existence, __ State, __ Locative state, __ Action, __ Locative action, __ Dative
- ❏ Coordinated categories: __ Specifier, __ Possession, __ Time, __ Negation, __ Attribution, __ Quantity, __ Recurrence
- ❏ Superordinate category: __ Causation, __ Coordination

Morphosyntactic Core
- ❏ MLU greater than 2.70
- ❏ Elaborated simple sentence: __ (subject + verb + complement)
- ❏ Noun modifiers: __ *the*, __ *a*, __ *an*, __ *that*, __ *this*, __ other (_____)
- ❏ Inflections: __ *-ed*, __ *-ing*, __ other (_____)

Source: Based on Stockman, 1996; Schraeder, Quinn, Stockman, & Miller, 1999.

glish, such as Developmental Sentence Scoring (DSS; Lee, 1974), but language analysis with BESS (Nelson & Hyter, 1990) removes this source of bias.

Informal Assessment Probes for Guiding Intervention and Measuring Progress

Naturalistic communication samples using repeatable probes offer good choices for selecting intervention targets and measuring progress for diverse groups of children. Several informal language-sampling and analysis procedures are particularly appropriate for children functioning at preschool levels.

Gathering Language Samples in the Preschool Years

Gathering spoken language samples from preschool-age children with language impairments requires clinical skill. Like parents, clinicians are most successful when they avoid direct questions, especially those of the *yes/no* variety. Rather than ask direct questions (e.g., "Where is the car going?"), it is better to use comments (e.g., "Uh oh, the car is about to crash") and open-ended questions (e.g., "What is happening here?") or indirect invitations to comments that do not obligate a response (e.g., "I wonder what Spider-man will do next"). *Yes/no* and test questions are especially problematic because they pressure a child to communicate and require only single-word answers (e.g., "Is your car big?"). Even indirect, child-centered techniques may put pressure on a child who is sensitive about talking, possibly leading to withdrawal. When that happens, the clinician must withdraw and approach the child more gently. It is better to prevent such occurrences than to recover from them.

Skilled clinicians achieve a delicate balance between waiting for children to initiate and encouraging them to respond. If a child seems to withdraw when adults attempt to engage him or her in play or communication, a time of silent parallel play may reduce the pressure. Clinicians can comment intermittently on a child's object of focus and wait for a response, or they may introduce an element of interactive play (e.g., bumping the child's car with their car), comment, and wait. If the child is verbalizing, clinicians can expand or extend any verbalizations and wait for a response.

Discourse interaction and contingency techniques, called *recasts* (discussed in Chapter 8), have varying degrees of directness and focus. They can expand the child's sentence structures or extend the child's meaning. Research has shown that extending the child's meaning works better for eliciting output than expanding the child's grammatical structures (e.g., Cazden, 1983; Girolametto et al., 1999).

Play contexts with toys that lend themselves to dramatic play (e.g., replica cars and fire trucks, play houses and barns, animal and people figures) tend to work better for encouraging language production than manipulatives (e.g., blocks, clay) and drawing materials (e.g., crayons and paper). Manipulative and drawing activities may result in long stretches of silent fine motor activity with little talking, unless symbolic and dramatic elements can be introduced into the play. In the context of dramatic play with miniature figures, choices can be offered for elaborating the play (e.g., "Do you think the dog wants to play with the boy or chase the car?"). Another less directive technique is to make "I wonder" statements, encouraging the child to make the next move but without obligating a response (e.g., "I wonder what the big lion is going to do next"). As the child becomes more comfortable, he or she may be drawn into pretend play scenarios by the clinician, perhaps including talking for the animals or play people (e.g., "Oh no, our house is on fire. What should we do?"). Children often work out their fears in play and may introduce scary themes.

Older preschool-age children are capable of longer segments of discourse. They may be able to produce connected discourse, such as narratives, with more complex syntactic structures and longer turns. Wordless picture books, such as Mercer Mayer's *Frog* books, can be used to elicit fictional narratives (Petersen, Gillam, & Gillam, 2008). Such books can support repeated assessment probes using similar conditions for children learning both Spanish and English (Miller et al., 2006). Story retelling contexts also can provide useful information about a child's language comprehension, memory, recall, and reformulation capabilities. Young children with language delays, however, may have difficulty cooperating with such complex task demands.

To elicit original narratives, clinicians can use a *high-point technique* (Bliss & McCabe, 2008; McCabe & Rollins, 1994) of telling a story with a problem (e.g., getting stung by a bee) to elicit a similar story from the child. Older preschool-age children may generate narratives when dictating a text to be acted out later in play or as part of a book they are creating and illustrating with the clinician's help. Paley (1990) transcribed samples of children's discourse in play and showed how dramatic play was associated with the development of more literate language forms when children dictated their stories for later dramatization. For example, Figure 10.4 shows peer-interaction discourse samples in two independent but related contexts—one in dramatic play and the other a dictation of a related story to be acted out formally.

Analyzing Language Production and Comprehension in Language Samples

Full transcripts of communicative interactions (both verbal and nonverbal) can provide information about a child's expressive language skills if transcribed and analyzed using quantitative (counting or other forms of measurement) and qualitative (descriptive and other ethnographic) techniques. Software transcription and analysis tools include the Systematic Analysis of Language Transcripts (SALT; Miller & Chapman, 2008), the Child Language Data Exchange System (CHILDES; MacWhinney, 1991, 1996), and the Language Assessment Remediation and Screening Procedure (LARSP; Crystal, Fletcher, & Garman, 1976). Many of these and related tools, including DSS and BESS scoring criteria, are incorporated into computerized profiling (Long & Fey, 2002). These tools can be downloaded at websites such as Computerized Profiling (2008). Other options are available as part of the SALT software package (Miller & Chapman, 2008).

Brief, targeted language samples may be gathered as well. Researchers in the United Kingdom have found evidence supporting the use of a 10-minute screening tool for identifying preschool and early elementary school children who need further in-depth assessment for language difficulties. The screening tool, called the Grammar and Phonology Screening (GAPS) test, involves a direct imitation task with 11 test sentences and 8 test nonsense words (Gardner, Froud, McClelland, & van der Lely, 2006).

figure *10.4*

Two Discourse Samples Showing How a Young Child's Discourse in Play with Peers Can Influence the Content and Structure of a Subsequent Narrative

Sample A[a]	Sample B[b]
[Katie, Simon, Alex, and Arlene are pretending to be four cats in a spaceship, all contributing to the discussion of cat beds and related concepts.] "Where do I sleep?" Simon asks. "In the waterbed because you're the dad." "The water turned into a bed?" "Turn the bed so it won't squeak." "And leak. Squeak and leak. And peek." "Only dads and moms can peek down there." "Meow! The water's coming down!" "Help! Help! We can't swim. A monster!" "In the water he is." "The bed's in the waterbed!" "Here's the floaters, jump in the floaters."	"Once there was a little squirrel, And his mother said, 'Go sleep in a waterbed.' So he did. And he drownded inside. And he got not-drownded because it leaked out and he leaked out. The mother told him to swim home. But he couldn't swim."

[a]Interactive discourse produced during dramatic play

[b]Story later dictated by Simon

Source: From Paley, 1990, pp. 20–21.

Rather than transcribe and code all aspects of a complete communication sample, a clinician may code a subset of features in a single probe or series of progress-monitoring probes. For example, play contexts (e.g., playing "house" or "school") might be designed to probe a child's *hi/bye* routines. Another example is to observe a child with social communication and turn-taking difficulties in a 10-minute play sample with a peer to assess the proportion of assertive or responsive communication acts. Fey's (1986) *communication acts profiling* (*CAP*) technique is designed to support this analysis. It and other appropriate techniques for analyzing features of communication in targeted areas are discussed in Chapter 11.

Language samples also may be used to document a child's language comprehension. Skarakis-Doyle and Dempsey (2008) reviewed literature on children's story comprehension, a skill critical both to preliteracy development and social interaction. Important developments occur during the preschool years from 3 to 5. At age 3, children tend to describe isolated states and actions and comprehend only portions of events in the stories of others. As they approach age 5, children understand goal–action–outcome sequences and use story grammar structure to organize their story retellings and picture narrations, particularly when they have experienced shared book reading. Language sampling can be used to document children's growing story comprehension abilities using a variety of specialized techniques, including comprehension questions and story retelling procedures (independent or joint, accompanied by pictures or not). Skarakis-Doyle and Dempsey also described an *expectancy violation detection task (EVDT)*, in which adults purposefully change a detail (e.g., character or event) in a familiar story and observe whether the child detects the discrepancy, as signaled by a nonverbal response or verbal protest. The ability to detect discrepancies in familiar stories is a positive indicator of literate language comprehension.

Context-Based Assessment of Early Language, Literacy, and Play

Interdisciplinary teams can apply the four questions of context-based assessment and intervention with children in early stages of language and literacy development. Application of these four questions presumes that a planning team already has identified at least one important setting and discourse context for assessment and intervention. This selection occurs in consultation with the family using the ethnographic techniques described in Chapter 1. Then observations are set up in those contexts to answer the four questions:

1. What language and communication abilities are required for this young child to function well in the selected developmentally appropriate context (e.g., playtime, interactive book reading, or storytime)?
2. What are the child's current levels of functioning within this naturalistic context?
3. What new abilities should be targeted to close gaps between what the child can do currently and what would represent better functioning in this context?
4. How might the context be modified to facilitate the child's development and to support more effective functioning?

The answers to these four questions can guide the development of a child's IFSP or IEP. In Chapter 11, more detailed suggestions are given for analyzing the cognitive–linguistic and social interaction aspects in naturalistic and functional contexts.

SUMMARY

A range of formal diagnostic tools and less formal assessment probe techniques may be used to assess early communication and language development and related systems. Although formal tests are better suited for diagnostic purposes, they can lead to misdiagnosis or inaccurate prognosis for early risks or for children whose cultural linguistic experiences do not match the expectations of the test. Less formal probe techniques include communication and language samples and dynamic assessment. They can provide baseline data and suggest context-based intervention goals and methods that are well suited to family-centered, culturally sensitive service delivery. Comprehensive assessment often includes administration of an age-appropriate formal test (unless culturally or linguistically inappropriate), a parent report measure, analysis of an informal sample of the child's communication gathered in naturalistic contexts, and a story comprehension and retelling task. Preschool-age children also should have an emergent literacy assessment documenting their interaction with books and ability to listen attentively to a story read aloud and to answer questions about it.

CHAPTER SUMMARY

This chapter has described service delivery and assessment activities for children functioning at preschool levels of language and literacy development. Policies and practices were described for children transitioning from IFSPs under Part C in the years from birth to age 3 to IEPs (or continued IFSPs but with preliteracy experiences added) under Part B, Section 619, at their third birthday. Formal and informal assessment tools and procedures were described that are appropriate for preschool-age children and others functioning at preschool levels of development.

EXERCISES *and* STUDY QUESTIONS

1. Describe at least three options for service delivery for preschool-age children (3 to 5 years) under IDEA '04.

2. Outline the basic components of an initial eligibility assessment for a preschool-age child, and justify the need for each component.

3. How do formal and informal assessment procedures differ, and which would be better for measuring progress in a specific goal area?

CHAPTER *eleven*

Preschool Intervention

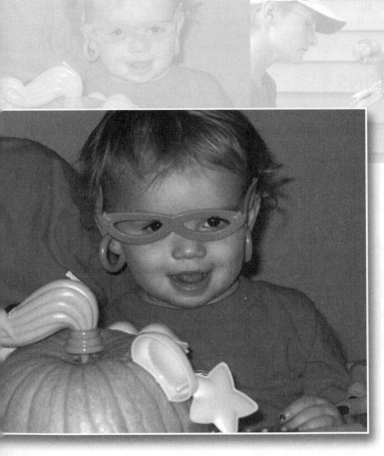

LEARNING *objectives*

After studying this chapter, you should be able to do the following:

1. Describe assessment procedures for sounds, words, and vocabulary concepts; early sentence and discourse development; social interaction and play; and emerging literacy.

2. Describe intervention procedures for sounds, words, and vocabulary concepts; early sentence and discourse development; social interaction and play; and emerging literacy.

Chapter 11 is organized into four goal areas appropriate for children functioning at a preschool level—sounds, words, and vocabulary concepts; early sentence and discourse development; social interaction and play; and emerging literacy. Goals in these four areas are discussed separately to highlight features of each. Typical development flows in an integrated and synergistic manner, however, and integration across domains should be targeted directly in intervention.

Sounds, Words, and Vocabulary Concepts

Vocabulary development and intelligible word production are two types of sound-/word-level goals addressed in this section. Phonological awareness also is a word-level goal, but it is addressed later in the section on emerging literacy.

Vocabulary

Assessing Early Vocabulary Development

For young children with language delay, baseline rates of vocabulary learning can be documented by asking parents to complete an inventory of early vocabulary development using the MacArthur-Bates Communicative Developmental Inventories (CDIs; Fenson et al., 2006) or the Language Development Survey (LDS; Rescorla, 1989). Progress can be monitored by having parents continually update the inventory, adding new words after observing them to meet the criteria of appearing at least three times spontaneously in a child's lexicon in three different contexts (Lederer, 2001).

As the pace of vocabulary acquisition picks up, measuring rate of word learning and identifying the full set of new words learned may not be feasible. At that point, a goal could be for a child to acquire a corpus of target words within a particular timespan, measured with periodic comprehension and production probes. The expectation would be that many words would be learned through natural exposure, along with words that are specifically targeted.

Vocabulary growth also can be measured by taking periodic language samples and transcribing and analyzing them by counting the ***number of different words (NDW)*** in the sample. NDW can be counted most easily with a computerized language sample analysis tool, such as Systematic Analysis of Language Transcripts (SALT; Miller & Chapman, 2008). When entering transcripts into SALT, the root word is always spelled the same way, and an inflectional morpheme follows a slash (e.g., *walk, walk/ing, walk/ed, walk/3s* [for third-person singular] and *walk/s* [for plural noun form, as in *taking walk/s*]). That way, all tokens with the root word *walk* are counted as the same type, regardless of inflection. Missing obligatory morphemes can be indicated in this transcription coding scheme with an asterisk, such as *walk/*3s* (e.g., *He walk/*3s home every day*) or *walk/*ed* (*He walk/*ed home yesterday*) so each occurrence is counted as a token of the word *walk* and the evidence of the child's morphological development can be documented.

The NDW measure is preferable to the more traditional ***type/token ratio (TTR)*** as a measure of vocabulary diversity, because TTR tends to drop as children use repeated tokens of the small set of function words and TTR is not sensitive to language growth. For example, a child producing the same word two times in a 10-minute sample would have a TTR of 0.50 (1 type/2 tokens), and so would a child producing 100 different words in a 200 word sample (100 types/200 tokens).

When pioneer child language researcher Mildred Templin (1957) reported data from language samples gathered for 480 children (ages 3 to 8 years), she found they showed remarkable consistency in TTR (around 0.50) across early childhood. Based on Templin's data, Miller (1981) recommended that a TTR of less than 0.50 be used as a threshold for concern for language disorder in this age range, noting that "if a normal hearing child's TTR is significantly below 0.50 we can be reasonably certain the sparseness of vocabulary use is not an artifact of SES but is probably indicative of a language-specific deficiency" (p. 41). On the other hand, research comparing language samples of children with specific language impairment (SLI) with age- and language-equivalent-matched children has shown that NDW is a more sensitive measure for discriminating language ability than TTR (Watkins, Kelly, Harbers, & Hollis, 1995). The ratio of the TTR measure cannot capture the evidence of vocabulary diversity the NDW measure can.

Several formal tools have been designed to assess conceptual vocabulary associated with the preschool curriculum. Examples are the Boehm Test of Basic Concepts-Preschool (BTBC-P3; Boehm, 2001) and Bracken Basic Concept Scale—Revised (BBCS-R; Bracken, 1998). These tools contain class charts that preschool teachers can use to monitor the acquisition of conceptual vocabulary by all members of the class.

Targeting New Words and Concepts in Comprehension and Production

Goal 11.1. The child will show increased rates of adding new words productively and will demonstrate comprehension of new vocabulary by responding appropriately in new contexts. The normal acquisition of new vocabulary is thought to occur in two phases (Carey, 1978). The first is *fast mapping* (also called *quick incidental learning,* or *QUIL),* which occurs when a child forms a preliminary association of a new word with a known or new concept using episodic and contextual cues. The second phase is more gradual. It occurs as the child cognitively maps additional information about the word's meaning in additional encounters in meaningful contexts.

Children with language impairment (LI) tend to show slower mapping of new vocabulary, possibly due to perceptual-processing difficulties. Evidence from studies of children with SLI shows they need more models and a slower speaking rate to incorporate new words into their vocabularies (Ellis Weismer & Hesketh, 1996). Studies of QUIL by children with SLI show them to need more time and intensive support, as well as more frequent exposure to infer meanings of words in context (Rice, Oetting, Marquis, Bode, & Pae, 1994). Children with LI apparently need to experience new words more times (at least 10 times per session) in meaningful contexts and over several sessions, with heightened focus on perceptual cues achieved by using a slower speaking rate and more pauses.

When targeting vocabulary, it is important to remember that there is more to knowing a word than simply being able to point to a referent or repeat the word in highly supported activities. Children must be able to use words functionally and generatively in novel situations for communicative purposes. Children learning a second language and children who rely on sign language (signed English or American Sign Language) or augmentative and alternative communication (AAC) techniques also may need additional opportunities to engage in rich experiences in which they learn to comprehend and express new words for conveying content and supporting social interaction and play. The recommendation to use pauses and slight slowing and simplification without distorting naturalness is appropriate for children who use hearing aids or cochlear implants as well. Adults are cautioned not to exaggerate articulatory production, however, as it can distort words and make them more difficult to recognize in other contexts.

Another caution is that too many massed repetitions out of context actually can reduce recognition of a word's meaning, rather than enhance it. This phenomenon can be experienced by producing phrases such as "This is a *book;* this is a *brush*" 10 times each in massed trials while pointing to the appropriate object—a technique sometimes used to teach words to children with autism (e.g., Lovaas, 1981). Most people find that massed repetitions soon lead to reduction in meaning. Although children with severe communication disorders may require many more repetitions of words to acquire them, the repeated opportunities should be in meaningful contexts, not meaningless ones. Proctor-Williams and Fey (2007) also found that, compared to natural conversations, dense recasts of verbs did not help children with SLI (ages 7 to 8 years); in fact, dense recasts actually slowed verb learning for children with typical language. Studies with toddlers have confirmed that distributed presentations are more efficient and preferable to massed presentations for promoting initial word acquisition by typical language learners (Childers & Tomasello, 2002).

Focused stimulation can be used to teach vocabulary as well as grammatical form. It involves the arrangement of repeated opportunities to experience preselected vocabulary but in meaningful contexts. Leonard and colleagues (1982) studied the approach with preschool-age children (2 years, 8 months to 4 years, 2 months) in play activities that specifically targeted labels for 16 unfamiliar objects and actions. Clinicians structured play to provide five repetitions of each novel, low-frequency word, always in the sentence-final position (e.g., "Here's the *shell*. Watch the doll *kneel*.") in ten 45-minute play sessions over one month. Word-learning results were compared with results for control children who had the same number of play sessions but no models of unfamiliar object and action labels. Dramatic differences were found in the mean number of target words comprehended and produced by children in the experimental group (7.14 and 3.50, respectively) compared with the control group (0.02 and 0.01, respectively), supporting the use of focused stimulation with multiple lexical models for teaching new vocabulary.

In meaningful contexts, adults frame cues about the meaning of new vocabulary in environments that convey meaning in relationship to neighboring semantic fields. Many semantic features (e.g., perceptible attributes, locations, emotions) are particularly distinguishable when contrasted to their polar opposites using exemplars. Preschool vocabulary teaching should begin with baseline testing of children's existing vocabulary knowledge. To take advantage of the principle of contrast, vocabulary words can be selected and introduced in contrasting pairs, perhaps constituting "concepts of the week" (e.g., *hot–cold; big–little; high–low; in–on; happy–sad; give–take; numbers; letters; colors*). Unfamiliar concepts then can be introduced weekly during circle time and recycled as needed. Three sets at a time is a good rate of introduction. Pairs of pictures representing contrasted exemplars of concepts might be hung from hooks on each of three branches of a "learning tree." Preschool teachers can review the concepts at the start of each session, with opportunities for choral responses to questions about which words apply to which concepts.

Repeated opportunities to experience the words can then be embedded in experiential activities to highlight features of meaning throughout the week. Thus, focus on content vocabulary can be integrated with goals targeting syntactic structures. For example, multiple opportunities to practice paired conceptual vocabulary (*hot* and *cold; red* and *green; one* and *two*) can be embedded in activities targeting the *-ing* present-progressive morpheme. These could include cooking activities, with talk about "stir/*ing* red and *green* Jell-o" and "cool/*ing* the *hot* Jell-o," or playing "Simon Says touch *one* ear" and "Simon says touch *two* ears." To extend the vocabulary-teaching activities to the home setting, children can be given "concept of the week" handouts to take home, with suggestions about how to create opportunities to work on concepts of the week in everyday routines—cooking and eating activities (e.g., choosing *round* or *square* crackers for a snack), dressing (e.g., putting shoes and socks *on* and taking them *off*, and counting *one* or *two* [*both*] hands and feet), bathing (e.g., making sure the water is not too *hot* or *cold*), and bedtime (e.g., deciding whether a stuffed animal should go *on* the covers or *under* them). Periodic probes can be used to update the class vocabulary chart to make sure that all children in the class are generalizing the new vocabulary.

Wilcox, Kouri, and Caswell (1991) investigated preschool word learning within two service delivery models by comparing word learning for 20 children (ages 20 to 47 months), all with language delay. Children were assigned randomly to a classroom-based program or to one-on-one sessions with a clinician. A set of 10 core vocabulary words was selected individually for each child to meet three criteria: (1) words contained initial phonemes already in each child's phonetic inventory; (2) both action words and object words were included; (3) words could be represented in functional interactions in classroom or clinic room. A focused stimulation approach was used, which meant that no imitative production prompts were used, nor were requests made to label items representing a target word.

Five principles guided the intervention: (1) establish joint attention by following the child's lead; (2) use simplified models to map single-word vocabulary onto the focus of the child's attention; (3) respond to the communicative function of spontaneous imitations and provide a semantic expansion with a related two-word combination; (4) respond conversationally (not punitively) with a correct label if a child mislabels an object (e.g., "No, that's not a cow; it's a pig"); and (5) use semantic–pragmatic contingent responses when a child produces a target word spontaneously. The results showed that both approaches were effective, but children in the classroom-based instruction generalized target words better to home.

Lexical comprehension grows along with expressive vocabulary and in most cases precedes it. But not all indicators of a child's comprehension represent actual *language* comprehension. Figure 11.1 summarizes how typically developing children may appear to comprehend more relational terms than they actually do because they can use nonlinguistic strategies to respond. Although the use of nonlinguistic comprehension strategies is normal during this period, assessment and intervention should aim at increasing linguistic comprehension without nonverbal support. To assess children's *language* comprehension, clinicians must carefully monitor and limit any nonverbal cueing in their gestures or direction of eye gaze that could signal to a child what to do without comprehending the words.

As children begin to use more words, growth in vocabulary comprehension and production can be assessed and scaffolded as necessary. Two normal vocabulary development processes are semantic **overextension** and **underextension.** Children with LI may use both processes in typical ways but may overuse them as well. This could signal a need not only for a larger vocabulary but also for more accurate mapping of lexical items onto conceptual categories. Semantic overextension occurs when a child applies a label to a broader conceptual domain than is appropriate (e.g., when a child calls a *horse* a *doggie*). It may be that the child lacks specific vocabulary for the concept and simply selects the best-fitting word from the available lexicon (e.g., Clark, 1993). Semantic underextension occurs when a child applies a label to a concept that is too limited. This may indicate that a child has an overly specific concept about the meaning of a word. For example, a child might conceive that the only referent for the general concept of *cookie* is an Oreo-brand cookie and reject all other exemplars. Demonstrating underextension, a 23-month-old boy protested that he had not watched a *video* but rather a *movie.* Overly specific meanings are modified easily for most children as their experience with multiple exemplars grows, but children with autism spectrum disorders may have particular difficulty with overly specific vocabulary use.

In typical development, overextension, such as calling a *horse* a *dog,* actually may represent strength in analogical processing for applying a reasonably close (analogical) term when an exact label is unavailable. This process may be used also by second-language learners who have a relatively large vocabulary in their first language but a smaller one in their second or by a child using an AAC device with a limited set of vocabulary symbols (Nelson, 1992). Applying inexact terms from a second language or from a communication board should prompt adults to offer appropriate words in the new language or to add options to a child's communication board.

figure *11.1* ————————————————————————————————————

Observation Tool for Contextualized Comprehension for Relational Vocabulary

Observation of Comprehension Strategies	Assessment and Intervention Suggestions	Observational Evidence (date and context)
Spatial terms (***in, on, under, over, beside***) ❑ Probable location strategy: Put object where you expect to see it in real life. ❑ Preference for containers and surfaces: ❑ If container present, put object in. ❑ If not, place object on surface. ❑ Motor ease strategy: Do the easiest thing. ❑ Preferred location strategy: When hearing *here* or *there*, *this* or *that*, always pick the object closest to self (child-centered strategy) or speaker (speaker-centered strategy). ❑ Fronted reference object strategy: When hearing *in front, in back, beside, behind,* look for the object to have a clear front (e.g., *car, people, animals*) to aid comprehension.	Create a scenario in which multiple positions are equally probable (e.g., Put object *in/on/under* the truck). Provide multiple containers with options for placing objects *in, on,* or *under*. Make all response choices equally easy to accomplish. Credit comprehension only when the child can demonstrate both ends of the contrast. Teach terms with fronted objects first and then with nonfronted objects (*tree, table, can*).	
Amount terms (***more, less, long, short***) ❑ Preference for greater amount strategy: When asked to pick the referent showing *less* or *short*, select the choice representing the greater amount. ❑ Judge by height strategy: When asked to pick the *tallest, largest,* or *oldest,* select the item with more height.	Assess both sides of antonym pairs to credit understanding and teach them in pairs to highlight contrasting features. Present choices in which the greatest height does not coincide with the *largest* or *oldest*.	
Dimensional adjectives (*big, little, short, tall, thin, thick, wide, narrow*) ❑ Big/little synonym strategy: Treat words like *thin, short,* and *low* as little and words like *tall, wide,* and *thick* as big.	Use test objects that differ in more than one dimension (e.g., ask for the *thick pencil* but make sure that it is shorter than the thin one).	
Temporal terms (*before, after*) ❑ Probable sequence strategy: Do things in the order they usually occur in life.	Use less predictable materials and events (e.g, "Before you feed the baby, give me the pencil.").	

Source: Based on Edmonston & Thane, 1992.

Producing Sounds in Words

Children who have difficulty learning to produce speech sounds and words with all their hierarchical features may need a comprehensive assessment and intervention program focused directly on speech production. A full description of assessment and intervention procedures for disorders of phonology/articulation is beyond the scope of this book, but it is the topic of numerous other sources (e.g., Bernhardt & Stemberger, 2000; Bernthal & Bankson, 2004; Kamhi & Pollack, 2005).

Assessing Speech Production in Words

Assessment for speech sound disorder (SSD) should include a standardized test of articulation/phonology (e.g., the Goldman-Fristoe Test of Articulation, 3rd ed.; GFTA-3; Goldman & Fristoe, 2000), accompanied by analysis of the child's developmental patterns (Tyler, 2005a). For example, the Khan-Lewis Phonological Analysis, 2nd ed. (KLPA-2; Khan & Lewis, 2002) might be used in conjunction with the GFTA-3. Screening of hearing and peripheral oral mechanisms should be conducted for all children but particularly for children with SSD.

Clinicians also need ways to quantify growth in phonological production accuracy within samples of speech production gathered during intervention. One approach is to compute a child's *phonological mean length of utterance (PMLU;* Ingram & Ingram, 2001) for a corpus of 25 of the child's words. To do this, clinicians count all *segments* (i.e., *C*s and *V*s) in a child's production (correct or not) of a word. For example, pronouncing *sock* as [tak] counts as three segments, awarding one point for each segment (phoneme) the child produces. Then, the total number of accurately produced consonants (i.e., those matching the adult model) is added to this count. In this example, the child's production [tak] would count 4 points because 1 point is added for the correct consonant /k/ but no point is awarded for the developmental /t/. Correct vowel production points are not added because research has shown that such judgments cannot be made reliably. The child's PMLU (in words) is computed by dividing the total score by the total number of words (usually 25) in the corpus.

As a child's phonological system develops, his or her speech production accuracy should increase along with intelligibility. This indicates that the child is approximating more features of the phonological structure of adult targets. Ingram and Ingram (2001) suggested measuring the *proportion of whole-word proximity (PWP)* by dividing the child's PMLU by the PMLU for the same words in their mature forms. The PWP is computed as a ratio of whole-word scores for the total corpus. For example, if the child's PMLU for the 25-word corpus is 3.5 but the PMLU for the correct adult forms of the words is 6.5, the child's PWP would be computed by dividing 3.5 by 6.5, which equals 0.54. This suggests that the child can represent approximately half of mature representation of phonetic information in words. Quantification methods can provide objective tools for measuring progress, but they do not necessarily indicate which aspects of word phonology should be targeted.

When a child's phonological systems are underdeveloped, the developmental phonology approaches introduced in Chapter 5 may be helpful for describing his or her speech production system and selecting intervention targets (Kamhi, 2006). Examples are as follows:

- *Nonlinear phonology* (e.g., Bernhardt & Stemberger, 2000) involves analyzing a corpus of phonetically transcribed words to identify features that are specified or as yet unspecified in the child's sound system (e.g., syllable stress, onset and rime, or phonetic features) relative to the mature targets.
- *Natural phonology* (e.g., Hodson & Edwards, 1997) involves analyzing the child's phonological simplification processes and selecting words to target in alternating

treatment cycles to highlight contrasts (e.g., *bow* versus *bone* so that the final consonant alters meaning).

- A *complexity approach* (e.g., Gierut, 2001) involves analyzing the child's productions
  and selecting multiple targets, including sounds representing a consistent error, a later
  acquired sound, and two new sounds paired for contrast.
- A *language-based approach* (e.g., Norris & Hoffman, 2005) involves studying words
  in a meaningful context, such as shared book reading; words are selected with consistent phonological characteristics that can be used to strengthen neural networks and
  links among a constellation of phonological concepts.
- When *whole-word production* is the target, as it generally is when combined speech
  and language problems are suspected, specialized assessment techniques may be used
  to quantify baseline levels and target the next higher levels of ability. One approach
  is to compute the *percent consonants correct* (*PCC*) in a sample of a child's speech
  (Shriberg & Kwiatkowski, 1982).

Targeting Intelligible Phonetic and Prosodic Structure and Phonological Awareness

*Goal 11.2. The child will produce speech with words that are intelligible and demonstrate
growing phonological maturity.* As reviewed in Chapter 5, preschool-age children with
marked SSD have somewhat higher risks for SLI, particularly affecting morphosyntax
(Rapin & Allen, 1983; Tyler, 2005b). Some researchers have found that approximately
60 percent of children with SSD have comorbid problems in language development (e.g.,
Bishop & Edmundson, 1987; Shriberg & Kwiatkowski, 1994). It makes sense, therefore, to
focus assessment and intervention on both language and speech when symptoms of difficulty appear in both domains (Tyler, 2005a). Case Example 11.1 provides a description of a
kindergarten-age child whose word concept confusions were intertwined with phonological
concept confusions, presenting risks for literacy difficulty as well.

When children have disorders affecting both speech and language, the initial focus
should be on producing a wider variety of words that are intelligible but not necessarily

---

CASE example *11.1*

Lisa's Phonological Confusions

Lisa was in kindergarten when her teacher noticed early signs of learning disability. The SLP, who asked Lisa to tell the story of "Goldilocks and the Three Bears," noted that Lisa was able to convey the gist of the story but showed phonological/word-level difficulties. She used the word *soup* (rather than *porridge*) and at various points pro-nounced it as *soup, thoup, thoot,* and *suit,* sug-gesting that her categories of /θ/ and /s/ and /t/ and /p/ were not well differentiated.

Later in the story, after talking accurately about the bowls of soup being *hot* and *cold,* Lisa told about Goldilocks trying out Daddy Bear's chair. She searched overtly for the correct word, saying

"Haaard [drawing the word out with question into-nation] or cold? I think cold." This segment seemed to reflect short circuiting of word meanings and sounds. Lisa's phonological confusions affected her word retrieval and word choice and may have played a role in her substitutions of objective for subjective case pronouns (*him* for *he; her* for *she*) and other word production difficulties (e.g., *aminal*).

These phonological confusions suggested a greater risk for literacy-learning difficulty than if Lisa had consistently misarticulated particular phonemes. The team decided to provide early intervention services and follow-up diagnostic testing as needed.

correct. As Velleman and Vihman (2002) pointed out, children start at a middle-unit level in speech production by producing whole words, rather than small-unit phonemes or large-unit sentences. An ***intelligible*** production is one that is recognizable enough that most listeners can respond to the word as having meaning. Context can play a role in rendering words intelligible, suggesting that early intervention for SSD should be embedded in reciprocal contextualized communication, rather than in nonmeaningful drills. As for syntax, elaboration should precede correctness. Correctness can be a target in the future.

For older preschool-age children, whose speech production is largely intelligible but delayed in complexity and accuracy, traditional articulation therapy might be appropriate. Such an approach targets the production of individual phonemes in isolation first, then moves to production in syllables, words, structured phrases, and eventually to naturalistic sentences in discourse contexts. Preschool-age children (from 3 to 5 years) can have "speech notebooks" that include letters to represent target sounds, contrasted with related but different sounds make the children focus on the distinguishing features of sounds, while introducing the alphabetic principle.

For example, if analysis of a corpus of the child's speech indicates consistency of /f/ pronounced as /p/, the clinician might create a side-by-side page with two pictures (and related graphemes) to elicit onomatopoetic productions of the two distinct target sounds and highlight the feature of distinction. The clinician then might teach the child to point to the letter *P* on a page with pictures of popcorn surrounding it when the clinician produces the /p-p-p/ stop consonant and to point to the letter *F* on a page with a picture of a "mad kitty" when the clinician produces the sustained continuant /f/) (see Figure 11.2).

Based on their recommended system for computing PMLU and PWP (see earlier discussion), Ingram and Ingram (2001) suggested intervention objectives targeting a higher proportion of phonological completeness, such as the following:

> John will produce 10 target words with an average PWP score of .8 or higher using his current phonological and word shape inventory. Today's session: *boy, bunny, lamb, hair, wool, barn, eat, hop, run, hay.* (p. 282)

This example illustrates embedding work on speech sound production in a language lesson with a theme and targeted vocabulary. Clinicians could use a play scenario with a story about a *bunny* who *hops* and a *lamb* who *lives in a barn* and *eats hay* and gives *wool*. Intervention around this objective might start with play with toy objects and then support co-construction of a simple storybook about the featured animals, attributes, actions, and objects to be used in repeated readings in the therapy setting and at home.

If a child is functioning at an even earlier developing level or has a severe impairment of speech sound production (perhaps diagnosed as childhood apraxia of speech), preverbal vocalizations (e.g., *wheee* or *woa*) might be targeted first as a bridge to word production. Even more basically, Davis (2005) noted that for a child who is not communicating consistently with voice, "the primary initial goal may be 'use of the voice for intentional communication' and targets may be related to facilitating communication interactions based on the vocalizations and pragmatic intentions noted to occur in the assessment process" (p. 91).

Some children with SSD become so sensitive about speech sound production and intelligibility problems that they avoid talking in intervention sessions. Such children may be engaged in play, with opportunities to produce vocalizations as sound effects using phonemes but not real words. For example, a child might learn to differentiate articulatory features, such as the presence or absence of the continuant feature in the "mmmm" of a car's motor versus the "t-t-t" of a clock, reducing communicative pressure for word production. The acquisition of more elaborate phonology can benefit from a period of experimentation

p   f

figure *11.2*

Illustration of Page from Child's Speech Notebook Contrasting the Continuant
Sound /f/ with the Stop Consonant /p/

and constructive learning, in which the child is led to explore different sound options without a requirement to say specific sounds or words correctly.

Researchers have studied whether speech sound production improves when the intervention focus is on language. For example, Fey et al. (1994) implemented a five-month
focused stimulation program (based on Leonard, 1981) with 25 children with dual speech
sound production difficulties and language problems. The children's grammar improved,
but their speech did not (measured as percent consonants correct [PCC]; Shriberg & Kwiatkowski, 1982).

Other evidence also supports the need for explicit focus on speech *and* language
targets. Tyler, Lewis, Haskill, and Tolbert (2002) alternated treatment focused on phonology and morphosyntax and found positive results for both language and speech. The study
by Tyler and her colleagues involved 27 preschool-age children with difficulties both in
speech sound production and grammar. Ten children were assigned randomly to a 12-week
block of intervention focused first on speech and then followed by a 12-week block of
intervention focused on language; 10 children had the same treatments in reverse order;
and 7 children were randomized into a wait list control group. The sessions that focused
on morphosyntax structures (e.g., third-person singular verb endings) included auditory
awareness (e.g., "The bear *sees* a blue horse"), a song (e.g., "The bear *sees* all his friends"),
focused stimulation (e.g., "John *tapes* feet on the dog"), and production elicited with a cloze
procedure (e.g., Adult: "The bear ___" Child: "*sees* a bird"). Sessions that focused on phonology (e.g., final /f/) included auditory awareness (e.g., *huff, puff, wolf* in "The Three Little
Pigs"), target sound identification (e.g., /f/ associated with picture of a *fan*), conceptual
(e.g., "Long sounds are like long spaghetti"), production practice (e.g., final /f/ pictures *fed*
to a puppet), a naturalistic activity (Be a *chef; puff* and *fluff* dough; make a *loaf* of bread),

and phonological awareness (e.g., select odd one out: *huff, puff, star*). The results showed that both phonology and morphosyntax interventions led to significant improvements in targeted domains. Unlike the Fey and colleagues (1994) study, however, children who received the morphosyntactic treatment first also showed improved phonological skills. An implication is that a language focus may be the place to start in intervention.

The primary conclusion to be drawn from these multiple studies is that if one wants to change speech, language, or communication, then intervention should target the area of concern directly. It is possible, however, to target skills from more than one domain in an integrated fashion, with potential benefits across domains. A general rule of thumb is to start with the largest units with which children can be successful and to switch attention between wholes and parts (sentences, words, and sounds) until children can manage larger units independently and with communicative competence.

SUMMARY

Language intervention during the preschool years may target sounds, words, and vocabulary in integrated activities at the word level. Research evidence shows that children who have difficulty producing intelligible words can benefit from a focused stimulation approach with repeated opportunities to hear a core vocabulary of words in meaningful contexts emphasizing contrasts in targeted phonological features. When a child exhibits a speech sound disorder as a component of a language disorder in the preschool years, the goal is for the child to increase word intelligibility rather than complete correctness.

Other word-level targets include the ability to comprehend and produce a greater variety of vocabulary words and to use words to represent abstract concepts as well as to name objects and animals. Semantic features can be taught using contexts and materials to exemplify contrasts in word meaning (e.g., *hot–cold, big–little*). Some research shows that new vocabulary can be learned both in preschool classroom settings and individual intervention, but children generalize better when taught in classrooms. A home program can be added to help children generalize new vocabulary using focused stimulation in meaningful contexts at home.

Sentence- and Discourse-Level Development

As typically developing children move through the preschool years, they produce sentences of increasing variety and complexity. These are not just isolated sentences but are embedded in a range of discourse structures, from conversation to narrative, and for performing a variety of communicative functions.

Premises of Early Syntax Intervention

More complex syntax comes from the need to represent more complex ideas. Therefore, the intervention techniques in this section are based on two premises: (1) syntax goals that target elaboration over correctness are more consistent with a natural developmental progression and reduce cultural–linguistic bias, and (2) syntax goals that are integrated with discourse goals are more likely to help children express their ideas cohesively.

A primary reason for avoiding premature focus on syntactic correctness is that errors are a natural part of grammatical learning. Elaboration of structures to represent more complex ideas may not be error free, but they should be valued as signs of growth both in the preschool (Johnston, 2007a) and school-age years (Weaver, 1982). No child uses fully mature adult grammar, even by age 5 when entering school. Language specialists at least since

Brown (1973) have observed that children may go through a period of incorrect regularization of forms, such as *wented,* after using irregular forms correctly for a time. It is normal for children in the early elementary years still to be developing regular and irregular verb inflections and higher-level forms. Research with typically developing children has shown associations between higher error rates and faster grammatical learning (Horgan, 1980; Ramer, 1976).

Another reason to target elaboration over correctness is to reduce the potential for bias in evaluating language advances. Elaboration is easier to detect across dialects of English and for dual language learners, whereas judgments of correctness are specific to particular language standards. Standard language use is defined by power structures in a political system. For example, the official standard language of instruction in most North American, African, and South American countries is the language of the European country that was in power during the period of world colonization (e.g., English, French, Dutch, Spanish, or Portuguese). This creates bias for children whose home language experiences are different from those of the mainstream culture and language.

In the preschool years, children's primary job is to learn the language of their homes; hence, they should be acquiring forms that are *appropriate* for home contexts, not necessarily *correct* by standard definitions. The recommendation to support elaboration over correctness applies particularly for dual language learners. It is now widely accepted that children can be exposed to more than one language without disadvantage and that exposure to two languages may even facilitate a child's language learning (Cole, Maddox, & Lim, 2006; Langdon & Cheng, 2002; Tabors, 1997). Nevertheless, dual language learning often brings grammatical glitches that are signs of difference (or language mixing), not disorder. Language clinicians should be interested foremost in helping preschool-age children develop communicative competence within their home communities before helping them acquire language consistent with the correctness standards of schooling.

The second premise is that children learn to comprehend and formulate more complex sentences when they need them to communicate in meaningful discourse contexts (e.g., conversational and narrative discourse of play and storytelling). This premise leads to procedures that involve engaging children in interactive construction of meaning to create a natural need for more complex linguistic forms for talking about complex ideas and performing higher-level communicative functions. Clinicians should embed scaffolding intervention in the natural contexts of play, storytelling, and shared book interactions, highlighting perceptual cues but without exaggeration or massed trials that are overly dense.

Syntax

Assessing Syntactic Growth Using Language Sample Analysis

The preschool years from age 3 to 5 are characterized by rapid advances in the ability to produce and comprehend longer and more complex sentences when children are developing typically. Figure 11.3 summarizes developmental advances as children move from Brown's Stage I, with an MLU of 1.5 (indicating that at least some two-word utterances are present), at about 24 months to Brown's Stage IV, with an MLU of 3.0, by about 36 months. In typical development, most children have reached Brown's Stage V (MLU of 3.75) by the time they are 3.5 years old (42 months). It is considered a sign of concern if children are not forming any three-word constructions by their third birthday (36 months).

As documented by Miller (1981), growth in MLU can be detected through analysis of a spontaneous language sample of 50 to 100 utterances. MLU continues to be a good measure of morphosyntactic development throughout the preschool years. Table 11.1 presents Miller's MLU and standard deviation data for children in the age range from 18 to 60 months. This growth occurs not by adding words onto the ends of sentences in linear

figure *11.3*

Observation Tool for Brown's Stages and 14 Morphemes

Stage	MLU	Sentence-Level Changes and 14 Morphemes
Prestage I		
Stage I	1.0–1.49	❑ Single-word utterances
Late Stage I	1.5–1.99	❑ Basic semantic relations (two-word utterances appear)

Stage II	2.0–2.49	❑ Modulation of meaning
		  ❑ *-ing* (no auxiliary)
		  ❑ *in*
		  ❑ *on*
		  ❑ regular plural *-s*
		  ❑ irregular past (imitated)
		  ❑ possessive *-s*

Stage III	2.5–2.99	❑ Modalities of sentences
		  ❑ uncontractible copula *be*
		  ❑ articles *a, the*
		  ❑ regular past *-ed*
		  ❑ regular third-person singular *-s*

Early Stage IV	3.0–3.49	❑ Embedding and coordination

Late Stage IV		❑ Embedding, coordination, and subordination
		  ❑ irregular third-person singular *does, has*
		  ❑ uncontractible auxiliary *be*
		  ❑ contractible copula *be*
		  ❑ contractible auxiliary *be*

Early Stage V	3.5–3.99	
Late Stage V	4.0–4.49	
Poststage V	4.5+	

Source: Based on Brown, 1973.

fashion but as hierarchical elaborations of the noun phrases and verb phrases that serve as the major constituents of sentences. Almost simultaneously, children begin to combine more than one proposition syntactically by embedding, coordinating, or subordinating the meaning of one sentence within or appending it to another. When applying MLU data to make judgments about disorder, it is important to use norms that are appropriate for the members of a particular sociolinguistic community.

Comparison databases appropriate for multiple populations, including Spanish-language and dual-language learners, are available in the SALT software program (Miller & Chapman, 2008). Stockman's (1996) Minimal Competency Core (MCC) provides alternative criteria for assessing language of 3-year-olds learning African American English (AAE). As described in Chapter 10, the MCC includes observation of multiple language components and sets a minimum MLU expectation of 2.70 for 3-year-olds learning AAE, with a recommendation for further assessment of children who do not reach this threshold.

As children move from a preponderance of two-word to three-word utterances (typically by 3 years of age), most children start by using all three components of basic sentence structure (i.e., agent + action + object). Then they begin to demonstrate other forms of elaboration, and the syntactic boom has begun. New semantic cases are added, such as instrumental (e.g., *Eat [with] fork*) and dative case forms (e.g., *Give me baby*). Brown's 14

table *11.1*   Predicted MLU Ranges within 1 Standard Deviation (SD)
of Predicted Mean for Each Age Group

Age ±1 Month	Predicted MLU[a]	Predicted SD[b]	Predicted MLU ±1 SD (Middle 68%)
18	1.31	0.325	0.99–1.64
21	1.62	0.386	1.23–2.01
24	1.92	0.448	1.47–2.37
30	2.54	0.571	1.97–3.11
33	2.85	0.633	2.22–3.48
36	3.16	0.694	2.47–3.85
39	3.47	0.756	2.71–4.23
42	3.78	0.817	2.96–4.60
45	4.09	0.879	3.21–4.97
48	4.40	0.940	3.46–5.34
51	4.71	1.002	3.71–5.71
54	5.02	1.064	3.96–6.08
57	5.32	1.125	4.20–6.45
60	5.63	1.187	4.44–6.82

[a]MLU is predicted from the equation MLU $= -0.548 + 0.103$ (age).
[b]SD is predicted from the equation $SD_{MLU} = -0.0446 + 0.0205$ (age).

Source: Jon F. Miller, *Assessing language production in children: Experimental procedures,* 1/e (p. 27). Published by Allyn and Bacon/Merril Education, Boston, MA. Copyright © 1981 by Pearson Education. Reprinted by permission.

morphemes also begin to emerge with a fair degree of predictability as the MLU advances for children learning standard English.

Complex sentences, which incorporate two or more propositions (e.g., *I wanna rock baby; I know what to color*), appear relatively early—long before children have mastered all regular and irregular inflections for producing basic noun phrase (NP) plus verb phrase (VP) constituents of simple sentences. This is one reason that limited elaboration may be a more valid indicator of risk of language disorder than grammatical error, especially for diverse groups of children with varied cultural–linguistic experiences. For example, Oetting and Newkirk (2008) found that children with SLI used fewer relative clauses (e.g., *He's the one that's my friend*) and relative clause markers (e.g., *who, that, which*) than typically developing children across three dialect groups (AAE, Southern White English, and Mainstream American English).

The construction of complex syntax is signaled by the presence of more than one verb phrase in the sentence. (Recall from Chapter 2 the key role played by the VP in prepositions.) New clinicians may have difficulty identifying the parts of a VP (i.e., one or more auxiliary verbs + main verb), confusing the multiple words that make up the auxiliary portion of a single VP as representing more than one verb. It is helpful, therefore, to analyze the auxiliary verb construction of each VP first and then to look for multiple VPs as a sign of syntactic complexity. Figure 11.4 illustrates these components.

figure *11.4*

Observation Tool for the Development of Auxiliary Verb Constructions and Showing Related Developmental Sentence Score (DSS) Points

C^a + (modal) + (have + en) + (be + ing) + V^b Person — *can could* Number — *will would* Tense — *shall should* *may might* *must must* He — *should* — *have* — *be + en* — *go + ing.* Third-person Singular Past		Developmental Examples	DSS Points
❏ Uninflected main verb/copula V ❏ Progressive *-ing* with no aux V + *ing* ❏ Contractible aux *be + ing* *is* V + *ing*		*I play. It is good. It's big.* *I playing. He playing.* *I is playing. You is playing.* *He is playing.*	1 0 0 1
❏ Third-person singular present *-s* ❏ Regular past *-ed* ❏ Inflected copula or aux: *am, are, was, were* V + *ing*		*He plays. He played.* *I am playing. He was playing.* *We are good. They were good.*	2

❏ Present tense modals: *can will may*   V
 ❏ "Dummy do" appears when no other aux for:
    ❏ negatives
    ❏ questions
    ❏ emphasis[c]
		I can play. She will play.
		 I can't play. Will she play?
		 I don't play. They don't play.
		 Do you play?
		 They do play!
			4

❏ Past-tense modals: *could, would, should, might* V ❏ Inflected third-person and past-tense forms of *do* V		*She might play. He could play.* *He doesn't play. Doesn't she play?*	6
❏ Passive with *be* or *get* (colloquial) V + *en* ❏ Modals *must* or *shall* (rare) V ❏ Present perfect (*have*), past perfect (*had*) V + *en*		*The game was played. The ball got hit.* *He must play. She shall play.* *She has gone. He had played.*	7
❏ Present-perfect progressive *have been* V + *ing* ❏ Past-perfect progressive *had been* V + *ing* ❏ Other aux combinations: (modal) *have been* V + *ing*		*I have been playing.* *He might have been playing.* *She could have been playing.*	8

[a]The C marker describes the proposition of the sentence in terms of person (first, second, or third), number (singular or plural), and tense (present or past). This information is marked on the next item in the string. Only the main verb is obligatory (parentheses indicate that all other components are optional); thus a third-person singular present-tense form with only a main verb would be *He walks,* but if the progressive (*be + ing*) form is used, it would be *He is walking.*

[b]The arrows show that inflectional morphemes for the perfective (*have + en/ed*) and progressive forms (*be + ing*) actually appear on the item that follows them in the string.

[c]Auxiliary verbs are required for forming questions, negatives, and emphatics; if none is already present, "dummy do" appears to serve this syntactic role.

Source: Based on Chomsky, 1957 (developmental examples) and Lee, 1974 (DSS points).

The auxiliary VP construction rule can be used to generate verb forms that communicate fine variations of meaning, including verb tense (present or past), sentence modality (future tense, possibility, certainty, etc.), and verb aspect, indicating completed or ongoing action (present or past perfect; present or past progressive). Figure 11.4 outlines the obligatory (no parentheses) and optional (in parentheses) components of a fully developed verb phrase in English. It shows the developmental steps taken by children progressing to full competence with VP production. An example of a fully formed adult VP—using the rule C + (modal) + (have + en) + (be + ing) + V with all optional parts included, is *I would have been going*. This example is structured using first person, singular, past tense (components of the *C* marker), influencing the modal auxiliary *will* (creating the past form *would*), followed by the present perfect (*have + en*), with the *-en* marked on *been,* and the present progressive (*be + ing*) forms, with the *-ing* marked on the main verb *to go*. Notice that the past tense is only marked on the first item in the string and that each additional bound morpheme appears on the component that follows it. It would be anomalous to mark tense on more than one element in the string (e.g., *I would had been went*). This is true for standard English and any dialect of English.

AAE includes options for expressing semantic aspects of verb tense that standard English does not allow (e.g., *I been done gone*). Such forms emphasize the completive meaning of the VP. AAE allows other variations in the auxiliary VP construction rule, such as an optional *be* in the auxiliary and copula (e.g., *She coming; He my friend*) and third-person singular inflection (e.g., *He drive a bus*). As Wyatt (1996) pointed out, systematic grammatical and pragmatic constraints influence whether the "zero copula" rule applies or not. The copula is more likely to be understood and not expressed when it follows a pronoun (especially plural) or word that ends with a voiceless consonant or when it precedes a locative, predicate adjective, or word beginning with a consonant. Table 11.2 outlines some features of AAE grammar and discourse traits.

Auxiliary verbs play a central role in forming questions, negatives, and emphatic utterances for all dialects of English (also illustrated in Figure 11.4). In each linguistic context, the first auxiliary (Aux) in the string plays an important role. In forming a question, the first Aux moves to the front of the sentence, representing the Aux inversion rule (e.g., ***Are*** *you going?* ***Will*** *you go?*). In forming a negative, the first Aux carries the negative marker (e.g., *I* ***am*** *not going; He* ***won't*** *go*). In forming an emphatic, the first Aux carries extra stress (e.g., *She* ***is*** *going! He* ***should*** *go!*). If there is no auxiliary verb already present, the "dummy do" assumes this syntactic role, as in questions (e.g., ***Did*** *she go?*), negatives (e.g., *He* ***didn't*** *go*), and emphatics (e.g., *We* ***did*** *go!*). Dialects of English also use auxiliaries to form negatives and questions, but most dialects allow variations. For example, *I am not* becomes *I ain't, I have got some* becomes *I got some,* and *He doesn't see it* becomes *He don't see it*. Many dialects allow multiple negatives, rather than just marking negatives on the first auxiliary in the string, such as *He don't got none*.

As illustrated in Figure 11.4, development of the VP occurs systematically. One of the earliest steps occurs when children add an auxiliary to the main verb to convey modality with a modal verb (*can* or *will*), usually in the negative form *can't* or *won't*. Later, children produce analyzed forms (Aux + neg) *cannot* and *will not* without contraction and *can* and *will* in their positive forms. Early forms of infinitives, such as *gonna, wanna,* and *gotta* (e.g., *Him gonna bite me, She wanna go,* and *I gotta climb up*), are called semiauxiliaries (i.e., concatenated, or "stuck together" forms), because they function more like auxiliaries than infinitives. True secondary verb (infinitive) forms come later.

Bliss (1987) offered guidelines for intervention for auxiliary verbs, including designing environments in which contexts lead children to talk about ability (*can*) and intention (*will*). Negative forms can be contrasted with positive ones (e.g., *I can reach it* versus *I can't reach it*). Modals also become more perceptually salient when they occur at the ends

table *11.2*   Selected African American English Grammatical Features and Discourse Traits

Form or Feature	Example
Zero Morpheme Markers	
Grammatical morphemes are not obligated in some contexts:	
Plural -*s*	*He wore two sock on his left foot.*
Possessive -*z*	*She put on her mama dress.*
Past tense -*ed*	*He walk to school yesterday. This car crash.*
Progressive -*ing*	*The lady is sleep.*
Third-person singular -3*s*	*He drive a bus. He do want some.*
Copula or auxiliary *is, am, are, was, were*	*She coming today. He my friend. I tired.*
Zero *to* in infinitives	*She try find him.*
Existential *it*	
Parallel to SAE *there is/are/were* to indicate existence	*It's two dimes stuck to the table.* *It was a lot of thing happening yesterday.*
Indefinite article	
a regardless of vowel context	*We pick a animal to write about.* *He stay for a hour.*
Pronoun in apposition	
Noun + pronoun reference same person or object	*My mama, she be mad at me.*
Aspectual Options	
Habitual: *be* + verb/*ing*	*She be watching me. (She is always watching me.)*
Remote past: *been* + verb/*ing*	*He been sleeping. (He has been sleeping for a long time.)*
Remote past completion: *been* + verb/*ed*	*We been ate. (We ate a long time ago.)*
Remote past perfect: *had* + *been* + verb/*ed*	*We had been ate. (We had eaten a long time ago.)*
Resultant state: *done* + verb/*ed*	*We done ate. (We have already eaten.)*
Combinations of the above with modal auxiliaries: multiple possibilities	*We should'a done ate. (We should have already eaten.)* *We been done ate. (We finished eating a long time ago.)* *We be done ate. (We usually have already eaten.)*
Discourse Traits	
Rhythmic, dramatic, evocative language	*Darkness is like a cage bird in black around me, shutting me off from the rest of the world.*
Use of proverbs, aphorisms, biblical verses	*People might shut me off from the world cause of a mistake, crime, or a sin . . .* *Judge not others, for you will have you day to be judged.*
Sermonic tone, especially in vocabulary, imagery, metaphor	*I feel like I'm suffering from being with world.* *I'm fightin, prayin for someone to find me.*
Direct address–conversational tone in formal contexts	*I think you should use the money for the railroad track.* *Please change your mind and pick the railroad tracks for the people's safety, okay.*
Cultural references	*How about some chitterlings tonight?*

Form or Feature	Example
Discourse Traits (*continued*)	
Ethnolinguistic idioms	*It will run me crazy. A fight broke loose.*
Verbal inventiveness, unique nomenclature	*[The settlers] were pioneerific.*
Signifying (verbal art of insult in which speaker humorously puts down another; similar to "playing the dozens")	*You so fat the door scream when it see you coming.*
Woofing (boasting used to intimidate opponent and avoid violent confrontation or to win woman's attention)	*Last dude try that be in the hospital.*
Rapping (rhythmic, braggadocios, or assertive statements put to music; originally referred to creative talk from man to woman to win affection)	*She be mine and she be lookin so fine.*

Source: Based on Green, 2003; Washington & Craig, 1994; Wyatt, 1996 (grammatical features) and Green, 2003; Smitherman, 2000a, 2000b (discourse traits); with contributions by Brandi Newkirk.

of sentences. For example, the clinician might put napkins, cups, a juice bottle, and cookies in the middle of a preschool classroom snack table, ask "Who can reach the napkins?" and then model responses, such as "I can" or "I can't," building such forms into a daily routine. Contexts for the auxiliary *will* are introduced after children demonstrate success with *can* by setting up occasions for expressing willingness or intention. A question such as "Who *will* pass out the napkins/cups/etc.?" could establish the need for the form "I *will*."

Compound or complex sentence use can be documented when children begin to incorporate two or more propositions (indicated by two or more VPs) in the same sentence. This often starts with the coordination of two independent clauses (T-units) joined with *and* (e.g., *The dog jump **and** he scare me*). The compounding of two independent clauses may be treated as an early developing complex sentence, although it does not represent true complexity. Truly complex sentences may be observed at or near the same time, in which the child embeds one proposition within another or uses a subordinating conjunction to convey a relationship that is logical (e.g., *He got in timeout because he hitted me*) or temporal (e.g., *I slide after you done*). Figure 11.5 provides an observational tool for documenting ability to combine more than one semantic proposition into a single compound or complex sentence.

As a rule of thumb, whenever a sentence includes two or more VPs, it can be considered compound or complex, depending on which of the following conditions is observed:

- A compound sentence is made up of two independent clauses joined with one of the four coordinating conjunctions—*and, but, or, so*. (*For* is also a coordinating conjunction but is rarely used.)
- A complex sentence is made up of a combination of independent and dependent clauses, which may be related in several ways:
  1. A relative clause is an embedded clause that modifies a NP constituent of another sentence; right-branching forms (e.g., *He saw the horse who won the race*) usually develop at the end of a sentence before center-embedded forms (e.g., *The boy who called is my friend*) appear in the middle.
  2. A complement clause serves as the object NP, becoming a constituent of another sentence (e.g., *I know that she can run fast*).
  3. A subordinate clause is conjoined to an independent clause with a subordinating conjunction (e.g., *when, if . . . then, after, because*) that conveys a logical or temporal

figure *11.5*

Observation Tool for the Development of Compound and Complex Sentences, with Associated Brown's Stage and DSS Points

Construction	Developmental Examples	Brown's Stage/DSS Points
Catenative (semiauxiliary) forms: *gonna, wanna, gotta* Children learning southern American dialects or AAE also may use /fɪntə/ "fixin' to" for *gonna*.	*I'm gonna make some.* *He's fixin' to come too.*	**Stage II** 2 DSS points in secondary verb column
Early forms: *let's, lemme* These forms act similar to unanalyzed catenatives in that they involve the obligatory omission of the infinitive *to* and *let* functions as an semiauxiliary.	*Let me do it.*	**Early Stage IV** 2 DSS points in secondary verb column
Simple infinitives with equivalent subjects in both clauses	*I have to see.* *He wants to come.*	**Early Stage IV** 3 DSS points in secondary verb column
Compound sentences conjoined by *and* These are sentences in which two independent clauses are joined.	*He looked out the door, and he saw a big dog.*	**Early Stage IV** 3 DSS points for *and* in conjunction column
Full propositional complements These involve use of one sentence (proposition/dependent clause) as the object of another, often following mental verbs (*know, wonder, guess, think, pretend, hope, show, forget*). *That* is optional as introducer but *what* does not yet appear.	*I know (that) he is.* *I think (that) that's mine.* *Pretend (that) you can.*	**Early Stage IV** 0 DSS points for conjunction unless *that* appears
Simple *wh-* **clauses with finite verbs** Some early dependent clauses are introduced by the subordinate conjunctions *what, where, why,* and *how.*	*That's why it happened.* *That's what I thought.* *She knows how it works.*	**Early Stage IV** 8 DSS points for conjunctions
Double embeddings These forms are credited when one clause is embedded within another, often with a catenative form.	*I'm gonna think about how to do it.* *You hafta let me come.*	**Late Stage IV/Early Stage V** Varied DSS points for each primary or secondary verb
Infinitive clauses with differing subjects or obligatory deletion In these sentences, the subject of the embedded sentence differs from that of the main clause or is a later form with obligatory deletion of *to* with a verb, such as *let, make, watch, help.*	*I want you to be my friend.* *How do you get this to work?* *He made her fall down.*	**Late Stage V/Stage V+** 5 DSS points in secondary verb column

Construction	Developmental Examples	Brown's Stage/DSS Points
Coordinating conjunctions Child coordinates two main clauses with *but* (conveying disjunction), *or* (conveying alternatives), or *and so* (conveying logical sequence).	*He can come <u>but</u> you can't.* *It happened <u>and so</u> I felt sad.*	**Late Stage V/Stage V+** 5 DSS points in conjunction column
Subordinating conjunctions Early subordinating conjunctions *if* and *because* are used to convey conditional and causal relationships between a main clause and a subordinated clause. Later ones are used to convey other relationships.	*I can come <u>if</u> you invite me.* *He fell <u>because</u> he was going too fast.* *He said yes <u>after</u> I did.*	**Late Stage V/Stage V+** *If* scores 5 DSS points, *because* scores 6, in conjunction column. *Where, when, how, while, whether, as_X_as, like, until, unless, since, before, after, that* score 8 DSS points.
Gerunds A gerund is a verb phrase used as a noun. It is a later-developing nonfinite verb form.	*<u>Falling down</u> is a problem when children first learn to ride their bikes.*	**Stage V++** Gerunds score 8 DSS points in the secondary verb column.
Relative clauses Any center-embedded clauses are considered more complex but especially if they are embedded in a clause that already is subordinated to another.	*The officer replied by saying "the man <u>who killed your daughter</u> admitted that he was just getting a ride home."*	**Stage V++** Relative pronouns earn 6 DSS points in the personal pronoun column.
Left-branching clauses with later developing subordinate conjunctions and multiple forms Sentences with left-branching clauses or with two levels of subordination or with multiple clauses are more complex.	*<u>Although they only searched for 15 minutes</u>, they found the cat.* *The boy ran from the boy <u>who was chasing</u> them <u>after he yelled</u>.*	**Stage V++** Higher DSS points are earned in multiple columns in highly complex sentences.

Source: Based on Lee, 1974; Miller, 1981; with contributions by Cheryl Scott.

relationship; it may use a left-branching (e.g., *After he fed the dog, they played catch*) or right-branching structure (e.g., *I saw her after she swam*). Left-branching forms are considered more complex to process and formulate, and they usually develop later.

4. Three types of secondary (i.e., nonfinite) verbs are used to embed one proposition within another as phrases rather than clauses:
   - An infinitive phrase (*to* + V) (e.g., *He likes to color pictures; Apples tend to fall*).
   - A participle (V + *ing* or V + *ed/en*) is a verb used as an adjective (e.g., *She saw him coloring pictures; She found the picture colored; He found the apply fallen off the tree*).
   - A gerund (V + *ing*) is a verb used as a noun (e.g., *He likes coloring pictures; Falling on the ground is not good for apples*).

A variety of formal and informal tools can be used to assess morphosyntactic abilities in the preschool years. Some formal tests reflect recent research on grammatical language acquisition. Examples are the Test of Early Grammatical Impairment (TEGI; Rice & Wexler, 2001) and the Diagnostic Evaluation of Language Variance (DELV; Seymour, Roeper, & de Villiers, 2003). In assessing syntactic development, language sample analysis can contribute information about forms a child is or is not using productively, especially relative to his or her MLU. The outline of developing syntax that appears in Table A in the Part III Appendix may be helpful in conducting such inventories.

Miller (1981) suggested an approach for analyzing early syntactic development, which he termed *assigning structural stages*. Scarborough (1990a) adapted Miller's approach to create an Index of Productive Syntax (IPSyn). The IPSyn is a measure of grammatical complexity based on a 100-utterance child language corpus (from which unintelligible, imitative, and self-repetitive utterances have been omitted). An IPSyn score is derived by crediting up to 2 dissimilar tokens of 56 types of syntactic and morphological forms; these are partially summarized in Figure 11.6. It can serve as an observation tool for comparison with evidence of age of acquisition data reported by Scarborough and Dobrich (1990).

Other observational measures of developmental syntax assign variable points for forms that develop earlier (lower scores) or later (higher scores). Laura Lee's (1974) *developmental sentence scoring (DSS)* analysis uses this technique. Points are assigned for forms in the eight grammatical categories outlined by Lee (i.e., indefinite pronouns and noun modifiers, personal pronouns, main verbs, secondary verbs, negatives, conjunctions, auxiliary inversion, and *wh-* questions) (see Table G in the Part III Appendix). A child's mean DSS is computed by analyzing a minimum of 50 sentences (defined as a NP + VP, or a compound sentence with a maximum of two independent clauses). Scores are totaled for individual sentences (including a sentence point if the entire structure is correct); then scores for all 50 sentences are totaled and divided by 50 to compute the child's mean DSS.

DSS captures evidence of growing syntactic maturity in two ways: (1) scores of increasing value (from 1 to 8 points) are assigned to each instance of a later developing form, and (2) total scores for each sentence add up to higher totals based on incorporation of more elements as well as higher scoring elements across the eight grammatical categories. Thus, children are rewarded both for using higher scoring structures that develop later and for elaborating sentences by packing more into them. Lee (1974) provided a chart with percentiles (see Figure 11.7) based on language samples produced by 200 children from ages 2 years to 6 years, 11 months playing with a set of toys (e.g., barn with farm animals; furniture and doll family; transport truck with cars) and using pictures to elicit the story of "The Three Bears." Lee's recommendation was that children who scored lower than the tenth percentile should be considered at risk for language disorder. Such children would require assessment with additional tools to decide whether they should receive language intervention services. Koenigsknecht (1974) added means and standard deviations for 20 males and 20 females (all White children from Illinois, Maryland, Michigan, and Kansas) "from monolingual homes where Standard English of general American dialect was spoken" (p. 224) (see Table 11.3).

DSS is appropriate for children in standard English-learning environments, but it penalizes children using dialectal forms. A two-pronged solution is (1) to give credit for dialectal forms and (2) to compare children's response to data for an appropriate peer group. Table F in the Part III Appendix provides criteria for Lee's original scoring scheme. Table H in the Part III Appendix provides criteria for adding points based on Black English Sentence Scoring (BESS; Nelson & Hyter, 1990). Figure 11.8 shows an example in which sentences are scored using DSS criteria, after which points are added for AAE forms (using BESS criteria). DSS scoring is completed first; then BESS points are added for AAE forms that receive "attempt makers" and thus would be treated as errors under DSS. Table 11.4 provides the means and standard deviations for 64 typically developing African American children,

figure *11.6*

Observation Tool for Index of Productive Syntax (IPSyn)

This chart shows the age at which nine of twelve (and all twelve) typically developing children used forms productively (rated as 0 = never occurred; 1 = occurred once in sample; 2 = occurred twice or more).

Rating	Morphosyntactic Form	Example	Age (in mos.) of Productive Use 9/12 (12/12)
❏	subject + verb + object	*Boy see me.*	27 (33) mos.
❏	prepositional phrase	*In box. On table.*	31 (33) mos.
❏	plural -*s*	*Two dogs. More cookies.*	31 (33) mos.
❏	*no(t)* + X	*No bed. Not baby.*	31 (33) mos.
❏	2-word predicate NP	*Jamie baby.*	31 (40) mos.
❏	catenative	*Gonna eat. Wanna read.*	31 (40) mos.
❏	progressive -*ing*	*Going bye bye.*	31 (40) mos.
❏	copula	*Baby is big.*	31 (40) mos.
❏	present tense modal	*Him can crawl.*	39 (40) mos.
❏	NP + negative + VP	*Him not crying.*	39 (45) mos.
❏	*Wh-* (+ NP) + VP	*What you doing? What doing?*	39 (45) mos.
❏	present tense *do/be* aux	*Me don't go. Him is scary.*	39 (45) mos.
❏	third-person singular -*s*	*Him bites.*	39 (45) mos.
❏	inverted *Wh-* question	*Where is it?*	39 (55) mos.
❏	aux + neg + V	*Him can't jump.*	39 (55) mos.
❏	inverted *yes/no* question	*Is it big?*	39 (55) mos.
❏	*Let's* + predicate	*Let's read.*	39 (55) mos.
❏	infinitive	*It's hard to do.*	39 (55) mos.
❏	propositional complement	*I think it can roll.*	39 (55) mos.
❏	conjoined clauses	*I coming and you read book.*	44 (55) mos.
❏	det + mod + N	*This my book.*	44 (55) mos.
❏	pre-verb NP	*The big dog bite me.*	44 (55) mos.
❏	past tense -*ed*	*He hitted me.*	44 (60) mos.
❏	past-tense auxiliary	*She was crying.*	50 (60) mos.
❏	3-VP sentence	*She is walking, jumping, and singing.*	50 (60+) mos.
❏	gerund	*She likes singing.*	59 (60+) mos.
❏	relative clause	*It's the best song that he knows.*	59 (60+) mos.
❏	tag question	*You want to come, don't you?*	60+ (60+) mos.

Source: Based on Scarborough, 1990a; Scarborough & Dobrich, 1990.

with eight children (four boys and four girls) at each six-month interval. A minimum of 50 sentences is required for DSS/BESS analysis.

The child in the example, Eric (age 4), earned a mean BESS of 6.55 for the full sample (see the partial sample in Figure 11.8); this score would be compared with the data in Table 11.4. The mean BESS for children in the 4 years to 4 years, 5 months age range is

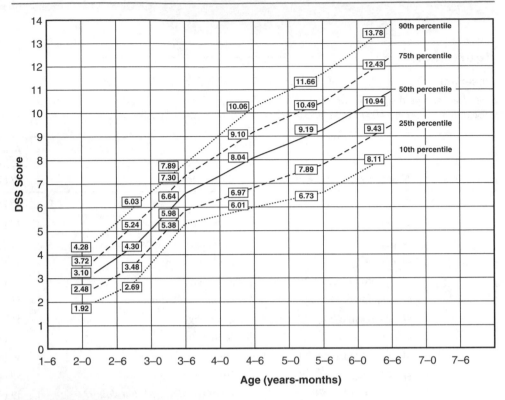

figure *11.7*

Norms for Developmental Sentence Scoring

The percentiles are based on data for typically developing children.

Source: From Lee, Laura Louise. *Developmental sentence analysis: A grammatical assessment procedure for speech language clinicians.* Evanston, IL: Northwestern University Press. 1974. p. 167. Adapted and reprinted by permission of the publisher.

table *11.3* DSS Means and Standard Deviations (SDs)

Age Group*	Males		Females	
	Mean DSS	*(SD)*	*Mean DSS*	*(SD)*
2;0–2;11	3.67	(1.11)	3.78	(1.41)
3;0–3;11	6.59	(0.97)	6.68	(1.00)
4;0–4;11	7.74	(1.61)	8.32	(1.59)
5;0–5;11	8.49	(1.93)	9.89	(1.53)
6;0–6;11	9.99	(2.04)	11.89	(2.00)

Note: The data are from 200 subjects, with 20 males and 20 females in each of five one-year age groups.

*Age ranges are shown in years;months (e.g., 2;0 is 2 years, 0 months).

Source: From Koenigsknecht, R. A. (1974). Statistical information on developmental sentence analysis. In L. Lee, *Developmental sentence analysis: A grammatical assessment procedure for speech and language clinicians* (p. 261). Evanston, IL: Northwestern University Press. Reprinted by permission of the publisher.

figure 11.8

Example Scoring Form and Partial Sample for Black English Sentence Scoring

A sample has been scored first using DSS criteria, and then points have been added for penalized AAE forms that are credited with the BESS scoring criteria found in Table H in the Part III Appendix.

Name Evic **Age** 4;0

Date May 31, 2009 DSS 3.73 BESS 6.55

	Indef. Pron.	Pers. Pron.	Prim. Verb	Sec. Verb	Neg.	Conj.	Inter. Rev.	WH Ques.	Sent. Point DSS	Sent. Point BESS	Total DSS	Total BESS
1. That the food that grandma ate.	1	6	1/– , 2						0	1[c]	9[a]	11[b]
2. I goin' to nursery school.		1	1/–						0	1	1	3
3. I putting my sister on a motorcycle.		1, 1	1/–						0	1	2	4
4. I listening.		1	1/–						0	1	1	3
5. I watched him yesterday,		1, 2	2						1		6	
6. I like these.		1, 3	4/–						1		6	
7. I push all these buttons, ok?	3	1, 3	2/–						0	1	7	12
8. They try catch me.		3, 1	2/–	5/–			–		0	1	4	12
9. I had a spoon.		1	2						1		4	
10. Who this on the phone?	1		1/–				1/–	2/–	0	1	1	6
11. Where the gun?			1/–				1/–	2/–	0	1	0	5

Total DSS for this partial sample: __41__ divided by 11 = __3.73__   Total BESS for this partial sample: __72__ divided by 11 = __6.55__

[a] Sentence total for DSS.
[b] Sentence total for BESS.
[c] Point earned for BESS but not DSS. (Numbers above DSS attempt markers (–) represent credit awarded for BESS but not DSS.)

Source: From *Black English Sentence Scoring: Development and Use as a Tool for Nonbiased Assessment* by N. W. Nelson and Y. C. Hyter, 1990, unpublished manuscript, Western Michigan University, Kalamazoo. Copyright 1990 by N. W. Nelson. Reprinted by permission.

table *11.4* Means and Standard Deviations (SDs) Showing Both the DSS and BESS Scores Computed on the Same Samples

Age Group*	N	Mean DSS (SD)		Mean BESS (SD)	
3;0–3;6	8	5.63	(0.91)	7.44	(1.15)
3;6–4;0	8	5.73	(1.04)	7.71	(0.98)
4;0–4;6	8	7.47	(1.58)	9.33	(1.26)
4;6–5;0	8	7.51	(1.68)	8.85	(1.48)
5;0–5;6	8	8.86	(1.93)	10.79	(1.92)
5;6–6;0	8	8.31	(2.04)	10.02	(2.16)
6;0–6;6	8	9.12	(2.43)	11.08	(1.61)
6;6–7;0	8	9.47	(1.72)	11.17	(2.17)

Note: The data are from 64 African American children, with 4 males and 4 females at each six-month age group.

*Age ranges are shown in years;months (e.g., 3;0 is 3 years, 0 months).

Source: Based on Nelson & Hyter, 1990.

9.33 (standard deviation [SD] = 1.26). Eric's mean BESS score could be compared with this benchmark using this formula: 6.55 − 9.33 = −2.78 / 1.26 = −2.2. This indicates that Eric's score was 2.2 SDs below the mean for his peer group (constituting a *z*-score of −2.2). A score this low would suggest significant cause for concern and need for further diagnostic testing using other age and culturally–linguistically appropriate measures and parent and teacher interviews. Based on DSS and BESS analysis, a clinician may identify patterns of forms a child is using or that are not appearing but obligated by the context.

Targeting Complete and Complex Sentences in Multiple Discourse Contexts

Goal 11.3. The child will use targeted syntactic and morphological structures and increased MLU in spontaneous language samples gathered in natural contexts. Intervention promoting more mature syntactic and morphological structures starts with an assessment of forms that the child is using, not using, or using inaccurately or intermittently (i.e., within the child's ZPD). A complete inventory may not be necessary, but the informal assessment process should identify the best short-term targets (highly functional, frequently needed forms) involving components such as (a) major sentence constituents (NPs and VPs); (b) sentence combining and embedding; and (c) function words and bound morphemes (e.g., articles *a, the;* auxiliaries; verb endings; plural and possessive markers).

Morphosyntactic forms are targeted frequently within conversational discourse, often in playlike settings with a clinician, teacher, or parent who uses a child-centered focus. The context can be manipulated to increase the functional–semantic need for targeted forms, and clinicians can use models and recasts to highlight targeted forms and scaffold their use by the child, usually without direct request for imitation. Three approaches that are appropriate for preschool-age children with morphosyntax problems are enhanced milieu teaching, focused stimulation, and conversational recast intervention.

Enhanced milieu teaching (Hancock & Kaiser, 2006) is designed for "preschool children with significant cognitive and language delays; children with autism spectrum disorders; and children from high-risk, low-income families" (p. 203). It uses a hybrid of three techniques: (1) environmental arrangement for supporting language learning and teaching; (2) responsive interaction (RI) for following the child's lead, responding to verbal and nonverbal initiations, providing meaningful semantic feedback, and expanding the child's utterances; and (3) milieu teaching (MT) techniques—modeling, mand modeling, time delay, and incidental teaching. The program relies on eliciting and reinforcing imitations and providing natural consequences. It is most effective with children who have at least 10 productive words and whose MLU is between 1.0 and 3.5 morphemes. Hancock and Kaiser (2006) summarized a body of research on EMT that supports its effectiveness when delivered either by clinicians or parents.

Focused stimulation (Leonard, 1981) targets specific vocabulary and forms. Language input exposes the child to multiple exemplars of a particular grammatical target, with no direct expectation for imitation. Naturalistic conversational contexts are arranged to attempt to elicit spontaneous productions of targeted form, content, or use. The effectiveness of focused stimulation is supported by a number of studies, as reviewed by Ellis Weismer and Robertson (2006).

Conversational recast intervention (Camarata & Nelson, 2006) parallels natural language acquisition. Clinicians respond to limited initiations using models that reflect children's forms but add something. For example, *Dog bark* would be recast as *The dog is barking* by adding the article *the,* auxiliary *is,* and progressive *-ing.* Parental recast of copulas has been associated with higher use of targeted forms. Some forms, such as passives, are more suited to conversational recasts, and others (e.g., the inverted auxiliary in questions or articles) appear less suited to recast approaches (Proctor-Williams, Fey, & Loeb, 2001).

Summarizing literature on grammar facilitation, Fey, Long, and Finestack (2003) outlined 10 principles. The first was that (1) all grammatical interventions should aim at facility in "comprehension and use of syntax and morphology in the service of conversation, narration, exposition, and other textual genres in both written and oral modalities" (p. 4). The second was that (2) "grammatical form should rarely, if ever, be the only aspect of language and communication that is targeted in a language intervention program" (p. 4). The third, fourth, and fifth principles were to target (3) syntactic processes (not just single forms); (4) structures that will support children's functional communication needs; and to manipulate (5) social, physical, and linguistic factors to arrange contexts necessitating targeted forms. The sixth, seventh, and eighth principles addressed the use of (6) multiple discourse contexts, written as well as spoken; (7) stress and positioning strategies to make grammatical features more salient, such as placing targeted forms at the ends of utterances; and (8) to use adult recasts of immature forms to model differences. The final two principles indicated that adults (9) should avoid telegraphic forms and always present "grammatical models in well-formed phrases and sentences," and (10) "use elicited imitation to make target forms more salient" (p. 4).

In summary, intervention scaffolding procedures for syntax are designed to highlight cues about linguistic features (phonological and morphological). They also should help children connect structures with semantic content and relationships represented in the environmental context (immediately present or being talked about). Models and other scaffolds can be implemented to support children to encode more relationships syntactically to accomplish authentic communicative functions. Although children with disorders need more opportunities, heightened cues, and extra time to acquire morphosyntactic forms, they still can benefit from approaches that are child centered, relatively naturalistic, communicative, and meaningful.

Narratives

Narratives—including scripts, stories, and personal narratives—play an important role in helping children develop skills for comprehending higher-level language forms and connecting with peers and adults (Boudreau, 2008; Johnston, 2008). Narratives organize experience into interpretable wholes that are more than just a series of connected sentences. They present opportunities for facilitating more complex language comprehension and production and for engaging young children in literate language experiences as well.

Personal narratives occur in all cultures. Narratives occur as isolated discourse events. Conversational partners also may switch from the *participant* discourse mode of interaction to the *spectator* discourse of narration (Britton, 1984). A personal narrative can be framed as an **account,** telling about an experience to someone who was not there (e.g., *Tell Nana what you did today*); a **recount,** telling about a past event in the presence of someone who was there (e.g., *Remember how funny it was when we . . .*); or an **eventcast,** describing an ongoing activity and planning for the future (e.g., *I'm going to be the mommy, and you be the dad*) (Westby, 1994). In all of these forms, narration is more than just a telling of events. It involves interpretation of personal experience, including attempts to understand the nature of motivation, goal setting, and responses to adversity.

Narration for younger preschool children in play incorporates metatalk for negotiating roles, which is an important skill in social interaction. The language of narratives (e.g., *Pretend you sleepy*) in play also predicts later literacy ability (e.g., Roskos & Christie, 2000). By age 4 to 5 years, the ability to use metaverbs, such as *think* and *know,* to talk about talking and thought processes in play is even more predictive of later literacy skills than the complexity of language embedded in the fantasy frames of play (Pellegrini, Galda, Bartini, & Charak, 1998). In their longitudinal "Home–School Language Study," Snow and Dickinson (1990) and Tabors, Snow, and Dickinson (2001) reported that narrative abilities of 3-, 4-, and 5-year-olds predicted later literacy development and school success. The findings held whether children demonstrated their narrative abilities in formal story retelling contexts or naturalistic dinner table conversations.

Narrative development is at risk for children with language delays and disorders. Paul and Smith (1993) reported both association and dissociation in the development of narratives and expressive syntax in preschoolers with language delay. They followed children with specific expressive language delay (SELD) from age 2 to 4 and gathered measures of productive syntax using DSS (Lee, 1974) and MLU and narrative development using the Bus Story Language Test (Renfrew, 1991). The Bus Story Language Test was developed for use in the United Kingdom. It requires children to retell a story with pictures about a naughty bus that runs away and gets stuck in the mud. By age 4, more than half (57 percent) of the children with SELD continued to show delay both in expressive syntax and narrative production (as predicted), but even those who appeared to have caught up to their peers in the production of expressive syntax continued to function at a level that was not significantly better in the area of narration. Paul and Smith interpreted difficulty with narrative skills as an ongoing risk factor for academic performance during the school-age years, even for children whose syntactic abilities have reached age-level expectations.

The task requirements of narration can be described based on their cognitive and linguistic demands and roles in supporting memory (Boudreau, 2008). In terms of cognitive demands, narratives are defined as decontextualized talk about the past or future (Snow & Dickinson, 1990). In terms of linguistic demands, narratives are defined as at least two utterances produced in temporal order about an event or experience (Hughes, McGillivray, & Schmidek, 1997). In terms of their role in memory, narratives are described as a natural way that children think about experience, making it more memorable (Bruner, 1986; Mandler, Scribner, Cole, & DeForest, 1980). Analysis techniques for targeting components of story grammar (e.g., Stein & Glenn, 1979) and high-point narrative macrostructures (e.g., McCabe & Bliss, 2003) are described in Chapter 13.

Bruner (1985) described narratives as representing a "landscape of consciousness" as well as a "landscape of action." This distinction is consistent with attributing a central role for narratives in helping children form a theory of mind. In telling stories, narrators must take account of their listeners' perspective (Wood, 1998) and tell about what characters are thinking and feeling. Thus, narratives interpret individual as well as cultural experience. Traditional fairy tales and fables offer a context for helping young children understand the concept of false belief. For example, Little Red Riding Hood does not at first recognize the wolf in her grandmother's clothing but gradually becomes more and more suspicious; Brer Rabbit begs not to be thrown into the briar patch, concealing that he knows it is his best chance of escape.

Themes of adversity, trickery, and resourcefulness characterize fables across ethnic groups, but not all cultures structure their stories the same (Au, 1980; Bliss & McCabe, 2008; Gee, 1989; McCabe & Bliss, 2003; Michaels, 1991; Westby, 1994). Hester (1996) reviewed research that oral narratives of children learning AAE are characterized by "topic-associating style, audience participation, and implicit cohesive relations, while the white children's narratives were characterized by a single topic, specific lexical references, and explicit relationships between characters" (p. 230). Westby (1994) described cultural socialization differences in how children are introduced to stories through their families:

- Mainstream middle-class Americans engage in frequent story reading, in which comprehension is negotiated, and production of imaginative stories is encouraged.
- White working-class Americans tend to listen to stories read with little negotiation of comprehension.
- Black working-class Americans tend to convey narratives in Bible stories and personal experience but rarely through children's storybooks.
- Mexican Americans tend to tell stories about real events and historical characters but rarely convey narratives through children's storybooks.
- Chinese Americans tend to tell tales about historical figures and events and show preference for informational texts over storybooks.

Assessing Narrative Development

Early narrative abilities can be assessed using the observation tools for assessing play and emergent literacy, which appear later in this chapter. Tools for assessing narratives also appear in Chapter 13. The need to consider cultural and familial differences in narrative experiences, particularly during the preschool years, has implications for assessment. *Dynamic assessment* (*DA*) is a good option whenever a clinician is concerned that an assessment procedure may not be part of the current child's experiences. Dynamic assessment approaches contrast with static ones that presume that all children of a particular age should know the same things. That presumption may be particularly unfounded for children from culturally and linguistically diverse backgrounds. DA approaches involve test–teach–retest sequences, so the clinician can control what a child has experienced and gauge how readily the child responds to the new experience when provided with controlled levels of scaffolding.

Narratives serve as an appropriate discourse context (although not the only one) that can be probed within a DA paradigm. DA uses graded levels of scaffolding, called ***mediated learning experience*** (***MLE;*** Gutiérrez-Clellen & Peña, 2001), to determine how children respond to language-learning experiences controlled by an examiner. Gutiérrez-Clellen and Peña (2001) based their targets and scaffolds on evidence from Gutiérrez-Clellen, Peña, and Quinn (1995) about qualities of culturally influenced narratives that tend to make mainstream teachers confuse them with disorders. The MLE, therefore, focused on helping the culturally diverse children learn to organize stories into basic components (e.g., setting, events, consequences, and reactions) and to respond to direct questioning about story facts (e.g., *what, where, when, who*), which were skills valued by teachers. Questions were designed to require attention to narrative structure, rather than specific story content.

For example, an examiner using DA might ask children to think about important features of each episode and to discuss interconnections among episodes (e.g., the three little pigs and their varied building materials), as well as relationships to the moral of the story (e.g., hard work pays off) and how to respond to story comprehension questions. For posttesting, children retell a different narrative, followed by questions about each episode and relationships among them to see how well they generalize their new abilities. Assessment of children's learning should focus on the ability to summarize information and monitor comprehension of events, as well as gains in correct answers to story comprehension questions. This DA approach also includes consultation with preschool teachers to interpret results. Teams decide collaboratively which children benefited sufficiently from the MLE to signify typical language learning and which children might need additional mediation and intervention.

Gutiérrez-Clellen and Peña (2001) continued to formalize techniques for documenting children's responsiveness to MLE and provided evidence supporting application of Peña's scale for rating examiner effort and child responsivity on a four-point Likert scale with these categories: 0 = slight, 1 = moderate, 2 = high moderate, and 3 = extreme. Transferability to new contexts can be rated similarly as 0 = low, 1 = medium, and 2 = high. These techniques constitute a form of response to intervention activity at the preschool level.

Miller, Gillam, and Peña (2001) developed formal materials for a DA approach called *Improving Children's Narrative Abilities*. Within this approach, the child tells a story based on a wordless picture book to provide information about his or her ability to use story components, episode structure, ideas, and language. DA data include test–retest gains and ratings of listener effort and student responsiveness. These measures of modifiability are used within MLEs designed to target two areas of difficulty identified with the baseline measure. The DA process is used to differentiate children with and without disorders, not on the basis of standardized scores but on the basis of their modifiability and generalization to other narrative tasks.

Targeting Ability to Comprehend Stories and Narrate Events

Goal 11.4. The child will produce narratives that show higher-level discourse levels and component skills than observed in baseline samples. Narratives provide an ideal context for targeting higher-level discourse and emergent literacy abilities and for encouraging more mature syntax to represent more complex and interrelated meanings. A problem with personal narratives (accounts) in preschool or clinic rooms is that children with limited language may lack sufficient cognitive–linguistic proficiency to communicate about there-and-then events. Thus, exchanges may be nonproductive and frustrating. Recounts carry advantages in that a person who was present can scaffold more details of the narrative.

A ***preschool journaling approach*** can be used to bridge the gap in event knowledge between the clinician and child and convey the value of print for assisting memory and communicating experience. This activity involves forming a partnership in home–school communication and using a spiral notebook to keep it going. In a preschool language classroom (described in Nelson, 1981), preschool journaling was explained to parents in a group meeting and a handout similar to Figure 11.9 was provided. Parents were asked to spend a few minutes each evening interacting with their child talking about events of the day and selecting a particular event to tell about in the journal. Examples were offered, ranging from memorable events (e.g., got a new puppy, ate dinner at McDonald's, dog got sick and threw up, got a new owie, attended a birthday party) to mundane events that were part of everyday routines (e.g., brushed teeth and went to bed; played trucks). Parents were asked to write

figure *11.9*

Memo for Parents of Children in a Preschool Language Classroom Introducing Preschool Journaling

Dear parents,

Here is a preview of the steps we will use in home-school journaling.

1. Talk with your child about something that happened during the day. It can be something exciting or scary or anything your child wants to talk about.

2. Open up the language notebook to a new page, write the date, and ask your child what he or she wants you to write for that day. Write down exactly what your child says in his or her exact words. Don't add anything or fix your child's sentence structure. (We should see that improve as the year goes on.) Use regular spelling, even if your child has trouble saying the words. Here is an example:

Me feeded doggie. Her liked it.

3. Draw a stick figure picture to go along with the story. Make the drawing very simple. Here is an example to go with the sample story:

4. Be sure to put the notebook in your child's backpack to bring the next day. We will help your child retell the story and use it to work on language goals. More about that at our meeting!

Thanks for working with us all year long. This will be fun!

down what his or her child said in his or her exact words on one page of the spiral notebook that traveled back and forth each day in the child's backpack. Parents also were invited to write a little more in their own words if that was needed to explain the event. Parents were encouraged to record their children's words exactly as they said them, spelled normally but without adding word endings or function words that were not yet present.

One rationale for this activity was to encourage parents (many of whom were from working-class families or receiving public assistance) to interact with their children at least once per day using *optional talk,* as described by Hart and Risley (1995, 1999). Parents needed to listen carefully to what their children were saying to write down their words. This produced a written record of each child's growing syntax that was rewarding to see. Parents were not taught any special expansion or other recast techniques, but in the process of getting the child's words written down exactly and seeking to understand his or her message, conditions were set for natural scaffolding, with the parents as an authentic audience. To help children connect the activity with the words and to support recall and representation the next day, parents were asked to draw a simple stick figure representation of the event as they talked with their children. So as not to intimidate parents, primitive stick figure drawing was modeled in the explanation memo (Nelson, 1981).

Children participated in narrating the event three times: (1) in a recount with the parent who was there; (2) in an account to the teacher, supported by the parent's written representation of the event; and (3) in an account to peers in the story circle using a new picture created by the teacher for support. The narrative account to the teacher occurred each day in the preschool during individual rotation through the storytelling center and other centers (e.g., fine motor and free play). In the one-on-one storytelling center, the teacher opened the book to the page with the new narrative and initiated a conversation about the event, referring to the parent's picture for support and reading the child's words as recorded by the parent. While talking about the event and scaffolding the child's retelling of the narrative, the instructor redrew the picture on a larger piece of paper and invited the child to retell the story so the instructor could write it at the bottom of the paper. This took about five minutes.

With the teacher's scaffolding, the dictation discourse became somewhat more formalized into a more literate *spectator discourse* form (Britton, 1984). The child also had an opportunity to see how spoken words can be represented with print. The teacher scaffolded the child's retelling and again wrote down exactly what he or she said, thus supporting metalinguistic awareness that print represents spoken words. The children then moved to the next center, where they could add details to their pictures or color parts of them while the teacher worked with other children. Later in the same half-day class session, the children reconvened in the story circle and retold their stories (while the teacher held up the redrawn pictures). This time the stories were retold to an audience of peers, who were amazingly quiet and attentive when listening to each others' stories.

When one of the special education preschool teachers observed that the children rarely initiated questions in any context, it was decided to invite each storyteller to call on one or two other children who had a question about his or her story. The question–answer exchange emulated the ***author's chair*** activity of writer's workshop for school-age children. With the storyteller taking center stage and controlling the discourse exchange that followed, opportunities arose to develop pragmatic skills for being sufficiently informative. Children also could practice syntactic forms and interrogative and declarative sentence types and become aware of heightened cues about conversational turn taking.

This preschool journaling approach was embedded along with other intervention activities in a comprehensive language preschool. In Nelson (1981), pre–post data were reported on changes for six special-needs preschool-age children. The overall purpose and measurable goal of the program was to help children catch up to peers by making as much or more gain on objective language measures during their time in the program. Children attended this program five half-days per week.

Gain scores over a three-month time period for MLU in spontaneous language samples produced by the six children ranged from –0.83 to 2.56 morphemes ($M = 1.2$ morphemes). Gain scores on the Test of Auditory Comprehension of Language (TACL; Carrow-Woolfolk, 1973) ranged from 0 to 30 months ($M = 10$ months). Gain scores on the expressive portion of the Sequenced Inventory of Communicative Development (SICD; Hedrick, Prather, & Tobin, 1975) ranged from 4 to 12 months ($M = 6$ months), and on the receptive portion of the SICD, gain scores ranged from 0 to 10 months ($M = 5$ months). Gain scores also ranged from 8 percent to 18 percent ($M = 12.7$ percent) of phonemes produced correctly on the Goldman-Fristoe Test of Articulation (Goldman & Fristoe, 1969).

Another indication of the success of the approach in supporting home–school connections was that the children liked the activity so much that they reminded their parents about working on their stories each night at home so they would have something new to share the next day at school. There was almost 100 percent participation in this activity among families (many of whom had extremely low incomes and faced multiple socioeconomic challenges), which provided another sign of the success of the approach.

Paley (1990) promoted narrative development in her early childhood classrooms through play, story dictation, and dramatization. She saw storytelling as an integral part of play but also somewhat separate from it. Paley described how children in her early childhood classroom developed their storytelling and thinking skills and also how she gained access to their ways of thinking, feeling, and relating to one another through stories:

> I listen to the stories three times: when they are dictated, when we act them out, and finally at home, as I transcribe them from my tape recorder. After that, I talk about them to the children whenever I can. The stories are at the center of this fantasy of mine that one day I will link together all the things we do and say in the classroom. (p. 3)

In Paley's classroom, the children developed their fantasy stories in play but also put their names on a list at the "story table" to take turns dictating them formally. Paley transcribed the children's stories, and later children invited peers to act out their stories with them in "a taped square in the center of the story room rug." Paley described this area as "sacrosanct when stories are performed; the children learn to keep off the stage unless they are in the story" (p. 37). In the process of first dictating and then fine-tuning their scripts and elaborating on them in the process of acting them out, the children engaged in an essentially social enterprise. Doing so promoted more advanced narration and emergent literacy. Not all children engaged readily in storytelling or social play. Case Example 11.2 tells of a child named Jason who began the year with many play and communication difficulties. It shows how he learned through storytelling to leave the safety of his repetitive play routine and to explore other options for interaction (Paley, 1990).

Ukrainetz (2006b) suggested that children be engaged by clinicians in retelling personal events or familiar stories with scaffolding and with picture supports. One structured prompting sequence has been described as *reciprocal reading* (Kirchner, 1991). It involves reading a familiar story aloud multiple times and then pausing and using a cloze technique, cuing the child to first fill in short segments of text and then longer ones. The goal is for the child to retell the story in its entirety.

McGregor (2000) described intervention for narrative skills among children with diverse cultural–linguistic backgrounds in a preschool classroom. She engaged peers as mediators in this intervention, noting that they might be more attuned to the children's cultural–linguistic experiences than their teachers, who tended to come from the mainstream culture. McGregor established goals for narrative components and cohesive devices to include six main components: (1) main characters; (2) feelings (i.e., emotional states of main characters); (3) setting (i.e., time and place of the story action); (4) complicating action (i.e., problem facing the main characters); (5) dialogue (i.e., reported speech of story characters); and (6) coda (i.e., ending resolving the action of the story and closing the story). Additional goals targeted cohesive devices for connecting the discourse, including conjunctions that were additive (i.e., conjunctions that link clauses through addition, such as *and*), temporal (i.e., with conjunctions that link clauses temporally, such as *then, next*), and causal (i.e., conjunctions that relate clauses causally, such as *because, so that*). McGregor reported pilot data for two less able storytellers, who practiced book narration following clinician-prompted models by peer tutors. She showed that stories incorporated more elements when told by concordant pairs of peers (i.e., pairs with similar abilities) and that more complete stories resulted when older peers worked with younger ones or when peers without disabilities worked with children with disabilities.

Most children like to hear stories being told by others. An orally told story with a simple plot, sometimes with characters named after the child, can encourage active listening and higher-level comprehension abilities. Comprehension can be facilitated, especially

---

CASE example *11.2*

Jason: Part 1

Jason is the central figure in Paley's (1990) account of how storytelling can be used in early childhood classrooms to connect purpose and emotion. Paley described her initial concerns about Jason and his solitary repetitive play:

> He plays alone; he tells stories to himself; he seems unaware of our habits and customs. Ask him a question and he says his helicopter is broken. Suggest an activity and he rushes away to fix his helicopter, sometimes knocking over a building in his path. (p. 29)

Paley did not want to label Jason's unusual behaviors. When her student teacher suggested the term *perseveration*, Paley noted its similarity to the word *persevere*, which would be considered a positive quality, rather than a symptom of disability:

> "Look, Trish, I'll admit I've little faith in your lists of so-called learning disabilities. But, in any case, none of these labels apply in a classroom that sees children as storytellers. These labels don't describe the imagination. A storyteller is always in the strongest position; to be known by his or her stories puts the child in the most favorable light." (p. 54)

Jason at first did not understand the social conventions of storytelling, including the rule of staying off the stage unless a player in someone's story. Paley wrote:

> Jason refuses to abide by the rule and it upsets everyone. His motor tunes up as each story begins, and within a sentence or two he is flying around the stage. (p. 37)

A turning point occurred one day when Jason forged "loudly onto the stage" and Paley asked:

> "Simon, is there a helicopter in your story? Do the squirrels see a helicopter?" Simon can barely hear me over Jason's tumult.
> "No . . . uh, yeah, they do. They heered it flying over there. Then it lands on *this* spot. Right here."
> Jason winds down and stops on the designated place. "Bru-ur-umpt! I turned off the motor," he says. Jason has deliberately furthered another child's story. (pp. 37–38)

A few days later, Paley heard Jason posing her question to Arlene, whose story concerned a little girl, a mother, and a crocodile. Jason asked, "Do you have a helicopter in your story?" Paley was surprised and noted that Arlene must have been too. Jason had to repeat the question three times before Arlene asked, "Is it too noisy?" Jason, in response, said, "It's already going to land. I turned off the motor" (p. 49).

---

when the story structure is controlled so as not to exceed the child's capacity for processing complex information (Boudreau, 2008; Just & Carpenter, 1992) and by stopping periodically to discuss the story, interpret the events, reflect on how the characters feel, and ask for predictions of what might happen next.

It is artificial to separate narrative discourse from play and literacy in preschool-age children. Children with disabilities, who are most at risk for demonstrating *dis*-integration across systems, may benefit most from intervention approaches deliberately aimed at fostering intersystemic *integration*. These discussions of narrative and the remaining objectives and discussions of this chapter target those integrated abilities.

SUMMARY

Language intervention at the sentence-level for preschool-age children is based on a set of premises that emphasize elaboration over correctness and embedding intervention focused on syntax in meaningful discourse contexts (e.g., conversations and storytelling). These premises emphasize the communicative uses of language structures and reduce bias for members of diverse cultural–linguistic communities.

Language sample analysis techniques were described, including computation of mean length of utterance (MLU) in morphemes, analysis of phrase and sentence complexity, developmental sentence scoring (DSS), and the index of productive syntax (IPSyn). Modifications were described for students learning dialectal forms of African American English, including the minimal competency core (MCC) approach and Black English Sentence Scoring (BESS) adaptations of DSS.

Three primary approaches were described for preschool-age children, including enhanced milieu teaching, focused stimulation, and conversational recasts. Narrative discourse is an important context for helping children to comprehend more complex syntax as well as to produce it (e.g., in story retelling). Dynamic assessment techniques, also called mediated learning experiences (MLEs), assess the storytelling capabilities of diverse learners. A preschool journaling approach enhances home–school scaffolding of children's combined syntax and narrative language development.

Social Interaction and Play

Dramatic play provides an appropriate context for assessing and encouraging social skills and language, including emergent literacy. Play provides opportunities to tell and act out stories and can serve as an intervention context for promoting integration among cognitive–linguistic skills and social–emotional development. Piaget (1959) and Vygotsky (1962) both linked symbolic play to representational skills, characterized by causal relationships in both directions. Patterson and Westby (1998) concluded that "at least some cognitive and social skills develop in the context of play" (p. 137). Summarizing the research relationships of language, play, and literacy, Roskos and Christie (2000) noted that play and literacy require similar mental processes and that children naturally incorporate literacy activities in play. They concluded that research supports children's ability to benefit from literacy-enriched physical play environments and adult assistance.

Play and Language

The ability to integrate language, thinking, and communication in the context of play is a primary developmental accomplishment of early childhood. Once toddlers reach the point of *functional play,* they use common objects functionally but in a pretend manner. From there, it is only a small step to *symbolic play,* in which children use objects arbitrarily to symbolize other things (e.g., a block for a cell phone), and then to *dramatic play,* in which children use words and props to create a scene and invite peers to join them in elaborating events and creating stories (see Figure 11.10).

From its earliest forms, play has special qualities that differentiate it from other forms of discourse. Although similar schemas are involved in play and nonplay activity (e.g., pretending to eat and eating for real), differences are clearly recognizable as well. Patterson and Westby (1998) identified eight qualities that differentiate play from real-life activities, including intrinsic motivation, process over product, child structured, active engagement, intrinsic rules and structure, free choice, positive affect, and nonliteralness. Within playful activities, children move from manipulating objects to using them symbolically and then dramatically, all within the first few years of life. This sets the stage for continued elaboration and understanding of others' motives and reactions in their play and thinking. In the process of learning to play, children acquire new vocabulary and complex sentences for developing cohesive narratives with characters who have thoughts, motivations, and plans.

In pretend play, children create a variety of imaginary personas as they explore ways to cope with the ordinary and superordinary challenges of living. They can pretend to be

figure *11.10*

Children Engaged in Different Types of Play

During early childhood, children advance in the ability to play with peers, use objects symbolically, and create dramatic scenes with language. The infants (upper-left) engage in parallel (noninteractive) focus on a stuffed toy; the toddlers (upper-right) share focus on a balloon; the preschool-age girls (lower-left) have an elaborated tea party, incorporating dress-up and emergent literacy (e.g., "Here's what I want to order for tea"); and the boys in their early elementary school years (lower-right) engage in hypothetical thinking (e.g., "What if your guy transforms into a monster?").

grown-ups, animals with human traits, or superheroes with superhuman traits. They learn how to pose "What if . . . ?" questions to themselves and their peers and to explore alternative responses to life's challenges and scary events. They can set up pillows as stepping stones to avoid a swamp full of crocodiles or pretend to build a treehouse to protect themselves from monsters who do not know how to climb trees. In the process, children need language forms and growing pragmatic competence to fulfill the social interaction discourse functions of suggestion, persuasion, collaboration, argument, and narration.

Assessing Language and Play

Context-based assessment for language and play involves arranging to observe an age-appropriate play scenario, in which a child with communication difficulties can be observed interacting with a more able peer. To gain a clear picture of the child's abilities with more than one type of communication partner, it may be necessary to observe interactions with different partners in different contexts. Clinicians can learn something about a child's abilities by playing with him or her themselves (and all clinicians should work on finding their inner child), but they also need to observe the child interacting with other children.

The observational tool in Figure 11.11, which summarizes key features from West-by's (1988) eight stages of play and parallel advances in language and communication, can be used to assess levels of play and language in preschool-age children. Descriptions by others (e.g., Howes, 1985; McCune-Nicholich, 1981) are embedded in Figure 11.11, as well, for observing the development of peer interactions in social play. Typically developing children demonstrate early play, language, and peer-interaction abilities in their infant and toddler years, but preschool-age children with disabilities are likely still to be mastering them. At the preschool level, children learn to separate their imaginary play from the immediate context using real toys and props, to develop themes that demonstrate increasing ability to integrate world knowledge and extend it in imagination, to organize play with forethought and in collaboration with others, and to integrate language and play, using each to support the other.

This observational tool can be used to address the first question of context-based assessment: What does the context require? Data gathered by using the tool as an observational checklist can be used to answer the second and third questions: What does the child currently do in the context, and what might the child learn to do differently? Insights can also be gleaned from such observations for answering the fourth question: How could the play context be altered to support higher-level functioning by the child?

Targeting Integration of Linguistic Forms and Functions with Symbolic Concepts and Discourse Scripts in Play

Goal 11.5. The child will demonstrate both play and language at least one level higher than baseline. Play is both the context of intervention and its goal. Preschool-age children who can play effectively and recruit others to fantasize with them in the context of dramatic play are preparing for other important connections in life—forming relationships, linking complex thoughts, understanding emotions, and communicating across cultures. Play is the context in which narratives develop and within which storytellers can exert maximum control. Paley (1990) described "play and its necessary core of storytelling" as "the primary realities in the preschool and kindergarten." She added that play and storytelling "may well be the prototypes for imaginative endeavors throughout our lives" (p. 6) (see also Personal Reflection 11.1).

PERSONAL reflection *11.1*

"This is why play feels so good. Discovering and using the essence of any part of ourselves is the most euphoric experience of all. It opens the blocked passages and establishes new routes. Any approach to language and thought that eliminates dramatic play, and its underlying themes of friendship and safety lost and found, ignores the greatest incentive to the creative process."

Vivian Gussin Paley (1990, p. 6), an early childhood educator, transcribes and interprets children's discourse in her classrooms and in their stories, play, friendships, and thinking.

Children with limited play skills need opportunities to develop more mature play in supportive and accepting contexts with children whose play is slightly more advanced than theirs. The play scale in Figure 11.11 can suggest intervention contexts and materials that are slightly above a child's current level of functioning for stretching the child's ZPD.

figure *11.11*

Observation Tool for Assessing Symbolic Play

Stage (approx. age)	Thematic Content, Decontextualization, and Organization	Self/Other Relations	Language	
			Function	Forms and Meanings
Westby's Stage I (17–19 months)	☐ Demonstrates tool use (e.g., pulling on yarn or using stick to retrieve toy) ☐ Uses lifelike props for pretending to participate in familiar, everyday activities (e.g., sleeping, eating, reading books)—in short, isolated schemas ☐ Begins to use one object to represent another	☐ Acts are based on self as agent (called *autosymbolic play*) (e.g., pretends to drink from cup or comb own hair) ☐ Noninteractive parallel play	☐ Directing ☐ Requesting ☐ Commanding ☐ Interacting ☐ Self-maintaining ☐ Protesting ☐ Protecting self-interests ☐ Commenting ☐ Labeling object or action ☐ Indicating personal feeling	☐ True verbal communication begins (example semantic categories and words): ☐ Recurrence (*more*) ☐ Existence (*there*) ☐ Nonexistence (*all gone*) ☐ Rejection (*no*) ☐ Denial (*no*) ☐ Agent (*Daddy*) ☐ Object/entity (*book*) ☐ Action or state (*going; is*) ☐ Location (*outside*) ☐ Attribute (*hot*) ☐ Possession (*mine*)
Westby's Stage II (19–21 months)	☐ Combines two actions in pretending but still in single schema (e.g., rocking baby doll and placing in bed; getting pretend food out of bowl and feeding it to bear with spoon; turning wheel and pushing buttons on pretend steering toy)	☐ Begins to act on another (e.g., doll, stuffed toy) ☐ May perform same play act with multiple recipients (e.g., gives sip of "tea" to mother, sister, and bear)	☐ Talks about things not immediately present (e.g., "Daddy bye-bye.")	☐ Begins to combine words into two-word utterances (example semantic–grammatic forms and words): ☐ Agent + action (*me go*) ☐ Action + object (*kiss baby*) ☐ Agent + object (*Mommy baby*) ☐ Attribute + entity (*big book*) ☐ Dative + object (*me book*)

Westby's Stage				

Westby's Stage III (2 years)	❑ Elaborates schemas by adding details and associated items (e.g., creating building for truck to knock over, putting plastic food on tray and placing it in play oven; putting doll in highchair before feeding)	❑ Simple social play (takes turns with another)
		❑ Shows awareness of performing action for benefit of another (e.g., cooking breakfast for doll; getting pillow for stuffed toy to sleep on)
			❑ Gives accounts of actions while performing them (e.g., "Me washing baby," "Me cooking")	❑ Uses phrases and short sentences
				❑ Morphological markers emerge:
				  ❑ Progressive -ing
				  ❑ Plurals
				  ❑ Possessives

Westby's Stage IV (2½ years)	❑ Includes thematic content that is less familiar but memorable as particularly pleasurable or scary (e.g., trip to emergency room, airplane ride, fighting monsters)		❑ Seeks information from another who is involved in the play (e.g., "What baby doing? Where kitty sleeping?")	❑ Asks and responds appropriately to some wh- questions in context:
				  ❑ What
				  ❑ Whose
				  ❑ Where
				  ❑ What . . . do
				❑ Asks why questions and responds appropriately in well-known routines; but at other times, asks inappropriate why questions, may fail to attend to answer, and may fail to respond when asked "Why?" by others

Westby's Stage V (3 years)	❑ Reenacts experienced events but with modified outcomes
	❑ Schemas show emerging sense of sequence, with "what next?" unplanned quality (e.g., doctor checks patient, calls ambulance, takes patient to hospital)
		❑ Cooperative social pretend play
		❑ Talks to another about third participant in play (e.g., "Is you baby sick?")
			❑ Uses language to create scenes and for:
			  ❑ Reporting
			  ❑ Predicting
			  ❑ Narrating or storytelling
				❑ Uses past tense (e.g., "I ate the cake; I pushed the truck")
				❑ Uses future aspect forms to express planning (e.g., "I'm gonna wash dishes")

(continued)

figure **11.11**

Continued

Stage (approx. age)	Thematic Content, Decontextualization, and Organization	Self/Other Relations	Language	
			Function	**Forms and Meanings**

Westby's Stage VI (3 to 3½ years)	❑ Reenacts observed events and scripts from movies or TV shows (e.g., superheroes, police, firefighters)
	❑ Uses replica toys (e.g., toy barn, doll house, garage, airport) or objects symbolically (e.g., chair as car; stick as gun)
	❑ Arranges blocks to form boundaries (e.g., fences or walls of houses)
		❑ Uses strategies to recruit others into play
		❑ Uses doll, puppet, or action figure as participant in play
		❑ Talks for doll and then takes reciprocal role as parent or other character to interact with doll
			❑ Projects desires, thoughts, and feelings to characters
			❑ Uses indirect requests (e.g., "Mommy lets me have cookies for breakfast.")
				❑ Uses vocabulary to describe objects' perceptual attributes (not always accurately):
				  ❑ Shapes
				  ❑ Sizes
				  ❑ Colors
				  ❑ Textures
				  ❑ Spatial relations
				❑ Uses metalinguistic and metacognitive language (e.g., "He said; I know")

Westby's Stage VII (3½ to 4 years)	❑ Plans schemas and invents scripts, arranges scenes (e.g., three-dimensional structures with blocks to provide setting for play) ❑ Hypothesizes (e.g., What would happen if . . .)	❑ Child or doll may play multiple roles in story (e.g., mother and wife; fireman, father, and husband)	❑ Uses language to invent props, set scenes, and create stories with plots	❑ Uses modals (*can, may, might, will, would, could*) ❑ Responds appropriately to *how* and *why* questions that require reasoning
Westby's Stage VIII (5 years)	❑ Plans highly complex events that add imaginative novel components to known experiences and schemas (e.g., traveling to distant planet, eating strange food, encountering aliens)	❑ Works with peers to coordinate complex scripts and integrate schemas	❑ Uses language totally to set scene, actions, and roles in dramatic play	❑ Uses relational terms (e.g., *then, when, first, next, last, while, before, after*)

Source: Based on Howes, 1985; McCune-Nicholich, 1981; Westby, 1988.

Preschool and kindergarten settings provide rich opportunities for children to develop their play, thinking, emotional skills, social skills, and language and literacy skills in an integrated, peer-supported environment. Paley's (1990) account of Jason's development through play and dramatic story telling continues in Case Example 11.3.

Teachers play important roles too, helping children socialize in group participation activities while encouraging their creativity and ability to put ideas into words; doing so develops concepts and language in tandem. Teachers and SLPs who fantasize with children in play can set up facilitative contexts for helping children elaborate play scenarios and related language.

Girolametto and Weitzman (2007) described professional development activities for helping early childhood educators and preschool teachers promote peer interactions in play. They drew on materials developed by the Hanen Centre, such as the Preschool Language and Literacy Calendar (which may be retrieved from www.hanen.org). These materials outline indirect suggestions teachers might use for inviting children to interact together in play, including to assign a role, use toys and proximity, select cooperative play activities, pair children strategically, and use snacktime. Teachers also can scaffold children to direct conversations to other children in play, including to provide a model of what to say, interpret one child's meaning to another by recasting it, give a suggestion, refer to a peer for help,

---

CASE example *11.3*

Jason: Part 2

As the schoolyear progressed, Jason began to expand his play and social communication options with his helicopter in the doll corner, eventually leaving his familiar script to participate in stories generated by others. He first adapted his helicopter script to other children's play and then was able to play without it. The transition began when Simon's pretend squirrel hole caved in.

In the following excerpt, Paley transcribed the children's discourse and described her reaction to it:

"This hole is caving in," Simon calls out.

"I'll call the police," Jason responds, to Simon's surprise.

"Helicopter police?"

Jason pretends to dial. "Helicopter police, helicopter police, answer the phone six, seven, eight."

"Tell them I'm caving in."

"He's caving in."

"Never mind. I dug myself out. Oh oh oh this hole is caving in again! Oh oh oh help!"

"Helicopter police, helicopter police, answer the phone. He's caving in." Jason dials rapidly.

"Never mind. I dug myself out."

I want to cheer and shout [Paley writes], "You've got it! You've really got it!" The helicopter has heard a cry of distress and called for help. No matter how deep the hole or high the wall, the voices of other children will penetrate. The children's manipulation of one another's play provokes a genuine self-awareness that the adult cannot emulate. Now that Jason is on his way, there is so much to learn. (pp. 128–129)

Later, Jason was flying his helicopter when Paley recorded the following discourse exchange:

"Meow meow," Samantha licks her paws. "Meow meow I'm a kitty now meow meow."

"It's a kitty airport," Jason says eagerly. "Yeah, a kitty airport. For kitties. Samantha, where's kitty?"

Samantha is momentarily puzzled. This is a new Jason; she is not entirely sure how to react. Then she trusts her instincts. "Meow meow, here's your kitty." (p. 129)

Paley reported that several turns later, "Jason bends down to whisper, 'Okay, the lady isn't going to lock you out. If you get out, I'll put you back in. Here kitty meow meow'" (pp. 129–130).

comment on similarities, and praise peer interaction. Girolametto and Weitzman provided evidence that teachers who received training learned to use the naturalistic environment and verbal support strategies to facilitate peer interactions. Measurable outcomes were found for typically developing children (the only children who had been studied at that point) in their ability to extend interactions beyond two conversational turns.

Children differ widely in their ability and interest in play. Children with autism spectrum disorders (ASD) and pragmatic language impairment demonstrate difficulty with symbolic play that is symptomatic of their difficulty in imagining and relating (Frith, 1989). The Floortime approach (also called DIR; Greenspan & Wieder, 2005) is designed to help parents relate to their children in play, especially when one member of the parent–child pair does not play easily. Floortime is part of a comprehensive approach that Greenspan and Wieder developed to help parents relate to their hard-to-reach children. As described previously, the DIR approach stands for its three primary components—developmental, individual difference, and relationship based. Parents take time each day to literally join their child on the floor, so they can play with him or her at a developmentally appropriate level while attempting to stretch that level. Videos and books are available to help parents learn to use interactions in play to promote shared attention and regulation, engagement and relating, purposeful emotional interaction, social problem solving, creation of ideas, and connecting ideas and thinking logically.

Language for Social Interaction

Assessing Assertive and Responsive Communication Acts

Play and social interaction are not identical, but they are closely intertwined. Assessment of children's language in conversation and play includes analysis of their ability to use both assertive communication acts (in which children initiate the interaction by making a statement or comment or asking a question) and responsive acts (in which children's communication is contingent on the acts of others). Competence with both assertive and responsive acts is important for children to be perceived as capable and desirable conversational partners across contexts and age groups.

Recognizing the close ties between communicative competence and social skills, Brinton and Fujiki (1989) suggested that assessment for children with language disorders should focus on the discourse level as well as the sentence level. These researchers recommended a series of questions for guiding informal assessment in this area: Does the child initiate topics or mostly respond to questions asked by the conversational partner? Does the child stay on topic or make frequent switches without preparing the listener? Does the child have presupposition skills to judge how much information the listener needs? Does the child have strategies to repair communication when it breaks down?

Communication acts profiling (*CAP;* Fey, 1986) can serve as a helpful tool for addressing these questions. CAP involves gathering a communication sample, coding it for the child's communication acts, and relating the findings to a matrix of profiles based on relative proportions of assertive and responsive acts. Figure 11.12 shows the codes for the communication acts a child makes relative to the acts made by an adult or child communication partner. Although individual differences are expected, a balance of assertive and responsive acts is desirable.

No firm rules are prescribed for judging how much of a discrepancy represents an imbalance of assertive and responsive acts. Decisions are based on a pattern of interaction across contexts, rather than data gathered in a single communication sample. Individual samples can be influenced significantly by interaction choices of adult partners or peers. In

figure *11.12*

Observation Tool for Tallying Assertive and Responsive Communicative Acts in a Conversation Sample

Assertive Acts	Speaker 1	Speaker 2	Responsive Acts	Speaker 1	Speaker 2
RQIN–Request information			RSIN–Response to RQIN		
RQAC–Request action			RSAC–Response to RQAC		
RQCL–Request clarification			RSCL–Response to RQCL		
RQAT–Request attention			RSAT–Response to RQAT		
ASCO–Assertive comment			RSAS–Response to ASST or ASCO		
ASST–Assertive statement					
ASDA–Assertive disagreement			RSPF–Response to PERF		
PERF–Performative					
Total			**Total**		
Discourse Codes			IMIT–Imitate		
IT–Initiate topic			**Total**		
MT–Maintain topic					
ET–Extend topic					
ETT–Extend topic tangential					
Total					

Assertive Acts

RQIN: Question (including tags) used to solicit new information from partner

RQAC: Utterance that solicits performance of action by partner

RQCL: Question that seeks clarification of a prior utterance

RQAT: Utterance that seeks attention or acknowledgment from partner but adds no new information

ASCO: Description of observable objects or events

ASST: Report of nonobservable mental states, opinions, rules, explanations, etc.

ASDA: Comment or statement that denies or objects to prior assertion

PERF: Claim, joke, tease, warning, *please, thank you,* etc. that is accomplished just by being uttered

Responsive Acts

RSIN: Attempt to provide new information requested by partner

RSAC: Verbal accompaniment to action requested by partner

RSCL: Attempt to clarify prior utterance following request by partner

RSAT: Response to request for attention that signals partner may continue

RSAS: Simple acknowledgment of prior partner utterance that adds no new information

RSPF: Response to a performative, such as saying *You're welcome,* after *Thank you*

Discourse Codes

IT: Introduces new information not related to prior utterance

MT: Relates to prior utterance but fulfills speaker obligation without adding any unsolicited information

ET: Relates to prior utterance and adds new semantic details or shades appropriately to related topic

ETT: Relates tangentially to some aspect of prior utterance but does not extend topic in adequate manner

Source: Based on Fey, 1986.

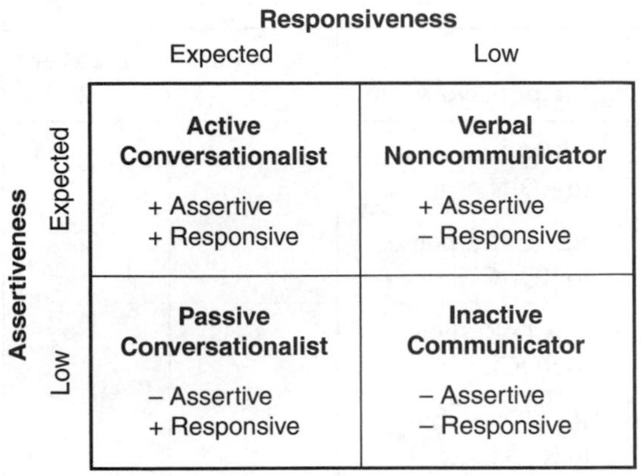

Responsiveness

	Expected	Low
Expected	**Active Conversationalist** + Assertive + Responsive	**Verbal Noncommunicator** + Assertive − Responsive
Low	**Passive Conversationalist** − Assertive + Responsive	**Inactive Communicator** − Assertive − Responsive

Assertiveness (vertical axis label, Expected / Low)

figure 11.13

Patterns of Assertiveness and Responsiveness for Fey's Communication Acts Profile of a Child's Discourse Interaction Style

Source: Adapted from Fey, 1986.

judging proportionality, therefore, clinicians must consider whether the sample context offered ample opportunity for both type of acts. Figure 11.13 illustrates the four quadrants that are predicted when different communication acts profiles are observed.

Any of the approaches appropriate for addressing language content and form also could be used to scaffold children's communication acts and social interaction skills. Options discussed previously include enhanced milieu teaching (Hancock & Kaiser, 2006), focused stimulation (Ellis Weismer & Robertson, 2006; Leonard, 1981), and conversational recast intervention (Camarata & Nelson, 2006).

One problem with using an analysis framework for pragmatic social skills that codes verbal communication acts exclusively is that it gives inadequate attention to nonverbal signals of communicative intent. Such systems also may not indicate clearly whether the particular act was appropriate for the context. Adaptations can be made in CAP coding to address these concerns (e.g., by coding for nonverbal turn taking or indicating the absence of an obligatory response, such as by coding RSIN−, or "response to request for information-missing;" see Figure 11.12). Another problem may be the misinterpretation of culturally determined socialization for interacting with adults, such as how much value is placed on children's talking or asking questions within a particular culture (e.g., Crago, 1990; Heath, 1983).

Hyter (2007a) suggested a framework for adapting observational tools for children with diverse experiences. She described a set of tools that are currently under development for assessing social engagement and social cognition among children who are being socialized for school in diverse ways, including a social engagement scale, communication functions checklist, and narrative assessment tool. The tool also includes an elicitation task for assessing social–cognitive skills to conceive another person's perspectives and a parent report form.

Olswang, Coggins, and Svensson (2007) described a procedure for assessing children's social interaction behaviors in classroom contexts during ongoing interactions. They developed a *social communication coding system* (*SCCS*) to capture evidence of problematic verbal and nonverbal social behaviors as well as prosocial ones, including categories labeled *hostile/coercive, prosocial/engaged, assertive, passive/disengaged, adult seeking,* and *irrelevant.*

Intervention starts with assessment to identify components that might be missing or underdeveloped. It also involves attempts to understand underlying factors that may be contributing to the problem. Framing this approach with the four questions of context-based assessment and intervention used across this book, Girolametto and Weitzman (2007) addressed the question about demands of the context by summarizing the demands of engaging in healthy peer relationships. They identified six abilities that are necessary for successful peer interaction in young children: (1) joint attention, making it possible to establish a shared mental focus with peers; (2) emotional regulation, allowing children to control negative feelings; (3) inhibitory control, making it possible to manage impulses, such as to grab toys from others; (4) imitation, allowing children to copy the play behavior of peers; (5) causal understanding of antecedent–consequent events, allowing children to weave narrative elements into their play; and (6) adequate language development, allowing children to comprehend others' ideas and intentions and to communicate their own.

Targeting a Range and Balance of Assertive and Responsive Communication Acts

Goal 11.6. The child will achieve an appropriate balance of assertive and responsive communication acts in supportive conversational contexts. Goals for improving balance between assertive and responsive communication acts are based on several forms of baseline evidence that contribute to identification of a particular child's profile.

Goals for ***active conversationalists*** (who already show an appropriate balance of assertive and responsive acts) are to produce new content–form interactions for achieving available conversational acts and new forms to fill alternative communication acts. Goals for ***passive conversationalists*** are to use available assertive conversational acts more frequently, to use available forms to produce a greater variety of assertive conversational acts, and to add new linguistic forms for performing available assertive acts. Intervention goals for ***inactive communicators*** are to increase the frequency of positive social bids (verbal and nonverbal) in a variety of social contexts and then to begin to target the same goals as for passive communicators. Intervention goals for ***verbal noncommunicators*** are to increase the frequency of responses related to assertive acts of communication partners and to produce sequenced utterances that are topically related to one another.

Intervention for social interaction difficulty involves attention to language development but also must take into consideration other aspects of the child's diagnostic condition, familial and cultural factors, and influences on the child's social–emotional development. An interdisciplinary approach is appropriate, especially when children exhibit marked difficulties of social cognition and social interaction with peers or seem excessively angry and unable to control their emotional responses to frustration.

Typically developing peers can be involved in intervention to improve the social and communicative interactions of children with social communication problems who have autism or other developmental disabilities. For example, Goldstein, Schneider, and Thiemann (2007) mediated more able peers to implement a variety of techniques to scaffold higher-level social skills by less able peers, including facilitative initiation and responsive interaction strategies, sociodramatic scripts, and written text and graphic cueing, such as in social stories. In addition to peer mediation, approaches for teaching social skills can involve teacher or clinician mediation and environmental arrangement. Timler, Vogler-Elias, and McGill (2007) recommended collaborative planning to help children transfer newly developed language and social interaction skills from clinician-mediated sessions to more naturalistic free play in preschool classrooms.

SUMMARY

Dramatic play and language are elaborated in tandem as children move through the preschool years as they progress from mostly functional play to symbolic play to dramatic play. Play and language can be assessed together, with implications for guiding intervention.

Assessing communication within social interaction contexts can also document the balance between the child's assertive and responsive communication acts, as a part of communication acts profiling (CAP). Four patterns were described, including the desired pattern of active conversationalist, as well as problematic patterns of passive conversationalist, verbal noncommunicators, and inactive communicator. Intervention plans for emphasizing content, form, and use vary depending on the nature of a child's communication profile.

Emergent and Early Literacy

The term *emergent literacy* refers to "children's developing knowledge about print and sound in the years prior to receiving formal reading and writing instruction" (Justice, Skibbe, & Ezell, 2006, p. 390). Emergent literacy development is deeply intertwined with other areas of language and communication development but should receive direct attention early in the intervention process (see Chapter 9).

Components of Emergent Literacy

Figure 11.14 summarizes key components of emergent literacy to provide an observation tool for guiding preventive interventions with infants and toddlers and assessment and intervention activities with preschool-age children. As noted previously, cultural differences in storytelling and play influence how children are socialized for formal literacy experiences in school. Commonalities across cultures and socioeconomic groups can be highlighted as well (Mandler, Scribner, Cole, & DeForest, 1980). In a review of studies of home literacy, van Kleeck (1990) indicated studies "have found literacy artifacts and print-related events to be pervasive in all kinds of homes in literate societies" (p. 27). However, print-related events in low-income families may occur more through activities of daily living, such as making lists and completing forms, rather than through storybooks.

Many aspects of early spoken language experiences (not just shared book reading) can provide a background for learning to read and write. Not all children have parents who can read and write or do so frequently. Conflicting results have been found in research on the role of shared book reading with preschoolers in predicting later language and literacy development (Johnston, 2007b; see Personal Reflection 11.2). When Scarborough and Dobrich (1994) reviewed 30 years of research on the effects of shared book reading on later development, they identified 31 evidence-based articles, with results showing only weak correlations. The strongest associations showed parental book reading to account for at most 6 percent to 8 percent of the variance and even less when SES was factored into the analysis.

PERSONAL reflection *11.2*

"Mothers who are nonreaders could help their children build scrapbook records of family adventures and then use them to tell and retell personal narratives. Likewise, mothers from cultures that do not expect young children to read may have a rich heritage of religious and/or historical tales that would invite retelling, anticipation, and constructive inference. Our challenge as interventionists is to determine whether book reading is good advice for particular families, given cultural and personal preferences, and to be creative in finding alternative paths to learning when books aren't available or valued."

Judith R. Johnston (2007b, p. 6), a speech–language pathologist and language scientist, provides commentary on best practices for children with language disorders.

Cultural–Linguistic Diversity in Literacy Practices

Hammer, Miccio, and Wagstaff (2003) compared reading outcomes for families who had emigrated from Puerto Rico and spoke both Spanish and English. Based on a questionnaire about family literacy practices, families were differentiated based on whether they used English at home or spoke only Spanish prior to their children entering Head Start. Families

figure *11.14*

Observation Tool for Emergent Literacy

Components of Emergent Literacy	Observational Evidence (example, date observed)

The child demonstrates knowledge about:
 	
❑ Books:
  ❑ Held in certain way and read from front to back
  ❑ Describe events outside of real time
  ❑ Represent fictional world
  ❑ Chosen for repeated reading by adult
  ❑ Used for pretend reading by child
❑ Pictures and printed words in books:
  ❑ Are for pointing and naming
  ❑ Represent other things
  ❑ Can represent events even though they are static	

The child demonstrates metalinguistic awareness about:
 	
❑ Environmental symbols (e.g., golden arches, stop signs)
❑ Print representing words (e.g., *What does this say?*)
  ❑ Scribbling as means for creating print messages
  ❑ Dictating stories for adult to write down and reread
❑ Alphabetic letters:
  ❑ Some letter names (especially in their names)
  ❑ Some sounds that letters make	

The child demonstrates narrative knowledge about:
 	
❑ Components of story grammar episodes:
  ❑ Main characters
  ❑ Feelings (emotional states of main characters)
  ❑ Setting (time and place of story action)
  ❑ Complicating action (problem facing main characters)
  ❑ Dialogue (reported speech of story characters)
  ❑ Coda (ending resolving action of story)
❑ Cohesive devices for connecting parts of discourse:
  ❑ Additive (using and comprehending conjunctions, such as *and*, that link clauses through addition)
  ❑ Temporal (using and comprehending conjunctions, such as *then*, *next*, that link clauses temporally)
  ❑ Causal (using and comprehending conjunctions, such as *because*, *so*, that relate clauses causally)	

Source: Based on Justice et al., 2006; McGee & Richgels, 1990; McGregor, 2000; Snow & Ninio, 1986; Strickland & Morrow, 1989; van Kleeck, 1990.

that used more English were more likely to report reading to their children and teaching them preliteracy skills, such as knowing the alphabet and counting. Just doing more of these things, however, did not lead to different results on the Test of Early Reading Ability (TERA; Reid, Hresko, & Hammill, 1989). The TERA tests knowledge of the alphabet and print conventions, as well as ability to attribute meaning to printed symbols. It was discouraging to find that both groups of children fell increasingly behind the norms of the TERA across the preschool years.

Roberts, Jurgens, and Burchinal (2005) measured early literacy and language development between the ages of 2 and 5 for 72 African American children from infancy. They gathered data using a combination of formal tests (i.e., Peabody Picture Vocabulary Test-Revised, Dunn & Dunn, 1981; Clinical Evaluation of Language Fundamentals–Preschool, Wiig, Secord, & Semel, 1992; and Test of Early Reading Ability (TERA; Reid, Hresko, & Hammill, 1989), maternal reports of book reading frequency, and direct evidence from videotaped mother–child shared book reading experiences. Annual test results revealed strong within-family consistency across the three-year period in the frequency with which mothers (or other caretakers) read to preschoolers and made child-sensitive comments about texts. Frequency of book reading, however, was not predictive of language or literacy test scores. With the exception of moderate correlations between receptive vocabulary and book strategies/sensitivity, none of the maternal book reading variables (frequency, book strategies, or sensitivity) predicted later language or literacy outcome measures.

Other researchers (van Kleeck, Gillam, Hamilton, & McGrath, 1997) focused on the quality (rather than frequency) of parent–child book-sharing interactions. The researchers videotaped 35 mothers and fathers in their homes reading books with their preschool-age children. The results showed gains correlated significantly with parental input (frequency of comments about the story) but not syntactic development, nonverbal IQ, or preliteracy abilities. Measures included the TERA but also the Preschool Language Assessment Instrument (PLAI; Blank, Rose, & Berlin, 1978), which was used to measure decontextualized categorical descriptions, connections, and inferences.

To what should these conflicting outcomes be attributed? Johnston (2007b) observed that family literacy practices involve more complex variables than the frequency of shared book reading and even the frequency of commenting within those experiences. For example, mothers in the two groups of families described by Hammer and colleagues (2003) reported engaging in similarly infrequent (less than once per month) adult literacy activities (e.g., reading a book or magazine or writing a letter) and having fewer than 10 books in the home. Johnston pointed to research with families who had emigrated from China or Southeast Asia that also showed the practice of reading books to children to be rare but without negative effects on learning to read (e.g., Johnston & Wong, 2002).

A more important and universal practice may be the telling of stories and other optional talk (Hart & Risley, 1995, 1999). Cultures vary in their expectations for children to play more active roles in telling stories to appreciative adults in the family or church community or more passive roles as listeners (e.g., Heath, 1983). Culturally diverse environments can contribute to the development of connected discourse abilities (especially narration), providing a foundation for literate language development in school. Wells (1986) found storytelling within the homes of socioeconomically diverse families in Bristol, England, to be the best predictor (compared to other emergent literacy experiences, including drawing and interaction with books) of later literacy success in school.

The goals in this section on emergent literacy are based on the two components that constitute a simple model of reading and writing—phonological skills and word-level knowledge that contribute to reading decoding and spelling, and more comprehensive nonphonological aspects of literacy awareness, including sentence- and discourse-level skills that contribute to comprehension and formulation.

Phonological Skills and Word-Level Knowledge

Phonemic awareness is required for engaging in essential cognitive operations of phonological processing—speech sound storage, retrieval, and manipulation (Catts & Kamhi, 2005a, 2005b). Evidence of phonemic awareness is observed when children can manipulate individual phonemes, usually in a progression that starts with awareness of initial phonemes in words, followed by awareness of final phonemes, then phoneme blending, and later segmentation of single-syllable words into component phonemes. Early forms of these abilities can be observed among typically developing children in the preschool years, but research suggests that at least some phonemic awareness develops in the process of learning to read and write, rather than preceding it (e.g., Ehri & Wilce, 1986; review by Ukrainetz, 2006b).

Assessing Phonological Awareness and Word Knowledge

Sound and word play at the whole-word level provides an important bridge to helping preschool-age children attend to metalinguistic concepts that are critical for literacy learning, starting with vocabulary development (discussed previously in this chapter). Both formal (e.g., Wagner, Torgesen, & Rashotte, 1999) and informal assessment activities can be used to observe a child's awareness of words and their sound structures. Because the focus in this area during the preschool years should be on prevention as much as intervention, assessment and intervention focused on word form become integrated into activities of dynamic assessment.

At school or home, the preschool-age child can benefit from listening to books with a rhythm and refrain (e.g., *Brown Bear, Brown Bear, What Do You See?* by Bill Martin, Jr.; *Chicka Chicka Boom Boom,* by Martin & Archambault, 1989; and *Goodnight Moon,* by Brown, 1975), and clinicians can observe how quickly they are able to learn those features. Young children also can be engaged in playing with the sounds of words, such as changing the first sounds of their names in a friendly playful manner (e.g., *Jonathon = Bonathon*), tapping out the syllable patterns of words, or generating rhyming words in play or storytelling. Dynamic assessment can also focus on how quickly children learn to associate letters with their names. For example, *Chicka Chicka Boom Boom* is a rhyming book that introduces children to the names of the letters of the alphabet. Knowledge of nursery rhymes in the preschool years is associated with later reading ability (Bryant, MacLean, & Bradley, 1990).

Targeting Phonological and Print Awareness and the Alphabetic Principle

Goal 11.7. The child will demonstrate phonological awareness, print awareness, and knowledge of the alphabetic principle. Broader concepts of phonological awareness develop into concepts of individual phonemes during typical development when children are engaged in emergent literacy activities. Phonemic awareness can be targeted along with speech sound production among preschoolers (e.g., Tyler, Lewis, Haskill, & Tolbert, 2002). Tasks focusing on phoneme identification and letter knowledge can result in gains in speech intelligibility for children with SSD as young as 3 to 4 years of age (Gillon, 2004, 2005).

Although preliterate children are not expected to have mastered phoneme segmentation and manipulation skills, SSD intervention approaches may rely on such knowledge while also fostering their early development (Hesketh, Dima, & Nelson, 2007). Hesketh et al. assigned 42 children with SSD (ages 4 years, 2 months to 4 years, 6 months) randomly to receive either an intervention program that emphasized phonemic awareness or a comparison treatment program that provided language stimulation without the phonemic awareness component. Children were assessed on four measures of phonemic awareness before and after treatment—alliteration awareness, phoneme isolation, word segmentation, and phoneme addition/deletion. Results showed that preschool-age children could develop phonemic awareness with explicit instruction, particularly for isolating word-initial phonemes, and more children in the phonemic awareness group improved on the phonemic awareness measures than in the general language stimulation group. However, Hesketh et al. also found that only those children who were older and more cognitively able showed improvement for the two most advanced phonemic awareness tasks (segmentation and addition/deletion).

Bergen and Mauer (2000) studied the relationship of low and high phonological abilities with play. Although children with low and high ability showed similar levels of overall play, those with higher phonological awareness abilities demonstrated more literacy-related play, including looking at a book, talking about each page, asking for help writing and reading their names, as well as "putting 'letters' in the 'mailbox,' calling out numbers on the toy cash register, counting marbles, matching numbers, proclaiming 'I got my name on here'" (pp. 56–57). Based on their research, Bergen and Mauer recommended that children still lacking phonological awareness capability in kindergarten should receive more teacher encouragement of pretend narratives, rhyming, and other language play. They also should receive "more time blocks for elaborated and literacy-related pretend play; and more teacher interaction in scaffolding literacy discussions" (p. 61).

Given that phonemic levels of phonological awareness are not expected to be developed fully by typically developing children until they reach school age, intervention activities for promoting phonemic awareness in the preschool years should be viewed as prevention more than intervention. Letters can be associated with speech sounds in therapy materials, and print can be associated with the words and phrases children are generating in the context of other activities. A comprehensive preschool language intervention program should make use of active interdisciplinary collaboration, with SLPs consulting with early childhood teachers to implement combined instruction and intervention representing characteristics of high-quality instruction (Justice et al., 2008; reviewed in Chapter 10).

Literate Language Comprehension and Formulation

Some children lack foundation skills for comprehending and producing language at sentence and discourse levels within activities that require the integration of social–cognition with other high-level cognitive–linguistic abilities. Social–dramatic play offers opportunities to integrate knowledge and skills across language, literacy, and social systems.

Assessing Emergent Literacy in Sentence-/Discourse-Level Contexts

Addressing the question of how children's profiles can change over time relative to increasing demands of literacy learning contexts, Scarborough and Dobrich (1990) followed four children with early language delay (ELD) and compared them to a control group of 12 children with typical development. The researchers measured children's language abilities at several points from age 2.5 to 5 years and their verbal and reading skills at the end of second grade. The language-delayed children, who initially showed severe and broad impairments in syntactic, phonological, and lexical production, progressed to the point that their deficits were milder and more selective. Most of the children exhibited normal or nearly normal speech and language proficiency by age 5 when they entered school.

At follow-up testing three years later, however, three of the four children demonstrated severe reading disability (Scarborough & Dobrich, 1990). The implication is that it is important to provide effective intervention early but also to monitor children's progress as they move through transition points and face more complex language demands of schooling. Interventions should directly address integration of abilities across language levels, modalities, and contexts and monitor change over time.

Targeting Integration of Language Skills in Play, Storytelling, and Early Literacy

Goal 11.8. The child will demonstrate the ability to construct narratives for storytelling and in dramatic play and will retell stories that have been read aloud. The interventions described previously in this chapter for developing narrative skills are also appropriate for encouraging integration of spoken and written language in the preschool years. Examples are the preschool journaling approach and Paley's (1990) story-dictating and play-acting approach.

Fein, Ardila-Rey, and Groth (2000) used an experimental design to compare approaches targeting narrative processes in two classrooms. One, characterized as the *author's chair* (*AC*) classroom, used an approach similar to preschool journaling, in which the child dictated a story to the teacher, who then read it to the group, after which children discussed it with the author. The other classroom used a *shared enactment* (*SE*) approach similar to Paley's (1990), in which stories were read and then socially recreated. Fein et al. described these "mediated interactions in a collaborative social setting":

> During SE sessions, the children gathered along two sides of a large space used for circle time and the teacher sat among them. The empty space before them became the stage. The teacher summoned the author to her side and read the story out loud to the group. The teacher then asked the author what characters were needed for the enactment. The author identified the characters (often with the eager help of other children) and chose a peer to portray each one. When the actors had assembled, the teacher read the story slowly as a narrator would, stopping to allow for action and omitting dialogues so that the actors could improvise. The players dramatized the story, following the lead of the author who acted as director. At the completion of the enactment and the applause, another story was selected for dramatization. (p. 31)

Fein and colleagues observed that "regardless of format, the children were riveted by the words of their peers when the stories were read aloud" (p. 33). In both classrooms, the peer audience comprehended and appreciated the stories, even though they might have seemed incomplete to an adult. Differences also appeared between the two classrooms as the schoolyear continued. Children in the AC classroom started to incorporate their stories into books, whereas those in the SE classroom focused more on the story itself and the integration of character with action. One approach was not necessarily better than the other, but they influenced different types of development, suggesting value for both.

Another integrative intervention approach targeting preschool language and literacy development is shared storybook reading. Kaderavek and Justice (2002) described shared storybook reading as an intervention context consistent with social interactionist perspectives at both theoretical and practical levels, because it places book sharing in a social context. This technique involves repeated readings of favored books in one-on-one interactions. As the child develops familiarity with the language and story of a book, the adult partner gradually transfers some of the book "reading" responsibilities to the child. When the child is able to produce longer portions of the text and participate more actively, it is appropriate to infer that his or her language comprehension and vocabulary are growing as well as language production. Retelling evidence should be analyzed to determine if the child is learning to construct a landscape of consciousness and develop a theory of mind as well.

Many aspects of early language and emergent literacy intervention at the preschool level address goals of prevention. Early intervention also aims to help children and families develop language and communication skills to support a happy, healthy early childhood, filled with positive interactions with siblings and peers as well as with parents and other adults.

SUMMARY

Preschool-age children continue to progress in their development of emergent literacy abilities that begin even earlier. Emergent literacy includes the development of knowledge about print and speech sounds before formal literacy instruction begins. Clinicians need to be aware of cultural–linguistic differences in home literacy practices and encourage oral storytelling whether or not parents are comfortable reading books with their young children.

The promotion of early literacy development can be viewed as a form of secondary prevention for children with disorders of spoken language in their preschool years. Interactions with stories and books can help all children develop language comprehension skills that are essential for learning to read. Sound-/word-level skills, including phonemic awareness, can be targeted in integrated tasks, aimed also at helping children learn the alphabetic principle (i.e., that speech sounds and letters go together) during speech–language intervention activities. This is consistent with research evidence that shows that learning to read can enhance phonemic awareness as well as vice versa.

CHAPTER SUMMARY

This chapter has described informal assessment practices and intervention approaches for addressing four goal areas—sounds, words, and vocabulary concepts; early sentence and discourse development; social interaction and play; and emerging literacy. Effective intervention is contextualized but based on explicit goals that target specific language content, form, and use. Techniques include focused stimulation and scaffolding recasts by clinicians and by parents and peers.

Intervention approaches vary in the degree to which they are child centered or adult directed. The four questions of context-based assessment and intervention can be used to keep intervention relevant to the natural and meaningful events of children's and families' lives. For some children (e.g., those with cognitive–communicative impairments), some goal areas (e.g., syntax), and some content (e.g., vocabulary and phonemic awareness), more direct elicitation techniques may be appropriate to provide evidence of a child's expressive and receptive language abilities. Social–dramatic play and shared book and storytelling experiences offer natural contexts for language and literacy development that can support the development of integrated abilities in culturally and linguistically sensitive ways.

EXERCISES *and* STUDY QUESTIONS

1. List four goal areas that might be particularly difficult for children with language impairments to achieve in their preschool years.

2. Name and describe three approaches for targeting morphosyntactic difficulty.

3. When children have symptoms of speech sound disorder along with morphosyntactic difficulty, what area should be targeted first? What does the research evidence suggest about the need to target phonology and morphosyntax explicitly and separately?

4. Describe a comprehensive program for targeting emergent literacy in the preschool years.

CHAPTER twelve

School-Age Policies and Practices

After studying this chapter, you should be able to do the following:

1. Discuss service delivery under IDEA '04 for school-age students.

2. Outline a comprehensive diagnostic evaluation protocol for school-age students.

3. Apply the four questions of curriculum-based language assessment and intervention (CBLAI).

Although developmental changes are not as well defined in the age range from 5 to 21 as they are from birth to age 5, steady advances still occur. Developmental charts in the Part III Appendix include signs of growth in cognitive development, receptive language, expressive language, social interaction/play, and literacy for school-age children and adolescents. Major influences on development during this period come from school and peers, as well as home. Chapter 12 provides an overview of evaluation practices for determining eligibility for services, followed by a discussion of curriculum-based language assessment and intervention.

Policies and Practices in the School-Age Years

School-age students with disabilities receive services under IDEA '04, Part B, which must be aligned with the No Child Left Behind Act (NCLB) and may include response to intervention (RTI) activities. This section also outlines procedures for individualized education programs (IEPs) and transitions.

IDEA '04, NCLB, and Response to Intervention Activities

As introduced in Chapter 4, service delivery to school-age students is influenced by two key pieces of legislation—IDEA '04 (Part B), known as the access law, and NCLB, known as the accountability law. IDEA '04 guarantees students with disabilities the right to a free, appropriate public education (FAPE). Under IDEA '04 children may receive early intervening services and, if necessary, special education and related services to enable them to progress in the general education curriculum.

Response to Intervention for Prevention and Identification

Early intervening services are part of **response to intervention** (also called *responsiveness to intervention*) activities, abbreviated RTI (e.g., Graner, Faggella-Luby, & Fritschmann, 2005; Moore-Brown, Montgomery, Bielinski, & Shubin, 2005). The term *response to instruction* also has been recommended to emphasize that RTI programs are part of general education (Griffiths, Parson, Burns, VanDerHeyden, & Tilly, 2007).

RTI programs serve at least two purposes—prevention and identification. According to the National Association of State Directors of Special Education (NASDSE, 2005):

> Response to Intervention (RTI) is the practice of providing high-quality instruction and intervention matched to student need, monitoring progress frequently to make decisions about changes in instruction or goals and applying child response data to important educational decisions. RTI should be applied to decisions in general, remedial and special education, creating a well-integrated system of instruction/intervention guided by child outcome data. (p. 3)

The primary prevention goal of RTI is to help children avoid learning failure. Its success can be measured by whether reductions occur in the number of students who need special education services, especially for learning disability (LD) but also for language impairment (LI) (Ehren & Nelson, 2005). RTI programs also address the goal to identify students who should be referred for comprehensive, individualized evaluation that may find them eligible for special education services as LD and/or LI. In addition, RTI programs provide the opportunity to differentiate students whose cultural–linguistic experiences are mismatched with school expectations but who learn quickly with adequate instruction.

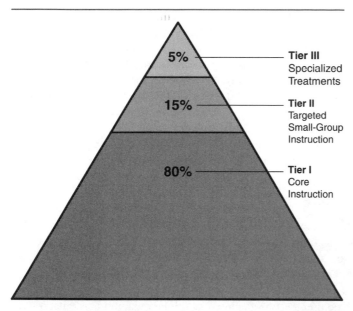

figure *12.1*

Three-Tier Model of School Supports in a Typical Response to Intervention (RTI) Program

This model shows the approximate percentages of the total group of students in a particular grade level who are expected to respond adequately at a particular level. Some of the 5 percent of students in Tier III who continue to show need will be tested and placed in special education with an IEP.

Source: Adapted from Troia, 2005.

RTI programs often assess and target early literacy abilities but may be designed for students at any grade level and any part of the curriculum, including social skills. RTI formats vary, but most involve three tiers of instructional activities (e.g., Griffiths et al., 2007; Troia, 2005). As illustrated in Figure 12.1, Tier I generally constitutes high-quality universal instruction for all students, accompanied by frequent probes of students' progress to measure whether they are responding well or not. Approximately 80 percent of students respond adequately to this first tier of basic instruction. Tier I activities commonly focus on literacy instruction in the early elementary years but can be used at any grade level to address multiple areas of concern. The 20 percent or so of children who show consistent difficulty on Tier I assessments move to Tier II (still general education), where they receive intensified small-group instruction. Another 10 to 15 percent are likely to respond at this level, and the 5 to 10 percent who continue to respond slowly receive more intensive individualized interventions in Tier III. Children are evaluated formally for LD/LI if they continue to exhibit learning or behavioral difficulties after Tier III services.

RTI activities should not be used to delay identification of students with clear signs of disability. A team may decide (or parents may request) to move a child to formal evaluation for special education services before a child moves through all three RTI tiers. IDEA '04 regulations make it clear that screening does not constitute evaluation for eligibility for special education and related services. Students who have difficulty through several tiers in RTI programs cannot be placed directly in special education but need comprehensive multidisciplinary evaluation to determine their eligibility.

Special Education Eligibility Evaluation Procedures

Parent notification and consent are required prior to any assessment that may identify a child as needing (or no longer needing) special education. Parents also "may initiate a request for an initial evaluation to determine if the child is a child with a disability" (34 CFR 300.301[b]) (20 U.S.C. 1414[a][1][B]). An initial evaluation must be completed within 60 days of receiving parental consent for the evaluation.

Regulations specify that a child must *not* be found eligible for special education based on difficulties related to "lack of appropriate instruction in reading, including the five essential components of reading instruction (as defined in section 1208[3] of the ESEA)"—phonemic awareness, phonics, reading fluency, vocabulary, and text comprehension. This is one reason that many Tier I services target the five essential components of reading in the early elementary grades, in which universal instruction is provided by general education teachers, perhaps in consultation with language and literacy specialists.

Assessment must be "provided and administered in the child's native language or other mode of communication and in the form most likely to yield accurate information on what the child knows and can do academically, developmentally, and functionally, unless it is clearly not feasible to do so (34 CFR 300.304[c][1][ii]) (20 U.S.C. 1414[b][3][A][ii]). Reevaluation of the child to determine continued need for special education services "must occur at least once every 3 years, unless the parent and the public agency agree that a reevaluation is unnecessary," and it "may occur not more than once a year, unless the parent and the public agency agree otherwise" (34 CFR 300.303[a]).

IEP Procedures and Content

If formal assessment procedures indicate that a school-age child or adolescent has a disability that qualifies him or her for special education services, the IEP team must proceed in a timely fashion to develop an IEP. Diagnostic and planning decisions are made by an interdisciplinary team, including the child's parents. A mere stapler (for fastening together separate multidisciplinary team member reports) is not an adequate tool of collaborative interdisciplinary planning. Requirements for the interdisciplinary team indicate that it must include a regular education teacher of the child (if the child is or may be participating in the general education environment); a special education teacher or other special education provider of the child; a representative of the public agency; an individual who can interpret the instructional implications of evaluation results (who also may represent one of the other categories); other individuals who have knowledge or special expertise regarding the child, including related services personnel; and, whenever appropriate, the child with a disability.

Changes with IDEA '04 define options for IEP team members to provide input in writing rather than attend the meeting if the parents and agency representatives agree. Flexibility is helpful, but IEP team meetings are more likely to function as problem-solving experiences if team members participate actively (both contributing and listening) to group discussions. The expectation to include the child in an IEP meeting may be appropriate for some younger students, but it is particularly important for adolescents.

A student with a disability *must* be invited to the IEP team meeting if one of the purposes for meeting is to consider postsecondary goals and transition services. Such components must be considered for the IEP that will be in effect when the student turns 16, or younger if appropriate. At least one year before reaching the age of majority under state law, students must be informed of the rights that will transfer to them at that age, although the law provides for situations in which young adults still need guardians. When the student is invited to the IEP meeting, he or she should be adequately prepared for the meeting and included as an active discussant, rather than the object of discussion. Chapter 14 describes planning strategies designed specifically for long-range planning for students with severe disabilities and cognitive–communicative issues that present complex communication needs.

The IEP team must review the student's IEP periodically but at least once per year. The purpose of the annual review is to determine whether goals for the child are being achieved and if the child is progressing in meeting general education curricular standards. If problems are identified, the team must revise the IEP. Under IDEA '04, teams may experiment with a multiyear IEP if members agree that is appropriate and if changes are made at required transition points or if progress is unsatisfactory.

The following requirements support the primary goal of IEPs to help school-age students with disabilities to participate actively in the general education curriculum:

1. A statement of the child's present levels of academic achievement and functional performance
2. A statement of measurable annual goals, including academic and functional goals designed to meet the child's needs that result from his or her disability, to enable the child to be involved in and make progress in the general education curriculum, and to meet each of the child's other educational needs that result from his or her disability
3. A description of benchmarks or short-term objectives for children with disabilities who take alternate assessments aligned to alternate achievement standards
4. A description of how the child's progress toward meeting the annual goals will be measured and a schedule for making periodic reports on the progress he or she is making toward meeting the annual goals (e.g., through quarterly reports, concurrent with the issuance of report cards)
5. A statement of the special education and related services and supplementary aids and services, based on peer-reviewed research to the extent practicable, to be provided to the child or on behalf of the child
6. A statement of any appropriate accommodations necessary to measure the academic achievement and functional performance of the child on state and districtwide assessments, and if the IEP team determines that the child must take an alternate assessment, a statement of why he or she cannot participate in the regular assessment and why the particular alternate assessment selected is appropriate

Under IDEA '04, districtwide testing is viewed as the primary measure of progress. Therefore, only goals (not short-term objectives) are required to appear on a child's formal IEP. That assumes that the formal testing will provide enough information to gauge the student's progress, however, which is not always the case. Clinicians may need more information from assessment probes to guide intervention planning and measure progress. Figure 12.2 provides an example IEP, with goals targeting and tracking progress for written language across multiple language levels (discourse, sentence, and word). The supplementary (optional) assessment plan for this IEP illustration involves gathering and analyzing periodic story-writing probes.

Although not a requirement of IDEA '04, it also is good practice to scaffold students to put IEP goals in their own words on a page of intervention *tool books* to build awareness and ownership. All children (and adults) can have goals, not just those receiving special education services. Tool books (also called *author notebooks* and *speech–language notebooks*) are loose-leaf binders with sections designed to support students' varied intervention activities and to hold such items as practice materials, minilesson handouts, and completed assignments. As students engage in curriculum-based language intervention activities, such as completing a writing assignment, they can be asked to open their tool books and identify which of several IEP language goals they might work on while completing the assignment (e.g., "I will plan before I write, so I can use all the parts of a story," "I will use sentences that combine more than one idea and make sense to others," "I will listen to my friends and make comments that fit the conversation").

Transition planning is required for school-age students under IDEA '04, beginning with the IEP that will be in effect on the child's sixteenth birthday. From that point, measurable postsecondary goals must be related to training, education, employment, and, where appropriate, independent-living skills. *Transition services* are defined as "a coordinated set of activities for a child with a disability" that are designed "to facilitate movement from school to post-school activities." They include services to prepare a student for "independent living, or community participation" (34 CFR §300.43). Transition goals are generated from context-based language assessment and intervention activities that go

figure *12.2*

Illustration of Goals, Objectives, and Reporting Format for an IEP Supplement

Area of Need Written Language   **Person(s) Responsible for Goal** SLP & Teacher

Present Levels of Academic Achievement and Functional Performance

Shaquela's district test scores in the area of written language are in the 5th percentile. She has difficulty at the discourse, sentence, and word levels. At the third-grade level, she should be producing narratives with at least abbreviated episode structure, but her story probe was written as a temporal sequence. The mean length of her sentences (in *T*-units) should be in the range of 5.5 to 9.5 words per *T*-unit (Nelson & Van Meter, 2007), but her MLTU was 4.5 and included 55% simple sentences (25% were simple incorrect; 30% were simple correct). S misspelled almost 30% of her words, while her classmates misspelled an average of 12%, and she lacked rules for common morpheme endings (e.g., she wrote *-t* for *-ed* in 3/3 opportunities).

Goals and Objectives	Evaluation Criteria	Date Met
Goal 1—Discourse level S will include a problem and attempt in her end of grading period probe story to raise it to the level of abbreviated episode.	Story includes: ___ problem ___ attempt ___ implied goal	_____ date
a. S will use a planning template to indicate the problem in stories planned in class. **b.** S will include cause and effect in her story. **c.** S will describe her character's attempt to solve an explicitly stated problem.	___ Included in plan independently. ___ Included in story. ___ Included in story with moderate scaffolding.	_____ date _____ date _____ date
Goal 2—Sentence level S will increase her MLTU to 5.0 or above when writing and will attempt more than 50% complex sentences. SI = simple incorrect SC = simple correct CI = complex incorrect CC = complex correct	___ MLTU in probe ___ % SI ___ % SC ___ % CI ___ % CC	_____ date
a. S will use simple combining strategies to show relationships between sentences in personal minilessons. **b.** S will use subordinating and embedding when scaffolded while drafting.	Number: ___ *and* ___ *but* ___ *or* ___ *so* Number: ___ *when* ___ *because* ___ *who* ___ (other:)	_____ date _____ date
Goal 3—Word level S will demonstrate knowledge of final morphemes by spelling *-ed* and *-ing* accurately in the probe.	85% of opportunities ___ *-ed* ___ *-ing* ___ (other:)	_____ date
a. S will add correctly spelled inflections in personal minilessons. **b.** S will revise to include morphemic spellings while scaffolded in works in progress. **c.** S will include morphemic spellings as she writes.	___ 4/5 words for 3 sessions ___ 8/10 corrected with minimal scaffolding ___ 6/10 opportunities with no scaffolding	_____ date _____ date _____ date

Note: Only measurable annual goals are required to appear in IEPs according to the regulations of IDEA '04; including short-term objectives is optional.

beyond curriculum-based assessment and into assessment of language and communication needs for participating in community-based, employment-based, and independent-living situations.

Service Delivery Options for School-Age Children

Students with either primary or secondary disorders of language and literacy require IEPs with services from interdisciplinary teams that include a general education teacher, special education teacher, and speech–language pathologist (SLP). Students with comorbid sensory or motor disabilities, depending on the nature of their disabilities, require consultation from other specialists, such as educational audiologists, low-vision orientation and mobility specialists, and occupational therapists (OTs). School social workers participate in assessment and intervention for children with environmental risks, autism spectrum disorders, and emotional and behavioral disorders. School psychologists often play roles in formal assessment and in designing, reviewing, and revising educational plans. Other health care providers and paraprofessionals may participate in meeting needs of students who are medically fragile or have other complex needs.

Team members work collaboratively to provide services that are coordinated and interactive—in other words, *interdisciplinary*. In some cases, service delivery plans are thoroughly integrated and *transdisciplinary* role release occurs (see Chapter 4), as when SLPs, reading specialists, and general and special education teachers educate each other to perform aspects of their unique roles. *Multidisciplinary* service delivery also may occur, as when professionals work in isolation of each other. This option carries the risk of providing a mixture of services that make students feel as if they are coming and going from one service or educational activity to the next. This feeling is expressed well by a third-grade student called Barbie in Case Example 12.1. Her comments provide a window into how patchwork scheduling is experienced by students who must move among three different teachers (general education, special education, and SLP), with little coordination among them.

As outlined in Chapter 4, service delivery options vary by setting (e.g., inclass or pull-out) and schedule (e.g., daily, weekly, or other, and for varying lengths of sessions), as well as by people and roles. ***Traditional models*** for students with complex needs include self-contained special education classrooms (full-time, five days per week), resource rooms (part time, most or all days per week), and center-based programs in separate facilities (full time, five days per week, sometimes year round). ***Inclusion models*** (sometimes called ***mainstreaming***) involve providing special education services in general education classroom settings.

A common traditional model for speech–language service delivery by an SLP is pull-out, usually in small groups scheduled for half-hour sessions two days per week. Although this service delivery model is widely used, its choice appears to be based on tradition and convenience more than evidence. Pull-out services predominated when SLPs traveled among several schools and were in a particular building to provide articulation interventions for most students one or two days per week (still all too common in many systems). However, little scientific evidence exists for deciding whether the pull-out model, or any other model of service delivery, is preferable and for which purposes. It is difficult to find any studies that directly compare one model of service delivery to another.

McGinty and Justice (2006) conducted a literature search (based on a PICO question [see Chapter 1]) for the population of children with speech–language impairment, in which they compared pull-out service delivery with classroom-based models of language intervention to evaluate outcomes of improved spoken communication skills. The researchers found a few studies reporting positive language outcomes for classroom-based interventions but

┌───┐

─CASE **example** *12.1*────────────────────────

Barbie Provides Insights into Patchwork Scheduling from a Student's Perspective

This language sample/ethnographic interview was gathered by a graduate clinician. It provides the personal reflections of a third-grade girl with language-learning disability (LLD) and her perception of having a patchwork schedule when she would rather be "a homework person," like the other third-grade students in her "real" classroom.

C = Clinician
B = Barbie

C We just got done with a holiday. Did you have a good holiday?

B Mhm.

C Yeah. Did you do anything special or fun?

B Not really.

C Not really. Would you rather be in school?

B Yeah [laughing].

C Than have the big break at home? At least at school you get to see all your friends, right?

B Oh no, I wanna do homework.

C You want to do homework?

B [Nods yes]

C Oh my goodness!

B I'm a homework person.

C I kind of like homework too but not all the time. I get kind of tired of it after a while.

B Yeah, X about (cur) cursive. I'm getting tired of that.

C You're getting tired of cursive writing?

B Yeah. And I (I) (XX) usually have to press down hard and I / hurts my hand.

C After awhile you get a little dent right here?

B Mhm. (I, I) I write with this hand. It's really hard.

C Is that the hardest thing about school is your cursive?

B Mhm. And I hate everything [laughing as she talks]. I can't even do anything. But I like to . . . [doesn't finish . . . laughs]

C What's your favorite thing about school?

B I don't know [laughs].

C You don't know.

= Clinician starts to talk about agenda for therapy; Barbie changes topic back.

B I don't know about Mrs. Y. She doesn't even let me take my books (in in) anywhere.

C Really?

B Yeah, (she) she's my second teacher. I have three teachers. My first one is Mrs. B. (She) she's my real teacher. Mrs. Y, she's the resource room. Mrs. M, she's my speech teacher.

C Oh.

B So, it's hard. You have to go, hurry, and go back, uh uh uh [motioning with her hands like she is traveling back and forth], and get XX.

C Like you're coming and going all the time.

B Yeah [laughs]. Like in eighth grade.

C Yeah, like they do in eighth grade.

B They do nu nu nu nu nah [motioning hands]. Say bye hi bye hi."

C Trading classrooms. See, you'll be ready for eighth grade then, won't you, because you're used to it?

B (But) But sometimes I have to in the same room so [laughs] it's hard. Like, ugh, you're getting dizzy and your head ache.

C Really.

B And sometimes I don't even eat lunch. I just pass.

Source: Clinical sample provided by Janet Sturm.

└───┘

essentially no experimental or quasi-experimental studies that directly compared pull-out with classroom-based service delivery models.

According to IDEA '04, service delivery choices must be individualized. There is no one-size-fits-all when it comes to IEPs. The principles for decision making should emerge from mutual goals and good questions, such as What is the best mix of services and best delivery model for helping this student achieve in the general education curriculum? More specific questions might include the following:

- Does this child need intensified, individualized practice with a subset of language/literacy skills, such as sound–symbol association, that might be best addressed in an individual or small-group setting?
- Does this child need a block of intensive, short-term services to correct an articulation problem, followed by monitoring to ensure that literacy learning is proceeding on schedule?
- Does this child need a classroom-based service delivery model to help him or her integrate and apply language across levels (sound, word, sentence, and discourse) and modalities (listening, speaking, reading, and writing)?
- Does this child need a social skills group outside the academic arena to work specifically on pragmatic skills for social interaction with peers?

These are examples of questions that might influence service delivery decisions for individual students with disabilities. The dual principles of least restrictive environment (LRE) and goals for students to function and progress in the general education curriculum should guide choices for particular children and adolescents. An ongoing need exists for high-quality research.

Special Services in General Education Classrooms

Being included full time in age-appropriate general education classroom programs might seem like the ideal LRE, and it does have advantages. However, classroom-based models are not ideal for everyone (e.g., Beck & Dennis, 1997). Classroom-based services require careful planning and coordination to support some students while not disrupting others and to provide therapeutic services that directly address students' needs (e.g., Ehren, 2000; Westby, 1994).

What is *not* appropriate is having a general education teacher stand at the front of the room teaching while a special service provider stands at the back of the room watching. It is not appropriate for students with special needs to be included in classrooms in body only, with little attention to whether their minds also are engaged (Westby, 1994). Classroom-based approaches can be relevant to students' needs and helpful for avoiding pitfalls of patchwork scheduling, but they require careful collaborative planning.

Bland and Prelock (1996) differentiated ***consultative models*** from ***collaborative models*** in describing different ways SLPs can work with teachers toward mutual goals. The distinction is based on the degree of shared involvement in the delivery of services (less in the former, more in the latter). Russell and Kaderavek (1993) described ***peer coaching*** as bidirectional sharing, in which teachers and SLPs coach each other in their knowledge and roles. It is different from ***co-teaching,*** which involves collaborative planning and implementation of instruction and intervention for all students. Elksnin and Capilouto (1994) outlined seven variations in classroom-based service delivery:

1. ***One teach, one observe,*** gathering onlooker observation data to inform future planning
2. ***One teach, one "drift,"*** providing assistance to individual students in need
3. ***Station teaching,*** moving students through stations to work with different adults at each station
4. ***Parallel teaching,*** introducing the same content to different groups of students by different professionals
5. ***Remedial teaching,*** involving a specialist working with students who need extra mediation of general education concepts

6. *Supplemental teaching,* involving a specialist teaching basic content to support acquisition of the general education curriculum
7. *Team teaching,* involving professionals who share responsibility for whole-class, small-group, and individual instruction

According to current terminology, fully integrated and transdisciplinary co-teaching constitutes a form of ***universally designed instruction.*** That means that it incorporates leveled opportunities and activities for simultaneously meeting the needs of a wide range of learners, including some with special needs (Merritt & Culatta, 1998). As teachers gain confidence in supporting language and literacy learning by students with special needs, SLPs can move from being fully collaborative co-teachers to serving a consultative role, freeing the language specialists' time to work more intensively with other classrooms and teachers.

Cirrin and Penner (1995) reviewed research on classroom-based direct and indirect services. They found some evidence in support of classroom-based models at the preschool level but concluded that classroom-based models "have not been put to any adequate test to determine their effectiveness in facilitating development of specific language abilities in school-age children" (p. 345). This situation has changed little in over a decade. Cirrin and Penner concluded, "No comprehensive language intervention plan can be considered complete without a plan that will enable the student to use newly learned target skills in the classroom and other natural environments" (p. 358). Both policy and evidence-based practice (EBP) indicate that choices of service delivery models should be based on children's individualized profiles and needs. Again, there is no "one-size-fits-all."

As reviewed by McGinty and Justice (2006), a few experimental or quasi-experimental studies have been reported for providing language intervention in classroom contexts that meet EBP standards, but only a very few. For example, Bland and Prelock (1995) studied a *language in the classroom (LIC)* service delivery model for 14 matched pairs of students with communication disorders, ranging in age from 6 years, 2 months to 9 years, 2 months at the beginning of the study. Their LIC model involved inservice training about language in the classroom; mutual goal setting, planning, and problem solving in weekly or bimonthly meetings (depending on schedules); and inclassroom language lessons co-taught once per week. Bland and Prelock analyzed language samples gathered over a three-year period and found few differences in syntax, semantics, or morphology for students in the LIC compared with those in the pull-out model. They did find significant advantages for communication skills in completeness and intelligibility in favor of students in the LIC model.

Throneburg, Calvert, Sturm, Paramboukas, and Paul (2000) evaluated three service delivery models in the elementary school setting—a collaborative approach, a classroom-based intervention model with the speech–language pathologist (SLP) and classroom teachers working independently, and a traditional pull-out model. Participants were kindergartners through third-graders who qualified for speech or language services. Outcomes were curricular vocabulary targeted across all interventions both for special-needs and general education students. Comparisons were made for the collaborative approach (general education teacher plus SLP), the independent classroom-based model (teacher and SLP working separately), and instruction from classroom teachers only (i.e., without the SLP's involvement). The collaborative model produced better results both for students with speech–language impairment (than a traditional pull-out model) and for general education students (than a classroom-based model provided by teachers without SLP collaboration). These results were interpreted as supporting integrated service delivery models for combined language instruction and intervention in the school setting.

With consultation, general education teachers can support learning by students with LI in their classrooms, but many lack confidence (see Case Example 12.2). Special service

─CASE **example** *12.2*─

Spencer's Transition from Visitor to Member of the Classroom

"He can't even read!" was the comment made by Spencer's third-grade teacher to communicate her dismay when the SLP indicated that Spencer would be included in her class for all writing lab activities as part of the writing lab outreach project. Spencer was introduced in Case Example 2.1 (based on a case study that appeared in Nelson, Bahr, & Van Meter, 2004). The SLP reassured this teacher that they would work together to identify the best ways to teach Spencer to read and write and to communicate better orally.

An early breakthrough came when Spencer (with SLP scaffolding) used a simile, "It looks like a beach ball," to describe a watermelon as part of the teacher's assignment to select a fruit and describe it in writing. The teacher was impressed and used Spencer's work as a positive example for the rest of the class. Spencer's SLP used the "shared pencil" technique in that early written language effort, but it was Spencer's ideas and words that caught the teacher's attention. Spencer continued to develop both his language skills and literacy abilities for independent decoding and spelling.

Another turning point came for Spencer and his teacher on the day that he wrote a story about being angry at his sister: "And then my temperature rised," he wrote (with scaffolded spelling help). "It's getting hot in here." Spencer's sense of audience and the importance of receiving his general education teacher's positive review of his work became apparent as he prepared to read the story to his teacher. He drew her attention prior to reading the story by saying, "You're going to love this!" and she did.

providers can be most active and helpful in classrooms with students working individually or in small groups on projects to target IEP objectives in the context of general curricular activities. This philosophy provided the primary motivation for developing the ***writing lab approach (WLA)*** (Nelson, Bahr, & Van Meter, 2004; Nelson & Van Meter, 2006b), which integrates language *instruction* for all students with individualized *intervention* for students with disabilities. The WLA is a flexible model that is guided by a set of ***BACKDROP principles*** outlined in Table 12.1. It incorporates three major components: (1) writing process instruction, targeting spoken and written communication for all students in the context of curriculum-based projects and using all stages of the writing process (planning, organizing, drafting, revising, editing, presenting); (2) computer supports for all stages of the writing process; and (3) collaborative, individualized instruction, in which special-needs students are included in the general education classroom for all writing lab activities. In the WLA, SLPs use a team-teaching model with general education teachers. Writing lab project activities are scheduled in the classroom at least two days per week (three, if possible) for an hour per session.

The WLA can be implemented within a single classroom or by all teachers at a particular grade level collaborating in developing a curriculum-based project their students can work on simultaneously over several weeks (with sharing across classrooms at the same grade level). Everything students do in school involves language and communication. Therefore, language intervention goals (both spoken and written) can be targeted in any segment of the curriculum. Teachers can work across grade levels to plan language arts, science, and social studies projects involving story writing, poetry, personal timelines, core democratic values, business plans, animal reports, weather reports, geography reports, and classroom practice of districtwide testing procedures. Special-needs students receive intensified scaffolding by SLPs within writing process instruction to address goals selected individually based on strengths and needs across language levels and modalities. Evidence

table *12.1* BACKDROP Principles for the Writing Lab Approach and Other Forms of Curriculum-Based Language Intervention

Principle	How It Applies
Balance	Balance applies to part/whole; spoken/written; teacher-directed/child-centered; assistance/independence; and so on.
Authentic audience	Serving as an authentic audience for students' ideas is a powerful scaffolding technique.
Constructive learning	Clinicians can scaffold learners, but students must construct their own knowledge.
Keep it simple	If teams keep projects simple, they will have more time for scaffolding deeper learning in targeted areas.
Dynamic	Classroom-based interventions are necessarily dynamic and flexible to respond to teachable moments.
Research/Reflective	The writing lab approach is based in research, ongoing data gathering, and collaborative reflection.
Ownership	Students participate in setting goals and are allowed ownership for their choices as authors.
Patience	Professionals need patience in collaborating with each other and allowing students ownership for authorship choices.

Source: Based on Nelson, Bahr, & Van Meter, 2004.

for the effectiveness of this approach comes from analysis of written story probes at three points across a schoolyear, with results showing improvements in written language expression that bring students with special needs closer to general education peers at the sound/word, sentence, and discourse levels (Nelson et al., 2004; Nelson & Van Meter, 2006b).

Pull-Out Services

Pull-out services may seem more restrictive than classroom-based services, but they have some advantages. Chief among these are opportunities for practicing massed trials of a targeted skill with immediate feedback, as appropriate for well-defined expressive language goals and motor speech production skills. It may be easier to practice production of speech sounds in words, build automatic associations of sounds and symbols, and work on reading decoding skills (when classmates are beyond that level) in pull-out sessions. On the other hand, language comprehension (listening or reading) and academic vocabulary learning might be addressed more effectively in co-taught classroom settings, where intervention can be contextualized in meaningful activity (e.g., Throneburg et al., 2000).

A major disadvantage of half-hour pull-out services is that they isolate the student from the general education experiences that are ongoing while he or she is out of the room. Transitions from one setting to another take time, and they may not be as automatic or smooth as they appear (as Barbie communicated in Case Example 12.1). To lessen this impact, some teachers appoint ***learning buddies*** to take explicit responsibility for reorienting peers who return to the classroom after pull-out sessions.

Integration of spoken and written, receptive and expressive language across multiple levels is taxed at higher levels in the classroom than in a pull-out session. If ***curriculum-based language assessment and intervention (CBLAI)*** is not provided in an integrated setting, it should be contextualized using curriculum standards and materials drawn from that setting. Curriculum-based language intervention can be accomplished in pull-out settings by bringing pieces of the student's general education curriculum to the pull-out room (e.g., textbooks, worksheets, practice problems, written works in progress). Kits and games rarely (if ever) are preferable to situating intervention in contexts and materials drawn from the student's actual curriculum. In intervention programs addressing phonological and morphological systems of sounds within syllables and words, integrated spoken–written language activities can be used to teach the principles of phonics, word decoding, fluent pattern recognition, and spelling. Figure 12.3, for example, shows how a warm-up syllable drill might be constructed to support multiple levels of practice, including the primary goal of producing the initial /s/ in syllables but also for associating sounds with symbols and CV syllables with orthographic patterns that include alternative spellings of vowel patterns, long and short.

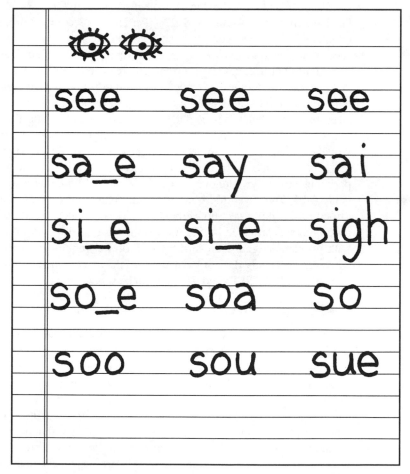

figure *12.3*

Sample Page from a Child's Speech Notebook

This sample shows how a "warm-up" page might be used to help the child learn to recognize orthographic patterns that represent alternative spellings of syllables pronounced the same way.

When children have isolated residual speech sound substitutions, one option is to provide intensive daily (or four-day-per-week) intervention in brief (e.g., five-minute) pull-out sessions. Clinical trials are needed to evaluate the effectiveness of this model, but clinicians have reported anecdotal success in using it with students with isolated speech sound disorders (SSDs) and no comorbid language-/literacy-learning difficulties. The five-minute daily articulation intervention model offers the advantages of efficiency and limited time spent away from general education classroom activities.

One *randomized controlled trial (RCT)* has investigated aspects of service delivery with school-age students. Researchers in Scotland (Boyle, McCartney, Forbes, & O'Hare, 2007) conducted a large RCT to evaluate the effectiveness and economic advantage of direct versus indirect and individual versus group language intervention for children with primary language impairment. Posttest results were available for 152 children from ages 6 to 11 years with primary LI. None of the children had hearing loss or moderate to severe speech production difficulties requiring individual therapy. The investigators assigned students randomly to receive either direct speech–language therapy (i.e., by a trained speech–language therapist, as the SLT role is identified in the United Kingdom) or indirect services (i.e., through a speech–language therapy assistant, or SLTA). Participants were randomized to individual or group treatment in schools. A control group of students received existing levels of community-based speech–language services. Language intervention was conducted according to a manual prepared for the project based on current research and the professional literature.

Primary outcome data came from standardized expressive and receptive language tests that were scored by clinicians blind to students' groups. Secondary measures were scores on a receptive vocabulary test and data from session audits, questionnaires, rating scales, and focus group responses. Results showed no significant advantage for direct or indirect, individual or group models. Some advantages were found based on secondary measures for direct services delivered by an SLT three times per week for 30 to 40 minutes over a 15-week period in expressive but not receptive language. Children with specific expressive language delay (SELD) showed more improvement than children with mixed receptive–expressive difficulties, regardless of nonverbal IQ. Boyle and colleagues (2007) concluded that indirect group therapy provided by SLTAs was the least costly model and appropriate for children with primary language impairment who do not require the specialized skills of an SLT. However, this study did not yield clear results about which children needed direct services by qualified SLTs/SLPs and which could be served adequately by trained assistants.

Special Education Classrooms and Related Services

Some special services are delivered in pull-out classrooms by special education teachers, rather than in cliniclike rooms by SLPs or related service providers. That is, some students with disabilities receive services in self-contained special education classroom programs, mostly taught by special education teachers, who are responsible for teaching all or part of the students' curriculum. Historically, some local or state policies mandated that special education teachers should teach only a special education curriculum, based on the rationale that otherwise the education would not be *special.* It followed that only general education teachers should teach the general education curriculum. Problems resulted with this model, however, in that students who were taught exclusively in a special curriculum tended to fall further and further behind in the general education curriculum. Such problems motivated changes in the IDEA and NCLB legislation described in Chapter 4 and earlier in this chapter.

Self-contained special education classrooms also have been called *categorical,* indicating that students with a diagnosis in a particular category (e.g., autism spectrum disorder, cognitive impairment, or learning disability) are placed in such rooms. Alternatively, such classrooms may be called *self-contained* because students may be placed in them for full days, five days per week (except maybe for subjects such as physical education and music). Some special education classrooms are called *resource rooms,* in that students spend only a portion of each schoolday receiving special resources in these classrooms but spend the majority of their time in *mainstream, inclusive,* or *push-in* settings (i.e., general education classrooms and activities). In resource rooms, students with a range of relatively mild disabilities receive remediation or more intensified instruction than in the general education curriculum. Such rooms may be called *noncategorical,* including students with a variety of high-incidence disabilities, such as a learning disability, mild intellectual disability, or emotional impairment. Special education classrooms for students with more severe cognitive impairments or multiple impairments (i.e., low-incidence disabilities) are more likely to be self-contained. These classrooms for students with severe and multiple comorbid disabilities, which often involve complex communication needs, may be housed in *center programs* in separate buildings from general education schools, although such programs now are somewhat controversial.

Questions remain about the best way to deliver language and communication intervention services for students with comorbid disabilities who are placed in special education classrooms for all or part of their day. Professionals have debated the merits and challenges of providing special education in separate classrooms (and buildings) for years. Can a separate classroom (or separate building) constitute the LRE for any student with a disability? It is not acceptable for a student to be segregated from the opportunity to be educated in the general curriculum, nor is it acceptable for a student to be included in body only in a general education classroom, with little opportunity to learn (Westby, 1994). Deliberate efforts must be made to foster learning in the general education curriculum and participation with peers who do not have disabilities.

Options exist for making special education services in separate classrooms more relevant to the general education curriculum. Some SLPs co-teach with special education teachers in their classrooms several hours per week to provide intensive language and literacy intervention activities. Others "push in" special-needs students to general education classrooms or "pull in" general education student volunteers to act as peer mentors.

Some self-contained language classrooms are developed specifically to target the language- and literacy-learning needs of students with a range of special education labels and moderate levels of functional limitations. Nelson (1981) reported on self-contained language classrooms for students in the early elementary school years (first through third grade) who had not acquired basic literacy and oral communication skills in general education classrooms or with traditional special education services, in spite of receiving targeted instruction. The goal was to enroll students with LI (some of whom had comorbid cognitive and emotional–behavioral conditions) in the special *language impaired/learning impaired (LILI)* classroom for only as long as needed to develop basic reading, decoding, spelling, social communication, and language comprehension skills. This intervention model focused on providing integrated spoken and written language instruction, with highly structured teacher-directed (form-oriented) activities focused on sound–symbol association and phonics at the sound/word level combined with child-centered (function-oriented) activities focused on written language as communication (e.g., students wrote communicative journals and shared them with classmates and teachers). Positive results were documented by gains on standardized tests using age scores that showed students with marked special needs catching up to age expectations by making at least as much growth on age scores on the tests as months in the program.

Services for Middle and High School Students

Middle and high school students with complex schedules involving multiple teachers and room changes present special service delivery challenges. Larson, McKinley, and Boley

(1993) identified three categories of service delivery options for adolescents with language disorders: (1) ***traditional pull-out services*** could be provided individually or in small groups; (2) a ***course for credit*** could be offered either by a clinician or clinician as part of a team; and (3) a classroom-based ***consultation model*** could be used either directly with the student in the classroom or indirectly through the classroom teacher.

Anderson and Nelson (1988) described an *alternative adolescent language class (AALC)* as an example of a course-for-credit option. The class was designed for middle school special-needs students with a variety of disability labels, such as LI/LD, hearing impaired, and emotionally impaired. With school board approval, the class became the source of language arts credit for this diverse group of students with special needs. Students attended the special class in a regularly scheduled time slot, one hour per day, five days per week. This model solved a number of problems for both the students and the system. It addressed the stigma and confusion reported by students when they were being pulled out of other classes, and it consolidated their speech–language homework with the general education curriculum.

At the beginning of the program, the students in the AALC showed little confidence in their abilities and few executive control strategies (Anderson & Nelson, 1988). Their teachers saw them as problem students, and their peers rarely selected them as partners for collaborative learning activities. The AALC was designed to help students achieve in the general education curriculum, not only in language arts but in other aspects of the curriculum as well. The SLP who taught the class held a secondary teaching certificate and based her language instruction on general curriculum standards; she used textbooks and curricular content selected in consultation with other teachers. Along with language and literacy skills focused on academic language, the SLP taught students to use self-talk and other executive control strategies. These included study skills and self-organization and -regulation strategies. For example, students began each class session by reminding themselves of the purpose "to improve enough not to need the special class anymore." Students also learned that teachers expected them to follow the unspoken student–teacher contract to attempt each assignment and turn something in. When students fulfilled their part of the contract, teachers were willing to help them when they were having trouble.

Outcomes of the AALC were better grades across classes and successful transitions back to general education classrooms for the majority of the students after one year. Qualitative data also showed changes in how teachers and peers viewed the students; teachers reported they were a pleasure to have in class, and peers chose them as cooperative learning partners (Anderson & Nelson, 1988).

Participation of Parents, Peers, Teachers, and Students with Learning Impairments

Parents are less centrally involved in language intervention programs for school-age students, but they still play an important role in supporting children's instructional and intervention needs. Nye, Turner, and Schwartz (2006) conducted a systematic review of literature on parent involvement and children's academic performance (for all children, not necessarily children with disabilities) in the elementary school years. Parent involvement was defined in four categories of out-of-school activities—collaborative reading, education and training, games, and reward and incentives. Meta-analysis showed that all forms of parent involvement had a "positive and significant effect on children's overall academic performance" (p. 25).

Westby (2006) emphasized the nature of the demands that students face in "learning to do school" (p. 320). She pointed out that many expectations of school participation are implicit and thus particularly challenging for students with different cultural–linguistic experiences or children with LI. Both groups may need more explicit classroom communication cues from their teachers about appropriate participation than students who come prepared with mainstream experiences to "do school." All students "must learn how to negotiate the multiple official and unofficial curricula of the classroom, which involve dealing with teachers, peers, and materials" (p. 320).

Westby (2006) illustrated her description of changing expectations in classroom *scripts* across the elementary years with examples from three classrooms. She characterized the second-grade script as "learning to participate" (p. 349), the third-grade script as "developing self-control" (p. 352), and the fifth-grade script as "developing self-regulation" (p. 355). Westby presented case study evidence for a fifth-grade classroom that included a majority of English language learners (ELLs) and eight students with LD. The service delivery model chosen for the students with LD was full-day inclusion. A special education teacher team taught with the general education teacher, and an educational assistant also was in the room. Although dynamic assessment showed that the ELLs could comply after minimal exposure to the high levels of expectation for independent functioning, the students with LD still struggled. Their greater need for external scaffolds for attention and behavior could not be met with the full-inclusion model. Westby concluded:

> For the students with special needs, even with the presence of a special education teacher and an aide, the gap between independent performance and assisted performance was too large, and negatively affected both groups of students. This classroom could be considered beyond the zone of proximal development for these students. (p. 357)

After reflecting on the difficulty in meeting the students' needs adequately in a single classroom, even with team teaching and an assistant, the two teachers collaboratively decided to terminate the full inclusion aspects of the program (Westby, 2006). They returned to a partial-inclusion model, in which the students were grouped for multicultural education, social studies, and science. The hybrid model seemed to work better for this grade level and situation. Although the evidence was largely anecdotal, this is an example of local evaluation of an experimental practice.

Peers can be involved in supporting communication intervention goals, but special scaffolding is required. Peer interventions may benefit from recruiting more able peers to welcome the overtures of children with LI. Peers also can be scaffolded to let peers with disabilities know directly but kindly when they violate social rules, such as proximity rules. Approaches for engaging peers in intervention approaches are described in the next two chapters. Case Example 2.1 (the Spencer example, which appeared in Chapter 2) also offers an illustration of this type of intervention embedded in the writing lab approach (WLA).

Social and cooperative learning groups can be designed to help students with disabilities gain access to communicative interactions with peers. Specific targets include age-appropriate ways of talking and interacting and gaining entrance to groups of peers. These goals are targeted most effectively in integrated service delivery models. Brinton and Fujiki (2006) noted the irony of pulling students out of situations with their peers when the goal is to work on social skills so they can interact better (see Personal Reflection 12.1).

PERSONAL reflection *12.1*

"The intuitive notion that students with language impairments should be learning with and from their peers is sometimes suppressed as they are pulled out of their classes for special services. Individualized learning models may be adopted that emphasize the interaction between the student and the clinician, but not the interaction among students. This is understandable considering that students with language impairments need highly individualized programs of intervention. The necessity of individualized intervention programs, however, is sometimes misconstrued as a need for solitary learning contexts."

Bonnie Brinton and **Martin Fujiki** (2006, p. 291), both speech–language pathologists and language scientists, have conducted extensive research on peer interactions and social skills.

....

Brinton and Fujiki (2006) applied Johnson and Johnson's (1999) framework of collaborative interaction (introduced in Chapter 1) to engage students in cooperative learning groups to work on curriculum-based projects, citing the three modes in which peers may interact as *competitive, individualistic,* and *cooperative.* As illustrated in Personal Reflection 12.1, some children with LI are prone to functioning in the individualistic mode, lacking competence for gaining access to groups. Such students need explicit scaffolding to acquire basic communication skills and higher-level strategies for interacting with peers that are unlikely to be acquired in pull-out interventions. Research evidence illuminates approach–avoidance barriers that cause students with LI to be "both eager and wary about interacting with peers" (p. 296). Brinton and Fujiki described an intervention approach (discussed more fully in Chapter 13) for teaching students to gain access to groups.

A recommendation for school-age children and adolescents is to involve them directly in planning, implementing, and evaluating their own intervention programs. Tattershall (2002) described this as a "shoulder-to-shoulder" approach (see Personal Reflection 12.2); it involved using interviews to help students describe their own situations. Interviews convey respect for students' perspectives while providing critical information to augment formal assessment activities. Tattershall described the first step as helping students "become aware of and to clearly define their language processing and learning needs" (p. 2). Once adolescents gain a deeper awareness and understanding of their problems, the next step is to help them "develop expertise in making appropriate, workable plans and in implementing, evaluating, and revising those plans" (p. 2). Through such processes, adolescents become full partners in planning and conducting their own interventions and are set on the pathway to becoming fully independent learners and adults.

PERSONAL reflection *12.2*

"As I worked with more and more adolescents, I began to think of a 'shoulder-to-shoulder' interaction, in which the adolescent and adult, side-by-side, consider and try to understand the client's language and learning, his or her strengths and weaknesses with the purpose of developing appropriate personalized plans and strategies."

"In this stance, shoulder-to-shoulder, the role of the clinician, teacher, special educator, vocational counselor, and so forth, is to respect what only the adolescent can contribute. Their perspectives, insights, specific experiences, feelings, and evaluations provide information that cannot be obtained in any other way. Without this contribution, the professionals cannot do their part in guiding creative planning, and utilizing skills, information and insight appropriately for each adolescent."

Sandra Tattershall (2002, pp. 10, 12), a speech–language pathologist in private practice, was describing the specialized approaches she has developed for working with adolescents, emphasizing the principles of ownership and partnership in the process.

....

SUMMARY

A need exists for high-quality research on service delivery models for school-age students with LI and related disabilities. Preliminary evidence supports classroom-based models addressing comprehensive language and literacy learning within the general curriculum (e.g., vocabulary, writing processes, written language), perhaps augmented by pull-out models to address spoken expression and related individual needs (e.g., speech sound production; sound–symbol associations that all the other children in the class have mastered). Little is known about the best contexts for addressing listening and reading comprehension, but a combination of whole-class instruction supplemented with individualized scaffolding may be the best option for most children with LI and related literacy-learning difficulties. Children with social interaction difficulties need to be scaffolded, at least some of the time, in social groups with peers. Adolescents, in particular, need to be engaged directly in planning, implementing, and evaluating their own intervention programs.

Comprehensive Assessment in the School-Age Years

Comprehensive assessment of school-age children requires data from multiple sources. Periodic brief assessment probes may serve preventive functions as part of RTI activities. Formal tests and data from referral sources are used to complete diagnostic evaluation for determining disability and eligibility for special services. Additional in-depth probes and informal assessment procedures are used to construct a comprehensive picture of a child's strengths and needs to inform intervention planning and to document progress. These are some of the varied assessment purposes that are appropriate for students in their school-age years.

Assessment for diagnostic purposes differs fundamentally from assessment for designing intervention and measuring progress. Diagnostic testing generally requires a norm-referenced test, although (as discussed in Chapters 5 through 7) diagnosis should never be based on a single indicator of disorder. Diagnostic criteria are based on multiple sources of data, including observation and parental input. Input from parents and teachers regarding a child's contextualized needs is required by IDEA '04. Assessment probes conducted as part of RTI activities may provide diagnostic information as well, particularly regarding a student's response (or lack thereof) to increasingly intense tiers of early intervening activities.

Formal tests are less well suited for the purpose of informing intervention planning. Some marker variables, such as nonsense word repetition, rapid naming, and short-term memory for digits, are particularly sensitive to disorder but particularly ill suited to intervention planning. Curriculum-based and other contextualized language assessment activities provide more relevant information for designing intervention and marking progress. In the remainder of this chapter, formal tests are discussed first, followed by informal, contextualized assessment approaches.

Formal Assessment Tools and Activities

Table D in the Part III Appendix identifies a range of formal tests designed for children and adolescents in the school-age years, from ages 5 to 21. It includes selected norm-referenced and criterion-referenced assessment tools for measuring language and literacy abilities. As recommended throughout this book, instruments that are valid for their intended purpose should be selected based on a careful review of the test's psychometric properties, as described in the test's technical manual (McCauley & Swisher, 1984). Among the language tests for school-age students reviewed by Spaulding, Plante, and Farinella (2006), only a few met sensitivity and specificity criteria for diagnosing language disorder among school-age students.

The Comprehensive Evaluation of Language Fundamentals (CELF–4; Semel, Wiig, & Secord, 2003) is one of these. It is a comprehensive measure of school-age students' spoken language abilities that satisfies such criteria. Its sensitivity is reported at 1.0 and its specificity at 0.89 when a cut score of –1.5 standard deviations (SDs) (standard score of 77.5) is used; sensitivity is reported at 0.87 and specificity at 0.96 when a cut score of –2.0 SDs (standard score of 70) is used. Other formal tests that meet criteria for diagnosing spoken language deficits include the Test of Narrative Language (TNL; Gillam & Pearson, 2004), with sensitivity of 0.92 and specificity of 0.87 using a cut score of –1.0 SDs (standard score of 85), and the Test of Language Competence–Expanded Edition (TLC–E; Wiig & Secord, 1989), with sensitivity of 0.90 and specificity of 0.85 (based on a regression analysis that does not make the cut score clear) (Spaulding et al., 2006).

Formal assessment should consider all potential areas of impairment. For school-age students, this includes spoken language comprehension and expression but also reading decoding and comprehension and written language composing and transcription. Assessment across language modalities involves contributions by multidisciplinary evaluation team members, who may divide responsibility for assessing spoken and written language and other cognitive abilities and then reconvene to interpret the results. A collaborative *multidisciplinary evaluation team* (*MET,* as defined by IDEA '04) combines results from multiple tests to construct a cohesive profile, remembering the caution that results cannot be compared directly for multiple tests standardized on different samples of school-age children.

Students with comorbid sensory and motor deficits need special accommodations and interdisciplinary contributions to ensure that formal and informal testing reflects their language/literacy skills, not functional limitations imposed by sensory–motor deficits at the peripheral input/output level. Comprehensive assessment of language skills of children with hearing impairment requires contributions from a team of specialists, including an educational audiologist, teacher of hearing-impaired students, and SLP, to ensure that students can hear any auditory stimuli at an optimal level and have access to facial expressions and speech reading and sign language interpretation, as appropriate. Interpretation of results should consider the possibility that a child may have missed certain items due to not hearing the words clearly, rather than not understanding the language conveyed. Teams assessing language skills for students with visual impairment should include a low-vision specialist with expertise in the technology for augmenting visual input and, if necessary, for transforming print into braille. Teams assessing students with motor impairments should include an SLP who assesses the student's speech motor control capabilities in addition to language and an OT who assesses other aspects of sensory–motor integration. If motor control problems are interfering with spoken or written language output, technology supports may be required to compensate. When standardized tests are administered in nonstandardized ways, caution always must be exercised in scoring and interpreting the results.

A language-levels-by-modalities model can guide comprehensive assessment for school-age students. Data should be gathered regarding children's knowledge of sound, word, sentence, and discourse levels across all four modalities—listening, speaking, reading, and writing. The *simple model* proposed by Gough and Tunmer (1986) for characterizing reading as involving decoding and comprehension was introduced in Chapter 2 (Figure 2.8) as a language-levels-by-modalities model. This model contrasts difficulties involving phonological aspects of language at the sound/word level with difficulties involving nonphonological aspects of language at the sentence/discourse level. Different combinations of high and low abilities predict four profiles of functioning that were illustrated in Figure 5.3. As discussed in Chapter 5, evidence for this model comes from a growing body of research (e.g., Catts, Hogan, & Adlof, 2005; Nation & Snowling, 2004; Snowling, Gallagher, & Frith, 2003).

Differential diagnosis requires tests to measure language across all levels and modalities. It is particularly challenging to diagnose disability when students have specific deficits in relatively isolated domains. For example, a student with dyslexia needs specialized intervention to learn to read and spell but may not qualify for language intervention services based on scores from a broad comprehensive test of spoken language only. A child with Asperger syndrome or pragmatic language impairment (PLI) needs intervention focused on social skills and higher-level comprehension, but such a student also might score within normal limits on a broad test of language and literacy ability.

This is one reason why no single measure should be used to evaluate a child's need for language and communication intervention services and why the input of teachers and others is so important for making the diagnosis and decisions about the need for special services (see Personal Reflection 12.3). If a test's psychometric properties support the use of subtest scores, profiles that indicate discrepancies across abilities might provide more meaningful information than full-scale scores, as full-scale scores may obscure difficulties in a specific area of functioning that are evened out by the student's areas of strength.

PERSONAL reflection *12.3*

"I do not have the training that you people [speech–language pathologists] have. However, I've been in the business a long time, and I think I know when I see a child with a language problem. So I make all the referrals. Now I don't know what happens in the 1:1 session, or what kinds of tests you give the kids, but my speech person keeps sending these children back to me saying they don't have a language problem. Finally, I just said to her, 'Then you get in the classroom and see what is wrong.'"

Frustrated teacher, whose comments were reported by Catherine Constable (1987, pp. 347–348).

Some formal tests are designed to assess selected language systems and modalities. For example, the Woodcock Reading Mastery Test-Revised–Normative Update (WRMT–R/NU; Woodcock, 1998) assesses word-level decoding and fluency. It assesses nonsense word reading as well as real-word reading fluency. The Gray Oral Reading Test, 4th edition (GORT-4; Weiderhold & Bryant, 2001) assesses auditory comprehension of written language (read aloud by the examiner) as well as reading comprehension. The Woodcock-Johnson III Tests of Achievement and Tests of Cognitive Ability (WJ-III; Woodcock, McGrew, & Mather, 2005) incorporates a range of subtests that may be administered by one professional (e.g., the school psychologist) but interpreted by an interdisciplinary team, including a language specialist. That way, the transdisciplinary team can compare perspectives based on their areas of unique expertise. The Comprehensive Test of Phonological Processing (C-TOPP; Wagner, Torgesen, and Rashotte, 1999) assesses phonological awareness and other word-level skills. The Oral-Written Language Scales (OWLS; Carrow-Woolfolk, 1995, 1996) assess both spoken and written language using a variety of sentence-level tasks. The Test of Word Finding-2 (TWF-2; German, 2000), Test of Word Finding in Discourse (TWFD; German, 1991), and Test of Adolescent/Adult Word Finding (TAWF; German, 1990) are designed for in-depth assessment of word retrieval and to provide profile information about cueing systems that are more or less accessible when children have difficulty. Other word-level measures focused on assessing vocabulary knowledge include the Peabody Picture Vocabulary Test, 3rd edition (PPVT-III; Dunn & Dunn, 1997), the Receptive One-Word Picture Vocabulary Test-Revised (ROWPVT-R; Brownell, 2000b), and the Expressive One-Word Picture Vocabulary Test-Revised (EOWPVT-R; Brownell, 2000a).

Based on the language-levels-by-modalities model, Nelson, Helm-Estabrooks, Hotz, and Plante (2007) are in the process of developing a curriculum-relevant, comprehensive measure of spoken and written language, which shows promise for offering information about profiles that will be informative for planning intervention. It is a Test of Integrated Language and Literacy Skills (TILLS). The TILLS is designed for differential diagnosis of students with varied profiles using the subtests outlined in Table 12.2 according to the primary levels and modalities assessed by each. Preliminary evaluation results and subsequent modifications using sophisticated analysis techniques have allowed the removal of biased items and supported the test's potential as a tool with high reliability and validity for diagnosing language/literacy disorders. The test also shows promise for developing profiles of strengths and needs that are relevant for informing curriculum-based language intervention. As a formal tool, the TILLS is a *curriculum-relevant* test, but it does not take the place of *curriculum-based* assessment and intervention activities using a student's actual curriculum. Those are discussed in the section that follows.

Rigid adherence to formulas, criteria, or the outcomes of any single measure should not supersede an evaluation team's judgment that incorporates clinical expertise and family values about the student's individualized needs. Diagnosis of disability should be made by a team of qualified professionals with reference to a set of published criteria and with parental and student input. Similarly, questions about eligibility and the need for special education must be made by a student's IEP team, which includes at least one of his or her teachers, his or her parents, and, when appropriate, the student himself or herself.

Curriculum-Based Language Assessment and Intervention

Learning and interacting in school exerts many demands on children's language/literacy and communication abilities. Reducing disability is not just a matter of targeting and "fixing" impaired processes (the communication processes model). It also involves providing

table *12.2*   Language-Levels-by-Modalities Model Showing Subtests in the Beta Research Edition of the Test of Integrated Language and Literacy Skills (TILLS)

Modality	Language Level	
	Sound/Word Level *(Word meaning and form)*	*Sentence/Discourse Level* *(Comprehension and formulation)*
Listening	1. **Semantic awareness** (What Goes Together) 2. **Phonemic awareness** (Code Game) 11. **Auditory memory** (Digit Span)	4A. **Listening comprehension** (Yes, No, Maybe: Listening Only) 6. **Following directions**
Speaking	5A. **Nonsense Word Imitation**	3. **Narrative discourse** (Story Retelling) 10. **Social communication** (Acting a Scene)
Reading	9. **Reading decoding** (Nonsense Word Reading) 7. **Reading fluency** (Reading the News)	4B. **Bimodal comprehension** (Yes, No, Maybe: Listening + Reading) 4C. **Reading comprehension** (Yes, No, Maybe: Reading Only)
Writing	5B. **Nonsense Word Spelling**	8. **Written sentence combining** (Writing the News)

Source: TILLS is being developed by Nelson, Helm-Estabrooks, Hotz, & Plante, 2007.

intervention and technological supports to meet a student's functional needs (the communication needs model) and systemwide efforts to increase communication opportunities (the participation model).

Curriculum-Relevant Language Assessment and Intervention

Curriculum-relevant language assessment and intervention uses tasks that *relate* to tasks of the general education curriculum (as when administering the TILLS, as described earlier). *Curriculum-based language assessment and intervention (CBLAI)* is conducted using *actual* materials drawn from the student's own general education curriculum.

RTI activities are an example of curriculum-relevant procedures. SLPs, teachers, and other specialists select screening tools and probe techniques that are efficient, sensitive, and specific for identifying children with language- and literacy-learning risks. School systems often use early literacy tasks (e.g., DIBELS; Good & Kaminski, 2002) to measure phonemic awareness, letter identification, and word reading fluency as part of RTI screening activities in the early elementary grades. SLPs can supplement word-level screening protocols with sentence- and discourse-level screening of listening comprehension. Story retelling procedures offer one tool for accomplishing this purpose.

Culatta, Page, and Ellis (1983) described a story-retelling procedure (Figure 12.4) for screening language in early elementary school students. They used the procedure to decide on one of three recommendations: (1) enrollment in language intervention for children unable to retell the story or if significant changes appeared in sequencing or content; (2) further evaluation for children whose stories were "sketchy but relevant and properly sequenced" (p. 68); or (3) no need for special attention for children whose stories were detailed and properly sequenced. Culatta and colleagues found the story-retelling task to be more sensitive than standardized screening procedures for identifying children who were in kindergarten or readiness classes. Figure 12.4 provides the stimuli and Table 12.3 summarizes the data reported by Culatta and her colleagues (1983) that could be used as a template for establishing local norms. The original article provides a fast-food story as an alternative to the birthday party story, which might be culturally more appropriate for children whose families do not celebrate birthdays with parties.

Curriculum-Based Language Assessment and Intervention

Table 12.4 shows how the four context-based language assessment and intervention questions used throughout this book apply to curricular contexts. It also reflects the three questions motivated by the World Health Organization's *Internal Classification of Functioning* (WHO/ICF, 2001) regarding communication processes, needs, and opportunities. *CBLAI* is defined as the "use of curriculum contexts and content for measuring a student's language intervention needs and progress" (Nelson, 1989, p. 171). This definition highlights differences between CBLAI and other forms of context-based assessment, as well as other forms of *curriculum-based measurement (CBM)*.

The basic question addressed with CBM (Deno, 1989) is whether the child is learning the general education curriculum. One might ask, for example, whether a student is learning the grade-appropriate curriculum in social studies or math. In contrast, the basic question addressed with CBLAI is whether the child has the *language* skills to learn the grade-appropriate curriculum in social studies or math.

In some cases, a child with a disability functions almost but not quite like same-age peers. In other cases, the severity and nature of a child's developmental challenges are such that he or she functions in ways that are clearly different from peers, possibly justifying modifications in the curriculum or the way in which it is taught. In either case, as described

figure *12.4*

Story Retelling as a Screening Tool in the Early Elementary Grades

Administration
- Introduce the story-retelling task by saying, "I'm going to tell you a story. You listen and when I'm finished you tell me the same story."
- Read the story to the child.
- Say, "Now you tell me the story."
- If the child does not begin, say, "Can you tell me the name of the little boy in the story?" Provide additional open-ended prompts if necessary, such as: "That's OK, what's the rest of the story?" "What did Tommy want?" "Really—what else happened?"
- Present the ten comprehension questions.

Make One of Three Disposition Decisions
1. *To enroll the child for language intervention.* Legally, under IDEA, a comprehensive multidisciplinary evaluation should be conducted at this point—children cannot be determined to have a handicapping condition on the basis of a single procedure administered by a single professional. The story-retelling activity is judged to support a diagnosis of language impairment if the child is unable to relate the story or if the child's version deviates significantly from the original version in either sequencing or content.
2. *To re-evaluate the child's language.* Children who seem to be "on-the-borderline" may be observed carefully in the regular education context or rescreened before receiving a comprehensive multidisciplinary evaluation if that seems more appropriate. This decision is made if the child tells a story that is sketchy but relevant and properly sequenced.
3. *To terminate contact.* Children whose integrated language skills are clearly adequate may be considered to have passed the screening. This decision is made if the child tells a detailed version of the story that is properly sequenced.

Stimulus Story with Number of Events

             1   2   3   4
Tommy was five years old, but his birthday was coming soon. He wanted a puppy for his birthday, but his mother
            5   6
said he was too little to take care of it. Tommy didn't think he was too little. When his birthday came Tommy had
   7 8   9   10   11   12
a party. Five of his friends came to his house. They played games, ate animal crackers and cokes, and Tommy
      13   14   15   16   17
opened his presents. He got a GI Joe, a fire truck, some comic books, and a baseball bat. He liked the presents,
18   19
but he was disappointed because he didn't get a puppy. All of Tommy's friends were getting ready to go home
 20   21   22
when his daddy brought out another present for him to open. Inside was a little black puppy. Tommy was really
   23   24
happy because he got the present he wanted.

Comprehension Questions

1. Who was the boy in the story?
2. How old was he?
3. Who said he was too little for something?
4. What was he too little for?
5. How many friends came to Tommy's house?
6. Why did the friends come over?
7. Name two presents Tommy got.
8. What did they eat at the party?
9. Who gave Tommy the puppy?
10. What color was the puppy?

Note: This is a nonstandardized procedure whose interpretation rests largely on clinical judgment. When the procedure is used within a particular school district, local norms might be established by quantifying some of the observations and performing statistical analyses to compute cutoff scores for children who fall more than 1 or 1.5 standard deviations below the mean for children when judged within the context of the normative group in their own linguistic and sociocultural community (see Saber & Hutchinson, 1990).

Source: From B. Culatta, J. L. Page, and J. Ellis, 1983. Story retelling as a communicative performance screening tool. *Language, Speech and Hearing Services in Schools, 14*, pp. 68, 73. Copyright 1983 by American Speech-Language-Hearing Association. All rights reserved. Reprinted by permission from p. 73; adapted by permission from p. 68.

table 12.3 Means and Standard Deviations (SDs) for the Story-Retelling Measures for Children at Three Grade Levels

Language Measure	Kindergarten n = 66		Readiness n = 16		First Grade n = 117	
	Mean	SD	Mean	SD	Mean	SD
Receptive measure of story retelling	7.20	2.10	7.43	1.78	7.96	4.80
Expressive measures of story retelling						
Number of prompts	5.75	3.70	4.25	3.15	5.02	4.80
Length complexity index	5.56	2.18	5.71	1.73	6.20	1.53
Total N words	55.46	30.79	45.37	29.67	68.95	34.93
N different words	29.80	13.90	25.06	14.25	36.90	13.99
N events	6.86	3.79	6.25	3.51	8.67	3.75
Events out of sequence	.72	1.25	.62	1.14	.91	1.16
Events added	1.10	1.27	.93	1.06	.60	1.05

Note: "Readiness" was included as a special grade level for children who had completed kindergarten but were not yet ready for first grade.

Source: From B. Culatta, J. L. Page, & J. Ellis. 1983. Story retelling as a communicative performance screening tool. *Language, Speech, and Hearing Services in Schools, 14,* pp. 68–73. Reprinted by permission of the American Speech-Language-Hearing Association. All rights reserved.

table 12.4 Four Questions of Curriculum-Based Language Assessment and Intervention and Their Relationship to the Three Questions Regarding Communication Processes, Needs, and Opportunities

Question	What It Yields	Procedures	Relationship to Broader Questions
1. What language skills are required?	Expected response [ER]	Consider language skills and strategies that effective language users employ.	*Communication needs model:* What does the student need to be able to do?
2. What does the student currently do?	Observed response [OR]	Describe by working with the student using dynamic assessment procedures.	*Communication processes model:* What strengths and weaknesses are evident in the student's current performance?
3. What might the student learn to do differently?	Mismatch: ER ←/→ OR	Establish instructional goals and benchmarks to target mismatch.	*Communication processes and needs models:* What abilities should be developed to better meet functional needs?
4. How should the curricular task or broader context be modified?	Bridge from OR → ER	Use scaffolding and task modifications, as necessary.	*Communication opportunities model:* Are systemic modifications needed to increase the student's opportunities to participate?

Note: OR = observed response
     ER = expected response

earlier, clinicians and other members of a child's educational team must focus on the general education curriculum when arranging contexts for learning and social interaction. For children with severe multiple disabilities, a curriculum-relevant approach may be as appropriate as a curriculum-based approach.

CBLAI approaches differ in several ways from earlier philosophies of special education that tended to focus on developmental level alone and emphasize the uniqueness of special education. One problem with teaching school-age children with disabilities using an entirely separate curriculum is that it may be guided by a low level of developmental expectation. Special educators and other specialists may target "baby steps," conveying little expectation for dramatic change, and provide few opportunities for children to learn the general education curriculum. The goal to get children ready for the curriculum while not actually engaging them in it (see Personal Reflection 12.4) is insufficient. While special-needs children are getting ready, general education students may be taking "giant steps" forward in learning.

If intervention is not designed to help students with disabilities meet the demands of the general education curriculum, they will likely fall further and further behind expected abilities for their chronological age group. The challenge is to design assessment and intervention activities using actual contexts of the general education curriculum and setting the goals of keeping students with disabilities as close as possible to their same-age peers and actively learning in the general education curriculum. Providing intentional and intensive scaffolding and other intervention will allow students to achieve those goals.

PERSONAL reflection *12.4*

"Life is not a dress rehearsal!"

Sarah Blackstone (1989, p. 1), editor of *Augmentative Communication News,* was commenting on the faulty assumptions of serving people with severe disabilities in segregated settings in order to get them "ready" to enter integrated settings later on.

Identifying Curricular Contexts for Assessment and Intervention

Interviewing prior to initiating CBLAI activities is designed to narrow the focus of the assessment to a manageable level. Ethnographic interviews and formal and informal questionnaires are used to identify and select school curricular contexts that students, teachers, and parents view as most problematic. By selecting areas of mutual concern, higher levels of joint ownership for remediation can be generated among participants. Mutual goal setting is the first step of collaborative problem solving that was introduced in Chapter 1.

In gathering ethnographic data, a selective focus on a particular student's individualized needs should be balanced with a broad view of the multiple curricula for which students are held responsible—some official and obvious, others less so (Nelson, 1989, 1998; Westby, 2006). Table 12.5 outlines six kinds of curricula, any of which might present difficulty for a student with language/literacy-learning difficulties and related conditions. This list starts with the official curriculum, which is established within district and state standards, but it also includes the so-called *underground curriculum,* involving the transmission of age-appropriate social expectations primarily through interactions with peers.

Following ethnographic principles, "The goal in interviewing is to have participants talk about things of interest to them and to cover matters of importance to [the clinician] in a way that allows participants to use their own concepts and terms" (Stainback & Stainback, 1988, p. 52). Table 12.6 suggests questions for use in ethnographic interviewing of school-age students, their parents, and teachers. As introduced in Chapter 1, structural questions

table *12.5* Summary of Six Curricula Students Must Master to Succeed in School

Official Curriculum	The outline produced by curriculum committees in many school districts. May or may not have major influence in a particular classroom.
Cultural Curriculum	The unspoken expectations for students to know enough about the mainstream culture to use it as background context in understanding various aspects of the official curriculum.
De Facto Curriculum	The use of textbook selections rather than an official outline to determine the curriculum. Classrooms in the same district often vary in the degree to which "teacher manual teaching" occurs.
School Culture Curriculum	The set of spoken and unspoken rules about communication and behavior in classroom interactions. Includes expectations for metapragmatic awareness of rules about such things as when to talk, when not to talk, and how to request a turn.
Hidden Curriculum	The subtle expectations that teachers have for determining who the "good students" are in their classrooms. They vary with the value systems of individual teachers. Even students who are insensitive to the rules of the school culture curriculum usually know where they fall on a classroom continuum of "good" and "problem" students.
Underground Curriculum	The rules for social interaction among peers that determine who will be accepted and who will not. Includes expectations for using the latest slang and pragmatic rules of social interaction discourse as diverse as bragging and peer tutoring.

Source: © 1992 N. W. Nelson. Shared by permission of the author.

table *12.6* Examples of Ethnographic Interviewing Questions Appropriate for Teachers, Parents, and School-Age Students

Teacher Interviews	Parent Interviews	Student Interviews
Objective information about the student's academic performance, both from achievement tests and classroom levels of performance.	Early development (Did they have any concerns early on?)	The student's description of what is hardest about school.
Descriptions of the student's classroom strengths.	Medical history (especially middle ear problems).	The student's description of what is easiest or best about school.
A prioritized review of the problems the teacher identifies as most important.	Educational history	The student's prioritized list of changes to be made.
Anecdotal descriptions of recent classroom events with which the student has experienced difficulty.	When did problems first show up at school? Did decoding problems show up early? Or did the problems show up in third or fourth grade when it became more important to read longer texts for meaning?	Anecdotal evidence—accounts of recent classroom events that made the student feel really bad or good.
Descriptions of aspects of the curriculum that present the greatest difficulties to the student and the most concern to the teacher.	Anecdotal evidence of specific problems within the past year or so.	The student's ideas about the future.
The teacher's view of the student's potential within the current school year and in the future.	A prioritized review of the problems the parents view as most critical. The parents' goals for their child's future.	

Source: © 1992 N. W. Nelson. Shared by permission of the author.

figure *12.5* —————————————————————————————————

Excerpt from an Ethnographic Interview with a Fourth-Grade Boy with LLD

Sample	Commentary
$ D'Angelo, Clinician + Grade: 4th + CA: 9;9	
C Tell me how school is going for you.	C [Begins with a grand tour descriptive question, which requires an expository response]
D School is boring.	D [Provides a label without elaboration]
C What about school is boring?	C [Asks a structural question using native language, again setting the context for expository discourse, but no response is forthcoming]
D [no response]	
C Are you bored with the assignments that are given? C Like, the types of things. C Are those boring?	C [Asks a series of <u>yes/no</u> questions (not usually the best approach); again, no response]
C What makes it boring?	C [Asks a mini-tour descriptive question]
D Sometimes it's boring. D Well, sometimes she gives out something. D I don't know.	D [Attempts an expository response but trails off into his standby "I don't know"]
C (Well, um) Let's think about today when you were in school. C Can you think of a time when you were bored today?	C [Asks two descriptive questions; first for experience, and then an example—the request for anecdotal discourse elicits a brief narrative]
D Yeah.	D [First, answers the literal <u>yes/no</u> question]
C Okay, tell me about it.	C [Provides descriptive prompt for narrative]
D We were doing math. D And I had no idea what to do. D So I was bored, I guess.	D [In this brief anecdote, D puts into words his concern about math and takes ownership for not knowing what to do as a cause for feeling bored. This sets the stage for curriculum-based language assessment and intervention]

Note: This excerpt illustrates how questions can be designed to elicit different styles of discourse and insight into problems and how to address them.

tend to elicit lists and labels, expressed with expository discourse; descriptive questions are more likely to elicit narrative anecdotes about a specific event in which the problem was evident. Both offer valuable insights into participants' views of the problem. They also describe a student's strengths as well as needs. Narrative anecdotes offer a particularly rich picture of specific problems and how informants feel about them. Figure 12.5 provides an illustration of how different types of questions elicit different types of discourse and insights.

Another example of how interviews inform CBLAI appears in Case Example 12.3. Matt's interviews were first introduced in Chapter 1 (Case Example 1.3) to illustrate principles of ethnographic interviewing. When Matt, his parent, and teacher were interviewed, "trouble on the playground" was on everyone's list. Similar to what happened in the interview with D'Angelo in Figure 12.5, it was only when Matt's clinician asked a descriptive experience question about a specific time when trouble arose on the playground that Matt provided the narrative about Desmond calling him names ("window-pane eyes" and "four eyes"). It

─CASE **example** *12.3*────────────────────────────────

Matt and How to Deal with Bullies

Matt was first introduced, along with the ethnographic interviewing process, in Chapter 1, Case Example 1.3. It was clear that Matt's most critical initial concern centered around his problems on the playground. It was not feasible to conduct a direct observation of the playground activities, but Matt was old enough and his spoken language skills were good enough that he could describe the nature of the problem.

During the interview, Matt had raised the issue of the playground problem and indicated that a peer, Desmond, had called him "four eyes" and "window-pane eyes." In addressing this concern, the clinician mentioned the conference with Matt's teacher, noting his teacher's positive comments about Matt as a person and his mentioning of the same problems with recess that Matt had reported. "This really seems to be a problem for you," the clinician commented. "Maybe we can work together to figure out something to do about it." In response, Matt fidgeted with his notebook and sucked his fingers.

Matt was asked to describe what he usually does—for example, what he did that day—when Desmond called him names. Matt said that he cried and reported the incident to the playground monitor, who in his eyes did nothing. Matt concluded that he wanted to go back to his previous school.

The clinician indicated that it sounded like Desmond was acting like a bully. She indicated that dealing with bullies could be a hard problem. She added that she was not sure what to do about bullies either but wished she did, because bullying is a problem for a lot of kids. The clinician did suggest that perhaps Matt might try an experiment using different ways to deal with Desmond's teasing. For example, Matt might try doing the opposite of what he usually does. Then the clinician helped Matt think about what that might look like. He said he usually cried and told someone. Then he decided that the opposite would be not crying and walking away. The session ended with everyone agreeing that this was a tough problem that might take some time to deal with.

The next session, when asked how the experiment had gone, Matt's immediate response was "Desmond and I are cool now!" Although Matt did not think he had done anything very different from before, he readily agreed to work with his clinician to create a "tool book" page on "How to Deal with Bullies." It appears in Figure 12.6.

──

was at that point that the clinician had a clearer understanding of the problem and some possible approaches for addressing it. Case Example 12.3 shows what was done and introduces the idea of the *experiment* as a useful technique in working with older students in pull-out sessions to address pragmatic communication difficulties that occur in other contexts.

Conducting ethnographic interviews taps into that part of the triad of EBP that represents *client and family values*. In Matt's case, Matt, his teacher, and mother all identified "rushing to finish his work" as a secondary concern (beyond the trouble during recess). Reading comprehension also was problematic and most central to Matt's language-learning disability, but it was not necessarily most important to target first.

Based on the interviews and initial assessment activities, the instructional team in Matt's case decided to target social difficulty on the playground first, while also helping Matt develop executive skills for reviewing his work critically and not rushing. These two goals would address immediate functional needs and the ownership principle because they were Matt's goals too. Figure 12.6 shows the "do the opposite" strategy sheet Matt developed (with clinician scaffolding) as a plan for dealing with bullies, although by then he was no longer being taunted by Desmond. Figure 12.7 shows how the information from CBLAI was used to scaffold Matt to construct a goal page for his "tool book," addressing goals for

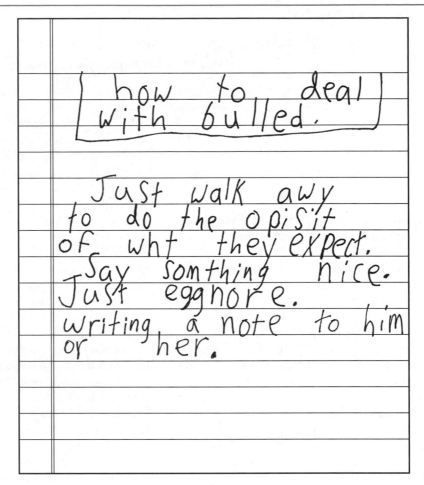

figure *12.6*

Matt's First "Tool Book" Page Describing His Plan for Dealing with the Playground Problem

not rushing through his work and finding books he liked to read. Matt's specific comprehension deficits and longer-term goals targeting reading and listening comprehension would be emphasized later.

A good summarizing question for any interview aimed at identifying CBLAI priorities is What one thing would you most like to change? It is quite different for a clinician to say "I gave you these tests and have decided that we should focus first on reading" than it is for a student to say "I don't like school, but I really hate reading." In the first scenario, the student may remain a passive participant in the intervention process; in the second, the student is more likely to take ownership and play an active role in fostering change as well. The clinician can say "It is awful to hate something that you need to do a lot, like reading. I can help you with reading. Will you work with me on that? Then you won't have to hate it any more."

It is particularly important to engage adolescents in the planning process. Tattershall (2002) offered a variety of interview tools to help adolescents pinpoint their areas of difficulty. Her *learning interview* starts with mini-tour questions asking the student to reflect on "What are usually your best subjects in school?" and "What are usually your hardest

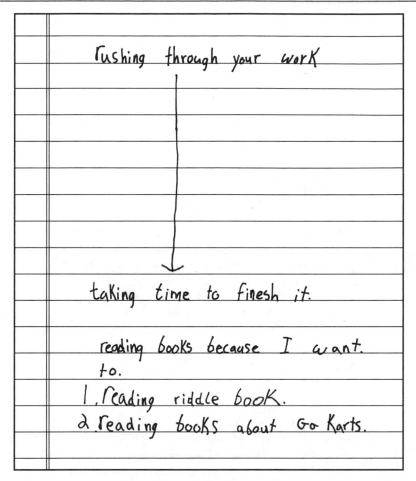

rushing through your work

↓

taking time to finesh it.

reading books because I want.
to.
1. reading riddle book.
2. reading books about Go Karts.

figure *12.7*

Matt's Second "Tool Book" Page Describing His Goals

subjects?" (p. 62). Tattershall also recommends asking directly "How often are you bored in class?" followed with the options "often," "sometimes," and "not very much" and with a further question "What do you do to pay better attention?" (p. 62). Questions such as these can help students see opportunities for gaining control over their own learning. Tattershall also asked students how often and in what circumstances they ask questions in class and what might make them not want to ask questions in class (e.g., embarrassment, not enough time, not paying attention). She also recommended asking students to describe a teacher who really helped them learn and what exactly the teacher did that was helpful, as well as a teacher whose way of teaching was not good for them—again, providing specific examples.

Westby (2006) recommended contextualizing student interviews by helping students reflect on the curricular products (*artifacts,* in the ethnographic framework) they completed in response to recent assignments. She recommended asking students to explain their understanding of what they needed to do to complete the assignment, what they were expected to learn, and what they should do if confused. She also suggested asking teachers how typical a student's performance was during an observed segment and whether instructional goals for that student differed from those of his or her classmates.

As shown in the Matt example, CBLAI may address the underground curriculum of social skills and the official curriculum of academic goals. The school-age years encompass a range of communication expectations and contexts. Although families exert the overriding influence in early childhood (ages 3 to 8), by middle childhood (ages 9 to 12), peers assume greater importance. Children spend increasing time in pursuits that do not directly involve their families. When children reach puberty, dramatic changes occur in their bodies, abilities, and attitudes (see Personal Reflection 12.5). Although families remain important, adolescents generally seek identities as unique, independent individuals. Ironically, most adolescents simultaneously yearn not to stand out from their peers in dress, action, music preferences, speech (e.g., social slang), and technocode skills, such as text messaging "R U OK?"

PERSONAL reflection *12.5*

"When the apostle Paul said, 'I put away childish things,' he reduced to five words a period of growth that psychologists and pediatricians eagerly study, parents anxiously anticipate, and children inevitably undergo. This is the period called adolescence. Although Paul's description is admirably succinct, it hardly does justice to the process that begins with the early subtle stirrings of the 10- or 11-year-old and does not end until mature independence is achieved in the mid-20s. The course of adolescence can be orderly and serene, or it can be turbulent and unpredictable. So can the experience of working with adolescents."

Harry E. Hartzell (1984, p. 1), a clinical professor of pediatrics at Stanford Medical School, was writing on the challenge of adolescence.

Interventions should target students' need for access to the underground curriculum, including what it takes to be "cool" (or "phat," or whatever term is currently in vogue). Although the underground curriculum is more likely to be conveyed through peers than teachers or clinicians, it may require deliberate arrangement of the environment and scaffolding of more able peers to facilitate learning. Children and adolescents may be more creative and resourceful than adults at arranging environments in the school lunchroom and athletic events to enhance communication opportunity and address participation goals. If parents and student agree, it may be appropriate to engage a peer culture informant to a special IEP meeting designed to focus on participation goals.

Contextual demands of academic language and literacy expectations evolve as well. The potential for mismatch between home and school language may widen as language expectations of academic curricular language increase during in the middle and secondary school years. Regarding students with cultural–linguistic differences, Iglesias (1985) commented:

> The problems children in higher grades encounter are more often attributed to low intellectual capacity and/or to a communication disorder. What teachers at this level often fail to realize is that the communicative demands of their classrooms are different from those of earlier grades, and that many of these children have not been taught, either at home or in their previous classes, the particular skills required for success in the higher grades. (p. 37)

Risks of disproportionate overidentification and underidentification of children in diverse cultural–linguistic groups persist. It is critical to select and apply assessment tools and procedures to yield accurate information about special needs, but clinicians must avoid equating racial or ethnic difference with language difference. Race and language are not isomorphic (i.e., not in a 1:1 relationship). For example, many African Americans do not use dialectal forms of African American English (AAE), and some White Americans use AAE forms extensively. Numerous other dialects are used throughout the United States. Loban (1976) conducted a longitudinal study of language development of school-age children from kindergarten through grade twelve. His analysis showed that is was lower socioeconomic status—not race or ethnicity—that correlated most directly with lower school success (see Personal Reflection 12.6).

PERSONAL reflection *12.6*

"Minority students who come from securely affluent home backgrounds did not show up in the low proficiency groups. The problem is poverty, not ethnic affiliation."

Walter Loban (1976, p. 23), a sociolinguist, was describing the results of an early longitudinal study of the language of school-age students.

The mismatch between experience and curricular language may account for academic difficulties of many students with disabilities, regardless of whether cultural–linguistic differences are involved. Rapid increases in the need to comprehend complex and abstract language are problematic, and "the intensity of the current high school curriculum often overwhelms the adolescent with learning disabilities who cannot read textbooks and has poor writing skills" (Trapani, 1990, p. x). Students with disabilities need explicit intervention to prepare them for the language and literacy demands of school. They may need extra time to complete assignments, accompanied by goals to keep them academically competitive with peers and scaffolding aimed at increased independence.

Applying the Four Questions of CBLAI

After input is gathered from parents, teachers, and students using ethnographic interviewing techniques (see Chapter 1), information from multiple sources is integrated to isolate a specific aspect of the curriculum for focus. At this point, the four questions of CBLAI are used to guide recursive assessment and intervention processes. The "pinball wizardry" model, which was introduced in Chapter 3, can be used to organize an effort to understand the cognitive linguistic demands of the task, gaps between the expected and observed demands of the task, and areas to target in intervention.

Figure 12.8 shows the data produced for fifth-grader Samantha when her clinician used the pinball wizardry model to analyze responses gathered using the four questions of CBLAI. Case Example 12.4 describes how the information was used in providing assessment and intervention services for Samantha.

The first CBLAI question asks about the ***expected response (ER)*** demanded by the task. A clinician can assume the perspective of the student, attempting the curricular task and reflecting on skills needed to complete it successfully. Ukrainetz (1998a, 2006a) also described an analysis framework for understanding the nature of curricular tasks, which she called ***activity analysis*** (based on post-Vygotskyan *activity theory*). Activity analysis involves consideration of five components:

- ***Motive*** is the basic underlying force that students must activate to be willing to attempt academic activities of any type.
- ***Goal*** is the purpose of the activity, which is usually established by the teacher, but not necessarily explicitly, and must be detected and assimilated by the student.

figure *12.8*

Samantha's Responses to Curriculum-Based Language Assessment Tasks

---

Excerpt from "A Voyage that Changed History," Read Aloud by Clinician

Have you ever read a book over and over again? About 500 years ago, Christopher Columbus did. The book told of faraway countries where people dressed in brightly colored silks. It described a beautiful gold palace. The book had been written by an Italian named Marco Polo in 1298, more than 150 years before Columbus was born. It described the 17 years Marco Polo spent in India, China, and Japan. Columbus hoped one day to see those Asian countries for himself. In the 1400s, however, the trip to Asia was as long and difficult as it had been in Marco Polo's day. The only routes Columbus knew crossed huge deserts and tall mountains. Still, Columbus felt sure there was a faster, shorter way to Asia. He planned to find it.

Transcript of Samantha's Oral Retelling	**Transcript of Samantha's Written Retelling**
$ Samantha	$ Samantha
+ Grade: 5th	+ Grade: 5th
+ CA: 11;3	+ CA: 11;3
+ Oral retelling	+ Written retelling
S Columbus, he um.	S Columbus [Clumbus] sail/ed to Asia [Aisa] with [whith] Marco Polo [Marko Polo] I think in the 1800 hundred/s [hunderes] for 100 and some then 1 day/s they stay/*ed in India [Indan].
S Columbus was sail/ing Marco Polo to Asia.	
S And he was try/ing to find a different route / to Asia and >	
S A hundred year/s they spent.	
S A hundred something year/s they spent in India or something>	S Columbus [Clumbus] found a different [diffent] route [rout] to Asia [Aisa] than [then] the other one [won] he had.
S Somewhere around there.	
S And um>	S Columbus [Clumbus] was look/ing for gold [Gold] and other thing/s.
S Can't remember.	

Notes for Responding to the Four CBLAI Questions with Reference to the "Pinball Wizardry" Model

1. **What does the task require?**
   - Receptive language task requires information processing and memory: attending, listening, deciding to remember, comprehending the narrative gist (complex temporal, motivational, and causal relationships, with a planned attempt, but no outcome), relating it to prior world knowledge, comprehending sentences with use of cohesive devices that connect them, perceiving spoken words, recognizing known vocabulary, inferring probable meaning for any new vocabulary, and constructing a mental model of places, people, events, and things that semantic/syntactic/discourse symbols represent.
   - Spoken retell task requires reformulation based on prior world knowledge and comprehension at the discourse, sentence, and word levels; memory for factual details and vocabulary; a mental plan for organizing the discourse; syntactic formulation of paraphrases that accurately represent the original meaning; retrieval of vocabulary for conveying the meaning, and articulating it clearly enough to be understood.
   - Written retell task requires the same, with the addition of being able to transcribe spoken words into their written (spelled) forms and to write them on the page.

2. **What does the student currently do?**
   - Starting with strengths, in both samples, S has used the main characters' names and has maintained the gist of the quest to find a different route to Asia. In the written sample, she added the detail about looking for gold.
   - It is apparent that S has not fully comprehended some of the complex syntax and did not use all syntactic cues, such as past-perfect tense (e.g., "had been written") and relative clauses (e.g., "more than 150 years before Columbus was born"), to reconstruct narrative temporal relationships in comprehending the text.
   - Expressively, S had difficulty organizing her discourse and formulating sentences (perhaps reflecting memory, retrieval, and processing difficulties), including case grammar confusions (Columbus sailing with Marco Polo to Asia) that reflected her comprehension difficulties. Her written sentences were more

complete but still awkwardly constructed. They had a knowledge-telling oral expression quality typical of younger children. Her spelling showed correct function word use but reflected incomplete representation of syllables that appeared in her speech as well (e.g., *Clumbus, diffent*).

3. **What might the student learn to do differently?**
   - S has difficulties at all three levels (discourse, sentence, word), but her functional limitations in comprehending complex discourse interfered the most and was the symptom that caused her teacher to refer her for evaluation. She needs to detect the discourse organization of texts so she can reconstruct them mentally as she comprehends relationships among key characters and events, developing a spatial and temporal mental model using a graphic organizer or timeline.
   - At the sentence level, S needs to construct fully formed sentences to represent complex relationships and to paraphrase sentences she hears or reads to represent complex relationships. She has strengths with bound morpheme use.
   - As comprehension and sentence formulation improve, S could focus on word- and syllable-level analysis and orthographic pattern representation in her spelling and speech.
   - Although S shows metacognitive and self-regulation strengths in her willingness to attempt complex tasks, she needs strategies for online processing, working memory, retrieval of key pieces of information, and recognizing when she has not understood.

4. **How should the task be modified or scaffolded?**
   - Dynamic assessment should be designed to probe ability to make use of syntactic and discourse cohesion cues.
   - Breaking text into shorter chunks, conducting intermittent comprehension checks, and then scaffolding S to do this herself may help.
   - Using graphic representations (semantic webs, outlines, timelines) may help S learn to analyze discourse-level structures and will help the clinician pinpoint areas of breakdown and potential deficits in basic relational vocabulary.

- *Conditions* are the features of the activity, which may be both facilitating and constraining, such as the complexity of textbook or teacher language and cues to macrostructural organization that might be detected by the student.
- *Actions* are the conscious behaviors or strategies that students must utilize to perform the task.
- *Operations* are the unconscious (pre-established) processes or skills that usually occur at an automatic level and underlie the student's ability to attempt new learning.

The second question asks about student's strengths and needs when attempting the task. It is called the ***observed response (OR).*** Observational data can be gathered through using ***onlooker observation*** techniques in actual classroom contexts, such as watching and taking notes while a student attempts to follow the teacher's directions in class. ***Participant observation*** techniques also may be used by working with the student in the classroom or by bringing a piece of the curriculum (textbook or completed assignment) out of the classroom. The clinician then works side by side with the student, collaborating to figure out the demands of the task and how the student is currently approaching it. The activity analysis framework also guides observation of a student's OR in terms of motivation, goal orientation, actions, and operations relative to the particular set of conditions associated with the curricular task.

This leads to the third question, which asks about gaps between the ER and OR. Information about missed cues (*action limitations*) and inadequate language knowledge of a particular type (*operations limitations*) can inform intervention and scaffolding to support construction of new cognitive–linguistic connections to bridge the gaps. Problems with motivation or goal orientation may be identified by asking the student to reflect on the task, its goal, and how he or she approached it.

—CASE **example** *12.4*—

Samantha's Retelling of "A Voyage that Changed History"

Samantha was a fifth-grade girl whose teacher had noted that she was falling behind in the curriculum, even though she was trying hard to keep up. Sam's teacher reported that the most pressing concern was her difficulty comprehending and remembering curricular concepts, in spite of working hard and seeming smart about other things. Sam also was having some difficulty with reading decoding, spelling, and pronouncing complex, multisyllabic words. Based on these concerns, Samantha's SLP decided to assess Sam's listening comprehension for written text without the confounding influence of possible reading decoding difficulties. Figure 12.8 shows the excerpt from the fifth-grade social studies text that the clinician read aloud, along with transcripts for spoken and written retelling samples that provided a window into Sam's comprehension processes.

The remainder of the table shows how the data were analyzed in relationship to the four questions of CBLAI. By first attempting the task herself, the clinician reflected on its complex demands. She then referred to the parallel-processing components of the "pinball wizardry" model to outline the demands of the task and Sam's approach to it. This addressed the first two assessment-focused CBLAI questions. The clinician then used the last two intervention-focused CBLAI questions to conceptualize approaches for targeting and scaffolding change in response to the first two questions. The clinician and Sam's teacher took an additional collaborative step in answering the fourth question by placing Sam's retold and rewritten versions of the text next to the original text. Looking at the data together, the clinician and teacher shared their hypotheses about what language systems Sam was using with more or less competence and discussed how they might work on the problem together.

They decided that the clinician would conduct further dynamic assessment and scaffolding using classroom materials in individual pull-out sessions, and the teacher would find a few minutes each day to read a paragraph and do a comprehension check or have Sam paraphrase what she read or heard read aloud in writing. The paraphrasing method worked so well that the teacher decided to have her whole class work in cooperative learning pairs to paraphrase what they read orally or in writing and then comparing notes to see how closely their own words agreed with each other and the original passage.

As the year progressed, students became aware that there could be more than one interpretation of the deeper meaning of a text. They used their new skills at note taking in writing reports on topics they had selected. Sam moved to higher levels of independent processing and memory for the language of the school curriculum, and the clinician was able to spend time in the classroom with Sam on both note taking and on her word-level difficulties as Sam worked on her report.

The fourth question asks whether a problematic task or broader system should be modified or scaffolded in some way. This question focuses on the *conditions* aspect of activity analysis and requires collaboration with others in the broader systems of the student's world. For example, if a teacher has indicated that following directions in the classroom is the greatest area of concern for a particular student, the clinician can sit down with the teacher after an onlooker observation session in the classroom and review the data from an observational session to decide what to do next.

Assessing Samples of Reading and Written Language

As children move through the school-age years, they move from learning to read and write to using reading and writing to learn. Children with LI may show varied patterns of difficulty that are consistent with their relative strengths and needs in the phonological sound/word aspects or nonphonological sentence/discourse aspects of language. Language assessment and intervention can be designed to focus on any of the component skills a student needs to learn to read, write, and communicate through spoken language in the grades K–12.

It is through samples of a student's actual reading and writing that clinicians can gain the most comprehensive picture of students' pinball wizardry skills for pulling together integrated knowledge of language and orthography to perform authentic academic tasks. Observation worksheets and other summary forms for analyzing read aloud samples and samples of students' writing were described by Nelson and Van Meter (2002) and available online (www.wmich.edu/hhs/sppa, then select Special Projects; Writing Lab Outreach Project). Nelson, Bahr, and Van Meter (2004) provided additional detail regarding assessment and intervention for students' written language production.

Gathering Reading Samples

To gather evidence of a child's decoding and comprehension abilities, it is necessary to observe him or her reading aloud. This can be done by selecting a short passage from one of the student's textbooks (e.g., science or social studies) or a narrative text (e.g., language arts text or library book). The material should be new to the child (to avoid memorized responses) and sufficiently above his or her current comfort level to allow observation of miscues and any strategies the child may be using currently to decode difficult text. The length of the sample may vary widely with the ability of the child and the time allotted. For younger children, two to three pages are generally sufficient. For older children, two to three paragraphs may be sufficient.

The clinician should read the selected passage first to be sure there is enough coherent information in the short passage to probe the child's comprehension. If the student has significant decoding difficulties or shows distress, the clinician can read part of the text aloud to him or her and probe comprehension separately for the part the child read independently and the part that was read by the clinician. It should be possible to gather an appropriate sample of the child's reading decoding and comprehension in 10 to 15 minutes. The sample should be audiorecorded to provide an accurate record of the child's responses for transcription of both the decoding and comprehension portions of the sample.

Marking Reading Samples to Reflect Decoding

Assessment of the student's reading decoding abilities is done in three steps. First, a printout (or photocopy) is marked to allow comparison between what the student said (OR, or observed response) and what the text said (ER, or expected response) (Figure 12.9 shows coding techniques). Second, miscues are numbered and analyzed to create a tally of the degree to which they match (indicated with +, –, or ~) language cues in three domains—*meaning, syntax,* and *graphophonemic (M, S, GP).* Third, data from the miscue analysis are used to complete relevant sections of the reading assessment worksheet and to compute the percentage of words read correctly and fluently. The goal in analyzing decoding miscues is to figure out the student's current and potential ability to integrate knowledge of graphophonemic relationships with knowledge of language meaning and syntax for decoding words in context.

For example, one student read the sentence *Harold taught Lizzie how to do cat's cradle* as *Harold choose, choose[1] Lizzie how to be, how to do[2], cat's crible[3].* The superscript numbers show that the student's reading of this sentence included three miscues. The first miscue is coded with a minus sign (–) in all three columns, M, S, and GP, because *choose* changes the meaning, is not syntactically acceptable, and bears no graphophonemic resemblance to the target word *taught.* The second miscue is coded with a plus sign (+) in all three

Omissions	(circled)	He made ⓐ kite...
Substitutions		
1. Text item substitutions		Her She didn't want him to be sad.
2. Involving reversals		said "Why?" asked ⌐Jane.⌐
3. Involving bound morphemes		ing ...and make kiteⓈ
4. Involving nonwords		Kansas　　　　/kɔɛnd/　/kɑkoni/ A city is a special kind of community.
5. Misarticulations		$specific He had a specific thing in mind.
6. Intonation shifts		récord He will record her voice.
7. Split syllables		You should try cut|ting hair.
8. Pauses		⌐15 sec. Cities are/crowded.
Insertions　(indicate with a ∧)		her Jane wanted to help∧Grandfather.
Repetitions and **corrections**		‖One day, Grandfather was sad. likeⓓ
Dialect and other language variations		...just about everybody likes babies.
Assistance from the examiner		Kansas There are four special things about a[city.]

figure *12.9*

Codes for Marking Miscues on Oral Reading Transcripts

Coding conventions: Underline omitted words and write substituted words above them; use a caret to insert an added word; circle words or morphemes that are omitted entirely; note potential dialectal influences with a superscript *d*; use editing marks for transpositions; mark text that is repeated (circled *r*) or corrected (circled *c*) with a tail to indicate amount of text involved; write nonwords using traditional orthography.

Source: K. S. Goodman, 1973; Y. M. Goodman et al., 1987. © 1992 N. W. Nelson. Reprinted by permission of the author.

columns because it was self-corrected. The third miscue is coded with a minus sign (–) in the first two columns because it is an uncorrected nonword, but it is coded with a tilde (~) in the GP column because it bears partial similarity to the target word *cradle*.

This tiny sample (taken from a more complete sample in Nelson & Van Meter, 2002) indicates that reading decoding is an area of possible concern for this student. Because the remainder of the sample and other input supported this initial hypothesis, further probing and dynamic assessment were conducted to look more closely at the student's knowledge of phoneme–grapheme and morpheme–orthographic pattern associations. Strategies for using meaning and sentence structure to aid in decoding and checking for sense making also were targeted in intervention.

Gathering and Analyzing Reading Comprehension Samples

Reading comprehension can be assessed with a variety of techniques, depending on the student's age, ability, and willingness to cooperate. Retelling is a good first step, as illustrated for Samantha, who retold a segment from her social studies book (see Figure 12.8). The clinician can follow the retelling with probe questions, asking about both literal and inferential meanings. It is helpful to transcribe comprehension retelling samples and responses to questions as further evidence of the student's ability to communicate in spoken language as well as to comprehend written language. If difficulties in either decoding or comprehension are prominent, the clinician might read a subsequent passage aloud to the student to assess whether listening comprehension is better than reading comprehension (as in the profile for dyslexia). If the child has difficulty retelling the story or has misrepresented relationships from the original text, as occurred in the example shown in Figure 12.8, the clinician might probe using dynamic assessment questions and framing cues, such as pronouns and other cohesive devices (e.g., "Where it says 'those Asian countries,' what does that mean?") and asking the student to identify anaphoric (previous) or cataphoric (upcoming) referents.

Gathering Writing Samples

A variety of techniques can be used to gather samples of students' written language, but original stories offer particularly rich glimpses into students' social–cognitive skills and language. Students in third grade or higher can usually write cohesive original stories in 45 to 50 minutes (with an additional 10 to 15 minutes for instruction and planning). Younger children (or less able children) may not be able to sustain writing for such a long period.

Following is a version of instructions that have been used for gathering written story probes with students in the writing lab approach, generally at three points across the school-year (Nelson et al., 2004; Nelson & Van Meter, 2002):

> We are interested in the stories that children/students write. You probably know something about stories. Stories tell about a problem and what happened. A problem doesn't have to be something bad your character did. It can be any kind of problem your character has to face. The characters and problem in your story can be real or imaginary. When you are done with your story, we will have you read it to one of your teachers.

Students are given a plain piece of paper to make a plan for their story. They are given about five minutes to think about their ideas and to make any kind of plan they want. Then, the instructors give each student a sheet of lined paper. Students are reminded that this is just a rough draft and that it is okay to cross out and make changes. They are asked to make changes by crossing out parts they do not want with one line and using arrows to add new information. Students are reminded that is how real authors work on rough drafts, and it will help the teachers to know how students think while they write.

Students who stop writing prematurely can be reminded that there is more time to reread and add more details to make the story better. When a student has clearly finished writing, he or she is asked to read the story aloud. Low-functioning children might read back (i.e., tell) a different story than they wrote, so it is helpful to make an audiorecording of the sample or make a separate online transcript of the dictated story. During drafting, students are encouraged to spell the best they can without help. If a student exhibits distress about not knowing how to spell a particular word, it can be scaffolded as a form of dynamic assessment. Students can be reminded that this is a draft and that the clinician can help them later with dictionary spellings.

Transcribing and Coding Writing Samples

A distinct advantage of gathering written story samples (compared with spoken ones) is that they are already transcribed. Original stories can be photocopied for coding (keeping the original clean for the student's portfolio), or samples can be transcribed for analysis with a program such as SALT (Miller & Chapman, 2008), so the clinician can reflect on them with the student.

Stories are divided into *T*-units for analysis. (Refer to Chapter 2, if necessary, for information about *T*-units.) Sentences are coded as being either **simple,** if they consist of a single *T*-unit with only one verb phrase, or **complex,** if a single *T*-unit incorporates more than one verb phrase, through embedding or subordination or two independent clauses are combined with one of the coordinating conjunctions (*and, but, or, so*). Sentences are further coded as being either incorrect or correct depending on whether any morphosyntactic forms are used that are inconsistent with standard edited English. This yields four sentence codes: simple incorrect [SI], simple correct [SC], complex incorrect [CI], and complex correct [CC]. The run-on [ro] code is used when a third independent clause is coordinated with two others. A third coordinated *T*-unit is treated as a new sentence and coded as [SI] or [SC], or

table 12.7   Mean Word per *T*-unit Levels from Multiple Studies

Grade Level	Spoken	Written
3	7.62[a] 8.73[b] 9.5[i] (narr) 10.5[i] (exp)	7.60[a] 7.67[b] 7.45[g] 9.3[i](narr) 9.9[i](exp)
4	9.00[a] 8.52[d]	8.02[a] 8.60[e] 5.21[f]
5	8.82[a] 8.90[b]	8.76[a] 9.34[b] 8.81[g] 10.7[h](male) 11.4[h](fem)
6	9.82[a] 9.03[c] 8.10[d] 10.03[i](narr) 11.4[i](exp) LLD 9.1[i](narr) 9.7[i](exp)	9.04[a] 7.32[f] 8.53[g] 10.4[i](narr) 12.1[i](exp) LLD 8.9[i](narr) 8.9[i](exp)
7	9.72[a] 9.80[b]	8.98[a] 9.99[b]
8	10.71[a]	10.37[a] 11.50[e] 10.34[f] 11.68[g]
9	10.96[a]	10.05[a]
10	10.68[a] 10.15[c]	11.79[a] 10.46[f]
11	11.17[a]	10.67[a]
12	11.70[a]	13.27[a] 14.40[e] 11.45[f]

[a]Loban, 1976. $N = 35$ at each grade. Data were also provided for high and low ability groups. Spoken: adult–child informal interview; Written: school compositions.
[b]O'Donnell et al., 1967. $N = 30$ at each grade. Spoken and written retelling/rewriting of silent fable (narrative).
[c]Klecan-Acker & Hedrick, 1985. $N = 24$ at each grade. Retelling of a favorite film (narrative).
[d]Scott, 1984. $N = 25$ 10-year-olds, $N = 29$ 12-year-olds. Retelling of a favorite book, TV episode, film (narrative).
[e]Hunt, 1965. $N = 18$ at each grade. School compositions.
[f]Hunt, 1970. $N = 50$ at each grade. Sentence combining exercise.
[g]Morris & Crump, 1982. $N = 18$ at each age (9.6, 11.25, 12.54, 14.08 years). Rewriting of silent film (narrative).
[h]Richardson et al., 1976. $N = 257$ 11-year-old boys, $N = 264$ 11-year-old girls. School compositions.
[i]Scott & Windsor, 2000. $N = 20$ students in each of three matched groups; 20 students with LLDs (mean age 11;5), 20 CA matched peers (mean age 11;6 years), and 20 LA matched peers (mean age 8;11).

Note: The scores listed above represent the mean scores for mean length of *T*-unit measures for spoken and written discourse from a variety of studies with differing sampling conditions. The studies labeled "d, f, g," and "i" reported data for age only. The data from these studies were entered in the table using the formula: grade = age (rounded) − 6 years.

Source: Adapted and expanded from Scott, 1988a, including additions from more recent studies.

it may be coded as complex if coordinated with an additional *T*-unit that follows. A number of studies have provided normative data on mean length of *T*-units (MLTU) for comparative purposes. These are summarized in Table 12.7.

Figure 12.10 provides an illustration of coding conventions using a story probe gathered for a third-grade boy with a history of speech sound disorder (SSD) and ongoing difficulties with language and literacy learning. The narrative in this sample was evaluated as an *abbreviated episode* (see Chapter 13), because it incorporated planning by the main character, the events of the story were only loosely connected, and the story did not have an ending that clearly resolved the main issue. Data from SALT showed that the story included 64 main body words (NDW = 32) in 9 *T*-units, yielding an MLTU of 7.11 (in words). The tally of word-level codes showed that 11 of the 64 words (17 percent) were misspelled, a high proportion that reflects this student's difficulty with the phonological level of language. Additionally, two obligatory morphemes were omitted (the copula *was* and the superlative morpheme *fast*/*est*). A sentence code summary showed 0 [SI], 3 [SC], 1 [CI], and 2 [CC] sentences. Overuse of sentence coordination with *and* (four times) and *but* (two times) led to three codes of run-on [ro]. Data from research (Nelson & Van Meter, 2007) has shown run-on sentences to be a prominent feature among typically developing second-grade students, but their use diminishes by third grade.

Integrating Findings from Reading and Writing Samples

Integrated analysis of probe data is different from listing every detail that can be quantified. Reading and writing sample worksheets and summary and goal sheets (Nelson & Van Meter, 2002) can be used to summarize the data for planning intervention and monitoring progress. Patterns can be described in terms of strengths and needs at language levels that cross modalities and discourse contexts.

figure *12.10*

Coded Transcript of a Written Language Sample for a Student with Language-Learning Disability (LLD)

```
$   CHILD, EXAMINER
+   Name: Carter
+   Gender: M
+   CA: 9;3
+   Race/ethnicity: Caucasian
+   {The dritbicke race} [t]

C   One there {ther} [sp] was a boy name/d David
C   and he had 20 trophy/s {trofes} [sp] [cc].
C   [ro] And he want[v] to be a millionaire {millnyer} [sp].
C   but {bet} [sp] he had to wait {what} [sp] until {untl} [sp] he was a grown {gron}
    [sp] up [cc].
C   [ro] And he was a great {grat} [sp] rider.
C   but he *was last {las} [sp] to {till} [sp] the next {nast} [sp] race he win [v] [ci].
C   [ro] and he was the fast/*est rider on the team [sc].
C   Then he was a grown {gown} up [sc].
C   He was {ws} [sp] a millionaire {millnyer} [sc].
C   {the End}.
```

Sound-/word-level symptoms, for example, may include difficulty remembering complex word forms when listening, pronouncing them when speaking, decoding them when reading, and spelling them when writing. Intervention that aims at building increased fluency for associating sounds and symbols (and syllables and orthographic patterns) across modalities can have benefits that reach further than focusing on specific areas in isolation for such students. Students with sound-/word-level difficulties also might receive scaffolding to associate morphemes with print, such as the *-ed* endings on verbs, or to say words in syllables before attempting to spell them so they can hear and feel all the sounds in sequence before attempting to represent them in spelling.

Sentence-/discourse-level symptoms may include difficulty comprehending complex syntax when listening or reading and difficulty organizing discourse and formulating complex sentences when talking or writing. As students participate in curriculum-based interventions, such as report writing, with opportunities for scaffolded reading and notetaking (paraphrasing passages), students with sentence-/discourse-level needs can be scaffolded to acquire higher-level syntactic abilities.

SUMMARY

Comprehensive assessment for school-age students may be designed for varied purposes—differential diagnosis, designing intervention, and measuring progress. Formal and informal tools may be used for all of these purposes. However, formal tests are better suited to diagnostic purposes, and informal assessment procedures are better suited to informing intervention and documenting change. Curriculum-based language assessment and intervention activities are appropriate for meeting the integrated language, literacy, and communication needs of school-age students with a variety of disabilities. Analyzing reading and writing samples offers particularly rich opportunities for understanding how a student's language abilities affect learning and literacy across modalities.

CHAPTER SUMMARY

School-age students with special needs are a heterogeneous group. Some can almost but not quite keep up with their peers in the general education curriculum, and some need extensive special education, related services, and accommodations. All students should be educated in the LRE, which is determined individually for each student by his or her IEP team. IEP teams should include the student whenever appropriate but *must* involve the student when developing the IEP that will be in effect when he or she turns 16. At that point, postsecondary goals and transition services become required components of the IEP as well.

This chapter has addressed formal evaluation for the purpose of diagnosis and for determining eligibility, as well as informal assessment procedures for designing intervention and documenting progress. The procedures of CBLAI were discussed as a special case of contextually based assessment and intervention, adapting the four questions for asking what the curricular context requires, what the student currently does when attempting the curricular activity, what the student might learn to do differently to perform better in the future, and how the context and other external systems should be modified to support better functioning and participation. Methods were described for collecting and analyzing samples of integrated discourse with reference to the language-levels-by-modalities model of spoken and written language disorders.

EXERCISES *and* STUDY QUESTIONS

1. List six kinds of curricula, and provide an example from your own experience that would illustrate the processing demands of each.

2. Select a specific curriculum-based task, and use some actual curriculum materials to construct a rich description of what a student of that age/grade level would need to "bring online" (using the pinball wizardry metaphor) to complete the task successfully.

3. Apply the four questions of CBLAI with a student with special needs by gathering reading and writing samples in an area of concern. Then use the pinball wizardry model to analyze the results and plan intervention.

CHAPTER thirteen

School-Age Intervention

LEARNING *objectives*

After studying this chapter, you should be able to do the following:

1. Describe procedures to address discourse-level goals to improve academic and social interaction conversational discourse, narration, exposition, and executive functions and self-regulation.

2. Describe procedures to address sentence-level goals to improve higher-level syntax production and comprehension and cohesive devices.

3. Describe procedures to address word-level goals to improve word knowledge required for reading decoding and spelling and vocabulary.

The school-age years are filled with expectations for higher-level uses of language in both spoken and written modalities. Decelerating growth curves mean that change occurs more gradually as age advances. Thus, developmental advances are grouped into larger age chunks within the upper ranges of the developmental charts in Tables A and B of the Part III Appendix. Communicative demands also vary within the social and academic contexts in which school-age children and adolescents participate. Intervention goals and methods for school-age students are organized in this chapter based on language level. Discourse-level abilities are discussed first, followed by sections discussing sentence-level and word-level abilities.

Discourse-Level Knowledge and Skills

By the time children reach school age, most are capable of functioning in diverse social situations and discourse events, although they still may be relatively dependent on nonverbal context to support language comprehension and use. As children gain literate language competence, they rely less on nonverbal context and more on language to convey or comprehend meaning. This process is known as *decontextualization* or *lexicalization* (see Table 13.1). Decontextualization becomes marked when children have to learn to communicate in the less familiar contexts of school. It continues when students can learn about unfamiliar topics and abstract concepts through language alone, with few contextual supports. Four discourse genres are addressed in this section—academic, social interaction, narration, and exposition.

Academic Discourse

Students need awareness and competence for engaging in the formal conversations of classrooms. Many formal classroom interactions involve typical sequences of initiate/inquire-respond-evaluate (I-R-E; Cazden, 1988) or initiate-respond-feedback (I-R-F; Mehan, 1979). Figure 13.1 provides a sample of discourse following this pattern. Students rarely receive

table *13.1* Terminology for the Continuum of Contextualization Differences between Home and School Language and between Less Literate and More Literature Language

Meaning in Context	Meaning in Words
Basic interpersonal communication skills (BICS)[a]	Cognitive academic language proficiency (CALP)[a]
Situated meaning[b]	Lexicalized meaning[b]
Exophoric meaning[c]	Endophoric meaning[c]
Particularistic (implicit) meaning[d]	Universalistic (explicit) meaning[d]
Typical of language at home[e]	Typical of language at school[e]

Source: [a]Cummins, 1992; [b]Cook-Gumperz, 1977; [c]Gregory & Carroll, 1978; [d]Bernstein, 1972; [e]Wells, 1986.

explicit instruction in how to interpret the conventions of academic discourse, and they may miss cues embedded by teachers in the discourse, such as those illustrated in Figure 13.1. Thus, intervention may need to target classroom discourse explicitly.

Research on formal classroom discourse has shown that students must be prepared to listen more than talk and to answer questions succinctly in classroom discussions (Sturm & Nelson, 1997; Westby, 2006). Because the school culture curriculum is conveyed through implicit rather than explicit means, it is sometimes called *hidden*. A distinction is made in this book, however, between the school culture curriculum, which Westby (2006) called "learning to do school," and the hidden curriculum, which is the subtle expectations about particular teachers' attitudes and values about what makes a good student (Nelson, 1989).

Violations of classroom communication, attention, and behavioral expectations can arise from multiple causes, including neurobiological difficulties with attention and impulse control, as well as from misunderstanding the language of instruction and culture of the classroom. Thus, an interdisciplinary approach to intervention is necessary. Classroom communication assessment begins with application of curriculum-based language assessment and intervention (CBLAI) procedures to gauge the student's awareness of the demands of the school culture curriculum and how to function within it. Intervention may require direct attention to the inner discourse of self-regulation (addressed in a later section) and understanding the outer expectations of classroom discourse.

Assessing Classroom Discourse Knowledge and Skill

Once classroom interaction is identified as an area of concern by a student, parent, and teacher, the clinician should conduct a preliminary analysis of the school culture curriculum at the student's grade level. Both common and unusual factors should be identified, such as linguistic **registers** (i.e., special-use vocabulary and phrasing) that are unique to a particular school or system. One school, for example, adopted a schoolwide system for referring to

figure *13.1*

Example of Teacher (T)–Student (S) Discourse Recorded in a First-Grade Classroom

Classroom Discourse Sample	Commentary
$ Teacher, Student + First-grade classroom	
T What sound does /cat/ begin with?	T inquires, starting the I-R-E exchange.
S "C."	S responds briefly with letter name.
T No, that's not what I asked.	T evaluates.
T I asked what sound.	T inquires, framing the missed cue.
S /k/.	S responds in the specified category.
T Good.	T evaluates.
T We have two letters that make a /k/ sound: k and c make that same sound.	T conveys content [CC].
T How do you know that /cat/ does not begin with a k?	T inquires about metacognitive component.
T Because I didn't put a k on the paper, so you know it has to begin with a c.	T conveys procedure [CP] with explicit cues about the school culture curriculum.
T Use your sounds and figure out the other words.	T requests action and conveys procedure [CP].

A behavior as negative traits of *anarchy* and *D* behavior as positive traits of *democracy.* This attempt to blend social studies content with classroom behavior management was admirable on one level but confusing to anyone who had problems with abstraction or different concepts of *A*-level and *D*-level abilities. Special scaffolding was required both for clinicians and students.

The second question of CBLAI asks about a student's current level of performance in the context. The student's explicit knowledge of the school culture curriculum (i.e., metapragmatic awareness) can be assessed by asking him or her to describe and explain communicative expectations of the classroom. Silliman (1987) contrasted ***declarative knowledge*** for knowing about things such as classroom rules from ***procedural knowledge*** for knowing how to do things, such as how to comply with those rules. Interviews with students should probe into their declarative knowledge of the conventions of classroom discourse and what it takes to be a good student in a particular teacher's eyes. Observation is needed to gauge procedural knowledge.

Figure 13.2 includes questions that can be used to interview students about classroom discourse, nonverbal communication, and classroom routines. To probe students' grasp of the hidden curriculum, for example, they might be asked what makes a particular teacher happy or unhappy and how the teacher responds and conveys such feelings in certain circumstances.

Targeting Awareness of and Participation in Classroom Discourse

Goal 13.1. The student will show awareness of classroom discourse by describing classroom rules and demonstrate appropriate classroom communication skills through observation and teacher report. After conducting an inventory of what a student knows and does not know, can do and cannot yet do, clinicians use information about gaps to judge the degree to which the student needs to develop metapragmatic awareness versus basic skills to improve classroom discourse.

When students show limited awareness of classroom discourse and nonverbal communication, one approach is to give them an assignment to observe more carefully (e.g., "You've told me who the good students are in your classroom; see if you can observe what they do while the teacher is giving directions; we'll talk about it next time") (Anderson & Nelson, 1988). Clinicians can characterize this as being a "scientist" in the classroom, thus raising the level beyond remedial and conveying a sense of ownership and control to the student.

Whole-class instruction can be used in the early grades. For example, a clinician might use the observational checklist in Figure 13.2 to organize a series of sessions, each designed to build students' awareness of an aspect of classroom discourse. Dodge and Mallard (1992) described a communication lab for making the expectations of classroom discourse more explicit for all students. Topics ranged from conventions of opening and closing activities in the classroom to how to read nonverbal cues from teachers about what to do or not do.

Once awareness is raised, a student with difficulties in this area can receive scaffolding to construct goals and a plan for what he or she might do differently in future situations that are similar. An action plan can be characterized as an *experiment,* with lists of options the student might try as new approaches and then discuss. For example, if a teacher does not like students coming to her desk with questions during certain times of the day, the student might identify when questions are acceptable and experiment with raising his or her hand and waiting for the teacher to come to his or her desk. When an experiment works, new learning can occur and stabilize within a single event. When it does not work, awareness can yet be raised and the stage is set to try something different without viewing the attempt as failure or inadequacy.

figure *13.2*

Observation Tool for Assessing Metapragmatic Awareness of the Classroom Routine and Rules

| Child _____ | Partner _____ |
| Context _____ | Date _____ |

Knowledge of Classroom Routines and Discourse	+ Confident – Don't know ~ Partial response	Descriptive Evidence
❑ **Openings and closings** ▪ What are you supposed to do when you arrive in class in the morning? ▪ What is the first thing you should do when class begins? ▪ What does your teacher do and say when it is time for a lesson to begin? ▪ What does your teacher say when it is time for a lesson to end? ▪ What is the last thing you should do before you go home for the day?		
❑ **Class discussion** ▪ What do you have to do to get a turn in class discussions? ▪ When is it okay to talk out loud without raising your hand? ▪ How do you know if you have given a correct or incorrect answer? ▪ When is it all right to ask a question in class? ▪ How does your teacher want you to ask for help?		
❑ **Teacher attitudes (hidden curriculum)** ▪ How do you know when your teacher is unhappy with the class? ▪ What makes your teacher unhappy with students? ▪ How do you know when your teacher is joking or teasing? ▪ What is the best time to talk to your teacher about problems with your work? ▪ What is the most important thing you should never do in class? ▪ What are some of the things that good students do in class?		

Source: Based on Creaghead & Tattershall, 1985; Tattershall, 2002; Westby, 2006.

The experiment approach worked for Matt in dealing with his playground issues with Desmond, as described in Chapters 1 and 12. To prepare for the experiment, students are scaffolded to list options they might try in their tool book, which provides a written record of intervention activities that should be reviewed periodically. Matt's tool book page for "How to Deal with Bullies" appeared as Figure 12.6.

When using a whole-class approach, clinicians can collaborate with teachers in a minilesson format to introduce topics and do some initial instruction. This also works for small-group instruction. For example, a small group (usually five to six) of middle school students participated in an after-school homework lab at a university clinic. Each session began with a brief group minilesson regarding a topic that arose from curriculum-related issues while students were working on their individual intervention goals. The group context of the minilessons simulated school discourse interactions but allowed discussions to reflect on discourse (e.g., hand raising or whether a student's words were encouraging or discouraging). The minilessons presented opportunities to assess students' abilities dynamically and to scaffold them in the so-called teachable moment. Minilessons also were used extensively in the inclusive writing lab approach, combining instruction and intervention in general education classrooms.

This minilesson format involves three steps—introducing a topic, holding a discussion using open-ended questions that allow multiple appropriate answers (different from I-R-E "teacher-talk" exchanges, which use known-answer questions), and ending with a hands-on opportunity to practice applying the new knowledge or skill. Some general education sources have described minilessons as teacher explanation only (e.g., Weaver, 1996), but group discussion can support assessment and intervention goals on classroom communication (e.g., Nelson, Bahr, & Van Meter, 2004; Nelson, Van Meter, Chamberlain, & Bahr, 2001).

Topics for minilessons arise out of assessment data and contextualized needs. In the context of minilessons in the homework lab it became clear, for example, that students had different approaches to hand raising in formal classroom lessons, and that some were dysfunctional. Variation in expectations about the need to raise hands to be called on in class is not surprising, as conventions vary across schools and classrooms, but some of these variations appeared individualistic and related to students' communication difficulties. Case Example 13.1 shows how concerns were addressed about hand raising and turn taking in the homework lab. This work was consistent with recommendations by Silliman and Lamanna (1986) to provide systematic instruction in classroom turn taking for students who are less skilled.

When using minilessons within the writing lab approach in inclusive classrooms, general education teachers collaborate in planning and implementing the minilessons (Nelson et al., 2004). Students particularly enjoy minilessons in which their general education teachers act out what *not* to do. For example, in a minilesson on reading from the author's chair, the teacher might slouch into position, hold a paper over his or her face while reading, never look at the audience, chew gum, mumble, and talk too low to be understood. Such a dramatization can trigger a lively discussion about "do's and don'ts" when reading from the author's chair. It also can lead to other minilessons, such as "Use your public voice." Then the term *public voice* can be used in later sessions when children need to be reminded to speak up.

The process of helping students gain proficiency with basic skills underlying academic discourse is multifaceted. Students with language impairment (LI) often need intervention to develop higher-level syntactic and inferencing skills, as well as skills for self-regulation (Westby, 2006), both of which are targeted later in this chapter. Consistent with the fourth question of CBLAI (How should the learning context be modified?), environmental accommodations may be needed. Westby (2006) listed potential changes to the physical or social environment, including modifying seating or providing written reminders, making tasks shorter or the steps more explicit, providing procedural cues and supports, dividing the day into scheduled activities and posting the schedule, and arranging the workspace for different routines.

Social Interaction Discourse

Social communication can be particularly difficult for students with LI who are unable to abstract social cues from conversational contexts and integrate them with insufficient language skills. Problems with social interaction constitute a central diagnostic feature for

Hand Raising in the Homework Lab

The need for a minilesson on hand raising in formal classroom discussions became apparent when several issues arose in the context of prior minilessons. Rick loved to express his opinion and waved his hand wildly to take a turn—that is, unless the turn involved reading. Then, he literally sat on his hands. Another student, Sahara, always raised her hand, but she rarely had a response prepared when called on. Sahara exhibited strengths in sensitivity to social pragmatic cues but difficulty with language comprehension. When interviewed about hand raising, Sahara said that she raised her hand so that the other students would think she knew the answer. A third student, D'Angelo (see Figure 12.5 in the previous chapter), almost never raised his hand.

When clinicians interviewed the children's fourth- and fifth-grade teachers about their students' classroom communication skills, including hand raising, the teachers' reports were consistent with what the clinicians had observed in the pull-out sessions. In Sahara's case, the interview process uncovered a silent conspiracy. Sahara's teacher reported that Sahara always raised her hand but never was prepared with an answer, so the teacher rarely called on her. D'Angelo's teacher was aware that he was having difficulty with math, but she was not sure how to help him with it.

To address these concerns, two minilessons were planned for the homework lab to work directly on hand raising and what is required to take a turn and answer questions in class. A tool book handout was created based on the students' discussion, which included such steps as "Listen to the question and what it asks," "Think about your answer," "Only raise your hand when you know what you want to say," and "Keep your answer short and on the topic." Students could start by practicing the skills in the minilessons of the homework lab, but they could also observe more closely and experiment with their new skills in their regular classrooms and come back and report to the group in the second minilesson. Using this multisession approach, students gained ownership over issues they all faced but in different ways, increasing metapragmatic awareness for themselves and their group mates.

Rick, the student whose hand-waving "me, me, me" approach often disrupted group discussions,

learned to temper his attention-getting behavior in the first minilesson. When called on during the introductory discussion about hand raising, Rick contributed that sometimes the teacher does not see a student who is raising his hand. At that point, the clinicians asked Rick whether there could be other reasons that the teacher might not call on a student who is raising his hand, besides not seeing him. Rick reflected for a moment and then said, "She might want to know what the other kids think." Rick's overactive hand waving was never a problem in the minilesson sessions again. As Rick improved his reading decoding skills in another part of his intervention program, he set a goal for himself to raise his hand for a turn to read aloud when a lesson called for it and accomplished this personal goal as well.

Depending on circumstances and grade level, classroom teachers can be made aware of intervention focused on classroom communication skills and recruited to collaborate in helping students generalize new skills. This addresses the fourth question of CBLAI, which asks about how the context should be modified. For example, the clinicians scheduled a collaborative discussion with Sahara's teacher to let her know that Sahara was working on developing her answer in her mind before raising her hand. Knowing this, the teacher arranged to formulate some questions at a level she knew would be within Sahara's competency zone, to call on her when she raised her hand, and to give adequate wait time to allow her to formulate a response.

If attention, memory, or other information-processing difficulties are acting as barriers to participating in classroom discussions, self-talk goals may be used to target self-regulation skills. In most cases, children pay better attention and find the curriculum less boring when they understand it better (as D'Angelo did). Components of linguistic processing may require direct assessment and intervention as well. For example, Rick needed to work on his reading decoding skills, Sahara on her vocabulary and comprehension strategies, and D'Angelo on the vocabulary and sentence structure of math. The comprehensive approach of the intervention, which included both group and individual activities, enabled the clinicians to use a balanced approach that targeted both basic skills and their application in complex curricular contexts.

students with autism spectrum disorders (e.g., Schopler & Mesibov, 1985) and for students with emotional and behavioral disorders. Sensory input deficits, such as loss of hearing (e.g., Gagne, Stelmacovich, & Yovetich, 1991) and vision, and motor output impairments, such as cerebral palsy, also present barriers to interaction and participation that require direct attention and accommodation. Problems with peer acceptance are reported widely in the literature on learning disabilities (LD) (e.g., Vaughn, McIntosh, & Spencer-Rowe, 1991) and communication disorders (Gallagher, 1991).

Language difficulties constitute a direct barrier to establishing social relationships. Fujiki, Brinton, Hart, and Fitzgerald (1999) reported that students with LI often have few or no friends and may be poorly accepted or even actively rejected. Students with LI also may have difficulty using language skills to negotiate with peers (Brinton, Fujiki, & McKee, 1998; Grove, Conti-Ramsden, & Donlan, 1993) and to resolve conflicts (Stevens & Bliss, 1995). Conti-Ramsden and Botting (2004) followed 242 children in England longitudinally who originally were identified with language risks at age 7. At age 11, 36 percent were regular targets of social victimization (three times higher than the 12 percent found for comparison children), and it was early pragmatic checklist scores (not language scores or nonverbal IQ scores) that predicted which children would have social difficulties.

Children with LI are more likely to seek adults for interaction and avoid social situations with peers (Rice, Sell, & Hadley, 1991). Even students who want to interact socially with peers may lack the social skills for doing so (Brinton & Fujiki, 2006). Many children with LI do not know how to enter a social group or cooperative learning group and often work alone during group activities. They may need direct intervention about how to join and participate in social activities with peers (see Personal Reflection 13.1).

PERSONAL reflection *13.1*

"Peer interaction is an essential component of the individual child's development. Experience with peers is not a superficial luxury to be enjoyed by some children and not others, but is a necessity in childhood socialization. And among the most sensitive indicators of difficulties in development are failure by the child to engage in the activities of the peer culture and failure to occupy a relatively comfortable place within it."

William Hartup (1983, p. 220), a child development specialist, writing about the role of peer interaction in the development of the individual child.

Assessing Social Interaction Discourse Knowledge and Skill

Students' social conversation discourse skills should be assessed when social interaction is identified as a primary concern. This can trigger a decision to conduct context-based assessment using interviews or onlooker or participant observation in problematic contexts, such as the lunchroom or playground. Interviews with the student are often used to gather baseline information. This context has the advantage of introducing a metapragmatic discussion, but it does not capture direct evidence of what happens when the student attempts to converse with peers. Onlooker observation may be required for gathering spoken samples of peer communication—directly, through recordings, or via student report.

Videorecording is particularly helpful for assessing social interaction discourse because it captures nonverbal elements as well as verbal ones. Most younger elementary school children interact fairly naturally in play or cooperative learning groups in the presence of audio- or videorecording equipment; older students may be self-conscious about being videorecorded, however, so alternative methods may be required (although the YouTube experience may be changing that). One option is to code for specific social behaviors online (i.e., during live observation) using low-technology methods (e.g., checklists on clipboards). Olswang, Coggins, and Svensson (2007) developed technology, however, for gathering data in a time-sampling approach using a personal data assistant (PDA) device. Their system used the authors' *social communication coding system (SCCS)* to code duration and frequency for the behavioral dimensions—hostile/coercive, prosocial/engaged, passive/disengaged, adult seeking, and irrelevant.

When students with LI have played a role in identifying talking with peers as a personal goal area, they may be willing to allow clinicians to gather samples of peer-interaction discourse to discuss in intervention. When students listen to or read samples of their own recorded discourse, they can be scaffolded to develop metapragmatic awareness of conversational conventions and how to use them and to practice alternative ways to say things. A socially mature peer might be recruited to hold practice conversations with the student and offer comments about what "most guys/girls like or don't like" when interacting with peers.

Some social communication discourse is written, rather than spoken. Letters and social notes constitute one side of a written conversation, allowing more time for reflection but missing the feature of immediate response contingency. E-mail and text messaging, for example, result in written social communication products that can become the context for assessment and intervention activities.

Figure 13.3 provides an observation tool for assessing students' knowledge of verbal and nonverbal pragmatic conventions and skills for engaging in conversational discourse. It combines items based on Fey's (1986) communication acts profiling (CAP; see Chapter 11), Grice's (1975) conversational maxims (see Chapter 2), and a pragmatic assessment protocol developed by Prutting and Kirchner (1987). If problems occur in one or more of these broad areas, more in-depth analysis can be conducted (e.g., by using the full CAP coding system described in Chapter 11). Students' pragmatic capabilities can be evaluated based on direct or recorded samples of communicative interactions. Metapragmatic abilities (i.e., awareness of pragmatic conventions and violations of them) can be assessed by engaging students directly in analyzing samples of their own discourse.

Targeting Pragmatic Skills for Interacting with Peers and Adults

Goal 13.2. The student will demonstrate changes in social pragmatic skills that were problematic during baseline samples. The observational chart in Figure 13.3 can serve as a worksheet for profiling pragmatic communication skills, identifying gaps, selecting intervention targets, and designing contextualized intervention opportunities.

A unique feature of intervention with older school-age students who are almost but not quite like their peers is their need for meta-awareness of the communication skill of focus. Students with mild to moderate disabilities usually have sufficient cognitive abilities to acquire awareness when clinicians provide explicit scaffolding. Such students can be engaged in analyzing their own communication samples. To make this manageable and nonthreatening, the clinician and student might focus on a single aspect at a time, discussing what the student might try to do differently the next time a similar situation arises. Intervention activities should shore up the student's confidence in using existing skills that are present but wobbly. *Wobbly* is a kid-friendly term that can be used with a student to describe abilities that are still a stretch within his or her zone of proximal development (ZPD), without labeling the skills as disordered or impaired. It signals to students that they can do this, just not all the time or in all circumstances. Regardless, they can learn to make the skills more stable.

Social skills interventions can make use of varied intervention approaches. Three common approaches are ***direct instruction, structured situations,*** and ***group-training programs***

figure *13.3*

Observation Tool for Assessing Pragmatic Discourse Abilities Used in Conversation

| Student _____ | Partner _____ | |
| Context _____ | Date _____ | |

Observation of Conversational Discourse	+ **Appropriate** – **Inappropriate** ~ **Semiappropriate** n/o **No opportunity**	**Descriptive Evidence**

Linguistic/Verbal aspects
 	
❑ Speech acts
   ❑ Assertive–responsive balance
   ❑ Speech act variation		

❑ Grice's maxims
   ❑ Quantity/informative
   ❑ Quality/truthful/supportable
   ❑ Relation/relevance
   ❑ Manner/organized, clear, and concise		

❑ Topic management
   ❑ Selection
   ❑ Introduction
   ❑ Maintenance
   ❑ Shading/switching		

❑ Turn taking
   ❑ Initiation
   ❑ Response
   ❑ Repair/revision
   ❑ Pause time/interruption/overlap
   ❑ Feedback to speakers
   ❑ Adjacency/contingency
   ❑ Quantity/conciseness		

❑ Lexical selection
   ❑ Specificity/accuracy
   ❑ Cohesion		

❑ Style
   ❑ Slang use with peers
   ❑ Informal with peers/familiar adults
   ❑ Formal with employers/unfamiliar adults		

Paralinguistic aspects ❑ Intelligibility ❑ Vocal intensity/quality ❑ Prosody/fluency		
Nonverbal aspects ❑ Physical proximity/contact ❑ Body posture/limb movement ❑ Gestures/facial expression ❑ Eye gaze		

Source: Based on Fey, 1986; Grice, 1975; Prutting & Kirchner, 1987.

(Bryan, 1986). Based on her review of the literature, Bryan concluded that direct instruction of a particular verbal ability within an isolated intervention context was the least effective because new skills taught this way often did not generalize to complex real-life settings. Structured situations that used peer modeling were more effective. For example, students with learning disabilities were able to adopt the open-ended and contingent questioning style of a talk-show format after listening to relatively few examples. Students with learning disabilities appeared to learn best within the parameters of semistructured interactions in which they received explicit scaffolding.

Peer mentors must be actively recruited and trained, and their interactions must be scaffolded initially within the context. The goal is to recruit socially mature peer partners who have a caring attitude and enough social status to become a model for other peers and not feel threatened that they will lose status by helping. For example, the clinician might say, "I've been watching how good you are at talking with other students. That is not so easy for Cindy. I wonder if you would be willing to be her partner on the next project and work with me to help her learn better ways for talking to other kids." After recruiting peers and describing the social skills intervention, clinicians may need to provide specific training using techniques such as prompting, modeling, rehearsing, and reinforcement. Clinicians also should prepare peer partners for possible rejection when they first approach peers with special needs (Elksnin & Elksnin, 1995).

Differences that make some children with LI seem odd to their peers and open to teasing might include such features as standing too close, not knowing how to make appropriate requests, and not answering obligatory questions (Brinton, Robinson, & Fujiki, 2004). Figure 13.4 provides an observation tool based on research on the nature of appropriate request behaviors of school-age students with peers (Ervin-Tripp & Gordon, 1986; Wilkinson, Milosky, & Genishi, 1986). It outlines component skills that should be targeted for interacting with peers in ways that are appropriately direct, designated for a particular listener, sincere, revised if unsuccessful, relevant to the task, and responded to appropriately.

Peer role models can help students with LI fit in socially in their choices of words and phrasing. The ability to use slang—from guys calling guys "dude," to girls sprinkling sentences with modifiers, as in "I'm just, like, so happy"—can signal the degree to which a student may be accepted as belonging in a preadolescent or adolescent peer group (Delpit, 2002; Donahue & Bryan, 1984; Tagliamonte, 2005).

Students with learning disabilities have been observed to lag six months to a year behind typically developing peers in their use of slang, making them seem like outsiders (Donahue & Bryan, 1984). Based on evidence that the amount of slang used by students with learning disabilities relates to the amount of time students with disabilities spend with typically developing peers, Donahue and Bryan recommended increasing opportunities for adolescents with LI/LD to engage in satisfying peer interactions. Peers make the best coaches not only because they can serve as models for students with disabilities but also because "no adult could keep up with the rapid changes in slang nor fully appreciate the fine nuances of its meaning" (p. 19).

Hess and Fairchild (1988) used peer models in an intervention called *model, analyze, and practice (MAP)*, which combined direct instruction, structured situations, and group training. In the modeling step, students view videorecorded simulations of peer-interaction discourse scripted to contrast more and less effective peer interactions. In the analysis step, students receive scaffolding to identify cues that signal the difference, as illustrated in Figure 13.5. In both samples, Speaker 1 starts by asking an open-ended question. In Sample A, however, the first speaker does not listen to the partner and just runs down a list of questions without tailoring them to the conversational context. In Sample B, Speaker 1 listens to the peer's response to the question and asks contingent follow-up questions based on the

figure *13.4*

Observation Tool for Making and Responding to Requests in Classroom Contexts

Student _____   Partner _____

Context _____   Date _____

Characteristics of Effective Requests/Responses	+ Observed – Not observed ~ Partial evidence	Descriptive Evidence

❑ Request is appropriately direct.
  ❑ Younger students may ask directly, such as "Where's the green marker?"
  ❑ Older students should be able to use more indirect forms, such as "Do you have a green marker I can use?"
  ❑ Degree of directness may vary with child's racial/ethnic identity.		

❑ Request designates listener.
  ❑ Verbal designation by calling name.
  ❑ Unambiguous nonverbal designation, such as looking directly at peer while requesting.		

❑ Request is sincere.
  ❑ Action, purpose, and need for request are clear.
  ❑ Listener can be assumed to have knowledge and skill to respond.
  ❑ Speaker has a right to make request.
  ❑ Request is not just rhetorical or sarcastic, such as "Can't you work any faster?"		

❑ Request is revised if unsuccessful.
  ❑ Request is restated to listener who did not respond appropriately.
  ❑ Request is directed appropriately to different listener.		

❑ Request is on task. ❑ Request is relevant to academic activity.		

❑ Student responds appropriately to others.
  ❑ Requested action or information is given.
  ❑ Reason is given for why action or information could not be given.		

Source: Based on Ervin-Tripp & Gordon, 1986; Wilkinson, Milosky & Genishi, 1986.

peer's prior response. After analyzing and discussing such features, students practice by videotaping themselves in similar conversations with peers. Then, the analysis step is scaffolded again, this time to analyze the students' recordings. Students take notes and record new practice conversations in which they try to incorporate peers' suggestions. The cyclical approach is repeated as needed.

Typically learning peers can be engaged as peer partners in cooperative learning groups. Simply putting students together in groups, however, does not mean they will

figure *13.5*

Two Samples for Analysis by Adolescents as Part of the MAP Approach to Conversational Intervention

Sample A	Sample B
S1 What are your hobbies? S2 I like to build models and play basketball. S1 Do you go to movies? S2 Yes. S1 How is your marching band doing?	S1 What are your hobbies? S2 I like to build models and play basketball. S1 Do you play basketball for your school? S2 No, I play for fun with my friends. I'm not tall enough for the school team. S1 Yeah, me too, but I play on one of the YMCA teams. S2 Oh yeah, how did you get on that team?

Note: S1 = Speaker 1; S2 = Speaker 2
Source: Adapted from Hess & Fairchild, 1988.

interact. In fact, research has shown that placing children with LI in a cooperative learning group (i.e., without scaffolding) may highlight their exclusion (Brinton, Fujiki, Spencer, & Robinson, 1997). Beilinson and Olswang (2003) described a collaborative teacher/clinician intervention program for teaching peer-group entry skills to kindergartners with social interaction and communication deficits. They used modeling and prompting to teach the children to use props and verbal statements to gain entry into peer groups and engage with peers in cooperative play. After treatment, the children's social behaviors more closely resembled those of comparison peers in use of props and verbal statements to enter peer groups and more time in cooperative play with peers.

Brinton and Fujiki (2006) analyzed the demands of seeking entrance to a group, including selecting a group to approach, observing to evaluate what is going on, waiting for a break in the conversation, and making a bid to join the conversation. A bid might include agreeing with something someone has just said, making a comment on the current topic, or asking a relevant question. Pragmatic judgment is required to recognize both when to make a bid and whether it has been accepted or not.

To teach the fine points of group entry to older elementary and middle school students, Brinton and Fujiki described a six-step approach:

1. *Introduce the social objective* by explaining that this is about learning how to join groups that are doing things together.
2. *Walk* closer to others to know what they are doing (prompted with a 5 × 7-inch card with the word *Walk* and a picture of a stick figure walking).
3. *Watch* (printed on a card illustrated with two eyes) is taught through role-play about the need to be patient and watch for a while so they will know what is going on before trying to enter the group's conversation.
4. *Talk* (printed on a card illustrated by two stick figures talking) requires students to practice contributing something that supports the activity.
5. *Try again* is used to help children understand that they should stay close and look for another opportunity if their first bid is not accepted.
6. *Reflect* involves facilitating discussion of the scenario with all group members (usually three), again scaffolded by the clinician.

Working on social skills can be a long process because the expectations of social contexts change with age. Evidence for this comes from longitudinal case studies that illustrate how individualized intervention focused on social skills can transition over the school-age years and into adolescence (Brinton, Fujiki, & Robinson, 2005; Brinton, Robinson, & Fujiki, 2004).

Participating actively in social interactions with peers requires skills for negotiating conflicts and engaging in verbal arguments, as well as for entering social conversations. Not all the skills required would be considered positive by adults. Brenneis and Lein (1977) listed verbal argument behaviors exhibited by third- and fourth-grade students as including threats, bribes, insults, praise, commands, moral persuasion, contradictions of prior assertions, simple assertions, denials, ironic affirmations (e.g., "yea, right"), supportive assertions (e.g., "because it's mine"), demand for evidence (e.g., "prove it"), and nonword vocal signals (e.g., "na-na-na the boo-boo-boo").

Stevens and Bliss (1995) compared the conflict resolution abilities of third- to sixth-grade students with specific language impairment (SLI) with those of typically developing peers in two contexts: (1) role-playing an argument (e.g., who is the strongest) and (2) discussing options a character in a hypothetical story might use to try to resolve a conflict. Students with SLI could handle the communication demands of the first context similarly to typically developing peers but not the second, more abstract context. Based on this finding, Stevens and Bliss recommended that intervention begin with role-play and then move to discussions of hypothetical scenarios.

Students can learn explicit "win/win" guidelines for resolving personal disputes. Drew (1987) recommended using six steps: (1) cool off and find alternative ways to express anger; (2) use *I*-messages by stating feelings with no blaming, name calling, or interrupting; (3) take the other person's perspective by stating the problem as he or she sees it; (4) take responsibility by having each person state how he or she is responsible for the conflict; (5) brainstorm possible solutions; and (6) affirm by each stating something positive about the other. These steps can be written on a chart or in a student's tool book, taught first in role-play, and then scaffolded in the context of actual disputes that arise in natural contexts.

By adolescence, typically developing students can engage in social reasoning that involves *role taking,* which is "the ability to assume the thoughts and perspectives of others" (Elksnin & Elksnin, 1995, p. 142). Concepts of friendship evolve from a focus on shared activities to a focus on shared values, to the point where "adolescents count as their friends those individuals with whom they can share their innermost thoughts without fear of rejection or judgment" (p. 142).

Students with disabilities may be unable to demonstrate mature forms of social cognition without intervention. Brion-Meisels and Selman (1984) described four levels:

Level 0 behaviors are **unreflective physical strategies** (i.e., acting on "fight or flight" impulses), which are common among younger children, older students with conduct disorders, and other adolescents under extreme stress.

Level 1 behaviors involve the issuance of **one-way commands,** which arise when students can engage in differentiated and subjective role taking but can consider only one perspective at a time.

Level 2 behaviors are **reciprocal,** signaling that the adolescent now "understands how to negotiate fairly and uses strategies such as making deals, trades, or exchanges" (p. 143).

Level 3 behaviors involve **mutual collaboration,** in which adolescents and adults learn to use strategies of compromise, collaboration, and cooperative goal setting.

Nippold (1994) outlined developmental changes in the ability to use persuasive discourse based on studies about what one could say to convince someone else to do something or buy something. From age 5 to 18, children and adolescents gain skill in adjusting to listener characteristics, such as age and authority; stating an advantage as a reason to comply; anticipating and replying to counterarguments; using more positive strategies (e.g., politeness and bargaining) and fewer negative strategies (e.g., nagging and begging); generating a wider variety of arguments; and controlling the interaction. Nippold recommended teaching students with LI to analyze the persuasive appeals of others and respond appropriately. This includes teaching students how to decline attempts to persuade them to engage in negative behaviors, such as using delaying tactics to resist negative peer pressure (e.g., "I don't want to smoke now; maybe I'll change my mind later").

Although most intervention approaches for social skills are set in spoken language contexts, social notes offer a written alternative. Lindfors (1987) pointed out the irony of teachers trying to stamp out note passing when it is a form of written interpersonal communication at its very best. In a homework lab session, the clinicians discovered that two of the seven middle school students with LI had never exchanged social notes. The clinicians and students discussed what one might write in a social note and then set up mailboxes so they could all practice writing notes and leave them for each other. Peer mentoring included how to fold notes into complex patterns used by typical adolescents. During the discussion, one student commented that she had a lot of experience with social notes—specifically, with using them to get back at other girls when they made her angry. The clinicians swallowed their urge to lecture and suggested an experiment to see what would happen if the student used an *I*-message to tell how the other girl's behavior made her feel instead of saying something hurtful back. The next session, the student came in bubbling with the news that she had conducted the experiment and "It worked!" Another girl had written a note about feeling insulted and angry. The student experimenter responded by writing back that she had not meant to hurt the other girl's feelings. The peer wrote a friendly note in return. The homework lab group benefited from an active learning lesson that was more powerful than any role-play or adult lecture could ever be on the virtues of saying nice things in social notes.

Narrative Discourse

Narration emerges in toddlerhood with the ability to combine more than one utterance to talk about the there-and-then events, interpret experiences, and share stories with an interested audience. Personal narratives vary based on whether they are *event cast* narrations of ongoing events, *accounts* of personal experience told with relative independence, or *recounts* of shared experience told with support from someone who shared the experience (Westby, 1994b). Fictional stories also may take many forms (e.g., science fiction, horror stories, mysteries, romances). When gathering written probe stories (see Chapter 12), students can be given the option to write stories that are real or imaginary.

Most researchers report that narrative texts are easier to comprehend and remember than expository ones, partly due to their greater familiarity to children, relevance to life experience, and recognizable structure (Gersten, Fuchs, Williams, & Baker, 2001). Stories are used often in beginning reading instruction and provide a natural transition from oral to written language. They play a role in helping children develop important cognitive and social skills, as well as academic skills (Westby, 1985).

As noted in Chapter 11, cultural differences occur in the forms of stories and in how children are socialized to tell them (e.g., Au, 1980; Bliss & McCabe, 2008; Gee, 1989; Hester, 1996; McCabe & Bliss, 2003; Michaels, 1991; Westby, 1994b). During the school-age years, cultural differences continue to influence how children comprehend stories and structure them in spoken and written narration. In all cultures, the ability to comprehend and tell stories draws on experience with narratives through hearing stories told orally. In highly literate cultures, children also experience stories through hearing them read aloud and later by reading stories independently.

Learning to tell stories can help children with listening and reading comprehension (Boudreau, 2008), as shown by a positive relationship between early narrative abilities and later reading comprehension in several longitudinal studies (e.g., Feagans & Applebaum, 1986; Griffin, Hemphill, Camp, & Wolf, 2004). The extensive Home-School Study of Language and Literacy Development (Dickinson & McCabe, 2001; Tabors, Snow, & Dickinson, 2001) also showed narrative performance in kindergarten to be a good predictor of vocabulary and reading comprehension in seventh grade. In one exception to this pattern, it was thought that the reading decoding difficulties of some children might have obscured their early grade discourse comprehension abilities (Roth, Speece, & Cooper, 2002).

The ability to produce narrative discourse fulfills multiple functions. Narratives are used to organize and communicate about experience, evaluate it, regulate it, and interpret its influence on human emotions. "Not only do we talk in stories, but we think in them" (Ukrainetz, 2006b, p. 197). Narrative discourse makes a complex but productive context for intervention because it requires integration among a range of cognitive–linguistic skills that can be targeted together, as summarized by Milosky (1987):

> When narrating, the child must recall and organize content, take into account the listener by determining shared background, formulate new utterances, relate them to what already has been said, and introduce referents and distinguish unambiguously among them in subsequent utterances. The need to balance all these demands makes narration cognitively demanding and requires extensive mental resources. (p. 331)

Johnston (1982b) identified four distinct knowledge bases children must activate to engage in narration: (1) the ***content*** of the narrative (both its general nature and specific details); (2) the ***framework*** of the narrative macrostructure (such as the high-point framework of personal narratives, as described by McCabe and Bliss [2003], or the story grammar structure of episodes, as described by Stein and Glenn [1979]); (3) the ***linguistic grammar*** for formulating complex sentences, including cohesive devices to form connections across sentence boundaries; and (4) ***communicative adequacy*** for taking into account listeners' prior knowledge and the need for explicit new information. Updating this framework, Johnston (2008) added a fifth component, (5) ***cognitive processing,*** for activating the other four knowledge sources simultaneously and strategically.

Most studies report that students with language-learning disability (LLD) have some sense of story grammar. They usually include aspects of each story grammar element but with fewer causal or temporal connectives to tie events in the story together, fewer elements related to characters' goals and inner nature, and fewer complete episodes, (e.g., Goldstein, Harris, & Klein, 1993; Klecan-Aker & Kelty, 1990; Merritt & Liles, 1987, 1989; Roth & Spekman, 1986; Vallecorsa & Gariss, 1990). Students with LLD have particular difficulty understanding the personal/social themes of narratives (Williams, 1993). The tendency to convey concrete actions with little mention of characters' goals has been interpreted as a deficit in metacognitive theory of mind capabilities among students with LLD (Gersten et al., 2001; Montague, Maddux, & Dereshiwsky, 1990).

Narrative comprehension and production deficits are closely intertwined with reading comprehension deficits. At least 80 percent of students with LD experience serious difficulties learning to read (Kavale & Reece, 1992), including problems with reading comprehension. This is especially likely when efficiency of reading comprehension is measured, not just accuracy (Fuchs, Fuchs, Mathes, & Lipsey, 2000).

Assessing Narrative Discourse Knowledge and Skills

Narrative comprehension and production draw on discourse-level skills and can be assessed in tandem by asking a child to listen to a story and then retell it. Contexts include retelling a story after listening to one, telling a story with the support of a wordless picture book, telling a story after taking a "picture walk" through a book (Paris & Paris, 2003), telling a story based on a video, answering questions about a story, and filling in missing information when co-constructing a story from a familiar text (e.g., Skarakis-Doyle & Dempsey, 2008; Ukrainetz, 2006b). Students also can be asked to generate original stories, using probe techniques such as the written story probe that was described in Chapter 12 or using story dictation strategies (Paley, 1990), as discussed in Chapter 11.

The narrative framework can be represented cognitively as a *schema* (i.e., macrostructure) for a classical story. Children who can activate a narrative schema may find it easier to organize and construct a story expressively or to make sense of a story in comprehension. Figure 13.6 provides an observation tool for the most frequently recognized schema.

Stein and Glenn's (1979) schema, which is used widely, captures key elements of the other versions in its six components: (1) *setting* (characters, place, and time), (2) *initiating event* (challenge or problem that must be faced by the main character), (3) *internal response* (main character's internal emotional and cognitive response to the initiating event, part of Bruner's [1986] landscape of consciousness), (4) *attempt* (a planful, goal-directed action taken by the main character to address the problem, also part of the landscape of consciousness), (5) *consequence* (outcome of the attempt to address the problem), and (6) *reaction* (again focusing on the thought life of the character and drawing the episode to a logical conclusion).

Hedberg and Westby (1993) used the Stein and Glenn (1979) components of a complete episode to build a developmental sequence that could be used to guide assessment. From least to most mature, each developmental level incorporates one additional component of a complete episode: (1) an *isolated description* consists only of heaps of information that describe the setting; (2) a *descriptive sequence* adds some related statements; (3) an *action sequence* (also called a *temporal sequence*) adds information about temporal relationships; (4) a *reactive sequence* (also called a *causal sequence*) adds causal relationships or consequences; (5) an *abbreviated episode* incorporates implied intentions on the part of the main character and an attempt to address the problem; (6) a *complete episode* adds a clear goal and plan by the main character to address the problem; and (7) a *complex episode* adds obstacles to implementing the plan.

Real stories, also called personal narratives, often fit the high-point description best (McCabe & Bliss, 2003) and may be stimulated by telling a story to get a story, such as a story about a bee sting or a trip to the hospital. Stories drawn from the child's own experience or imagination have many advantages over story-starters in helping children develop narrative confidence and competence. A high-point framework (McCabe & Rollins, 1994; Peterson & McCabe, 1983) incorporates similar components for describing personal narratives. According to this framework, a classic high-point narrative "is complete in that the narrator orients the listener to who, what, when, and where something occurred, builds actions up to a high point, and then resolves them" (Bliss & McCabe, 2008, p. 163).

The developmental sequence based on high-point analysis uses slightly different terminology (e.g., McCabe & Bliss, 2003): (1) a *one-event narrative,* with one past-tense event; (2) a *two-event narrative,* with two past-tense events; (3) a *miscellaneous narrative,* with more than two past-tense events; (4) a *leap-frog narrative,* with logical or causal sequencing of events; (5) a *chronological narrative,* with events mirroring the real-life sequence; (6) an *end-at-high-point narrative,* including a high point but no resolution; and (7) a *classical narrative,* with a resolution after the high point that wraps up the crisis.

figure *13.6*

Observational Tool for Narrative Macrostructure Components

Student _____ Context _____ Date _____		
Narrative Maturity Evaluation Options	**Evidence of Story Comprehension**	**Evidence of Story Production**

❑ **Applebee analysis**
  ❑ Heap (no relationship among elements)
  ❑ Sequence (central theme, with structure of *X* does *A*, *X* does *B*, and *X* does *C*, but superficial sequence in time)
  ❑ Primitive narrative (narrative elements bear relationship to each other; feelings may be included)
  ❑ Unfocused chain (events are linked logically)
  ❑ Focused chain (organization shows both center and sequence)
  ❑ True narrative (well-developed plot with clear ending, in which intentions and goals flow from attributes or feelings of characters)		

❑ **High-point analysis**
  ❑ One-event narrative
  ❑ Two-event narrative (two past-tense events)
  ❑ Miscellaneous narrative (more than two past events)
  ❑ "Leap frog" narrative (partial logical or causal relationships)
  ❑ Chronological narrative (accurate temporal sequencing and logical relationships)
  ❑ End-at-high-point narrative (includes a high point but no resolution)
  ❑ Classical narrative (full plot with resolution)		

❑ **Story grammar analysis**
  ❑ Isolated description (descriptive elements)
  ❑ Descriptive sequence (related components)
  ❑ Action sequence (temporal relationships)
  ❑ Reactive sequence (causal relationships)
  ❑ Abbreviated episode (implied intentions)
  ❑ Complete episode (clear goal setting and resolution)
  ❑ Complex episode (adds obstacle character must overcome)		

Source: Based on Applebee, 1978; Botvin & Sutton-Smith, 1977; Hedberg & Westby, 1993; McCabe & Bliss, 2003.

Another approach that is used commonly to describe children's growing narrative maturity comes from Applebee (1978) and is based on work by Botvin and Sutton-Smith (1977). Applebee described narrative development as the process of acquiring skill at maintaining a central theme, while simultaneously communicating temporal and logical relationships among the surrounding events, with closure resolving the initiating event (see Figure 13.7).

figure *13.7*————————————————

Criteria for Rating Narrative Maturity

1. Heaps
- Text organization comes from whatever attracts attention.
- No story macrostructure.
- No relationship or organization among elements or individual microstructures.

2. Sequences
- Narrative has macrostructure with central character, setting, topic.
- Activities of central character occur in particular setting.
- Story elements are related to central macrostructure through concrete associative or perceptual bonds.
- Superficial sequences in time.
- No transitions.
- May use format *A* does *X, A* does *Y, A* does *Z,* or *A* does *X* to *N, A* does *X* to *O, A* does *X* to *P.*
- No ending to narrative.
- Trip stories may be in this category if events lack logical sequence or trip theme.

3. Primitive Narratives
- Characters, objects, and events of narratives are put together because they are perceptually associated and complement each other.
- Elements of the narrative follow logically from attributes of the center.
- Attributes of the center are internal to the character, objects, and events, and they determine the types of events that occur.
- May use inference in narrative.
- Narrative goes beyond perceptual and explicit information but stays concrete, with links forged by shared situation rather than abstract relationship.
- May talk about feelings.
- Interactive narrative elements.
- Organized trip stories fall in this category if they include multiple comments on events, including interpretive feelings.

4. Unfocused Chains
- Events are linked logically (cause–effect relationship).
- Elements are related to one another.
- No central theme or character, and no plot or story theme.
- Lack of evidence of complete understanding of reciprocal nature of characters and events.
- True sequence of events.

5. Focused Chains
- Organized with both center and sequence.
- Actual chaining of events that connect elements.
- Does not have a strong plot.
- Events do not build on attributes of characters.
- Characters and events of narratives seldom reach toward goal.
- Weak ending, no ending, or ending does not follow logically from the beginning.
- May be problems or motivating events that cause actions.
- Transitions are used.
- More *because–then* chains are used.
- May be trip story if events follow logically from each other, more than just occurring next on same trip.

6. True Narratives
- Integrated chaining events with complementary centering of primitive narrative.
- Developed plot.
- Consequent events build out of prior events and also develop central core.
- Ending reflects or is related to issues or events presented in beginning of narrative.
- Intentions or goals of characters dependent on attributes and feelings.

Source: Based on Applebee, 1978; Botvin & Sutton-Smith, 1977.

Other techniques for assessing discourse comprehension include ***comprehension questions (CQs)*** and ***joint story retelling (JSR)*** (Skarakis-Doyle & Dempsey, 2008). Although designed for preschool-age children, most of these techniques can be used with school-age children with LI functioning at a variety of levels. As with younger children, the challenge is to assess the completeness of a student's mental representation of the gist and events of the story and also the student's grasp of the underlying feelings, motives, goals, and plans of the main characters.

Clinicians analyze telling or retelling of narrative samples by looking for the inclusion of key macrostructural components, perhaps augmented with answers to questions used to gauge the depth and completeness of a child's comprehension. The process of retelling a story is different from repeating it verbatim. Skilled retelling requires story reconstruction and reinterpretation, not just memory, although working memory plays an important role in recalling a story's gist or details. By using dynamic assessment techniques, clinicians can gauge how well a student has comprehended a particular story and identify gaps in understanding that signal where intervention should begin (e.g., Gillam, Peña, & Miller, 1999). Clinicians also can gauge whether a student can add missing components with minimal scaffolding. If so, organization and retrieval processes might need attention but may be within the student's ZPD.

Some formal tests are available for assessing narrative discourse capabilities. The Test of Narrative Language (TNL; Gillam & Pearson, 2004) is a standardized, norm-referenced test that is designed to assess narrative comprehension and production in children between ages 5 and 12 years. Three narrative formats are used to elicit children's abilities to listen to a story, create a new story, and answer questions about it—a fast-food script with no picture support, personal events supported by sequenced pictures, and fictional events supported by a single picture. Examiners score the audiorecorded samples for story content, macrostructural elements, and microstructural elements (such as sentences and cohesive devices). Spaulding, Plante, and Farinella (2006) reported the TNL to be one of only five formal tests with acceptable sensitivity (0.92) and specificity (0.87) for diagnosis of LI.

One formal criterion-referenced test of narrative ability is an American version of the British Renfrew Bus Story Test (Cowley & Glasgow, 1997; Renfrew, 1988, 1991), in which young children (up to age 7 years) retell a story using a set of pictures showing a naughty bus going off course and getting stuck in the mud. Another is the Strong Narrative Assessment Procedure (Strong, 1998), which uses three equivalent illustrated stories and criterion-referenced scoring to assess a variety of narrative components.

To measure progress in storytelling, a series of storytelling probes might work better than a structured test. To quantify changes, Petersen, Gillam, and Gillam (2008) suggested a four-point (0, 1, 2, 3) *index of narrative complexity (INC)*. Rubrics were provided for assigning a score of 0 (absence of the targeted component), 1 (a single unelaborated example of the component), 2 (more than one example of the component), or 3 (multiple elaborated examples of the component). Additional descriptors were proposed for crediting narrative components: character, setting, initiating event, internal response, plan, action/attempt, complication, consequence, formulaic markers, temporal markers, causal adverbial clauses, knowledge of dialogue, and narrator evaluations.

Targeting Comprehension of Narrative Discourse

Goal 13.3. The student will retell stories and answer questions in a manner that shows growth in narrative comprehension over baseline. The ability to comprehend and interpret narrative discourse can be scaffolded by interacting with school-age students to construct meanings in scaffolded discussions of stories drawn from the general education curriculum.

Narratives and language comprehension skills can be targeted in literature-based units. Gillam and Ukrainetz (2006) outlined a three-step approach for using literature, beginning with *prestory knowledge activation* using a graphic organizer and discussion based on pictures. Also in this step, the clinician or teacher scaffolds students to construct the main storyline. The second step involves shared reading of the story, stopping occasionally to use dialogic book-sharing techniques. The third step involves a poststory comprehension discussion, with questions about the most important characters of the story, what they look like, how they think, what they did and why, what main problem they had to face, what happened to solve the problem, and how the story ended. Gillam and Ukrainetz suggested a fourth step, using the book as a model for constructing a parallel story, starting with a graphic organizer and then reviewing the story so as to produce another similar story. They also described constructing a pictographic record of the story as an environmental scaffold to support retelling.

Davies, Shanks, and Davies (2004) reported results for an intervention study aimed at teaching discourse-level narrative skills to early elementary school children with language/literacy risks. The participants were 34 children from low-income families in the United Kingdom in the first two years of schooling (ages 5 to 7 years) who had been identified by their teachers as struggling with language but who were not diagnosed with LI. Initial assessments using the Action Picture Test (Renfrew, 1988) and Bus Story Test (Renfrew, 1991) confirmed the children's low abilities in the area of narrative discourse. Children participated in small-group activities for three sessions per week over eight weeks. The goal was to "help children recognize the structure of their own and other narratives" (p. 279). Cue cards were used to draw students' attention to the various story grammar elements, and a *Wh*-question framework was used to scaffold responses (e.g., Who was in the story? What happened?). Children also audiotaped and listened to their own stories, acted out stories with puppets, sorted pictures, and drew pictures to represent the various story grammar components. Change was measured at the discourse (i.e., macrostructure) level in terms of story grammar **coherence** and at the sentence (i.e., microstructure) level in terms of *communication units (C-units)* and **cohesive devices** linking story components. Such devices are contrasted with the examples (Davies et al., 2004):

> **Child A:** 'He was driving and he said I'm tired and he jumped over the gate and the cow went moo and the bus said hello.'
> **Child B:** 'And he said I'm tired *of going on the road* so he runned over the fence and he met a cow and the cow went moo, *I can't believe my eyes.*' (p. 273)

Davies and colleagues (2004) pointed out, "It is the macrostructure rather than the microstructure of these two utterances that is different" (p. 273). Although the two samples are similarly complex at the microstructure level, Child B's utterances are more coherent at the macrostructure level because they represent two story grammar components not encoded in the utterances of Child A—goal orientation in the bus's decision to jump over the fence and an internal response by the cow in the words "I can't believe my eyes." Another way to look at this is that Child A encoded only what Bruner (1986) called the *landscape of action,* whereas Child B also encoded a *landscape of consciousness* both for the bus and the cow. Comparison of pre- and posttest performance for the 34 children in this study showed improvement on information recall and grammar scores on the Renfrew Action Picture Test (Renfrew, 1988) and in teachers' comments.

Gersten and colleagues (2001) conducted a systematic review of research on reading comprehension strategy instruction with students with learning disabilities. The majority of discourse comprehension research with older school-age students used expository texts rather than narrative ones, but the researchers did identify 11 intervention studies that used narratives. Most instruction followed what the authors called the "proven effective paradigm of teacher explanation and modeling, guided practice, and independent practice" (p. 295). Intervention techniques specific to narrative discourse for which positive effects were found included approaches that taught students to analyze story grammar structure as an organizational framework, to identify story themes (e.g., greed, perseverance), to conduct prereading activities using advanced organizers, and to monitor their comprehension by paraphrasing or restating the author's words after each paragraph. Based on their systematic review, Gersten and colleagues concluded that the "use of story-grammar elements to improve comprehension of narrative text should be considered best practice for students with learning disabilities" (p. 296).

As an example of the story grammar approach, Idol and Croll (1987) taught five students in middle-elementary school with poor reading comprehension and IQs in the high 80s to use a story map to guide their identification of the structural components of stories: setting (characters, time, and place), problem, goal, action, and outcome. Students read a practice story out loud for 20 minutes each day (at a reading level at which comprehension was poor but rate and accuracy were relatively high) and then retold the story from memory and answered 10 comprehension questions orally. Results for four of the five students showed strong gains on responses to the comprehension questions, length and quality of retold stories, and performance on standardized reading and listening comprehension tests. The fifth student improved marginally on some of the measures. All four successful students maintained their mastery level of 80 percent correct comprehension even when no longer directed to use the story-mapping strategy, and three of them showed generalization to classroom reading materials, suggesting that they had internalized the framework.

Advance organizers and prereading strategies can be used to teach students to recognize themes of stories and improve their comprehension. Idol-Maestas (1985) used the acronym TELLS: study the story **T**itle; **E**xamine and skim pages for clues as to what the story may be about; **L**ook for important words; **L**ook for difficult words; think about the **S**tory setting and decide whether it is fact or fiction. Idol-Maestas implemented the procedure with four elementary school students with learning disabilities, ages 8 to 12, using a single-subject multiple baseline design. During the intervention phase, students received scaffolding to complete the advance organizer, read each probe, and respond to questions (e.g., "What is the title?" "Does it give a clue as to what the story is about?"). All four participants improved their performance on the Gray Oral Reading Test (Weiderhold & Bryant, 2001) when using the advance organizer. Three of the four improved on a test of listening comprehension.

Carnine and Kinder (1985) taught four generic questions aimed at highlighting the macrostructural components of narratives: Who is the story about? What are they trying to do? What happens when they try to do it? and What happens at the end? Results showed that the students improved their ability to recall the story and to answer comprehension questions, with gains maintained two to four weeks after intervention.

Another technique for assessing and working on comprehension is paraphrasing. Paraphrasing provides a means for both the clinician and the student to monitor comprehension. Jenkins, Heliotis, Stein, and Haynes (1987) taught students in grades three to six to restate what happened in each paragraph of a story immediately after reading it. The students learned to formulate and then write their paraphrases in answer to the two generic questions Who? and What's happening? on lines printed below each paragraph of text. To evaluate the approach, 16 matched students were assigned randomly to the experimental or a control condition. On posttesting, students in the experimental group used the procedure and answered more comprehension questions correctly, even when using paper without the lines as cues. They also transferred the skill to new contexts.

Peer-supported interventions also have been used to improve narrative comprehension. Fuchs, Fuchs, Mathes, and Simmons (1997) developed ***peer-assisted learning strategies (PALS)*** as a classwide, one-to-one, peer-tutoring program for high school students. PALS uses activities such as partner reading, paragraph summary, and prediction. Fuchs and colleagues reported that students in 20 PALS classrooms demonstrated greater reading progress on words read correctly during a read-aloud, more comprehension questions answered correctly, and more missing words identified correctly in a cloze (maze) test than students in 20 comparison classrooms.

In a subsequent study, Fuchs, Fuchs, and Kazdan (1999) studied the effects of PALS on reading comprehension with 102 students, most of whom had disabilities. PALS improved performance in reading comprehension when paired readers engaged in three key collaborative activities: reading passages aloud with partner modeling and peer coaching; formulating a general understanding by asking and answering questions about each paragraph; and working with partners to predict and confirm or disconfirm predictions.

Targeting Construction of Spoken and Written Narratives

Goal 13.4. The student will construct narratives orally and in writing that demonstrate competence with narrative discourse. Goals for discourse production can be targeted in the same activities as goals for comprehension.

Storytelling goals are particularly suited to writing process instruction—planning, organizing, drafting, revising, editing, and presenting (Bashir & Singer, 2006; Flower & Hayes, 1980; Harris, Graham, Mason, & Friedlander, 2008; Nelson, Bahr, & Van Meter, 2004). Even when students are functioning at an emergent writing level, dictation and "shared pencil" techniques and technology supports can be used to get a child's story written down (Sturm & Koppenhaver, 2000). The value of conveying expectations that all students have stories to tell and can learn to read and write is conveyed in Case Example 13.2 (based on Swoger, 1989).

Englert (1992) incorporated the recursive phases of writing processes in her POWER mnemonic: **P**lan, **O**rganize, **W**rite, **E**dit, **R**ewrite/**R**evise. Englert emphasized the communicative aspects and awareness of audience by using preparatory think sheets that prompted students to think about *who* they are writing for, *why* they are writing, and *what* they know.

Harris and colleagues (2008) recommended writing process steps for writing stories: **P**ick my idea; **O**rganize my notes; **W**rite and say more. These three POW steps are followed with a series of question prompts: "Who is the main character? When does the story take place? Where does the story take place? What does the main character do or want to do? What do other characters do? What happens then? What happens with other characters? How does the story end? How does the main character feel? How do other characters feel?" (p. 77).

Story grammar graphic organizers can be used to scaffold the inclusion of narrative macrostructure components during prewriting. Scaffolding for story production could be conversational (asking for details about precipitating events), historical (supporting sequencing of events), or psychological (focusing on the landscape of consciousness) (Ninio & Snow, 1996). If assessment indicates that a student is producing an isolated description with unrelated information heaps, for example, a series of pictograph frames (Ukrainetz, 1998b, 2006b) might help the student tell a story with features of an action sequence. Once the student can maintain temporal order, "I wonder why . . ." questions can be designed to elicit information about causality. At upper levels, clinicians might ask theory of mind questions about characters' goals and choices and how they must feel about the events of the story. Figure 13.8 shows a graphic organizer that was completed with scaffolding by a third-grade student with language and literacy risks in the writing lab approach (Nelson et

Scott's Writing Workshop Experience and Broader Outcomes

Peggy Swoger was a general education English teacher who previously had taught English to ninth-grade honor students. In an article in the *English Journal*, Swoger (1989) described what happened when she developed a writer's workshop and taught reading and writing to students with special needs, focusing on one student, Scott, whose "disability had been diagnosed as Attention Deficit Disorder (ADD) with hyperactivity and speech difficulties" (p. 63). Swoger noted that these issues, "paired with an IQ of 74," were "terrible hurdles" for Scott to overcome. In describing Scott at the beginning of the year, she wrote:

> His special-education teacher said that last year Scott became so depressed and withdrawn that they considered special counseling for him. He rarely tried to communicate; in fact, Scott's problems had always been complicated by his language and speech difficulties. He seemed not to be able to generate sentences, even orally. (p. 61)

It is not uncommon for students with disabilities to have few opportunities to write original pieces in their special education classrooms. So-called story starters are often deemed necessary, especially for students with low cognitive abilities, as Scott's IQ score suggested. So, when initially engaged in the writer's workshop approach (Atwell, 1987) that Swoger used with her new students, Scott had no experience generating his own ideas. Swoger's approach was to show patience and confidence that Scott did have stories to tell. In fact, it was this article that first stimulated Nelson and colleagues (2004) to make the "Patience principle" one of the key tenets of BACKDROP in their writing lab approach. Swoger wrote that, because it was her first experience with students with learning disabilities, she did not know what to expect, so she just "accepted whatever they could do and praised it" (p. 61). Describing this initial process further, she wrote:

> If they did not perform, I waited, but I revisited each desk every day. "Tell me about your story," I would say while looking with interest into their eyes at the person somewhere within. Scott was shy, but his soft brown eyes said that he liked my visits to his desk. He stumbled over each word and started over repeatedly. After three days, he had written three sentences. (p. 61)

Scott's first story was about how when he was 6 years old, his dog, Hambone, had been missing. When Scott and his friend found the dog, it was dead. Scott, who received some help with spelling, ended his first story with these words: "So we buirded him in that hole and we covered it up, Tom and me. We were pretty sad" (p. 62).

After enjoying initial success, Scott's writing about his second story topic, snow skiing, came easier. He also began to revise in the process of drafting. After reading his first draft to Swoger, he returned to the page and added the word *steep* to the sentence, "I was real afraid of the *steep* mountain" (p. 62). Swoger's patience, combined with the ownership Scott had been granted for coming up with his own ideas, were working. Scott not only bloomed at the discourse level but also at the sentence and word levels. He began to need and notice new words associated with details in his environment and then write about them. Swoger described this process:

> One day, later in the year, he came to my desk and asked if there were two meanings of the word "hospital." He wrote: "The friend's sister had a lot of people over to celebrate Mardi Gras. I met a lot of them and they were very hospitable." Scott seemed to be noticing words. He needed words; he was a writer.
>
> He also needed details. "Scott notices everything," his mother told me. His writing began to show his attention to detail. He wrote: "It was the first time I ate crawfish. You suck the inside of the head and eat the tail. It was very spicy." These details were certain to entertain his classmates. (pp. 62–63)

Scott's reading improved along with his writing. His scores on the Stanford Reading Diagnostic Test increased from 2.8 to 7.3 (over four years' growth) in eight months. Swoger attributed much of this growth to the time Scott spent reading. Two periods were devoted to sustained, silent reading each week in English class and five periods a week in reading class. Swoger also attributed Scott's growth in using language for both spoken and written communication to the fact that "Scott was telling his own story in his own way from what he knew" (p. 64).

Characters	Who or what is in your story?
	me mom and a man
Setting	Where does your story take place?
	in my car I was 6 in the spring
Problem	What problem is going on here?
	car axadint
Events	What events happen in the story? What are some of the things that bring the problem closer to a solution?
	I am prod that I was savde
Solution THE END ☺	How do the characters solve the problem?
	The person That crashd in to me savde my Life

figure *13.8*

Story Grammar Graphic Organizer Completed by a Third-Grade Student
with Language-Learning Difficulties

al., 2004) as she planned an original story based on a personal narrative about a serious car accident she had been in as a younger child.

When working with preadolescents and adolescents, Hyter and Westby (1996) suggested three goals focused on the landscape of consciousness:

(1) to develop the social-cognitive knowledge essential for perspective taking that underlies the landscape of consciousness, (2) to develop an appreciation of the stylistic variations necessary to convey the landscape of consciousness, and (3) ability to translate between oral style and the literate style approaches to presenting the landscape of consciousness in narratives. (p. 272)

Students need a reason and audience for telling stories. Peers can be scaffolded to show their interests (which usually comes naturally) in specific details (e.g., "I liked the part where you told about being scared") and not just general appreciation (e.g., "I liked your story"). This can take place in the context of partner editing, author groups, or a whole-class author's chair experience.

In support of discourse-level intervention, Nelson and Van Meter (2006b) reported data for pre- and posttest written story probes gathered in fall and spring by 41 third-grade students (32 with typical language and 9 with a variety of special written-language needs) who were participating in the writing lab approach. The baseline data for the story grammar scores in the fall samples showed that the special-needs students produced stories with a mean score of 1.40 (standard deviation [SD] = 0.84), signaling a level partway between an isolated description and action sequence (using an adaptation of a story grammar scoring). Meanwhile, typically developing children produced baseline stories with a mean story grammar score of 2.47 (SD = 0.86), signaling a level halfway between a temporal and causal sequence. After eight months of intervention with the writing lab approach, the students with special needs had improved their story grammar level to a mean of 3.50 (SD = 1.08), which represented a difference of 2.10 story grammar levels with an effect size of 2.85 SD. The students with typical language who received instruction in the same context also improved their performance an average of 1.77 story grammar levels to a mean of 4.23 (SD = 1.04) with an effect size of 1.97 SD units.

The lack of a no-treatment control group makes it difficult to attribute the changes made by both groups of students purely to the activities of language instruction and intervention. On the other hand, the fact that students with special needs who received extra individualized scaffolding moved closer to their peers (rather than further away) supports a conclusion that they benefited specifically from the inclusive intervention approach and not from development alone.

Expository Discourse

Expository discourse presents unique challenges and opportunities as an intervention context. Most content-area textbooks (e.g., science, social studies) use an expository genre to convey information. Expository texts often use complex syntactic structures, higher-level and abstract vocabulary, and assumptions for background knowledge that increase with grade level (Norris, 1995). This presents challenges to students with LI/LD and students with other language-learning challenges (see Personal Reflection 13.2).

PERSONAL reflection *13.2* ————————————————————————

"It's just written the way adults read it. . . . And they have the knowledge to do that. . . . And they write it in their own little language. Like you said, there's different ways to write a sentence. . . . Well, they write it in their language that only them can understand because they graduated, they have a diploma and everything. And we don't get that. The words are big that you're like, 'Okay.' You gotta go look it up. . . . You read the word and you try to translate it and you can't. . . . It's like, oh, it gives you a head ache. . . . So it gets you brain dead."

These interview comments from **Yolanda,** a 16-year-old, first-generation Latina immigrant to the United States, were gathered in an ethnographic study by Elizabeth Birr Moje (2006, p. 12).

To process expository discourse, students need to bring online multiple resources to receive the input, process the perceptual data, understand the words and sentences, detect the discourse structure, relate it to background (world) knowledge, and use it to organize concepts into a framework of relationships that makes sense. Students who are aware of the macrostructures of texts are able to use the information to comprehend and paraphrase or summarize a text, whereas less proficient readers seem to approach expository text without a plan and provide disjointed retellings (Meyer, Brandt, & Bluth, 1980).

In a systematic review, Gersten and colleagues (2001) found that students with learning disabilities have difficulty reorganizing disorganized text, identifying information that is essential and nonessential (e.g., they may highlight everything as important when reading), comprehending what they read, and organizing information for retelling. Gersten and colleagues concluded that text structure awareness is a developmental skill, that some structures are easier to detect than others, and that skill for detecting expository macrostructure (e.g., compare–contrast, hierarchical categories, cause–effect) is important for comprehension. Englert and Thomas (1987) also showed that students with learning disabilities lacked awareness of text macrostructures and that the difficulties affected their ability to understand expository discourse. Wong (1980) found that students with learning disabilities were able to recall as many main ideas as their peers when provided with prompting questions but were unable to organize information on their own for retelling.

Both cognitive and metacognitive processes are required to grasp the macrostructure of expository discourse. Identification of expository macrostructures both requires and supports working memory. Visual–spatial mental models can be used to chunk, organize, retain, and recall information from texts. For his updated model of working memory, Baddeley (2003) described four components: (1) a phonological loop for keeping active auditory–verbal information while processing it; (2) a visual–spatial sketchpad, which serves a parallel function for visual–spatial information; (3) a central executive unit that is limited by attention and controls the allocation of information-processing resources; and (4) an episodic buffer to hold partially processed information. Detecting macrostructures of expository text may make it easier to maintain key information in buffer storage while the student is working on understanding the microstructures of a text and getting to underlying conceptual relationships. Speed of processing, capacity limitations, and integration difficulties make it difficult for students with LI to process auditory–verbal and visual–spatial input simultaneously and efficiently (e.g., Hoffman & Gillam, 2004; Leonard et al., 2007). Such difficulties place limits on understanding and reconstructing the meaning of expository texts.

Assessing Expository Discourse Knowledge and Skills

CBLAI procedures for expository discourse follow the usual sequence of identifying contexts of concern, selecting curricular materials, analyzing demands of the task (the expected response, ER), and observing gaps between the ER and the student's observed response (OR). Similar to making story grammar structure explicit to help students comprehend and produce narrative discourse, macrostructure features can be used as a template for assessing students' ability to abstract organizing structures for conveying information in expository texts (see Figure 13.9). This is a skill that has been identified consistently by researchers as facilitating expository text comprehension (Gersten et al., 2001).

To gain access to a student's inner thought processes for making sense of expository text, the clinician can model the think-aloud process and encourage students to do the same while engaging in targeted curricular activities. Another technique is to ask students to draw a sketch of what they think a segment of expository text means. This approach is particularly helpful for assessing understanding the discourse of story problems in mathematics, as illustrated in Case Example 13.3.

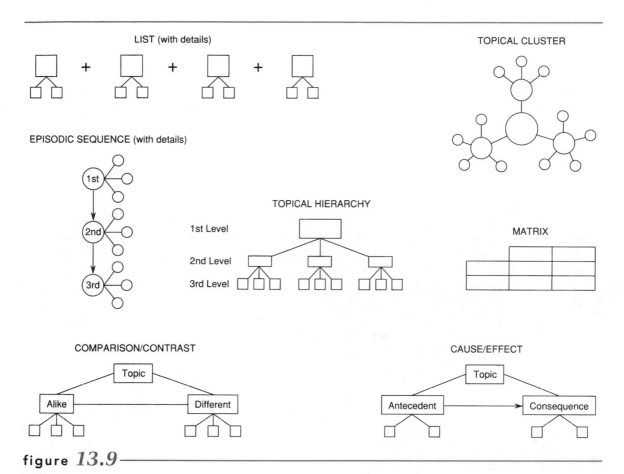

figure *13.9*

Expository Discourse Macrostructures

Source: Based on Calfee & Chambliss, 1988; Westby, 1991.

If a student seems unaware of expository structures, the clinician might offer a fitting graphic organizer template, such as one of those illustrated in Figure 13.9, and conduct dynamic assessment to see how well the student can fit content from the text into the components of the graphic structure with scaffolding. Retelling, summarizing, and paraphrasing techniques also can be used to assess comprehension of expository texts. Scott and Windsor (2000) gathered spoken and written language samples of students summarizing narrative and expository texts. Analyzing language samples can help teachers gain insights into how well students are understanding material from their expository lessons (Westby, 2006). The goal in retelling is to get inside students' thought processes by asking them to think aloud, sketch what they think texts mean; or summarize, paraphrase, or retell the information they heard, read, or experienced. Combinations of probe techniques can be used to gain a more complete picture. Time spent in assessment transitions directly into intervention.

Based on the observational and language sample data, the clinician analyzes mismatches between the ER and OR to know where to begin to scaffold a better match between the discourse and the student's concepts. For some students, it may be necessary to provide basic instruction about vocabulary and phrases that may have been misunderstood (e.g., *each* bike rack, *all together*), syntactic devices that are ignored or misrepresented in memory, and executive strategies that could be helpful as well.

---CASE **example** *13.3*---

Monica and the Language of Math

Monica was a fifth-grade girl who was having difficulty with the language of school—particularly expository discourse and, even more so, the language of math. A dynamic assessment approach was used to attempt to understand the source of the difficulty and what might be done to help. Monica had difficulty both with story problems and computation problems. She struggled with computation, especially on pages in her math book that required her to copy and work problems with a variety of operations (addition, subtraction, multiplication, and division). Monica made copying and computation errors, often selecting the wrong operation for the nature of the problem in seemingly random fashion.

Having observed this, the clinician mediated the experience by modeling the think-aloud approach and then asked Monica to think out loud while attempting to solve a page of mixed computation problems. The clinician observed Monica's tendency to use nonexact language to talk about the problems, with overuse of the conjunction *and* in contexts in which specific terms, such as *minus*, *plus*, and *divided by*, fit the mathematical symbols on the page. Intervention was designed to be sure that Monica knew and could retrieve more precise terminology to talk herself through each problem and then do what the problem said.

The think-aloud protocol also was used to assess Monica's ability to understand the discourse of story problems. In addition, Monica was asked to sketch what she thought the words of a specific problem meant. One difficulty was ruled out when she was able to read aloud the words of the problems without difficulty, but it soon became apparent that she was not actively generating mental pictures that matched the words, possibly because of problems at the level of basic vocabulary that fifth-grade students were assumed to know. For example, Monica read this problem: "There are seven bike racks. If each bike rack will hold eight bikes, how many bikes will the racks hold all together?" After reading, she thought a moment and then said, "Eight." The clinician then asked Monica to go back and read each part of the problem and sketch what it meant, framing the first sentence for Monica to focus on first. Monica's drawing suggested that she had understood the sentence. It looked something like this:

—— —— —— —— —— —— ——

When asked to sketch the part about each rack holding eight bikes, Monica simply added a single line to each rack.

╱ ╀ ╀ ╱ ╀ ╀ ╀

The clinician attempted to help Monica bridge the gap between the observed response (OR) and expected response (ER) by providing scaffolding feedback on the mismatch between what the words meant and what the picture Monica drew showed, first focusing on how to represent the words "If each bike rack will hold eight bikes" before discussing why multiplication was the best approach to solve the problem.

Targeting Expository Text Comprehension

Goal 13.5. The student will outline and summarize expository texts and answer factual and inferential questions about them to show comprehension. As in the goal area on narration, it makes sense to combine intervention on expository discourse comprehension and formulation. Gersten and colleagues (2001) described a transition from a traditional three-phase instructional approach (modeling, guided practice using controlled materials, and independent practice) to more flexible cognitive constructivist approaches. Dynamic dialogic approaches view comprehension instruction as "an attempt to teach students how to think while they read" (p. 307). To improve reading comprehension, students can be taught to recognize expository macrostructures. Outlining, summarizing, and answering factual and experiential questions all can be targeted while working on expository text formulation in a writing process approach or other curriculum-based activities.

Even if grade-level expository texts are above the student's current reading level, there are advantages to using the student's actual textbooks (rather than packaged commercial materials) for intervention. Advantages include relevance, preparation for high-stakes tests, exposure to higher-level vocabulary and concepts, and the status of using the same textbooks as peers. If the reading level is too high, students can be scaffolded to find information in the text using macrostructure cues (e.g., the table of contents, major and minor headings, bold text or italics for key words) and to read at least some sections independently. The clinician can take a turn at reading and can scaffold the student to figure out the meanings of unfamiliar vocabulary and to decode highly complex sentence structures by requesting summaries after each paragraph. The overriding goal is to help the student move toward greater independence. That goal should remain at the forefront and be discussed explicitly with the student.

In addition to textbooks, other authentic options can be used as intervention contexts. Ukrainetz (2006c) listed daily-life examples of expository subgenres that could be used in intervention, including description (classified ad), enumeration (table of contents, nutrition label), procedure (technical manual, recipe), explanation (nature magazine), comparison/contrast (consumer report), and persuasion (editorial, letter of complaint). Students can become aware of *signaling devices* that characterize cohesion for a particular type of expository text.

An early approach to teaching reading comprehension strategies was developed during World War II to teach soldiers to comprehend training manuals (Robinson, 1941/1970). Known as **SQ3R,** for **Survey, Question, Read, Recite, Review,** this approach encouraged readers to take multiple passes through expository texts (Just & Carpenter, 1987). The first two steps, survey and question, are advance organizers to be used prior to reading. They involve surveying a text's topics and organizational structure (e.g., based on headings) and formulating questions the text might answer. The next step is to read the text, while keeping active the questions the text is expected to answer. The final two steps, recite and review, occur after reading to solidify understanding.

Schumaker and colleagues (1984) developed Multipass as an adaptation of SQ3R. In this approach, students make three passes through expository material to **survey, size-up,** and **sort-out.** In the *survey pass,* students seek information about main ideas and organization by reading the chapter title and introductory paragraph, reviewing the relationship to adjacent chapters, reading major subtitles, looking at illustrations and captions, reading summary paragraphs, and paraphrasing the information. In the *size-up pass,* students skim the text to seek specific information for answering questions at the end of the chapter or questions they have formulated in their minds. In the *sort-out pass,* students test themselves by reading each question at the chapter's end and checking off those they can answer immediately. If not, they return to the text section where the answer might be found and read until they can answer the question.

In research on this approach, teachers worked individually with students to model the strategic approach while thinking aloud and then supported the students in guided practice until they reached 100 percent criterion on each step using controlled materials. This was followed by practice using grade-level materials. Schumaker and colleagues (1984) found improved posttest performance on 20-item tests of expository materials in both instructional and grade-appropriate material.

Consistent with the Multipass and SQ3R approaches, Tierney and Cunningham (1984) described four purpose-driven, constructivist steps that instructors could use to mediate students' comprehension (listening or reading) with the goal of transferring the steps to students' control:

Step 1: Establish purpose(s) for comprehending.

Step 2: Have students read or listen for the established purpose(s).

Step 3: Have students perform some task which directly reflects and measures accomplishment of each established purpose for comprehending.

Step 4: Provide direct information feedback concerning students' comprehension based on their performance of that (those) task(s). (p. 625)

Background knowledge plays an important role in helping students understand what they read. One approach for helping students become conscious of old and new information in expository texts is to develop three-column *K-W-L charts* to serve as reading guides. Students receive scaffolding to identify what they *Know* before reading, what they *Want* to know, and what they *Learned* after reading the passage (Carr & Ogle, 1987). Raphael and Pearson (1982) taught students to analyze whether textbook questions require students to locate an answer in the text *(right there questions),* derive an answer from their own background knowledge *(on my own questions),* or infer an answer based on both processes *(think and search questions).*

Other approaches to teaching reading comprehension have incorporated peer-mediation techniques. Palincsar and Brown (1984) developed a constructivist dialogic approach to teach peers to mediate discussions about texts for peers. They called it *reciprocal teaching.* Using this approach, typically learning students learned to lead discussions about short sections of text using four strategies—*predicting, questioning, clarifying,* and *summarizing.* In a variation, Englert and Mariage (1991) taught fourth-, fifth-, and sixth-grade students with learning disabilities to use a graphic organizer with the acronym *POSSE* to *Predict* ideas, *Organize* predicted ideas and background knowledge based on text structure, *Search* for the text structure, *Summarize* the main ideas, and *Evaluate* your comprehension (see Figure 13.10). Teachers modeled the strategies with the graphic organizer and gradually transferred control to students using the reciprocal teaching paradigm. Dialogue transcripts showed that students with learning disabilities had not fully internalized the strategies during the two-month treatment, but they did increase their strategy knowledge more than control students, and they performed better on recall of novel expository passages. Students performed best when teachers transferred more control for the dialogue to students.

Collaborative strategic reading (CSR) is a variation on reciprocal teaching (Vaughn & Edmonds, 2006). It involves teaching students to use four strategies:

- *Previewing* involves recalling what students already know and predicting what the text might be about.
- *Clunking* involves monitoring comprehension for areas that "clunk" because of difficult words and concepts and using fix-up strategies when text does not make sense.
- *Getting the gist* includes restating the most important idea in a passage while reading.
- *Wrap up* involves summarizing what has been learned and generating questions that a teacher might ask on a test.

Questions can be generated that are considered "easy," "harder," and "hardest." CSR combines cooperative learning techniques and reciprocal teaching so that students develop skills for using executive strategies in the group context. Students work collaboratively in groups of three to five to read the assigned text and practice the strategies. Preliminary evidence indicates that peer-assisted learning can have a positive effect on the reading comprehension of struggling high school students.

POSSE

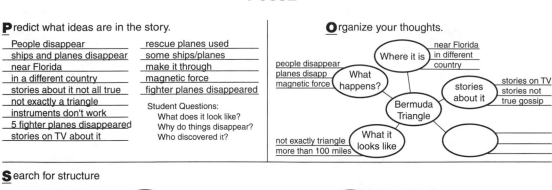

Predict what ideas are in the story.

People disappear
ships and planes disappear
near Florida
in a different country
stories about it not all true
not exactly a triangle
instruments don't work
5 fighter planes disappeared
stories on TV about it

rescue planes used
some ships/planes
make it through
magnetic force
fighter planes disappeared

Student Questions:
What does it look like?
Why do things disappear?
Who discovered it?

Organize your thoughts.

Search for structure

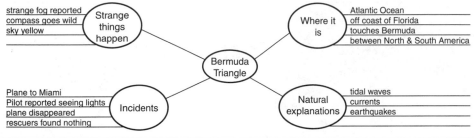

Summarize. Summarize the Main Idea in your own words. Ask a "Teacher" Question about the Main Idea

Evaluate. Compare. Clarify. Predict.

figure *13.10*

Partially Completed POSSE Strategy Sheet

Source: From "Making students partners in the comprehension process: Organizing the reading 'POSSE,'" by C. S. Englert & T. V. Mariage, 1991, *Learning Disability Quarterly, 14*, p. 129. Copyright by The Council for Learning Disabilities. Reprinted by permission.

Targeting Expository Text Construction

Goal 13.6. The student will construct spoken and written expository texts that are more mature than at baseline. Writing process instruction can help students construct mental models for expository text structures to improve comprehension at the same time they are planning and organizing varied expository texts—reports, essays, editorials, business plans, and so on. Paper-and-pencil graphic organizers can be used to support learning of expository macrostructures, but computer software supports (e.g., Inspiration and Kidspiration software) offer alternative planning and organizing possibilities. Computer supports are popular with students, and they can compensate for some of the difficulties of students with disabilities (Nelson et al., 2004).

In collaborating with general education teachers to implement the writing lab approach, Nelson and colleagues (2004) have worked with second-graders to plan and construct personal timelines, with third-graders to write animal reports, with fourth-graders to do research and prepare PowerPoint presentations on weather phenomena, and with fifth- and sixth-graders to write reports on outer space. In each case, the topics and projects were developed to address goals of the general education curriculum. Each curricular project began by discussing with teachers the communicative purpose and structure of the relevant subgenre, which were then explained to students. Next, templates were used to scaffold students to find information to achieve a particular expository communication purpose. Intervention sessions were held over several weeks to allow students to move through all stages of the writing process and to share their products with peers. Students with special needs had language development goals at all levels and across all modalities.

The need to seek information from other sources when constructing an expository text brings the added opportunity to locate and read expository texts for a purpose, both online and in print. When working on weather reports, for example, a graduate clinician developed a minilesson on note taking that started with the generation of a set of questions about the nature of tornados. Figure 13.11 shows the overhead transparency that laid out the questions in a semantic map. Then the clinician read a segment of text from the students' science textbook that explained that tornadoes are produced when a cold front meets rap-

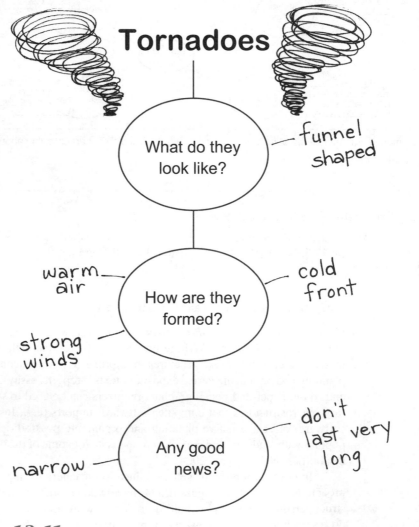

figure *13.11*

Note-Taking Template about Tornadoes Used in Minilesson

Source: Contributions by Frazier Jordan.

idly rising warm air so that more air moves in to replace it. The text went on to explain that when the air begins to rotate, it produces a funnel cloud that can touch the ground. The brief paragraph ended with a sentence about how tornadoes usually only touch a narrow area and do not last very long. Following this introduction, the clinician modeled the process of rephrasing relevant points from the text and led the class in a discussion about how to find answers to the questions that were noted on the plan. Then students conducted their own searches and took notes. In subsequent sessions, the students organized their information in PowerPoint slides and made oral presentations on their topics.

Numerous other sources recommend using writing process contexts to teach students to produce expository texts. Harris, Graham, Mason, and Friedlander (2008) described how to implement ***self-regulated strategy development (SRSD),*** using steps to develop background knowledge, discuss the strategy goals and significance, model the strategy, have students memorize the strategy, support strategy practice, and provide opportunities for students to engage in independent performance (e.g., Graham, Harris, & Troia, 2000). Harris and colleagues (2008) suggested a combination of mnemonic acronyms accompanied by cue cards, scaffolding, and transfer tools. For example, Harris and colleagues offered a strategy and a web for organizing notes on "What I Know and What I Want to Learn," with these steps: brainstorm what you know and what you want to learn; organize your information in a web; gather new information and revise your web; use the web as you write; and keep planning as you write. The clinicians taught macrostructure components for a persuasive essay using the acronym ***DARE***, for **D**etermine your premise, **A**ssemble reasons to support your premise, **R**eject arguments for the other side, and **E**nd with a conclusion. Ukrainetz (2006c) described a case study in which the DARE mnemonic was used, noting that the student with language impairment showed more interest and intervention when taught the strategy in the context of assignments drawn from the general education curriculum.

Bashir and Singer (2006) also identified writing process instruction as a prime context for developing self-regulation abilities. Their **EmPOWER** acronym captures the complex elements that students need to plan and write discourse in the expository genre. In this approach, students learn to **E**valuate the writing assignment by first reading the instructions carefully, **M**ake a **P**lan that is based on communicative purpose and will help the student get started, **O**rganize their ideas graphically using templates specific to the intended genre, **W**ork from the plan to represent the idea with written language, and **E**valuate and **R**ework the draft with the purpose and audience in mind.

Executive Control and Self-Regulation Discourse

Executive control and self-regulatory "thinking language" grow out of social mediation (scaffolding) from supportive, attentive others. Mediators convey confidence in a student's ability to learn and frame cues in the environment to make learning more effective. The process of learning self-regulation is complete when the student internalizes social talk, making it self-talk (Englert, 1992; Feuerstein, 1980; Rogoff, 1990). Feuerstein's (1979) terminology for social mediation refers to "framing, selecting, focusing, and feeding back environmental experiences" to produce in the child "appropriate learning sets and habits" (p. 179). The desired outcome is a set of integrated operations a student can use automatically and flexibly.

The ability to call on background knowledge and skills that have reached an automatic level of proficiency plays a critical role in strategic, efficient approaches to problem solving. With expertise, less effort is needed to recognize patterns, and perception becomes automatic (Bransford, Brown, & Cocking, 2000). When people can cluster concepts and organize information into patterns, they can remember more with shorter exposure. Miller's

(1956) classic study of short-term memory capacity showed that the consistent limit of 7 ± 2 for unrelated items (e.g., numbers) could be expanded considerably if people learned to chunk information into larger units that made sense to them (e.g., patterns of numbers that are higher and lower).

In this goal area, executive control and self-regulation of strategies are targeted separately. Bashir and Singer (2006) described "executive functions as distinct from, but central to and supportive of, self-regulated learning" (p. 573). *Executive functions* are invoked when a student faces a complex task and allocates such cognitive resources as attention, inhibition, planning, organizing, and working memory. *Self-regulation abilities* are strategies used to accomplish a specific information-processing goal. Another way to think about this is that executive functions are generic reason and control mechanisms that allocate limited capacity resources to achieve a goal, whereas strategies are active tools of self-regulation that are used for specific tasks (e.g., rehearsal, association, chunking, filling in mental slots, self-talk, summarization, and decisions to store information in long-term memory).

For executive control, students need adequate motivation and attention to attempt academic tasks and take an active approach to learning. *Attention,* as defined by Smith (1975), was described in Chapter 1 as "questions being asked by the brain" (p. 28). The demands of integrated curricular tasks are particularly challenging for students with LI/LD and other comorbid disabilities. Students with learning disabilities often appear to be *inactive learners* and show erratic ability to use newly acquired skills, such as how to underline selectively to increase retention of material they have read (Torgesen, 1982). The ZPD for students with disabilities may seem wide and full of wobbly skills, in which partial competence is evident and only in certain circumstances (see Personal Reflection 13.3). The clinical process involves helping such students acquire efficient executive functions so they are able to do more, remember more, and learn more.

PERSONAL reflection *13.3*

"A child is not a computer that either 'knows' or 'does not know.' A child is a bumpy, blippy, excitable, fatiguable, distractible, active, friendly, mulish, semi-cooperative bundle of biology. Some factors help a moving child pull together coherent address to a problem; others hinder that pulling together and tend to make a child 'not know.' "

Sheldon White (1980, p. 43), a psychologist at Harvard, was describing how cognitive competence and performance are influenced by everyday environments.

Taking an active approach to academic and social challenges requires a belief that one is capable of change and growth. Dawson and Guare (2004) described two sets of executive skills. The first set—planning, organization, time management, working memory, and metacognition—is used "to select and achieve goals or to develop problem solutions" (p. 1). The second set—response inhibition, regulation of affect, task initiation, flexibility, and goal-directed persistence—is needed "to guide or modify our behavior as we move along the path" (p. 2).

Metacognition is the ability to monitor and understand one's own learning capabilities (strengths and needs) and to analyze the demands of a learning task (Bransford et al., 2000). Consciously or not, most children form concepts regarding their intelligence and ability to learn. Students who see their intellectual capacity as static and unchangeable (based on entity theories of intelligence) are less likely to expend effort to learn than those who see their intellectual capacity as dynamic and open to change (based on incremental theories) (Dweck, 1989; Feuerstein, Rand, & Rynders, 1988). Gersten and colleagues (2001) characterized students with learning disabilities as having difficulties more in the area of metacognitive awareness and efficiency than in deficits of basic skills:

> In other words, while students with learning disabilities possess the necessary cognitive tools to effectively process information, for some reason they do so very inefficiently. Most researchers suspect that the breakdowns occur in the domain of strategic processing and metacognition (i.e., students' ability to control and manage their cognitive activities in a reflective, purposeful fashion). (p. 280)

Persistence in the face of obstacles is an important trait, especially for learners who may require more time and additional assistance to learn. When students with LI/LD experience repeated unsuccessful efforts to solve academic problems, they have difficulty sustaining their motivation to work hard at learning. Stanovich (1986) noted that when students experience failure at learning to read, they soon begin to avoid classes that require large amounts of reading and rarely engage in after-school recreational reading. Gersten and colleagues (2001) noted that a "major movement in the field of comprehension has been to develop teaching approaches that actively encourage students to persist in figuring out what the text is saying" (p. 286) and to monitor how well they are doing.

Bandura (1977) theorized that ***personal efficacy*** derives from four information sources: performance accomplishments, vicarious experience, verbal persuasion, and physiological states. All four must be activated to support children and adolescents with language and communication problems to function more effectively in school. Expectations of personal efficacy play an essential role in the face of aversive experiences and obstacles for determining whether coping behavior will emerge, how much effort will be expended, and how long it will be sustained.

Assessing Metacognitive Awareness and Executive Functions

CBLAI procedures can be designed to assess the degree to which students can use self-talk as an executive control mechanism for solving academic and social problems. Self-talk is both a tool of assessment and a goal of intervention. Clinicians can start by modeling the think-aloud procedure and asking students to engage in it while they attempt curriculum-based tasks in an area of primary concern. Interview techniques also can be used to gain insight into a student's inner messages. Figure 13.12 summarizes executive functions and self-regulation skills for use as a tool for guiding observations of students engaging in curricular tasks and other types of problem-solving behavior.

Simply asking a student in the midst of a curriculum activity "What's your goal here?" can be revealing. Students with limited self-awareness may say "I don't know." Those with partial self-awareness may be able to express something like "I'm doing math" or "I can't figure out what to do." Students who have a higher level of metacognitive awareness will be able to express a more specific goal, such as "I'm trying to decide how to start" or "I'm looking for the section that will help me answer this question."

It is not only self-talk about how to work through academic or social interaction problems that may be problematic but also negative "I can't" messages that students incorporate in stories they tell themselves about their capabilities (see Personal Reflection 13.4). Simply counting the number of times a student says "I can't" in the midst of a curriculum-based assessment activity can yield a means of measuring the baseline level of functioning in this area to target in intervention.

figure *13.12*

Observation Tool for Executive Skills and Self-Regulation

Context _____	Date _____
Student _____	Observer _____

Skills for Executive Function and Self-Regulation	+ Observed – Not observed ~ Partial evidence	Descriptive Evidence
❑ **Preparing for challenging tasks** ❑ Shows motivation for making effort. ❑ Plans with forethought. ❑ Organizes approach to task. ❑ Gathers essential materials and does not lose them. ❑ Manages time well. ❑ Shows adequate working memory. ❑ Can use metacognition to analyze tasks and reflect on personal efficacy.		
❑ **Guiding and modifying behaviors in context of tasks** ❑ Initiates task without delay or procrastination. ❑ Inhibits responses to irrelevant stimuli. ❑ Shows flexibility when new approach is needed. ❑ Shows goal-directed persistence for completing task. ❑ Works through frustration when having difficulty.		

❑ **Using strategies to perform specific tasks**
 ❑ Uses positive self-talk.
 ❑ Uses self-talk strategically.
 ❑ Uses all levels of Bloom's taxonomy:
    – Knowledge
    – Comprehension
    – Application
    – Analysis
    – Synthesis
    – Evaluation
 ❑ Learns strategies for specific curricular tasks quickly.
 ❑ Transfers learned strategies to new contexts.
 ❑ Shows independence in selecting and applying appropriate strategy for task.		

Source: Based on Bandura, 1977; Bashir & Singer, 2006; Bloom, 1956; Dawson & Guare, 2004; Ukrainetz, 2006a; Zimmerman, Bonner, & Kovach, 1996.

PERSONAL reflection *13.4*

"We not only are continuously learning language, but, in our interactions in language, we are constantly developing the narratives that comprise who we are, how we think of ourselves, and how we present ourselves to others."

Barbara Hoskins (1990, p. 60), a language-learning disabilities consultant in Pasadena, California, was writing about the importance of personal narratives as a form of self-talk.

Targeting Executive Functions (Including Inner Language and Awareness)

Goal 13.7. The student will demonstrate the application of executive skills for improving problem-solving capabilities over baseline. Through the dialogic discourse of intervention, students can gain ownership for their goals for change and the executive functions for persisting in the face of adversity. The focus of scaffolding, as always, must be on helping students develop increased independence in challenging situations, and caution is required to judge how much to scaffold and when to intervene (see Personal Reflection 13.5).

PERSONAL reflection *13.5*

"This common error, providing too much help, focuses on task completion as an end in itself, rather than on revealing to the student the underlying goal and processes needed for task completion."

Teresa A. Ukrainetz (2006a, p. 41), a speech–language pathologist and language scientist, described the finer points of scaffolding PreK–12 literacy achievement in her book on contextualized language intervention.

To engender in students a sense of self-efficacy, clinicians must convey that they are interested in and respect students' goals for change and capacity for reaching them. In addition, clinicians must convey that they have expertise for helping students reach their goals if they work together. This is particularly critical when signs indicate that the vicious cycle of negative intersystemic causation has begun, in which failure begets failure and reduced willingness to try. When someone suggests a student "could if he would," it is helpful to remember that most students "would if they could." Fear of failure and a wobbly ZPD can cause children and adolescents not to be able to do something they might manage in a more supportive environment. Some students feign not caring or even express outright hostility to learning because it is better to be thought bored or to feel angry than to think one is not smart enough to learn. Clinicians can play a role in reversing this cycle.

Decisions to target self-talk for regulating emotional and motivational states may be triggered by symptoms of difficulty with self-regulation. When children exhibit an exaggerated emotional or behavioral response to circumstances that ordinarily would not elicit such an extreme response, interdisciplinary intervention teams should gather assessment data and help students develop new ways to regulate their emotional states and impulsive actions. Social workers, psychologists, and medical professionals often collaborate with teachers to address such needs. Communication specialists may play a less central role in the intervention, unless obvious speech–language impairments are involved. Regardless, communication (external and internal) aspects should not be overlooked as part of the problem and potentially as part of the solution.

For example, one fourth-grade boy with an explosive temper was asked what it felt like when he was about ready to lose control. He thought about several different terms to describe the feeling but decided that *volcano* described it best. He then made a page in his "tool book" to describe the feeling, talking about how he could gain control of it rather than let it control him. He wrote several descriptive phrases about what it felt like when pressure was building up before his volcano "blew," and he illustrated the page with an erupting volcano. Then he worked on a second page with a picture of a resting volcano and a list of things he could experiment with to try to keep the volcano from blowing. The clinician helped the boy create a rating scale with rubrics so that he could score his own eruptions, from 0 points (for a full-force explosion) to 4 points (for keeping calm in a situation that usually made him blow his top). Creating a new way to communicate about a familiar problem can be shared across settings to help all involved take a fresh look at the student's outbursts as a problem he or she is trying to control from within, rather than bad behavior that must be punished externally.

When assessment shows that students are sending themselves (and others) negative messages about their capabilities, it is tempting to say "Oh yes, you can do it" or "Oh no, you're not stupid," but such responses often play into long-standing patterns of negativity and thus do little good. Taking a proactive approach to this problem may work best for addressing discouraging talk. Figure 13.13 presents a minilesson that can be used to help later elementary and middle school students see how the messages they communicate to themselves and others might be discouraging (e.g., "I can't," "I'm so stupid") and how they might change the negative messages to more positive ones, such as "This is hard, but I can try."

Executive functions are required for monitoring and controlling aspects of learning and interaction beyond the social–emotional domain. Bloom's (1956) taxonomy can be used to expand objectives for promoting higher levels of language and thinking. Using this taxonomy for assessment and planning purposes, teachers and clinicians can collaborate to develop universally designed instruction and intervention to meet a variety of learning needs. Students with higher-level abilities can be challenged with goals that are further up the hierarchy, while those functioning at lower levels can be challenged to move to the next level. Bloom's taxonomy might be used to generate different levels of questions within a social studies lesson on ecological disasters (Westby, 2006), as in the following example:

Knowledge: What do you know about hurricanes? When did Hurricane Katrina occur?

Comprehension: Describe why Hurricane Katrina affected so many people.

Application: What did people learn from the Katrina disaster that they can use in the future?

Analysis: Name at least one problem before and one problem after the hurricane that made matters worse.

Synthesis: What recommendations would you make to the state and local governments in places that have hurricanes?

Evaluation: Discuss the barriers and successes when people tried to clean up after Hurricane Katrina.

Students can have many patterns of cognitive strengths and needs. Most people demonstrate higher levels of executive function in areas where they are more competent (Bransford et al., 2000). When a language clinician focuses exclusively on a student's areas of weakness without pointing out his or her strengths as well, the student can develop a lower perception of his or her intellectual skills than justified. Gardner's (1983) theory of multiple intelligences can be used to help students construct more realistic (i.e., positive) profiles of all the ways they are smart. Miller (1993) developed a procedure for consulting with learners and scaffolding them to develop a "Smart Profile" of areas in which they are functioning more like beginners and more like experts to guide intervention planning.

Assessing Self-Regulation and Strategic Learning

Strategies for *self-regulation* are defined as "specific, learned procedures that foster active, competent, self-regulated, and intentional learning" (Trabasso & Bouchard, 2002, p. 176). The social interaction roots of strategy instruction were emphasized by Palincsar and Brown (1988) in their dialogic approach of reciprocal teaching. Self-regulated learners are able to demonstrate the ability to establish attainable goals, use effective strategies to

Step One
Write the word "courage" in the middle of a whiteboard. Have the students brainstorm what the word means and add key words in a semantic web.

Step Two
Add the prefix "dis-" to the beginning of the word in a different colored marker. Ask what happens to the meaning then. Students generally say things like, "It takes away your courage," and "You don't try." Cross out related qualities out on the semantic web to dramatize the meaning.

Step Three
Replace the "dis-" prefix with "en-," also in a different color. Ask the students what they think the word means now and rebuild the semantic web.

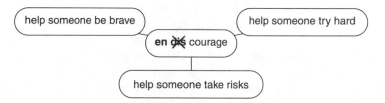

Step Four
Break into smaller groups of two to three students. Help the students list nonverbal and verbal ways they communicate messages to themselves and others in a chart with two columns.

Encouraging Things I Say and Do	**Dis**couraging Things I Say and Do

figure *13.13*

Encourage/Discourage Minilesson for Teaching Students about Derivational Morphology and Value of Positive Self-Talk

Source: © 1996 by N. W. Nelson. Used by permission of author.

achieve goals, self-monitor and evaluate, maintain motivation, use supports, and mediate performance with language (Bashir & Singer, 2006).

Interview and dynamic assessment techniques are appropriate for assessing executive and self-regulation skills together, as outlined in Figure 13.12. Observation of self-talk can be an important window into both. Guided by the four questions of CBLAI, the clinician can use participant observation and questioning to identify the degree to which a student is able to learn new strategies, call on specific strategies to address an area of concern, and decide what strategies to use for addressing which types of problems.

Targeting Self-Talk, Self-Regulation, and Strategic Approaches to Problem Solving

Goal 13.8. The student will demonstrate the use of self-talk and other self-regulation strategies to address academic and social problems. Intervention for improving self-regulation provides a classical example of scaffolding. What starts as social mediation can be transferred to personal, independent mediation as a means of self-regulation.

Students internalize the words of their mediators while constructing new cognitive–linguistic approaches for more mature problem solving in the future. Bruner (1983) differentiated "handover" of control from aid or assistance. Clinicians can foster independence by teaching students to use structural supports in the environment as scaffolds. Options include tool books with tabbed sections for minilesson handouts, personal dictionaries, and other reminders; mnemonic devices, such as acronyms, and steps students can follow sequentially; word walls with example words that illustrate common orthographic patterns; and printed schedules for organizing time.

Teaching strategies for self-regulation of learning processes for school-age students can be viewed along a continuum. Highly structured sequences fall at one end of the continuum, often involving mnemonic acronyms that students memorize and then follow step by step. Research has shown that acronyms can be effective in reminding adolescents with learning disabilities of the required steps in a strategy (e.g., Schumaker, Deshler, Alley, Warner, & Denton, 1984; Wolgemuth, Cobb, & Alwell, 2008). A concern, however, is that memorizing mnemonics is demanding in term of mental capacity (e.g., Gersten et al., 2001), and learning costs should not be overlooked (Ukrainetz, 2006c).

At the other end of the continuum are approaches to help students build inner purpose and rationale for using a fluid set of processes strategically. These more dynamic approaches teach students to have an authentic audience in mind, and they foster ownership for decisions so that steps of strategic processes flow naturally from the purpose and from mental models the student has constructed with scaffolding. For example, Dawson and Guare (2004) recommended that, rather than assign cues, clinicians should teach students to design their own cues and put systems in place to use them.

Students also can be taught to use self-talk as a generic problem-solving strategy or tool. This includes teaching them that people use self-talk when they think out loud and that students can use self-talk to guide their thinking about school problems by asking and answering questions one step at a time. A tool book handout might include a series of general self-talk questions that students can consult while working through a variety of curriculum-based activities, such as Do I understand what this problem is about? How can I solve this problem? What information will help me to solve this problem? What is the first step I need to do? What is the next step? Does the answer seem right? Am I done? (Nelson et al., 2004).

SUMMARY

Assessment and intervention for discourse-level skills can support other levels of communicative and academic functioning. Macrostructures and communication-processing demands vary for academic and social interaction conversational discourse forms and for narrative and expository forms. Assessment and intervention techniques should address metacognitive awareness and executive skills as well as basic skills.

Sentence-Level Knowledge and Skills

Students need syntactic skills both for combining semantic components into meaningful sentences and for decombining syntactic structures to analyze components and comprehend an author's or speaker's message. Sentence-level goals for school-age children are divided into goals for comprehending and producing higher-level syntactic structures and for using cohesive devices to understand and express complex semantic–syntactic relationships in discourse.

Higher-Level Sentence Comprehension and Production

Teachers' instructional language becomes syntactically more complex with increasing grade level (e.g., Sturm & Nelson, 1997), and so does textbook language (Biber, 1988; Eisenberg, 2006; Scott, 1994). The ability to comprehend and formulate complex sentence structures and to infer semantic relationships among the concepts they encode is an essential component of competence with higher-level language. The most active period for developing productive syntax occurs during the preschool years from ages 3 to 5, but development of syntactic abilities continues throughout childhood and adolescence before stabilizing at around age 20 (Nippold, Hesketh, Duthie, & Mansfield, 2005).

Limited morphosyntactic development is a central problem for children with specific and nonspecific language impairment (SLI and NLI, respectively) that affects production and comprehension in both spoken and written language. Rice and her colleagues (2004) tracked the use of grammatical tense markers by children with SLI and NLI from kindergarten through fourth grade and found that children with NLI lagged behind peers with SLI in grammatical performance during grades two and three but reached the same level by grade four. In the Epi-SLI study, children diagnosed with LI in kindergarten continued to produce stories in second and fourth grade with shorter and less complex *C*-units than peers and also more grammatical errors (Fey et al., 2004). Grammatical difficulty also is a factor in the profiles of students with difficulty learning to read and write, which explains variance beyond that associated with word-level phonological skills (Catts, Fey, Zhang, & Tomblin, 1999; Juel, 1988; Windsor, Scott, & Street, 2000). Additionally, grammatical difficulty can present barriers to social interaction (Donahue, 1987; Leonard & Fey, 1991; Mentis, 1994).

Assessing Higher-Level Syntax Comprehension and Production

Assessment of syntactic ability in samples of spoken and written language in the school-age years can employ many of the techniques described previously for preschoolers. Hewitt, Hammer, Yont, and Tomblin (2005) identified measures that differentiated kindergarten-age children (mean age 6 years) with and without SLI. Discriminating techniques included Scarborough's (1990a) IPSyn measure (see Chapter 11), number of different words in 50 utterance samples, and mean length of utterance (MLU) in morphemes. A difference is that normative studies of language development in the school-age years (Hunt, 1965; Loban, 1963) tend to use MLU counts in *words,* rather than morphemes. Counts using words rather than morphemes have advantages for school-age students in that the counts can be compared with data from normative studies and are less likely to reflect cultural–linguistic bias for students whose dialectal forms are less marked with inflectional morphemes.

Language samples for school-age children require special rules for dividing utterances. Due to the potential for run-on sentences, the samples are divided into *T*-units or *C*-units prior to computing MLU. Hunt (1965) defined the *T*-unit syntactically as "one main clause with all the subordinate clauses attached to it" (p. 20). He promoted using *T*-units as the best method for segmenting and analyzing the utterances of school-age children. It preserves the

table *13.2* Data from a Longitudinal Study of Oral Language Development for a Group of Children Followed from Kindergarten through Sixth Grade

	Lowest Group		Highest Group		Total Group	
Grade	*Mean*	*SD*	*Mean*	*SD*	*Mean*	*SD*
K	4.18 (*N* = 22)	1.29	5.76 (*N* = 30)	1.53	4.81 (*N* = 338)	1.33
1st	4.89 (*N* = 22)	1.36	6.89 (*N* = 30)	1.39	6.05 (*N* = 260)	1.37
2nd	5.49 (*N* = 22)	1.18	7.04 (*N* = 30)	1.18	6.57 (*N* = 261)	1.18
3rd	6.08 (*N* = 22)	1.82	7.73 (*N* = 30)	1.33	6.65 (*N* = 259)	1.81
4th	6.42 (*N* = 24)	1.20	8.77 (*N* = 25)	1.08	7.70 (*N* = 246)	1.26
5th	6.90 (*N* = 24)	0.93	8.85 (*N* = 25)	0.95	7.89 (*N* = 243)	1.10
6th	7.19 (*N* = 24)	0.88	9.48 (*N*= 25)	1.12	8.37 (*N* = 236)	1.25

Source: Data from Loban, 1963.

student's subordination and coordination between words but does not overcredit the less mature strategy of coordinating main clauses. Loban (1963) defined the *C*-unit similarly but with a focus on meaning as "a group of words which cannot be further subdivided without the loss of their essential meaning" (p. 6). *C*-units are designed to include elliptical utterances that are common in spoken communication. The terms *T-unit* and *C-unit* can be used essentially interchangeably, with incomplete or elliptical *T*-units included in counts of average length (MLTU). Loban reported MLCU data for oral language samples gathered in a longitudinal study, starting with 388 students in kindergarten and ending with 236 students in sixth grade. Data for low- and high-functioning groups from this study are summarized in Table 13.2. Data from other studies of developing syntax compared for spoken and written samples over the school-age years appear in Chapter 12 (Table 12.7).

Spoken language samples include not only sentences that are elliptical but also evidence of hesitation, formulation glitches, rephrasing, word-finding difficulties, and so forth. Loban (1963) labeled these linguistic nonfluencies ***mazes.*** Hunt (1965) called them ***garbles.*** Children with LI and word-finding difficulties, in particular, may have a higher frequency of mazes in their spoken discourse (see Table 13.3 for an example). Mazes never completely disappear, even from the spoken communication of highly accomplished adult speakers, but they do become less frequent as language proficiency advances. Table 13.4 summarizes the data reported by Loban (1963) based on his longitudinal study, which show higher rates of linguistic nonfluency for children in the low-functioning group than in the high-functioning group.

At all developmental levels, the *verb phrase (VP)* plays a key role in propositions conveying the state or action around which all other sentence parts (agents, instruments,

table _13.3_ Spoken Language Sample from a 10-Year-Old Fifth Grade Girl with Language Impairment and Attention-Deficit/Hyperactivity Disorder (ADHD)

Classroom Discourse Sample	Commentary
$ Child, Examiner	The child's spoken language shows a high rate of linguistic nonfluency (mazes) and several abandoned utterances.
E What kind of music do you like listening to?	
C (oh um) Hannah Montana [SC].	
E Oh, I don't know who that is.	
C It's (um) a TV show.	
C and (um this) this girl <u>named</u> Miley Cyrus and has a wig [CI].	The mazes include both syntactic and semantic (word-finding) hesitancies. Pauses filled with _um_ and _like_ or linguistic revisions are coded as mazes and do not influence judgment of syntactic correctness.
C And it's a blonde wig.	
C and (um, she, um) she is Miley when (uh, um) with {sigh} [CI]>	
C (Lola um) Lily is Miley's friend.	
C and (um) she does/n't have it on [CC].	Other problems involve pronoun cohesion clarity (e.g., "doesn't have <u>it</u> on") and a high rate of general, all-purpose words (_stuff, put, make_).
C And (um) she has a concert [SI].	
C She (um) has the wig on.	
C and she (um) is Hannah Montana [CC].	
E Oh, okay that sounds cool.	

E What have you been doing in art lately?	
C Making (like making like) stuff [SC].	
C (like um) drawing stuff like (um) scarecrow/*s but only with the pumpkin head and (um) with corn on the side and a rose [SC].	Syntax coding shows nonfluent simple sentences and some attempts at coordination (coded as "simple" because of only one verb). The most complex elements are the two examples of embedding using participles (_named, jumping_).
C And (um) then (one with a um) I made (a um) a landscape but only with water [SC].	
C We (put um we like put we) can make (like) a dolphin <u>jumping</u> out of the water [CC].	

Note: Mazes are enclosed in parentheses, following SALT coding conventions, and utterances are divided into _T_- and _C_-units, coded for complexity and correctness.

Source: Miller & Chapman, 2008 (SALT coding) and Nelson & VanMeter, 2002 (sentence-type coding).

table _13.4_ Data for Mazes Based on the Samples and Groupings Reported in Table 13.2

Grade	Percentage of Words in Mazes in Relation to Total Words			Percentage of Words in Mazes in Relation to Communication Units		
	Low	_High_	_Total_	_Low_	_High_	_Total_
K	11.92	9.17	12.30	32.07	22.55	25.38
1st	15.51	7.57	9.97	39.29	21.80	25.16
2nd	10.49	6.65	8.88	26.30	14.69	19.90
3rd	10.62	4.98	6.15	25.54	13.69	18.67
4th	9.74	5.43	7.11	31.63	23.82	28.33
5th	9.27	5.17	7.41	32.51	23.27	29.74
6th	9.49	5.17	7.53	32.09	25.75	32.06

Source: Data from Loban, 1963, p. 33.

locations, objects, etc.) revolve. To judge sentence complexity (i.e., embedding, subordination, coordination), one can begin by identifying verbs as the best indicator of whether more than one proposition is combined in the syntactic unit. Every complete *T*-unit includes at least one VP. (See Chapter 2 for a description of *T*-units and Figure 11.4 for an outline of the components of the mature VP in standard English.) The presence of more than one embedded or subordinated VP within a *T*-unit is an indication of greater syntactic embedding or subordination and hence complexity.

As discussed in Chapter 5, one prominent theory of SLI assigns a critical role to problems with verbs, particularly for using inflectional morphemes on verbs to fit particular syntactic contexts (e.g., Gopnik & Crago, 1991; Rice, 2004; Rice, Wexler, & Cleave, 1995). Related theories focus on problems of verb diversity, suggesting that the language of preschool and school-age children with LI is characterized by overreliance on a relatively few *general all-purpose (GAP)* verbs, including *come, do, eat, get, go, have, know, like, make, put, say, see, take, think, try* (Thordardottir & Ellis Weismer, 2001). All children around the age of 8 years use high rates of GAP verbs, such as *do, put,* and *make,* as prototypes for major categories of meaning (e.g., acting, affecting things, creating things). Because of this, GAP verb frequency should not be viewed as a symptom for diagnosing disorder, but it could be used for assessing periodic language samples to monitor change.

Other measures of syntactic variability can be used to assess children's growing syntactic abilities. Chapter 12 presented a sentence-coding scheme for assessing syntactic complexity and correctness in the written language probes for the writing lab approach (Nelson, Bahr, & Van Meter, 2004; Nelson & Van Meter, 2002). This analysis involves transcribing a written language sample into *T*-units using SALT (Miller & Chapman, 2008), as exemplified in Figure 13.3. Using this coding scheme, sentences incorporating up to two coordinated *T*-units are then coded as one of four types: simple incorrect (SI), simple correct (SC), complex incorrect (CI), and complex correct (CC). Proportions of types of sentences are computed in baseline probes and then monitored in subsequent samples as a means for documenting change.

As this coding scheme suggests, sentence-level difficulties can be signaled both by *errors* and as *limited variety and complexity* of syntactic structures. The frequency of grammatical errors per *T*-unit has been found to differentiate students with LI from those with typical language (Gillam & Johnston, 1992; Scott & Windsor, 2000). Nippold and her colleagues (2005) reported that MLTU and relative clause production were the two best indicators of growth in syntactic maturity in conversational and expository spoken discourse, and they and others reported expository discourse as incorporating particularly complex syntax (Eisenberg, 2006; Scott & Windsor, 2000).

Grammatical error rates should be interpreted with caution, both because they occur developmentally in the language of all school-age children (Loban, 1976; Scott, 1988; Tomblin, Zhang, Weiss, Catts, & Ellis Weismer, 2004) and because "errors" occur more frequently in dialects that differ from standard English. For students whose spoken dialects allow variations in subject–verb agreement or plural forms (e.g., as in African American English, or AAE), sentence elaboration may be a better measure than syntactic "correctness." Nelson and Van Meter (2007) analyzed written language samples for a diverse group of students with and without special needs, and found that MLTU was significantly shorter in the written story samples of students with special needs across racial/ethnic groups (approximately half African American) but that grammatical errors per *T*-unit did not differentiate students with and without special needs. The proportion of sentences coded simple incorrect (SI) (i.e., which included grammatical errors but no coordinated or subordinated clausal elements), however, was significantly higher for students with special needs compared to those with typical language, regardless of racial/ethnic category.

To address concerns about bias in inflectional morphemes for speakers of AAE, other forms of syntactic elaboration, such as the inclusion of relative clauses, can be used as an index of syntactic difficulty (Oetting & McDonald, 2001; Oetting & Newkirk, 2008). Craig and Washington (2004) coded features of African American English development and measured the frequency of their use (using a *morphosyntactic dialect density measure, MorDDM*) among African American children from grades one through five. The researchers found that students who included fewer dialectal features as they progressed through elementary school performed better on tests of reading achievement and vocabulary breadth, perhaps representing greater metalinguistic strength.

Many students with LI have difficulty with both receptive and expressive syntax, but their receptive problems may be more subtle and more easily overlooked (Snowling & Hayiou-Thomas, 2006; Stothard, Snowling, Bishop, Chipchase, & Kaplan, 1998). Some students have specific comprehension impairments, with relative strengths for processing language at the sound/word level compared with weaker sentence-/discourse-level skills. Those stronger phonological-level abilities may mask difficulties in the early grades. If students' speech sounds normal, no one may notice that their expressive language is limited in syntactic complexity. When students begin to show comprehension difficulties while reading or listening, it is often assumed that they are not paying attention or simply not trying. It is difficult to sustain persistence for a task one does not understand, so those may be secondary symptoms. Semantic/syntactic demands also are intertwined. If clinicians look closely into the language skills of children with syntax problems, they may find evidence of difficulty with semantic judgment tasks, poor semantic fluency (rapid word naming and recall), and reduced semantic priming of categorically associated items, as well as subtle deficits on tests of grammatical awareness (Nation, 2005).

As most students become literate, their written discourse becomes syntactically more complex than their spoken language. Perera (1986), for example, found the written language of 9-year-olds to include more elaborate noun phrases than the spoken language of 12-year-olds. Students with LI, however, persist in showing greater complexity in their spoken than written language (Gillam & Johnston, 1992). Windsor, Scott, and Street (2000) found that students with LI omitted the past tense *-ed* morpheme only in their written samples. Other research has supported the finding that students with language difficulties use fewer morphemes and produce syntactic structures with shorter mean length of *T*-unit (MLTU) in their written compositions compared with peers (Lewis, O'Donnell, Freebair, & Taylor, 1998; Nelson & Van Meter, 2007).

Although syntactic production abilities may be assessed using either spoken or written discourse tasks, Eisenberg (2006) observed that complex syntactic forms (e.g., passive structures) may not be represented frequently enough in spoken discourse to allow assessment of a student's ability to handle the complex syntactic demands of schooling. Thus, she recommended using written language contexts (reading and writing) for curriculum-based assessment activities. Students' written compositions also carry the advantage of already being transcribed (i.e., written down).

Targeting Comprehension and Formulation of Complex Sentences and Discourse

Goal 13.9. The student will increase the proportion of syntactically correct, complex sentences in spoken and written discourse samples over baseline. For school-age students, language and literacy intervention at the sentence level involves creating meaningful contexts requiring higher-level structures. Clinicians, acting as interested, sensitive communicative partners, can make communication-learning (whether spoken or written; involving play, drama, or academic learning) interesting, fun, and functional. More complex ideas create a need for more complex syntactic structures and higher-level vocabulary.

Culatta and Horn (1982) implemented a four-step program with children in early elementary school to teach targeted grammatical structures (e.g., copula or auxiliary forms of *be,* past tense *went,* and modal *will*). The first step involved modeling by the clinician in 75 percent to 100 percent of utterances in contexts structured to require the target form. The second step involved engineering occasions for the targeted structure to occur in 50 percent to 75 percent of utterances in meaningful play (e.g., playing "store"), with modeling by the clinician occurring at a corresponding lower rate. The third step elicited target structures at a 25 percent to 50 percent frequency, accompanied by less direct clinician scaffolding. The fourth step required the target structure in less than 25 percent of utterances, with similarly reduced clinician modeling. In all steps, clinicians evoked targeted structures using five strategies: (1) require the child to convey information, (2) request information by specifying the reason for the information, (3) create a situation that dictates the need to request action or attention, (4) create an unusual or novel event, and (5) provide inaccurate information that requires correction. Four students (ages 4 years, 6 months to 9 years, 2 months) participated in the multiple-baseline study to compare trained and untrained rules. The results supported the effectiveness of the intervention because trained target rules increased in frequency but untrained rules did not. When therapy was initiated later on untrained forms, they increased in frequency, and the first targeted structures were maintained at mastery level.

Connell and Stone (1992) studied the role of imitation in language intervention targeting morphemes, also with early elementary school students. They taught novel morphemes under controlled experimental conditions to three groups of children: 32 with SLI (ages 5 to 7 years); 24 typically developing, matched for age and nonverbal ability; and 20 typically developing, matched for language age and nonverbal ability. Two interventions were compared that differed only in whether the child was asked to imitate new language forms or just observe them in modeling. Imitation supported production but not comprehension for the children with SLI but not for the language- or age-matched controls.

Eisenberg (2006) summarized syntactic intervention approaches for students in the school-age years. Under the heading *minilesson procedures,* she included the following:

- *Observational modeling,* in which clinicians present 10 to 20 model sentences and pictures illustrating targeted form-meaning relationships (Fey & Proctor-Williams, 2000)
- *Content alterations,* in which students shift a grammatical component, such as changing the pronoun *he* to *she,* to fit a different picture (e.g., Killgallon, 1998)
- *Contrastive modeling and imitation,* in which contrasting structures are used to highlight the target feature and meaning conveyed by the structures (e.g., Cleave & Fey, 1997; Connell, 1982)
- *Sentence expanding* to teach students to elaborate a simple sentence (Gould, 2001; Killgallon, 1998)
- *Sentence combining* to practice combining two simple sentences into a more complex sentence (Hunt, 1977; Strong, 1986)

Eisenberg (2006) also summarized scaffolded approaches for fostering more complex syntax that can be embedded into what she called *microlessons* (which might also be called *minidrills*), including *expansions, extensions,* and *paraphrasing* (contingent on a student's less elaborate or grammatically incorrect written syntax), *vertical structuring* (which involves the use of sequenced scaffolding questions to get a student to elaborate on an idea), and *prompting, multiple-choice modeling,* or *partial modeling.*

Scaffolding and minidrills targeting syntax are easily incorporated in writing process approaches to instruction and intervention. Graham and Harris (2002) described possibilities for addressing multiple language targets by focusing on students' written language.

Nelson and colleagues have employed many of these techniques in the writing lab approach (Nelson et al., 2001, 2004) and found that students with LI/LD respond well to sentence-level scaffolding while drafting their stories (not just during revising and editing). Drafting and revising with computerized word-processing programs makes it easy to add words and make changes. Younger and less skilled students may need scaffolding to formulate a spoken sentence out loud before attempting to write it and then to remember what they said during the transcription process. When revising, students can learn to move their cursor to insert more interesting descriptive terms to respond to something an audience member wants to know, to move phrases around to communicate more clearly, to correct grammatical errors, and so forth. Grammatical sensitivity can be developed by teaching students to ask the self-talk question "Does this sound right?" Speech synthesis tools can be particularly helpful in developing this sensitivity, as students may be more likely to hear that morphemes are missing or that they need to add final punctuation to get the computer to read a text as intended when the computer makes mistakes.

Cohesive Devices Connecting Sentences in Discourse

Assessing Comprehension and Production of Cohesive Devices in Discourse

The second target in this section addresses acquisition of higher-level syntactic/semantic skills for processing relationships across sentence boundaries within larger units of discourse. Irwin (1988) defined *linguistic cohesion* as the "set of semantic and syntactic relationships that link sentences together in a piece of text," so that "interpretation of one unit in the text depends on another" (pp. 14–15).

Cohesive devices make it possible for a component of one sentence to refer across sentence boundaries either backward (anaphoric reference) or forward (cataphoric reference). Halliday and Hasan's (1976) framework for categorizing cohesive devices was introduced in Chapter 2. Cohesive devices include pronoun reference, word substitution, ellipsis, conjunction, lexical reiteration, and lexical collocation. Correlative conjunctions signal symmetrical and contrastive relationships of concepts within sentences (e.g., *both . . . and, either . . . or*). Transition terms and phrases signal similar relationships across sentences and even paragraphs (e.g., *however, as well as, therefore, in conclusion*). Figure 13.14 provides an observation chart summarizing component skills students need for grasping how sentences fit together and how units refer to each other across texts.

The ability to extract meaning from multiple related syntactic structures in order to actively reconstruct an author's or speaker's intended message is essential to academic and social success. Students with literacy-learning difficulties often have difficulty with grammatical structure (Catts, Fey, Zhang, & Tomblin, 1999; Juel, 1988) and drawing inferences by integrating information from many sources. Liles, Duffy, Merritt, and Purcell (1995) analyzed stories produced by students with and without LI and found that microstructure problems with cohesive devices and complex grammatical structures contributed more than macrostructure difficulties to identifying students with LI. Eisenberg (2006) pointed to connections between syntactic ability and pragmatic skills. She noted that students with LI may have difficulty adapting sentence forms to meet varied pragmatic demands, in which "the specific grammatical form is partly determined by discourse needs and presuppositional inferences" (p. 153).

Dynamic assessment techniques can be used to assess comprehension of cohesive devices by asking questions that require inferences or asking about causal and temporal relationships (Nelson & Van Meter, 2002). To probe students' ability to make sense of other cohesive devices, clinicians can ask students to point out referents for pronouns in text and questions. In retelling tasks, clinicians can observe students' ability to paraphrase

figure *13.14*

Observation Tool for Comprehending and Producing Syntactic/Semantic Cohesive Devices
That Connect Meanings across Texts

Student _____ Context _____ Date _____		
Targeted Cohesive Device	**Evidence of Comprehension**	**Evidence of Production**

❑ **Cohesion using lexical strategies**
  ❑ Reference (*The <u>dog</u> ran slowly. <u>He</u> was an old dog.*)
  ❑ Substitution (*The squirrel <u>got away</u>. It always <u>did</u>.*)
  ❑ Ellipsis (*The girl tried to see.*)
  ❑ Lexical reiteration (*The squirrel flicked its <u>tail</u>. It teased the dog with its <u>tail</u>.*)
  ❑ Lexical collocation (*The dad yelled at the <u>squirrel</u>. He yelled at the <u>pest</u>.*)		

❑ **Cohesion using conjunctions**
  ❑ Temporal or spatial relationships (*before, after, while, during, first, next,* etc.)
  ❑ Logical or causal relationships (*because, although,* etc.)
  ❑ Correlative conjunctions (*both . . . and; not only . . . but also; either . . . or; neither . . . nor,* etc.)		

❑ **Transition terms and phrases**
  ❑ Comparative (e.g., a*s well as, also, similarly)*
  ❑ Contrastive (e.g., *however, on the other hand*)
  ❑ Logical (e.g., *therefore, in summary*)		

Source: Based on Eisenberg, 2006; Halliday & Hasan, 1976; Irwin, 1988; Westby, 2006.

successfully and to convey appropriate inferences. In observing writing processes, clinicians can observe whether students refer to planning, pause periodically, and revise while drafting—which suggest the use of sentence-level processes under executive control. Clinicians also can observe whether students use writing processes for rereading, adding information, rewording ideas, clarifying references, reorganizing content, and correcting grammar, either spontaneously or with scaffolding.

Targeting Cohesion in Comprehension and Expression of Complex and Nonliteral Language

Goal 13.10. The student will employ devices for connecting and embedding multiple propositions and nonliteral forms in spoken and written discourse. Intervention for sentence cohesion should focus on helping students develop skill at linking syntactic structures to convey meaningful complex relationships when talking or writing. It also should target the development of figurative language (idiom, simile, and metaphor) and paralinguistic awareness (e.g., sarcasm and irony).

When targeting sentence-/discourse-level skills, it is important to use materials that are drawn from the student's own curriculum and age-level social groups. Expository textbooks are rich sources of complex and interconnected syntactic structures; narrative texts can be used as well. Cues about cohesive devices can be framed while scaffolding comprehension of curricular texts, asking students to explain relationships and scaffolding understanding as necessary.

To be able to comprehend and formulate higher-level sentences and discourse, students must be able to handle both literal and figurative meanings. Cain and Oakhill (2007) noted that subtle deficits of short-term memory, nonverbal IQ, and social–cognitive limitations in SLI and pragmatic language impairment (PLI) might contribute to comprehension deficits in written and spoken language. They reviewed research showing that weaknesses in all three areas can lead to difficulties with higher-level skills for drawing inferences and understanding figurative expressions such as idioms.

Nippold (1998) has studied the ability to comprehend and produce complex, abstract forms, including idioms (e.g., *getting caught in a storm*), similes (e.g., *as high as a kite*), and metaphors (e.g., *a sunny disposition*). Intervention starts with helping students become aware of nonliteral language structures, but many actual items have to be learned as vocabulary entries through experience with higher-level language forms. Therefore, Nippold emphasized the need for mediated exposure to abstract forms of language in meaningful contexts as a key to successful intervention. Deeper levels of inferential comprehension may not be fully realized until students learn to reflect at metalinguistic and metacognitive levels on alternative potential meanings. These were skills that Piaget (1969) described as part of *formal thought* for processing information on two levels simultaneously. Students can be asked to paraphrase both figurative and literal meanings in texts to assess and enhance their reading and listening comprehension of higher-level forms (Jenkins et al., 1987).

Sentence-combining techniques often are recommended for helping students develop embedding and subordination skills for conveying complex semantic relationships and saying more in fewer words (Hunt, 1977). Eisenberg (2006) recommended targeting sentence combining within the context of minilessons, perhaps using books with refrains and other literary devices that model clustered examples of cohesive devices or particular grammatical forms. Through repeated readings and strategic pausing, younger children can be scaffolded to fill in cohesive devices using a cloze procedure.

Writing process approaches with computer supports and instructor or peer scaffolding can be used to promote skill for communicating relationships across units of meaning. Table 13.5 shows changes in one student's use of cohesive devices in excerpts from a baseline story and end-of-schoolyear story (adapted from Nelson et al., 2004). At baseline, Josh, an eighth-grader with learning disabilities, tended to write only simple sentences, even though he showed the ability to use more complex structures when speaking. One day, while reading a draft of his story on the computer screen, Josh used the word *until* to describe how his horse was moving along the trail calmly *until* it saw a deer. The clinician commented on how much the word *until* helped readers to understand the importance of the event but noted that the word was not on the computer screen. Josh reread his last few sentences and combined clauses with a subordinating conjunction. Later in the schoolyear, Josh wrote a story about colonization in space, demonstrating his new skill for relating concepts within and across sentence boundaries.

SUMMARY

Assessment and intervention for sentence-level skills involves targeting abilities to comprehend and produce syntactic structures and build cohesion across texts. Many assessment tools and intervention techniques appropriate for younger children remain appropriate in the school-age years. As children mature, most become better at meeting the multilevel demands of complex integrated tasks. Written language contexts, both reading and writing, can be used to work on sentence-level skills in spoken language and vice versa.

table *13.5*   Spoken Language Sample Showing a Middle School Student's Growing
Ability to Use Syntactic Combining and Cohesion across a Schoolyear

Written Discourse Sample	Commentary
$ Student + Excerpt from baseline written story probe produced early in eighth-grade year S ONE MORNING <u>DUKE</u> WOKE <u>ME</u> UP. S <u>WE</u> PLAY/ED WITH <u>HIS CHEWY TOY</u>. S I THREW <u>IT</u> UP. S AND <u>HE</u> CAUGHT <u>IT</u>. S <u>WE</u> DID <u>IT</u> A COUPLE OF TIMES. S THEN <u>WE</u> ATE BREAKFAST.	In his baseline story (which continued for several more lines), Josh showed skill in using personal pronouns (*I, we, it*) to create cohesion. Except for the use of coordinating conjunctions, however, all his sentences were simple, with little cohesion and a feeling of choppiness. The sample included no grammatical errors. Josh's original approach was safe in more than one way. By using "Caps Lock" on the keyboard, Josh did not have to worry about capitalization.
$ Student + Excerpt from written story probe produced in April of eighth-grade year. S One morning <u>my squad</u> found <u>some pirates</u> firing on a <u>smaller</u> colony. S <u>We</u> fired on <u>them</u>. S <u>Before</u> <u>they</u> left <u>we</u> got five of <u>them</u>. S <u>But</u> this time <u>they</u> fought back. S <u>So</u> <u>we</u> attack/ed <u>them</u>. S <u>They</u> lost 11 of the 12 ships. S <u>We</u> lost 2 of the 10. S <u>We</u> let <u>the one</u> get away to tell <u>the pirates</u>.	In this portion of his later story, Josh's use of the comparative word *smaller* implies that there were a number of colonies that needed protection. *Them* shows pronoun cohesion, changing to *they* in later sentences. *My squad* becomes *we*. The subordinating conjunction *before* conveys time; the adversative coordinate conjunction *but* conveys contrast; the causal coordinate conjunction *so* conveys cause–effect. Males often use numbers in their stories. This example shows ellipsis in the two sentences with parallel structure using numbers. In the final sentence in this excerpt, *them* is replaced by the indefinite pronoun *the one,* and lexical reiteration is used to reintroduce *the pirates.* Also, the definite article *the* replaces the indefinite determiner *some* when referring to pirates.

Note: The student participated twice weekly in an after-school, computer-supported writing lab approach.

Source: From Nelson, Bahr, & Van Meter, 2004, pp. 474, 476; commentary added.

Word-Level Knowledge and Skills

Word-level abilities comprise sensitivity to the phonological and morphological forms of words and knowledge of vocabulary concepts and relationships they represent. Both aspects of word knowledge develop first in spoken language and later in association with print. As in other areas, spoken language influences literacy learning and vice versa. Clinicians can take advantage of the relative permanence of print symbols and the reciprocal nature of developmental relationships to help children with LI put together all the pieces of the puzzle to develop language proficiency across modalities (illustrated in Figure 13.15).

Word Form and Associated Print Concepts

By the time children reach school age, they can produce most phonemes in isolated imitation and most phonetic patterns in words. By age 9, the period of normal development for speech sound production is considered complete (Shriberg, 1997). Long before school

figure *13.15*

Elements of Early Literacy Learning

Early literacy learning involves putting together multiple pieces to create a mental picture that has meaning.

age, most children can fast map the structural characteristics of novel words well enough to represent them accurately in imitation, memory, and retrieval. This includes the ability to represent multisyllable words that incorporate consonant clusters and inflectional and derivational morphemes.

Children with prior emergent literacy experience come to school with phonological awareness, concepts of phonemes, and understanding of the ***alphabetic principle*** (i.e., that letters represent speech sounds), preparing them to learn ***phonics*** (i.e., sound–symbol relationships). As students develop concepts of printed word shapes and understand the ***orthographic principle*** (i.e., that patterns of letters represent syllables and morphemes), they acquire greater speed and word recognition fluency based on automatic pattern recognition (visual and auditory). This allows them to associate meaning chunks (i.e., morphemes) and syllable shapes with patterns of letters (e.g., *-ight, -ed,* long vowel + silent *-e*). Knowledge of morphology and associated orthographic patterns continues to develop into the secondary grades as students learn the derivational morphology of scientific language with Greek and Latin roots, such as *-ology, -itis, hyper-*, and *hypo-* (Carlisle & Stone, 2005; Henry, 1989).

Children with primary or secondary language and literacy difficulties can have difficulty with any aspect of this knowledge base. Deficits in the knowledge of (and memory for) word form interferes with learning to read and spell (e.g., Wagner & Torgesen, 1987). Severe and specific difficulty in this area constitutes a cardinal symptom of dyslexia (e.g.,

Catts, Hogan, & Fey, 2003; Snowling, 1995). Delay in recognizing and treating sound-/word-level difficulties can have negative effects on early literacy development; early treatment can have preventive and protective effects, however, when incorporated into a comprehensive instructional approach (e.g., Moore-Brown, Montgomery, Bielinski, & Shubin, 2005; Troia, 2004). Even when intensive individualized treatment is provided, as in upper tiers of RTI programs, some students have difficulty responding (e.g., Torgesen, 2000), justifying referral for learning disability testing.

Students with sensory deficits involving hearing or vision may have difficulty accessing adequate perceptual data about relationships of orthographic images to spoken words to support concept development. Unless students have comorbid language deficits, however, those who are deaf or hard of hearing or who have low vision should be able to move past sensory input barriers (auditory or visual) with supportive technology, as long as they have adequate exposure to language. Similarly, children with isolated motor system deficits should be able to understand speech and read print without excessive difficulty, although they may need technological supports for producing spoken and written words.

Assessing Phonological and Morphological Awareness

Difficulty with word phonology and sound–symbol association may be signaled by the presence of speech sound production difficulties, especially when speech perception weaknesses are observed as well (Rvachew, Ohberg, Grawburg, & Heyding, 2003). Comprehensive assessment for school-age children with articulation disorders should incorporate screening for phonological processing along with speech sound production and perception. Difficulties at the level of word knowledge are more likely to go undetected among children whose speech production capabilities are within normal limits.

Knowledge of the phonological and morphological structures of words appears to be necessary (though not sufficient) for developing the analysis and synthesis skills for reading decoding and spelling. This is one reason that widespread early screening and intervention programs have been instituted in many elementary schools using the Dynamic Indicators of Basic Early Literacy Skills (DIBELS; Good & Kaminski, 2002). DIBELS tasks assess word-level skills (and some phrase- and sentence-level skills), mostly in the area of reading. Separate measures are included for assessing Letter Naming Fluency (LNF), Phoneme Segmentation Fluency (PSF), Nonsense Word Fluency (NWF), Oral Reading Fluency (ORF), Retell Fluency (RTF), and Word Use Fluency (WUF). These tasks (which can be downloaded at http://dibels.uoregon.edu/measures.php) are used as repeated measures in many early elementary schools to assess children's response to instruction/intervention aimed at early literacy development.

Standardized tests of awareness of the phonological and morphemic structures of words in both spoken and written language include the Comprehensive Test of Phonological Processing (CTOPP; Wagner, Torgesen, & Rashotte, 1999), which is designed to assess phonological awareness, phonological memory, and rapid naming from ages 5 through 24 years. Difficulties at the sound/word level also can be assessed with the Lindamood Auditory Conceptualization Test (LACT; Lindamood & Lindamood, 1979). The LACT assesses children's concepts of phonemic word structure without requiring alphabetic knowledge by teaching them first to select colored blocks to represent particular sounds. The use of colors is arbitrary, but the same color always represents the same phoneme. For example, the CVC pattern /p/-/o/-/p/ could be represented with red-blue-red blocks to signal that the first and last sounds are the same. The sounds are presented one at a time and then blended, for example, into /pop/. At that point the clinician might ask, "If that shows /pop/, what goes with /op/?" A student with mature phonemic awareness should be able to remove the first red block in the string to represent ***elision*** (removal) of the first sound in the spoken word.

Masterson, Apel, and Wasowicz (2002) developed a diagnostic test of children's ability to represent word-level knowledge in their spelling of real words. Called the Spelling Performance Evaluation for Language and Literacy (2nd ed.; SPELL-2), this test assesses students' (from grade two to adult) phonemic awareness and knowledge of phonics, vocabulary, word parts, and related words. It also assesses student's mental images of words. The test provides a profile of word form knowledge components that students must draw on for effective word decoding and spelling and that clinicians can use to inform intervention planning.

German (1990, 1991, 2000) has developed assessment tools for diagnosing word retrieval difficulties, which may be associated with having unstable (i.e., wobbly) concepts of word structure despite having an adequate vocabulary. One theoretical explanation of interrelated phonological and word-level concepts in reading deficits points to difficulties with the speed of retrieval. Many children who are delayed in learning to read exhibit double-deficits involving phonological awareness and *rapid automatic naming (RAN;* Denckla & Rudel, 1976; Wolf & Bowers, 1999). The phonological hypothesis suggests that a common deficit of phonological representation and retrieval is at the root of both deficits and can explain difficulties in learning to read and spell.

For assessment purposes, it is helpful to sort out vocabulary knowledge from word form knowledge as much as possible. To reduce the influence of vocabulary knowledge, assessment tasks often use nonsense words rather than real words. Nonsense words can be controlled for ***phonotactic probability*** and frequency (i.e., how often certain sound patterns occur in words) and for ***neighborhood density*** (i.e., how many similarly shaped words are likely to be in the vocabulary a child is likely to know). Ironically, words that have many close perceptual neighbors may take longer to perceive because closely related words may be competing for the child's mental recognition capacity (Munson, Edwards, & Beckman, 2005).

Targeting Phonological and Morphological Awareness for Reading Decoding and Spelling

Goal 13.11. The student will demonstrate phonological and morphological awareness skills when decoding and spelling words in curriculum-based, grade-level activities. Intervention focused on word-level knowledge may be appropriate (and necessary) for students at any grade level but particularly for students in the initial stages of reading and spelling.

The five essential components of early reading instruction targeted in the No Child Left Behind Act (NCLB, PL 107-110) are phonemic awareness, phonics, vocabulary, reading fluency, and comprehension. These five components were highlighted based on systematic reviews of the scientific literature on early reading instruction conducted by the National Research Council (1998) and the National Institute of Child Health and Human Development (2000). Four of the five—phonemic awareness, phonics, reading fluency, and vocabulary—are word-level targets. They both promote and draw on abilities to analyze, synthesize, associate, remember, and rapidly retrieve spoken and written word parts, while relating them to whole-word patterns and meanings. The fifth component—comprehension—relates to discourse- and sentence-level knowledge and skills addressed previously in this chapter.

The general rule of thumb for children with literacy-learning risks is the earlier the intervention, the better the chance of long-term benefits. Children with speech sound disorders (SSD), some of whom receive services in the preschool years, continue to make up a large part of speech–language pathologist (SLP) caseloads in the early elementary school years. Kirk and Gillon (2007) followed children who had demonstrated SSD from their preschool years into elementary school (ages 7 to 9 years). They found that children who had received intervention that incorporated phonemic awareness and orthographic awareness performed significantly better on tasks requiring nonword decoding and spelling of morphologically complex words than those whose intervention focused on speech only.

Ukrainetz, Cooney, and Dyer (2000) embedded instruction in phonemic awareness targeting first and last sound identification, sound segmentation, and deletion within meaningful literacy experiences of shared reading and writing for small groups of 5- and 6-year-old children. Benefits of embedding phonemic awareness activities within naturalistic instruction were found across general language and literacy systems, and children in the treatment group showed better first-sound identification, last-sound identification, and sound segmentation than those in a no-treatment control group.

Torgesen and colleagues (1999) compared three instructional approaches for preventing reading disabilities in young children with weak phonological skills. Two approaches targeted phonemic decoding but varied in intensity; a third, less intensive approach was designed to support the children's regular classroom reading program. From the last half of kindergarten through second grade, children received 88 hours of individual instruction with one of the three programs. Results showed that the most phonemically explicit condition produced the strongest growth in word-level reading skills, but no differences were found between groups in reading comprehension.

Children who are dual language learners also may need heightened cues to help them develop phonemic awareness and phonics. Moore-Brown, Montgomery, Bielinski, and Shubin (2005) described a program of comprehensive intervention that was designed as a third-tier RTI program in an urban school district with 96 percent minority (mostly Hispanic) students. The program was conducted by SLPs and resource teachers in a 45-hour intensive instructional program that was based on the five essential components of reading instruction. Pre–post testing showed that these high-risk students, who had struggled in prior learning tiers, made significant reading progress with moderate effect sizes. Additionally, most students demonstrated improvement on the statewide assessment, and only 8 of the original 123 at-risk students required special education services two years later.

Word knowledge can be particularly challenging for English language learners (ELLs). Questions are often raised whether instruction should be provided in the child's first or second language. Pollard-Durodola and colleagues (2006) summarized four large-scale experimental studies they had conducted with first-grade ELLs whose primary language was Spanish. The children received explicit instruction in shared storybook reading using one oral language (Spanish or English, depending on group assignment). Both groups made progress in phonemic awareness, letter–sound identification, word attack, and comprehension skills. Results showed that knowledge of word structure should be taught explicitly, but knowledge may transfer from one language to the other with moderate assistance.

Children with more severe language-learning risks need intervention that is both phonemically and alphabetically explicit to learn phonics. Many sound-/word-level intervention programs are based on the premise that interdomain associations are necessary if children are to develop automatic recognition of sound–symbol relationships in either direction (i.e., hear a sound and write its letter, or see a letter and say its sound). Figure 13.16 provides an observation tool that can be used to document a student's ability to respond quickly to a segmental stimulus in one modality with an associated response in another, so that stimuli become associated with responses in multiple directions.

An early example of an approach based on this intersystemic association hypothesis is the ***Orton–Gillingham approach.*** It was developed by physician Samuel Orton, after whom the Orton Dyslexia Society was named (now called the International Dyslexia Association), in collaboration with reading clinician Anna Gillingham (Gillingham & Stillman, 1997). The Orton–Gillingham approach is based on multisensory principles, with the expectation that associations in one sensory system—auditory, visual, tactile, or kinesthetic—

figure 13.16

Observation Tool for Documenting Sound–Symbol Associations

Sound	Primary Spelling	"Say /sound/"	"Point to /sound/." (Aud + Vis)	"Point to /sound/." (Aud only)	"Point to /sound/." (Vis only)	"What does this letter say?"	"Write the letter that says /sound/."
/p/	p						
/ɑ/	o						
/m/	m						
/f/	f						
/u/	oo[1]						
/ʊ/	oo[2]						
/b/	b						
/i/	ee						
/ɑɪ/	i_e						
/t/	t						
/oʊ/	o_e						
/θ/	th						
/s/	s						
/æ/	a						
/g/	g						
/ɔ/	aw						
/ʃ/	sh						
/eɪ/	a_e						
/l/	l						
/w/	w						
/æʊ/	ou						
/ɪ/	i						
/ɝ/	r						
/ɛ/	e						
/n/	n						
/oɪ/	oi						
/d/	d						
/k/	k						
/ʤ/	j						
/u/	u						
/ʧ/	ch						
/u/	u_e						
/h/	h						

[1]The first pronunciation for "oo" that the students learn is /u/ as in *tool*.
[2]The second pronunciation for "oo" is /ʊ/ as in *took*.

can support another. For example, to learn letter shapes, children can be encouraged to use large movements to make letter shapes in the air to enhance kinesthetic feedback or to make small movements with a finger in a tray of dry rice to enhance tactile feedback. The goal is to help children enhance the concept of letter shape through the kinesthetic and tactile senses to augment the concepts of print on the page and phonemes they hear. Similar multi-sensory approaches include the Wilson Reading System (n.d.), which teaches decoding and encoding (spelling), beginning with phoneme segmentation and working toward other levels and contexts with controlled language texts.

Another early approach that still holds promise is the ***association method.*** McGinnis (1963) developed the association method originally for children with symptoms of auditory agnosia (i.e., with intact peripheral hearing accompanied by inability to make sense of spoken language input) who were receiving services at the Central Institute for the Deaf in St. Louis. Variations of the association method (also called *structured language*) have been described (e.g., DuBard, 1974; Monsees, 1972) for use with children with severe but specific disorders of spoken language (e.g., developmental apraxia of speech) and who seem unable to learn to talk through naturalistic methods alone. Nelson (1981) used a modified association method in classrooms for children with language and learning impairments as a key component of a more comprehensive approach that also targeted sentence-/discourse-level comprehension and formulation skills.

In the association method, listening and precise direction-following skills are taught first so that children learn to inhibit anticipatory responses and wait to initiate a response until after the clinician gives a direction. This is followed by an articulation step in which the student is shown a letter, such as *p,* and is told to "Say /p/" while pointing to the letter on the page. Scaffolding is provided, as necessary, to teach the child to articulate the sound correctly (with minimal schwa vowel plosion, /pə/), and a page is added to the student's sounds and letters book. A small letter chip is added to a "My Sounds" envelope taped inside the student's notebook when the student completes seven Level I teaching steps. The first three association steps target sounds and symbols one at a time: (1) attention and articulation training; (2) saying in imitation (articulation practice); and (3) tracing the letter while saying the sound. The other four association steps use multiple letters arrayed on marker board for (4) lip-reading and pointing, (5) auditory only, (6) saying from memory ("reading") and pointing, and (7) writing from memory.

Letters are presented in lowercase only, with vowels in one color and consonants in another. Traditional orthography is used, but spelling is regularized using symbols from the Yale spelling charts, which were designed originally for children with hearing loss. These include long vowel notations (*i_e, a_e, o_e,* and *ee*) where _ indicates a place for a consonant with a silent e after. Short vowel notations can be added (e.g., *_o_* for /ɑ/; *_a_* for /æ/) with a _ on either side for consonants, indicating the vowel is short. Clinicians teach students to associate sounds with symbols and mostly avoid using letter names. Accurate records are kept of students' progress, and students are held responsible for prior learning of motor and sensory associations of sounds with letters. Phonemes are introduced in an order designed to maximize their discriminability (visual and auditory). For example, long vowels are usually taught before short vowels (/ɪ/ /æ/ /ɛ/ /ʌ/), and continuants (e.g., /m/) are contrasted with stops (e.g., /p/).

Level II is introduced after a student shows competence with 15 to 20 sound–symbol associations across all seven steps. At that point, unblended consonant–vowel (CV) combinations (e.g., *b ee t i_e*) are taught using the same seven steps. Then variations are introduced using drills in blending syllable structures, in which the child learns to point and say each phoneme—first separately and then blended, while dragging the pointing finger from sound to sound within an array (see Figure 13.17). A progression is used, starting with CV

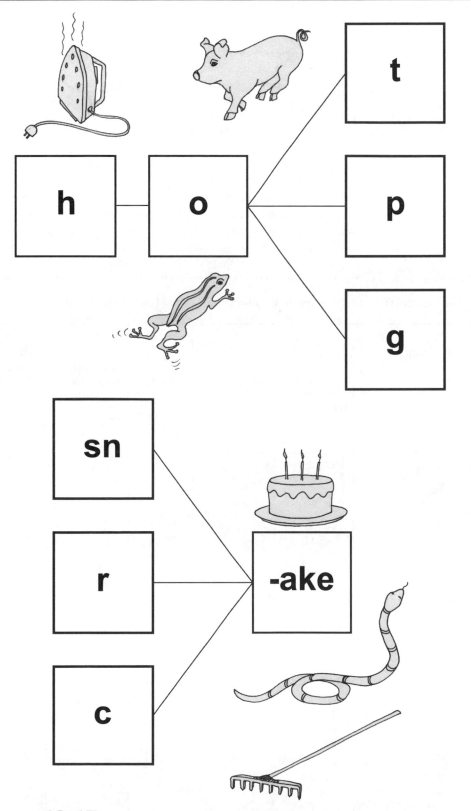

figure *13.17*

Syllable Drill for Teaching CV and VC Blending with Associated Orthographic Patterns

variations—single consonant to multiple vowels and multiple consonants to single vowel—followed by VC combinations—single vowel to multiple consonants and multiple vowels to single consonant. Later, CVC combinations and onset-to-rime combinations are used to transition into common word families; after which morphology–orthography associations may be used to teach common word chunks (e.g., *-ing, -tion, un-, dis-*). Figure 13.18 provides an observation chart for documenting syllable and word-level decoding.

Later in Level II, words are taught using nine steps: (1) articulation drill; (2) association with meaning; (3) writing from immediate memory; (4) listening; (5) copying or tracing; (6) lip reading; (7) auditory; (8) reading (oral memory); and (9) writing (written memory). In the oral memory step, the student first reads words on the board and then turns around and repeats them from memory to a small audience of peers, with the goal of improving revisualization and transition to whole-word recognition and fluent recall. The written memory step

figure *13.18*

Observation Tool for Documenting Syllable and Word-Level Associations

Spelling/ Sound Pattern	Examples	Unblended	Blended	Alternative Spelling Cross Drill	Alternative Spelling Words	Memory for Cross Drill
C – Vs	to_ ta_e					
Cs – V	ti_e pi_e ki_e					
V – Cs	om op ot					
Vs – C	eet ate					
C – V – C	hot mom					
CC – V – (C)	blu_e brake					
C – V – CC	barb					
Word families	-ight -oot -ike					
Words with varied orthographic patterns	see, sea, say it, at, eat					
Words in phrases	I like ___ I see a ___					

is similar, except the student rewrites a short list of words without looking at them. Children are taught explicitly that sounding out is an inefficient way to read and that they should be looking for chunks and whole words that they know. Secondary spellings are introduced in cross drills (e.g. *ra_e, rai, ray*), in which students learn that alternative spellings for the same vowel sound may be pronounced the same way. In Levels III and IV, new sounds continue to be taught in isolation, while students begin to strengthen their sound-blending skills, read simple sentence patterns (e.g., *A mouse can run; Can a fish swim?*), expand their vocabulary, and begin to read for meaning in authentic grade-appropriate texts.

Reading is not reading unless it includes both decoding and comprehension, but these two skills draw on different levels of ability. To sort out the advantages of working on word-level phonological processing skills prior to targeting sentence-level semantic–syntactic skills, Gillon and Dodd (1995) assigned 10 school-age students (10- to 12-year-olds) with specific reading disabilities randomly to receive either (1) a structured phonological training program followed by a semantic–syntactic training program or (2) the same two programs in the reverse order. The goal was to improve both reading accuracy and comprehension. Results showed that training at the sound/word level had a greater impact on reading accuracy, but intervention at both levels contributed to improvements in reading comprehension. This suggests that it may be most efficient to target the related abilities in separate activities but on the same day, which was the approach used by Nelson (1981).

The Lindamood Phonemic Sequencing (LiPS) Program (Lindamood & Lindamood, 1998; formerly called Auditory Discrimination in Depth [ADD]; Lindamood & Lindamood, 1984) also begins at the level of the individual spoken phoneme and helps students associate phonemes with print symbols. The LiPS approach uses multisensory experiences but adds a metafocus on speech production to help learners become aware of articulatory features of individual phonemes and selecting labels to describe articulatory and phonological features. This feature makes the LiPS approach appropriate for older learners who have not yet developed basic competence in phonemic awareness. For example, participants learn to differentiate the features of voiceless and voiced production of cognates produced in the same place, such as /t/ and /d/, calling /t/ the "quiet tip tapper" and /d/ the "noisy tip tapper." Such labels highlight similarities and differences in voicing, tongue placement, and manner of production.

The predecessor program, ADD (Lindamood & Lindamood, 1984), was one of two intensive intervention programs compared by Torgesen and colleagues (2001) in a large randomized controlled trial comparing ADD with an embedded phonics approach. The trial was conducted with 60 students with severe reading disabilities in third through fifth grade who had been receiving services in learning disablility resource rooms with little improvement. All children received 67.5 hours of one-to-one instruction in 50-minute sessions twice per day for eight weeks. Large gains were measured in generalized reading skills for both groups (with effect sizes of 4.4 for the ADD approach and 3.9 for the embedded phonics approach), and growth was retained over a two-year follow-up period. Most (but not all) children could perform in the average range on reading accuracy and comprehension at follow-up. Difficulties with reading rate, however, continued for most of the children. Almost half (40 percent) no longer needed special education services within one year following the intervention. Factors that predicted long-term growth in addition to response to the intervention included teacher ratings of attention/behavior, general verbal ability, and prior levels of component reading skills.

When the context becomes more difficult in the upper grades, older students with learning impairment are likely to show difficulty at the word level, even if they have not before (Scarborough, 2005). This is the point at which academic language may involve more frequent use of derived forms of morphemes with Latin or Greek roots. All students can benefit from explicit instruction in how words work. For example, a middle school vocabulary might include words such as *fend,* which are difficult to memorize, define, and spell when viewed in isolation. When associated with better-known words, such as *fender, defender,* and *defend,* the new word *fend* (as in *fend for yourself*) might be easier to remember. Clinicians should keep in mind that adolescents with reading comprehension difficulties may have difficulty with word decoding, vocabulary and sentence knowledge, discourse comprehensions, or all of these skills, especially in integrated contexts. Deshler, Hock, and Catts (2005) summarized research data that showed that large numbers of readers (especially from inner-city urban areas) "may require both word-level and comprehension interventions in order to make it over the fourth-grade hump" (p. 21).

Spelling can be particularly challenging for students with difficulty acquiring word-level knowledge. Spelling is the reciprocal of word decoding, but it requires productive knowledge, not just recognition (Ehri, 2000), and thus can be even more challenging. Spelling is one of the language levels that can be targeted with the writing lab approach (Graham, 2000; Nelson et al., 2004). Children who have authentic reasons to spell words accurately enough so peers and parents can read their work will be motivated to learn to spell better.

Spelling requires comprehensive word knowledge, including phonemic awareness, but also knowledge of phonics, vocabulary, word parts, and related words (Apel & Masterson, 2001b). In addition, students need to be able to form mental images of the orthographic patterns of words (called ***mental graphemic representations, MGRs***), so they can recognize when words do not appear to be correct and alternative spellings are needed. To spell words while composing text, students need to use working memory to hold the intended words in mind while attempting to spell them (Berninger, 2000). Within the context of writing lab activities (Nelson et al., 2004), children can be engaged in one-on-one or small-group minidrill experiences, such as the one illustrated in Figure 13.19, to help them form mental pictures and recognize common orthographic patterns. They also may need scaffolding to acquire the strategy to "Say the word slowly, hear it, feel it, and then spell it."

Knowing where to start in spelling intervention requires analysis of which developmental spelling strategies a student is and is not using (Apel & Masterson, 2001b; Bourassa & Treiman, 2001; Ehri, 2000; Gentry, 1982; Moats, 2000). Young children may start by scribbling and then generating random sequences of letters or using a letter name approach (e.g., *ne = any*). Children with phonemic awareness and other linguistic knowledge soon begin to use phonetic and orthographic strategies to generate recognizable spellings for words they do not know how to spell. In fact, a child's generated spellings can provide an important window into his or her speech perception and level of phonemic awareness. In older children, spelling provides insight into their knowledge of other linguistic factors, such as inflectional and derivational morphemes, which also contribute to knowing how to spell. Spelling intervention approaches (e.g., Bear, Invernizzi, Templeton, & Johnson, 2000; Wasowicz, Apel, Masterson, & Whitney, 2004) take advantage of word knowledge and teach it explicitly. Such approaches have advantages for all students over the traditional approach of teaching children to memorize the spellings of 10 words per week for a weekly spelling test (Scott, 2000).

Caravolas, Hulme, and Snowling (2001) recommended targeting spelling early and in tandem with reading decoding, based on their finding that early phonological spelling ability predicts later reading but early reading ability does not predict later phonological spelling ability. Blachman and colleagues (2004) examined the effectiveness of explicit instruction on phonologic and orthographic associations in words and text-based reading for second- and third-grade children with poor word-level skills. Children were randomly assigned either to eight months of explicit word-based training or received usual remedial reading services. At posttest, children in the experimental treatment showed significantly greater gains than control children in real-word and nonword reading, reading rate, pas-

figure *13.19*

Minidrill for Spelling

This minidrill support was designed to teach orthographic pattern recognition among word families and was added to the student's tool book.

sage reading, and spelling. Gains were maintained at a one-year follow-up, indicating that explicit word-level instruction could significantly improve reading and spelling outcomes when targeted together. Similarly, Apel and Masterson (2001b) described a multilevel, intermodality intervention program using a case study report for a 13-year-old student with spelling difficulties who made clinically significant gains in phonemic and morphological awareness, orthographic knowledge, spelling, and word-level reading. This supports the value of approaches that work across the modalities—listening, speaking, reading, and writing—to build higher-level word knowledge and skill.

Vocabulary Knowledge and Skill

Vocabulary knowledge is a powerful predictor of reading comprehension (Anderson & Freebody, 1981), which correlates with reading frequency (Cunningham & Stanovich,

1998; Stanovich, 1986). Vocabulary is one area of language that continues to develop across a person's lifetime (Anglin, 1993). Experts suggest that students know about 40,000 words by the time they graduate from high school and many times that number if the total includes proper nouns, idiomatic phrases, and morphological variants of word roots (Miller & Gildea, 1987).

Although some words are learned earlier than others (e.g., function words and words for everyday concepts, such as *hot/cold* and *big/little*), new vocabulary is typically learned in the meaningful contexts in which it occurs and varies with a child's experiential history. Exposure to spoken vocabulary also varies greatly across socioeconomic and cultural–linguistic groups, so that children come to school with different word-learning backgrounds (e.g., Hart & Risley, 1995).

Children with specific language impairment (SLI) may have a limited lexicon. Rice, Oetting, Marquis, Bode, and Pae (1994) studied factors contributing to problems with ***quick incidental learning (QUIL)*** among 5-year-old children with SLI and age- and MLU-matched controls. To examine immediate versus long-term memory, they tested children's word comprehension immediately following viewing of video story presentations with varied wordtype (nouns or verbs) and word-input frequency (0, 3, or 10 encounters); the children were tested again several days later. Children with SLI could map the words quickly, but they needed more encounters to learn new words and had difficulty storing them in long-term memory.

Assessing Vocabulary Comprehension and Production

Formal vocabulary tests can be used to measure whether an individual child's receptive or expressive vocabulary is commensurate with that of same-age peers. Frequently used instruments include the Peabody Picture Vocabulary Test, Third Edition (Dunn & Dunn, 1997), Receptive One-Word Picture Vocabulary Test–Revised (ROWPVT–R; Brownell, 2000b), and Expressive One-Word Picture Vocabulary Test–Revised (EOWPVT–R; Brownell, 2000a). Vocabulary diversity measures, such as number of different words, also are used to document vocabulary richness in a spoken or written language samples and for documenting change over time (see Chapter 12; Nelson & Van Meter, 2002). When reading a segment from a curriculum-based text, a student's vocabulary knowledge can be assessed by watching for words that he or she mispronounces without correction, signaling that the student is not monitoring comprehension or does not have a mental entry for that word in his or her lexicon. The clinician then can probe word knowledge by asking for a definition or paraphrase or offering multiple choices and asking the student to select the best meaning.

Comprehensive assessment should address the student's processes for learning new words and estimate the size of the vocabulary of words the student already knows. The test–teach–test steps of dynamic assessment can be used to assess a student's vocabulary-learning potential. For example, when an unknown word is identified in context, the clinician shows the student how to seek clues from the sentence and discourse contexts and to think about words that look and sound similar. Scaffolding can be provided as needed to help the student accurately construct the meaning of a particular word, and then the clinician can probe how well the student learned, retained, and retrieves the new word by establishing a context that requires it again.

Targeting Basic- and Grade-Level Academic Vocabulary

Goal 13.12. The student will demonstrate the appropriate comprehension and expression of new vocabulary in academic contexts. Rice and colleagues (1994) recommended that intervention targeting word learning for children with LI should provide multiple opportunities for mediated encounters with word meanings, not only within single sessions but across several sessions. School-age children need to be able to learn vocabulary through both spoken and written language experiences.

Although good readers have larger vocabularies and larger vocabularies support better reading, simply increasing a student's reading time may not have the desired effects on vocabulary learning. Beck and McKeown (1991) concluded, "Research spanning several decades has failed to uncover strong evidence that word meanings are routinely acquired from context" (p. 799), at least not reading contexts (Scarborough, 2005). This suggests that, as in other areas, clinicians (and teachers) need to target vocabulary learning directly and explicitly, especially when the goal is to support word learning by children with LI and other language-learning risks. This can include discussion and paraphrasing of what was read to ensure that students are understanding the words and larger units of text.

Justice, Meier, and Walpole (2005) studied the difference between merely exposing at-risk kindergarten children to novel vocabulary words in repeated storybook readings and providing elaborated discussions about the meanings of words in context. They used a pretest–posttest comparison group research design with 57 kindergartners in high and low vocabulary skill groups (based on standardized receptive vocabulary scores). Students were randomly assigned to a treatment ($n = 29$) or comparison ($n = 28$) group. The treatment group participated in 20 small-group storybook reading sessions and were exposed to 60 novel words experienced in nonelaborated or elaborated conditions. The quality of children's definitions for the 60 words were measured with pre–post tests. The treatment group improved more than the comparison group but only on elaborated words, and those who started with the poorest skills made the greatest gains. Storybook reading without elaboration did not influence the ability to define words. Children seem to need dialogic discussions with adults to abstract the meanings of new words.

Other research shows that the number of encounters with a new word can help students with learning disabilities learn new words, but learning may be enhanced even further if word meanings are primed in discussions immediately prior to reading a passage. Pany, Jenkins, and Schreck (1982) found that active practice using new words in sentences was more effective than having students read sentences containing target words and synonyms or definitions of target words. Jenkins, Stein, and Wysocki (1984) found that students with learning disabilities learned the meanings of words after encountering them six or ten times within a text, but two encounters could produce positive effects when meanings of unfamiliar words were explained before reading the passage.

Older students may be able to enhance their capabilities for learning new vocabulary while reading. To be able to learn new words in context, students must first heighten their awareness of words they do not recognize by identifying words that "clunk" for them while reading. Then they can receive scaffolding to use word-learning strategies to figure out the meanings. Harmon (2000) recommended teaching adolescents to use three types of cues. *Contextual cues* are found in the local context (before or after the word or elsewhere in the sentence containing the word), distant contexts, and other locations within the text. *Discourse cues* are found in immediate story events, knowledge of the storyline, ideas beyond the text, and the author's style of writing. *Word-level cues* involve sounding out, structural analysis, and attention to word appearance. All of these cues can be framed and scaffolded to teach a student to become a successful word learner.

Word-level processing difficulties also can be expressed as word-finding delays and the substitution of general, all-purpose words or circumlocutions that talk around an intended word that cannot be retrieved. Some students with severe word-finding impairments have extensive vocabularies, yet their word-level processing difficulties create word retrieval delays and interfere with their communicative and academic functions (German,

1983). Interventions can be designed to help such students build rich associations of meaning among words and concepts, as well as with word forms (Kail & Leonard, 1986). Writing lab activities can be ideal for giving students more time to reflect on word choice and to use computer software tools, such as a dictionary and a thesaurus, to support higher-level vocabulary choices, activating the student's natural "vocabulary sponge" (Nelson & Van Meter, 2006a). This happens when students need new words to communicate more complex ideas to an audience of parents and peers (Swoger, 1989).

When SLPs work collaboratively with general education teachers, learning goes both ways. SLPs become familiar with the vocabulary of instruction at a student's grade level, and they can show teachers how to help students with LI construct meanings and form associations for relating spoken and written words. Farber and Klein (1999) described a collaborative intervention program called *Maximizing Academic Growth by Improving Communication (MAGIC),* which they implemented weekly as a pilot classroom intervention program in 12 kindergarten and first-grade classes. Children involved in the MAGIC program performed significantly better than control peers on subtests of listening, writing, and understanding vocabulary and cognitive–linguistic concepts. They also showed increased writing skill for producing relevant sentences with correct mechanics and spelling.

Hadley, Simmerman, Long, and Luna (2000) also evaluated a collaborative service delivery model in which an SLP worked with general education teachers in two inner-city primary grade classrooms. Their results showed that experimental students showed significantly better gains than students in standard practice control classrooms in receptive vocabulary, expressive vocabulary, beginning sound awareness, and letter–sound associations as well as generalization to a novel phonological awareness task.

SUMMARY

Words and the phonemes and morphemes within them are the building blocks of language. Alphabetic letters and orthographic letter patterns provide graphic representations of spoken words. Mature, literate language use requires the ability to analyze and synthesize language at multiple levels. Children with extensive vocabularies and related orthographic knowledge have an essential knowledge base for comprehending language fluently when listening and reading and for retrieving spoken words and spelling patterns fluently when speaking and spelling.

Some students benefit from intervention techniques that focus initially on word form (associating sounds with symbols and syllables with orthographic shapes) in isolation from word, sentence, and textual meaning in early stages of intervention. Doing so may help them detect perceptual features that they would otherwise miss. Any minidrills at the sound/word level, however, soon should give way to intervention experiences that present not only the demands but also the opportunities of intersystemic parallel processing of sentence- and discourse-level language in meaningful contexts.

CHAPTER SUMMARY

This chapter targeted areas that require integration in the minds and skill sets of school-age children and adolescents. One of the functions of special services is to identify profiles of strengths and needs so that specialized intervention can be integrated with instruction to keep all students active in the general education curriculum at grade level or as close to it as possible. The sections in this chapter on discourse described assessment and intervention that target academic and social conversational discourse, narrative, expository, and thinking language discourse for executive control and self-regulation. Sentence-level and word-level goal areas target language units that are combined to form discourse that is communicative and meaningful, both for comprehension and expression of complex, socially appropriate messages. The explicit nature of intervention scaffolding requires clinicians to analyze complex and integrated behaviors for assessment and intervention and sometimes to frame smaller chunks of perceptual spoken and written language input. Students have a clear need to be able to integrate knowledge and skills across language levels and modalities and to be able to apply them with wizardlike proficiency. To promote knowledge and skill integration and to mobilize them in curriculum-based experiences, clinicians must collaborate actively with classroom teachers and work side by side with students.

EXERCISES *and* STUDY QUESTIONS

1. Describe the use of the four questions of CBLAI in the school-age years. If possible, apply them with a student who is struggling to learn to read, write, and communicate in spoken language.

2. Describe what is meant by a language-levels-by-modalities model and how it influences the goals and methods of this chapter.

3. Name two advantages of working on spoken and written language in tandem at each level.

4. Discuss several reasons that executive function goals are critical to working on all other goals.

CHAPTER *fourteen*

Interventions for Special Populations

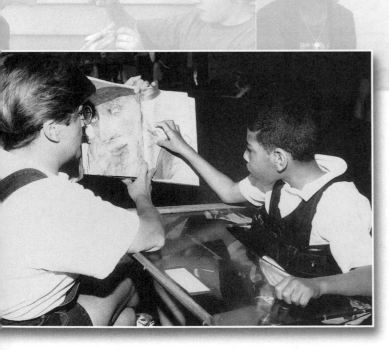

LEARNING *objectives*

After studying this chapter, you should be able to do the following:

1. Describe comprehensive planning options for children and adolescents in special populations.

2. Describe intervention options for children with complex communication needs, including severe physical and speech impairments; children who are deaf or hard of hearing (D/HH), have cochlear implants, or have auditory-processing disorders (APD); and children with autism spectrum disorders (ASD) and other cognitive-communicative needs.

This chapter focuses on methods for promoting communication, language, and literacy development in the face of significant barriers to learning and participation. The groups of individuals described in this chapter arc not homogenous. Even those who share a common diagnosis (e.g., ASD, Down syndrome, traumatic brain injury) can exhibit a wide range of cognitive–linguistic and sensory–motor abilities and disabilities.

To describe students "who have traditionally been labeled as having mental retardation, autism, developmental disabilities, traumatic brain injury, and multiple disabilities," McSheehan, Sonnenmeier, Jorgensen, and Turner (2006) suggested the term *students with significant disabilities* (p. 266). This phrasing is not entirely satisfactory, however, because it seems to imply that milder forms of disability are somehow *not* significant. As indicated throughout this book, disabilities can be subtle but significant. In this chapter, the term *significant disabilities* is used with reservations, along with the term **complex communication needs** (**CCN;** Beukelman & Mirenda, 2005). Other, more specific diagnostic terms are used where appropriate, including terminology related to sensory and motor problems that require specialized intervention methods, even though children's underlying cognitive-processing systems seem to be basically intact.

This chapter describes comprehensive planning approaches and interventions to promote intentional communication, reduce challenging behaviors, and develop speech, language/literacy, and social communication abilities for children in special populations. It does *not* cover treatments and technologies that support communication but do not directly involve it, such as breathing (e.g., tracheotomy and ventilation tubes) and feeding (e.g., oral or gavage) systems for children with severe physical impairments; sensory integration for children with neurosensory system difficulties; hearing aids, assistive listening devices, and cochlear implant inputs for children with D/HH; orientation and mobility for children with low vision; technological supports for augmenting communication; and considerations related to pharmaceutical or dietary interventions. These are important components of comprehensive service delivery that require diverse expertise, but they are beyond the scope of this book (see Personal Reflection 14.1).

PERSONAL reflection *14.1*

"An autistic boy who has food allergies deserves to be relieved of the stomachaches caused by certain foods. And while a stomachache-free autistic boy is a much happier boy, he is still an autistic boy."

Edward R. Ritvo, M.D. (2006, p. 101), has led attempts to understand many aspects of autism, focusing on the need for scientific evidence and critical appraisal of fads and promised cures.

Comprehensive Planning for Comprehensive Needs

When children and adolescents face challenges that make them dependent on others for basic needs, parents worry about many things, including what will happen when they can no longer care for their adult children with disabilities. Communication and related systems are best targeted as a mutual concern of all members of an interdisciplinary team, who pool their expertise and design comprehensive, intersystemic approaches. Parent and student values are the essential third leg on the evidence-based practice (EBP) triad. Without it, the best scientific evidence and clinical expertise are insufficient. Planning efforts also should involve general education teachers who can provide input about the general education curriculum and keep it in focus as an authentic goal.

No Prerequisites to Communication

As addressed in the communication processes, needs, and participation model (introduced in Chapter 1), some communication processes are impossible to fix. A person's disability may be as much a function of societal barriers as personal inability (Duchan, 2006). Earlier models that located impairment within the person included criteria for determining readiness for certain types of developmental interventions. Such models are inappropriate because they reduce educational and social interaction opportunities (see Personal Reflection 14.2). By addressing communication needs and facilitating participation, disability can be reduced.

PERSONAL reflection *14.2*

"It became increasingly clear that when people were excluded from AAC services because of their 'inadequate' capabilities, they were also usually excluded from the experiences, instruction, and practice necessary to improve those capabilities."

David Beukelman and **Pat Mirenda** (2005, p. 135) were writing about the importance of a policy of no prerequisites for AAC as being critical to improving access to all forms of learning and interaction.

A principle of "no prerequisites" is in direct contrast to cognitive-referencing formulas that require cognitive–communicative discrepancies as a prerequisite to intervention services. Cognitive-referencing policies, simply put, are wrong. Based on a *zero exclusion philosophy,* Calculator (1994) emphasized that "there are no minimal criteria or prerequisites that must be in place to justify communication services" (p. 120).

Another facet of the "no prerequisites" principle is to recognize that it is impossible *not* to communicate (see Personal Reflection 14.3). Children who communicate at a presymbolic level should receive adequate and appropriate services regardless of their age and degree of disability. Working at the societal level, teams can reduce functional impairment and increase communication opportunities, thus reducing disability. This does not mean pulling out students with significant disabilities from their classrooms for traditional speech therapy twice per week. It does mean that speech–language pathologists (SLPs) should participate with other members of a transdisciplinary team to plan and implement comprehensive interventions.

PERSONAL reflection *14.3*

"No matter how one may try, one cannot *not* communicate. Activity or inactivity, words or silence all have message value: they influence others and these others, in turn, cannot *not* respond to these communications and are thus themselves communicating. It should be clearly understood that the mere absence of talking or of taking notice of each other is no exception to what has just been asserted."

This classic quotation by **Paul Watzlawick, Janet Helmick Beavin,** and **Don D. Jackson** (1967, p. 49) in their book on the *Pragmatics of Human Communication* established that it is impossible for living, breathing human beings to not communicate.

Views of Cognitive Ability as Dynamic, Not Static

Reuven Feuerstein (1979) challenged assumptions that intelligence sets limits on development that cannot be changed. He introduced *dynamic assessment* as a technique for working with a child one on one to teach a novel concept, with intelligence measured based on how well the child learns the novel task. Feuerstein developed a mediated learning approach to guide students' learning, which he termed *instrumental enrichment (IE)*. He described the IE approach as an interactional process between a developing individual and "an experienced, intentioned adult," in which the adult mediates the world to the child by "framing, selecting, focusing, and feeding back environmental experiences" to produce in the child "appropriate learning sets and habits" (p. 179). Feuerstein, Rand, and Rynders (1988) wrote the book *Don't Accept Me as I Am: Helping "Retarded" People to Excel,* describing application of the IE approach with children with biologically based developmental intellectual disabilities, such as Down syndrome.

IE and other mediational approaches convey the expectation that students can change. Donnellan (1984) called this the "least dangerous assumption," and Biklen (1999) called it "presumed competence." Master clinicians convey confidence in their clients' abilities to acquire new knowledge and skills, while working to support their learning directly and intentionally. This involves identifying missed cues in meaningful contexts and framing them to focus students' attention on those cues.

Planning for Participation

Several models have been proposed to facilitate planning for inclusion and participation of people with significant disabilities. The McGill Action Planning System (MAPS; Vandercook, York, & Forest, 1989), now called Making Action Plans (MAPS; Falvey, Forest, Pearpoint, & Rosenberg, 1994), is designed to engage students, families, and friends in planning that focuses on students' positive characteristics as individuals, rather than their impairments as people with disabilities. MAPS questions include Who is this person? (described in regular words, not special education language) What is this person's history? What is his or her dream? What is the nightmare? What are the person's gifts? What does the person need right now to have a good life? What needs to be done by students, parents, teachers, peers, and others to help the person realize those needs?

Another planning approach, the COACH model, for Choosing Options and Accommodations for Children with Handicaps (Giangreco, Cloninger, & Iverson, 2000), starts with a student/family interview. Quality-of-life indicators are explored, including a student's current living situation, health status and well-being, and how and with whom he or she spends free time. Based on this discussion, the team establishes priorities for change to facilitate the student's participation within the general education curriculum.

Goals for increasing participation should be active, not passive. Newer planning models emphasize active participation and actual learning of the general education curriculum, not just access to it. Although access is critical for participation, access alone (e.g., placement in a general education classroom with typically learning peers) is not enough. Based on the requirements of IDEA '04 and the No Child Left Behind Act (NCLB), children with significant disabilities are expected to meet general education standards along with peers. McSheehan and colleagues (2006) described the *beyond access model* (see Personal Reflection 14.4) as incorporating three key changes: (1) students are treated as full members of the classroom; (2) they pursue the same learner outcomes as students without disabilities; and (3) augmentative and alternative communication (AAC) systems are developed, monitored, and expanded so students can "communicate the same messages—and to the same extent socially and academically—as students without disabilities" (p. 267).

PERSONAL reflection *14.4*

"Communication access has come to be seen not as the goal but the means by which students are able to engage socially and academically at school."

The interdisciplinary team of **Michael McSheehan, Rae M. Sonnenmeier, Cheryl M. Jorgensen,** and **Karen Turner** (2006, p. 267) from the University of New Hampshire, Institute on Disability were describing shifts in perspective associated with their beyond access model of planning for inclusion and participation in the social and academic contexts of school.

Teams using this model write instructional objectives to promote family–school partnerships, with shared responsibility by all members of the team. Table 14.1 contrasts three forms of objectives to show changes in planning philosophy over recent decades. The earlier shift (Jorgensen, 1994) transformed a goal that targeted sequencing in isolated sessions into a goal for sequencing within the general curricular activities of the classroom. It did not, however, target the actual learning of curricular content. The newer beyond access objective (based on principles recommended by McSheehan et al., 2006) targets the application of improved sequencing skills to learn academic content, not just the generic process of sequencing. This approach builds on the framework introduced in Chapter 1, including the comments by the mother in Personal Reflection 1.2, who said, "You listen to me politely, but you never write it down!" This was the mother who, when invited to contribute in writing, wrote to the IEP team, "I know that this is a major request, but it's really time for academics to start showing up on his IEP as a *real* goal."

Large-scale controlled studies of collaborative planning and beyond access models are difficult to conduct due to individual differences and ethical concerns. Some evidence, however, supports collaborative planning and implementation as an effective way of serving students with complex communication needs. Hunt, Soto, Maier, Muller, and Goetz (2002) evaluated the effectiveness of collaborative intervention for three students who used AAC in general education classrooms. Each team consisted of a general education teacher, an inclusion support teacher, an instructional assistant, an SLP, and one of the student's

table *14.1* Applying Participation Principles to Access to Academic Learning

Old Short-Term Objective	New Short-Term Objective	Newer Short-Term Objective (Based on Beyond Access Model)
"Matt will sequence 5–6 pictures depicting a familiar activity correctly 9 times out of 10." (p. 92)	"During classroom activities, such as science lab, Matt will improve his skills in sequencing by assembling dissection trays or by documenting the steps of the experiment by taking instant photos and pasting them in order along the corresponding steps of the written report." (p. 92)	During science lab, Matt will show understanding of conceptual vocabulary by pointing to at least 4 animal body parts named by his lab partner and will use his full AAC options to help his team members perform the sequence of steps in the dissection process.

Note: This chart shows three ways of designing instructional objectives for Matt, a student who was included in the eighth-grade science class but had no academic goals on his IEP.

Source: The "Old" and "New" objectives are from Jorgensen, 1994, p. 92; the "Newer" objective was constructed for this example based on principles of the beyond access model of McSheehan et al., 2006.

parents. The teams collaborated in developing and implementing unified plans of support that incorporated academic adaptations and communication and social supports. Outcomes measured using behavioral observations and team interviews showed that the unified plans of support model resulted in improved academic skills, social interactions with peers, engagement in classroom activities, and use of AAC supports.

Interventions for Special Populations Incorporating Family and Peers

Based on a comprehensive review of intervention research with children with ASD, the National Research Council, Committee on Educational Interventions for Children with Autism (2001) concluded that parental involvement is a key component of effective intervention programs. Planning should *involve* family members but not dictate to them to avoid adding to a plate that already is overflowing (see Personal Reflection 14.5).

PERSONAL reflection *14.5*

"The speech therapist says, 'Do half an hour of therapy after dinner.' The physical therapist says, 'Do 30 minutes of therapy in your spare time.' What spare time?! I have two other kids and a husband! I finally said, 'no' to all that therapy. I had to choose between being my child's extension therapist and being his mother. And I chose being his mother."

A parent of a child with complex developmental needs expressed her frustration with the multiple demands she experienced from diverse professionals using a multidisciplinary (rather than an interdisciplinary model) of service delivery (quoted by Simons, 1987, p. 51).

Tétreault, Parrot, and Trahan (2003) studied parental perceptions of their roles in implementing **home activity programs** with children with global developmental delay. Individualized home activity programs were developed for 41 families, each guided by an interdisciplinary team that included an occupational therapist, physical therapist, and SLP. Results showed high adherence to programs, which was influenced by degree of support from professionals. After seven months, 31 families were still using the home activity programs, but high compliance was associated with high stress, so intervention teams were reminded of the need to consider demands home programs place on parents, especially mothers.

Families experience widespread changes when children are diagnosed with life-long disabilities such as deafness. A large body of literature supports early identification of hearing loss accompanied by high-quality, family-centered services (Moeller, Schow, & Whitaker, 2007; Yoshinaga-Itano, Sedey, Coulter, & Mehl, 1998). Jackson, Traub, and Turnbull (2008) interviewed parents of children with severe or profound sensorineural hearing loss and found they placed a high value on family-centered planning with support from professionals who cared about them as well as their children. Parents felt stressed by pressure to integrate therapy into daily activities, to make decisions about modes of communication, and to make decisions whether to seek cochlear implantation. They were sensitive to judgmental responses about their choices. One mother reported negative responses from someone who "jumped all over me about how I ruined all of her chances for her ever being able to be normal because I took her hearing away and gave her an implant" (p. 87). Another reported being judged by professionals when she decided to have her daughter *not* get an implant, saying, "They were looking at me like, why not?" (p. 87). Impact of the child's deafness also was felt on family interactions and leisure time and on the child's friendships, access to hearing and Deaf communities, and self-perception and identity. All parents worried about the future. The authors concluded by recommending that professionals provide family-centered supports, not just child-specific supports.

Emergent literacy should be included in programs for students in special populations. Buckley and Johnson-Glenberg (2008) cited case studies and other evidence that showed that children with Down syndrome have better spoken language outcomes when they are introduced to reading prior to age 5. The authors hypothesized that the relative permanence and visual supports offered by language in print were needed to overcome barriers introduced by hearing problems and language form deficits. Early literacy and communication supports from families using visual symbol systems also may be particularly important for children with ASD (e.g., Charlop-Christy & Jones, 2006; Kanner, 1943; Minshew, Goldstein, & Siegel, 1997).

Studies show that generalization of language skills (e.g., vocabulary learning) benefits from group intervention (Oliver & Scott, 1981) and interactions with peers, but children with significant disabilities may have difficulty establishing sincere friendships. To address this concern, Falvey et al. (1994) described the Circle of Friends approach as a procedure to help general education students assume the perspective of a student with disability. The approach uses a diagram of concentric circles to engage potential friends in a dialogue. Students start by writing their own names (and family members' names) in the center circle. In the next circle, they place an X to represent each of their most intimate friends (i.e., friends with whom they share all their secrets); in the next ring out, they place an X to represent each of their good friends (i.e., people who almost fit in the previous circle); in the next, they list people and groups that are important but not best friends (e.g., sports teams or clubs); and in the outside ring, they list roles for people who are paid to do things for them (e.g., doctors, teachers, other care providers). Then, the facilitator shows the students a Circle of Friends diagram for a student with a disability, whose inside circle includes only family with few Xs in the inner two or three circles, but many people in the outside ring, who are paid. Students are specifically *not* asked if they want to be the target student's friend but rather to discuss ideas for planning specific next steps. Scaffolding questions are asked, such as "Who knows Jane and is willing to brainstorm ways with me ideas for getting Jane more involved? For example, if Jane likes films, maybe we can identify someone who would invite her to the film club" (Falvey et al., 1994, p. 352).

SUMMARY

Children with complex communication needs who have disabilities beyond language impairment require comprehensive planning by members of interdisciplinary teams. Planning should be based on assumptions of the potential for competence being greater than it may seem (the least dangerous assumption). There should be no prerequisites for providing AAC supports or working directly on language and literacy skills with any student, including a student with complex communication needs.

A number of planning, assessment, and intervention approaches were described, including instrumental enrichment (a form of dynamic assessment and mediated learning), which emphasizes intelligence as dynamic and modifiable rather than static; the McGill action planning system (MAPS); choosing options and accommodations for children with handicaps (COACH); and the beyond access model. Home activity programs and the circle of friends model are approaches for engaging family and peers in helping the student with complex needs gain skills and participate in age-appropriate activities.

Preverbal to Intentional Communication

Some children with cognitive–communicative impairments, such as autism spectrum disorders (ASD), are significantly delayed in intentional communication acts. They may express preferences, protest when they are unhappy, or place an adult's hand on a desired object in a seeming act of requesting, but none of these actions represents a clear sign of ***intentional communication.*** As described in Chapter 9, intentional communication begins in typical development when infants learn to coordinate shared attention to objects with communication partners to achieve joint focus and shared messages (Adamson & Chance, 1998). Circles of communication (Greenspan, Wieder, & Simmons, 1998) do not develop naturally for some children with complex diagnoses (ASD, in particular), but they can be encouraged with explicit and direct facilitation.

This section describes intervention options for children with significant developmental delays who need particularly explicit cues to learn the power of communication. Methods include social responsivity interventions delivered primarily by parents, responsivity education and prelinguistic milieu teaching (RE/PMT), the picture exchange communication system (PECS), and applied behavioral analysis (ABA; also called *discrete trials training*).

Social Responsivity Interventions

Prelinguistic commenting is an important signal that a child is beginning to understand the social function of communication. It involves actively soliciting another's attention on an object of interest, which is a key prognostic indicator for language and communication development (Wetherby, Yonclas, & Bryan, 1989; Woods & Wetherby, 2003). Thus, joint attention and closed communication circles are important goals for early communication intervention.

Greenspan and his colleagues developed Floortime to help parents support their children's development by literally joining them on the floor in play. With coaching, parents learn to scaffold their children's participation in circles of communication and to be assertive in initiating communication in a way that is sensitive to their children's developmental uniqueness and social–emotional needs. This represents the three components—development, individualization, and responsiveness (DIR; Greenspan & Wieder, 2005; see Chapter 8 in this book). Developmental milestones characterize the six phases of shared attention and regulation, engagement and relating, purposeful emotional interaction, social problem solving, creating ideas, and connecting ideas and thinking logically. Individuality characterizes the goal for parents to understand their child's unique way of "taking in the world—sights, sounds, touch, etc.—and responding to it," including understanding that the "child's individual differences can interfere with his or her ability to relate, communicate, and think" (p. 1). Relationship-based parental interactions are modified to fit a child's current state of development and individual differences.

Elder (1995) studied the effects of an inhome communication-training program based on MacDonald's (1989) *ecological* (called *ECO*) parent-training approach. Nurses implemented the social interaction principles by teaching four mothers in two inhome training sessions to use animated imitating to match their children's actions, followed by expectant waiting. After training, the mothers conducted videotaped training sessions in their homes for 10 minutes, three times per week, for 8 to 12 weeks. The ECO Scales Interaction Profile showed significantly improved interactions for the parent–child dyads. Increases were documented in four child behavior frequencies (i.e., vocal utterances, social responding, social initiating, and intelligible words spoken). Although mothers often are the presumed parental participants in home-training approaches, fathers can be actively engaged in social reciprocity training as well. Seung, Ashwell, Elder, and Valcante (2006) taught fathers to use the same imitation with animation and expectant waiting techniques studied by Elder. Positive results included decreases in the ratio of father-to-child utterances, increases in fathers' imitations of children, and increases in the number of single words and different words produced by the children.

Bernhardt, Smith, and Smith (1992) also evaluated a two-year collaborative language intervention program involving parents, an SLP, and teachers of a 4-year-old boy with a pervasive developmental disorder with autistic features. The transdisciplinary intervention goals addressed social, cognitive, and behavioral areas, as well as specific communication development needs, incorporating both direct therapy and indirect facilitation. Results showed improvements in the boy's language, communication, and social skills in preschool contexts, but "they did not replace his acting out behaviors" (p. 265).

Koegel, Bimbela, and Schreibman (1996) investigated parent training to promote naturalistic language development supports to identify any collateral positive effects in other areas of family life. They compared two parent-training paradigms, both implemented during unstructured dinnertime interactions using random assignment. One group of parents learned an ***individual target behaviors (ITB)*** paradigm using discrete trial training; the other learned a ***pivotal response training (PRT)*** paradigm, aimed at developing motivation and responsivity to multiple cues. These responses are called *pivotal* because they play a role across many learning contexts. Imitation is another example of a pivotal response. Videotapes were scored by judges blind to the phase of treatment. Families in both conditions scored in the neutral range at baseline on four social–emotional dimensions—happiness, interest, stress, and style of communication. Only the parents who received the PRT showed significantly more positive interactions on all four scales after intervention.

Responsivity Education with Prelinguistic Milieu Teaching

Incidental teaching approaches (Hart & Risley, 1968) were designed to provide instruction in naturalistic contexts to overcome a key limitation of behaviorist approaches—lack of generalization of newly acquired behaviors. Within an incidental teaching paradigm, learning trials are initiated by the child showing interest in a toy or routine. Often the item of interest is withheld, using time delay to avoid direct prompting of the desired requesting behavior. When requests occur, natural reinforcers (i.e., the desired toy or action) are used to reinforce them. A problem is that incidental learning trials might be too dispersed to support the learning of new behaviors, and children might require more direct models to know what to do. Activities can be engineered to increase the likelihood that a child will initiate.

An example of an incidental teaching exchange is set in a preschool activity for making pudding. In this example, the trainer gives a peer a turn at stirring while the target child looks on, prompting the child to initiate:

> **Child:** Me! [Child initiates and reaches for ladle.]
> **Trainer:** Stir pudding. [model]
> **Child:** Stir pudding.
> **Trainer:** All right. You stir the pudding too. [verbal acknowledgment + expansion + activity participation] (Warren & Bambara, 1989, p. 461)

Milieu teaching (Warren & Bambara, 1989) was developed as a variation on incidental teaching to keep the intervention situated in relatively naturalistic routines but included *mand model* (Rogers-Warren & Warren, 1980) components to increase adult control and the rate of teaching–learning opportunities. The following is an example of a mand model exchange set in a playful milieu in which a child is scooping dry beans into a pot:

Trainer: What are you doing? [target probe question]
Child: (no response)
Trainer: Tell me. [mand]
Child: Beans.
Trainer: Say, "Pour beans."
Child: Pour beans.
Trainer: That's right, you're pouring beans into the pot. [verbal acknowledgment + expansion] (Warren & Bambara, 1989, p. 461)

Further development of milieu teaching approaches has led to inclusion of social interactionist components, including parent (or teacher) *responsivity education* (*RE*). In RE training adults are taught to respond contingently to children's messages, expanding beyond their role as deliverers of reinforcement to increase the authenticity of communication. In RE/PMT two-component models, prelinguistic milieu teaching (PMT) "is delivered by the clinician to the child" and RE "is delivered by the clinician to the parents" (Warren et al., 2006, p. 47). ***Enhanced milieu teaching*** (***EMT;*** Hancock & Kaiser, 2006), as it is also called, incorporates the three components of environmental arrangement, responsive interaction, and milieu teaching. Hancock and Kaiser indicated that "more than 50 empirical studies have provided evidence for the efficacy and effectiveness of EMT for preschool children with significant cognitive and language delays; children with autism spectrum disorders; and children from high-risk, low-income families" (p. 203).

Fey and colleagues (2006) used a randomized controlled trial (RCT) to evaluate the efficacy of a six-month course of RE/PMT for children with significant developmental delay by measuring learner outcomes and parental stress. Participants were 51 children (ages 24 to 33 months; 13 in each group had a diagnosis of Down syndrome) who had fewer than 10 expressive words or signs at entry. Children in the RE/PMT treatment group exhibited superior gains in communication compared with the no-treatment group, and the diagnosis of Down syndrome had no effects on child outcomes. Parents of children without Down syndrome in the RE/PMT group made modest increases in treating their children's preintentional acts as intentional.

Picture Exchange Communication System

The ***picture exchange communication system*** (***PECS;*** Bondy & Frost, 1994, 1998; Frost & Bondy, 1994) jumpstarts interpersonal communication by teaching children to exchange picture symbols for desired objects or actions. PECS takes advantage of discrepancies between low verbal and relatively higher visual abilities by children with autism (e.g., Charlop-Christy & Jones, 2006; Kanner, 1943; Minshew, Goldstein, & Siegel, 1997). Children learn to hand an adult a picture to make requests in the behaviorist sense of *mands* (i.e., requesting behaviors that specify the reinforcer, as in "I want juice"). No requirements are made for eye contact, facial orientation, and imitation or vocalization to signal intentionality.

To implement PECS, an intervention team must first identify potential reinforcers (e.g., food items or toys) that can be represented with pictures (usually, black-and-white or colored drawings) on cards. The intervention occurs in six phases. In Phase 1, an adult assistant sits behind the child and uses physical prompts to help the child pick up the pictured symbol and hand it to the communication partner, who sits in front of the child; the partner accepts the pictured object and gives the child the desired object in exchange. This approach explicitly avoids the problems of prompt dependency because the assistant refrains from using such verbal prompts as "What do you want?" Any prompting is nonverbal, provided by the assistant, and faded as soon as possible. Time-delay procedures increase the "likelihood of prompt independence and independent use of PECS" (Charlop-Christy & Jones, 2006, p. 107). The assistant also plays a role at the beginning of Phase 2, but the goal of the second phase is for the child to find the picture and take it to the communication partner without help. In Phase 3, symbol pictures are organized in a loose-leaf notebook and new symbol choices are added. In Phases 4 to 6, the child learns to use carrier phrase symbols, such as "I want," along with the pictured symbols. The child also learns to label objects (i.e., to exhibit the "tact" function when asked "What is this?") and to answer *yes/no* questions about choices.

Conspicuously absent from this group of communication acts are *comments* to solicit another's attention on objects of interest. Commenting is a critical prognostic indicator for later communication development (Wetherby, Yonclas, & Bryan, 1989; Woods & Wetherby, 2003). Commenting acts, as targeted in Floortime (Greenspan & Wieder, 2005), may be needed to help children conceptualize communication as a means of social *interaction* as well as *transaction.* Symbolic picture exchange methods, such as PECS, however, can provide a critical first step for children who show limited understanding of the function of communication.

Some parents and others have expressed another concern about using PECS. Parents universally want their children to talk, but children with autism who have not begun to speak prior to age 5 (often, the majority—up to 80 percent, as reported by Bondy & Frost, 1994) have a limited prognosis for talking (e.g., Schreibman, 1988). Because PECS uses a nonvocal means to get communication going, some express concerns that it may interfere with speech development during a critical learning period (Charlop-Christy & Jones, 2006). Research results suggest, however, that such concerns are unfounded. Bondy and Frost (1994, 1998) described results for using PECS with preschool-age children with autism. Of 19 children who used PECS for less than one year, 2 acquired independent speech, 5 developed some functional speech along with PECS, and 12 used PECS as their sole communication modality. Of 66 children who used PECS for more than one year, 39 developed independent speech, 20 used speech plus PECS, and 7 used only PECS to communicate. These results are more positive than would be predicted by the prognosis of 80 percent of children with autism showing limited or no speech by age 5 years. Charlop-Christy, Carpenter, Le, LeBlanc, and Kellet (2002) also showed that children who learn to exchange picture symbols for desired objects have a better chance of learning to exchange words. They found that a majority of children (59 percent) learned to speak after using PECS for a year or more, compared with the poorer prognosis of around 20 percent.

Howlin, Gordon, Pasco, Wade, and Charman (2007) conducted a randomized controlled trial in which children with ASD were engaged in immediate PECS training, delayed training, or no training. After five months, children whose teachers received training and consultation showed higher use of symbols and communication initiations. Other areas of communication did not improve, however, and the changes were not maintained after the intervention stopped. This study suggested the need for longer interventions and perhaps the support of other methods for helping children understand the social functions of communication.

Some practical concerns ensue if children continue to use PECS as their primary means of communication, requiring a larger number of symbols. Barbera (2007) wrote, "The PECS book has to accompany the child everywhere he goes, and it can be nearly useless for practicing mand trials while a child is in a pool or bouncing on a trampoline" (p. 85). This was one of the reasons that Barbera recommended adding sign language as soon as feasible when children with autism learn to communicate with PECS but remain nonspeaking.

Applied Behavioral Analysis/Discrete Trial Interventions

Applied behavioral analysis (ABA) approaches are based in behaviorist explanations of language learning (e.g., Skinner, 1957). Kearney (2008) prepared an accessible book to explain

ABA to parents, teachers, and other professionals, calling it an ABC approach, in which the alphabetic letters are used not only to signify a primer introducing a complex topic but also stand for the three "building blocks that B. F. Skinner referred to as the contingencies of reinforcement—the antecedents, behaviors, and consequences" (p. 10). Anderson (2007) emphasized the functional aspects of behaviorist approaches, based on the principle that all individuals acquire behavior through interaction with their environments. Anderson added, "We learn behaviours that are helpful to us in any given situation" (p. 9).

The classical form of ABA, or ***discrete trial training (DTT),*** for teaching speech and language to children with autism was developed at the University of California at Los Angeles (UCLA) by O. Ivar Lovaas (1977). In a controlled study, Lovaas (1987) showed that children with autism who began treatment using an ABA approach prior to age 4 gained apparently typical intellectual and educational functioning after two years of intensive 40-hour-per-week, one-on-one, face-to-face treatment. Lovaas (1993) reported that the DTT led to lasting social and intellectual gains measured when the children were assessed later at ages 7 and 13 (see Personal Reflection 14.6). This evidence of generalization and sustainable results was in response to other reports that skills learned in DTT sessions failed to generalize to more naturalistic interactions.

PERSONAL reflection *14.6*

"When I was little I couldn't speak properly and I didn't listen well to people. I used to be a bit of a whirlwind and never sat still (except for dinner). The activities we did helped me overcome this. I remember a looking game which helped me look at people. This is called good eye contact. Now I really like conversations and my interests include reading newspapers, playing video games, watching action movies, swimming and walking with my Dad and my youngest sister. My favourite subjects at secondary school are technology, art, history and home economics. I feel very comfortable about having autism (sometimes I make a joke about Asperger's syndrome and call it hamburger syndrome). The good thing about autism it that, when I want to, I can concentrate really hard and I find learning quite easy."

Colin was described by Dillenburger and Keenan (2006) as "the first child in Northern Ireland to benefit from ABA in 1995 and who today attends the same grammar school as his brothers and sisters" (p. 17).

DTT is conducted sitting face to face with the child at a table, so the stimuli can be tightly controlled and each trial is a separate event (Anderson, 2007). Trials are massed, usually in groups of 10, and tangible reinforcers, often food snacks, are used to increase target responses, which also are tightly defined. An example of a Lovaas (1981) training sequence (to train hugging) goes as follows:

Step 1. Say, "Hug me," and prompt (e.g., physically move) the child so that his cheek makes momentary contact with yours. Reward him with food the moment his cheek makes contact.

Step 2. Gradually fade the prompt while keeping the instruction ("Hug me") loud and clear.

Step 3. Gradually withhold the reward contingent on longer and longer hugs. Move in slow steps from a 1-second hug to one lasting 5 to 10 seconds. At the same time, require a more complete hug such as placing his arms around your neck, squeezing harder, etc. Prompt these additional behaviors if necessary.

Step 4. Generalize this learning to many environments and many persons. Gradually thin the reward schedule so that you get more and more hugs for less and less reward. (p. 50)

Some of the problems with a one-on-one training protocol that involves 40 hours per week are prohibitive monetary costs as well as removal from other social contexts. Lovaas (1993) acknowledged the high financial and personal costs and difficult practicalities of the approach. Cohen, Amerine-Dickens, and Smith (2006) attempted to replicate DTT by providing *early intensive behavioral treatment (EIBT)* for children with autism in community settings. They used a three-year, quasi-experimental design in which children were assigned to groups based on parental preference. In one group, 21 children received 35 to 40 hours per week of EIBT from a community agency, replicating most aspects of Lovaas's model. In the comparison group, 21 age- and IQ-matched children received services in special education classes at local public schools. Repeated measures were compared (with baseline scores as covariates) for three yearly assessments. Students in the EIBT group earned significantly higher IQ and adaptive behavior scores than students in the comparison group, but no significant differences were found between groups in language comprehension or nonverbal skill. At the end of the third year, 6 of the 21 EIBT children could be fully included in general education classrooms without assistance; 11 others were included with support. Only 1 comparison group child could function primarily in general education.

Eikeseth, Smith, Jahr, and Eldevik (2002) examined the use of ABA techniques in school programs with 4- to 7-year-old children with autism. The researchers compared the results for one year of intensive behavioral treatment for 13 children with the results for 12 comparison group children receiving eclectic intervention, both in school settings. The two treatment groups received similar amounts of treatment for an average of 28.52 hours per week. Rather than randomly assigning children to treatments, an independent clinician assigned children in a way that was "not influenced by child characteristics or family preference" (p. 49). Results showed that children in the behavioral treatment group made significantly larger gains on standardized tests than those in the eclectic group, and some of the gains were quite large. The authors concluded that aspects of behavioral treatment (beyond intensity) may account for favorable outcomes.

In a follow-up study with the same children reported five years later, Eikeseth, Smith, Jahr, and Eldevik (2007) found that at a mean age of 8 years, 2 months, the behavioral treatment group continued to show larger increases in IQ and adaptive functioning than the eclectic group, and they also displayed fewer aberrant behaviors and social problems. To investigate the variable of intensity further, Eldevik, Eikeseth, Jahr, and Smith (2006) retrospectively compared the results of training when the intensity was reduced for two years to an average of 12 hours per week (from the earlier mean of 28.5). Although the behavioral group again made larger gains than the eclectic group, the gains were more modest than those reported in previous studies in which children received more intensive behavioral treatment (up to 40 hours per week). The authors questioned whether the gains were clinically significant.

Intensity can be influenced not only by total contact hours with a clinician, teacher, or other specialist but also by how close together discrete trials occur. Koegel, Dunlap, and Dyer (1980) measured the effects of varying the time between massed trials. They found that more closely spaced trials (with one-second intervals) produced higher levels of correct responding and more rapid acquisition compared to trials with four or more seconds between trials. Massed trials, however, can lead to loss of meaning.

Koegel, Glahn, and Nieminen (1978) studied varied methods for training parents how to use ABA methods. Initially, they found that four mothers of autistic children could learn to teach their children specific behaviors after only a brief demonstration but did not generalize the ability to train new child target behaviors. A second parent-training program was designed to teach general behavior modification procedures, rather than specific child behaviors. In this case, watching videotaped illustrations was sufficient for participants to learn the techniques, but participants needed to view the entire set of tapes.

Considering the Evidence for Varied Approaches

Preferences for one approach over another are influenced by clinicians' theoretical orientations and prior experience, as well as by scientific evidence and parent and client values. Both professionals and parents may be confused about whether one approach is always better than another. Parents of children with autism may be especially susceptible to claims about best methods, only methods, or methods that promise a cure. Ritvo (2006) addressed this concern by indicating that parents should be advised against many treatments, not because they are harmful or dangerous but "because they have yet to be scientifically proven, they needlessly squander limited family resources, and they give vulnerable parents false hope of a cure" (p. 118).

Charlop-Christy and Carpenter (2000) conducted a study in which they compared three approaches reviewed previously in this section—traditional incidental teaching, modified incidental teaching (milieu teaching), and discrete trial training (DTT). The incidental teaching approach required the child to initiate, using only a time delay procedure. For example, a parent entered the child's room in the morning and waited for him or her to say "Good morning, Mom" before providing a model (if an initiation was not forthcoming) and reinforcing the child with a greeting, praise, and desired activity. The milieu teaching approach involved engineering the environment (e.g., placing a toy out of reach, withholding a favorite video) to increase the number of learning and practice trials within a day. The DTT involved 10 massed trials in one sit-down, face-to-face session in the same location in the house and time each day; food reinforcers were provided for producing a targeted response. For example, the parent, using two dolls, would wait to see if the child would spontaneously ask "How are you?" within 10 seconds; if not, the parent would model having one doll ask, "How are you?" Correct responses were reinforced with food and praise. After a baseline period, in which data were taken with no intervention, the three intervention approaches were implemented in alternating one-week intervals, each with a different target. Results were compared for three boys with autism from age 6 years, 2 months to 9 years, 8 months in racially/ethnically diverse families (Caucasian, East Indian, Hispanic). The best acquisition and generalization results were found with the milieu teaching procedure. One boy acquired targeted responses with incidental teaching, and two did not acquire the targeted responses with this frequency (called dosage) of DTT. Generalization occurred for all three boys only with the milieu teaching program. Parents evaluated all three programs positively and thought all were reasonable to implement.

In another study of varied approaches, Yoder and Stone (2006) compared the efficacy of RE/PMT and PECS using a randomized controlled trial with 36 preschoolers with ASD. They measured changes in spoken communication from pre- to posttreatment and maintenance at six-month follow-up. Children in both groups received treatment for a maximum of 24 hours over a six-month period. Results showed that PECS was more successful than RE/PMT in increasing the number of nonimitative spoken communication acts and the number of different nonimitative words at posttesting. Maintenance results varied based on the degree of interest children showed in exploring objects prior to the initiation of treatment. Children who began treatment showing relatively high interest in object exploration showed faster growth in the number of different nonimitative words in the PECS group than in the RE/PMT group. Children who began treatment with relatively low object exploration showed faster learning in the RE/PMT group than in the PECS group.

Other research has investigated uses of ABA techniques to target commenting and joint action routines, goals traditionally associated with social interactionist theory. Training joint attention and symbolic play can yield positive results and better expressive language outcomes than treatment with ABA alone (Kasari, Freeman, & Paparella, 2006). Ingersoll and Schreibman (2006) also reported success in teaching reciprocal imitation to young children with autism using a naturalistic behavioral approach, in which they taught imitation of actions on toys as a pivotal skill. Gains were found in spontaneous imitation, joint attention, pretend play, and language.

Rocha, Schreibman, and Stahmer (2007) used behavior analytic techniques to teach parents to initiate more frequent bids for joint attention with their children. They used massed trials and discrete trial training (DTT), accompanied by pivotal response training (PRT) involving elements of child choice and motivating toys. Parents learned to allow one full minute of play after a child's correct response but only 20 seconds after a prompted response. In Phase 1 of this approach, *response to hand on object,* parents place their child's hand on a new toy while the child is engaged with a previous object. In Phase 2, *response to object tapping,* parents solicit their child's attention by presenting a new toy and tapping on it. In Phase 3, *response to showing of object,* parents show the child a toy and provide verbal cues (e.g., "Look, I have a car that seems fun") or nonverbal cues (e.g., "zooming" the car along the floor). Correct responses are judged if the child's attention shifts to the new toy within five seconds and is sustained for five seconds. Prior to moving to Phases 4 and 5, parents learn to use DTT prompting and fading techniques to teach their child to make eye contact prior to receiving a desired toy as a reinforcer. In Phase 4, *following a point,* a parent draws the child's attention by saying "Look" or holding a toy up near the parent's face; the parent then turns his or her head and points to another object in the room. A correct response is judged if the child follows the point; prompting is provided as necessary. In Phase 5, *following a gaze,* a response is required (prompted if necessary) when parents shift their gaze to another toy but do not point. Although the focus of this study was on parental initiations, researchers found that by the end of the treatment, children in the study were initiating bids for joint attention and responding to the bids of their parents, which is a huge step beyond requesting only actions or objects.

The finding that children increase their bids for attention along with their parents is consistent with explanations of naturalistic learning. The difference in intervention contexts relates to the clarity of cues, which seem necessary for some children with autism and other complex communication needs to learn to communicate and relate. Studies have confirmed the importance of providing direct instruction with clear goals and clear response expectations. Ritvo's (2006) summary applies broadly: "One thing all professionals agree upon today is that autistic children, severe to middle to high-functioning, need active teaching intervention. Teachers and therapists must get right in their faces and force relating and participation" (p. 104).

SUMMARY

This section described intervention approaches for targeting intentional communication, particularly for children with autism and other pervasive developmental disorders. The range of approaches includes some that are based more on fostering interpersonal relations, such as floortime (also referred to as DIR); some that use applied behavioral analysis (ABA) techniques to teach communication transactions, such as the picture exchange communication system (PECS) and discrete trial training (DTT); and some that represent a hybrid of social-interactionist and behaviorist techniques, such as combined responsivity education for parents and prelinguistic milieu teaching (RE/PMT) for children. Some research evidence is available to support each of these approaches, although controversies continue to surround questions of generalizability and which children need which approaches. Clinician expertise and family preference plays a primary role in making evidence-based practice decisions for children with complex needs at early stages of communication development.

Echolalia, Challenging Behaviors, and Nonsymbolic Communication

Developmental disabilities with varied etiologies, especially autism, may lead to unconventional forms of communication. Unconventional communication can range from unusual communication traits, such as echolalia, to severely debilitating and isolating forms of aggressive or self-abusive behavior. A general intervention principle for addressing such problems is to discover the underlying message value in the behavior. Thus, goals and techniques in this area mirror the perlocutionary stages of communication in infancy (discussed in Chapters 8 and 9), in that adults treat actions as communicative, whether they seem intentional or not, and gradually scaffold to help children to transition from preintentional to intentional communication.

Replace Echolalia with Generative Communicative Utterances

Imitation is encouraged in language intervention based on a variety of theoretical models, but echolalia in place of functional communication is problematic. *Echolalia* occurs when a child imitates all or part of an utterance, immediately or after a time delay, without shifting components to fit the reciprocal speaker–listener context. Prizant and Rydell (1993) termed echolalia a form of *unconventional verbal behavior.* Echolalia that occurs frequently in place of more normal reciprocal interactions is a symptom of ASD (Prelock, 2006; Prizant & Rydell, 1993).

Laski, Charlop, and Schreibman (1988) differentiated appropriate imitation of models (e.g., "This is red" in response to "This is red") from inappropriate echoes (e.g., when a partner asks "What do you want?" and the child echoes "What do you want?"). Prelock (2006) provided the following example of *immediate echolalia* (i.e., occurring immediately following the model) by a 4-year-old child with ASD:

> **Father:** Give that to me, Joshua.
> **Child:** Give that to me Joshua. (p. 171)

Delayed echolalia is an echoed response that appears after some time has passed, often in circumstances that evoke similar strong feelings. For example, the father in the prior example might have been expressing alarm because Joshua was holding something dangerous, such as a kitchen knife. Having formed an association of the exclamation with the event, Joshua might produce a delayed echo, saying "Give that to me, Joshua" with similar intonation when he sees the knife later in the week. Delayed echolalia provides a window into the child's focus of attention and emotional state. A responsive parent, noting this, might respond contingently, "Yes, it scared me to see you hold the knife. Knives can be dangerous. Dangerous." If the child repeats the final word, saying "Dangerous," the father might model the two-word utterance, "Knife dangerous," working toward a more functional two-word utterance in response and in later similar circumstances.

To convey the properties of words as building blocks, rather than gestalt phrases, the father might then produce a relevant but different two-word combination, such as "Knife sharp." ***Mitigated echolalia*** is the term used when a child varies the imitated utterance, perhaps as simplification or partial contextualization. It is a positive sign that the child is beginning to integrate some of the generative recombinatorial properties (i.e., words as building blocks) of language. Generative communication can be credited when a child begins to produce new one- or two-word utterances spontaneously in the appropriate contexts without immediate models.

To capture differences in echolalic responses, it is helpful to analyze where they fall along continua for exactness of the repetition, degree of comprehension, and communicative intent (Fay & Schuler, 1980; Prizant, 1987). In providing intervention, clinicians can help others detect and respond to the message value of echoed utterances. Prizant (1987) described interactive functions of immediate echolalia as including turn taking, declarative commenting, *yes* answers, and requests. Noninteractive functions of immediate echolalia include nonfocused responses (e.g., conveying fear or pain arousal), rehearsal, and self-regulation. Even noninteractive echolalic language can be functional. Prizant and Rydell (1984) described interactive functions of delayed echolalia as turn taking, verbal completion, providing information, interactive labeling, protest, request, calling, affirmation, and direction of actions by others. They described noninteractive functions of delayed echolalia as nonfocused expressions of inner states (including self-stimulatory function), situation association, self-direction, rehearsal, and noninteractive labeling.

Although echolalia is considered problematic, the tendency of human beings to imitate each other is a pivotal skill for learning language. This suggests a conflict between goals, but evidence shows that parents of children with autism can learn to use naturalistic techniques to increase their children's communicative speech, in which children learn to imitate without increasing their echolalia. Laski, Charlop, and Schreibman (1988) studied speech production outcomes after training parents to play with their nonverbal or echolalic children using a variety of toys. They taught the parents to use a *natural language paradigm (NLP),* in which they modeled words and phrases in meaningful contexts and prompted answers to questions and other speech. Posttest results showed that all children increased the frequency of their verbalizations in three nontraining settings, and that "increases in children's appropriate speech were not accompanied by increases in echolalia." These findings suggested that the "NLP took advantage of the children's echolalia by converting it to appropriate imitative speech" (p. 399).

Replace Aggressive Behaviors with Functional Communication

When severe cognitive impairment and multiple comorbid conditions are present, it may be difficult to help children reach the stage of intentional communication using words or other conventional symbols. In such cases, communication partners need to glean intended messages from idiosyncratic signals associated with the perlocutionary stage. Then prelinguistic communication can be targeted using intervention goals to nudge the child or adolescent into intentional signaling, taking them into the illocutionary stage. At that point, more conventional symbols—spoken, signed, printed, or pictured—may be targeted as indicators of the locutionary stage.

Some children with severe disabilities exhibit ***self-injurious behaviors*** (e.g., head banging, scratching, or throwing) that are aggressive and potentially dangerous to themselves and others. In such cases, it is essential to identify components of the problem and form a comprehensive intervention plan. This requires an interdisciplinary and multipronged approach. Both behavioral and social–emotional principles are relevant.

—CASE **example** *14.1*————————————————————

| **Reba and the Challenges and Benefits of Full Inclusion** |

Reba was a fifth-grade girl with autism who had complex communication needs. Her new IEP specified that she would be included in a general education classroom for the first time, but she exhibited a behavior that interfered with the plan. She intermittently emitted extremely loud, long, high-pitched squeals. When Reba squealed, it was hard for anyone to think about anything else. The noise effectively stopped all other teaching and learning, so the usual consequence was to remove Reba from the classroom and to bring her back when she stopped squealing.

The intervention team conducted an ABC (Antecedent, Behavior, Consequence) assessment but could not identify a clear pattern of antecedent events that were stimulating and consequences that were reinforcing Reba's squealing behavior. Team members considered too much pressure or not enough attention as triggers, but the squealing seemed more a response to an internal state than to predictable environmental stimuli, although it may have signaled "I need a break." The team continued to use removal as a response to this presumed message and also to preserve the learning environment for other students. The team was able to conclude from the assessment that removal was not acting as an inadvertent reinforcer for the squealing, because the frequency of squealing decreased over time, rather than increased. What seemed to be asso-

ciated with the decrease in the frequency of the negative behavior was an increase in Reba's communicative repertoire, as she received facilitation to point to letter and number symbols on a communication board as a mode of communication and could participate academically.

The special education teacher consultant who worked with Reba from elementary school into high school noted that Reba quieted especially when the paraprofessional read to her from her textbooks. Reba remained unable to express herself using spoken language but continued to use facilitated pointing to spell words and to compute math problems. Because her pointing was facilitated, the team could not be sure whether Reba was the sole author of any of the messages she expressed in this manner. (See Calculator & Hatch [1995] and Shane [1994] for evidence regarding problems with facilitated communication, and see Mirenda [2003] for a perspective on facilitation as a route to independent pointing.) By middle school, Reba did learn to carry her books from class to class in her backpack like all of the other students, to focus on the pages of her textbooks, and to appear to answer comprehension questions correctly using facilitated communication. In high school, with facilitation, she wrote her term paper on autism. In spite of improvements, however, the squealing remained a mystery, never disappearing entirely.

The behavioral component involves an observational inventory of environmental conditions that may be triggering, reinforcing, and maintaining an undesired behavior. As Halle, Ostrofsky, and Hemmeter (2006) pointed out, behavior is not random; it serves a function for the person engaging in it. To analyze what that function is, it may be helpful to adopt an ABC framework to set up an observational chart in three sections, with the headings Antecedent, Behavior, and Consequence. Halle et al. called this a *functional behavioral assessment* (*FBA*) that results in a statement with "(1) an operational definition of the challenging behavior, (2) events that trigger it, (3) its maintaining consequences, and (4) its likely function" (p. 527). It is the likely function (i.e., message component) that rounds out the ABC analysis to incorporate social interaction principles. As illustrated in Case Example 14.1, the objective is to identify antecedent stimuli or consequences that may be inadvertently triggering or reinforcing the unconventional behavior. Reichle and Wacker (1993) summarized the process:

First, the function of challenging behavior must be identified; we must identify the reinforcers maintaining behavior. Second, the identified reinforcers must be available only for one or more acceptable communicative responses and withheld for the challenging behavior. (pp. 2–3)

Exclusive use of behavioral approaches to analyze maladaptive behaviors is viewed by many to be problematic (e.g., Donnellan, Mirenda, Mesaros, & Fassbender, 1984; Schuler & Goetz, 1981). When only the surface-level behavioral aspects of the problem are analyzed and addressed, both the message value and deeper emotional needs of the individual are missed. Another problem is that desperate situations may lead to temptation to adopt aversive consequences to punish (as a means of reducing) dangerous behaviors. Aversive treatments used in the past have included extreme punishments, such as electric shock, squirting a child in the face with vinegar, and shouting "No!" Figure 14.1 presents the position statement of the Autism Society of America, calling for the cessation of such approaches.

What is needed is an approach that recognizes the social–emotional aspects of unconventional and maladaptive behavior. This involves interpreting the communicative messages that underlie unconventional behaviors in terms of their likely function and personal meaning. Schuler and Goetz (1981) noted that communication analysis may reveal some nonsymbolic behaviors to be function specific (i.e., conveying only one message); whereas others serve a variety of functions. For example, self-injurious behaviors may serve the varied functions of sensory stimulation, eliciting attention from others, and terminating undesirable situations. These functions might correspond with the respective messages "I'm bored," "Pay attention to me," and "I don't want to do this any more" (Donnellan et al., 1984, p. 202). Based on the analysis, teams may design interventions to reduce maladaptive behaviors by manipulating antecedent contexts and teaching alternative communicative behaviors or other functionally related behaviors.

Targeting Alternative Communicative Behaviors to Replace Aberrant Behaviors

A first approach is to identify the message value of an aberrant behavior and to replace it with a more conventional way to communicate the same message. This is a form of ***functional communication training (FCT),*** which is supported by a body of research (Halle et al., 2006). After identifying the message value of aberrant behaviors, clinicians seek to teach conventional and functional signals to replace unconventional ones. If new signals make underlying messages more intelligible to a wider audience, positive benefits can be realized both in communication and behavior. For example, Frea, Arnold, and Vittemberga (2001) reported that PECS instruction had a positive effect in eliminating severe aggressive behavior in a preschooler with autism while teaching appropriate requesting.

Donnellan and colleagues (1984) provided an example of FCT with Don, an 18-year-old with severe intellectual disabilities. Don's formal communication repertoire was limited to about 15 signs, which he rarely used spontaneously. His head banging, head punching, and face slapping elicited attention from his teacher, which apparently was reinforcing the behavior whose message seemed to be "Pay attention to me, I need help" (p. 518). Don's intervention program used prompt fading and modeling techniques to teach more conventional communication in three steps. First, Don was taught step by step to seek the teacher's attention by visually scanning the room, going over, tapping him on the shoulder, and making the sign for "Help" to request assistance. Don also learned to specify the type of help needed, for example, by walking back to the work area and pointing to the part that needed help. After six weeks, "Don regularly performed the request-for-assistance sequence whenever he encountered task difficulty, and the self-injurious behavior was virtually eliminated" (p. 203).

figure *14.1*

Excerpt from Autism Society of America Resolution on Abusive Treatment and Neglect

The Society calls for a cessation of treatment and/or intervention that results in any of the following:

1. Obvious signs of physical pain experienced by the individual;

2. Potential or actual physical side effects, including tissue damage, physical illness, emotional stress, or death;

3. Dehumanization of an individual with autism by the use of procedures that are normally unacceptable for non-handicapped persons in all environments;

4. Ambivalence of discomfort by family, staff, and/or caregivers regarding the necessity of such extreme strategies or their involvement in such intervention; and

5. Revulsion or distress felt by handicapped and non-handicapped peers and community members who cannot reconcile extreme procedures with acceptable human conduct.

Source: "Resolution on Abusive Treatment and Neglect" by the Autism Society of America, July 16, 1988, *The Advocate, 20*(3), p. 17. Reprinted with permission of the Autism Society of America.

Robinson and Owens (1995) reported a similar situation for a 27-year-old woman with moderate to severe intellectual disabilities, who used stomping, head banging, biting, and assaultiveness when stressed. Analysis suggested that the message underlying her behaviors was primarily a request for medicine to relieve her headaches, allergies, and constipation, but her behaviors also expressed her fears and anxieties about changes in her routine. Although this young woman had been taught a few signs, she did not use them spontaneously. Intervention involved developing a temporal sequencing and "Wants and Needs" board so she could use photographs to communicate about upcoming activities and to request medication. A few days after the board was introduced, the woman was able to detach and replace photographs representing transitions in activities. Although the stomping did not disappear entirely, it was reduced from pretreatment levels.

Targeting Other Functionally Related Behaviors to Replace Aberrant Responses

The second technique is to teach functionally related behaviors that are not necessarily communicative. Donnellan and colleagues (1984) illustrated this technique with the case of Sam, a 12-year-old boy with autism and moderate intellectual disability. Sam had a fairly extensive sign language repertoire, which he used spontaneously. Sam's unconventional behaviors were triggered when he was in crowded or noisy conditions, such as shopping malls and recreational facilities. In response, Sam used several auditory self-stimulatory behaviors, such as loud, repetitive vocalizations and finger snapping, which seemed to convey the message "I'm anxious/tense/excited/overwhelmed by the input available" (p. 204). Sam was taught to use a portable audio player with earphones to serve the calming function in two phases. First, he learned to operate the device and use it to listen to soothing music in any situation in which he felt overstimulated; then he learned to remain in stimulating situations for increasing periods of time before using the audiosystem. The first phase took only a few weeks, but the second took three months. After that, "Sam was able to tolerate exposure to novel environments for up to one hour at a time before using the tape set for a 10-minute period" (p. 204). Sam would fit right in with today's youth, who carry personal audio devices and wear earbuds almost constantly when the situation permits.

Manipulating Antecedent Contexts

A third technique involves manipulating antecedent conditions to reduce aberrant behavior. This approach is appropriate when the message seems to be "I don't want to do this anymore." To illustrate this technique, Donnellan and colleagues (1984) described Sarah, a 7-year-old girl with autism and severe intellectual disabilities. Sarah's aberrant behaviors consisted of being aggressive to staff members and throwing objects in the classroom. Intervention for Sarah included assessment of her learning strengths, needs, and modality preferences, so that learning tasks could be matched more closely to her abilities. The result was that Sarah's "aggression and tantrum behaviors decreased as they became unnecessary for terminating the activity" (p. 205).

Providing Comprehensive Interventions

When selecting communication approaches to replace aberrant responses for people with autism and other complex communication needs, it is helpful to consider methods that will support nonsymbolic message comprehension as well as expression, taking advantage of visual system strengths. Visual strategies include enhanced gestures and facial expression, cartoon drawings, lists with pictures, time limits with clock drawings, communication schedules, signs posted with environmental reminders, cards that divide big jobs (e.g., "Clean your room") into small parts (e.g., "Make the bed, put the dirty clothes in the hamper, etc."), and other supports to help children feel less anxious and more aware of upcoming events (Hodgdon, 1999).

Siegel-Causey and Guess (1989) described a comprehensive approach for enhancing nonsymbolic communication based on these five principles: nurturance, sensitivity, opportunities, sequencing, and movement. The approach makes use of matching techniques and multiple modalities (auditory, visual, tactile, kinesthetic, and olfactory) to teach symbolic and nonsymbolic communication. Case Example 14.2 provides an example of an exchange in which Wendy, a new teacher, used nonverbal communication to establish reciprocal communication with Jennifer, an adolescent with autism and intellectual disabilities.

Another comprehensive ***intensive habilitation program (IHP)*** was implemented in a residential program in Sicily, Italy, with 18 participants ranging in age from 16 to 38 years (Polirstok, Dana, Buono, Mongelli, & Trubia, 2003). Many were long-time residents who had been treated with discrete behavior plans using an ABA approach accompanied by mood-stabilizing or neuroleptic medications. Few gains had been observed in functional skills, however, and participants continued to exhibit high rates of maladaptive behavior.

The IHP used positive behavioral methods, including the gentle teaching approach (McGee & Menolaschino, 1991; McGee, Menolaschino, Hobbs, & Menousek, 1987) and humanistic applied behaviorism (Hall, 1992). Each client's weekly goals and intervention plan was posted in work areas. ***Errorless learning*** and ***backward chaining*** techniques were used to engage participants in functional skills as part of daily living and occupational activities. As an example of errorless learning, participants learned to stencil paint designs on towels and to assemble materials for packaging and sale in local markets. Using backward chaining, they learned to complete the final step first and then they learned each prior step, keeping frustration low and success and rewards high. Social rewards of human closeness and bonding were emphasized, consistent with McGee's gentle teaching philosophy that individuals with challenging behaviors need to experience human interaction as positive, not punitive. Alternatives to punishment included ignore-redirect-reward and interrupt-ignore-redirect-reward sequences. Staff members learned to use gentle redirection consistently, to treat residents with respect, and to avoid using loud voices or showing their anger. As described by Polirstok and colleagues (2003):

CASE example *14.2*

Jennifer and the Use of a Nonsymbolic Communication Approach

Siegel-Causey and Guess (1989) provided the following case example, describing how a new teacher, Wendy, used a nonsymbolic communication approach with Jennifer, an adolescent with complex communication needs.

Jennifer: Walks around the room stopping to look closely and intently at things with patterns. Sometimes she stops for long periods and rocks, shakes her head, and giggles. She smiles the entire time. Finally, she sits down at the table.

Wendy [using nurturance]: Goes over to the table and sits down. In order to avoid threatening Jennifer, she does not look at her or say anything.

Jennifer: Immediately stops rocking and smiling. She seems to be waiting for something. After a few minutes, when Wendy does not do anything, Jennifer goes back to rocking and smiling, though she keeps her eye on Wendy.

Wendy [using movement]: Begins to imitate Jennifer's movements, because she knows this is an effective way of getting the student's attention as well as a good way to break the ice. She rocks, drums her fingers, picks up a book, examines it closely, stands up, and rocks while standing as Jennifer performs these actions. Of course, Wendy does not imitate any socially unacceptable behaviors such as eye poking, face slapping, light gazing, or light playing (e.g., moving arms/hands to play with shadows and brightness or light sources) because she does not want to encourage Jennifer's use of stereotypical behaviors.

[a little later in the interaction]

Wendy [using movement and nurturance]: Begins drawing and talking, but without addressing Jennifer. "I'm drawing Wendy," and points to herself. Wendy didn't really expect Jennifer to understand her words, but she continues to talk because she thinks it might be soothing to Jennifer. "I'm drawing Wendy's hair," and runs her hands through her hair. "I'm drawing Wendy's face," and points to her face. Wendy draws the nose and the mouth, but no eyes.

[providing opportunity] She puts the pen down and waits to give Jennifer a chance to participate without intruding on her.

Jennifer: Who has been watching the drawing very closely, picks up the pen and draws the eyes.

Source: From E. Siegel-Causey and D. Guess, 1989 (pp. 145–147).

If a client began to engage in self-stimulatory behavior, the teacher would simply redirect the resident to a task or activity, wait for him or her to engage, and then give praise for appropriate behavior. . . . [Or] if a resident was engaging in food preparation for a meal and began to behave aggressively, throwing food, or screaming out of control, the teacher would begin talking to the resident about the meal that was being prepared. As soon as the resident stopped throwing the food, the teacher would begin to walk him or her away from the food preparation area. (p. 149)

A short (five-minute) timeout would be provided as an opportunity for the resident to calm down and return to the task. Otherwise, he or she would be escorted to a relaxation room with soothing music, lighting, and comfortable pillows. When calm, the resident would again be escorted back to meal preparation.

Results of the IHP program (Polirstok et al., 2003), as measured with the Vineland Adaptive Behavior Scales (VABS; Sparrow, Balla, & Cichetti, 1984), showed increases in functional communication and habilitation accompanied by decreases in maladaptive behaviors. "Functional communication was the task compliance area that showed the greatest magnitude of change, increasing 31.2% across the study" (Polirstok et al., 2003, p. 151).

SUMMARY

Some idiosyncratic forms of communication are challenging to understand. Self-injurious behaviors and nonsymbolic communication may be unclear in their intent and may serve other, noncommunicative functions for the child (e.g., stress release or desire to escape an anxiety-producing situation). Such forms of communication can be treated as perlocutionary communicative acts. Intervention involves attempts to understand the message value and other language-learning or self-regulatory functions that echolalia, unconventional communication acts, or challenging behaviors may serve for a particular child. Techniques were described for targeting goals to replace echolalia (immediate, delayed, and mitigated) with generative symbolic communication; to replace aggressive behaviors with functional communicative ones; and to provide comprehensive interventions for children, adolescents, and young adults with mixtures of challenging behaviors.

Intervention for Severe Speech Production Disorders

Some children show severe speech production difficulties that clearly are primary to their language difficulties; others show speech production difficulties that are difficult to disentangle from their language problems. Language is only effective for communicative purposes if a child's words or other symbols can be understood, so speech production goals are particularly critical when intelligibility is low. Augmentative and alternative communication (AAC) options, including nonsymbolic communication, can be introduced either as a primary or secondary mode of communication.

The etiology of severe but specific speech impairment is not always clear. What one clinician might diagnose as severe phonological impairment, another might call childhood apraxia of speech (CAS). Research suggests that the two groups do not differ in the number of articulatory errors but in the coordination of articulatory gestures, such as movement of the velum and lips (Bahr, 2005). These gestures can be inferred but may be difficult to confirm in practice without sophisticated laboratory equipment. In practice, CAS is diagnosed when speech is slow to develop and resistant to treatment and when motor planning and sequencing are noticeably affected. Although CAS appears in relatively specific forms, children with autism or pervasive developmental disability and children with Down syndrome are particularly prone to CAS (Kumin, 2008).

In some cases, children with cerebral palsy (CP) and other forms of childhood dysarthria demonstrate frank neuromotor impairments accompanied by feeding problems and drooling, as well as articulatory difficulties. Dysarthric speech in childhood may occur as a specific deficit, leaving a child's language-learning system essentially intact, or comorbidly with other disorders, such as hearing loss, intellectual disability, and language-learning disability. Comorbidity adds to the complexity of intervention planning. Children with acquired brain injury have greater risk for dysarthric speech.

Intervention for Severe Speech Sound Disorders and Childhood Apraxia of Speech

When children are unable to abstract acoustic and articulatory features from completely natural models or have difficulty learning to speak at a developmentally appropriate level, they may need explicit, goal-oriented instruction and practice producing speech sounds and syllables. Intervention focused on speech production involves providing clear phonetic models and heightened auditory, visual, sensory, and kinesthetic cues about manner of speech production (e.g., stop or continuant; voiced or voiceless), as well as placement and coordination of the articulators, and focus on articulatory transitions.

Children need to use imitation and feedback to bring their imitative productions closer to clinicians' models. Mirrors often are used in therapeutic modeling, with the clinician positioned behind the child, rather than face to face, so the child can see the clinician's face and mouth next to his or her own, modeling a sound, syllable, or word to imitate. This provides immediate feedback regarding discrepancies in the visible aspects of speech production. Small, sterile instruments, such as tongue blades and applicators, also may be used to tickle a child's tongue to heighten tactile sensation on the tip for producing the /t/ and /d/ sounds, for example, and the corresponding contact point on the alveolar ridge (behind the upper teeth). The child can put one hand on the clinician's voice box and the other on his or her to feel the laryngeal vibration associated with voicing on /d/ but not /t/. Working directly on speech can have benefits in phonemic awareness as well as speech production. The addition of associated print symbols can add a stable concrete visual image to go with a fleeting abstract auditory or kinesthetic image of a speech sound.

Strand, Stoeckel, and Baas (2006) described a treatment approach based on principles of motor learning that used integral stimulation and dynamic ***temporal and tactile cueing.*** They used a single-subject, multiple-baseline design replicated across four children and found that three of the four children exhibited rapid change following treatment, with improvement maintained for all utterances. Performance was variable, however.

Several authors have offered general recommendations for working with children with CAS (e.g., Hall, Jordan, & Robin, 1993; Love, 2000; Price & Kent, 2008; Velleman, 2003; Velleman & Strand, 1994), but methods remain largely untested in the scientific literature (e.g., Love, 2000; Velleman, 2003). Recommendations include the following:

- Start with meaningful and functional but phonetically simple single words (e.g., *hi* and *bye*) to work on motor memory.
- Move from less to more complex linguistic levels (e.g., from single-syllable words to multisyllable words to words in carrier phrases to spontaneous speech).
- Provide multiple practice opportunities with a limited number of stimuli in each session.
- Target prosodic features of rate, rhythm, stress, and intonation, along with phonemes.
- Use multiple modalities (visual, motor, tactile, print) to heighten cues, and explore methods for associating speech production with rhythm, hand, and body movements.
- Vary the social and linguistic context and content of intervention to promote flexibility; avoid speaking telegraphically to children with CAS, so they will learn function words and morphology as well as content words.

One question that arises is the degree to which phonemes should be practiced in isolation versus in more natural contexts of real words and language. Crosbie, Holm, and Dodd (2005) hypothesized that different forms of underlying speech-processing deficits should respond to different treatment approaches. They identified two groups of children with severe speech sound disorder (SSD) (18 total, ages 4 years, 8 months to 6 years, 5 months) who differed by showing either consistent speech disorder affecting certain phonemes (primarily speech) or inconsistent speech disorder affecting sound patterns differently in varied words and contexts (primarily language). The children participated in two eight-week blocks of intervention comparing their response to two intervention approaches—phonological contrast versus core vocabulary. All the children increased consonant production accuracy during the interventions, measured as percent of consonants correct. As hypothesized, children with inconsistent speech disorder (phonology of language) benefited more from the core vocabulary approach, whereas children with consistent speech disorder (phonology of speech production) benefited more from the phonological contrast approach. When both speech and language are affected, it is important to give attention to both systems, either in tandem or beginning with language (morphosyntax) and then focusing on word forms (phonology). This finding also was supported by Tyler, Lewis, Haskill, and Tolbert (2003), whose work was discussed in Chapter 11 of this book.

Intervention for Dysarthria in Cerebral Palsy and Acquired Disorders

Intervention focused on speech production for children with neuromotor impairments can benefit from research on the development of speech motor control. By measuring lip and jaw coordination at ages 1 year, 2 years, and 6 years and in young adulthood, speech scientists (Green, Moore, Higashikawa, & Steeve, 2000) have found support for a theory of motor development that starts with integration of muscle control, followed by differentiation, and later refinement. Developmental constraints operate in the preschool years, even for typically developing children, but neuromotor deficits add extra constraints and challenges. Children with dysarthria have difficulty with muscle weakness or hypertonicity along with coordinating neuromotor actions.

Clark (2003) described *neuromuscular treatment* (*NMT*) for speech and swallowing. She also outlined the controversy over whether time spent in NMT exercises results in better speech production. Those in favor of NMTs say neuromotor exercises apart from speech are needed to develop the neuromuscular substrate. Others point out the lack of evidence for the efficacy of NMT that does not work on speech directly. These opponents emphasize that to learn to speak clearly, children need to practice speech. Working on speech intelligibility in meaningful language also is more consistent with goals to foster language and communication along with speech.

Pennington, Goldbart, and Marshall (2005) conducted a systematic review of the literature regarding the effects of direct speech and language therapy for children with cerebral palsy (CP). They reviewed 832 abstracts but identified only seven studies that met the criteria for their review. Many of those were conducted with children and adolescents with intellectual disabilities and communication impairments that added more challenges than CP alone. In fact, most of the studies addressed the establishment of intentional communication, as addressed previously in this chapter, rather than speech production. The findings were uniformly positive, however, showing the potential for intervention to "facilitate the development of pre-intentional communication skills (e.g., maintaining eye contact), functions of conversation (e.g., asking questions, providing information, repeating when misunderstood), and syntactic structure in expressive language (e.g., 'is/are' with verb)" (p. 60). Conspicuously missing were studies focused on speech production.

Pennington, Smallman, and Farrier (2006) sought to address this gap in the literature by studying the effects of intensive intervention on speech production and intelligibility for older children with CP. They worked with six students with CP (ages 10 to 18 years) to implement a program of intensive individual intervention targeting increased breath support for speech and setting the goal to maintain breath support and volume across utterances. Findings immediately after the block of therapy and again seven weeks later showed that intelligibility of single words improved but not intelligibility in connected speech.

SUMMARY

A variety of causal factors may underlie severe disorders of speech sound production. This section described intervention techniques for children with speech sound disorders associated with childhood apraxia of speech and with dysarthria secondary to neuromotor disorders such as cerebral palsy or acquired brain injury. Children with apraxia are likely to need explicit instruction at the individual phoneme level and practice with visual and auditory feedback on the blending of sounds into words, then moving to longer units of speech. It may be tempting to work on motor control exercises that do not involve speech for children with dysarthria because their motor control problems affect all forms of oral–motor control, but research has shown that such exercises are generally ineffective in improving speech. If the goal is to improve speech, it is necessary to work directly on speech. Intervention focused on speech for students with severe speech sound disorders should not ignore the need to target language and literacy development as well.

AAC for Children and Adolescents with Complex Communication Needs

When children and adolescents have severe physical and speech impairments, they may need *augmentative and alternative communication (AAC)* services. AAC is not just a device or a symbol system but a multiple-component system comprising symbols, aids, strategies, and techniques (Beukelman & Mirenda, 2005). People with complex communication needs (CCN) who are technically nonspeaking are not necessarily nonverbal. *Nonverbal* refers to inability to use words to communicate (not just speech). A person may be *verbal* with the support of AAC if he or she can use symbols to encode and represent meaning. In a comprehensive review, Wilkinson and Hennig (2007) noted, "One misconception about AAC is that it *replaces* spoken communication" (p. 74). AAC can be used both to support nonsymbolic forms of communication and to augment natural speech, but it is not intended to replace speech altogether.

Components of AAC Systems

The *symbols* used in AAC systems may be aided or unaided with external supports and may be graphic, auditory, gestural, tactile, or textured. Some symbols communicate individual words or parts of words; some represent phrases or larger chunks of meaning. Some are iconic (i.e., they look like the things they represent); others are more abstract, requiring special knowledge by one or both partners. Input symbols (e.g., letters on a keyboard) may differ from output symbols (e.g., synthesized speech).

Aids are devices that can transmit or receive messages (see Figure 14.2). Aids may be nonelectronic (sometimes called *light-tech*) or electronic (sometimes called *high-tech*) and come in many varieties. Some are dedicated to communication; others are more generic (e.g., laptop computers), serving multiple purposes for more than one person. *VOCA* is the acronym used to refer to a *voice-output communication aid* (also called an *SGD,* for *speech-generating device*) that produces synthesized speech and may use varied techniques and types of symbols. These devices make it possible to communicate with new partners and at a distance. However, unaided symbols and techniques (e.g., sign language) have the advantages of being portable, available in any context (e.g., swimming pools), and unsusceptible to mechanical breakage.

Techniques are used to encode and transmit messages. Some techniques do not require literacy skills, such as spelling, but others do. Literacy dramatically expands options for constructing unique messages and is an important target for other reasons. Some techniques, such as PECS, involve handing over a symbol; others involve pointing to symbols on an array, activating switches, or using a keyboard. Some children have limited movement

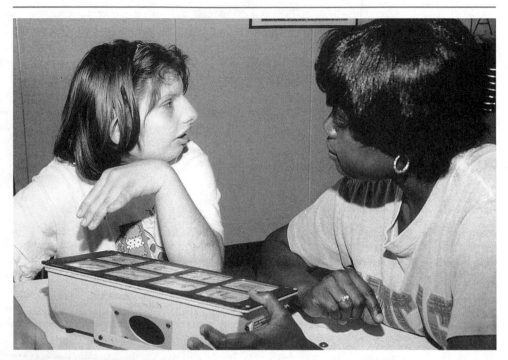

figure *14.2*

Example of Communication Aid

A conversation between a student with complex communication needs and similar age peer can be facilitated by an AAC device and also make use of gesture and eye contact.

options and need access and training to use innovative single switches activated with their knees, elbows, or a sophisticated *row-and-column scanning* method. This involves movement from row to row on a rectangular display by hitting a switch either to start or stop the scanning (often signaled with a light). After the intended row is selected, scanning begins again column by column within the selected row, leading to selection of an intended symbol when the switch is activated again. A nonelectronic technique might involve eye pointing to symbols on a translucent display held by the communication partner.

Strategies are used to convey messages in the manner that is most efficient and effective. This component emphasizes the need for training, practice, and metapragmatic instruction about strategies for using AAC in ways that increase the number of partners and frequency and the success of opening and closing communication circles and repairing breakdowns.

Intervention Using AAC Systems

Whether to provide high- or light-technological supports for communication should never be viewed as an *either/or* decision that involves giving up on speech. AAC provides a means of supporting language development and communication when motor and/or cognitive barriers make spoken communication or handwriting less functional. Concerns may arise that AAC options signal giving up on speech, but there is no evidence that the use of AAC reduces a child's potential to talk, read, and write. Studies show, in fact, that AAC may facilitate speech and language development (Beukelman & Mirenda, 2005).

Everyone needs a way to communicate at every stage in life. Technological communication aids also are more acceptable and less a sign of difference in the twenty-first century, because they are everywhere (e.g., cell phones with key pads) and not used only by people with disabilities. This may reduce the stigma that has been associated with assistive technology in the past.

Using a System for Augmenting Language

Romski, Sevcik, Cheslock, and Barton (2006) confirmed the central role of AAC in helping children with complex disabilities develop language and communication, not just serving as an output mode by which individuals can convey information. Their *system for augmenting language (SAL)* incorporates five integrated components:

> (1) a speech-generating device; (2) individually chosen visual-graphic symbols; (3) use in natural everyday environments that encourage, but do not require, the child to produce symbols; (4) models of symbol use by communicative partners; and (5) an ongoing resource and feedback mechanism. (p. 123)

These researchers reported the results of a longitudinal study with 13 school-age participants (mean age 12 years, 8 months) with moderate to severe cognitive disability and diagnoses including Down syndrome, CP, ASD, and unknown. They followed the youth through two years of intervention using the principles of SAL at home and school and measured two aspects of communication achievement—communication use and vocabulary mastery. Some students developed communicative use of a small number of symbols (20 to 35), and others learned more than 100 symbols and combined them syntactically. All of the students "integrated the use of their speech-output communication devices into their extant vocal and gestural repertoires" (p. 129).

Planning for the Future

AAC systems should be designed to be functional not only in the present but also for the future. To be able to make full use of AAC systems, people need competence that is linguistic, operational, social, and strategic (Beukelman & Mirenda, 2005). Plans should be in place for continual updating of technological supports and people skills at all stages of the child's development. Barbera (2007) suggested a series of assessment questions that a team could use to decide when to add other support options to children with complex needs, especially related to autism:

> Is the child able to use the system independently to request his wants and needs throughout the day (not just at snack time or when the device or book is placed within reach of the child)?; Is the child having tantrums or other problem behaviors because the system is overly cumbersome, breaks, or he is unable to use it fluently?; Does the child have access to the system across all environments and do both home and school providers use it consistently? (p. 85)

Keeping Communication Learning Natural and Options Open

Because children with complex communication needs have less access to the flexible system of spoken language, they and their communication partners need to be particularly attuned to the nonverbal aspects of communication. The raise of an eyebrow, a twinkle in the eye, or laughter while pointing to communication symbols might convey that a child is making a joke or being sarcastic, rather than conveying a literal meaning. Encouraging such elaborated and nonliteral communication abilities can influence a child's ability to function well socially and to progress academically. Intervention targeting small talk for purely social purposes is as important as helping students to express their wants and needs or to participate academically (see Personal Reflection 14.7).

PERSONAL reflection *14.7*

"With a voice output device people really do expect me to engage in idle chit-chat, a form of communication I used to abhor; after all, why go to all the work of communicating something that means nothing? It suddenly dawned on me one day that this chit-chat, small talk, shooting the breeze kind of communication was a large part of daily social interaction and I'd better start doing it if I wanted to be in the mix."

Michael Williams (quoted in King, Spoeneman, Stuart, & Beukelman, 1995, p. 260) is an adult who relies on AAC to communicate and who writes and speaks extensively about his experiences.

In one self-contained classroom for students with complex communication needs, clinicians worked with students who delighted in planning tricks while their special education teacher, Ms. K, was out of the room. For example, at Halloween, the students decided to hide a plastic spider in one of the students' hair and to wait for the teacher to discover it. It was hard for Ms. K to miss the eye pointing and hilarity of the joke in the students' laughter, and she responded with appropriate shock and surprise. The students used their AAC systems to construct a small book that told the story of hiding the spider and Ms. K's surprise when she discovered it. The book was then available for supporting storytelling to a new audience of other teachers and students in the building, generating comments and questions the students could answer with their communication boards. Another group of teachers who had participated in the writing lab outreach project (Nelson et al., 2004) used digital photography to create storybooks of field trips and other classroom events that their students could use as a support to retell the stories of their adventures to new audiences.

Selection of Service Delivery Models

Questions arise about the best service delivery models for students with complex communication needs. Hunt-Berg (2005) described a comprehensive service delivery model used by the Bridge School in the San Francisco Bay area to provide intensive short-term AAC services to students with severe speech and physical impairments, with the goal of returning them to their local inclusive schools. Hunt-Berg described outcomes for 16 former Bridge School students whose school records showed varied patterns of instructional focus, acquisition of AAC technologies, and levels of educational participation. After receiving intensive services, 13 participants made the transition to inclusive educational settings in their local schools. Educational teams in the students' home schools rated the transitions as successful, although not all students achieved independent use of AAC devices.

Murray-Seegert (1989) described an innovative approach for including students with disability in an inner-city high school in which many students were at risk for reasons other than disability (e.g., poverty, high-crime neighborhoods). In this program, peers volunteered to work with students with special needs, receiving course credit through enrollment in an *internal work experience (IWE)* program. Murray-Seegert conducted qualitative research on the program and found peer tutoring "to be an important variable influencing the development of social relations between disabled and nondisabled students" (p. 114). Personal Reflection 14.8 shows a portion of letter written by Preston, one of the peer tutors, to a friend about his experiences in the program.

PERSONAL reflection *14.8*

"In my third period class I have a Special Ed class. It's students with a disability. Like one student Juan he's a student that's a little slow in the mind and can't all the way speak yet. He's about 59 inches and black hair and he's Spanish and he dress average. Sometimes he likes to play games or go outside for a walk, but sometimes he just likes to Kick back. When he wants something, he yells and gives you sign language. He can go to the restroom by his self he know his way around the school and sometimes he goes to lunch with a peer tutor or to the wash house or to the store. He's kind of slow learning but he catches on sooner or later. He needs a little help with yelling out loud or whistling, and he needs help with his way of approaching people."

Preston (quoted in Murray-Seegert, 1989, pp. 112–113) was a general education high school student acting as a peer tutor for students in a special education class.

Supporting Literacy Learning by Children Who Use AAC

The first barrier to overcome when targeting literacy for students who use AAC is one of limited expectation. Changes in federal legislation and multiple studies showing students with CCN's limited access to literacy learning (e.g., Koppenhaver, Coleman, Kalman, & Yoder, 1991; Koppenhaver & Yoder, 1993; Light & Kelford Smith, 1993; Light & McNaughton, 1993) have emphasized the need for educators to take seriously the obligation to teach these students to read and write for authentic communicative and learning purposes—not just to discriminate "Exit" signs and labels on women's and men's room doors.

Literacy interventions for children and adolescents who rely on AAC to communicate start early with shared book experiences and learning to enjoy wordplay and rhymes, just as they do for any child. They must not stop there, however (Koppenhaver et al., 1991; Light, Binger, & Kelford Smith, 1994; Sturm, 2005). Phonological awareness (PA) plays a role in literacy development in this population, as it does for children who are typically developing (Blischak, 1994), although PA may be less predictive of reading success for children with limited speech (Dahlgren Sandbert & Hjelmquist, 1996). Learning graphic symbols in AAC systems and using them to convey meaningful messages, however, does have a positive association with learning to read (McNaughton & Lindsay, 1995; Rankin, Harwood, & Mirenda, 1994).

Fallon, Light, McNaughton, Drager, and Hammer (2004) described potential barriers to using code-oriented phonics programs that are designed to teach children to form sound–symbol associations and learn to sound out words, including limited access to articulatory and auditory feedback from producing sounds themselves and limited ability for others to monitor the children's learning based on what they say. To fill the knowledge gap, researchers conducted a single-subject study with multiple probes across five participants. Participants (ages 9 to 14) had severe speech impairments (defined as less than 30 percent intelligible at the single-word level). Two students were diagnosed with mental retardation, two with CP, and one with Down syndrome. The direct instruction program targeted single-word reading. Prior to word-level instruction, participants received training until they could point reliably to line drawings representing targeted vocabulary and identify 50 percent of the targeted letters in association with their sounds or names. The intervention made use of a controlled set of 14 targeted letters and corresponding sounds, selected based on their potential to be combined into multiple concrete, depictable vowel–consonant (VC) and consonant–vowel–consonant (CVC) words (75 words total). Letters were introduced in a sequence to be maximally dissimilar in their auditory and visual lowercase forms. The order of introduction of vowels was *a* as in *apple, e* as in *egg, i* as in *ill, o* as in *mop,* and *u* as in *up.* The order of introduction of consonants was *m, n, b, p, t, g, r, l, s.* The 75 words were randomly distributed, with 50 used for intervention and 25 reserved for generalization probes. All five participants reached criterion for matching targeted written words to corresponding pictures. Three of the five participants demonstrated generalization of reading skills to novel-word reading, and four of the five generalized reading skills to book contexts.

The *simple model* that emphasizes integrated roles for reading, decoding, and comprehension discussed in Chapter 5 of this book is relevant for students who use AAC, as it is for all literacy learners. It is important not to overlook the need for exposure to meaningful literate language and opportunities to associate text with pictures initially, using age- and curriculum-appropriate materials, so that later, transitions can be made to learn through reading alone, either independently or listening to others read aloud. Assistive technologies may be needed to support both the physical demands of reading (e.g., page-turning and row-scanning controls) and writing (e.g., picture as word generation supports at first, followed by word prediction software) (Sturm, 2005).

Learning to comprehend and construct language at the sentence and discourse levels involves reciprocal processes and results in mutual potential benefits as students learn to formulate written discourse. The preparation of written products can create a need to have words to communicate to a real audience (e.g., Nelson & Van Meter, 2006a) but without the time pressures of spoken communication interaction. Erickson and Koppenhaver (1995) described a transdisciplinary literacy intervention program for eight students in a classroom for students with multiple disabilities. The program was integrated with educational and related goals (e.g., physical therapy) and made use of light- and high-technology devices and techniques. Basic literacy components were targeted in calendar activities, directed reading in small groups, computer-assisted learning experiences (using off-the-shelf software), and group activities.

The group component illustrates the authentic audience and constructive learning principles emphasized throughout this book. Erickson and Koppenhaver (1995) described goals to keep reading and writing activities "child directed and constructive rather than teacher directed and reactive" (p. 680), including performances to act out stories of favorite books:

> Skits could be time consuming. Choreographing the movement of seven wheelchairs in a small classroom could be a feat in itself. In addition, several children had to use speech synthesis and loop tapes to say their lines, and the movements in general were slower. However, each child was provided with an opportunity to participate independently. (p. 679)

At the end of two years, four of the eight children returned to neighborhood schools. Even so, Erickson and Koppenhaver noted continued challenges in educators' tendencies to offer a reduced curriculum, "instead of providing alternative ways to participate in the standard curriculum" (p. 529).

SUMMARY

This section differentiated between conditions in which children and adolescents are *non-speaking* (i.e., incapable of producing speech intelligible enough to be functional) but not *nonverbal* (i.e., they still have words). Augmentative and alternative communication systems were described as comprising symbols, aids, techniques, and strategies. Intervention can aim at teaching more strategic use of AAC systems while also using AAC systems to help children learn language and literacy skills and to communicate more effectively. Principles addressed in this section included the need to plan for the future and to keep communication learning as natural as possible. Service delivery models include students who rely on AAC in school activities and engage peers to support them in doing so, some of whom may have academic risk–related factors other than disability. The need to support literacy learning by children who rely on AAC was emphasized, with a focus both on word decoding and comprehension, as for all children.

Intervention for Sensory Loss and Central-Processing Disorders

Sensory impairment, particularly deafness or hard of hearing (D/HH), makes it difficult to acquire intelligible spoken language. Visual impairment makes it difficult to acquire language by eye and to learn the subtle aspects of nonverbal communication. Central-processing deficits can interfere with communication learning and functioning, as well, but in less predictable ways. Auditory-processing disorder (APD) is difficult to disentangle from other issues, such as attention, memory, and phonological processing. Central processing of visual information also may be impaired beyond what a child's peripheral vision would explain, as characterized by difficulties learning to associate orthographic patterns automatically with morphemes. This may be classified as *dyseidetic* reading disability (Catts & Kamhi, 2005a), although the old, simplistic concept of dyslexia as a visual perception disorder has been largely discredited.

Intact, integrated systems support processing functions for receiving and integrating information from sensory organs, performing preliminary analyses of parts and wholes, holding phonological and/or visual–spatial information in working memory, processing it to make sense, and storing information intentionally and selectively for longer-term memory and retrieval. Multiple levels of information processing make use of dispersed but integrated neural mechanisms. What is controversial is the assumption that lower-level, bottom-up processing can be assessed in isolation from upper-level, top-down processing. This is problematic from an intervention perspective, because it implies that underlying processes must be fixed before upper-level spoken and written language processes can be addressed effectively. Such an approach ignores the top-down roles of constructive meaning making and prior knowledge in perceiving and remembering input data, particularly when signals are degraded by sensory impairments.

Limitations of sequential-processing models are addressed with the "pinball wizardry" model (see Chapter 3) in its representation of parallel and multidirectional aspects of intact information-processing systems. Unlike unidirectional models, the "pinball wizardry" model portrays information flowing in multiple directions, with multiple regions of the brain "lighting up" in parallel as well as in sequence (hence, the pinball metaphor). This model acknowledges the importance of clarity of input to the central-processing system (bottom up) but also the importance of having an intact cognitive–linguistic and metacognitive system for perceiving input and making sense of it, even when input information is incomplete (top down). The implication is that intervention methods for sensory- and central-processing deficits should be two pronged and bidirectional as well. On the bottom-up side, interventions must be designed to improve access to clear perceptual input data. On the top-down side, children need strong language systems that enable them to make sense of input even when it is less than optimal.

Interventions Focused on Auditory Input for Children with D/HH or APD

Interventions for children with D/HH or APD diagnoses need to include efforts to provide optimal listening environments. The ability to receive language input through hearing depends on clear acoustic signals reaching the ear or listening device. This is as true for children with typical hearing as it is for children with all forms and levels of D/HH, APD, or other disabilities.

Enhancing Listening Environments

Signal-to-noise ratios can be improved in classrooms by reducing sources of noise and increasing the audibility of signals (Smaldino & Crandell, 2001). Reducing noise includes steps to improve the physical properties of classroom acoustics, such as adding carpeting and other sound-absorptive materials to reduce noise and reverberation. Amplification options include installation of sound field and FM personal amplification systems.

Sound field amplification systems transmit amplified speech from a microphone worn by the speaker (usually the teacher) to several speaker units placed strategically around the classroom (Crandell & Smaldino, 2001). The sound is amplified only by about 10 to 15 decibels (dB), providing an improved signal-to-noise ratio but not risking overexposure to noise. It just sounds as if the teacher is standing nearby. Palmer (1998) observed eight students in acoustically similar kindergarten and first- and second-grade classrooms and found a decrease in inappropriate behaviors associated with activating the amplification system; inappropriate behaviors increased again when the sound field system was shut off. Massie and Dillon (2006) also reported that sound field amplification systems were associated with improved reading, writing, and numeracy for all students, including students who had hearing loss or spoke English as a second language.

Sound field systems often are recommended for classrooms with students who have mild to moderate losses, unilateral losses, conductive losses, or APD or who face other attentional or cognitive–communicative challenges. Children with all types of hearing loss (and with attention deficits and other special needs) may benefit from sound field amplification and also from preferential seating that places them closer to sound sources and to visual input from their teacher's face and information on a whiteboard or screen. Such accommodations are needed even if students use sign language interpreters, cochlear implants, or receive adequate access to language through other accommodations.

Children with hearing impairments in the moderate to severe range or lower need personalized FM systems to augment their personal amplification devices. FM systems differ from sound field systems in that the signal from the teacher's microphone is transmitted over a special FM frequency directly to an ear-level receiver connected to a child's hearing aid (Crandell & Smaldino, 2001) or cochlear implant speech processor (Thibodeau, 2006).

The choice of an inclusive classroom versus a self-contained classroom for a child with D/HH is complicated and requires careful consideration by the IEP team. Nelson and Camarata (1996) noted that educators must find the best "tricky mix" of options when providing optimal learning environments for children with D/HH. They described advantages of multimedia approaches and commented that visual input contributes information about social pragmatics as well, which is important for the development of the social–emotional maturity that goes beyond academic success.

To address concerns that visual distractions of mainstream (i.e., general education) classrooms might compete with speech perception for children with D/HH, Keetay (1996) studied whether students with D/HH could track auditorially and visually presented discourse samples in the presence of visual distractors typical of classroom activity. She found that students could cope with visual distractions and concluded that high control of the visual environment need not be a deciding factor in classroom placement for students with hearing impairment.

Modifying Speech Signals to Improve Auditory Processing

Some information-processing theories of LLD and APD suggest that temporal processing deficits impair the ability to process the phonological information of spoken language when it arrives at the brain at a normal rate, contributing to language-learning difficulties. According to this theory, if sequential input is slowed, the brain will be able to detect sequence and process the signals more effectively. Based on preliminary empirical support for the theory, Tallal and colleagues (1996) developed a computer software program called FastForword–Language (FFW–L; Scientific Learning Corporation, 1998) that modifies acoustic signals by amplifying fast transitional elements and slowing down rate. The modified speech signals then are incorporated into a training program that uses gamelike tasks to introduce changes in acoustic features of stimuli systematically, based on children's prior responses.

Exposure to modified speech has been shown to benefit children with LLD with respect to their language skills. Tallal and colleagues (1996) randomly assigned two groups of children with LLD; the experimental group received a four-week intensive training program using computer-based training exercises with modified speech, and the control group received the same four-week intensive training program but with unmodified speech. Children in both groups showed improvements in speech and language scores, but the group exposed to modified speech achieved significantly greater gains.

Attempts to replicate those original positive findings, however, have been less successful (Gillam, Crofford, Gale, & Hoffman, 2001). Gillam and colleagues (2008) reported results of a large randomized controlled trial with 216 children between 6 and 9 years of age. All participants received one hour and 40 minutes of treatment, five days per week for six weeks, based on random assignment to FFW–L, individual language intervention (ILI), academic enrichment (AE) using computer games, or computer assisted language intervention (CALI). The CALI treatment used Earobics software (Cognitive Concepts, 2000) and Laureate Learning software (Semel, 2000) designed to teach speech discrimination and word- and sentence-level skills. At a six-month follow-up, participants who received the FFW–L and CALI treatments earned higher phonological awareness scores than those who received comparison treatments. CALI did not involve modified speech, however, so the speech modification feature could not be credited for the advantage.

It also has been hypothesized that modified speech might improve the intelligibility of spoken language input for children with D/HH. To test the hypothesis, Uchanski, Geers, and Protopapas (2002) measured the effects of slowing down and amplifying speech input on speech intelligibility. They tested two groups of listeners—eight children with severe to profound hearing loss who wore sensory aids and five with normal hearing. Stimuli included language at three levels—words in sentences, isolated words, and syllables. The levels were altered consistently with the FFW–L paradigm in three ways (i.e., envelope-amplified speech, slowed speech, and both slowed and envelope-amplified speech) for comparison with discrimination of natural unprocessed speech. Normal-hearing children were tested in a background of noise to make the task more discriminative. Results from the children with D/HH showed that all varieties of modified speech yielded either equivalent or poorer intelligibility than unprocessed speech. For both groups, speech modification had no statistically significant effect on syllable discrimination.

Although the benefits of modified speech input are questionable, these and other studies have indicated that systematic computer-supported speech perception exercises may improve children's auditory perceptual abilities. Zwolan, Connor, and Kileny (2000) studied the effectiveness of the software program Foundations in Speech Perception (FSP; Brown, 1994) to improve perceptual skills for seven elementary school children with prelinguistic deafness and cochlear implants. The program was to be used at home, 15 minutes per day for six months. Children who used the program regularly at home (10 or more days per month) demonstrated gains in speech perception and production that exceeded those of the seven children in a matched control group, and students who used the program fewer than eight days per month still showed gains relative to the control group.

Speech–Language/Literacy–Communication Intervention for Children with D/HH

Children with diagnoses of D/HH face barriers for learning language even when the sensory loss is specific and other language-learning systems are basically intact. When comorbid conditions are present, planning must address those additional challenges as well.

Individual Technological Supports for Children with D/HH

One of the advantages of early identification of hearing loss is that it makes it possible to provide both early amplification and early intervention to enhance communication. Binaural high-quality, individually prescribed and monitored hearing aids are essential for children with hearing losses that range from mild to profound. Although FM systems are important in classrooms, personal aids have several advantages. [They] "allow student-to-student communication and self-monitoring by the child, and in small groups, they provide satisfactory amplification for teacher-to-student communication" (Moeller et al., 2007, p. 346). Some personal hearing aids now provide built-in FM systems.

Increasingly, children with profound hearing loss also have access to early cochlear implants (CI) (see Chapter 6). CI in young, prelingually deaf children can make it possible for them to gain an auditory foundation for learning language (Miyamoto et al., 2003). Research has shown that children who were prelingually deaf but have had a CI for at least three years perform better on language comprehension tasks administered in their preferred modality than prelingually deaf children without CI who are learning either sign or spoken language (Tomblin, Spencer, Flock, Tyler, & Gantz, 1999). Children with CI also are more likely to acquire intelligible speech than children with even moderate impairments and aided hearing, although not quite as well as children with normal hearing (Chin, Tsai, & Gao, 2003). Factors that influence the level of success in language and literacy learning for children with CI include their nonverbal cognitive abilities, the functioning of the technology, and the frequency of oral communication.

Children with CI still may need speech–language intervention services and auditory training and related services from specialists in aural habilitation. Children need to learn to use their technology effectively so that it can support their language development and other learning. Aural rehabilitation specialists often train teachers and parents to monitor whether a child's technology is working. For a traditional hearing aid, this includes doing a listening check and a battery check and checking cords for shorts or intermittencies. For a cochlear implant (see Chapter 6), steps include checking battery function (and keeping an extra supply of cords, magnets, and batteries on hand), monitoring the child's ongoing ability to detect sounds, using a signal check device to make sure that a signal is being transmitted, and checking cords (Moeller et al., 2007). Both CI and traditional hearing aids also are checked with Ling's (1989) six-sound test, in which children are asked to imitate (in random order) the sounds /u/, /a/, /i/, /ʃ/, /s/, and /m/ to assess whether they are receiving information across the sound spectrum.

Children with the congenital diagnosis of auditory neuropathy/auditory dyssynchrony (AN/AS) are difficult to treat with most traditional methods because of severe difficulties processing sound in spite of intact cochlear function. Stredler-Brown (n.d.) described the development of spoken language as the general treatment goal for such children, although every child's profile is different and a comprehensive interdisciplinary approach is required. Auditory training and amplification are of variable benefit, but CI may have better results (Zeng & Liu, 2006). Visual input methods (sign language and cued speech) may provide the best support for early language learning. Regarding prognosis, Stredler-Brown wrote:

We know that some children eventually process auditory information. Some children sponta-neously recover from the disorder and then have the ability to process auditory information that supports the development of speech. Other children are given the opportunity to process auditory information as a result of treatment, such as successful use of a cochlear implant. (pp. 6–7)

Early Intervention for Children with D/HH

Early identification and intervention are critical for achieving optimal outcomes for chil-dren with hearing loss of all etiologies, levels, and configurations. If identification occurs prior to 6 months of age and parents learn to intensify their support for communication development, children can make dramatic progress in social interaction skills and language development, regardless of degree of loss or communication mode parents choose to em-phasize (Moeller et al., 2007; Yoshinaga-Itano et al., 1998).

Professionals can adopt any of the methods described previously in this and prior chapters to establish mutual attention, joint action routines, and other components of early communication that are critical to later language learning. What must be added is special attention to provide access to amplification or CI as soon as possible. Parents can also be advised to talk to their child at close range, using heightened cues but naturalistic input. One widely used comprehensive approach for working with families of infants with hearing impairment is called **SKI-HI** (Watkins, 2004). SKI-HI is designed to help parents identify their child's early use of communicative signals and to respond interactively in the context of joint action routines, to organize the listening environment at home, to communicate frequently with eye contact and closeness, and to optimize communication using reciprocal (back-and-forth) turn taking and meaningful facial gestures and touch.

Communication Mode Choices for Children with D/HH

The debate over communication mode choices is old, complex, and ongoing (English, 2007). The primary choices are oral–aural, American Sign Language (ASL), and total com-munication. The oral–aural approach includes two major variations—auditory–verbal and cued speech.

Oral–aural communication was promoted by Alexander Graham Bell and continues to be emphasized by the association that bears his name. Intervention targeting oral–aural communication emphasizes oral speech production and comprehension, amplification, and optimal use of residual hearing and to some extent speechreading. Ling (1989), a primary proponent of the oral–aural approach, wrote, "With spoken language, opportunities for higher education are less restricted, a more extensive range of careers is open, and there is greater employment security. Those who can talk also face fewer limitations in the personal and social aspects of their lives" (p. 9). Variations on the oral–aural instructional approach differ based on the degree to which they emphasize or discourage the use of visual input, including speechreading. Relatively pure oral–aural approaches specifically avoid the use of sign language.

Auditory–verbal communication is a variation of oral–aural communication that is based on the premise that children will maximize their use of audition for perceiving and producing speech only if they learn to rely on audition alone. Those who favor this approach discourage all visual input, including speechreading, especially during auditory training. To make it necessary for children to rely on their hearing, in fact, clinicians cover their mouths with a porous cloth-covered hoop screen that does not distort sound (Estabrooks, 2004).

Cued speech is another variation on oral–aural emphasis in which the focus is on heightening visual input, not diminishing it. Cued speech is a system of eight hand signals, performed close to the head and mouth to convey hidden phonetic features as an aid to speechreading (Cornett, 1967). For example, the voiced–voiceless distinction between /g/ and /k/ is signaled by pointing with all five fingers to the larynx for /g/ but with only the index and middle finger for /k/. This variation of oral–aural communication focuses on visual input to supplement missing auditory information. The emphasis on articulatory features may support articulation as well as speech reception, but it places cognitive demands on both senders and receivers to learn.

American Sign Language (ASL) is advocated by members of the Deaf community (the capital *D* signifies the culture of Deafness) and thus may be called the *bilingual/ bicultural (bi/bi) approach* (English, 2007). Many Deaf adults express the view that children born with deafness have no disability if they learn American Sign Language (ASL) as their first language. Deaf children of Deaf parents learn ASL as a natural part of growing up in a community that uses ASL as the primary mode of communication. Language-learning difficulties arise, however, when children are born deaf but have hearing parents who are not part of a Deaf community proficient in sign language. Such parents tend to lack the proficiency to provide a rich enough sign language environment to enable their child to learn ASL naturally. Although sign can provide an important adjunct supporting family communication, it does not prepare children to use the phonological and grammatical systems of spoken language. ASL is a fully functional language, but it is not a direct translation of English and has no written form. Therefore, children whose primary communication mode is ASL face extra challenges when learning to read and write in English that are similar to those when learning to read and write in a second language (Paul, 1996).

Total communication represents attempts to bring sign language closer to English by incorporating English word order and additional hand signals to encode grammatical function words and bound morphemes. Fingerspelling also is employed. Variations include signed English, manually coded English (MCE), and signing exact English (SEE). Total communication programs are built on the premise that children need access to as much information as possible and that multiple modality input should be viewed as supportive rather than competitive.

Choices of communication modes for language input influence how speech–language services are provided. Although advocates of different philosophical camps express similar long-term goals—learning success within the general curriculum, literacy acquisition, social acceptance, and independence—they prioritize goals differently. In many cases, parents are left to sort out confusing mixed messages and feel conflicted about communication mode choices for their children (Jackson, Traub, & Turnbull, 2008), as described in Case Example 14.3.

Auditory and Language Training as Coordinated Activities

Auditory training often appears as a separate topic in textbooks on aural rehabilitation, but that implies that auditory training is separate from efforts to support speech–language development. Although some auditory-training efforts are aimed at helping children notice and discriminate environmental sounds, it is "people sounds" (i.e., speech) that will be most important to them (Moeller et al., 2007).

Auditory training often targets components of Erber's (1982) model of auditory skill development, including detection, discrimination, identification, and comprehension. A test based on this model is the Glendonald Auditory Screening Procedure (GASP; Erber, 1982), which was developed at the Glendonald Auditory School for the Deaf in Australia. The GASP includes three subtests—phoneme detection, word identification, and sentence comprehension. A frequently used auditory training program, Developmental Approach to Successful Listening (DASL; Stout & Windle, 1994), also includes a test for assessing sound awareness, phonetic listening, and auditory comprehension.

Moeller and colleagues (2007) expanded the list a bit, describing six levels that should be part of a comprehensive auditory skills development approach—auditory awareness (de-

─CASE **example** *14.3*─────────────────────────────────

Samantha and the Choice of Communication Method

Samantha was identified with a profound hearing loss at birth following her mother's prenatal bout with rubella. The family was working with a local clinic that had a strong commitment to auditory–verbal learning. Samantha's parents made certain that her hearing aids were working and that they bathed her in a rich environment of words and concepts. They had been told that she would need to hear a word hundreds of times in varied contexts to learn it and decided to make a game of learning the word *ball*. They hid balls of different sizes and colors all around the house (including the vegetable drawer in the refrigerator) and exclaimed with delight every time Samantha found a ball, labeling it and playing with it, hoping that Samantha would learn the word. Although Samantha seemed to delight in the game, *ball* was not her first word. Rather, her parents were surprised when they returned home in the car one day to hear a small voice from the back seat say "Home," echoing the

parents' "We're home," heard many times associated with that meaningful family routine.

As Samantha entered preschool, she became part of a public school program that encouraged total communication, including sign language as well as oral communication. Samantha's parents struggled with this choice at first. They worried about warnings by professionals devoted to auditory–verbal approaches that visual modes of communication might have negative effects on their daughter's learning to talk, but they also worried about having no way to convey abstract information to Samantha. For example, they wanted to be able to prepare her for visits to the dentist. As they embraced the total communication approach, Samantha developed well in all modes of communication, and her parents did not regret their decision to augment her spoken and written language development with another modality for gaining meaning.

───

tection) and attending, listening from a distance, locating, discriminating, identifying, and comprehending. Comprehension should be emphasized along with auditory awareness, not as a final step. Learning words such as *bottle, blanket,* and *bye-bye* can help infants with D/HH become aware that people sounds are meaningful and rewarding and worth their attention. Schery and Peters (2003) noted, "With multiple goals to address, it is helpful to know that auditory goals can be incorporated into other speech and language activities" (p. 6).

Ling's (1989) approach for targeting early vocal and phonological development among children with severe hearing impairments includes targeting the ***phonetic level,*** in which children learn to produce and to discriminate sounds but without assigning meaning to them, and the ***phonological level,*** in which children associate speech sounds with language. Ling emphasized the need to address both the phonetic and phonological levels during early development to help children with D/HH achieve natural speech. Meaning may be minimized in brief exercises to help children focus on the physical properties of sound, but such practice should occur in minidrills in selected learning contexts. The use of drill-and-practice techniques should neither interfere with nor delay close-contact naturalistic language interactions in meaningful contexts.

Children whose D/HH affects their perception of speech input often have difficulty acquiring fully intelligible speech. Moeller and colleagues (2007) recommended assessing functional auditory skills, phonetic skills, phonological skills, suprasegmental skills, and vocal behaviors, as well as stimulability for sound production or emergence of skills and speech intelligibility. In clinical contexts, technology can display acoustic properties of speech in sound spectrograms, providing visual feedback about features of speech that children with D/HH have difficulty detecting auditorily. A difference between CI and traditional hearing aids is that children with CI may find it easier to detect features of high-frequency sounds, such as /s/and /ʃ/, which are very difficult to detect through aided hearing. Thus, it is appropriate to vary practice stimuli to fit a child's needs.

Combined attention to clear auditory signals and specialized instruction can help children acquire basic and metalinguistic knowledge about phonology and other aspects of language that can prepare them for literacy learning (Yoshinaga-Itano & Downey, 1996). Working with children at the whole-word level brings advantages of developing vocabulary along with speech. Case Example 14.4 is based on a description of two boys with acquired D/HH, both of whom received CI but at different ages and with different preimplantation skills and age of onset (Ertmer, Leonard, & Pachuilo, 2002).

Targeting Literacy Learning by Children with D/HH

If hearing is compromised in any way, even by a relatively mild or unilateral loss (McKay, 2006), children are at risk for having difficulty learning auditory–oral language and for

---

CASE example *14.4*

Drew's and Bobby's Experiences after Cochlear Implantation

Ertmer, Leonard, and Pachuilo (2002) reported case studies for two boys, Drew and Bobby, who received cochlear implants (CI), but at different ages and with different preimplantation skills and age of onset.

Drew developed typically until he was 3, when meningitis left him with a moderate hearing loss in his right ear and a severe loss in his left. Drew's speech intelligibility and language comprehension both declined following his illness, but he continued to use speech for expression and learned to combine it with manually coded English (MCE) for reception at home and school. Approximately four years later, Drew's hearing level suddenly decreased to the profound range, and he became a candidate for CI. He received his implant at age 7 years, 6 months, which was followed by intervention incorporating analytic (bottom-up) auditory training to perceive phonetic features and synthetic (top-down) auditory training focused on the comprehension of meaningful speech. Because Drew was an avid sports fan, comprehension checks involved observing his responses to false assertions (e.g., "Michael Jordan can't jump," p. 208). Drew learned to use comprehension monitoring and to request clarification when he did not understand. By sixth grade, Drew was using a combination of FM amplification and sign interpretation for most of his classes. He needed sign interpretation particularly in classes in which new vocabulary and content

were being introduced. After four years, his first CI failed and he received a new implant, which improved his speech perception.

Bobby was deafened prelingually at 5 months of age, also by meningitis. He received his cochlear implant at age 3, but because of ossification, only 11 of 22 electrodes were inserted and activated. Following the first year of implantation, Bobby learned to alert to some environmental sounds but made limited progress in using the CI to process speech. Bobby was described as "an attentive yet highly cautious child. He was often reluctant to interact with clinicians and usually responded through eye gaze, pointing, or single signs—sometimes made under the table" (p. 210). He did respond better when his mother was in the room. Bobby's intervention program included a combination of structured auditory and speech training, accompanied by play-based language intervention. Early speech production goals were to increase the quantity and quality of his vocalizations, consonant and vowel productions, and spoken words. Bobby's skills for imitating speech improved, but after approximately one year of intervention, his vocalizations in play still were not clearly recognizable as words.

The experiences of these two boys illustrates the protective factor of longer exposure to language prior to deafness. They also provide examples of individual differences and the need for individualization of intervention plans and methods.

learning to read and write (Yoshinaga-Itano & Downey, 1996). Learning to read and write, conversely, has implications for learning language (see Personal Reflection 14.9). Historically, few children with severe hearing loss have exceeded a fourth-grade level of literacy, regardless of communication mode (Krose, Lotz, Puffer, & Osberger, 1986), but children with CI in grades K–12 have been found to score considerably above levels of reading found in prior studies with children who were prelingually deaf but had no CI (Spencer, Tomblin, & Gantz, 1997). Dillon and Pisoni (2006) also found that children with CI demonstrated higher-level phonological knowledge in nonword repetition and single-word reading tasks than children with other forms of auditory support and that the advantage could be found for sentence comprehension as well.

PERSONAL reflection *14.9*

"I would have a deaf child read books in order to learn language, instead of learning the language in order to read books."

Alexander Graham Bell (1847–1922), in addition to inventing the telephone, was a teacher of speech and a strong advocate for auditory–oral education for people who are deaf or hard of hearing. (He was quoted on the cover of the *Volta Review,* in 1965, with reference to the original publication which appeared in February, 1915, on p. 55.)

Connor and Zwolan (2004) used sophisticated analysis methods to identify factors that predict later literacy learning for children with prelingual and profound hearing impairments who receive CI at varying ages. The following factors emerged from analysis of results for 91 children that predict later reading comprehension:

- *Age at which the children received an implant*—Younger is better.
- *Method of communication*—Better overall language predicts better outcomes. Children who used total communication prior to implantation tend to have stronger pre-implant vocabulary scores, but the total effect of preimplant communication method on children's reading skills is negligible.
- *Vocabulary skills*—Postimplant vocabulary has a direct positive effect on reading, and preimplant vocabulary has an indirect positive effect on reading through post-implant vocabulary.
- *Socioeconomic status*—Lower status has negative effects.

Sterne and Goswami (2000) studied phonological awareness (PA) among children who were deaf (with a mean age of 11 years) using syllables, rhymes, and phonemes. Although "previous research has been equivocal about whether deaf children can develop phonological awareness" (p. 609), results showed that children with D/HH could draw on phonological skills in supportive conditions. Sterne and Goswami concluded that deaf children can develop PA, but their phonological skills lag behind those of hearing children and may develop in different ways.

Having a cochlear implant is not a panacea, but it can have a noticeable impact on a child's prognosis for language and literacy learning, including influence on PA, comprehension, and ability to benefit from interactive book reading. DesJardin, Ambrose, and Eisenberg (2008) conducted a longitudinal study with 16 children with CI and their mothers to investigate early book reading and its possible influence on PA and reading skills three years later. Mothers and children were videotaped during two storybook interactions. Children's language skills were assessed using a variety of measures, with results indicating that the use of early expressive oral language skills and open-ended questions by mothers during storybook reading each contributed uniquely to children's later literacy skills.

Speech–Language/Literacy–Communication Intervention for Children with B/LV

Language specialists can serve as members of interdisciplinary teams to assess general language abilities at the sound/word and sentence/discourse levels for children with visual impairment who are struggling with spoken or written language. Although children with blindness or low vision (B/LV) face some unique challenges with the nonverbal aspects of language learning, they face no special language acquisition risks due to the sensory loss alone. Andersen, Dunlea, and Kekelis (1984) described two key differences in language acquisition from birth to age 3 for children with B/LV: (1) a tendency to acquire vocabulary more as unanalyzed labels for specific referents than as hypotheses about classes of referents and (2) challenges in learning to understand shifting perspectives in social interactions.

The higher risk of multiple comorbid disabilities for children with B/LV, including cognitive impairment, also can influence language and literacy learning directly, underscoring the need for comprehensive interdisciplinary assessment of multiple systems that may be involved. Erin (2007) pointed out that more than 60 percent of children with B/LV have multiple disabilities that cause them to be identified by other diagnoses in federal counts, thus underrepresenting the number of children actually challenged by B/LV issues.

Reading (i.e., language by eye) is a special concern, but auditory language abilities provide important foundational skills for children with B/LV, as for all children. Erickson, Hatton, Roy, Fox, and Renne (2007) pointed out that the language skills of preschool-age children with B/LV may not be as mature as their teachers think. Durando (2008), on the other hand, reported results of a survey of teachers of children with visual impairments and other disabilities that suggested a need to raise expectations for children with multiple disabilities. Although evidence suggests that "measures of cognitive ability are neither static nor effective predictors of reading achievement," Durando found that "45% of the respondents agreed with the statement, 'braille is too difficult for students with multiple disabilties'" (p. 44). As self-efficacy theory suggests, confidence that change is possible is an essential ingredient to ensuring that it can occur. These figures suggest that some blind children with comorbid disabilities are not gaining access to instruction in braille because their IEP teams may be underestimating their potential to learn to read.

Supporting Literacy Learning by Children with B/LV

Many children with low vision can see well enough to learn to read using print when it is enlarged and presented with adequate contrast. When augmented visual processing is not possible, many children can learn braille (i.e., patterns of raised dots). Learning to read braille requires learning to access linguistic meaning by sensing how raised dots on a page represent orthographic symbols and how those in turn represent phonologically and morphologically structured words. This calls for a combination of instruction and practice.

Emergent print awareness for children with B/LV may need to include tactile sensitivity training and instruction in the concept of spatial representation (Steinman et al., 2006), especially for young blind children who are tactually defensive. Specially designed curricular materials are available from the American Printing House for the Blind (1987) to provide prereading experiences in detecting patterns through tactile sensation. Parents of children with B/LV also can use deliberate strategies to help their toddlers and preschoolers experience braille symbols in the environment (e.g., in elevators, on menus in fast food restaurants, on household items). These deliberate efforts are needed so children can access early print symbols as an introduction to reading, similar to exposure to environmental print experienced incidentally by children who are sighted (Craig, 1996; Steinman et al., 2006).

In the early stages of formal reading instruction, teachers of braille face a choice whether to use materials that show one-to-one correspondence between braille characters and alphabetic letters or to provide early exposure to the system of **contracted braille** that adult readers use to represent common morpheme and spelling patterns. For example, the word *can* is represented with *c,* and the word *have* is represented with *h.* Bound morphemes (e.g., *-er* and *-ed*) also can be represented with single symbols, as can high-frequency function words (e.g., *for* and *the*) (Steinman et al., 2006). Expanded and contracted choices both have proponents, but efforts are being made to collect evidence addressing questions related to best methods for teaching braille reading to children (Robert Wall Emerson, personal communication, May 25, 2007).

Monson and Bowen (2008) analyzed studies of PA and phonics by children learning braille and pointed to the "logographic nature of braille" (p. 217) as a factor to consider. Their analysis showed conflicting findings and variations in methodology (e.g., ages of participants and types of PA tasks) among the 11 studies, making it difficult to draw general conclusions about the ability of children with B/LV to develop PA. Pring (1994) found that children who were congenitally blind could learn to demonstrate similar levels of phonemic awareness as children who were sighted. Gillon and Young (2002) also found a strong relationship between the phonemic abilities by children with B/LV and their performance on reading tests, confirming the importance of working on phonological concepts to support reading development by children with B/LV.

Like all children, children with B/LV need opportunities to develop reading comprehension along with decoding. They must be able to construct mental models (i.e., *conceptual schemas*) to make sense of meaning in texts (e.g., Kintsch, 1994). When children with visual impairments are learning to decode written forms, either in enlarged print or braille, they need opportunities to read aloud texts about familiar concepts (Steinman et al., 2006). Similar recommendations are often made for helping all children transition smoothly and quickly from a phase of *learning to read* to one of *reading to learn.* Erickson and colleagues (2007) presented detailed case studies for three young children, showing that it is never too early to begin working on concepts about the world through interactions with books (see Personal Reflection 14.10).

PERSONAL reflection *14.10*

"With these guys, early literacy is preteaching for life. . . . Blind kids don't get knowledge of stuff delivered to their doorsteps the way sighted kids do. I just use early literacy as a chance to deliver background knowledge."

Ms. Heather (quoted in Erickson et al., 2007, p. 91) was an early intervention teacher of children with B/LV participating in a qualitative study of emergent literacy.

All receptive language, whether received through auditory, visual, or tactual modalities, involves processing perceptual input that is received sequentially, which means some components must be held in working memory and worked on simultaneously until meaning is grasped. As Wall Emerson (personal communication, June 27, 2007) pointed out:

> Braille adds another level of difficulty to this process since it is inherently slower than print reading. The tactual reader tends to process bits of information slower and must piece together words more laboriously than the print reader who takes in one or more words in a visual "gulp."

Comprehension of receptive language requires the contributions of parallel constructive processes in the mind of the listener or reader, as newly arriving input is integrated into a developing picture (schema) of the meaning of the discourse. When a mismatch occurs between perceptual data and the meaning being constructed by the listener or reader, an effective communicator implements repair strategies to locate the source and resolve the error. Older children and adolescents, if they are fluent readers, grasp literal meanings and also draw inferences about figurative and social meanings. Assessment of auditory language comprehension may be indicated if children with B/LV experience academic difficulties and unusual challenges comprehending literate language. All children need opportunities to formulate ideas into written discourse, and appropriate assistive technology should be provided to make that possible.

Assistive Technology for Children with B/LV

Numerous assistive technologies are available to support the language- and literacy-learning needs of children with B/LV. Auditory forms of books and other print materials can be checked out of any library and increasingly can be downloaded from the Internet or read (i.e., listened to) online. Other tools, such as a Kurzweil reader, use an omniprint scanning technology with print-to-speech capabilities to change print to spoken output for hard copies of printed materials. States typically offer support services for creating large-print and braille books for schoolchildren. This process is becoming centralized and even more efficient as textbook publishers provide electronic files to a central depository, the National Instructional Materials Accessibility Center, housed at the American Printing House for the Blind. These electronic files are downloaded at the agency, formatted using computers, and then embossed into braille or printed in large print. Federal law requires that all new editions of children's textbooks be made available in an electronic version, as well as a print version.

Children with B/LV need keyboarding instruction and writing software with speech feedback so they can monitor their keystrokes as they type, and with speech synthesis so they can review their written discourse for revising and editing. Such tools provide important accommodations supporting the physical aspects of language transcription, but they cannot teach students how to write. Students with B/LV need instruction in written language composition, just as all students do. The instruction should include scaffolding and practice in how to compose ideas in a written language style, even if a student is dictating his or her words for another to transcribe. In addition to direct work on writing, experience hearing published materials read aloud should help students develop an "ear" for written language forms and can be recommended for all students for supporting written composition and comprehension.

Supporting Social Skills Learning by Children with B/LV

When young children with B/LV show difficulty with social skills learning, they may benefit from explicit instruction. Gronna, Serna, Kennedy, and Prater (1999) combined script training and puppetry to teach social skills to a preschool child with B/LV. The child participated in treatment activities with three to four typically developing peers; the treatment was scaffolded by an adult using puppets to model a script that included a targeted social skill (i.e., greeting, initiating, responding). All the children then practiced the skill with their puppets. After training, they participated in free play on the playground, and adult prompting was eliminated. Following treatment, the child's frequency of interactions with peers and use of social skills both increased.

Speech–Language/Literacy–Communication Intervention for Children with Deafblindness

All populations discussed in this chapter face extra challenges learning to communicate, but the loss of both distance senses by children with deafblindness can be particularly isolating. As with D/HH, the age of onset of deafblindness is important in determining best choices for providing instruction and for supporting the development of language and communication. Postlingual deafness is an important protective factor. Any inner language that has been developed prior to loss of function can make a difference in the child's later development.

Literacy skills also open communication options that otherwise would be unavailable, adding to the imperative to help children challenged by loss (sometimes progressive) of both vision and hearing to learn to read fingerspelling in their hands, to read braille or enlarged print on the page, and to learn to write. Assistive technologies and specialized forms of communication are particularly critical for the wide range of people with deafblindness. Table 14.2 summarizes communication options for children and adolescents coping with both deafness and blindness.

When intellectual deficits co-occur with sensory deficits, challenges mount. When children with deafblindness are functioning at preintentional stages of communication, they may benefit from the intervention methods described previously in this chapter adapted for their sensory input difficulties by using near senses more than distance ones. Most children who are called *deafblind* have useful residual vision and/or hearing. Intervention involves teaching them to "integrate sensory input from the damaged distance senses with past experience and input from other senses" (McInnes & Treffry, 1982, p. 3).

To address the earliest stages of preintentional communication, Sternberg, Ritchey, Pegnatore, Wills, and Hill (1986) adapted a curriculum and an approach developed by van Dijk (1965). The program uses proximal senses of ***movement resonance*** (also called ***coactive movement***) to help a child understand the reciprocal nature of communication while being held in the lap of an adult, moving first in concert and later in reciprocal turns through five phases of development. Each phase uses receptive and expressive indices to gauge progress through the phase and to decide when the child is ready to move to the next phase of the program. These are summarized in the form of an observation tool in Figure 14.3.

SUMMARY

Children and adolescents may experience relatively specific forms of peripheral and central auditory and visual sensory loss, or such losses may be part of more complex comorbid cognitive–communicative conditions. The choice of intervention techniques varies with the profile of the individual child. Children with peripheral hearing loss or (central) auditory processing disorder need attention to their listening environments. Sound field amplification systems provide an improved signal-to-noise ratio for all students, increasing access to the phonological structure of words. However, the research on the effectiveness of modifying the acoustic features of speech has shown equivocal results. Explicit instruction using natural speech appears to be as effective as using modified acoustic signals for improving speech production and perception.

Children who are deaf or hard of hearing (D/HH) need high quality technological supports either in the form of personally fitted hearing aids or cochlear implants. They also need early intervention focused directly on establishing communication, regardless of communication mode emphasized (auditory–verbal, American sign language, or total communication). Auditory training should be coordinated with instruction and intervention targeting the comprehension and production of spoken and written language. Advantages

table _14.2_ Communication Supports That May Be Used by People with Deafblindness

Dependence on Added Technology and Literacy	Type	Description
Unaided Techniques		
Requires no literacy	Signals	Co-active rocking and interactive games can lead to the development of stop and start signals through body movement.
	Class cues	Concrete objects may be used to signal an upcoming event (such as presenting a bath towel to indicate that bath time is near).
	Gestures and gross signs	Conventional gestures, such as _yes, no, hi,_ and _bye,_ may be taught expressively and receptively. Deafblind manual sign uses a double tap on a person's hand to signal _yes_ and a brushing sign of erasure to signal _no._
	Speech and vision	Deafness is rarely complete, and some information can be communicated through natural speech and visual cues. Tadoma is a less used (and demanding) method, in which the person with deafblindness rests a hand on the face of a speaker to gather information by detecting cues as to speech rhythm, voicing, airflow, and place of articulation.
	Guide dogs	Guide dogs (which might be classified as skilled partners) can increase independence and safety. When placed off duty, dogs can become a topic of conversation, leading to broadened social contacts.
Requires literacy and skilled partner	Sign language options	People who learned sign language prior to becoming blind may prefer to read ASL by touching the arms and hands of those signing. Visual frame signing involves modifications in a restricted space to aid the receiver. Deafblind manual sign uses a combination of near signs and fingerspelling.
	Fingerspelling options	Manual fingerspelling on a person's left hand uses a special manual alphabet; block letters drawn on the left hand can be used as a temporary solution by those who have not learned fingerspelling.
Aided Techniques		
Requires no literacy	Raised tactile signs	Raised labels can be designed with shapes as well as braille or letters.
	Amplified speech	High-quality hearing aids and other listening devices are always appropriate.
	Implants	Cochlear implants (and retinal implants) can be considered.
Requires literacy but no special skill from partner	Braille	People who have adequate language skills can learn to read braille. Opticon is a device that changes print into a tactile representation. Teletouch uses standard keyboard input to change text to braille.
	Software options	Access to computers with amplified speech output can make reading and composing accessible.

Source: Based on Gallagher, 2007; McInnes & Treffrey, 1982.

figure *14.3*

Observation Tool for Documenting Advances in Co-Active Movement by Children with Deafblindness and Other Complex Disabilities

Phase	Receptive	Expressive	Descriptive Evidence
Preresonance	❑ Random movement ❑ Moves in same plane and motion with adult	❑ Undifferentiated cry ❑ Differentiated movements and vocalizations	
Resonance	❑ Responds to others' cues by participating in movement modification while facing adult ❑ Performs repetitive actions on objects and observes what happens	❑ Indicates recognition of familiar person or object ❑ Signals adult to continue desired activity (e.g., pulling or pushing)	
Coactive movement dialogue	❑ Responds to tactile signals for movement ❑ Anticipates next movement in sequence	❑ Imitates motion after movement stops (based on adult's position) ❑ Gives multiple signals to continue activities ❑ Duplicates different movements while adult is moving, with no physical contact needed	
Deferred imitation	❑ Responds to simple gestural commands without physical contact ❑ Anticipates routine events from cues ❑ Responds to functional gesture for object when object is present	❑ Imitates movement after adult finishes ❑ Uses gestures specific to certain situations ❑ Produces new movements in imitation of models	
Natural gestures	❑ Responds to functional gesture for object to locate object not present	❑ Uses gestures for objects and actions across situations ❑ Uses gestures rather than whole-hand pointing to refer to object	

Source: Based on Sternberg, Ritchey, Pegnatore, Wills, & Hill, 1986; van Dijk, 1965.

in acquiring spoken and written language have been documented for children who were exposed to auditory language prior to becoming deaf and children with cochlear implants.

Children with blindness or low vision (B/LV) need access to high quality instruction to develop literate language abilities (using braille or enlarged print and magnification). Some also may need intervention to extend their knowledge of visually supported vocabulary, cognitive–communicative concepts, and social interaction cues. Children with deaf-blindness need multiple supports for communication and language/literacy learning.

Intervention for Cognitive–Communicative Disorders

The population of children and adolescents with cognitive–linguistic impairments is large and heterogeneous. It varies with etiologies (genetic or not, acquired or not), degree of cognitive limitation, and other personality and familial factors. Children with cognitive limitations may require particularly clear cues, simplified structures, more repetitions, and additional opportunities to acquire language. Some children require AAC supports to communicate with spoken or written language.

Speech–Language–Communication Intervention for Children with Cognitive Limitations

Children and adolescents with Down syndrome and other etiological syndromes may need intervention focused on speech intelligibility as well as language/literacy abilities and social communication. Price and Kent (2008) described biological and cognitive factors that may affect speech intelligibility in children with Down syndrome and fragile X syndrome, "including oral-motor impairments, hypotonicity, impairments in fine motor coordination, chronic otitis media, difficulty planning motor sequences, general cognitive delay, and a specific language impairment" (p. 224). They noted that "intelligibility is a relatively global aspect of speech that combines syntax, lexical choice, phonological patterns, and execution of the motor plan for speech" (p. 228). Thus comprehensive assessment of multiple systems is needed to inform intervention.

Kumin (2008) emphasized that there is no single pattern of speech and language skills in individuals with Down or fragile X syndrome. She noted a higher risk for coexisting conditions in children with cognitive limitations, including sensory-processing disorders, autism, and CAS, and she described features of comprehensive language intervention approaches that could be used to target *complex language,* which she defined as the three-word stage and beyond (p. 193). Kumin recommended drawing on language intervention programs developed for other populations because of the limited literature addressing the needs of children with cognitive limitations specifically. Programs should be individualized based on comprehensive assessment of language strengths and needs across levels and modalities, coordinating across the school and home and making modifications relevant to the student's grade level while planning for the future.

Supporting Language/Literacy Learning by Children with Intellectual Disabilities

Like all children, students with cognitive limitations may benefit from phonemic awareness training to prepare them for language/literacy learning. Some children in special populations have visual skills that are notably better than auditory ones, including children with Down syndrome (Buckley & Johnson-Glenberg, 2008). Comprehensive approaches to language and communication development can make active use of visual strategies to support the acquisition of spoken and written language (e.g., Hoffman & Norris, 2006; Ukrainetz, 1998b, 2006b). Participation in meaningful learning activities, as described previously in this chapter for using AAC to act out stories (e.g., Erickson & Koppenhaver, 1995), also can contribute to literacy learning.

Research on the phonemic awareness skills of children with Down syndrome has supported their ability to acquire such skills. Fletcher and Buckley (2002) used a battery of tests to assess literacy and related skills for 10 male and 7 female children with Down syndrome (ages 9 years, 2 months to 14 years, 5 months). Phonemic awareness was tested, along with reading and spelling competence, nonword reading and spelling ability, and nonverbal communication skill. Similar to typically developing children, children with Down syndrome demonstrated varying competence with phonemic awareness; better ability correlated positively with reading and spelling competence, ability to spell nonwords, and performance on nonverbal communication measures.

Cupples and Iacono (2000) tested phonemic awareness, receptive language, cognitive function, and oral reading abilities for 22 children with Down syndrome (ages 6 years, 7 months to 10 years, 3 months). They reassessed reading and phonemic awareness approximately nine months later. Results showed that early segmentation ability predicted later nonword reading but not the reverse, suggesting a causal relationship. This has implications for prioritizing phonemic awareness in intervention for children in this population who may have difficulty with the processing of auditory linguistic information without special instruction.

Lovett, Barron, Forbes, Cuksts, and Steinbach (1994) implemented computer-supported literacy intervention targeting literacy skills for 17 students with significant neurological impairment with varied etiologies (e.g., spina bifida and hydrocephalus, seizure disorder, brain tumors, cerebral palsy, and head injury) and 5 students with developmental dyslexia. The program provided synthesized speech feedback. Three programs for training in word recognition and spelling were compared with a math-training control program. The language program taught spoken–written language relationships at three levels of language units—letter–sound (*train*—t/r/ai/n), onset–rime (*train*—tr/ain), and whole word (*train*—train). Although all the literacy-training groups made significant gains in word recognition and spelling, those who received letter–sound training showed the best transfer on uninstructed rhymes of instructed regular words. The authors concluded that the neurologically impaired children were able to profit from instructional procedures that segmented printed words into units corresponding to onsets, rimes, and phonemes and that the segmentation training (i.e., using individual speech *segments,* or *phonemes*) facilitated transfer to similar but novel words and contexts.

A focus on language comprehension plays a role that is at least as important as word-level decoding intervention for children with Down syndrome and other cognitive–communicative conditions, as for all children. Along with heightened cues about sounds, words, and their representation with letters and orthographic patterns, children and adolescents with cognitive impairments need heightened cues about the communicative value of written language and the meanings of written texts. This can be engendered through pleasurable experiences with books and story writing, as recommended for all children. To emphasize the communicative nature and authentic audience roles associated with writing, personal notes may also play a role. When a child receives a surprise written note from a parent or sibling, perhaps with a drawing and Xs and Os (i.e., conveying kisses and hugs), tucked in a lunch bag or taped to the mirror, the motivation to learn to read and write for communicative purposes may be enhanced, along with the expectation that literacy is a legitimate goal for children with cognitive–communicative disabilities.

SUMMARY

Children and adolescents with cognitive–communicative impairments face multiple challenges for acquiring basic communication skills. In the past, intervention efforts have stopped too often with attempts to teach functional communication only. Serious attempts to teach children with cognitive impairments to develop literacy skills beyond the recognition of environmental print have increased in recent years. That coupled with the heterogeneity of this population and their complex communication needs means that this is an area ripe for further exploration by clinical researchers. Studies of students with Down syndrome and other cognitive–communicative needs suggest that they can benefit from direct instruction in phonemic awareness as well as a focus on language comprehension (through both listening and reading). Children with cognitive–communicative impairments also may benefit from interventions aimed at helping them learn to write for an audience of interested peers.

Intervention for Autism Spectrum Disorders

Earlier sections of this chapter focused on intentional communication by children with autism by teaching communication acts aimed at soliciting attention, commenting, and making requests. Once intentional communication and speech are possible, imitation, modeling, and selective reinforcement can be used to shape the production of words.

Comprehensive Curricula for ASD

Comprehensive programs have been developed to address the speech–language communication needs of children with ASD. Several are described briefly prior to describing techniques for addressing specific concerns associated with ASD.

The TEACCH Language and Communication Curriculum

TEACCH (for Treatment and Education of Autistic Children with Communication Handicaps) (e.g., Schopler & Mesibov, 1985) is a statewide program developed in North Carolina to serve children with ASD and their families, but it is used more widely. The TEACCH language and communication curriculum targets the development of spontaneous communication in children with ASD using a model of integrated contextualized language learning across multiple systems.

Figure 14.4 shows an observational assessment tool (Watson, Lord, Schaffer, & Schopler, 1989) for documenting quantitative and qualitative information related to the five communication and language components targeted by the TEACCH curriculum—communication functions, communication contexts, semantic categories, units of communication (e.g., words, signed symbols, or gestures), and communicative modalities (e.g., signs, print symbols, speech). Outcome studies for children involved in the TEACCH program have documented higher IQ scores for students served in the preschool years (Lord & Schopler, 1989) and higher academic achievement for students with higher cognitive abilities (Venter, Lord, & Schopler, 1992).

The SCERTS Model

The **SCERTS** model is explained in two volumes by the interdisciplinary team of Prizant, Wetherby, Rubin, Laurent, and Rydell (2006). The acronym stands for Social Communication, Emotional Regulation, and Transactional Support. These are the key components of an integrated assessment and intervention approach for individuals with ASD and their families. The SCERTS model is implemented in natural learning contexts, rather than one-on-one training sessions, to encourage language and communication development and to support families in improving their quality of life.

Student: Ralph
Observer: Warren
Date: 1/17
Time began: 9:30
Time ended: 11:30

CONTEXT	WHAT STUDENT SAID OR DID	Request	Getting Attention	Reject	Comment	Give Information	Seek Information	Other	Object	Action	Person	Location	Other
① Makes mess while making breakfast	towel (signs)	✓							object wanted				
② Work-folding clothes	finish (signs)				✓					own action			
③ Free time-R. walks into kitchenette	touches teacher's arm		✓										
④ "	hands teacher a cup	✓											
⑤ T: "What?"	drink (signs)	✓							object wanted				
⑥ T. hands R. orange juice	pushes jar away			✓									
⑦ R. opens refrigerator	drink (signs)	✓											
⑧ T: "Drink what?"	R. picks up cola bottle												
	+ signs drink	✓							object wanted				
⑨ R. stands up T.: "What do you want?"	bathroom (signs)	✓										own location	
⑩ R's shoe untied; to T.	shoe (signs)	✓							object acted on				
⑪ " "	shoe (signs) + holds								object acted on				
	up untied shoe	✓											
⑫ finishes playing with comb	finish (signs)				✓					own action			

figure *14.4*

Illustration of a Charting Method That Combines Qualitative and Quantitative Observations

The observations are from a naturalistic communicative interaction between a teacher (observer) and a student with autism.

Source: From *Teaching Spontaneous Communication to Autistic and Developmentally Handicapped Children* (p. 29) by L. Watson, C. Lord, B. Schaffer, and E. Schopler, 1989, Austin, TX: Pro-Ed. Copyright 1989 by Pro-Ed, Inc. Reprinted by permission.

In the area of social communication, the authors emphasize the establishment of joint attention and symbol use as the key to further advances. In the area of emotional regulation, they note that children are most available for learning and interaction when they have the capacity and skills to (1) seek assistance and/or respond to others' attempts to provide support for emotional regulation when faced with stressful, overly stimulating, or emotional dysregulating circumstances (referred to as *mutual regulation*); (2) remain organized and well regulated in the face of potentially stressful circumstances (referred to as *self-regulation*); and (3) recover from being "pushed over the edge" or "under the carpet" into states of extreme emotional dysregulation or shutdown by using mutual and/or self-regulatory strategies (referred to as *recovery from extreme dysregulation*) (Prizant et al., 2006, Vol. I, p. 5)

Transactional support is the third major domain addressed within the SCERTS model. It incorporates interpersonal supports in the form of adjustments and accommodations made by communicative partners; learning supports, such as environmental arrangement to support social interaction; support to families; and support among professionals and other service providers. The term *transactional* signals a view of children as active learners, development as involving interrelationships across systems, the need for children with ASD to interact with children without special needs, and goals to engender feelings of trust, respect, and empowerment within children and families coping with autism.

The Do-Watch-Listen-Say Model

The ***Do-Watch-Listen-Say*** model (Quill, 2000) addresses the social, communicative, and repetitive behavior problems that define autism. It is leveled primarily to the needs of young children, but the principles apply to older students as well. The book of the same name provides assessment and intervention guidance for addressing unique developmental patterns of autism and includes activities and strategies for home and school, including children who use AAC. Quill addresses information-processing tendencies of children with ASD, such as overly selective attention, as in the case of Alex, a student with autism who was learning about money in first grade math:

> When asked to tell the class what he would do with a nickel, he explained, "A nickel is gray or silver. A nickel is a circle, and a nickel has a man on it with a jacket. The quarter has a man with no jacket." Alex recognized the Presidents' attire on U.S. coins, but he had concentrated on details that were not socially relevant and did not appear to understand the purpose of money. (p. 23)

To address such concerns, the Do-Watch-Listen-Say framework applies to any social or academic interaction. The components are aligned with other capacities:

Do aligns with the cognitive capacity to know what to do in a given situation.

Watch aligns with the social capacity to observe others and understand proximity and other nonverbal social cues, such as gestures and emotional expressions.

Listen aligns with language and the ability to assign meaning to verbal and nonverbal events, actions, and signaling.

Say aligns with communication, or the ability to know what to say in a given context so that messages will be relevant to the social context and informational needs of others.

Quill (2000) provided an example of how the framework applies to targeting social play for a preschool-age child playing blocks with his peers:

- DO—use the blocks in exploratory, functional, or creative ways
- WATCH—observe peers' play, observe peers' socioemotional behaviors, share blocks, take turns, and/or cooperate on a joint building project
- LISTEN—listen to what is said during the activity; respond to the verbal requests and comments of peers; and respond to the nonverbal requests, comments, and behaviors or peers
- SAY—initiate and maintain reciprocal communicative interactions. (p. 83)

Speech–Language/Literacy–Communication Intervention for Children with Autism

A high proportion of the evidence-based intervention literature about children with ASD targets prelinguistic or early intentional communication, often using the ABA paradigm influenced by behaviorist theory (as explained earlier in this chapter). Although some children with autism remain nonspeaking, at least half do learn to talk before the age of 5 years (Charlop-Christy & Jones, 2006). They may not necessarily talk clearly or form sentences without difficulty, however, and speech–language intervention may be needed to help children with autism develop spoken language skills at the word, sentence, and discourse levels. Many of the intervention approaches described in Chapter 13 are appropriate for children with autism as well; the emphasis should be placed on using visual input to compensate for deficits in auditory linguistic processing, taking advantage of visual-processing strengths that may be present.

Targeting Speech Intelligibility for Children with Autism

Lovaas (1981) used highly structured ABA programs to target speech development and language for children who might otherwise remain nonverbal. Intervention with this method starts at the level of the individual phoneme, which is shaped using operant procedures to move closer to a target in highly dense massed trials. Then syllables are targeted and finally words.

Focusing on communication success, Smith and Camarata (1999) targeted intelligibility by showing teachers of children with autism how to provide clear feedback regarding speech production within the context of naturalistic language intervention. Teachers in the study worked with three children with autism (two boys and a girl) between the ages of 4 years, 10 months and 6 years, 0 months in the school setting. All three children produced spoken language with limited intelligibility at baseline. Teachers learned to provide feedback for unintelligible utterances using one of two approaches. If teachers were able to decipher the child's intended utterance using contextual cues, they provided a conversationally appropriate correct model of the utterance and naturalistic reinforcement. If they were unable to figure out the child's intended meaning using contextual cues, they used repair strategies aimed at understanding the child's intentions. Results were measured by coding time intervals and counting those in which speech was intelligible (or not) to an unfamiliar observer. Frequency of verbal interactions and ratios of intelligible-to-unintelligible utterances went up for all three children after their teachers learned to provide clear feedback focused on message adequacy.

The use of naturalistic learning contexts and clear feedback also were supported in a study by Koegel, Camarata, Koegel, Ben-Tall, and Smith (1998). They compared a drill-based with a play-based phonological intervention for children with autism. The play-based intervention incorporated social and natural reinforcers. Listeners who were blinded to the treatment condition were asked to rate spontaneous speech samples, and only children who had received the play-based intervention increased intelligibility levels and correct production of target phonemes in conversation.

Targeting Morphosyntax for Children with Autism

A general principle of language intervention focused on morphosyntax is to arrange a linguistic context to require the use of a particular targeted form. Koegel, Carter, and Koegel (2003) reported the results of an intervention study in which they taught two boys with autism (ages 6 years, 3 months and 4 years, 4 months) to use the past-tense -*ed* morpheme (boy 1), or present-progressive -*ing* morpheme (boy 2). The researchers first taught both boys to initiate questions as a pivotal response using a different pop-up book chosen by each boy. Boy 1 learned to ask "What happen*ed*?" being prompted to initiate the question after the pop-up feature had been activated. Then the clinician would model an appropriate past-tense response (e.g., "He pinch*ed*," regarding a crab), after which the child learned to repeat "He pinch*ed*." Boy 2 learned the present-progressive morpheme through a similar modeling procedure. He was taught to ask "What's happen*ing*?" while the pop-up feature was being activated, setting the context for phrases such as "He's jump*ing*" (referring to a kangaroo hopping) to be modeled by the clinician and repeated by the child, "He's jump*ing*." Intervention sessions took place in a university clinic room, and generalization probes were taken at home and in a play room at the clinic.

Results were dramatic in that the intervention data documented almost immediate acquisition. In addition, high rates of generalization were documented in other contexts after only five or six sessions (Koegel et al., 2003). Additionally, although question asking is rare for children with autism, these two boys quickly "generalized use of the self-initiation into other question forms, and concomitant increases [were found] in mean length of utterance, verb acquisition, and diversity of verb use" (p. 134).

Targeting Literacy and Discourse-Level Skills for Children with ASD

Children and adolescents vary along the ASD spectrum in terms of their speech–language abilities, including literacy. By definition, all people with ASD share diagnostic traits of difficulty with social skills and unusually restricted interests, but they differ by definition in their acquisition of language. Whereas spoken language deficits are part of the triad of diagnostic symptoms for autism, language learning per se is not impaired in people with Asperger syndrome. As pointed out in Chapter 7, however, that simplistic view does not account for comprehension deficits and social perception difficulties that interfere with aspects of language learning for people with Asperger syndrome. Specifically, discourse-level skills and theory of mind issues make it difficult for people with ASD to interpret abstract and deeper meanings while reading (or being read to), to maintain audience perspective while writing, and to understand and express the landscape of consciousness in a narrative.

Some children on the autism spectrum have unusual strengths with word decoding and spelling aspects of learning to read and write relative to cognitive and language abilities measured in traditional ways. Mirenda (2003) summarized characteristics of hyperlexia (also discussed in Chapter 7) as including onset at ages 2 to 5 years in the absence of formal instruction, compulsive or indiscriminate reading of words, and a discrepancy between word-level reading abilities (high) and discourse comprehension abilities (low). Mirenda also described unusual developmental patterns for some individuals with autism, particularly those who became independent typists after receiving training in early facilitated pointing to letters on a keyboard. She noted that these case study examples provide evidence that "some individuals with autism who cannot speak or write can learn to read and spell" (p. 273). This led Mirenda to hypothesize (along with Crossley, 1993) that speech is not a prerequisite to literacy and that reading may be learned simply through exposure to print, as well as through formal teaching.

Intervention to support literacy learning by people with autism starts with assessment of current word-level reading decoding and spelling abilities and sentence- and discourse-level abilities for using written language to make sense. In Chapter 7 (Case Example 7.1), Hewetson (2005) described how her son, Mark, gained access to spoken language through print (including how the family started by labeling objects around the home with printed signs, through which Mark acquired the ability to name things) and then how she took the important step of coaxing him to listen to stories through books.

The role of phonemic awareness in learning to decode has been emphasized throughout this book, but analytical word decoding is only one of the skills that can be used by beginning readers to identify words. Mirenda (2003) noted the relevance of all four skills summarized by Ehri and McCormick (1998) as routes to word recognition, including decoding, reading words by analogy, predicting, and reading words by sight (i.e., memory for whole patterns). When children with ASD show an unusual interest in printed words (or even if they do not), instruction should be provided to help them develop their word-level skills further and to use those skills to formulate and comprehend connected sentences and discourse. When children write without a plan and without clear intention to communicate with an audience, their writing may suggest free association of thought. Individual words may appear to have some connections based on the child's own experiences but the writing will lack semantic, syntactic, and thematic connectedness. This window into the student's thinking can be extremely helpful for assessment purposes, however. The relative permanence of written words makes it possible for clinicians to use them to gain more access to the student's ideas and to encourage better integration and coherence of thinking and communication skills.

Writing process approaches to language intervention for students with autism take advantage of these strengths, while targeting multiple other areas of concern, including social skills. Bedrosian, Lasker, Speidel, and Politsch (2003) described an intervention with two eighth-grade boys with special needs. One had autism and used AAC; the other had mild cognitive impairment and intelligible speech. The pair learned to collaborate in planning and writing stories, and their final probe stories illustrated their learning of the narrative genre along with improvements in word- and sentence-level skills.

To examine the potential of written language to support social communication, Schairer and Nelson (1996) conducted a multiweek study with three adolescents with autism (Larry, Mark, and Becky). The clinician engaged in individual sessions with each student, alternating between conversing in spoken language and written language for 15 to 20 minutes in each session about photographs, books, and topics brought in by the student. The written conversations were held by passing a paper and pen back and forth. This provided a concrete signal for turn taking, as well as a stable record of the partner's comments or questions from the prior turn. All of the students showed strengths in the written over the spoken modality (except in number of words produced, which can occur more rapidly while speaking) (see Table 14.3). This adds to suggestions that written modalities may be used to support the development of spoken language communication, including social skills for children with ASD.

table *14.3* Examples of Spoken and Written Conversational Discourse for Two Adolescents with Autism

Spoken Conversation	Written Conversation	Commentary
Topic: videogames	Topic: videogames	In his oral conversations, Larry often used inappropriately elliptical forms and sometimes failed to respond to direct requests for information. In his written conversations, he was more assertive and produced more informative and nonobligatory utterances, and his topics better matched his prior utterances.
R: I'm an ace detective	R: It sounds like fun.	
= pause	L: Cody and Haggar are	
L: On the bonus round, eight different countries.	punching and jump-kicking.	
R: What's the bonus round?	R: Cool! I bet you're really good at it.	
L: Eight markers.	L: I have the new high score.	
R: How do you get to that?	(p. 175)	
R: 45 seconds. (p. 174)		
Topic: cooking	Topic: music class	Becky's utterances were on topic in both modalities, but she used more informative and complete sentences in writing than in speaking. She appeared to use the syntax of the prior sentence to help formulate her response when writing.
R: Why don't you tell me about some of the things you like to cook?	R: What do you do in music class?	
B: Brownies.	B: I do singing.	
R: What else do you like to cook? Your mom says you really like recipes.	R: That sounds like fun! I love to sing.	
B: Cake. (p. 176)	B: I love music because it's fun. (p. 176)	

Note: R = Researcher; L = Larry; B = Becky

Source: Adapted from Schairer & Nelson, 1996; commentary added.

Social Stories, Drama, and Peers Supporting Social Development for Children with ASD

Social skills difficulties are a cardinal feature of ASD, including Asperger syndrome. Children and adolescents with pragmatic language impairment (PLI) have difficulty with social cognition but do not have the other symptoms of ASD (i.e., restricted interests, repetitive behaviors, and insistence on sameness). They do, however, have difficulty reading social cues and may benefit from the intervention methods described in this section as well.

Social Stories and Comic Strip Conversations

To address social cognition concerns, particularly for children and adolescents on the high-functioning end of the autism spectrum and with Asperger syndrome, Gray (1994a, 1994b, 1998) introduced *social stories.* These are created for individual students by clinicians collaborating with them and their families to conduct context-based assessment of the circumstances that trigger the need for the story. As described by Gray (2005), "To write a Social Story is to create a bridge for information to cross between two minds that—while similar in many ways—may regard and perceive social situations from strikingly different vantage points" (p. 10). Gray also noted that those who write social stories should not assume the successful exchange of meaning. Rather, "it is a goal that we work very, very hard to achieve" (p. 10). Authors of social stories must carefully choose words and a format most likely to convey intended information.

As an example of word choice, Howley and Arnold (2005) noted the importance of using modifiers such as *usually* and *sometimes* to avoid problems stemming from the tendency to interpret messages too literally. This was illustrated with a story called "I go to Oak Tree House [a respite care facility]. Where are Mummy and Daddy? A Story for Harvey" (p. 56). It described what Harvey *usually* did and what his parents *usually* did during these times (e.g., go to work or the movies), and it ended "When my stay at Oak Tree House is finished, usually I go home. Sometimes I go to Granny's. Mummy and Daddy are happy to see me when I go home."

Some views of social stories focus on a directive function for addressing problems of social interaction or behavior, but this view is incomplete. Purposes of social stories include informing, reassuring, instructing, consoling, supporting, and praising—not just correcting and directing (Gray & White, 2002; Howley & Arnold, 2005). Social stories are used to help children with ASD develop social understanding. This is important, because it can be relatively easy to teach social skills in isolation, but a problem with discrete skill instruction is that it "may result in little more than a series of unrelated tricks and splinter skills if not placed into useful and meaningful contexts and developed with a degree of social understanding of how and when to use those skills" (Howley & Arnold, p. 17). For example, Howley and Arnold described one child who "was taught to hug, but knew nothing about who, when, how long for and where to hug" (p. 17). Social stories also can help family members and others to understand the perspective of the person with autism. "After all, social reciprocity and competence depend not only on the individual with an ASD but also on the neurotypical individuals within society" (Howley & Arnold, p. 25).

Social stories and comic strip conversations offer illustrated simplified and explicit explanations of what people expect in social contexts. Simple drawings and other visual symbols are added to make visual cues more salient. The stories address a personally relevant topic and are structured using a sequence of three types of sentences: (1) *descriptive sentences* incorporate information about events, including the where, who, what, and why of activities of focus; (2) *prescriptive sentences* describe the internal states of those involved, including their perspectives, wants, feelings, and motivations; and (3) *directive sentences* describe specific social cues and appropriate social responses, using such frames as "I will try to remember to . . ." to avoid demands for compliance (Gray, 1998; Howley & Arnold, 2005). Most social stories are written in the first-person point of view and remain available for repeated reading and review and for celebrating social success.

Scripts and Script Fading

McClannahan and Krantz (2005) described how the following scenario prompted them to ask new questions, which led them to develop new and more effective solutions for helping children with autism gain conversational skills and interact socially:

> A seven-year-old approached us, and when his teacher, one step behind, prompted "Say 'Good morning,'" he quickly repeated the greeting but did not wait for a reply.
>
> We knew him and the other youngsters well, and our minimal prompts (saying "Hi," taking a step toward a student, or raising an eyebrow) resulted in greetings, but when we did not prompt, the children were silent, although virtually all of them had learned to talk. When imitating teachers' verbal models or answering questions, they responded with words, phrases, or sentences, but if they were not instructed to talk, they did not do so. Obviously, we had a problem.
>
> The problem challenged us to ask questions, to reexamine intervention procedures for children with autism, and to undertake research. (p. x)

The solutions that McClannahan and Krantz (2005) developed to address this problem of prompt dependency involved the introduction scripts (video modeling, audio modeling, and printed scripts) to provide language, or nonverbal gestures if necessary, to show children what to say or do to engage in social interaction. The technique then involves systematically fading the scripts so that children can use the scripts independently. In their book, McClannahan and Krantz provided case examples and data to support the use of this technique with students across a wide range of ages and with varied levels of language, literacy, and cognitive development. The authors emphasized "It is important to note that scripts and script fading are not procedures for teaching children to *speak,* but procedures for teaching them to *interact*—to engage in the give-and-take of conversation" (p. xii). Using this technique, children are taught to imitate audiotaped scripts or to read printed scripts, which offer conversational comments, such as "I like trains." The fading process involves removal of each word in sequence, starting with the last word, and removing each previous word in turn, until only the blank tape or plastic sleeve (for printed scripts) remains, and then those cues are removed as well. For example, the audiotaped script, "I like trains," would be reduced to "I like," then to "I," then to the blank tape, which would be removed eventually. McClannahan and Krantz summarized the results of their research as follows:

> After many scripts have been presented and faded, most young people do one or more of the following:
>
> 1. they continue to say the scripts, although the scripts are absent;
> 2. they combine parts of the scripts with other scripts, or with language that was modeled by their conversation partners, thereby producing novel statements; or
> 3. they say things that were neither scripted nor modeled by their current conversation partners, but that were previously learned either via formal instruction or by imitating other people's conversations. (p. 6)

This use of scripts and script-fading is similar to the use of social stories and comic strip conversations. Both accentuate social cues and what to say without disrupting authentic acts of communication between two partners.

Dramatization

Schneider (2007) described the use of drama to improve social perception by people with ASD and related disabilities. She posed the question "What is acting all about? It is about reading and portraying emotions by using your voice as well as nonverbal communication" (p. 13). That makes play acting a rich context for helping students with ASD develop social perspective and the ability to read social cues, including nonverbal indicators, through constructivist learning. Schneider described the multiple benefits of planning, practicing, and producing performances with troupes of actors that include people with and without disabilities. When preparing an authentic performance for an authentic audience, the motivation and fun of learning to communicate becomes a goal for all and moves intervention into the opportunity for full participation.

Peer Supports for Social Communication

Thiemann and Goldstein (2001) studied the use of peer support along with social stories to provide written text cues and video feedback. Five students with autism (ages 6 years, 6 months to 12 years, 2 months) were paired with two peers each without disabilities to

---

─CASE **example** *14.5*────────────────────────

Mark and the Metaphoric Explanation of Multiple Labels

In Chapter 7, Mark, a person with autism, was introduced through the words of his mother, Ann Hewetson (2005). Hewetson shared information about their family's journey to understand the autism spectrum and Mark's needs. As Mark entered his twenties, he was diagnosed with psychiatric difficulties in addition to autism, including symptoms of depression with a concomitant drop in self-esteem. The family found a therapist who could address both aspects of Mark's dual diagnosis by engaging him in cognitive behavior therapy. Hewetson told this story:

> He has become very conscious now that he has two medical conditions—a developmental disorder and a co-existing psychiatric condition. In his own estimation he has two labels and this is a big issue for him. Listening to his concerns, his therapist decides to tap into his strong capacity for visual imagery. Some days later he wears a smart, new, grey jacket which he loves and feels good in. As he leaves, she says—"Mark I'm admiring your jacket. It's a wonderful colour and beautiful soft material. It must be very comfortable to wear and it's such a smart up-to-date style. You look so well in it. May I have a look?"
>
> Mark slips off the jacket to show her. Turning it inside out she finds the labels—two small discs of innocuous black cloth stitched on to the inside of the lining.
>
> "They're just the labels," says Mark, looking at her in puzzlement.
>
> "Yes, they're *just* the labels. Are they part of the jacket?"
>
> "No—not really I suppose."
>
> "Mark, when you go home this evening will you do something for me? Will you measure the area of the jacket and compare it with the area of the labels. Let me know what percentage the labels are." Showing his surprise he nods, wondering: does she need the measurements to make a similar one?
>
> This evening he spreads the jacket across the dining room table and running the measuring tape over it section by section he jots down his figures. Then he measures the labels and with a calculator in hand he works out the answer. The labels are 0.0001 percent of the jacket.
>
> He knows now why he has been asked to do it.
>
> It puts the question of labels into perspective for him. He views them now as something which may be necessary because they give information and they give insight. But they form no part of the jacket *per se* and the jacket is what matters. Compared to it, they are infinitesimal.
>
> Mark reaches the beginning of acceptance. (pp. 199–200)

receive 30-minute intervention sessions twice per week, with 10 minutes of systematic instruction using visual stimuli, 10 minutes of social interaction, and 10 minutes of self-evaluation using visual feedback. Results showed increases in targeted skills and partial generalization across behaviors and contexts.

Goldstein, Schneider, and Thiemann (2007) described other treatments that engaged peers as social communication partners, including techniques to prepare peers for taking an active role. One approach involved the use of sociodramatic play scripts to increase social interaction, such as a script for a hamburger stand theme that included gestural–motor and verbal responses divided equally among roles for a cook, salesperson, and customer. The script alone was not enough, but when prompts were added for children to stay in roles and then exchange roles, improvements were noted in the social and communicative interactions of students both with and without disabilities (Goldstein, Wickstrom, Hoyson, Jamieson, & Odom, 1988).

Although students with autism and Asperger syndrome have difficulty with abstract concepts and social perceptions by definition, they can benefit from using language to develop those perceptions (see Case Example 14.5). This is a case in which metapragmatic and metacognitive skills may be enhanced first to help students develop lower-level automatic abilities as an outcome of higher-level awareness.

SUMMARY

This section described methods for targeting the communication and social interaction needs for students with autism spectrum disorders. Comprehensive intervention approaches discussed included Treatment and Education of Autistic Children with Communication Handicaps (TEACCH); Social Communication, Emotional Regulation, and Transactional Support (SCERTS); and Do-Watch-Listen-Say. Also discussed were interventions for improving speech intelligibility, morphosyntactic structure, and literacy and discourse-level skills for children with autism. Children with autism spectrum disorders, including Asperger's syndrome, also may benefit from social stories and comic book conversations; dramatization; scripts and script fading; and interactions with peers who have received special training.

CHAPTER SUMMARY

This chapter described intervention methods for special populations, beginning with approaches for diverse populations functioning at preintentional and presymbolic levels. Then it addressed application of communication-based interventions for challenging and unconventional communication behaviors. The latter half of the chapter provided an overview of intervention techniques for targeting comprehensive speech, language/literacy, and communication concerns for children and adolescents in a variety of special populations. Sections were included targeting speech production, effective use of AAC, sensory and central processing, cognitive-communicative concerns, and language and social skills associated with autism spectrum disorders.

The point was made that there should be no prerequisites for speech–language–literacy service delivery. High expectations and interdisciplinary approaches both play an important role in keeping students in special populations participating socially and progressing in the general education curriculum, consistent with the message that *Problems are not just within children, and neither are solutions.*

EXERCISES *and* STUDY QUESTIONS

1. Some of the methods introduced in this chapter were primarily behaviorist; others were primarily social interactionist. Describe how intervention would vary if you used one approach versus another to reduce challenging behaviors or to target improved social perception.

2. How would a peripheral sensory or motor problem influence assessment and intervention choices? What are bottom-up and top-down approaches, and why is a two-pronged approach necessary to address both peripheral and central-processing deficits?

3. Discuss the meaning of this statement, "Problems are not just within children, and neither are solutions." Provide illustrations that relate to at least two of the special populations discussed in this chapter.

Part III Appendix

table A Developmental Summary Chart across the Age Span from Infancy through Preschool

Approx. Age	Cognition	Receptive Language	Expressive Language	Social–Emotional and Play	Emergent Literacy
0–8 months	Preintentional (Sensorimotor I, II, & III): Transitions from reflexive to goal-oriented behavior.	Startles to noise. Orients to sound source. Quiets when spoken to.	Has differentiated cry. Produces vocalizations. Produces syllabic babbling. Makes intentional gestures.	Shares attention and can self regulate. Recovers from distress within 20 minutes.	Shares reference on pages of book when engaged by caregiver.
8–12 months	Early Intentional (Sensorimotor Stage IV): Uses familiar means to achieve novel ends.	Laughs at familiar interaction sequences. Inhibits action in response to *no*.	Takes vocal and gestural turns. Uses conventional gestures (*bye bye, no*).	Cries when parent leaves. Plays nursery games. Recovers from distress within 10 minutes.	Looks at pictures in book with adult and listens to short segments of story. Imitates scribbling.
12–18 months	Late Intentional (Sensorimotor Stage V): Uses novel means to achieve familiar ends.	Points to objects (e.g., body parts) in response to "Show me _____."	Uses first words in intentional acts. Uses word + gesture to express a variety of functions.	Closes communication circles with words and gestures. Engages in solitary or onlooker pretend play.	Names pictures or makes sound effects in books. Scribbles spontaneously with crayon.
18–24 months	Representational Thought (Sensorimotor Stage VI): Internal problem solving using images, memories, and symbols.	Shows word recognition. Responds to two-word commands and questions about agent, action, object, and location.	Has vocabulary spurt. Onset of two-word utterances (MLU = 1.5). Talks more frequently.	Engages in parallel play. Combines two ideas in pretend play; acts on doll. Begins to reason about feelings.	Imitates literacy events in play. Listens to short story read aloud. Attempts to make shapes with crayon. Pretends to write name.

25–48 months	Early Preoperational Thought: Indicates what another person can see but cannot perform false belief tasks.	Answers *yes/no* questions. 30 months: Answers *what, what-do, where* questions. 36 months: Answers *whose, who, why, how many* questions.	Brown's Stages: I: MLU 1.75 (24 months) II: MLU 2.25 (28 months) III: MLU 2.75 (30 months) IV: MLU 3.50 (36 months)	Engages in parallel play, symbolic play, and associative group play (around 40 months). Uses pretend play to recover from distress.	Listens to longer stories. Demonstrates print awareness. Demonstrates phonological awareness in nursery rhymes. Makes letter shapes.
48–72 months	Late Preoperational Thought: Systematic trial and error. Can respond appropriately to false belief theory of mind tasks by around 48 months.	Demonstrates verbal comprehension of prepositional instrument or manner relations. Responds to two-part action commands.	Brown's Stage V: MLU 3.75 (42 months) Elaborates phrases and combines and embeds clauses.	Shows increased dramatization and realism in play. Develops friendships. Plays games in groups with rules (by 72 months). Spends extended time at one activity.	Comprehends longer texts. Retells story. Acts out stories in play. Expands phonological awareness and learns phonics. Decodes and spells words phonetically.

Source: Based on Brown, 1973; Greenspan, 1997; Hatzell, 1984; Larson & McKinley, 1987; Nelson, Silbar, & Lockwood, 1981; Piaget, 1965; Westby, 1988.

table _B_ Developmental Chart Showing Benchmarks across the Age Span from Infancy through Adolescence

Approx. Age	Cognition	Receptive Language	Expressive Language	Social–Emotional and Play	Emergent Literacy
0 to 3+ months	Preintentional (Sensorimotor Stages I & II): • Shows little evidence of goal oriented activities at beginning of period. • Assimilates new objects into reflex actions. • Explores objects by mouthing and banging. • Moves from being purely reflexive to initial goal-oriented behavior.	Precursors: • Startles to noise. • Orients to sound source. • Quiets when spoken to.	Motor foundations: • Drinks from bottle or breast. • Sneezes, coughs. Precursors: • Has undifferentiated cry. • Makes reflexive vocalizations and comfort sounds.	Shared attention and regulation: • Makes eye contact. • Alerts to sights and sounds and follows caregiver with eyes. • Engages, disengages, re-engages in short periods (e.g., smiles in response to interesting facial expressions). • Sobers at sight of strangers. • Quiets when picked up. • Recovers from distress within 20 minutes with help from caregiver.	Shares reference on pages of book when engaged by caregiver.
4 to 7+ months	Preintentional (Sensorimotor Stage III): • Gradually develops object permanence. • Early: Focuses on empty space where dropped object was last seen; fails to look under scarf for object. • Later: Eyes follow object when it drops; looks under scarf for object. • Anticipates object that was shown and then removed. • Works to reach toy. • Returns to activity after interruption.	Precursors: • Looks at person who calls name. • Responds within communicative exchanges with signs of engagement.	Motor foundations: • Handles semisolid foods. • Mouths objects. Precursors: • Has differentiated cries. • Performs syllabic babbling. • Blows bubbles. • Makes "raspberries" sound.	Engagement and relating: • Smiles to familiar faces and mirror image. • Responds to parental overtures with pleasure and interest. • Becomes distressed when caregiver is unresponsive during play. • Recovers from distress within 15 minutes with help from caregiver.	Engages in routines involving books.

Age		Precursors / Comprehension	Intentional Expression	Two-way / Complex Communication	Literacy
8 to 11+ months	Early Intentional (Sensorimotor Stage IV): • Uses familiar means to achieve novel ends (e.g., tries to repeat a new effect). • Imitates ongoing actions already in repertoire ("Peekaboo," "Kiss Mommy," "Pattycake"). • Reacts in anticipation prior to event. • Stares to gain information.	Precursors: • Looks at objects, sharing reference with caregiver. • Acts on objects noticed. • Imitates object or sound already in repertoire. • Laughs at familiar interaction sequences. • Inhibits action in response to *no*. • Begins to respond to caregiver gestures and to gesture in return.	• Drinks from cup; feeds self crackers. Intentional expression: • Takes vocal and gestural turns in communication games. • Initiates interactions and looks expectantly for response; points to show wants and desires. • Expresses anger by banging and throwing and later by mumbling privately. • Kisses, waves, holds out hands.	Two-way communication: • Initiates comforting and closeness by pulling on leg or initiating hug. • Cries when parent leaves. • Plays nursery games ("This little piggy," "Pattycake"). • Stacks rings on peg. • Cooperates in dressing. • Recovers from distress within 10 minutes by being involved in social interactions.	• Looks at pictures in book with adult. • Listens to short segments of text read aloud. • Holds crayon; imitates scribbling.
12 to 18+ months	Late Intentional (Sensorimotor Stage V): • Uses novel means to achieve familiar ends (e.g., communicative gestures and stereotypic vocalizations to achieve desired end). • Figures out ways to overcome some obstacles (e.g., opens doors, reaches high objects).	Nonverbal comprehension strategies: • Attends to object mentioned. • Gives evidence of notice. • Does what is usual with objects. Early verbal comprehension: • Shows knowledge of single words in sentence contexts with referents present. • Points to objects (e.g., body parts) in response to "Show me _____."	First words appear in intentional acts; child uses word + gesture to express a variety of functions: • Performatives: *hi/bye* routines, *thank you.* • Comment: *hot, pretty, dog.* • Rejection: *No* + hands outstretched for unwanted bed or food. • Request object: object name or vocalization + pulling or pointing. • Request action: *Up* + hands raised. • Attention: *Mom* (calling intonation). • Claims possession: *Mine.*	Complex communication: • Closes multiple communication circles in a row using words and gestures. • Engages in solitary or onlooker pretend play (hugs doll, crashes car, makes motor noise). • Reacts to emotions of others. • Can recover from anger and be cooperative; uses imitation to recover from distress (yelling after being yelled at).	• Points to objects in picture book response to "Show me _____," or "Where is the _____?" • Names pictures or makes sound effects in interactions with familiar books: "What does a doggy say?" "What noise does the truck make?" • Scribbles spontaneously with crayon.

Approx. Age	Cognition	Receptive Language	Expressive Language	Social–Emotional and Play	Emergent Literacy

18 to 23+ months	Representational Thought (Sensorimotor Stage VI):
	
	• Begins to replace sensorimotor schemas with internal problem solving using images, memories, and symbols to represent actions and objects mentally.
		Nonverbal comprehension strategies:
		
		• Locates object mentioned.
		• Gives evidence of notice.
		• Does what you usually do (e.g., puts things in container, brushes hair).
		
		Verbal comprehension:
		
		• Shows word recognition when referent not present.
		• Carries out two-word commands.
		• Responds to routine questions about agent, object, locative, and action.
			Transitions to two-word combinations:
			
			• Produces successive one-word utterances.
			• Encodes new semantic roles:
			  • Early: Action–object relations. Uses words to refer to agent, action, object, recurrence, disappearance.
			  • Late: Object–object relations. Uses words to refer to object location, possession, nonexistence.
			• Answers routine questions and asks "What's that?"
			• Has vocabulary spurt with rapid acquisition of new words.
			• Onset of two-word utterances (MLU = 1.5).
			• Increases frequency of talking.
				Creating representations (emotional ideas):
				
				• Engages in parallel play.
				• Talks to self in play.
				• Begins to distinguish real vs. pretend.
				• Combines two ideas in pretend play, although not necessarily related (e.g., trucks crash; trucks pick up sand).
				• Acts on doll as well as self (e.g., feeding, washing).
				• Follows rules and respond to limits.
				• Shows optimism and confidence (e.g., with early puzzles).
				• Begins to reason about feelings and connect them to behaviors.
				• Knows what to say or do to get a hug and other closeness.
				• Conveys emotions in pretend play and communication showing closeness, pleasure and excitement, assertive curiosity, fear, anger, and limit setting.
				• Uses pretend play to recover from distress (e.g., acting out eating a cookie or holding a bottle).
					• Imitates literacy events in play (e.g., "reading" newspaper, menu, books).
					• Listens to short story read aloud.
					• Attempts to make shapes with crayon.
					• Pretends to write name.

25 to 35+ months	Early Preoperational Thought:	Verbal comprehension strategies:	Brown's Stages:	Building bridges between ideas (logical thinking):	

	• Has preconceptual thought, but ability to represent one thing with another increases as language develops.
	• Shows new understanding of object relationships:
	  • Arranges objects in patterns but not categories.
	  • Matches identical objects.
	  • Matches similar objects.
	  • Sorts blocks of varying size, shape, color into groups based on one attribute (50% can do by 42 months).
	• May be able to indicate what another person can see or know but cannot yet perform false belief theory of mind tasks.
		• Accepts, rejects, confirms, or denies in response to yes/no questions.
		• By 2.5 years, can answer:
		  • *What* for object.
		  • *What-do* for action.
		  • *Where* for location.
		• By 3 years, can answer:
		  • *Whose* for possessor.
		  • *Who* for person.
		  • *Why* for cause.
		  • *How many* for number.
		• Gender contrasts for third person pronouns.
		• Comprehension strategies (2–3 years):
		  • Do what is usually done.
		  • Probable location strategy for *in, on, under, beside.*
		  • Probable event strategy for reversible sentences.
		  • Infer most probable speech act in context.
		  • Supply missing information (2 years).
		  • Supply explanation (3 years).
			• Stage I (MLU 1.75; basic semantic relations), age 24 months:
			  • Agent–action.
			  • Action–object.
			  • Agent–object.
			  • Possession.
			  • Entity–locative.
			  • Action–locative.
			  • Existence.
			  • Recurrence.
			  • Nonexistence.
			  • Rejection.
			  • Denial.
			  • Attributive.
			• Stage II (MLU 2.25; grammatical inflections), age 28 months:
			  • Some articles, plurals, possessives.
			  • *-ing* on verbs.
			  • Asks "What doing?"
			• Stage III (MLU 2.75; sentence differentiation), age 30 months:
			  • Modals (*can, don't*).
			  • Possession.
			  • Noun plurals.
			  • *In/on.*
			• Stage IV (MLU 3.50; sentence embedding of infinitive object complements), age 36 months:
			  • Immediate future (*gonna*).
			  • Other catenatives (*wanna; let's*).
			  • Regular past-tense *-ed* appears.
			  • Inflects verb *to be* (*am, are, was*).
				• Parallel play with peers predominates (25 months).
				• Engages in symbolic play; ties 2 or more ideas together logically in play; organizes props and plays imaginatively.
				• Builds on adult's pretend play idea.
				• Begins associative group play with peers (around 40 months).
				• Creates bridge with blocks.
				• Plays spatial and motor games with rules (e.g., taking turns on slide).
				• Conveys emotions in pretend play and communication showing closeness, pleasure and excitement, assertive curiosity, fear, anger, and limit setting.
				• Uses pretend play with logical ideas to recover from distress.
					• Listens to longer stories read aloud.
					• Pretends to read words on the page and to write notes to parents.
					• Shows awareness that print represents words.
					• Shows phonological awareness in nursery rhymes, songs, and rhythms.
					• Has increased control of writing tools:
					  • Imitates drawing of vertical line (by 30 months).
					  • Imitates drawing of horizontal line and circle (by 36 months).
					  • Draws two or more lines to imitate a cross (by 42 months).

(continued)

table _B_ Continued

Approx. Age	Cognition	Receptive Language	Expressive Language	Social-Emotional and Play	Emergent Literacy

3 to 7+ years	Late Preoperational Thought:
	• Still classifies on the basis of a single characteristic, but can switch set to focus on a different characteristic with greater ease.
	• Applies systematic trial-and-error problem solving to classification and seriation tasks.
	  • Sorts blocks by size, shape, or color into two piles (by one attribute) by 3.5–4 years.
	  • Arranges seven blocks in order of increasing height; then places three missing blocks in sequence by 4.5–5 years.
	  • Identifies member of set that does not belong and tells why.
	  • Identifies one of three pictures not in same category.
	  • Matches pictures that go together.
	• Develops concepts of time and space and shows concepts through drawing and shape identification.
	  • Closes shapes in drawings.
	  • Makes squares with corners by 4.5–5 years.
		• Responds to two-part, and later three-part action commands.
		• Understands contrasts for topological locatives (*in, on, under, beside*).
		• Answers *what/how* questions with manner or instrument (*What do we eat with?*).
		• Shows comprehension strategies:
		  • Early: uses word order strategies to understand agent + action + object as active sentences.
		  • Later: begins to understand nonreversible and reversible passive sentences.
		• Minimum distance principle in center embedded sentences (e.g., understands "Burt, after pushing Ernie, got in trouble" to mean that Ernie got in trouble).
		• Draws inferences based on context.
			• Stage V (MLU 3.75); syntactic elaboration and later forms:
			  • Sentence conjoining.
			  • Regular past-tense *-ed*.
			  • Third person singular.
			• Demonstrates multiple levels of embedding and subordination in a single sentence.
			• Develops event relations sequence from 3.5–7 years.
			  • *And* (coordinate and temporal).
			  • *Because, so* (causal).
			  • *But* (contrastive).
			  • *When* (conditional).
			  • *While* (simultaneity).
			  • *After* (sequential).
			  • *Before* (sequential).
			  • Past time (*-ed*).
			  • Possibility (*might*).
			• Demonstrates syntactic rule emergence from 4–6 years.
			  • N + cop + PN/PA/loc (*He's sick*).
			  • *There's* expleture (*There's cars on the table*; AAE: *Here go the cars*).
			  • Possessive/Adj + N + V (*Jim's big dog bites*).
			  • Obligatory and emphatic do (*He does not feel good. He does feel good.*).
			  • Continued regularization of irregular forms.
				• Establishes complex dramatic play scenes with words (*"Let's pretend . . . ; You be the . . . , and I'll be the . . ."*).
				• Repairs communicative breakdowns with peers.
				• Resolves social conflict with words.
				• Demands more realism in play.
				• Recovers from anger or emotional distress on own.
					• Masters phonics (sound–symbol associations).
					• Learns to apply the orthographic principle to recognize irregular spellings and connect them to syllables (e.g., *-ough; -ike*) and morphemes (e.g., *-tion, pre-, -ology*).
					• Reads simple texts with mostly known words fluently.
					• Comprehends complex texts read aloud by others.
					• Draws inferences about nonliteral meanings and meanings not explicit in the text.
					• Writes simple stories at advancing levels of maturity:
					  • Heaps.
					  • Isolated descriptions.
					  • Temporal sequences.
					• Writes social notes.
					• Reads sources and takes notes with support and drafts expository reports.

Age	Physical / Motor	Cognitive	Language	Social / Emotional	Literacy

	• Copies triangle by 5–5.5 years.
	• Draws person with two parts; gradually draws body, arms, legs, feet, nose, eyes.
			• Double negatives (optional in AAE).
			• Demonstrates syntactic rule emergence 6–7 years.
			• Forms passive sentences (*Miss Piggy was kissed by Kermit.*).
			• If . . . then subordination (*If it rains, we won't go.*).
			• Pronominalization (*John knew he would win the race.*).
			• Still perfecting auxiliary modal inversion in questions (*When's going to be the party?*).
				• Considers the perspectives and rights of others when making decisions.
				• Engages in genuine cooperative play.
				• Self-consciousness leads to formation of intense relationships with peers based on similarities.
				• Values approval of peers.
				• Home and family remain important social and emotional factors.
				• Displays emotional lability, which may lead to wide mood swings.
				• Displays conventional moral outlook in most cases.
				• Conforms to authority and obeys rules.
					• Uses reading for learning (acquires new vocabulary, concepts about the physical world, and insights into social relationships).
					• Reads chapter books.
					• Writes stories at advancing levels of maturity:
					  • Temporal sequence.
					  • Abbreviated episode.
					  • Complete episode.
					  • Multiple and embedded episodes.
					• Varies writing for social audiences (e-mail, social notes).
					• Plans expository reports, conducts research with print and online sources, takes relevant notes, writes a cohesive report.
					• Writes for other purposes:
					  • Persuasion.
					  • Procedures.
					  • Timelines/historical accounts.

7 to 12+ years		Concrete Operations:
		• Solves problem in egocentric and concrete ways.
		• Can perform multiorder theory of mind false belief tasks (*A believes that B will believe that C will hold a particular false belief.*).
		• Uses executive functions to maintain attention when distractions are present.
		• Imagines consequences before acting.
		• Can set goals and overcome obstacles to reach them.
		• Makes accurate toy replicas and working models.
		• Builds collections and categorizes components.
			• Understands conditional conjunctions with usual rather than logical sense.
			• Concludes probable relations in causal constructions.
			• Understands causal conjunctions *because* and *so* by 8 years.
			• Understands contrastive conjunctions *but* and *although* as meaning "and" (8 years).
			• Understands contrastive meaning of conjunctions *but* and *although* (10 years).
			
			Marks of maturity:
			• Forms longer sentences.
			• Uses more clauses per sentence.
			• Adverbial clauses (*He was sleeping while I watched.*).
			• Adjective clauses (*The girl with the red hair is my friend.*).
			• Nominals (*Flying airplanes is fun.*).
			• Sentence complements (*We elected Jim President.*).
			• Infinitive complements with new subject (*She told Maria to feed the dog.*).
			• Uses multiple speech acts and discourse types:
			  • Conversation.
			  • Persuasion.
			  • Teasing.		

(continued)

table *B* Continued

Approx. Age	Cognition	Receptive Language	Expressive Language	Social–Emotional and Play	Emergent Literacy
12 to 17+ years	Formal Thought: • Uses mental operations and hypothetical thinking to solve complex problems, weighing the pros and cons of varied solutions before acting. • Uses strategic, executive functions to organize and plan approaches to problem solving. • Introspection increases. • Thinks in more abstract, theoretical, and idealistic ways, but persists in finding simple solutions for complex problems.	• Comprehends complex language in academic lectures. • Abstracts main ideas and discourse structures from lectures and written texts. • Able to understand and tell jokes with appreciation of irony.	• Varies language effectively for varied purposes: • Uses slang with peers. • May overuse certain phrases (*you know*). • Has fewer mazes and tangles. • Develops ability to speak formally in public. • Develops literate complexity when speaking. • Uses more clauses per sentence (eighth-graders use 150% more clauses than fourth-graders).	• Persists in overcoming adversity. • Shows genuine cooperation in working on joint projects. • Reduces level of imaginary play but may develop theatrical drama or skills for entertaining others. • In middle adolescence (after physical changes of maturity are complete), boys and girls both show interest in working on their bodies and worry that they may not be normal. • May reject parental values earlier in period but return to them later. • Feelings of rebellion may be exhibited in dress styles, hair styles, adolescent slang, and fascination with teen music and performers. • Enjoys social life primarily with peers; dating is common by end of period. • Gets first job; participation in sports and music are important.	• Reads selectively and for a purpose. • Critiques what was read. • Can describe and compare literary genres. • Writes for multiple purposes. • Uses all stages of the writing process (planning, drafting, revising, editing, presenting).

| 16 to 21+ years | Formal Thought:
 • Gains higher-level skills for considering multiple perspectives held by different participants on a given situation.
 • Refines strategic, executive functions to organize and plan approaches to problem solving. | • Infers deeper meanings from texts read and heard, movies seen, etc.
 • Recognizes difference between scientific and fantastical explanations of phenomena. | • Refines formal spoken language expression for academic, social, and employment purposes. | • Develops personal identity and value systems in late adolescence.
 • Can make mature, independent judgments (often more like parents than in middle adolescence).
 • Has fewer feelings of rebellion.
 • Feels increased comfort with body maturity.
 • Is partially dependent on parents; this may be extended into young adult years.
 • Relies more on friends than family for support.
 • Experiences increase in sexual intimacy and ability to deal with interpersonal complexities. | • Reads and writes for complex academic purposes.
 • Reads for pleasure and discusses reading selections with peers.
 • Continues to develop skill in using all stages of the writing process, particularly for reflecting on own work and revising it to achieve a communicative purpose. |

Note that the progression of changes is relatively predictable, but chronological ages at which "stages" occur are less so; hence, overlaps and gaps appear in chronological ages for typical development of abilities and a decelerating growth curve is evident in the age-range shift from several months at the beginning to several years at the end of the scale.

table *C*   Selected Formal Tests for Assessing Language, Communication, and Other Development during the Preschool Years

Test	Author/Year/Publisher	Description	Age Range
Ages and Stages Questionnaire: A Parent-Completed, Child-Monitoring System, 2nd Edition (ASQ)	Bricker, D., & Squires, J. (1999). Baltimore: Paul H. Brookes.	This screening instrument uses a parent questionnaire to assess five categories: communication, gross motor, fine motor, problem solving, and personal/social.	4 to 60 months
Assessment, Evaluations, & Programming System, 2nd Edition (AEPS)	Bricker, D. (2002). Baltimore: Paul H. Brookes.	This criterion-referenced tool assesses fine motor, gross motor, adaptive, cognitive, and social–communicative developments. It includes a parent report measure.	Birth to 6 years
Bankson Language Test, 2nd Edition (BLT-2)	Bankson, N. (1990). Greenville, SC: Super Duper.	This norm-referenced expressive/receptive test is organized into three categories: semantic knowledge, morphological/syntactical rules, and pragmatics. It evaluates the child's ability to recognize and use language skills.	3 to 6 years, 11 months
Battelle Developmental Inventory, 2nd Edition (BDI)	Newborg, J., Stock, J., Wnek, L., Guidubaldi, J., & Svinicki, J. (2005). Chicago: Riverside.	This norm-referenced test uses observation in natural and structured settings and interviews with parents, caregivers, and teachers to assess personal–social, adaptive, motor, communication, and cognitive domains. A Spanish version is available.	Birth to 7 years, 11 months
Bayley Scales of Infant & Toddler Development, 3rd Edition (Bayley III)	Bayley, N. (2006). San Antonio, TX: Harcourt Assessment.	This norm-referenced tool uses observation and parent report to assess cognitive, language, motor, social–emotional, and adaptive development. It may be used with children with mild cognitive and sensory communication delays.	1 to 42 months
Boehm Test of Basic Concepts-Preschool, 3rd Edition (BTBC-P3)	Boehm, A. (2001). San Antonio, TX: Harcourt Assessment.	This norm-referenced test measures concepts and vocabulary relevant to preschool and early elementary curriculum. It includes a curriculum-based summary and parent report form.	3 to 5 years, 11 months
Bracken Basic Concept Scale, 3rd Edition: Receptive (BBCS-3:R) Bracken Basic Concept Scale, 3rd Edition: Expressive (BBCS-3:E)	Bracken, B. (2006). San Antonio, TX: Harcourt Assessment.	These norm-referenced measures evaluate the acquisition of basic concepts of a child, which is strongly related to cognitive and language development as well as early childhood academic achievement. Spanish versions are available.	3 to 6 years, 11 months
Brigance Infant & Toddler Screen Early Preschool Screen-II	Brigance, A., & Glascoe, F. (2003). North Billerica, MA: Curriculum Associates.	This criterion-referenced test also allows norm-referenced comparisons (correctly classifying 75% of at-risk children and 82% of typically developing children). The infant and toddler scales assess fine motor skills, receptive language, expressive language, gross motor skills, self-help skills, and	Birth to 11 months (infant)

Test	Author/Year/Publisher	Description	Age Range
		social–emotional skills. The preschool scales also assess reading readiness and other preacademic skills. Spanish direction books are available.	12 to 23 months (toddler)
Clinical Evaluation of Language Fundamentals-Preschool, 2nd Edition (CELF-P2)	Wiig, E., Secord, W., & Semel, E. (2006). San Antonio, TX: Harcourt Assessment.	This norm-referenced test assesses basic concepts, sentence structure, formulating labels, and word structure. Sensitivity is reported at 60% and specificity at 66%.*	3 to 6 years
Communication and Symbolic Behavior Scales Developmental Profile (CSBS-DP)	Wetherby, A., & Prizant, B. (2002). Baltimore: Paul H. Brookes.	This norm-referenced assessment tool uses a rating scale for language and symbolic development. Based on an infant–toddler checklist, caregiver questionnaire, and behavior sample (gestures, facial expressions, and play behaviors), a profile is built of the child's social, speech, and symbolic abilities.	6 to 24 months (functional communication age) 9 months to 6 years (atypical development)
Comprehensive Receptive and Expressive Vocabulary Test (CREVT-2)	Wallace, G., & Hammill, D. (2002). Austin, TX: Pro-Ed.	This test measures receptive and expressive strengths and weaknesses in oral vocabulary.	4 to 18 years
Diagnostic Evaluation of Language Variance (DELV)	Seymour, H., Roeper, T., & de Villiers, J. (2003). San Antonio, TX: Harcourt Assessment.	This criterion-referenced (and screening) test is designed to minimize effects of language variation in a comprehensive assessment of language, including pragmatics, syntax, semantics, and phonology. Sensitivity reported in the manual is 65% and specificity is 72%.*	4 to 12 years (language variation status) 4 to 9 years (diagnostic risk status)
Expressive One Word Picture Vocabulary Test, 2000 Edition (EOWPVT)	Brownell, R. (Ed.). (2000). Novato, CA: Academic Therapy.	This norm-referenced test provides an assessment of an individual's English speaking vocabulary. It requires children to name objects in pictures. A Spanish version is available.	4 to 18 years, 11 months
Expressive Vocabulary Test, 2nd Edition (EVT-2)	Williams, K. (2007). Circle Pines, MN: American Guidance Service/Pearson Assessment.	This norm-referenced assessment measures two types of expressive vocabulary (labels and synonyms) as well as word retrieval by comparing the standard score of the EVT with the PPVT.	2 years, 6 months to 90+ years
Hawaii Early Learning Profile (HELP) for Special Preschoolers, Assessment and Curriculum Guide	Furuno, S., O'Reilly, K., Hosaka, C., Inatsuka, T., & Zeisloft-Falbey, B. (1994). Palo Alto, CA: VORT Corporation.	This broad assessment tool uses a checklist format to assess (through observation, play interaction, and parent interview) self help, motor, communication, social, and cognitive skills. The communication portion assesses auditory perception/listening, receptive language, expressive language, sign language, and speech reading.	3 to 6 years

(continued)

table *C*   Continued

Test	Author/Year/ Publisher	Description	Age Range
Language Development Survey	Rescorla, L. (1989). Burlington, VT: ASEBA.	This checklist asks parents to check off words they have heard their children say (not just understand or imitate) from a list of 242 words arranged in 17 semantic categories.	18 to 35 months
MacArthur-Bates Communicative Developmental Inventories, 2nd Edition (CDIs)	Fenson, L., Marchman, V., Thal, D., Dale, P., Reznick, J., & Bates, E. (2007). Baltimore: Paul H. Brookes.	These questionnaires ask parents to check off words their child says or signs, including vocabulary relating to things in the home, people, action words, description words, pronouns, prepositions, question words, and also sentences and grammar.	8 to 18 months (words and gestures) 16 to 30 months (words and sentences) 30 to 37 months (vocabulary, grammar, and use)
MacArthur-Bates Inventario del Dessarrolo de Habilidades Comunicativas (Inventarios)	Jackson-Maldonado, D., Bates, E., & Thal, D. (2003). Baltimore: Paul H. Brookes.	The Spanish forms of the CDIs were developed separately from the English forms in order to reflect the vocabulary and grammatical structure of the Spanish language.	8 to 18 months (words and gestures) 16 to 30 months (words and sentences)
Peabody Picture Vocabulary Test, 4th Edition (PPVT-4)	Dunn, L., & Dunn, D. (2007). Circle Pines, MN: American Guidance Service/Pearson Assessment.	This norm-referenced receptive language test measures auditory comprehension of vocabulary in standard English by having the client point to the picture that the clinician names.	2 to 90+ years
Preschool Language Assessment Instrument, 2nd Edition (PLAI-2)	Blank, M., Rose, S., & Berlin, L. (2003). Austin, TX: Pro-Ed.	This norm-referenced test assesses how effectively a child integrates cognition, linguistics, and pragmatics to deal with communication with an adult. It offers formal and informal assessment parts and six subtests.	3 to 5 years, 11 months
Preschool Language Scale, 4th Edition (PLS-4)	Zimmerman, I., Steiner, V., & Pond, R. (2002). Austin, TX: Harcourt Assessment.	This norm-referenced test assesses receptive and expressive language, attention, social communication, and speech development. The manual reports sensitivity and specificity, both above 80%.*	Birth to 6 years, 11 months

Test	Author/Year/ Publisher	Description	Age Range
Receptive-Expressive Emergent Language Test, 3rd Edition (REEL-3)	Bzoch, K., League, R., & Brown, V. (2003). San Antonio, TX: Pro-Ed.	This norm-referenced test uses behavioral observations by caregivers to assess receptive and expressive language and to inventory vocabulary. The manual reports studies relating to norms, reliability, and validity.	Birth to 3 years
Receptive One Word Picture Vocabulary Test, 2000 Edition (ROWPVT)	Brownell, R. (Ed.). (2000). Novato, CA: Academic Therapy.	This individually administered, norm-referenced test provides an assessment of an individual's English hearing vocabulary. It uses a picture-pointing task with progressively harder vocabulary and concepts. A Spanish version is available.	4 to 18 years, 11 months
Reynell Developmental Language Scales (U.S. Edition)	Reynell, J., & Gruber, C. (1990). Los Angeles: Western Psychological Services.	This norm-referenced test uses toys for assessing expressive language structure, vocabulary, and content and for assessing receptive language when children can respond orally or only by pointing.	1 to 6 years, 11 months
Rossetti Infant-Toddler Language Scale	Rossetti, L. (2005). East Moline, IL: LinguiSystems.	This criterion-referenced scale uses observation, elicitation, and caregiver report to assess preverbal and verbal: interaction–attachment, pragmatics, gesture, play, language comprehension, and expression at three month intervals.	Birth to 36 months
Stanford-Binet Intelligence Scales, 5th Edition (SB5)	Roid, G. H. (2004). Chicago: Riverside.	This is a norm-referenced individually administered assessment of intelligence and cognitive abilities to be administered by a psychologist. Areas assessed include: fluid reasoning, knowledge, quantitative reasoning, visual–spatial processing, and working memory.	2 to 85+ years
Structured Photographic Language Test-Preschool, 2nd Edition (SPELT-P2)	Dawson, J., Stout, C., Eyer, J., Tattersall, P., Fonkalsrud, J., & Croley, K. (2005). DeKalb, IL: Janelle.	This norm-referenced measure probes early developing morphological and syntactic forms including prepositions, articles, plurals, possessive nouns and pronouns, subject pronouns, auxiliary verbs, copulas, present participles, past tense, third-person markers, as well as negatives, conjoined sentence, *wh*-questions, interrogative reversals, infinitive phrases, propositional complements, relative clauses, and front embedded clauses.	3 to 5 years, 11 months
Test for Auditory Comprehension of Language, 3rd Edition (TACL-3)	Carrow-Woolfolk, E. (1999). Austin, TX: Pro-Ed.	This norm-referenced test of spoken language comprehension uses a picture pointing task to assess vocabulary, grammatical morphemes, and elaborated phrases and sentences.	3 to 9 years, 11 months
Test of Early Grammatical Impairment (TEGI)	Rice, M. L., & Wexler, K. (2001). San Antonio, TX: Harcourt Assessment.	This criterion-referenced test assesses morphological and grammatical markers of specific language impairment. The manual reports sensitivity and specificity, both above 80%.*	3 to 8 years, 11 months

(continued)

table *C* Continued

Test	Author/Year/ Publisher	Description	Age Range
Test of Early Language Development, 3rd Edition (TELD-3)	Hresko, W., Reid, D., & Hammill, D. (1999). Austin, TX: Pro-Ed.	The norm-referenced language assessment tool yields standard scores with a mean of 100 and SD of 15.	2 to 7 years, 11 months
Transdisciplinary Play-Based Assessment, 2nd Edition (TPBA2)	Linder, T. (2008). Baltimore: Paul H. Brookes.	This criterion-referenced tool guides professionals across disciplines to observe a child in a 60- to 90-minute play session with his or her parent and to describe development across 4 domains—sensorimotor, emotional and social, communication and language, and cognition.	Birth to 6 years
Wechsler Preschool and Primary Scale of Intelligence, 3rd Edition (WPPSI-3)	Wechsler, D. (2002). San Antonio, TX: Harcourt Assessment.	This norm-referenced test assesses a child's cognitive abilities and measures language expression, comprehension, listening, and problem solving. The child responds orally to orally given stimuli.	2 years, 6 months to 7 years, 3 months

*The sensitivity and specificity data summarized in this table are based on Spaulding, Plante, and Farinella, 2006.

table *D* Selected Formal Tests for Measuring Language and Literacy Development during the School-Age Years

Test	Author/Year/Publisher	Description	Age Range
Clinical Evaluation of Language Fundamentals, 4th Edition (CELF-4)	Semel, E., Wiig, E., & Secord, W. (2003). San Antonio, TX: Harcourt Assessment.	This norm-referenced expressive/receptive language test looks at various areas of language including tests for semantic, syntactic, metalinguistic, and phonological aspects. It also has tests to assess working memory, pragmatics, and classroom performance/social interaction.	5 to 21 years
Comprehensive Assessment of Spoken Language (CASL)	Carrow-Woolfolk, E. (1999). Circle Pines, MN: American Guidance Service/Pearson Assessment.	This norm-referenced expressive/receptive test assesses the client's abilities in the areas of auditory comprehension, expression, and retrieval in the categories of lexical/semantic, syntactic, supralinguistic, and pragmatic skills. No reading or writing is required of the client, and the test is orally administered.	3 to 21 years
Comprehensive Receptive and Expressive Vocabulary Test (CREVT-2)	Wallace, G., & Hammill, D. D. (2002). Austin, TX: Pro-Ed.	This norm-referenced test measures receptive and expressive strengths and weaknesses in oral vocabulary. The receptive half of the test follows a "Point to the picture I name" format, while the expressive half asks the client to "Define the word I say," allowing for a more complete expressive sample.	4 to 89 years, 11 months
Comprehensive Test of Phonological Processing (CTOPP)	Wagner, R., Torgesen, J., & Rashotte, C. (1999). Austin, TX: Pro-Ed.	This norm-referenced expressive/receptive language test assesses phonological awareness, phonological memory, and rapid naming skills. Two separate versions are included, one for the 5- to 6-year-olds and one for the 7- to 24-year-olds.	5 to 24 years, 11 months
Diagnostic Evaluation of Language Variance (DELV)	Seymour, H., Roeper, T., & de Villiers, J. (2003). San Antonio, TX: Harcourt.	This criterion-referenced (and screening) test is designed to minimize effects of language variation in a comprehensive assessment of language, including pragmatics, syntax, semantics, and phonology. Sensitivity reported in the manual is 65% and specificity is 72%.*	4 to 12 years (language variation status) 4 to 9 years (diagnostic risk status)
The Expressive Language Test (ELT)	Huisingh, R., Bowers, L., LoGiudice, C., & Orman, J. (1998). East Moline, IL: LinguiSystems.	This norm-referenced expressive language test assesses many different aspects of verbal communication, including sequencing, defining, generating samples, grammar and syntax, concepts, categorizing, and describing.	5 to 11 years
Expressive One-Word Picture Vocabulary Test, Revised, 2000 Edition (EOWPVT)	Brownell, R. (Ed.). (2000). Novato, CA: Academic Therapy.	This norm-referenced test provides an assessment of an individual's English speaking vocabulary. It requires children to name objects in pictures. A Spanish version is available.	4 to 18 years, 11 months

(continued)

table *D* Continued

Test	Author/Year/ Publisher	Description	Age Range
Expressive Vocabulary Test, 2nd Edition (EVT-2)	Williams, K. (2007). Circle Pines, MN: American Guidance Service/Pearson Assessment.	This norm-referenced assessment measures two types of expressive vocabulary (labels and synonyms) as well as word retrieval by comparing the standard score of the EVT with the PPVT.	2 years, 6 months to 90+ years
Gray Oral Reading Test, 4th Edition (GORT-4)	Weiderhold, J., & Bryan, B. (2001). Austin, TX: Pro-Ed.	This norm-referenced test assesses a child's reading abilities in the following areas: rate, accuracy, fluency, comprehension, and overall reading ability.	6 to 18 years, 11 months
The Language Processing Test, 3rd Edition: Elementary (LPT-3)	Richard, G., & Hanner, M. (2005). East Moline, IL: LinguiSystems.	This norm-referenced receptive/expressive test assesses association, categorization, similarities and differences, multiple meaning, and attributes. It identifies receptive and expressive deficits in vocabulary acquisition, word-retrieval skills, inappropriate word usage, organization of knowledge, memory skills, imprecise verbal descriptions, and the inability to self-correct.	5 to 11 years
The Listening Comprehension Test, 2nd Edition	Huisingh, R., Bowers, L., & LoGiudice, C. (2006). East Moline, IL: LinguiSystems.	This norm-referenced test evaluates how students attend to, process, and extract meaning from what they hear. The five subtests include: main idea, details, reasoning, vocabulary, and understanding messages.	6 to 11 years
Oral and Written Language Scales (OWLS): Comprehension and Oral Expression Scale Written Expression Scale (WES)	Carrow-Woolfolk, E. (1996). Circle Pines: MN: American Guidance Service/Pearson Assessment.	This norm-referenced expressive/receptive test assesses listening comprehension, oral expression, and written expression. Some of the tests include answering questions, completing sentences, or generating answers in response to visual/verbal stimulus. The receptive part of the test has the client point to pictures in response to a verbal cue. The written version of the test assesses a client's abilities in handwriting, spelling, punctuation, syntax, relevance, cohesiveness, and organization.	3 to 21 years, 11 months (oral version) 5 to 21 years, 11 months (written version)
Patterned Elicitation Syntax Test (PEST)	Young, E., & Perachio, J. (1993). San Antonio, TX: Harcourt Assessment.	This norm-referenced receptive/expressive test determines whether a child's expressive grammatical skills are age appropriate. The student listens to sentences and phrases and is instructed to repeat the sentences back with the aid of pictures.	3 to 7 years, 6 months
Peabody Individual Achievement Test, Revised-Normative Update (PIAT-R/ NU)	Markwardt, F. (2007). Circle Pines, MN: American Guidance Service/Pearson Assessment.	This norm-referenced receptive language test assesses the student's ability to comprehend questions in six different areas of school achievement: general information, reading comprehension, reading recognition, written expression, mathematics, and spelling. Nearly all of the tests, save for the writing	5 to 22 years, 11 months

Test	Author/Year/ Publisher	Description	Age Range
		portion, are multiple choice. The test is good for children with limited expressive abilities or those who are considered to be low functioning.	
Peabody Picture Vocabulary Test, 4th Edition (PPVT-4)	Dunn, L., & Dunn, D. (2007). Circle Pines, MN: American Guidance Service/Pearson Assessment.	This norm-referenced receptive language test measures auditory comprehension of vocabulary in standard English by having the client point to the picture that the clinician names.	2 to 90+ years
Qualitative Reading Inventory, 4th Edition (QRI-4)	Leslie, L., & Caldwell, J. (2006). Boston: Pearson Education.	This measure is an individually administered informal reading inventory (IRI). It was designed to provide diagnostic information about decoding, reading fluency, and reading comprehension abilities and can be used to estimate an individual's reading level. It provides both narrative and expository passages at all levels. The qualitative information obtained can be used to design intervention.	Pre-Primer– High School
Receptive One Word Picture Vocabulary Test, 2000 Edition (ROWPVT)	Brownell, R. (Ed.). (2000). Novato, CA: Academic Therapy.	This individually administered, norm-referenced test provides an assessment of an individual's English hearing vocabulary. It uses a picture-pointing task with progressively harder vocabulary and concepts. A Spanish version is available.	4 to 18 years, 11 months
Structured Photographic Language Test, 3rd Edition (SPELT-3)	Dawson, J., Stout, C., & Eyer, J. (2003). DeKalb, IL: Janelle.	This norm-referenced test targets the child's use of morphology (preposition, plural, possessive noun and pronoun, reflexive pronoun, subject pronoun, direct/indirect object, present progressive, regular and irregular past, future, contractible/uncontractible copula, contractible/uncontractible auxiliary), and syntax (negatives, conjoined sentences, *wh*-questions, interrogative reversals, negative infinitive phrases, propositional complements, relative clauses, and front embedded clauses). The test is available in Spanish.	4 to 9 years, 11 months
Test for Auditory Comprehension of Language, 3rd Edition (TACL-3)	Carrow-Woolfolk, E. (1999). Austin, TX: Pro-Ed.	This norm-referenced test of spoken language comprehension uses a picture pointing task to assess vocabulary, grammatical morphemes, and elaborated phrases and sentences.	3 to 9 years, 11 months
Test for Examining Expressive Morphology (TEEM)	Shipley, K., Stone, T., & Sue, M. (1983). Austin, TX: Pro-Ed.	This norm-referenced expressive language test assesses a child's competency in the following areas: present progressives, plurals, possessives, past tenses, third-person singulars, and derived adjectives.	3 to 7 years, 11 months
Test of Language Competence, Expanded Edition (TLC-E)	Wiig, E., & Secord, W. (1989). San Antonio, TX: Harcourt Assessment.	This norm-referenced receptive/expressive test assesses a student's competency in the following areas: ambiguous sentences, listening comprehension, making references, oral expression, recreating speech acts, and figurative language. The test also comes with a supplemental memory subtest. The test meets an 80% criterion of acceptable sensitivity and specificity.*	Level 1: 5 to 9 years Level 2: 10 to 18 years

(continued)

table *D* Continued

Test	Author/Year/Publisher	Description	Age Range
Test of Language Development: Intermediate, 4th Edition (TOLD-I4)	Hammill, D., & Newcomer, P. (2007). Austin, TX: Pro-Ed.	This norm-referenced test examines various aspects of spoken language such as understanding and meaningful use of words and aspects of grammar such as semantics, syntax, and phonology. It profiles individual strengths in basic language abilities.	8 to 17 years, 11 months
Test of Language Development: Primary, 4th Edition (TOLD-P4)	Newcomer, P., & Hammill, D. (2008). Austin, TX: Pro-Ed.	The norm-referenced test is comprised of nine subtests that measure semantics (i.e., meaning and thought), grammar (i.e., syntax and morphology), and phonology (i.e., phoneme) skills. Three measure listening abilities; three measure organizing; and three measure speaking abilities.	4 to 8 years, 11 months
Test of Narrative Language (TNL)	Gillam, R., & Pearson, N. (2004). Austin, TX: Pro-Ed.	This norm-referenced test measures a child's ability to answer literal and inferential comprehension questions and how well they use language in narrative discourse. This test comes with three parts: no picture cues, sentence picture cues, and single-sentence cues. Data show 92% sensitivity and 88% specificity.*	5 to 11 years, 11 months
Test of Pragmatic Language, 2nd Edition (TOPL-2)	Phelps-Terasaki, D., & Phelps-Gunn, T. (2007). Austin, TX: Pro-Ed.	This standardized measure analyzes social communication in context to identifying individuals with pragmatic language deficits and determining individual strengths and weaknesses. It focuses on a student's ability to monitor and appraise the effectiveness of the response to resolve the social problem situation.	6 to 18 years, 11 months
Test of Problem Solving 2: Adolescent (TOPS 2: Adolescent)	Bowers, L., Huisingh, R., & LoGiudice, C. (2007). East Moline, IL: LinguiSystems.	This norm-referenced test addresses critical thinking abilities based on the student's language strategies using logic and experience. Questions focusing on a broad range of critical thinking skills, including making inferences, determining solutions, problem solving, interpreting perspectives, and transferring insights, have all been included in the test.	12 to 17 years, 11 months
Test of Problem Solving 3: Elementary (TOPS 3: Elementary)	Huisingh, R., Bowers, L., & LoGiudice, C. (2005). East Moline, IL: LinguiSystems.	This standardized measure provides information on how students integrate semantic and linguistic knowledge with critical thinking abilities. It assesses language strategies in the following areas: making inferences, sequencing, negative questions, problem solving, predicting, and determining causes.	6 to 12 years, 11 months
Test of Semantic Skills: Primary (TOSS-P) Test of Semantic Skills: Intermediate (TOSS-I)	Huisingh, R., Bowers, L., LoGiudice, C., & Orman, J. (P-2002, I-2004). East Moline, IL: LinguiSystems.	This norm-referenced receptive/expressive language test analyzes the skills that are important to conversation, reading comprehension, and academic achievement. The tests include labels, categories, attributes, functions, and definitions. The test results show standardized analyses of receptive, expressive, and overall semantic and vocabulary abilities, as well as a thorough discussion of performance.	Primary: 4 to 8 years, 11 months Intermediate: 9 to 13 years, 11 months

Test	Author/Year/Publisher	Description	Age Range
Test of Word Finding, 2nd Edition (TWF-2)	German, D. J. (2000). Austin, TX: Pro-Ed.	This test assesses word-finding abilities at the single-word level through four different naming sections: picture-naming nouns, sentence-completion naming, picture-naming verbs, and picture-naming categories.	4 to 12 years, 11 months
Test of Word Knowledge (TOWK)	Wiig, E., & Secord, W. (1992). San Antonio, TX: Harcourt Assessment.	This norm-referenced expressive/receptive test evaluates semantic and lexical knowledge through evaluating word definitions, multiple contexts, opposites, synonyms, and other parts of speech. The manual shows only 35% sensitivity, although specificity is 100%. (This means no typical language student is identified as having a disorder, but only 35% of students who do have a disorder are identified).*	5 to 17 years
Woodcock-Johnson III NU Complete (WJ III)	Woodcock, R., McGrew, K., & Mather, N. (2005). Chicago: Riverside.	This version features two distinct, co-normed batteries for achievement and cognition. They provide a comprehensive system for measuring general intellectual ability, specific cognitive abilities, scholastic aptitude, oral language, and academic achievement.	2 to 90+ years
Woodcock Reading Mastery Test (WRMT)	Woodcock, R. (1998). Circle Pines, MN: American Guidance Service/Pearson Assessment.	This norm-referenced test assesses the student's reading readiness, basic skills, and comprehension.	5 to 75+ years
The Word Test 2: Adolescent (WORD: 2-Adolescent)	Huisingh, R., Bowers, L., LoGiudice, C., & Orman, J. (2005). East Moline, IL: LinguiSystems.	This curriculum-based language test assesses expressive vocabulary and semantic skills critical to academic achievement in the secondary school environment. Subtests include associations, synonyms, antonyms, definitions, semantic absurdities, and flexible word use (multiple meanings). It provides comprehensive, standardized test results for each subtest.	12 to 17 years, 11 months
The Word Test 2: Elementary (WORD: 2-Elementary)	Bowers, L., Huisingh, R., LoGiudice, C., & Orman, J. (2004). East Moline, IL: LinguiSystems.	This curriculum-based language test examines students' grasp of the relationship among words and how effectively students store, recall, and use vocabulary. Subtests include associations, synonyms, antonyms, definitions, semantic absurdities, and flexible word use (multiple meanings). Raw scores can be converted to age equivalencies, percentile ranks, and standard scores for each subtest and the total test.	7 to 11 years, 11 months

*The sensitivity and specificity data summarized in this table are based on Spaulding, Plante, and Farinella, 2006.

table E Selected Materials for Assessment and Intervention of Auditory and Motor Skills

Test	Author/Publisher	Description	Age Range
Developmental Approach to Successful Listening (DASL II)	Goldberg Stout, G., & Van Ert Windle, J. Englewood, CA: Resource Point.	The DASL II is a sequential listening criterion-referenced curriculum focused on a hierarchy of listening skills in three sections: sound awareness, phonetic listening, and auditory comprehension.	Not specified
Early Listening Function (ELF)	Anderson, K. L. Available online at Phonak.com.	The ELF is an observation tool that parents/caregivers can use to monitor their young children's auditory development. It can be downloaded from www.phonak.com/com_elf_questionnaire_gb.pdf.	Infants and toddlers
Early Motor Control Scales (EMCS)	Hayden, D. A., Wetherby, A. M., Cleary, J. E., & Prizant, B. M. (2008). Baltimore: Paul H. Brookes.	This norm-referenced communication assessment is a tool that measures young children's motor control to identify impairments that may lead to a speech delay or disorder. Observation data are based on a 15–20 minute sample with caregiver interacting with toys to assess arm and hand control, motor speech control, and abnormal structure/function.	8 to 24 months (up to 72 months for children with atypical speech, motor, or cognitive development)
Early Speech Perception Test for Profoundly Hearing-Impaired Children	Moog, J. S., & Geers, A. E. St. Louis: Central Institute for the Deaf.	This text uses a picture pointing task to examine children's speech perception abilities according to four categories: no pattern perception, pattern perception, some word identification, and consistent word identification. It allows for vocabulary learning with items before being required to identify the pictures through audition alone. Results can be used to assist in developing auditory training objectives, to assess progress in auditory training, and to measure amplification effectiveness. It is not valid for children who use tactile aids or cochlear implants.	Not specified (but vocabulary tested is known by most children D/HH by age 6)
Functional Auditory Performance Indicators: An Integrated Approach to Auditory Development	Stredler-Brown, A., & Deconde-Johnson, C. American Academy of Audiology.	This criterion referenced assessment scale examines seven categories of auditory development: sound awareness, sound is meaningful, auditory feedback, localizing sound source, auditory discrimination, short-term auditory memory, and linguistic auditory processing. The examiner rates the child's skills as E = emerging (0–35%), P = in progress (36–79%), or A = acquired (80–100%) in a variety of conditions. For example the examiner can measure responses to auditory stimuli paired with visual cues versus auditory stimulus alone or while in close proximity to the child versus far away.	Not specified
Grammatical Analysis of Elicited Language, Pre-Sentence Level (GAEL-P)	Moog, J. S., Kozak, V. J., & Geers, A. E. St. Louis: Central Institute for the Deaf.	The GAEL-P uses standardized, structured play and pictures to elicit language specific to three areas: readiness skills, single words, and word combinations. It can be administered in spoken or signed English.	3 to 6 years

Test	Author/Publisher	Description	Age Range
HELP for Special Preschoolers, Assessment and Curriculum Guide	Santa Cruz County Office of Education. Palo Alto, CA: VORT Corporation.	This checklist includes developmental criteria to assess (through observation, play interaction, and parent interview) the areas of self help, motor, communication, social, and cognitive skills. The goal is to identify whether or not a child possesses various skills. The communication portion of the assessment includes developmental criteria related to auditory perception/listening, receptive language, expressive language, sign language, and speech reading.	3 to 6 years
INSITE Developmental Checklist	Watkins, S., & Morgan, E. North Logan, UT: HOPE.	This checklist was developed for use with D/HH children who have multiple disabilities. It contains information regarding milestone behaviors and is designed to be used in combination with the INSITE curriculum. The checklist covers nine developmental areas: communication, audition, vision, cognition, gross motor, fine motor, self-help, social–emotional development, and taction. There is a short version of this checklist that can be used to assess children 0 to 2 years and a longer version for children 0 to 6 years.	Birth to 6 years
Listening Skills Scale for Kids with Cochlear Implants (LSSKCI)	Phillips, A. L., Erber, N., Edward, C., & Estabrooks, W.	The LSSKCI uses a parent questionnaire format to assess the child's listening behaviors in four different levels: preverbal, verbal, comprehension, and figure ground.	Not specified
MacArthur-Bates Communicative Developmental Inventory (Sign Language Adaptation)	Fenson, L., Dale, P. S., Reznick, J. S., Thal, D., Bates, E., Hartung, J. P., Pethick, S., Reilly, J. S. Baltimore: Paul H. Brookes. Words, Gestures, and Sentences sections adapted by Allison Sedey for children who use sign language.	These questionnaires ask parents to identify words that their child either says or signs. It includes vocabulary relating to things in the home, people, action words, description words, pronouns, prepositions, and question words. It also asks about sentences and grammar.	Words and Gestures: Birth to 16 months Words and Sentences: 16 to 30 months Sentences and Phrases: 30 months and up
Minnesota Child Development Inventory (adapted at Gallaudet University for D/HH children)	Ireton, H., & Thwing, E. Minneapolis, MN: Behavior Science Systems.	This caregiver questionnaire asks parents to rate whether or not their child performs activities in areas such as language development, fine and gross motor development, and play behaviors.	9 months to 6 years

(continued)

table *E*   Continued

Test	Author/Publisher	Description	Age Range
SKI-HI Language Development Scale	Watkins, S. North Logan, UT: HOPE.	This parent rating scale assesses receptive and expressive language ability by asking parents to observe whether their children exhibit the behaviors listed on the scale. From birth to 2 years, skills are listed in two-month intervals; from 2 to 4 years skills are listed in four-month intervals; and from 4 to 5 years skills are listed in six-month intervals.	Birth to 5 years
SKI-HI Communication Interaction (SKI-HI Resource Manual)	Watkins, S. (Ed.). North Logan, UT: HOPE.	This test uses a checklist and data record forms to help parent and facilitator observe and record interaction between the parent and child regarding vocal and nonvocal utterances, verbal and nonverbal communication, and verbal and nonverbal skills of the parent.	Not specified

table *F* Selected Formal Tests for Diagnosing Autism Spectrum Disorders

Test	Author/Year/Publisher	Description	Age Range
Autism Diagnostic Observation Schedule-Generic (ADOS-G)	Lord, C., Rutter, M., DiLavore, P. C., & Risi, S. (1999). Los Angeles: Western Psychological Services.	The ADOS-G is a semistructured, standardized observation tool with strong psychometric properties. It is designed to probe communication, social interaction, and play. Four modules are used, depending on expressive language level.	2 to 5 years
Childhood Autism Rating Scale (CARS)	Schopler, E., Reichler, R. J., & Renner, B. R. (2002). Austin, TX: Pro-Ed.	The CARS uses structured observation and parent interview to differentiate children with autism from children without autism but with other forms of intellectual disability. It probes many areas of communication, sensation, intellectual functioning, and relating to people.	24 months and older
Communication and Symbolic Behavior Scales Developmental Profile (CSBS-DP)	Wetherby, A., & Prizant, B. (2002). Baltimore: Paul H. Brookes.	This norm-referenced assessment tool uses a rating scale for language and symbolic development. It is based on an infant and toddler checklist, caregiver questionnaire, and behavior sample (gestures, facial expressions, and play behaviors). A profile is built of the child's social, speech, and symbolic abilities.	6 to 24 months (functional communication age) 9 months to 6 years (atypical development)
Gilliam Asperger's Disorder Scale (GADS)	Gilliam, J. E. (2001). Austin, TX: Pro-Ed.	Parents, teachers, and practitioners (after sustained contact for at least two weeks) use this scale to rate behaviors to identify difficulties in the areas of social interaction, restricted patterns of behavior, cognitive patterns, and pragmatic skills. It includes an optional scale for rating early development and shows good discrimination accuracy for Asperger syndrome.	3 to 22 years
Gilliam Autism Rating Scale (GARS)	Gilliam, J. E. (1995). San Antonio, TX: Pro-Ed.	This scale uses a checklist completed by parents, teachers, and practitioners to identify symptoms and rate severity in the areas of stereotyped behaviors, communication, social interaction, and developmental disorders.	3 to 22 years
Modified Checklist for Autism in Toddlers (M-CHAT)	Robins, D. L., Fein, D., Barton, M. L., & Green, A. J. (2001). *Journal of Autism and Developmental Disorders, 31*(2), 131–144.	This checklist is completed by parents at a visit to the pediatrician. It probes areas of pretend play, social relatedness, communication, and sensory and motor function. The modified version resulted in improved psychometric properties over the original CHAT.	18 months

table G Developmental Sentence Scoring (DSS) Criteria

	Indefinite Pronouns or Noun Modifiers	Personal Pronouns	Main Verbs	Secondary Verbs
1	it, this, that	1st and 2nd person: I, me, my, mine, you, your(s)	A. Uninflected verb: I <u>see</u> you. B. copula, is, or 's: <u>It's</u> red. C. is + verb + ing: He <u>is</u> <u>coming</u>.	
2		3rd person: he, him, his, she, her, hers	A. -s and -ed: <u>plays</u>, <u>played</u> B. Irregular past: <u>ate</u>, <u>saw</u> C. Copula: <u>am</u>, <u>are</u>, <u>was</u>, <u>were</u> D. Auxiliary <u>am</u>, <u>are</u>, <u>was</u>, <u>were</u>	Five early-developing infinitives I wan<u>na</u> <u>see</u> (want <u>to</u> <u>see</u>) I'm gon<u>na</u> <u>see</u> (going <u>to</u> <u>see</u>) I got<u>ta</u> <u>see</u> (got <u>to</u> <u>see</u>) Lem<u>me</u> [to] see (let me [<u>to</u>] see) Let's [to] play (let [us <u>to</u>] <u>play</u>)
3	A. no, some, more, all, lot(s), one(s), two (etc.), other(s), another B. something, somebody, someone	A. Plurals: we, us, our(s), they, them, their B. these, those		Non-complementing infinitive: I stopped <u>to</u> <u>play</u>. I'm afraid <u>to</u> <u>look</u>. It's hard <u>to</u> <u>do</u> that.
4	nothing, nobody, none, no one		A. can, will, may + verb: <u>may go</u> B. Obligatory do + verb: <u>don't go</u> C. Emphatic do + verb: I <u>do</u> <u>see</u>.	Participle, present or past: I see a boy <u>running</u>. I found the toy <u>broken</u>.
5		Reflexives: myself, yourself, himself, herself, itself, themselves		A. Early infinitival complements with differing subjects in kernels: I want you to <u>come</u>. Let him [<u>to</u>] <u>see</u>. B. Later infinitival complements: I had <u>to</u> <u>go</u>. I told him <u>to go</u>. I tried <u>to go</u>. He ought <u>to go</u>. C. Obligatory deletions: Make it [<u>to</u>] <u>go</u>. I'd better [<u>to</u>] <u>go</u>. D. Infinitive with *wh*- word: I know what <u>to get</u>. I know how <u>to do</u> it.

6		A. *Wh*- pronouns: who, which, whose, whom, what, that, how many, how much
		    I know <u>who</u> came.
		    That's <u>what</u> I said.
		B. *Wh*- word + infinitive:
		    I know <u>what</u> to do.
		    I know <u>who(m)</u> to take.
			A. could, would, should, might + verb: <u>might come</u>, <u>could be</u>
			B. Obligatory does, did + verb
			C. Emphatic does, did + verb	

	Negatives	Conjunctions	Interrogative Reversals	*Wh-* Questions
1	it, this, that + copula, or auxiliary is 's, + not: It's <u>not</u> mine. This is <u>not</u> a dog. That is <u>not</u> moving.		Reversal of copula: <u>Isn't</u> <u>it</u> red? <u>Were</u> <u>they</u> there?	
2				A. who, what, what + noun: <u>Who</u> am I? <u>What</u> is he eating? <u>What</u> <u>book</u> are you reading? B. where, how many, how much, what . . . do, what . . . for <u>Where</u> did it go? <u>How</u> <u>much</u> do you want? <u>What</u> is he <u>doing</u>? <u>What</u> is a hammer <u>for</u>?
3		and		
4	can't, don't		Reversal of auxiliary be: <u>Is</u> <u>he</u> coming? <u>Isn't</u> <u>he</u> coming? <u>Was</u> <u>he</u> going? <u>Wasn't</u> <u>he</u> going?	
5	isn't, won't	A. but B. so, and so, so that C. or, if		when, how, how + adjective: <u>When</u> shall I come? <u>How</u> do you do it? <u>How</u> <u>big</u> is it?
6		because	A. Obligatory do, does, did: <u>Do</u> <u>they</u> run? <u>Does</u> <u>it</u> bite? <u>Didn't</u> <u>it</u> hurt? B. Reversal of modal: <u>Can</u> <u>you</u> play? <u>Won't</u> <u>it</u> hurt? <u>Shall</u> <u>I</u> sit down? C. Tag question: It's fun, <u>isn't</u> <u>it</u>? It isn't fun, <u>is</u> <u>it</u>?	

(continued)

table *G* Continued

	Indefinite Pronouns or Noun Modifiers	Personal Pronouns	Main Verbs	Secondary Verbs

7	A. any, anything, anybody, anyone
	B. every, everything, everybody, everyone
	C. both, few, many, each, several, most, least, much, next, first, last, second (etc.)
		(his) own, one, oneself, whichever, whoever, whatever:
		  Take <u>whatever</u> you like.
			A. Passive with <u>get</u>, any tense
			  Passive with <u>be</u>, any tense
			B. must, shall + verb: must come
			C. have + verb + en: <u>I've</u> <u>eaten</u>
			D. have got: <u>I've</u> <u>got</u> it.
				Passive infinitival complement:
				With <u>get</u>:
				  I have <u>to</u> <u>get</u> <u>dressed</u>.
				  I don't want <u>to</u> <u>get</u> <u>hurt</u>.
				With <u>be</u>:
				  I want <u>to</u> <u>be</u> <u>pulled</u>.
				  It's going <u>to</u> <u>be</u> <u>locked</u>.

8			A. have been + verb + ing
			  had been + verb + ing
			B. modal + have + verb + en: <u>may</u> <u>have</u> <u>eaten</u>
			C. modal + be + verb + ing: <u>could</u> <u>be</u> <u>playing</u>
			D. Other auxiliary combinations: <u>should</u> <u>have</u> <u>been</u> <u>sleeping</u>
				Gerund:
				  <u>Swinging</u> is fun.
				  I like <u>fishing</u>.
				  He started <u>laughing</u>.

	Negatives	Conjunctions	Interrogative Reversals	*Wh-* Questions

7	All other negatives:
	A. Uncontracted negatives:
	    I can <u>not</u> go.
	    He has <u>not</u> gone.
	B. Pronoun-auxiliary
	  or pronoun-copula
	  contraction:
	    I'm <u>not</u> coming.
	    He's <u>not</u> here.
	C. Auxiliary-negative
	  or copula-negative
	  contraction:
	    He was<u>n't</u> going.
	    He has<u>n't</u> been seen.
	    It could<u>n't</u> be mine.
	    They are<u>n't</u> big
				why, what if, how come, how about + gerund:
				<u>Why</u> are you crying?
				<u>What</u> <u>if</u> I won't do it?
				<u>How</u> <u>come</u> he is crying?
				<u>How</u> <u>about</u> coming with me?

8		A. where, when, how
		  while, whether (or not),
		  till, until, unless, since,
		  before, after, for, as +
		  adjective + as, as if,
		  like, that, than:
		    I know <u>where</u> you are.
		    Don't come <u>till</u> I call.
		B. Obligatory deletions:
		    I run faster <u>than</u> you
		    [run].
		    I'm <u>as</u> <u>big</u> <u>as</u> a man
		    [is big].
		    It looks <u>like</u> a dog
		    [looks].
		C. Elliptical deletions
		  (score 0):
		    That's <u>why</u> [I took it].
		    I know <u>how</u> [I can
		    do it].
		D. *Wh-* words + infinitive:
		    I know <u>how</u> to do it.
		    I know <u>where</u> to go.
			A. Reversal of auxiliary
			  have:
			    <u>Has</u> <u>he</u> seen you?
			B. Reversal with two or
			  three auxiliaries:
			    <u>Has</u> <u>he</u> <u>been</u> eating?
			    <u>Couldn't</u> <u>he</u> <u>have</u>
			    waited?
			    <u>Could</u> <u>he</u> <u>have</u> <u>been</u>
			    crying?
			    <u>Wouldn't</u> <u>he</u> <u>have</u> <u>been</u>
			    going?
				whose, which, which + noun:
				<u>Whose</u> car is that?
				<u>Which</u> <u>book</u> do you want?

Source: From Lee, Laura Louise. *Developmental sentence analysis: A grammatical assessment procedure for speech and language clinicians.* (p. 67) Evanston, IL: Northwestern University Press. Copyright 1974 by Northwestern University Press. Reprinted by permission of the publisher.

table *H* Black English Sentence Scoring (BESS) Criteria

	Indefinite Pronouns or Noun Modifiers	Personal Pronouns	Primary Verbs	Secondary Verbs
1	• these/this: <u>these</u> many.	• mine's/my, you/your: That <u>you</u> book? • y'all (plural <u>you</u>) • me/I (in compound subj.): Me and my brother went in it.	• θ copula <u>is</u>, <u>am</u>, <u>are</u>: That boy my friend. Or hypercorrect: I'm is six. • θ aux <u>be</u> + Ving: The girl singin'. • locational <u>go</u> or existential <u>it's</u>: Here <u>goes</u> the dog. <u>It's</u> two dimes stuck on the table. • got as uninflected <u>have</u>: You gotta take it home.	
2		• he, she (in apposition): My brother, <u>he</u> bigger than you. • they/he: They my uncle. • he, he's/his: He's name is Terry. • she, she's/her	• third person singular and regular past tense markers deleted. It <u>go</u> fast. • have/has: It have money on it. • Regularization of -s and -ed: Trudy and my sister hides. • Aux was/were: We <u>was</u> gon' rob some money. • Irreg. past tense—Uninflected: He <u>find</u> the money; Past form as participle: We <u>have</u> went; Participle as past form: He <u>done</u> it first.	• I'm, I'mon, I'ma pronunciation of I'm gonna + V: I'm play. I'ma be tired. • go pronunciation of gonna: His nose go bleed. • fixin' to (used like gonna): I'm fixin' to take him to jail. (sometimes pronounced as /f^tə/)
3	• <u>no</u> (when 2nd or 3rd neg. marker): He don't like me <u>no</u> more.	• we, they (in apposition): The boys, <u>they</u> get in trouble. • they/their: <u>They</u> name is Tanya and Brian. • them/they or their: I know what <u>them</u> is. One of 'em name is Caesar. • them/those: <u>them</u> kids.		
4	• nothing, nobody, none, no one (when 2nd or 3rd neg. marker): Ain't nobody got none.		• θ modal <u>will</u> or '<u>ll</u>: I be five when my birthday come. • don't + verb (3rd pers. sing.): My mama, she don't like it. • *do* uninflected: <u>Do</u> he still have it? (Score inc. in My sister <u>do</u>.) • θ <u>do</u> in questions: You still have it? • ain't (as copula or aux): Ain't no dirt in it. Nobody ain't got no more. • can't, don't, won't as preposed neg. aux.: Can't nobody do it. • could/can: He could climb that tree.	• participle with deleted -*en*: She has a state name Tennessee. (phonological cluster reduction rule) • I found the toy broke. (morphological difference)
5		• personal datives, me, him, her: I'm gonna buy <u>me</u> some candy. He make <u>him</u> a lot of 'em. • reflexives: hisself, theirselves, themself, theyselves		• deleted <u>to</u> in infinitival complements: My grandma tell me stay away from him. I like go shopping. My mommy used do it.

	Negatives	Conjunctions	Interrogative Reversal	*Wh-* Questions
1	• it, this, that + θ copula/aux + not/ain't: That <u>not</u> mine. It <u>ain't</u> on?		• rising intonation with deleted or unreversed copula: You my friend? Where the gas at? What that is? • is/are: Derrick, is you?	
2				• who, what, what + noun (with deleted aux or copula) • where, how many, how much, what . . . do, what . . . for (with deleted aux or copula): Where the man? • *Wh-* questions formed without interrogative reversal: What that is?
3		• and plus • θ and (when intonation makes sentence combination clear): *He pointed his finger at him* (with rising intonation); *he pointed his finger at him* (with falling intonation).		
4	• don't (with 3rd pers. sing. as 2nd or 3rd neg. marker): He <u>don't</u> want none. No, nobody <u>don't</u> live with me. • can't, don't (as preposed aux): Can't nobody make me. • θ copula/aux + not + V: My mama <u>not</u> gonna pick me up today. He <u>not</u> a baby. • ain't (as negative copula or aux. <u>be</u>): He <u>ain't</u> my friend.		• θ auxiliary be: My voice gonna come out of here? You gonna tell my mama? • was/were: Was you throwin' rocks?	
5	• won't (as preposed aux): <u>Won't</u> nobody help him.	• for/so: The dog make too much noise for they won't catch many fish. • conditional <u>and</u>: You do that <u>and</u> I'm gonna smack you. • <u>if</u> with phrase deletions: He lookin' if he see the money. • aux. inversion in indirect questions (instead of <u>if</u>): She ask me do he want some more.		• when, how (with deleted aux, copula or do): How you do this?

(continued)

table *H*   Continued

	Indefinite Pronouns or Noun Modifiers	Personal Pronouns	Primary Verbs	Secondary Verbs
6		• what (in apposition): My voice gonna come out of here <u>what</u> I said on that book? • what/that or who: He's the one <u>what</u> I told you about. • Deleted relative pronoun: I saw a little girl was on the street.	• did + nt + verb (when 2nd or 3rd neg. marker: Nobody didn't do it. • could, would, should + nt + verb (preposed neg. aux): Couldn't nobody do it. • θ contracted could or would (phonol. deletions): You('d) burn your head off. • might/will: Who might be the baby?	
7	• many a: <u>Many</u> a people likes to give him a nickel.		• passive verb + en with <u>getting</u> (aux deleted): Leroy <u>getting</u> dressed. • passive verb ± be ± en: One is name Brick. They named Chief and JoJo. • done + verb + en (completive aspect): I <u>done</u> <u>tried</u>. • ± (neg.) aux + supposed: He don't supposed to do it. What toy you supposed to play with? • ± have ± verb ± en: We seen him already. He have made him mad.	• passive with phonological deletions: I'm be dressed up real cute. I'ma be tired. She gonna be surprise, ain't she? I want it cut on.
8			• invariant <u>be</u>: My daddy know I skip school 'cause I be home with him. He be mad when somebody leave him home. • double modals: We might could come. • other expanded aux. forms: He be done jumped out the tub. He been going. (<u>have</u> has undergone phonological deletion) You shouldn't did that. • remote past aspect: She been whuptin' the baby. I been wanted this.	• gerund with <u>go to</u>, <u>got to</u>, <u>start to</u>: When I cry, she goes to whipping me. He started to crying. He got to thinking.

	Negatives	Conjunctions	Interrogative Reversal	*Wh-* Questions
6		• or either, or neither (as disjunctives): He will go <u>or either</u> he will stay. He told her that he wouldn't be bad <u>or neither</u> get in trouble. • preposed why phrase (with because): Why he's in here, cause baby scared the dog.	• θ do: You know that one with the tractor? Where you work? You got blue eyes? • do (with 3rd pers. sing.) Do he still have it? • θ or unreversed modal: Now, what else I be doin? Why you can't talk on that? • Tag question with ain't: It gonna be fun, ain't it?	
7	• ain't (for have + not) ± uninflected V: I <u>ain't</u> taste any. • ain't (for did + not) ± uninflected V: Yesterday, he <u>ain't</u> go to school. I ain't found Marge in the school. • couldn't, wouldn't, shouldn't (as preposed aux). • wasn't/weren't: The brakes wasn't workin' right. • weren't/wasn't: There weren't no money. • uncontracted, uninflected neg. aux.: Lester <u>do</u> <u>not</u> like it.			• why, what if, how come (with deleted or unreversed aux, copula or do, or with got): <u>Why</u> she turn that way? Hey, why you got a dress on mama?
8		• less'n (for unless) • to/till: I didn't get to sleep to I had to come in the morning. • ± as + adjective + as: He sock Leroy in the arm hard as he could.	• deleted have: He seen it? How you been? What you been doing? • have with 3rd pers. sing.: Have he seen you?	• whose, which, which + noun (with deleted aux, copula or do) • who/whose: Who this bed? Who baby is that?

Source: From *Black English Sentence Scoring: Development and Use as a Tool for Nonbiased Assessment* by N. W. Nelson and Y. D. Hyter, 1990, unpublished manuscript, Western Michigan University, Kalamazoo. Copyright 1990 by N. W. Nelson. Reprinted by permission.

References

Abbeduto, L., & Murphy, M. M. (2004). Language, social cognition, maladaptive behavior, and communication in Down syndrome and fragile X syndrome. In M. L. Rice & S. F. Warren (Eds.), *Developmental language disorders: From phenotypes to etiologies* (pp. 77–97). Mahwah, NJ: Lawrence Erlbaum.

Adams, M. J. (2002). Alphabetic anxiety and explicit, systematic phonics instruction: A cognitive science perspective. In S. B. Neuman & D. K. Dickinson (Eds.), *Handbook of early literacy research* (pp. 66–80). New York: Guilford Press.

Adamson, L. B., & Chance, S. E. (1998). Coordinating attention to people, objects, and language. In A. M. Wetherby, S. F. Warren, & J. Reichle (Eds.), *Transitions in prelinguistic communication* (pp. 15–37) Baltimore: Paul H. Brookes.

Administration on Children, Youth, and Families (ACYF). (2006). *Child maltreatment 2005.* Washington, DC: U.S. Department of Health and Human Services. Retrieved August 6, 2007, from www.acf.hhs.gov/programs/cb/pubs/cm05/cm05.pdf

Agocs, M. M., Burns, M. S., De Ley, L. E., Miller, S. L., & Calhoun, B. M. (2006). Fast ForWord language. In R. J. McCauley & M. E. Fey (Eds.), *Treatment of language disorders in children* (pp. 471–508). Baltimore: Paul H. Brookes.

Allington, R. L. (1980). Teacher interruption behaviors during primary grade oral reading. *Journal of Educational Psychology, 72,* 371–377.

Als, H., & Gilkerson, L. (1995). Developmentally supportive care in the neonatal intensive care unit. *Zero to Three, 15*(6), 1–10.

Als, H., Lester, B. M., Tronick, E., & Brazelton, T. B. (1982). Toward a research instrument for the assessment of preterm infants' behavior (APIB). In H. E. Fitzgerald, B. M. Lester, & M. W. Yogman (Eds.), *Theory and research in behavioral pediatrics* (Vol. 1, pp. 35–132). New York: Plenum Press.

American Association of Mental Retardation (AAMR). (2006). World's oldest organization on intellectual disability has a progressive new name. Press release from AAMR. Retrieved March 11, 2007, from www.aaidd.org/About_AAIDD/name_change_PRdreen.htm

American Foundation for the Blind. (2007). Key definitions of statistical terms. Retrieved January 1, 2008, from www.afb.org/Section.asp?SectionID=15&DocumentID=1280

American Printing House for the Blind. (1987). *Patterns prebraille program: Teacher's manual.* Louisville, KY: Author.

American Psychiatric Association (APA). (1980). *Diagnostic and statistical manual of mental disorders* (3rd ed.). Washington, DC: Author.

American Psychiatric Association (APA). (1994). *Diagnostic and statistical manual of mental disorders* (4th ed.). Washington, DC: Author.

American Psychiatric Association (APA). (2000). *Diagnostic and statistical manual of mental disorders* (text revision). Washington, DC: Author.

American Speech-Language-Hearing Association (ASHA). (1982). *Language* [Relevant paper]. Retrieved January 1, 2008, from www.asha.org/policy

American Speech-Language-Hearing Association (ASHA). (1993). *Definitions of communication disorders and variations* [Relevant paper]. Retrieved October 20, 2007, from www.asha.org/policy

American Speech-Language-Hearing Association (ASHA). (2004). *Roles of speech-language pathologists in the neonatal intensive care unit* [Position statement]. Retrieved October 20, 2007, from www.asha.org/policy

American Speech-Language-Hearing Association (ASHA). (2005a). *(Central) auditory processing disorders: The role of the audiologist* [Position statement]. Retrieved October 20, 2007, from www.asha.org/policy

American Speech-Language-Hearing Association (ASHA). (2005b). *Evidence-based practice in communication disorders* [Position statement]. Retrieved October 20, 2007, from www.asha.org/members/deskref-journals

American Speech-Language-Hearing Association (ASHA). (2007a). *Membership profile.* Retrieved December 3, 2007, from www.asha.org/about/membership-certification/member-data/member-counts.htm

American Speech-Language-Hearing Association (ASHA). (2007b). *Advocacy materials.* Retrieved May 31, 2007, from www.asha.org

Andersen, E. S., Dunlea, A., & Kekelis, L. S. (1984). Blind children's language: Resolving some differences. *Journal of Child Language, 11,* 645–664.

Anderson, G., & Nelson, N. (1988). Integrating language intervention and education in an alternate adolescent language classroom. *Seminars in Speech and Language, 9,* 341–352.

Anderson, M. (2007). *Tales from the table: Lovaas/ABA intervention with children on the autistic spectrum.* London: Jessica Kingsley.

Anderson, R. C., & Freebody, P. (1981). Vocabulary knowledge. In J. Guthrie (Ed.), *Comprehension and teaching: Research reviews* (pp. 77–117). Newark, DE: International Reading Association.

Angelman Syndrome Foundation. (n.d.). Angelman Syndrome Foundation website. Retrieved January 30, 2007, from www.angelman.org/angel

Anglin, J. M. (1993). Vocabulary development: A morphological analysis. *Monographs of the Society for Research in Child Development, 58*(10, Serial No. 238).

Apel, K. (2001). Developing evidenced-based practices and research collaborations in school settings. *Language, Speech, and Hearing Services in Schools, 32,* 149–152.

Apel, K., & Masterson, J. J. (2001a). *Beyond baby talk: From sounds to sentences—A parent's complete guide to language development.* Rockville, MD: American Speech-Language-Hearing Association.

Apel, K., & Masterson, J. J. (2001b). Theory-guided spelling assessment and intervention: A case study. *Language, Speech, and Hearing Services in Schools, 32,* 182–195.

Apel, K., Masterson, J. J., & Hart, P. (2004). Integration of language components in spelling: Instruction that maximizes students' learning. In E. R. Silliman & L. C. Wilkinson (Eds.), *Language and literacy learning in schools* (pp. 292–315). New York: Guilford Press.

Apel, K., Masterson, J. J., & Niessen, N. L. (2004). Spelling assessment frameworks. In A. Stone, E. R. Silliman, B. Ehren, & K. Apel (Eds.), *Handbook of language and literacy: Development and disorders* (pp. 644–660). New York: Guilford Press.

Applebee, A. N. (1978). *The child's concept of story*. Chicago: University of Chicago Press.

Aram, D. M. (1988). Language sequelae of unilateral brain lesions in children. In F. Plum (Ed.), *Language, communication, and the brain* (pp. 171–197). New York: Raven Press.

Aram, D. M. (1997). Hyperlexia: Reading without meaning in young children. *Topics in Language Disorders, 17*(3), 1–13.

Aram, D. M., & Ekelman, B. L. (1988). Scholastic aptitude and achievement among children with unilateral brain lesions. *Neuropsychologia, 26,* 903–916.

Aram, D. M., Ekelman, B. L., & Gillespie, L. L. (1989). Reading and unilateral brain lesions in children. In K. von Euler, I. Lundberg, & G. Lennerstrand (Eds.), *Brain and reading* (pp. 61–75). Hampshire, England: MacMillan Press.

Aram, D. M., Ekelman, B. L., & Nation, J. E. (1984). Preschoolers with language disorders: 10 years later. *Journal of Speech and Hearing Research, 27,* 232–244.

Aram, D. M., Hack, M., Hawkins, S., Weissman, B. M., & Borawski-Clark, E. (1991). Very-low-birthweight children and speech and language development. *Journal of Speech and Hearing Research, 34,* 1169–1179.

Aram, D. M., & Healy, J. M. (1988). Hyperlexia: A review of extraordinary word recognition. In L. K. Obler & D. Fein (Eds.), *The exceptional brain: Neuropsychology of talent and special abilities* (pp. 70–102). New York: Guilford Press.

Aram, D. M., & Nation, J. (1975). Patterns of language behavior in children with developmental language disorders. *Journal of Speech and Hearing Research, 18,* 229–241.

Aram, D. M., & Nation, J. (1980). Preschool language disorders and subsequent language and academic difficulties. *Journal of Communication Disorders, 13,* 159–170.

Archibald, L. M. D., & Gathercole, S. E. (2006). Short-term and working memory in specific language impairment. *International Journal of Language and Communication Disorders, 41*(6), 675–693.

Atchison, B. J. (2007). Sensory modulation disorders among children with a history of trauma: A frame of reference for speech-language pathologists. *Language, Speech, and Hearing Services in Schools, 38,* 109–116.

Attwood, T. (2007). *The complete guide to Asperger's syndrome*. London: Jessica Kingsley.

Au, K. H. (1980). Participation structures in a reading lesson with Hawaiian children: Analysis of a culturally appropriate instructional event. *Anthropology and Education Quarterly, 11*(2), 91–115.

August, D., Snow, C., Carlo, M., Proctor, D. P., Rolla de San Francisco, A., Duursma, E., & Szuber, A. (2006). Literacy development in elementary school second-language learners. *Topics in Language Disorders, 26*(4), 351–364.

Austin, J. (1962). *How to do things with words*. London: Oxford University Press.

Autism Society of America. (2007). *Improving the lives of all affected by autism*. Retrieved August 12, 2007, from www.autism-society.org/site/PageServer

Aydelott, J., Kutas, M., & Federmeier, K. D. (2005). Perceptual and attentional factors in language comprehension: A domain-general approach. In M. Tomasello & D. I. Slobin (Eds.), *Beyond nature-nurture: Essays in honor of Elizabeth Bates* (pp. 281–315). Mahwah, NJ: Lawrence Erlbaum.

Aylward, E. H., Richards, T. L., Berninger, V. W., Nagy, W. E., Field, K. M., Grimme, C., Richards, A. L., Thomson, J. B., & Cramer, S. C. (2003). Instructional treatment associated with changes in brain activation in children with dyslexia. *Neurology, 61*(2), 212–219.

Ayres, A. (1989). *Sensory integration and praxis tests*. Los Angeles: Western Psychological.

Baddeley, A. D. (2003). Working memory and language: An overview. *Journal of Communication Disorders, 36,* 189–208.

Baddeley, A. D., Gathercole, S., & Papagno, C. (1998). The phonological loop as a language learning device. *Psychological Review, 105,* 158–173.

Bahr, R. H. (2005). Differential diagnosis of severe speech disorders using speech gestures. *Topics in Language Disorders, 25,* 254–265.

Bailey, D. B., Roberts, J. E., Hooper, S. R., Hatton, D. D., Mirrett, P. L., Roberts, J. E., & Schaaf, J. M. (2004). Research on fragile X syndrome and autism: Implications for the study of genes, environments, and developmental language disorders. In M. L. Rice & S. F. Warren (Eds.), *Developmental language disorders: From phenotypes to etiologies* (pp. 121–150). Mahwah, NJ: Lawrence Erlbaum.

Bailey, D. B., & Simeonsson, R. J. (1988). Home-based early intervention. In S. L. Odom & M. B. Karnes (Eds.), *Early intervention for infants and children with handicaps* (pp. 199–215). Baltimore: Paul H. Brookes.

Bain, B. A., & Olswang, L. B. (1995). Examining readiness for learning two-word utterances by children with specific language impairment: Dynamic assessment validation. *American Journal of Speech-Language Pathology, 4*(1), 81–91.

Bandura, A. (1977). Self-efficacy: Toward a unifying theory of behavioral change. *Psychological Review, 84,* 191–215.

Barber, P. A., Turnbull, A. P., Behr, S. K., & Kerns, G. M. (1988). A family systems perspective on early childhood special education. In S. L. Odom & M. B. Karnes (Eds.), *Early intervention for infants and children with handicaps* (pp. 179–198). Baltimore: Paul H. Brookes.

Barbera, M. L. (2007). *The verbal behavior approach: How to teach children with autism and related disorders*. London: Jessica Kingsley.

Barbero, G. (1982). Failure-to-thrive. In M. H. Klaus, T. Leger, & M. A. Trause (Eds.), *Maternal attachment and mothering disorders (Pediatric Round Table: 1)* (pp. 3–6). Skillman, NJ: Johnson & Johnson.

Baron-Cohen, S. (1995). *Mindblindness: An essay on autism and theory of mind*. Cambridge, MA: MIT Press.

Barratt, J., Littlejohns, P., & Thompson, J. (1992). Trial of intensive compared with weekly speech therapy in preschool children. *Archives of Disease in Childhood, 67,* 106–108.

Bashir, A. S., & Singer, B. D. (2006). Assisting students in becoming self-regulated writers. In T. A. Ukrainetz (Ed.), *Contextualized language intervention: Scaffolding PreK–12 literacy achievement* (pp. 565–598). Eau Claire, WI: Thinking Publications.

Bates, E. (1976). *Language and context: Studies in the acquisition of pragmatics.* New York: Academic Press.

Bates, E., Benigni, L., Bretherton, I., Camaioni, L., & Volterra, V. (1979). *The emergence of symbols: Cognition and communication in infancy.* New York: Academic Press.

Bates, E., Camaioni, L., & Volterra, V. (1975). The acquisition of performatives prior to speech. *Merrill-Palmer Quarterly, 21,* 205–226.

Bates, E., & MacWhinney, B. (1987). Competition, variation, and language learning. In B. MacWhinney (Ed.), *Mechanisms of language acquisition* (pp. 157–194). Hillsdale, NJ: Lawrence Erlbaum.

Bateson, M. C. (1975). Mother–infant exchanges: The epigenesis of conversational interaction. *Annals of the New York Academy of Sciences, 263,* 101–113.

Batshaw, M. L. (2002). *Children with disabilities* (5th ed.). Baltimore: Paul H. Brookes.

Batshaw, M. L., & Shapiro, B. (2002). Mental retardation. In M. L. Batshaw (Ed.), *Children with disabilities* (5th ed., pp. 287–305). Baltimore: Paul H. Brookes.

Batshaw, M. L., & Tuchman, M. (2002). PKU and other inborn errors of metabolism. In M. L. Batshaw (Ed.), *Children with disabilities* (5th ed., pp. 333–345). Baltimore: Paul H. Brookes.

Baugh, J. (2000). *Beyond Ebonics: Linguistic pride and racial prejudice.* New York: Oxford University Press.

Baxendale, J., & Hesketh, A. (2003). Comparison of the effectiveness of the Hanen Parent Programme and traditional clinic therapy. *International Journal of Language and Communication Disorders, 38,* 397–415.

Bayley, N. (1969). *Bayley Scales of Infant Development.* New York: Psychological Corporation.

Bayley, N. (1993). *Bayley Scales of Infant Development II.* San Antonio, TX: Psychological Corporation.

Bear, D. R., Invernizzi, M., Templeton, S., & Johnson, F. (2000). *Words their way* (2nd ed.). Upper Saddle River, NJ: Merrill.

Beck, A. R., & Dennis, M. (1997). Speech-language pathologists' and teachers' perceptions of classroom-based interventions. *Language, Speech, and Hearing Services in Schools, 28,* 146–153.

Beck, I. L., & McKeown, M. (1991). Conditions of vocabulary acquisition. In R. Barr, M. Kamil, P. Mosenthal, & P. D. Pearson (Eds.), *Handbook of reading research* (Vol. 2, pp. 789–814). New York: Longman.

Beck, I. L., McKeown, M. G., Sandora, C., Kucan, L., & Worthy, J. (1996). Questioning the author: A year-long classroom implementation to engage students with text. *Elementary School Journal, 96,* 385–414.

Bedrosian, J., Lasker, J., Speidel, K., & Politsch, A. (2003). Enhancing the written narrative skills of an AAC student with autism: Evidence-based research issues. *Topics in Language Disorders, 23*(4), 305–324.

Beilinson, J. S., & Olswang, L. B. (2003). Facilitating peer-group entry in kindergartners with impairments in social communication. *Language Speech and Hearing Services in Schools, 34*(2), 154–166.

Beitchman, J. H., Nair, R., Clegg, M., & Patel, P. H. (1986). Prevalence of speech and language disorders in 5-year-old children in the Ottawa-Carleton region. *Journal of Speech and Hearing Disorders, 51,* 98–110.

Bennardo, G. (2003). Language, mind, and culture: From linguistic relativity to representational modularity. In M. T. Banich & M. Mack (Eds.), *Mind, brain, and language: Multidisciplinary perspectives* (pp. 23–59). Mahwah, NJ: Lawrence Erlbaum.

Bergen, D., & Mauer, D. (2000). Symbolic play, phonological awareness, and literacy skills at three age levels. In K. A. Roskos & J. F. Christie (Eds.), *Play and literacy in early childhood: Research from multiple perspectives* (pp. 45–62). Mahwah, NJ: Lawrence Erlbaum.

Bernhardt, B. H., Smith, D., & Smith, R. (1992). Language intervention with a "family-centered, collaborative, transdisciplinary, integrated" approach: An example. *Child Language Teaching and Therapy, 8*(3), 265–284.

Bernhardt, B. H., & Stemberger, J. P. (2000). *Workbook in nonlinear phonology for clinical application.* Austin, TX: Pro-Ed.

Bernhardt, B. H., & Stoel-Gammon, C. (1994). Nonlinear phonology: Introduction and clinical application. *Journal of Speech and Hearing Research, 37,* 123–143.

Berninger, V. W. (2000). Development of language by hand and its connection with language by ear, mouth, and eye. *Topics in Language Disorders, 20*(3), 65–84.

Bernstein, B. B. (1972). A critique of the concept of compensatory education. In C. B. Cazden, V. P. John, & D. Hymes (Eds.), *Functions of language in the classroom* (pp. 135–154). New York: Columbia University Teachers College Press.

Bernthal, J. E., & Bankson, N. W. (Eds.). (2004). *Articulation and phonological disorders* (5th ed.). Boston: Allyn & Bacon.

Bess, F. H., & Humes, L. E. (2003). *Audiology: The fundamentals* (3rd ed.). Baltimore: Lippincott Williams & Wilkins.

Betz, S. K., & Stoel-Gammon, C. (2005). Measuring articulatory error consistency in children with developmental apraxia of speech. *Clinical Linguistics and Phonetics, 19*(1), 53–66.

Beukelman, D. R. (1987). When you have a hammer, everything looks like a nail. *Augmentative and Alternative Communication, 3,* 94–96.

Beukelman, D. R., & Mirenda, P. (1992). *Augmentative and alternative communication: Management of severe communication disorders in children and adults.* Baltimore: Paul H. Brookes.

Beukelman, D. R., & Mirenda, P. (2005). *Augmentative and alternative communication: Supporting children and adults with complex communication needs* (3rd ed.). Baltimore: Paul H. Brookes.

Bialystok, E., & Hakuta, K. (1994). *In other words: The science and psychology of second-language acquisition.* New York: Basic Books.

Biber, D. (1988). *Variation across speech and writing.* Cambridge, MA: Cambridge University Press.

Bigelow, A. (1990). Relationship between the development of language and thought in young blind children. *Journal of Visual Impairment and Blindness, 84,* 414–419.

Bigelow, A. E., MacLean, K., & Proctor, J. (2004). The role of joint attention in the development of infants' play with objects. *Developmental Science, 7,* 518–526.

Biklen, D. (1999). The metaphor of mental retardation: Rethinking ability and disability. In H. Bersani, Jr. (Ed.), *Responding to the challenge: Current trends and international issues in developmental disabilities* (pp. 35–52). Cambridge, MA: Brookline.

Bishop, D. V. M. (1985). Age of onset and outcome in "acquired aphasia with convulsive disorder" (Landau-Kleffner syndrome). *Developmental Medicine and Child Neurology, 27*(6), 705–712.

Bishop, D. V. M. (2000). Pragmatic language impairment: A correlate of SLI, a distinct subgroup, or part of the autistic continuum? In D. V. M. Bishop & L. B. Leonard (Eds.), *Speech and language impairments in children: Causes, characteristics, intervention, and outcome* (pp. 99–113). East Sussex, England: Psychology Press.

Bishop, D. V. M., & Adams, C. (1989). Conversational characteristics of children with semantic-pragmatic disorder. 2. What features lead to a judgment of inappropriacy? *British Journal of Disorders of Communication, 24,* 241–263.

Bishop, D. V. M., & Adams, C. (1990). A prospective study of the relationship between specific language impairment, phonological disorders, and reading retardation. *Journal of Child Psychology and Psychiatry, 31,* 1027–1050.

Bishop, D. V. M., Byers Brown, B., & Robson, J. (1990). The relationship between phoneme discrimination, speech production and language comprehension in cerebral-palsied individuals. *Journal of Speech and Hearing Research, 33,* 210–219.

Bishop, D. V. M., & Edmundson, A. (1987). Language impaired 4-year-olds: Distinguishing transient from persistent impairment. *Journal of Speech and Hearing Disorders, 52,* 156–173.

Bishop, D. V. M., & Norbury, C. F. (2002). Exploring the borderlands of autistic disorder and specific language impairment: A study using standardized diagnostic instruments. *Journal of Child Psychology and Psychiatry and Allied Disciplines, 43,* 917–929.

Bishop, D. V. M., & Snowling, M. J. (2004). Developmental dyslexia and specific language impairment: Same or different? *Psychological Bulletin, 130,* 858–886.

Blachman, B. A. (1994). Early literacy acquisition: The role of phonological awareness. In G. P. Wallach & K. G. Butler (Eds.), *Language learning disabilities in school-age children and adolescents* (pp. 253–274). Boston: Allyn & Bacon.

Blachman, B. A., Schatschneider, C., Fletcher, J. M., Francis, D. J., Clonan, S. M., Shaywitz, B. A., et al. (2004). Effects of intensive reading remediation for second and third graders and a 1-year follow-up. *Journal of Educational Psychology, 96*(3), 444–461.

Blackstone, S. (1989). Life is not a dress rehearsal. *Augmentative Communication News, 2*(5), 1–2.

Bland, L. E., & Prelock, P. A. (1995). Effects of collaboration on language performance. *Journal of Children's Communication Development, 17*(2), 31–38.

Blank, M., Rose, S., & Berlin, L. (1978). *Preschool Language Assessment Instrument (PLAI).* Austin, TX: Pro-Ed.

Blischak, D. M. (1994). Phonological awareness: Implications for individuals with little or no functional speech. *Augmentative and Alternative Communication, 10,* 245–254.

Bliss, L. (1987). "I can't talk anymore; My mouth doesn't want to." The development and clinical applications of modal auxiliaries. *Language, Speech, and Hearing Services in Schools, 18,* 72–79.

Bliss, L., & McCabe, A. (2008). The clinical application of personal narratives for children with discourse impairments. *Topics in Language Disorders, 28*(2), 162–177.

Bloom, B. S. (1956). *Taxonomy of educational objectives. Handbook I: Cognitive domain.* New York: David McKay.

Bloom, L., & Lahey, M. (1978). *Language development and language disorders.* New York: John Wiley & Sons.

Blosser, J. L., & DePompei, R. (1994). *Pediatric traumatic brain injury.* San Diego, CA: Singular.

Boehm, A. E. (2001). *Boehm Test of Basic Concepts-Preschool* (3rd ed.) (BTBC-P3). San Antonio, TX: Harcourt.

Bogdashina, O. (2005). *Communication issues in autism and Asperger syndrome: Do we speak the same language?* London: Jessica Kingsley.

Bogdashina, O. (2006). *Theory of mind and the triad of perspectives on autism and Asperger syndrome.* London: Jessica Kingsley.

Bondy, A., & Frost, L. (1994). Picture Exchange Communication System (PECS). *Focus on Autistic Behavior, 9,* 1–19.

Bondy, A., & Frost, L. (1998). Picture Exchange Communication System (PECS). *Topics in Language Disorders, 19,* 373–390.

Boothroyd, A. (1982). *Hearing impairments in young children.* Englewood Cliffs, NJ: Prentice-Hall.

Botting, N., Simkin, Z., & Conti-Ramsden, G. (2006). Associated reading skills in children with a history of Specific Language Impairment (SLI). *Reading and Writing, 19,* 77–98.

Botvin, G. J., & Sutton-Smith, B. (1977). The development of structural complexity in children's fantasy narratives. *Developmental Psychology, 13,* 377–388.

Boudreau, D. (2008). Narrative abilities: Advances in research and implications for clinical practice. *Topics in Language Disorders, 28*(2), 99–114.

Bourassa, D. C., & Treiman, R. (2001). Spelling development and disabilities: The importance of linguistic factors. *Language, Speech, and Hearing Services in Schools, 32,* 172–181.

Boyd, F. B., & Brock, C. H. (Eds.). (2004). *Multicultural and multilingual literacy and language: Contexts and practices.* New York: Guilford Press.

Boyle, J., McCartney, E., Forbes, J., & O'Hare, A. (2007). A randomised controlled trial and economic evaluation of direct versus indirect and individual versus group modes of speech and language therapy for children with primary language impairment. *Health Technology Assessment, 11*(25), 1–158.

Bracken, B. A. (1998). *Bracken Basic Concept Scale-Revised* (BBCS-R). San Antonio, TX: Harcourt.

Bradshaw, M., Hoffman, P., & Norris, J. (1998). Efficacy of expansions and cloze procedures in the development of interpretations by preschool children exhibiting delayed language development. *Language, Speech, and Hearing Services in Schools, 29,* 85–95.

Bransford, J. D., Brown, A. L., & Cocking, R. R. (Eds.). (2000). *How people learn: Brain, mind, experience, and school* (Expanded ed.). Washington, DC: National Academy Press.

Brazelton, T. B. (1982). Mother-infant reciprocity. In M. H. Klaus, T. Leger, & M. A. Trause (Eds.), *Maternal attachment and mothering disorders (Pediatric Round Table: 1)* (pp. 49–54). Skillman, NJ: Johnson & Johnson.

Brazelton, T. B., Koslowski, B., & Main, M. (1974). The origins of reciprocity: The early mother-infant interaction. In L. M. Rosenblum (Ed.), *The effect of the infant on its caregiver.* New York: John Wiley & Sons.

Brenneis, D., & Lein, L. (1977). "You fruithead": A sociolinguistic approach to children's dispute settlement. In S. Ervin-Tripp

& C. Mitchell-Kernan (Eds.), *Child discourse* (pp. 49–65). New York: Academic Press.

Brinton, B., & Fujiki, M. (1989). *Conversational management with language-impaired children: Pragmatic assessment and intervention.* Rockville, MD: Aspen.

Brinton, B., & Fujiki, M. (2006). Improving peer interaction and learning in cooperative learning groups. In T. A. Ukrainetz (Ed.), *Contextualized language intervention: Scaffolding PreK–12 literacy achievement* (pp. 289–318). Eau Claire, WI: Thinking Publications.

Brinton, B., Fujiki, M., & McKee, L. (1998). The negotiation skills of children with specific language impairment. *Journal of Speech, Language, and Hearing Research, 41,* 927–940.

Brinton, B., Fujiki, M., & Robinson, L. A. (2005). Life on a tricycle: A case study of language impairment from 4 to 19. *Topics in Language Disorders, 25*(4), 338–352.

Brinton, B., Fujiki, M., Spencer, J. C., & Robinson, L. A. (1997). The ability of children with specific language impairment to access and participate in an ongoing interaction. *Journal of Speech, Language, and Hearing Research, 40,* 1011–1025.

Brinton, B., Robinson, L. A., & Fujiki, M. (2004). Description of a program for social language intervention: "If you can have a conversation, you can have a relationship." *Language, Speech, and Hearing Services in Schools, 35,* 283–290.

Brion-Meisels, S., & Selman, R. L. (1984). Early adolescent development of new interpersonal strategies: Understanding intervention. *School Psychology Review, 13,* 278–291.

Britton, J. N. (1984). Viewpoints: The distinction between participant and spectator role. *Research in the Teaching of English, 18*(3), 320–331.

Brown v. Board of Education, 347 U.S. 483 (1954).

Brown, C. (1994). Foundations in speech perception [Computer software]. Oakdale, IA: Breakthrough.

Brown, M. W. (1975). *Goodnight Moon.* New York: Harper Trophy.

Brown, R. (1973). *A first language: The early stages.* Boston: Harvard University Press.

Brownell, R. (Ed.). (2000a). *Expressive One-Word Picture Vocabulary Test-Revised (EOWPVT-R).* Novato, CA: Academic Therapy.

Brownell, R. (Ed.). (2000b). *Receptive One-Word Picture Vocabulary Test-Revised (ROWPVT-R).* Novato, CA: Academic Therapy.

Bruner, J. (1975). The ontogenesis of speech acts. *Journal of Child Language, 2,* 1–19.

Bruner, J. (1985). Narrative and paradigmatic modes of thought. In E. Eisner (Ed.), *Learning and teaching: The ways of knowing* (pp. 97–115). Chicago: University of Chicago Press.

Bruner, J. (1986). *Actual minds, possible worlds.* Cambridge, MA: Harvard University Press.

Bryan, T. (1986). A review of studies on learning disabled children's communicative competence. In R. L. Schiefelbusch (Ed.), *Language competence: Assessment and intervention* (pp. 227–259). Austin, TX: Pro-Ed.

Bryant, P., Bradley, L., Maclean, M., & Crossland, J. (1989). Nursery rhymes, phonological skills and reading. *Journal of Child Language, 16,* 407–428.

Bryant, P., MacLean, M., & Bradley, L. (1990). Rhyme, language, and children's reading. *Applied Psycholinguistics, 11,* 237–252.

Buckley, S., & Johnson-Glenberg, M. C. (2008). Increasing literacy learning for individuals with Down syndrome and fragile X syndrome. In J. E. Roberts, R. S. Chapman, & S. F. Warren (Eds.), *Speech and language development and intervention in Down syndrome and fragile X syndrome* (pp. 233–254). Baltimore: Paul H. Brookes.

Bunce, B. H. (1995). *Building a language-focused curriculum for the preschool classroom.* Baltimore: Paul H. Brookes.

Bus, A. G., van IJzendoorn, M. H., & Pellegrini, A. D. (1995). Joint book reading makes for success in learning to read: A meta-analysis on intergenerational transmission of literacy. *Review of Educational Research, 65,* 1–21.

Caffrey, E., & Fuchs, D. (2007). Differences in performance between students with learning disabilities and mild mental retardation: Implications for categorical instruction. *Learning Disabilities Research and Practice, 22,* 119–128.

Cain, K., & Oakhill, J. (2007). *Children's comprehension problems in oral and written language: A cognitive perspective.* New York: Guilford Press.

Cairns, H. W. (1996). *The acquisition of language* (2nd ed.). San Antonio, TX: Pro-Ed.

Calculator, S. N. (1994). Designing and implementing communicative assessments in inclusive settings. In S. N. Calculator & C. M. Jorgensen (Eds.), *Including students with severe disabilities in schools: Fostering communication, interaction, and participation* (pp. 113–181). San Diego, CA: Singular.

Calculator, S. N., & Hatch, E. R. (1995). Validation of facilitated communication: A case study and beyond. *American Journal of Speech-Language Pathology, 4*(1), 49–58.

Calfee, R., & Chambliss, M. (1988). Beyond decoding: Pictures of expository prose. *Annals of Dyslexia, 38,* 243–257.

Camarata, S., & Nelson, K. (1992). Treatment efficiency as a function of target selection in the remediation of child language disorders. *Clinical Linguistics and Phonetics, 6,* 167–178.

Camarata, S., & Nelson, K. (2006). Conversational recast intervention with preschool and older children. In R. McCauley & M. Fey (Eds.), *Treatment of language disorders in children* (pp. 237–264). Baltimore: Paul H. Brookes.

Camarata, S., Nelson, K., & Camarata, M. (1994). A comparison of conversation based to imitation based procedures for training grammatical structures in specific language impaired children. *Journal of Speech and Hearing Research, 37,* 1414–1423.

Campos, J. G., & de Guevara, L. G. (2007). Landau-Kleffner syndrome. *Journal of Pediatric Neurology, 5*(2), 93–99.

Cantwell, D. P., Baker, L., & Mattison, R. E. (1979). The prevalence of psychiatric disorder in children with speech and language disorder: An epidemiological study. *Journal of the American Academy of Child Psychiatry, 18,* 450–461.

Caravolas, M., Hulme, C., & Snowling, M. J. (2001). The foundations of spelling ability: Evidence from a 3-year longitudinal study. *Journal of Memory and Language, 45,* 751–774.

Carey, S. (1978). The child as word learner. In M. Halle, J. Bresnan, & G. Miller (Eds.), *Linguistic theory and psychological reality.* Cambridge, MA: MIT Press.

Carey, S., & Bartlett, E. (1978). Acquiring a single new word. *Papers and Reports in Child Language Development, 15,* 17–29.

Carle, E. (1995). *Brown bear, brown bear, what do you see?* New York: Henry Holt.

Carlisle, J. F. (1988). Knowledge of derivational morphology and spelling ability in fourth, sixth, and eighth graders. *Applied Psycholinguistics, 9,* 247–266.

Carlisle, J. F. (1995). Morphological awareness and early reading achievement. In L. B. Feldman (Ed.), *Morphological aspects of language processing* (pp. 189–209). Hillsdale, NJ: Lawrence Erlbaum.

Carlisle, J. F., & Stone, C. A. (2005). Exploring the role of morphemes in word reading. *Reading Research Quarterly, 40,* 428–449.

Carnine, D., & Kinder, B. D. (1985). Teaching low-performing students to apply generative and schema strategies to narrative and expository material. *Remedial and Special Education, 6*(1), 20–30.

Carr, E., & Ogle, D. (1987). KWL Plus: A strategy for comprehension and summarization. *Journal of Reading, 30,* 626–631.

Carroll, J. M., & Snowling, M. J. (2004). Language and phonological skills in children at high-risk of reading difficulties. *Journal of Child Psychology and Psychiatry, 45,* 631–640.

Carrow-Woolfolk, E. (1973). *Test of Auditory Comprehension of Language (TACL).* Bingham, MA: Teaching Resources.

Carrow-Woolfolk, E. (1995). *Oral-Written Language Scales (OWLS): Listening Comprehension (LE) and Oral Expression (OE) Scales.* Minneapolis, MN: Pearson Assessments.

Carrow-Woolfolk, E. (1996). *Oral-Written Language Scales (OWLS): Written Expression (WE) Scale.* Minneapolis, MN: Pearson Assessments.

Casby, M. W. (2003). Developmental assessment of play: A model for early intervention. *Communication Disorders Quarterly, 24*(4), 175–183.

Casby, M. W. (1992). The cognitive hypothesis and its influence on speech-language services in schools. *Language, Speech, and Hearing Services in Schools, 23,* 198–202.

Catts, H. W. (1993). The relationship between speech-language and reading disabilities. *Journal of Speech and Hearing Research, 36,* 948–958.

Catts, H. W., Fey, M. E., Tomblin, J. B., & Zhang, X. (2002). A longitudinal investigation of reading outcomes in children with language impairments. *Journal of Speech Language and Hearing Research, 45,* 1142–1157.

Catts, H. W., Fey, M. E., Zhang, X., & Tomblin, J. B. (1999). Language basis of reading and reading disabilities: Evidence from a longitudinal study. *Scientific Studies of Reading, 3,* 331–361.

Catts, H. W., Fey, M. E., Zhang, X., & Tomblin, J. B. (2001). Estimating the risk of future reading difficulties in kindergarten children: A research-based model and its clinical implementation. *Language, Speech, and Hearing Services in Schools, 32,* 38–50.

Catts, H. W., Hogan, T. P., & Adlof, S. M. (2005). Developmental changes in reading and reading disabilities. In H. W. Catts & A. G. Kamhi (Eds.), *The connections between language and reading disabilities* (pp. 25–40). Mahwah, NJ: Lawrence Erlbaum.

Catts, H. W., Hogan, T. P., & Fey, M. E. (2003). Subgrouping poor readers on the basis of individual differences in reading-related abilities. *Journal of Learning Disabilities, 36,* 151–164.

Catts, H. W., & Kamhi, A. G. (2005a). Classification of reading disabilities. In H. W. Catts & A. G. Kamhi (Eds.), *Language and reading disabilities* (2nd ed., pp. 72–93). Boston: Allyn & Bacon.

Catts, H. W., & Kamhi, A. G. (Eds.). (2005b). *The connections between language and reading disabilities.* Mahwah, NJ: Lawrence Erlbaum.

Catts, H. W., & Kamhi, A. G. (Eds.). (2005c). *Language and reading disabilities* (2nd ed.). Boston: Allyn & Bacon.

Cazden, C. B. (1983). Adult assistance to language development: Scaffolds, models, and direct instruction. In R. Parker & F. Davis (Eds.), *Developing literacy: Young children's use of language* (pp. 3–18). Newark, DE: International Reading Association.

Cazden, C. B. (1988). *Classroom discourse: The language of teaching and learning.* Portsmouth, NH: Heinemann.

Centers for Disease Control and Prevention (CDC). (1996). State-specific rates of mental retardation—United States, 1993. *MMWR Weekly, 45*(3), 61–65. Retrieved December 2, 2008, from www.cdc.gov/mmwr/preview/mmwrhtml/00040023.htm

Centers for Disease Control and Prevention (CDC). (2007). CDC releases new data on autism spectrum disorders (ASDs) from multiple communities in the United States. Press release from U.S. Department of Health and Human Services. Retrieved August 9, 2007, from www.cdc.gov/od/oc/media/pressrel/2007/r070208.htm

Chadwick, O., Rutter, M., Brown, G., Shaffer, D., & Traub, M. (1981). A prospective study of children with head injuries: II. Cognitive sequelae. *Psychological Medicine, 11,* 49–61.

Chall, J. S. (1967). *Learning to read: The great debate.* New York: McGraw-Hill.

Chamberlin, S. L., & Narins, B. (2005). Alcohol-related neurological disease. *Encyclopedia of Neurological Disorders.* Thomson Gale. Retrieved August 5, 2007, from http://health.enotes.com/neurological-disorders-encyclopedia/alcohol-related-neurological-disease

Chao, P.-C., Bryan, T., Burstein, K., & Ergul, C. (2006). Family-centered intervention for young children at-risk for language and behavior problems. *Early Childhood Education Journal, 34*(2), 147–153.

Chapman, R. S., Schwartz, S. E., & Kay-Raining Bird, E. (1991). Language skills of children and adolescents with Down syndrome: I. Comprehension. *Journal of Speech and Hearing Research, 34,* 1106–1120.

Chapman, R. S., Seung, H.-K., Schwartz, S. E., & Kay-Raining Bird, E. (1998). Language skills of children and adolescents with Down syndrome: II. Production deficits. *Journal of Speech, Language, and Hearing Research, 41,* 861–873.

Charlop-Christy, M. H., & Jones, C. (2006). The picture exchange communication system: Nonverbal communication program for children with autism spectrum disorders. In R. J. McCauley & M. E. Fey (Eds.), *Treatment of language disorders* (pp. 105–122). Baltimore: Paul H. Brookes.

Charlop-Christy, M., & Carpenter, M. (2000). Modified incidental teaching sessions: A procedure for parents to increase spontaneous speech in their children with autism. *Journal of Positive Behavior Interventions, 2*(2), 98–112.

Charlop-Christy, M., Carpenter, M., Le, L., LeBlanc, L., & Kellet, K. (2002). Using the Picture Exchange Communication System (PECS) with children with autism: Assessment of PECS acquisition, speech, social-communicative behavior, and problem behavior. *Journal of Applied Behavior Analysis, 35,* 213–231.

Chen, D. (1996). Parent-infant communication: Early intervention for very young children with visual impairment or hearing loss. *Infants and Young Children, 9*(2), 1–12.

Child Trend's Data Bank. (n.d.). Child maltreatment. Retrieved August 6, 2007, from www.childtrendsdatabank.org/pdf/40_PDF.pdf

Childers, J., & Tomasello, M. (2002). Two-year-olds learn novel nouns, verbs, and conventional actions from massed or distributed exposures. *Developmental Psychology, 38,* 967–978.

Children's Health Act, P.L. 106–310 (2000).

Chin, S. B., Tsai, P. L., & Gao, S. (2003). Connected speech intelligibility of children with cochlear implants and children with normal hearing. *American Journal of Speech Language Pathology, 12,* 440–451.

Chomsky, N. (1957). *Syntactic structures.* The Hague, the Netherlands: Mouton.

Chomsky, N. (1965). *Aspects of the theory of syntax.* Cambridge, MA: MIT Press.

Chomsky, N. (1968). *Language and mind.* New York: Harcourt, Brace.

Chomsky, N. (1980). *Rules and representations.* New York: Columbia University Press.

Chomsky, N., & Halle, M. (1968). *The sound pattern of English.* New York: Harper & Row.

Chua-Eoan, H. (1997, January 27). "He was my hero." *Time,* 23–27.

Cirrin, F. M., & Penner, S. G. (1995). Classroom-based and consultative service delivery models for language intervention. In M. E. Fey, J. Windsor, & S. F. Warren (Eds.), *Language intervention: Preschool through the elementary years* (pp. 333–362). Baltimore: Paul H. Brookes.

Clark, E. (1993). *The lexicon in acquisition.* Cambridge, England: Cambridge University Press.

Clark, H. M. (2003). Neuromuscular treatments for speech and swallowing: A tutorial. *American Journal of Speech-Language Pathology, 12,* 400–415.

Clay, M. M. (1967). The reading behavior of five-year-old children: A research report. *New Zealand Journal of Educational Studies, 2,* 11–31.

Clay, M. M. (1979). *The early detection of reading difficulties* (3rd ed.). Auckland, New Zealand: Heinemann.

Cleave, P. L., & Fey, M. W. (1997). Two approaches to the facilitation of grammar in children with language impairments: Rationale and description. *American Journal of Speech-Language Pathology, 6,* 22–32.

Cleaver, R. L., & Whitman, R. D. (1998). Right hemisphere, white-matter learning disabilities associated with depression in an adolescent and young adult psychiatric population. *Journal of Nervous and Mental Disease, 186,* 561–565.

Cochrane Collaboration. (2007). *Cochrane reviews.* Retrieved November 5, 2007, from www.cochrane.org/reviews

Cockerill, H., & Carroll-Few, L. (2001). Communicating without speech: Practical augmentative and alternative communication. In *Clinics in Developmental Medicine* (No. 156). Suffolk, England: MacKeith Press.

Coggins, T. B., Olswang, L. B., & Guthrie, J. (1987). Assessing communicative intents in young children: Low structured or observation tasks? *Journal of Speech and Hearing Disorders, 52,* 44–49.

Coggins, T., Timler, G., & Olswang, L. (2007). A state of double jeopardy: Impact of prenatal alcohol exposure and adverse environments on the social communicative abilities of school-age children with fetal alcohol spectrum disorder. *Language, Speech, and Hearing Services in the Schools, 38,* 117–127.

Cognitive Concepts. (2000). *Earobics Step 1 and Step 2* [Computer software]. Evanston, IL: Houghton Mifflin.

Cohen, H., Amerine-Dickens, M., & Smith, T. (2006). Early intensive behavioral treatment: Replication of the UCLA model in a community setting. *Journal of Developmental and Behavioral Pediatrics, 27*(Suppl.2), S145–S155.

Cohen, J. (1988). *Statistical power analysis for the behavioral sciences* (2nd ed.). Hillsdale, NJ: Lawrence Erlbaum.

Cohen, S. E., & Parmelee, A. H. (1983). Prediction of five-year Stanford-Binet scores in preterm infants. *Child Development, 54,* 1242–1253.

Cole, K., & Dale, P. (1986). Direct language instruction and interactive language instruction with language delayed preschool children: A comparison study. *Journal of Speech and Hearing Research, 29,* 206–217.

Cole, K. N., Dale, P. S., & Mills, P. E. (1992). Stability of the intelligence quotient–language quotient relation: Is discrepancy modeling based on a myth? *American Journal on Mental Retardation, 97,* 131–143.

Cole, K. N., Maddox, M. E., & Lim, Y. S. (2006). Language is the key: Constructive interactions around books and play. In R. J. McCauley & M. E. Fey (Eds.). *Treatment of language disorders in children* (pp. 149–173). Baltimore: Paul H. Brookes.

Cole, K. N., Mills, P. E., & Kelley, D. (1994). Agreement of assessment profiles used in cognitive referencing. *Language, Speech, and Hearing Services in Schools, 25,* 25–31.

Cole, M. (1981). Preface. In J. V. Wertsch (Ed.), *The concept of activity in Soviet psychology* (pp. vii–x). New York: M. E. Sharpe.

Computerized Profiling. (2008). Software transcription/analysis tools. Retrieved January 22, 2008, from www.computerizedprofiling.org

Connell, P. J. (1982). On training grammatical rules. *Language, Speech, and Hearing Services in Schools, 13,* 231–248.

Connell, P. J., & Stone, C. (1992). Morpheme learning of children with specific language impairment under controlled instructional conditions. *Journal of Speech and Hearing Research, 35,* 844–852.

Connor, C. M., & Zwolan, T. A. (2004). Examining multiple sources of influence on the reading comprehension skills of children who use cochlear implants. *Journal of Speech, Language, and Hearing Research, 47,* 509–526.

Constable, C. M. (1987). Talking with teachers: Increasing our relevance as language interventionists in the schools. *Seminars in Speech and Language, 8*(4), 345–356.

Conti-Ramsden, G., & Botting, N. (1999). Classification of children with specific language impairment: Longitudinal considerations. *Journal of Speech, Language, and Hearing Research, 42,* 1195–1204.

Conti-Ramsden, G., & Botting, N. (2004). Social difficulties and victimization in children with SLI at 11 years of age. *Journal of Speech, Language, and Hearing Research, 47,* 145–161.

Conti-Ramsden, G., Crutchly, A., & Botting, N. (2003). The extent to which psychometric tests differentiate subgroups of children with SLI. *Journal of Speech, Language, and Hearing Research, 40,* 765–777.

Conti-Ramsden, G., Hutcheson, G. D., & Grove, J. (1995). Contingency and breakdown: Children with SLI and their conversations with mothers and fathers. *Journal of Speech and Hearing Research, 38,* 1290–1302.

Cook, T. D., & Campbell, D. T. (1979). *Quasi-experimentation: Design and analysis issues for field settings.* Chicago: Rand-McNally.

Cook-Gumperz, J. (1977). Situated instructions. In S. Ervin-Tripp & C. Mitchell-Kernan (Eds.), *Child discourse* (pp. 103–124). New York: Academic Press.

Copeland, D. R., Fletcher, J. M., Pfefferbaum-Levine, B., Jaffe, N., Ried, H., & Maor, M. (1985). Neuropsychological sequelae of childhood cancer on long-term survivors. *Pediatrics, 75,* 745–753.

Cornett, R. (1967). Cued speech. *American Annals of the Deaf, 112,* 3–13.

Cossu, G., Rossini, F., & Marshall, J. C. (1993). When reading is acquired but phonemic awareness is not: A study of literacy in Down's syndrome. *Cognition, 46*(2), 129–138.

Cowan, N. (1996). Short-term memory, working memory, and their importance in language processing. *Topics in Language Disorders, 17*(1), 1–18.

Cowley, J., & Glasgow, C. (1997). *The Renfrew Bus Story.* Centreville, DE: Centreville School.

Crago, M. B. (1990). Development of communicative competence in Inuit children: Implications for speech-language pathology. *Journal of Childhood Communication Disorders, 13,* 73–83.

Crago, M. B., & Cole, E. B. (1991). Using ethnography to bring children's communicative and cultural worlds into focus. In T. M. Gallagher (Ed.), *Pragmatics of language: Clinical practice issues* (pp. 99–131). San Diego, CA: Singular.

Craig, C. J. (1996). Family support of the emergent literacy of children with visual impairments. *Journal of Visual Impairment and Blindness, 90,* 194–200.

Craig, H. K., & Washington, J. A. (2004). Grade-related changes in the production of African American English. *Journal of Speech, Language, and Hearing Research, 47,* 450–463.

Crain, S. (1994). Language acquisition in the absence of experience. In P. Bloom (Ed.), *Language acquisition* (pp. 364–409). Cambridge, MA: MIT Press. (Reprinted from *Behavioral and Brain Sciences, 14,* 1991).

Crais, E. R. (1990). World knowledge to word knowledge. *Topics in Language Disorders, 10*(3), 45–62.

Crais, E. R. (1995). Expanding the repertoire of tools and techniques for assessing the communication skills of infants and toddlers. *American Journal of Speech-Language Pathology, 4*(3), 47–59.

Crandell, C. C., & Smaldino, J. J. (2001). Acoustical modifications for the classroom. *Volta Review, 101*(5), 33–46.

Creaghead, N. A., & Tattershall, S. S. (1985). Observation and assessment of classroom pragmatic skills. In C. S. Simon (Ed.), *Communication skills and classroom success: Assessment of language-learning disabled students* (pp. 105–131). San Diego, CA: College-Hill Press.

Crosbie, S., Holm, A., & Dodd, B. (2005). Intervention for children with severe speech disorder: A comparison of two approaches. *International Journal of Language and Communication Disorders, 40,* 467–491.

Cross, T., Bazron, B., Dennis, K., & Isaacs, M. (1989). *Towards a culturally competent system of care* (Volume I). Washington, DC: Georgetown University Child Development Center, CASSP Technical Assistance Center.

Crossley, R. (1993). Literacy ad facilitated communication training. *Facilitated Communication Digest, 1*(2), 12–13.

Crystal, D., Fletcher, P., & Garman, M. (1976). *The grammatical analysis of language disability.* London: Edward Arnold.

Culatta, B., & Horn, D. (1982). A program for achieving generalization of grammatical rules to spontaneous discourse. *Journal of Speech and Hearing Disorders, 47,* 174–180.

Culatta, B., Page, J. L., & Ellis, J. (1983). Story retelling as a communicative performance screening tool. *Language, Speech, and Hearing Services in Schools, 14,* 66–74.

Culbertson, D. S. (2007). Language and speech of the deaf and hard of hearing. In R. L. Schow & M. A. Nerbonne (Eds.), *Introduction to audiologic rehabilitation* (pp. 197–244). Boston: Allyn & Bacon.

Cummins, J. (1992). Language proficiency, bilingualism, and academic achievement. In P. A. Richard-Amoto & M. A. Snow (Eds), *The multicultural classroom: Readings for content-area teachers.* Reading, MA: Addison Wesley.

Cunningham, A. E., & Stanovich, K. E. (1998). What reading does for the mind. *American Educator, 22,* 8–15.

Cupples, L., & Iacono, T. (2000). Phonological awareness and oral reading skill in children with Down syndrome. *Journal of Speech, Language, and Hearing Research, 43,* 595–608.

Curran, M., Colozzo, P., & Johnston, J. (2004, Nov.). *Narrative assessment: Form vs. content.* Poster session presented at the British Columbia Association of Speech-Language Pathologists and Audiologists, Kelowna, British Columbia, Canada.

Dahlgren Sandberg, A., & Hjelmquist, E. (1996). Phonologic awareness and literacy abilities in nonspeaking preschool children with cerebral palsy. *Augmentative and Alternative Communication, 12,* 138–153.

Damico, J. S. (1988). The lack of efficacy in language therapy: A case study. *Language, Speech, and Hearing Services in Schools, 19,* 51–66.

Data Analysis System (DANS). (2006). Early intervention services on IFSPs provided to infants and toddlers and their families in accordance with Part C. U.S. Department of Education, Office of Special Education Programs, OMB No. 1820–0556. Retrieved September 2, 2007, from www.ideadata.org/tables29th/ar_6–6.htm

Davies, P., Shanks, B., & Davies, K. (2004). Improving narrative skills in young children with delayed language development. *Educational Review, 56,* 271–286.

Davis, B. L. (2005). Goal and target selection for developmental speech disorders. In A. Kamhi & K. Pollock (Eds.), *Phonological disorders in children: Clinical decision making in assessment and intervention* (pp. 89–100). Baltimore: Paul H. Brookes.

Dawson, J., Stout, C., Eyer, J., Tattersall, P., Fonkalsrud, J., & Croley, K. (2005). *Structured Photographic Language Test-Preschool-Second Edition (SPELT–P2).* DeKalb, IL: Janelle Publications.

Dawson, P., & Guare, R. (2004). *Executive skills in children and adolescents: A practical guide to assessment and intervention.* New York: Guilford Press.

Dehaene-Lambertz, G., Hertz-Pannier, L., & Dubois, J. (2006). Nature and nurture in language acquisition: Anatomical and functional brain-imaging studies in infants. *Trends in Neurosciences, 29*(7), 367–373.

Delpit, L. (1995). *Other people's children: Cultural conflict in the classroom.* New York: New Press.

Delpit, L. (2002). No kinda sense. In L. Delpit & J. K. Dowdy (Eds.), *The skin that we speak* (pp. 33–48). New York: New Press.

Delpit, L. (2004). Foreword. In F. B. Boyd & C. H. Brock (Eds.), *Multicultural and multilingual literacy and language: Contexts and practices* (pp. ix–xii). New York: Guilford Press.

Denckla, M. B. (1983). The neuropsychology of social-emotional learning disabilities. *Archives of Neurology, 40,* 461–462.

Denckla, M. B., & Rudel, R. (1976). Rapid "automatized" naming (RAN): Dyslexia differentiated from other learning disabilities. *Neuropsychological, 14,* 471–479.

Denne, M., Langdown, N., Pring, T., & Roy, P. (2005). Treating children with expressive phonological disorders: Does phonological awareness therapy work in the clinic? *International Journal of Language and Communication Disorders, 40*(4), 493–504.

Deno, S. L. (1989). Curriculum-based measurement and special education services: A fundamental and direct relationship. In M. R. Shinn (Ed.), *Curriculum-based measurement: Assessing special children* (pp. 1–17). New York: Guilford Press.

Deshler, D. D., Hock, M. F., & Catts, H. W. (2005). Enhancing outcomes for struggling adolescent readers. *Perspectives (Newsletter of the International Dyslexia Association), 32*(3), 21–25.

DesJardin, J. L. (2006). Family empowerment: Supporting language development in young children who are deaf or hard of hearing. *Volta Review, 106,* 275–298.

DesJardin, J. L., Ambrose, S. E., & Eisenberg, L. S. (2009). Literacy skills in children with cochlear implants: The importance of early oral language and joint storybook reading. *Journal of Deaf Studies and Deaf Education, 14,* 22–43.

Diagnostic Classification Task Force. (1994). *Diagnostic classification 0–3: Diagnostic classification of mental health and developmental disorders of infancy and early childhood.* Arlington, VA: Zero to Three, National Center for Clinical Infant Programs.

Dick, F., Dronkers, N. F., Pizzamiglio, L., Saygin, A. P., Small, S. L., & Wilson, S. (2005). Language and the brain. In M. Tomasello & D. I. Slobin (Eds.), *Beyond nature-nurture: Essays in honor of Elizabeth Bates* (pp. 237–260). Mahwah, NJ: Lawrence Erlbaum.

Dickinson, D. K. (2006). Toward a toolkit approach to describing classroom quality. *Early Education and Development, 17,* 177–202.

Dickinson, D. K., & Caswell, L. (2007). Building support for language and early literacy in preschool classrooms through in-service professional development: Effects of the Literacy Environment Enrichment Program (LEEP). *Early Childhood Research Quarterly, 22,* 243–260.

Dickinson, D. K., & McCabe, A. (2001). Bringing it all together: The multiple origins, skills, and environmental supports of early literacy. *Learning Disabilities Research and Practice, 16,* 186–202.

Dickinson, D. K., McCabe, A., Anastasopoulos, L., Peisner-Feinberg, E., & Poe, M. D. (2003). The comprehensive language approach to early literacy: The interrelationships among vocabulary, phonological sensitivity, and print knowledge among preschool-aged children. *Journal of Educational Psychology, 95*(3), 465–481.

Dillenburger, K., & Keenan, M. (2006). Preface. In M. Keenan, M. Henderson, K. P. Kerr, & K. Dillenberger (Eds.), *Applied behaviour analysis and autism: Building a future together* (pp. 16–17). London: Jessica Kingsley.

Dillon, C. M., & Pisoni, D. B. (2006). Nonword repetition and reading skills in children who are deaf and have cochlear implants. *Volta Review, 106*(2), 121–146.

Dodge, E. P., & Mallard, A. R. (1992). Social skills training using a collaborative service delivery model. *Language, Speech, and Hearing Services in Schools, 23*(2), 130–135.

Dollaghan, C. A. (1987). Comprehension monitoring in normal and language-impaired children. *Topics in Language Disorders, 7*(2), 45–60.

Donahue, M. (1987). Interactions between linguistic and pragmatic development in learning-disabled children: Three views of the state of the union. In S. Rosenberg (Ed.), *Advances in applied psycholinguistics. Volume 1: Disorders of first language development* (pp. 126–179). New York: Cambridge University Press.

Donahue, M., & Bryan, T. (1984). Communication skills and peer relations of learning disabled adolescents. *Topics in Language Disorders, 4*(2), 10–21.

Donnellan, A. M. (1984). The criterion of the least dangerous assumption. *Behavioral Disorders, 9,* 141–150.

Donnellan, A. M., Mirenda, P. L., Mesaros, R. A., & Fassbender, L. L. (1984). Analyzing the communicative functions of aberrant behavior. *JASH (Journal of the Association for Persons with Severe Handicaps), 9,* 202–212.

Drew, N. (1987). *Learning the skills of peacemaking.* Rolling Hills Estates, CA: Jalmar Press.

Drews, C. D., Yeargin-Allsopp, M., Murphy, C. C., & Decouffle, P. (1992). Legal blindness among 10-year-old children in metropolitan Atlanta: Prevalence, 1985 to 1987. *American Journal of Public Health, 82,* 1377–1379.

DuBard, E. (1974). *Teaching aphasics and other language deficient children: Theory and application of the association method.* Hattiesburg: University Press of Mississippi.

Duchan, J. (2006). Issue editor foreword. *Topics in Language Disorders, 26*(3), 185–188.

Dunn, L. M., & Dunn, L. M. (1981). *Peabody Picture Vocabulary Test-Revised.* Circle Pines, MN: American Guidance Service.

Dunn, L. M., & Dunn, L. M. (1997). *Peabody Picture Vocabulary Test* (3rd ed.). Circle Pines, MN: American Guidance Service.

Duquette, C., Stodel, E., Fullarton, S., & Hagglund, K. (2006). Persistence in high school: Experiences of adolescents and young adults with fetal alcohol spectrum disorder. *Journal of Intellectual and Developmental Disability, 31*(4), 219–231.

Durando, J. (2008). A survey on literacy instruction for students with multiple disabilities. *Journal of Visual Impairment and Blindness, 102,* 40–45.

Dweck, C. S. (1989). Motivation. In A. Lesgold & R. Glaser (Eds.), *Foundations for a psychology of education* (pp. 87–136). Hillsdale, NJ: Lawrence Erlbaum.

Eckert, M. A., Leonard, C. M., Richards, T. L., Aylward, E. H., Thomson, J., & Berninger, V. W. (2003). Anatomical correlates of dyslexia: Frontal and cerebellar findings. *Brain, 126,* 482–494.

Edmonston, N. K., & Thane, N. L. (1992). Children's use of comprehension strategies in response to relational words: Implications for assessment. *American Journal of Speech-Language Pathology, 1*(2), 30–55.

Education for All Handicapped Children Act (EAHCA), P.L. 94-142, 89 Stat. 773 (1975).

Ehren, B. J. (2000). Maintaining a therapeutic focus and sharing responsibility for student success: Keys to in-classroom speech-language services. *Language, Speech, and Hearing Services in Schools, 31,* 219–229.

Ehren, B. J. (2007). Responsiveness to intervention: An opportunity to reinvent speech language services in schools. *The ASHA Leader.*

Ehren, B. J., & Nelson, N. W. (2005). The responsiveness to intervention approach and language impairment. *Topics in Language Disorders, 25*(2), 120–131.

Ehri, L. C. (2000). Learning to read and learning to spell: Two sides of a coin. *Topics in Language Disorders, 20*(3), 19–36.

Ehri, L. C. (2004). In J. Wasowicz, K. Apel, J. J. Masterson, & A. Witney, *SPELL-Links to reading and writing product sampler* (p. 2). Evanston, IL: Learning By Design. Retrieved January 1, 2008, from www.learningbydesign.com

Ehri, L. C., & McCormick, S. (1998). Phases of word learning: Implications for instruction with delayed and disabled readers. *Reading and Writing Quarterly, 14,* 135–163.

Ehri, L. C., & Wilce, L. (1982). Recognition of spellings printed in lower and mixed case: Evidence for orthographic images. *Journal of Reading Behavior, 14,* 219–230.

Ehri, L. C., & Wilce, L. S. (1986). The influence of spellings on speech. In D. B. Yaden & S. Templeton (Eds.), *Metalinguistic awareness and beginning literacy* (pp. 101–113). Portsmouth, NH: Heinemann.

Eikeseth, S., Smith, T., Jahr, E., & Eldevik, S. (2002). Intensive behavioral treatment at school for 4- to 7-year-old children with autism. A 1-year comparison controlled study. *Behavior Modification, 26*(1), 49–68.

Eikeseth, S., Smith, T., Jahr, E., & Eldevik, S. (2007). Outcome for children with autism who began intensive behavioral treatment between ages 4 and 7: A comparison controlled study. *Behavior Modification, 31*(3), 264–278.

Eisenberg, S. L. (2006). Grammar: How can I say that better? In T. A. Ukrainetz (Ed.), *Contextualized language intervention: Scaffolding PreK–12 literacy achievement* (pp. 145–194). Eau Claire, WI: Thinking Publications.

Ekman, P., & Friesen, W. V. (1969). The repertoire of nonverbal behavior: Categories, origins, usage, and coding. *Semiotica, 1,* 49–98.

Elder, J. H. (1995). In-home communication intervention training for parents of multiply handicapped children. *Scholarly Inquiry for Nursing Practice, 9*(1), 71–95.

Eldevik, S., Eikeseth, S., Jahr, E., & Smith, T. (2006). Effects of low-intensity behavioral treatment for children with autism and mental retardation. *Journal of Autism and Developmental Disorders, 36*(2), 211–224.

Elementary and Secondary Education Act (ESEA), P.L. 89-10, 79 Stat. 27 (1965).

Elksnin, L. K., & Capilouto, G. L. (1994). Speech-language pathologists' perceptions of integrated service delivery in school settings. *Language, Speech, and Hearing Services in Schools, 25,* 258–267.

Elksnin, L. K., & Elksnin, N. (1995). *Assessment and instruction of social skills.* San Diego, CA: Singular.

Ellis Weismer, S. (1996). Capacity limitations in working memory: The impact on lexical and morphological learning by children with language impairment. *Topics in Language Disorders, 17,* 33–44.

Ellis Weismer, S., & Hesketh, L. J. (1996). Lexical learning by children with specific language impairment: Effects of linguistic input presented at varying speaking rates. *Journal of Speech and Hearing Research, 39,* 177–190.

Ellis Weismer, S., & Robertson, S. (2006). Focused stimulation approach to language intervention. In R. McCauley & M. Fey (Eds.), *Treatment of language disorders in children* (pp. 175–202). Baltimore: Paul H. Brookes.

Englert, C. S. (1992). Writing instruction from a sociocultural perspective: The holistic, dialogic, and social enterprise of writing. *Journal of Learning Disabilities, 25*(3), 153–172.

Englert, C. S., & Hiebert, E. H. (1984). Children's developing awareness of text structures in expository materials. *Journal of Educational Psychology, 76,* 65–75.

Englert, C. S., & Mariage, T. V. (1991). Making students partners in the comprehension process: Organizing the reading "POSSE." *Learning Disability Quarterly, 14,* 123–138.

Englert, C. S., & Thomas, C. C. (1987). Sensitivity to text structure in reading and writing: A comparison between learning disabled and non-learning disabled students. *Learning Disability Quarterly, 10*(2), 93–105.

Englert, C. S., Raphael, T. E., Anderson, L. M., Anthony, H. M., Fear, K. L., & Gregg, S. L. (1988). A case for writing intervention: Strategies for writing informational text. *Learning Disabilities Focus, 3*(2), 98–113.

English, K. (2007). Audiologic rehabilitation services in the school setting. In R. L. Schow & M. A. Nerbonne (Eds.), *Introduction to audiologic rehabilitation* (5th ed., pp. 269–300). Boston: Pearson.

Erber, N. (1982). *Auditory training.* Washington, DC: Alexander Graham Bell Association.

Erickson, K. A., Hatton, D., Roy, V., Fox, D. L., & Renne, D. (2007). Literacy in early intervention for children with visual impairments: Insights from individual cases. *Journal of Visual Impairment and Blindness, 101,* 80–95.

Erickson, K. A., & Koppenhaver, D. A. (1995). Developing a literacy program for children with severe disabilities. *Reading Teacher, 48,* 676–684.

Erickson, K. A., Koppenhaver, D. A., & Cunningham, J. W. (2006). Balanced reading intervention and assessment in augmentative communication. In R. J. McCauley & M. E. Fey (Eds.), *Treatment of language disorders in children* (pp. 309–345). Baltimore: Paul H. Brookes.

Erikson, E. H. (1940). Studies in interpretation of play, I: Clinical observation of child disruption in young children. *Genetic Psychology Monograph, 22,* 557–671.

Erin, J. N. (1990). Language samples from visually impaired four- and five-year olds. *Journal of Childhood Communication Disorders, 13,* 181–191.

Erin, J. N. (2007). Identifying the primary disability: Are we speaking the same language? *Journal of Visual Impairment and Blindness, 101,* 582–585.

Ertmer, D. J. (2002). Challenges in optimizing oral communication in children with cochlear implants. *Language, Speech, and Hearing Services in Schools, 33,* 149–152.

Ertmer, D. J., Leonard, J. S., & Pachuilo, M. L. (2002). Communication intervention for children with cochlear implants: Two case studies. *Language, Speech, and Hearing Services in Schools, 33,* 205–217.

Ervin-Tripp, S., & Gordon, D. (1986). The development of requests. In R. L. Schiefelbusch (Ed.), *Language competence: Assessment and intervention* (pp. 61–95). Austin, TX: Pro-Ed.

Estabrooks, W. (2004). *The ABCs of auditory-verbal therapy.* Washington, DC: Alexander Graham Bell Association.

Ewing-Cobbs, L., Fletcher, J. M., & Levin, H. S. (1985). Neuropsychological sequelae following pediatric head injury. In M. Ylvisaker (Ed.), *Head injury rehabilitation: Children and adolescents* (pp. 71–89). Austin, TX: Pro-Ed.

Eyberg, S., & Pincus, D. (1999). *Eyberg Child Behavior Inventory and Sutter-Eyberg Student Behavior Inventory* (Rev. ed.). Odessa, FL: Psychological Assessment Resources.

Fallon, K. A., Light, J., McNaughton, D., Drager, K., & Hammer, C. (2004). The effects of direct instruction on the single-word reading skills of children who require augmentative and alternative communication. *Journal of Speech, Language, and Hearing Research, 47*(6), 1424–1439.

Falvey, M. A., Forest, M., Pearpoint, J., & Rosenberg, R. L. (1994). Building connections. In J. S. Thousand, R. A. Villan, & A. I. Nevin (Eds.), *Creativity and collaborative learning: A practical guide for empowering students and teachers* (pp. 347–368). Baltimore: Paul H. Brookes.

Farber, J. G., & Klein, E. R. (1999). Classroom-based assessment of a collaborative intervention program with kindergarten and first-grade students. *Language, Speech, and Hearing Services in Schools, 30*(1), 83–91.

Farrant, B. M., Fletcher, J., & Maybery, M. (2006). Specific language impairment, theory of mind, and visual perspective taking: Evidence for simulation theory and the developmental role of language. *Child Development, 77,* 1842–1853.

Fay, W., & Schuler, A. L. (1980). *Emerging language in autistic children.* Baltimore: University Park Press.

Feagans, L., & Applebaum, M. I. (1986). Validation of language subtypes in learning disabled children. *Journal of Educational Psychology, 78,* 358–364.

Fein, G. G., Ardila-Rey, A. E., & Groth, L. A. (2000). The narrative connection: Stories and literacy. In K. A. Roskos & J. F. Christie (Eds.), *Play and literacy in early childhood: Research from multiple perspectives* (pp. 27–44). Mahwah, NJ: Lawrence Erlbaum.

Feldman, H. M., Dollaghan, C. A., Campbell, T. F., Colborn, D. K., Janosky, J., Kurs-Lasky, M., Rockette, H. E., Dale, P. S., & Paradise, J. L. (2003). Parent-reported language skills in relation to otitis media during the first 3 years of life. *Journal of Speech, Language, and Hearing Research, 46,* 273–287.

Fenson, L., Marchman, V. A., Thal, D., Dale, P. S., Reznick, J. S., & Bates, E. (2006). *MacArthur-Bates Communicative Developmental Inventories (CDIs)* (3rd ed.). Baltimore: Paul H. Brookes.

Feuerstein, R. (1979). *The dynamic assessment of retarded performers.* Austin, TX: Pro-Ed.

Feuerstein, R. (1980). *Instructional enrichment.* Baltimore: University Park Press.

Feuerstein, R., Rand, Y., & Rynders, J. E. (1988). *Don't accept me as I am: Helping "retarded" people to excel.* New York: Plenum Press.

Fey, M. A. (1986). *Language intervention with young children.* Austin, TX: Pro-Ed.

Fey, M. A., Catts, H. W., Proctor-Williams, K., Tomblin, J. B., & Zhang, X. (2004). Oral and written story composition skills of children with language impairment. *Journal of Speech, Language, and Hearing Research, 47,* 1301–1318.

Fey, M., Cleave, P., & Long, S. (1997). Two models of grammar facilitation in children with language impairments: Phase 2. *Journal of Speech, Language, and Hearing Research, 40,* 5–19.

Fey, M., Cleave, P., Long, S., & Hughes, D. (1993). Two approaches to the facilitation of grammar in children with language impairment: An experimental evaluation. *Journal of Speech and Hearing Research, 36,* 141–157.

Fey, M. E., Cleave, P. L., Ravida, A. I., Long, S. H., Dejmal, A. E., & Easton, D. L. (1994). Effects of grammar facilitation on the phonological performance of children with speech and language impairments. *Journal of Speech and Hearing Research, 37,* 594–607.

Fey, M. E., & Frome Loeb, D. (2002). An evaluation of the facilitative effects of inverted yes-no questions on the acquisition of auxiliary verbs. *Journal of Speech, Language, and Hearing Research, 45,* 160–174.

Fey, M. E., Long, S. H., & Cleave, P. L. (1994). Reconsideration of IQ criteria in the definition of specific language impairment. In R. V. Watkins & M. L. Rice (Eds.), *Specific language impairment in children* (pp. 161–178). Baltimore: Paul H. Brookes.

Fey, M. E., Long, S. H., & Finestack, L. H. (2003). Ten principles of grammar facilitation for children with specific language impairments. *American Journal of Speech-Language Pathology, 12,* 3–15.

Fey, M. E., & Proctor-Williams, K. (2000). Recasting, elicited imitation and modeling in grammar intervention for children with specific language impairments. In D. V. M. Bishop & L. Leonard (Eds.), *Speech and language impairments in children: Causes, characteristics, intervention, and outcome* (pp. 177–194). East Sussex, England: Psychology Press.

Fey, M. W., Warren, S. F., Brady, N., Finestack, L. H., Bredin-Oja, S. L., Fairchild, M., Sokol, S., & Yoder, P. (2006). Early effects of responsivity education/prelinguistic milieu teaching for children with developmental delays and their parents. *Journal of Speech, Language, and Hearing Research, 49,* 526–547.

Fillmore, C. (1968). The case for case. In E. Bach & R. Harmas (Eds.), *Universals in linguistic theory.* New York: Holt, Rinehart, & Winston.

Finley, B. L. (2005). Rethinking developmental neurobiology. In M. Tomasello & D. I. Slobin (Eds.), *Beyond nature-nurture: Essays in honor of Elizabeth Bates* (pp. 195–218). Mahwah, NJ: Lawrence Erlbaum.

Fisher, S. A. (2006). Tangled webs: Tracing the connections between genes and cognition. *Cognition, 101,* 270–297.

Flavell, J. H. (1999). Cognitive development: Children's knowledge about the mind. *Annual Reviews of Psychology, 50,* 21–45.

Fletcher, H., & Buckley, S. (2002). Phonological awareness in children with Down syndrome. *Down's Syndrome Research and Practice, 8*(1), 11–18.

Fletcher, J. M., Morris, R. D., & Lyon, G. R. (2003). Classification and definition of learning disabilities: An integrative perspective. In H. L. Swanson, K. R. Harris, & S. Graham (Eds.), *Handbook of learning disabilities* (pp. 30–56). New York: The Guilford Press.

Florian, L., Hollenweger, J., Simeonsson, R. J., Wedell, K., Riddell, S., Terzi, L., & Holland, A. (2006). Cross-cultural perspectives on the classification of children with disabilities:

Part I. Issues in the classification of children with disabilities. *Journal of Special Education, 40*(1), 36–45.

Flower, L. S., & Hayes, J. R. (1980). The dynamics of composing: Making plans and juggling constraints. In L. W. Gregg & E. R. Steinberg (Eds.), *Cognitive processes in writing* (pp. 31–50). Mahwah, NJ: Lawrence Erlbaum.

Fombonne, E. (2007). Epidemiology of pervasive developmental disorders. In J. M. Perez, P. M. Gonzales, M. L. Comi, & C. Nieto (Eds.), *New developments in autism: The future is today* (pp. 14–32). London: Jessica Kingsley.

Foorman, B. R., & Nixon, S. M. (2006). The influence of public policy on reading research and practice. *Topics in Language Disorders, 26,* 157–171.

Forcada-Guex, M., Pierrehumbert, B., Borghini, A., Moessinger, A., & Muller-Nix, C. (2006). Early dyadic patterns of mother–infant interactions and outcomes of prematurity at 18 months. *Pediatrics, 118,* 107–114.

Foss, J. (1991). Nonverbal learning disabilities and remedial interventions. *Annals of Dyslexia, 41,* 128–140.

Fowler, W., Ogston, K., Roberts, G., & Swenson, A. (2006). The effects of early language enrichment. *Early Child Development and Care, 176*(8), 777–815.

Fox, L., Long, S. H., & Langlois, A. (1988). Patterns of language comprehension deficit in abused and neglected children. *Journal of Speech and Hearing Disorders, 53,* 239–244.

Fraiberg, S. (1979). Blind infants and their mothers: An examination of the sign system. *Before speech: The beginning of interpersonal communication* (pp. 149–169). New York: Cambridge University Press.

Fraiberg, S. (1980). *Clinical studies in infant mental health: The first year of life.* New York: Basic Books.

Fraiberg, S., Adelson, E., & Shapiro, V. (1987). Ghosts in the nursery: A psychoanalytic approach to the problems of impaired infant–mother relationships. In L. Fraiberg (Ed.), *Selected writings of Selma Fraiberg* (pp. 100–136). Columbus: Ohio State University Press.

Francis, D. J., Fletcher, J. M., Shaywitz, B. A., Shaywitz, S. E., & Rourke, B. P. (1996). Defining learning and language disabilities: Conceptual and psychometric issues with the use of IQ tests. *Language, Speech, and Hearing Services in Schools, 27,* 132–143.

Frea, W. D., Arnold, C. L., & Vittemberga, G. L. (2001). A demonstration of the effects of augmentative communication on extreme aggressive behavior of a child with autism within an integrated preschool setting. *Journal of Positive Behavioral Interventions, 3*(4), 194–198.

Freitag, C. M., Kleser, C., & von Gontardf, A. (2006). Imitation and language abilities in adolescents with autism spectrum disorder without language delay. *European Journal of Child and Adolescent Psychiatry, 15,* 282–291.

Freud, A. (1965). *Normality and pathology in childhood: Assessments of development.* New York: International Universities Press.

Frith, U. (1989). *Autism: Explaining the enigma.* Oxford, England: Basil Blackwell.

Frost, L. A., & Bondy, A. S. (1994). *The Picture Exchange Communication System (PECS) training manual.* Cherry Hill, NJ: Pyramid Educational.

Fuchs, D., Fuchs, L. S., Mathes, P. G., & Lipsey, M. W. (2000). Reading differences between underachievers with and without learning disabilities: A meta-analysis. In R. Gersten, E. Schiller, & S. Vaughn (Eds.), *Research syntheses in special education* (pp. 81–104). Mahwah, NJ: Lawrence Erlbaum.

Fuchs, D., Fuchs, L. S., Mathes, P. H., & Simmons, D. C. (1997). Peer-assisted strategies: Making classrooms more responsive to diversity. *American Educational Research Journal, 34*(1), 174–206.

Fuchs, L. S., Fuchs, D., & Kazdan, S. (1999). Effects of peer-assisted learning strategies on high school students with serious reading problems. *Remedial and Special Education, 20*(5), 309–318.

Fujiki, M., Brinton, B., Hart, C. H., & Fitzgerald, A. (1999). Peer acceptance and friendship in children with specific language impairment. *Topics in Language Disorders, 19*(2), 34–48.

Fulbright, R. K., Jenner, A. R., Mencl, W. E., Pugh, K. R., Shaywitz, B. A., Shaywitz, S. E., Frost, S. J., Skudlarski, P., Constable, R. T., Lacadie, C. M., Marchione, K. E., & Gore, J. C. (1999). The cerebellum's role in reading: A functional MR imaging study. *American Journal of Neuroradiology, 20,* 1925–1930.

Furuno, S., O'Reilly, K., Hosaka, C., Inatsuka, T., & Zeisloft-Falbey, B. (1994). *Hawaii Early Learning Profile (HELP) for Special Preschoolers—Assessment and curriculum guide.* Palo Alto, CA: VORT.

Gagne, J.-P., Stelmacovich, P., & Yovetich, W. (1991). Reactions to requests for clarification used by hearing-impaired individuals. *The Volta Review, 93,* 129–143.

Galaburda, A. M. (1989). Ordinary and extraordinary brain development: Anatomical variation in developmental dyslexia. *Annals of Dyslexia, 39,* 67–80.

Gallagher, A., Frith, U., & Snowling, M. J. (2000). Precursors of literacy delay among children at genetic risk of dyslexia. *Journal of Child Psychology and Psychiatry, 41*(2), 203–213.

Gallagher, J. (2007). *A–Z to Deafblindness.* Retrieved June 26, 2007, from www.deafblind.com/info-db.html

Gallagher, T. M. (1991). Language and social skills: Implications for assessment and intervention with school-age children. In T. M. Gallagher (Ed.), *Pragmatics of language: Clinical practice issues* (pp. 11–41). San Diego, CA: Singular.

Gallego, M. A., & Hollingsworth, S. (2000). Introduction: The idea of multiple literacies. In M. A. Gallego & S. Hollingsworth (Eds.), *What counts as literacy: Challenging the school standard.* New York: Teachers College Press.

Gamse, B. C., Bloom, H. S., Kemple, J. J., & Jacob, R. T. (2008). *Reading First impact study: Interim report* (NCEE No. 2008-4016). Washington, DC: National Center for Education Evaluation and Regional Assistance, Institute of Education Sciences, U.S. Department of Education.

Gardner, H. (1983). *Frames of mind: The theory of multiple intelligences.* New York: Basic Books.

Gardner, H., Froud, K., McClelland, A., & van der Lely, H. K. J. (2006). Development of the Grammar and Phonology Screening (GAPS) test to assess key markers of specific language and literacy difficulties in young children. *International Journal of Language and Communication Disorders, 41,* 513–540.

Gee, J. (1989). Two styles of narrative construction and their linguistic and educational implications. *Discourse Processes, 12,* 287–307.

Gee, J. (1990). *Social linguistics and literacies: Ideology in discourses.* Bristol, PA: Falmer Press.

Gee, K. (1995). Facilitating active and informed participation and learning in inclusive settings. In N. G. Haring & L. T. Romer (Eds.), *Welcoming students who are deaf-blind into typical classrooms* (pp. 369–404). Baltimore: Paul H. Brookes.

Gelo, J., & O'Malley, K. (2003). Family stress in parenting a child or adolescent with FASD. *Iceberg, 13*(1). Retrieved August 3, 2007, from http://fasiceberg.org/newsletters/Vol13Num1_Mar2003.htm

Genesee, F., Paradis, J., & Crago, M. B. (2004). *Dual language development and disorders: A handbook on bilingualism and second language learning.* Baltimore: Paul H. Brookes.

Genetics Home Reference. (n.d.). Cri-du-Chat Syndrome. Retrieved March 11, 2007, from http://ghr.nlm.nih.gov/condition=criduchatsyndrome

Gentry, J. R. (1982). An analysis of developmental spelling in GNYS AT WRK. *Reading Teacher, 36,* 192–200.

German, D. (1983). I know it but I can't think of it: Word retrieval difficulties. *Academic Therapy, 18,* 539–545.

German, D. (1990). *Test of Adolescent/Adult Word Finding (TAWF).* Minneapolis, MN: Pearson Assessments.

German, D. (1991). *Test of Word Finding in Discourse (TWFD).* Minneapolis, MN: Pearson Assessments.

German, D. (2000). *Test of Word Finding-2 (TWF-2).* Minneapolis, MN: Pearson Assessments.

Gersten, R., Fuchs, L., Williams, J., & Baker, S. (2001). Teaching reading comprehension strategies to students with learning disabilities: A review of research. *Review of Educational Research, 71,* 279–320.

Geschwind, N. (1984). The brain of a learning disabled individual. *Annals of Dyslexia, 34,* 319–327.

Geschwind, N., & Levitsky, W. (1968). Human brain: Left–right asymmetries in temporal speech region. *Science, 161,* 186–187.

Giangreco, M., Cloninger, C., & Iverson, V. (2000). *Choosing Outcomes and Accommodations for Children (COACH): A guide to educational planning for students with disabilities.* Baltimore: Paul H. Brookes.

Gibbard, D. (1994). Parental-based intervention with pre-school language-delayed children. *European Journal of Disorders of Communication, 29*(2), 131–150.

Gierut, J. (2001). Complexity in phonological treatment: Clinical factors. *Language, Speech, and Hearing Services in Schools, 32,* 229–241.

Gillam, R. B., Crofford, J. A., Gale, M. A., & Hoffman, L. M. (2001). Language change following computer-assisted language instruction with Fast ForWord or Laureate Learning Systems software. *American Journal of Speech-Language Pathology, 10,* 231–247.

Gillam, R. B., Frome Loeb, D., Hoffman, L. M., Bohman, T., Champlin, C. A., Thibodeau, L., Widen, J., Brandel, J., & Friel-Patti, S. (2008). The efficacy of Fast ForWord language intervention in school-age children with language impairment: A randomized controlled trial. *Journal of Speech, Language, and Hearing Research, 51,* 97–119.

Gillam, R. B., & Johnston, J. (1992). Spoken and written relationships in language/learning impaired and normally achieving school-age children. *Journal of Speech and Hearing Research, 35,* 1303–1315.

Gillam, R. B., & Pearson, N. (2004). *Test of Narrative Language (TNL).* Austin, TX: Pro-Ed.

Gillam, R. B., Peña, E. D., & Miller, L. (1999). Dynamic assessment of narrative and expository discourse. *Topics in Language Disorders, 20*(1), 33–47.

Gillam, R. B., & Ukrainetz, T. A. (2006). Language intervention through literature-based units. In T. A. Ukrainetz (Ed.), *Contextualized language intervention: Scaffolding PreK–12 literacy achievement* (pp. 59–94). Eau Claire, WI: Thinking Publications.

Gillette, Y. (1992). *CATCH guide to planning services with families: Coordinated transitions from the hospital to the community and home.* San Antonio, TX: Communication Skills Builders.

Gillingham, A., & Stillman, B. W. (1997). *Gillingham manual* (8th ed.). Cambridge, MA: Educators Publishing Service.

Gillon, G. (2004). *Phonological awareness: From research to practice.* New York: Guilford Press.

Gillon, G. (2005). Facilitating phoneme awareness development in 3- and 4-year-old children with speech impairment. *Language, Speech, and Hearing Services in Schools, 36,* 308–324.

Gillon, G., & Dodd, B. (1995). The effects of training phonological, semantic, and syntactic processing skills in spoken language on reading ability. *Language, Speech, and Hearing Services in Schools, 26,* 58–68.

Gillon, G., & Young, A. A. (2002). The phonological awareness of children who are blind. *Journal of Visual Impairment and Blindness, 96,* 38–49.

Girolametto, L., Pearce, P., & Weitzman, E. (1996). Interactive focused stimulation for toddlers with expressive vocabulary delays. *Journal of Speech and Hearing Research, 39,* 1274–1283.

Girolametto, L., Pearce, P. S., & Weitzman, E. (1997). Effects of lexical intervention on the phonology of late talkers. *Journal of Speech, Language, and Hearing Research, 40,* 338–348.

Girolametto, L., & Tannock, R. (1994). Correlates of directiveness in the interactions of fathers and mothers of children with developmental delays. *Journal of Speech and Hearing Research, 37,* 1178–1192.

Girolametto, L., Verbey, M., & Tannock, R. (1994). Improving joint engagement in parent–child interaction: An intervention study. *Journal of Early Intervention, 18,* 155–167.

Girolametto, L., & Weitzman, E. (2002). Responsiveness of child care providers in interactions with toddlers and preschoolers. *Language, Speech, and Hearing Services in Schools, 33,* 268–281.

Girolametto, L., & Weitzman, E. (2006). It takes two to talk—The Hanen Program for Parents: Early language intervention through caregiver training. In R. J. McCauley & M. E. Fey (Eds.), *Treatment of language disorders in children* (pp. 77–101). Baltimore: Paul H. Brookes.

Girolametto, L., & Weitzman, E. (2007). Promoting peer interaction skills: Professional development for early childhood educators and preschool teachers. *Topics in Language Disorders, 27*(2), 93–110.

Girolametto, L., Weitzman, E., Wiigs, M., & Pearce, P. S. (1999). The relationship between maternal language measures and language development in toddlers with expressive vocabulary delays. *American Journal of Speech-Language Pathology, 8,* 364–374.

Girolametto, L., Wiigs, M., Smyth, R., Weitzman, E., & Pearce, P. (2001). Children with a history of expressive vocabulary delay: Outcomes at 5 years of age. *American Journal of Speech-Language Pathology, 10,* 358–369.

Glenn, P., & Hurley, S. (1993). Preventing spelling disabilities. *Child Language Teaching and Therapy, 9,* 1–12.

Goffman, L. (2005). Assessment and classification: An integrative model of language and motor contributions to phonological development. In A. G. Kamhi & K. E. Pollack (Eds.), *Phonological disorders in children: Clinical decision making in assessment and intervention* (pp. 51–64). Baltimore: Paul H. Brookes.

Goldfield, B. A., & Reznick, J. S. (1990). Early lexical acquisition: Rate, content, and the vocabulary spurt. *Journal of Child Language, 17*(1), 171–183.

Goldman, R., & Fristoe, M. (1969). *Goldman-Fristoe Test of Articulation.* Circle Pines, MN: American Guidance Service.

Goldman, R., & Fristoe, M. (2000). *Goldman-Fristoe Test of Articulation* (3rd ed.) (GFTA-3). Circle Pines, MN: American Guidance Service.

Goldstein, A. P. (1988). *The prepare curriculum: Teaching prosocial competencies.* Champaign, IL: Research Press.

Goldstein, B. (2006). Clinical implications of research on language development and disorders in bilingual children. *Topics in Language Disorders, 26*(4), 305–321.

Goldstein, B., Harris, K. C., & Klein, M. (1993). Assessment of oral storytelling abilities of Latino junior high school students with learning handicaps. *Journal of Learning Disabilities, 26,* 138–143.

Goldstein, H. (1985). Enhancing language generalization using matrix and stimulus equivalence training. In S. Warren & A. Rogers-Warren (Eds.), *Teaching functional language* (pp. 225–249). Austin, TX: Pro-Ed.

Goldstein, H., Schneider, N., & Thiemann, K. (2007). Peer-mediated social communication intervention: When clinical expertise informs treatment development and evaluation. *Topics in Language Disorders, 27*(2), 182–199.

Goldstein, H., Wickstrom, S., Hoyson, M., Jamieson, B., & Odom, S. (1988). Effects of sociodramatic script training on social and communicative interaction. *Education and Treatment of Children, 11,* 97–117.

Good, R. H., & Kaminski, R. A. (2002). DIBELS Oral Reading Fluency Passages for First through Third Grades (Technical Report No. 10). Eugene: University of Oregon.

Goodman, K. (1986). *What's whole in whole language.* Portsmouth, NH: Heinemann.

Gopnik, M., & Crago, M. (1991). Familial aggregation of a developmental language disorder. *Cognition, 39,* 1–50.

Gordon, N. (2006). Williams syndrome. *Journal of Pediatric Neurology, 4*(1), 11–14.

Gough, P. B., & Tunmer, W. (1986). Decoding, reading, and reading disability. *Remedial and Special Education, 7,* 6–10.

Gould, B. W. (2001). Curricular strategies for written expression. In A. M. Bain, L. L. Bailet, & L. C. Moats (Eds.), *Written language disorders: Theory into practice* (2nd ed., pp. 185–220). Austin, TX: Pro-Ed.

Grace, J., & Malloy, P. (1992). Neuropsychiatric aspects of right hemisphere learning disability. *Neuropsychiatry, Neuropsychology, and Behavioral Neurology, 5,* 194–204.

Graham, S. (2000). Should the natural learning approach replace spelling instruction? *Journal of Educational Psychology, 92,* 235–247.

Graham, S., & Harris, K. R. (2002). The road less traveled: Prevention and intervention in written language. In K. Butler & E. Silliman. (Eds.), *The language learning disabilities continuum: Integration of research, technology, and education.* Mahwah, NJ: Lawrence Erlbaum.

Graham, S., Harris, K. R., & Troia, G. (2000). Self-regulated strategy development revisited: Teaching writing strategies to struggling writers. *Topics in Language Disorders, 20*(4), 1–14.

Graner, P. S., Faggella-Luby, M. N., & Fritschmann, N. A. (2005). An overview of responsiveness to intervention: What practitioners ought to know. *Topics in Language Disorders, 25,* 93–104.

Gray, C. (1994a). *The new social stories book.* Arlington, TX: Future Horizons.

Gray, C. (1994b). *Comic strip conversations.* Arlington, TX: Future Horizons.

Gray, C. (1998). Social stories and comic book conversations with students with Asperger syndrome and high-functioning autism. In E. Schopler, G. E. Mesibov, & L. J. Kunce (Eds.), *Asperger syndrome or high functioning autism?* (pp. 167–196). New York: Plenum Press.

Gray, C. (2005). Foreword. In M. Howley & E. Arnold, *Revealing the hidden social code: Social stories for people with autistic spectrum disorders.* London: Jessica Kingsley.

Gray, C., & White, A. L. (Eds.). (2002). *My social stories book.* London: Jessica Kingsley.

Green, J. R., Moore, C. A., Higashikawa, M., & Steeve, R. W. (2000). The physiological development of speech motor control: Lip and jaw coordination. *Journal of Speech, Language, and Hearing Research, 43,* 239–255.

Green, L. J. (2003). *African American English: A linguistic introduction.* New York: Cambridge University Press.

Greenspan, S. I. (1995). *The challenging child.* Reading, MA: Perseus Books.

Greenspan, S. I. (1997). *The growth of the mind.* Reading, MA: Perseus Books.

Greenspan, S. I., & Shanker, S. G. (2004). *The first idea: How symbols, language, and intelligence evolved from our primate ancestors to modern humans.* Cambridge, MA: Da Capo Press.

Greenspan, S. I., & Wieder, S. (1997). Developmental patterns and outcomes in infants and children with disorders in relating and communicating: A chart review of 200 cases of children with autistic spectrum diagnoses. *Journal of Developmental and Learning Disorders, 1,* 87–141.

Greenspan, S. I., & Wieder, S. (2005). *Floortime DVD training guide.* Floortime Foundation and Interdisciplinary Council on Developmental and Learning Disorders. Retrieved January 1, 2008, from www.floortime.org

Greenspan, S. I., & Wieder, S. (2006). *Infant and early childhood mental health: A comprehensive developmental approach to assessment and intervention.* Washington, DC: American Psychiatric Publishing.

Greenspan, S. I., Wieder, S., & Simmons, R. (1998). *The child with special needs: Encouraging intellectual and emotional growth.* New York: Perseus Books.

Gregory, M., & Carroll, S. (1978). *Language and situation: Language varieties and their social contexts.* London: Routledge and Kegan Paul.

Grice, H. P. (1975). Logic and conversation. In P. Cole & J. L. Morgan (Eds.), *Syntax and semantics 3: Speech acts* (pp. 41–58). New York: Academic Press.

Griffin, T. M., Hemphill, L., Camp, L., & Wolf, D. P. (2004). Oral discourse in the preschool years and later literacy skills. *First Language, 24,* 123–147.

Griffiths, A. J., Parson, L. B., Burns, M. K., VanDerHeyden, A., & Tilly, W. D. (2007). *Response to intervention: Research for practice.* Alexandria, VA: National Association of State Directors of Special Education.

Gronna, S. S., Serna, L. A., Kennedy, C. H., & Prater, M. A. (1999). Promoting generalized social interactions using puppets and script training in an integrated preschool. *Behavior Modification, 23*(3), 419–440.

Grove, J., Conti-Ramsden, G., & Donlan, C. (1993). Conversational interaction and decision-making in children with specific language impairment. *European Journal of Disorders of Communication, 28,* 141–152.

Gutiérrez-Clellen, V., Peña, E. (2001). Dynamic assessment of diverse children: A tutorial. *Language, Speech, and Hearing Services in Schools, 32,* 212–224.

Gutiérrez-Clellen, V., Peña, E., & Quinn, R. (1995). Accommodating cultural differences in narrative style: A multicultural perspective. *Topics in Language Disorders, 15*(4), 54–67.

Hack, M., Taylor, H. G., Drotar, D., Schluchter, M., Cartar, L., Wilson-Costello, D., Klein, N., Friedman, H., Mercuri-Minich, N., & Morrow, M. (2005). Poor predictive validity of the Bayley Scales of Infant Development for Cognitive Function of extremely low birth weight children at school age. *Pediatrics, 116,* 333–341.

Hadley, P. A., Simmerman, A., Long, M., & Luna, M. (2000). Facilitating language development for inner-city children: Experimental evaluation of a collaborative, classroom-based intervention. *Language, Speech, and Hearing Services in Schools, 31,* 280–295.

Hall, P. K., Jordan, L. S., & Robin, D. A. (1993). *Developmental apraxia of speech: Theory and clinical practice.* Austin, TX: Pro-Ed.

Hall, P. K., & Tomblin, J. B. (1978). A follow-up study of children with articulation and language disorders. *Journal of Speech and Hearing Disorders, 43,* 227–241.

Hall, P. S. (1992). Applied humanism: A model for normalized behavior programming. *Journal of Humanistic Education and Development, 31,* 22–31.

Hallahan, D. P., & Mock, D. R. (2003). A brief history of the field of learning disabilities. In H. L. Swanson, K. R. Harris, & S. Graham (Eds.), *Handbook of learning disabilities* (pp. 16–29). New York: Guilford Press.

Halle, J. W., Ostrosky, M. M., & Hemmeter, M. L. (2006). Functional communication training: A strategy for ameliorating challenging behavior. In R. J. McCauley & M. E. Fey (Eds.), *Treatment of language disorders in children* (pp. 509–545). Baltimore: Paul H. Brookes.

Halliday, M. A. K., & Hasan, R. (1976). *Cohesion in English.* London: Longman.

Hammer, C. S., & Miccio, A. W. (2006). Early language and reading development of bilingual preschoolers from low-income families. *Topics in Language Disorders, 26*(4), 322–337.

Hammer, C., Miccio, A., & Wagstaff, D. (2003). Home literacy experiences and their relationship to bilingual preschoolers'

developing English literacy abilities: An initial investigation. *Language, Speech, and Hearing Services in Schools, 14,* 20–30.

Hancock, T. B., & Kaiser, A. P. (2006). Enhanced milieu teaching. In R. McCauley & M. Fey (Eds.), *Treatment of language disorders in children* (pp. 203–236). Baltimore: Paul H. Brookes.

Handleman, J. S., & Harris, S. L. (1980). Generalization from school to home with autistic children. *Journal of Autism and Developmental Disorders, 10*(3), 323–333.

Hardy, J. (1983). *Cerebral palsy.* Upper Saddle River, NJ: Prentice-Hall.

Harmon, J. M. (2000). Assessing and supporting independent word learning strategies of middle school students. *Journal of Adolescent and Adult Literacy, 43,* 518–527.

Harris, K. R., Graham, S., Mason, L. H., & Friedlander, B. (2008). *Powerful writing strategies for all students.* Baltimore: Paul H. Brookes.

Hart, B., & Risley, T. (1995). *Meaningful differences in the everyday experience of young American children.* Baltimore: Paul H. Brookes.

Hart, B., & Risley, T. R. (1968). Establishing the use of descriptive adjectives in the spontaneous speech of disadvantaged preschool children. *Journal of Applied Behavioral Analysis, 1,* 109–120.

Hart, B., & Risley, T. R. (1999). *The social world of children learning to talk.* Baltimore: Paul H. Brookes.

Hartup, W. (1983). Peer interaction and the behavioral development of the individual. In W. Damon (Ed.), *Social personality development: Essays on the growth of the child.* New York: W. W. Norton.

Hartzell, H. E. (1984). The challenge of adolescence. *Topics in Language Disorders, 4*(2), 1–9.

Haskill, A. M., & Tyler, A. A. (2007). A comparison of linguistic profiles in subgroups of children with specific language impairment. *American Journal of Speech-Language Pathology, 16,* 209–221.

Hatcher, P. J., Hulme, C., Miles, J. N., Carroll, J. M., Hatcher, J., Gibbs, S., et al. (2006). Efficacy of small group reading intervention for beginning readers with reading-delay: A randomised controlled trial. *Journal of Child Psychology and Psychiatry, 47*(8), 820–827.

Hayward, D., & Schneider, P. (2000). Effectiveness of teaching story grammar knowledge to pre-school children with language impairment: An exploratory study. *Child Language Teaching and Therapy, 16,* 255–284.

Heath, S. B. (1983). *Ways with words: Language, life, and work in communities and classrooms.* New York: Cambridge University Press.

Hedberg, N. L., & Westby, C. E. (1993). *Analyzing story-telling skills: Theory to practice.* Tucson, AZ: Communication Skill Builders.

Hedrick, D. L., Prather, E. M., & Tobin, A. R. (1975) *Sequenced Inventory of Communicative Development (SICD).* Seattle: University of Washington Press.

Heilmann, J., Ellis Weismer, S., Evans, J., & Hollar, C. (2005). Utility of the MacArthur-Bates Communicative Development Inventory in identifying language abilities of late-talking and typically developing toddlers. *American Journal of Speech-Language Pathology, 14,* 40–51.

Heilmann, J., Miller, J. F., Iglesias, A., Fabiano-Smith, L., Nockerts, A., & Andriachhi, K. D. (2008). Narrative transcription accuracy and reliability in two languages. *Topics in Language Disorders, 28*(2), 178–188.

Helm-Estabrooks, N., & Albert, M. L. (2004). *Manual of aphasia and aphasia therapy* (2nd ed.). Austin, TX: Pro-Ed.

Henry, J., Sloane, M., & Black-Pond, C. (2007). Neurobiology and neurodevelopmental impact of childhood traumatic stress and prenatal alcohol exposure. *Language, Speech, and Hearing Services in Schools, 38,* 99–108.

Henry, M. K. (1989). Children's word structure knowledge: Implications for decoding and spelling instruction. *Reading and Writing, 1*(2), 135–152.

Hesketh, A., Dima, E., & Nelson, V. (2007). Teaching phoneme awareness to pre-literate children with speech disorder: A randomized controlled trial. *International Journal of Language and Communication Disorders, 42,* 251–271.

Hess, L. J., & Fairchild, J. L. (1988). Model, analyse, practice (MAP): A language therapy model for learning-disabled adolescents. *Child Language Teaching and Therapy, 4,* 325–338.

Hester, E. J. (1996). Narratives of young African American children. In A. G. Kamhi, K. E. Pollack, & J. L. Harris (Eds.), *Communication development and disorders in African American children: Research, assessment, and intervention* (pp. 227–245). Baltimore: Paul H. Brookes.

Hewetson, A. (2005). *Laughter and tears: A family's journey to understanding the autism spectrum.* London: Jessica Kingsley.

Hewitt, L. E. (1991). Narrative comprehension: The importance of subjectivity. In J. F. Duchan, L. E. Hewitt, & R. M. Sonnenmeier (Eds.), *Pragmatics: From theory to practice* (pp. 88–104). Englewood Cliffs, NJ: Prentice-Hall.

Hewitt, L. E., Hammer, C. S., Yont, K. M., & Tomblin, J. B. (2005). Language sampling for kindergarten children with and without SLI: Mean length of utterances, IPSYN, and NDW. *Journal of Communication Disorders, 38,* 197–213.

Hodgdon, L. A. (1999). *Solving behavior problems in autism: Improving communication with visual strategies.* Troy, MI: QuirkRoberts.

Hodson, B. W., & Edwards, M. L. (Eds.). (1997). *Perspectives in applied phonology.* Gaithersburg, MD: Aspen.

Hoffman, L. M., & Gillam, R. B. (2004). Verbal and spatial information processing constraints in children with specific language impairment. *Journal of Speech, Language, and Hearing Research, 47,* 114–125.

Hoffman, P. R., & Norris, J. A. (2006). Visual strategies to facilitate written language development. In R. J. McCauley & M. E. Fey (Eds.), *Treatment of language disorders in children* (pp. 423–434). Baltimore: Paul H. Brookes.

Hogan, K., & Pressley, M. (Eds.). (1997). *Scaffolding student learning: Instructional approaches and issues.* Cambridge, MA: Brookline Books.

Holmes, A. E., & Rodriguez, G. P. (2007). Cochlear implants and vestibular/tinnitus rehabilitation. In R. L. Schow & M. A. Nerbonne (Eds.), *Introduction to audiologic rehabilitation* (4th ed., pp. 77–112). Boston: Allyn & Bacon.

Hoover, W. A., & Gough, P. B. (1990). The simple view of reading. *Reading and Writing, 2,* 127–160.

Horgan, D. (1980). Nouns: Love 'em or leave 'em. In V. Teller & S. White (Eds.), *Studies in child language and multilingualism* (pp. 5–27). New York: New York Academy of Sciences.

Hoskins, B. (1987). *Conversations: Language intervention for adolescents.* Allen, TX: DLM Resources.

Hoskins, B. (1990). Language and literacy: Participating in the conversation. *Topics in Language Disorders, 10*(2), 46–62.

Howes, C. (1985). Sharing fantasy: Social pretend play in toddlers. *Child Development, 56,* 1253–1258.

Howley, M., & Arnold, E. (2005). *Revealing the hidden social code: Social stories for people with autistic spectrum disorders.* London: Jessica Kingsley.

Howlin, P. (1981). The results of a home-based language training programme with autistic children. *British Journal of Disorders of Communication, 16*(2), 73–88.

Howlin, P., Davies, M., & Udwin, O. (1998). Cognitive functioning in adults with Williams Syndrome. *Journal of Child Psychology and Psychiatry and Allied Disciplines, 39,* 183–189.

Howlin, P., Gordon, R. K., Pasco, G., Wade, A., & Charman, T. (2007). The effectiveness of Picture Exchange Communication System (PECS) training for teachers of children with autism: A pragmatic, group randomized controlled trial. *Journal of Child Psychology and Psychiatry, 48,* 473–481.

Hudson, J., & Shapiro, L. (1991). From knowing to telling: The development of scripts, stories and personal narratives. In A. McCabe & C. Peterson (Eds.), *Developing narrative structure* (pp. 89–136). Hillsdale, NJ: Lawrence Erlbaum.

Hughes, D., McGillivray, L., & Schmidek, M. (1997). *Guide to narrative language.* Eau Claire, WI: Thinking Publications.

Hunt, K. W. (1965). *Grammatical structures written at three grade levels.* Urbana, IL: National Council of Teachers of English.

Hunt, K. W. (1970). Syntactic maturity in school children and adults. *Monographs of the Society for Research in Child Development, 134.*

Hunt, K. W. (1977). Early blooming and late blooming syntactic structures. In C. R. Cooper & L. O'Dell (Eds.), *Evaluating writing: Describing, measuring, judging* (pp. 91–106). Urbana, IL: National Council of Teachers of English.

Hunt, P., Soto, G., Maier, J., Muller, E., & Goetz, L. (2002). Collaborative teaming to support students with augmentative and alternative communication needs in general education classrooms. *AAC: Augmentative and Alternative Communication, 18*(1), 20–35.

Hunt-Berg, M. (2005). The Bridge School: Educational inclusion outcomes over 15 years. *AAC: Augmentative and Alternative Communication, 21*(2), 116–131.

Huttenlocher, J., Vasilyeva, M., Cymerman, E., & Levine, S. (2002). Language input and child syntax. *Cognitive Psychology, 45,* 337–374.

Hutter, J. J. (1986). Late effects of children with cancer [Letter to the editor]. *American Journal of Diseases of Children, 140,* 17–18.

Hyter, Y. (2007a). Pragmatic language assessment considerations. *Topics in Language Disorders, 27*(2), 128–145.

Hyter, Y. D. (2007b). Prologue: Understanding children who have been affected by maltreatment and prenatal alcohol exposure. *Language, Speech, and Hearing Services in Schools, 38,* 93–98.

Hyter, Y. D., & Westby, C. E. (1996). Using oral narratives to assess communicative competence. In A. G. Kamhi, K. E. Pollack, & J. L. Harris (Eds.), *Communication development and disorders in African American Children: Research, assessment, and intervention* (pp. 247–275). Baltimore: Paul H. Brookes.

Iacono, T., & Cupples, L. (2004). Assessment of phonemic awareness and word reading skills of people with complex communication needs. *Journal of Speech, Language, and Hearing Research, 47,* 437–449.

Idol, L. (1987). Group story mapping: A comprehension strategy for both skilled and unskilled readers. *Journal of Learning Disabilities, 20*(4), 196–205.

Idol, L., & Croll, V. J. (1987). Story-mapping training as a means of improving reading comprehension. *Learning Disability Quarterly, 10,* 214–229.

Idol, L., Paolucci-Whitcomb, P., & Nevin, A. (1986). *Collaborative consultation.* Austin, TX: Pro-Ed.

Idol-Maestas, L. (1985). Getting ready to read: Guided probing for poor comprehenders. *Learning Disability Quarterly, 8,* 243–254.

Iglesias, A. (1985). Communication in the home and classroom: Match or mismatch? *Topics in Language Disorders, 5*(4), 29–41.

Individuals with Disabilities Education Act Amendments, P.L. 105-17, 11 Stat. 37 (1997).

Individuals with Disabilities Education Improvement Act, P.L. 108-446, 118 Stat. 2647 (2004).

Ingersoll, B., & Schreibman, L. (2006). Teaching reciprocal imitation skills to young children with autism using a naturalistic behavioral approach: Effects on language, pretend play, and joint attention. *Journal of Autism and Developmental Disorders, 36*(4), 487–505.

Ingram, D. (1997). The categorization of phonological impairment. In B. W. Hodson & M. L. Edwards (Eds.), *Perspectives in applied phonology* (pp. 19–41). Gaithersburg, MD: Aspen.

Ingram, D., & Ingram, K. D. (2001). A whole-word approach to phonological analysis and intervention. *Language, Speech, and Hearing Services in Schools, 32,* 271–283.

Interdisciplinary Council for Developmental and Learning Disorders (ICDL). (2005). *Diagnostic manual for infancy and early childhood mental health disorders, developmental disorders, regulatory-sensory processing disorders, language disorders, and learning challenges (ICDL-DMIC).* Bethesda, MD: Author.

International Dyslexia Association. (2002). Definition of dyslexia adopted by the IDA Board of Directors, Nov. 12, 2002. Retrieved February 4, 2009, from www.interdys.org/FAQ WhatIs.htm

Irwin, J. W. (1988). Linguistic cohesion and the developing reader/writer. *Topics in Language Disorders, 8*(3), 14–23.

Jackendoff, R. (1992). *Languages of the mind: Essays on mental representation.* Cambridge, MA: MIT Press.

Jackson, C. W., Traub, R. J., & Turnbull, A. P. (2008). Parents' experiences with childhood deafness: Implications for family-centered services. *Communication Disorders Quarterly, 29,* 82–98.

Jackson-Maldonado, D., Thal, D., Marchman, V. A., Fenson, L., Newton, T., & Conboy, B. (2003). *MacArthur-Bates Inventario del Desarrollo de Habilidades Comunicativas (Inventarios).* Baltimore: Paul H. Brookes.

Jakobson, R. (1968). *Child language, aphasia, and linguistic universals* (A. Keiler, Trans.). The Hague, the Netherlands: Mouton. (Original work published 1941).

Jenkins, J. R., Heliotis, J. D., Stein, M. L., & Haynes, M. C. (1987). Improving reading comprehension by using paragraph restatements. *Exceptional Children, 54,* 54–59.

Jenkins, J. R., Stein, M., & Wysocki, K. (1984). Learning vocabulary through reading. *American Educational Research Journal, 21,* 767–787.

Jerger, J., & Musiek, F. (2000). Report of the Consensus Conference on the diagnosis of auditory processing disorders in school-aged children. *Journal of the American Academy of Audiology, 11*(9), 467–474.

John-Steiner, V. (1984). Learning styles among Pueblo children. *Quarterly Newsletter of the Laboratory of Comparative Human Cognition, 6,* 57–62.

Johnson, C. J. (2006). Getting started in evidence-based practice for childhood speech-language disorders. *American Journal of Speech-Language Pathology, 15,* 20–35.

Johnson, D. W., & Johnson, R. T. (1999). *Learning together and alone: Cooperative, competitive, and individualistic learning* (5th ed.). Boston: Allyn & Bacon.

Johnston, J. (1982a). Interpreting the Leiter IQ: Performance of young normal and language-disordered children. *Journal of Speech and Hearing Research, 25,* 291–296.

Johnston, J. (1982b). Narratives: A new look at communication problems in older language-disordered children. *Language, Speech, and Hearing Services in Schools, 13,* 144–155.

Johnston, J. (1994). Cognitive abilities of children with language impairments. In R. V. Watkins & M. L. Rice (Eds.), *Specific language impairment in children* (pp. 107–121). Baltimore: Paul H. Brookes.

Johnston, J. (2007a, January 8). Second thoughts on error-free learning. Retrieved March 25, 2008, from www.speech pathology.com/articles/article_detail.asp?article_id=310

Johnston, J. (2007b, June 18). Reading to kids. Retrieved March 25, 2008, from www.speechpathology.com/articles/article_detail.asp?article_id=321

Johnston, J. (2008). Narratives: 25 years later. *Topics in Language Disorders, 28*(2), 93–98.

Johnston, J., & Wong, A. (2002). Cultural differences in beliefs and practices concerning talk to children. *Journal of Speech, Language, and Hearing Research, 45,* 916–926.

Johnston, P. H. (2004). *Choice words: How our language affects children's learning.* Portland, ME: Stenhouse.

Jorgensen, C. M. (1994). Modifying the curriculum and short-term objectives to foster inclusion. In S. N. Calculator & C. M. Jorgensen (Eds.), *Including students with severe disabilities in schools: Fostering communication, interaction, and participation* (pp. 75–111). San Diego, CA: Singular.

Juel, C. (1988). Learning to read and write: A longitudinal study of 54 children from first through fourth grades. *Journal of Educational Psychology, 80,* 437–447.

Just, M., & Carpenter, P. A. (1987). *The psychology of reading and language comprehension.* Boston: Allyn & Bacon.

Just, M., & Carpenter, P. (1992). A capacity theory of comprehension: Individual differences in working memory. *Psychological Review, 99,* 122–149.

Justice, L. M. (2006). Evidence-based practice, response to intervention, and the prevention of reading difficulties. *Language, Speech, and Hearing Services in Schools, 37,* 284.

Justice, L. M., Chow, S. M., Capellini, C., Flanigan, K., & Colton, S. (2003). Emergent literacy intervention for vulnerable preschoolers: Relative effects of two approaches. *American Journal of Speech-Language Pathology, 12,* 320–332.

Justice, L. M., & Ezell, H. K. (2000). Enhancing children's print and word awareness through home-based parent intervention. *American Journal of Speech-Language Pathology, 9*(3), 257–269.

Justice, L. M., Mashburn, A. J., Hamre, B. K., & Pianta, R. C. (2008). Quality of language and literacy instruction in preschool classrooms serving at-risk pupils. *Early Childhood Research Quarterly, 23*(1), 51–68.

Justice, L. M., Meier, J., & Walpole, S. (2005). Learning new words from storybooks: An efficacy study with at-risk kindergartners. *Language, Speech, and Hearing Services in Schools, 36*(1), 17–32.

Justice, L. M., & Schuele, C. M. (2004). Phonological awareness: Description, assessment, and intervention. In J. E. Bernthal & N. W. Bankson (Eds.), *Articulation and phonological disorders* (5th ed., pp. 376–405). Boston: Allyn & Bacon.

Justice, L. M., Skibbe, L., & Ezell, H. (2006). Using print referencing to promote written language awareness. In T. A. Ukrainetz (Ed.), *Contextualized language intervention: Scaffolding PreK–12 literacy achievement* (pp. 389–428). Eau Claire, WI: Thinking Publications.

Kaderavek, J. N., & Justice, L. M. (2002). Shared storybook reading as an intervention context: Practices and potential pitfalls. *American Journal of Speech-Language Pathology, 11,* 395–406.

Kaderavek, J. N., & Sulzby, E. (1998). Parent-child joint book reading: An observational protocol for young children. *American Journal of Speech-Language Pathology, 7*(1), 33–47.

Kaderavek, J. N., & Sulzby, E. (2000). Narrative production by children with and without specific language impairment: Oral narratives and emergent readings. *Journal of Speech, Language, and Hearing Research, 43,* 34–49.

Kail, R., & Leonard, L. B. (1986). Word-finding abilities in language impaired children. *ASHA Monographs, 25.*

Kaiser, A., & Hester, P. (1994). Generalized effects of enhanced milieu teaching. *Journal of Speech and Hearing Research, 37,* 1320–1340.

Kamhi, A. G. (1981). Nonlinguistic symbolic and conceptual abilities of language-impaired and normally developing children. *Journal of Speech and Hearing Research, 24,* 446–453.

Kamhi, A. G. (2004). A meme's eye view of speech-language pathology. *Language, Speech, and Hearing Services in Schools, 35,* 105–111.

Kamhi, A. G. (2006). Treatment decisions for children with speech–sound disorders. *Language, Speech, and Hearing Services in Schools, 37,* 271–279.

Kamhi, A. G., Minor, J. S., & Mauer, D. (1990). Content analysis and intratest performance profiles on the Columbia and the TONI. *Journal of Speech and Hearing Research, 33,* 375–379.

Kamhi, A. G., & Pollack, K. E. (2005). *Phonological disorders in children: Clinical decision making in assessment and intervention.* Baltimore: Paul H. Brookes.

Kanner, L. (1943). Autistic disturbances of affective contact. *Nervous Child, 2,* 217–250.

Karmiloff, K., & Karmiloff-Smith, A. (2001). *Pathways to language.* Cambridge, MA: Harvard University Press.

Kasari, C., Freeman, S., & Paparella, T. (2006). Joint attention and symbolic play in young children with autism: A randomized controlled intervention study. *Journal of Child Psychology and Psychiatry, 47*(6), 611–620.

Kaufman, S. Z. (1988). *Retarded isn't stupid, Mom!* Baltimore: Paul H. Brookes.

Kavale, K. A., & Forness, S. R. (2003). Learning disability as a discipline. In H. L. Swanson, K. R. Harris, & S. Graham (Eds.), *Handbook of learning disabilities* (pp. 76–93). New York: Guilford Press.

Kavale, K. A., & Reece, J. H. (1992). The character of learning disabilities. *Learning Disability Quarterly, 15,* 74–94.

Kayser, H. (1989). Speech and language assessment of Spanish-English speaking children. *Language, Speech, and Hearing Services in Schools, 20,* 226–244.

Kearney, A. J. (2008). *Understanding applied behavioral analysis: An introduction to ABA for parents, teachers, and other professionals.* London: Jessica Kingsley.

Keenan, M., Henderson, M., Kerr, K. P., & Dillenberger, K. (2006). *Applied behaviour analysis and autism: Building a future together.* London: Jessica Kingsley.

Keetay, V. (1996). The effect of visual distractions on speech perception in children. *Volta Review, 98*(2), 43–54.

Kelman, M., & Apel, K. (2004). The effects of a multiple linguistic, prescriptive approach to spelling instruction: A case study. *Communication Disorders Quarterly, 25*(2), 56–66.

Khan, L. L., & Lewis, N. (2002). *Khan-Lewis Phonological Analysis* (2nd ed.) (KLPA-2). Circle Pines, MN: American Guidance Service.

Killgallon, D. (1998). Sentence composing: Notes on a new rhetoric. In C. Weaver (Ed.), *Lessons to share: On teaching grammar in context* (pp. 169–183). Portsmouth, NH: Heinemann.

Kim, A., Vaughn, S., Wanzek, J., & Wei, S. (2004). Graphic organizers and their effects on the reading comprehension of students with LD: A synthesis of research. *Journal of Learning Disabilities, 37*(2), 105–118.

King, J., Spoeneman, T., Stuart, S., & Beukelman, D. R. (1995). Small talk in adult conversations: Implications for AAC vocabulary selection. *Augmentative and Alternative Communication, 11,* 260–264.

King, R. R., Jones, C., & Lasky, E. (1982). In retrospect: A fifteen-year follow-up report of speech-language-disordered children. *Language, Speech, and Hearing Services in Schools, 13,* 24–32.

Kintsch, W. (1994). Text comprehension, memory, and learning. *American Psychologist, 49,* 294–303.

Kirchner, D. M. (1991). Using verbal scaffolding to facilitate conversational participation and language acquisition in children with pervasive developmental disorders. *Journal of Childhood Communication Disorders, 14,* 81–98.

Kirk, C., & Gillon, G. T. (2007). Longitudinal effects of phonological awareness intervention on morphological awareness in children with speech impairment. *Language, Speech, and Hearing Services in Schools, 38*(4), 342–352.

Kirk, S. A. (1962). *Educating exceptional children.* Boston: Houghton Mifflin.

Kirk, S. A., McCarthy, J. J., & Kirk, W. D. (1968). *Illinois Test of Psycholinguistic Abilities.* Champaign-Urbana: University of Illinois Press.

Klecan-Acker, J. S., & Hedrick, L. D. (1985). A study of the syntactic language skills of normal school-age children.

Language, Speech, and Hearing Services in Schools, 16, 187–198.

Klecan-Aker, J., & Kelty, K. (1990). An investigation of the oral narratives of normal and language-learning disabled children. *Journal of Childhood Communication Disorders, 13,* 207–216.

Koegel, L. K., Carter, C. M., & Koegel, R. L. (2003). Teaching children with autism self-initiations as a pivotal response. *Topics in Language Disorders, 23*(2), 134–145.

Koegel, L. K., Koegel, R. L., Frea, W., & Green-Hopkins, I. (2003). Priming as a method of coordinating educational services for students with autism. *Language Speech and Hearing Services in Schools, 34*(3), 228–235.

Koegel, R. L., Bimbela, A., & Schreibman, L. (1996). Collateral effects of parent training on family interactions. *Journal of Autism and Developmental Disorders, 26*(3), 347–359.

Koegel, R. L., Camarata, S., Koegel, L. K., Ben-Tall, A., & Smith, A. E. (1998). Increasing speech intelligibility in children with autism. *Journal of Autism and Developmental Disorders, 28*(3), 241–251.

Koegel, R. L., Dunlap, G., & Dyer, K. (1980). Intertrial interval duration and learning in autistic children. *Journal of Applied Behavior Analysis, 13*(1), 91–99.

Koegel, R. L., Glahn, T. J., & Nieminen, G. S. (1978). Generalization of parent-training results. *Journal of Applied Behavior Analysis, 11*(1), 95–109.

Koenig, A. J., & Farrenkopf, C. (1997). Essential experience to undergird the early development of literacy. *Journal of Visual Impairment and Blindness, 91,* 14–24.

Koenigsknecht, R. A. (1974). Statistical information on developmental sentence analysis. In L. Lee, *Developmental sentence analysis* (pp. 222–268). Evanston, IL: Northwestern University Press.

Kohl, F. L., Wilcox, B. L., & Karlan, G. R. (1978). Effects of training conditions on the generalization of manual signs with moderately handicapped students. *Education and Training of the Mentally Retarded, 13*(3), 327–335.

Koppenhaver, D. A., Coleman, P. P., Kalman, S. L., & Yoder, D. E. (1991). The implications of emergent literacy research for children with developmental disabilities. *American Journal of Speech-Language Pathology, 1,* 38–44.

Koppenhaver, D. A., & Yoder, D. E. (1993). Classroom literacy instruction for children with severe speech and physical impairments (SSPI): What is and what might be. *Topics in Language Disorders, 13*(2), 1–15.

Kramer, J. H., Norman, D., Grant-Zawadzki, M., Albin, A., & Moore, I. (1988). Absence of white matter changes on magnetic resonance imaging in children treated with CNS prophylaxis therapy for leukemia. *Cancer, 61,* 928–930.

Kritikos, E. P. (2003). Speech-language pathologists' beliefs about language assessment of bilingual/bicultural individuals. *American Journal of Speech-Language Pathology, 17,* 73–91.

Kroeger, K. A., & Nelson, W. M., III. (2006). A language programme to increase the verbal production of a child dually diagnosed with Down syndrome and autism. *Journal of Intellectual Disability Research, 50*(2), 101.

Krose, J., Lotz, W., Puffer, C., & Osberger, M. J. (1986). Language and learning skills of hearing impaired children. *ASHA Monographs, 23,* 66–77.

Kumin, L. (1994). Intelligibility of speech of children with Down syndrome in natural settings: Parents' perspective. *Perceptual and Motor Skills, 78,* 307–313.

Kumin, L. (2008). Language intervention to encourage complex language use: A clinical perspective. In J. E. Roberts, R. S. Chapman, & S. F. Warren (Eds.), *Speech and language development and intervention in Down syndrome and fragile X syndrome* (pp. 193–218). Baltimore: Paul H. Brookes.

Kutas, M., & Schmitt, B. M. (2003). Language in microvolts. In M. T. Banich & M. Mack (Eds.), *Mind, brain, and language: Multidisciplinary perspectives* (pp. 171–209). Mahwah, NJ: Lawrence Erlbaum.

Labov, W. (1972). The transformation of experience in narrative syntax. In W. Labov (Ed.), *Language in the inner city: Studies in the Black English vernacular* (pp. 354–396). Philadelphia: University of Pennsylvania Press.

Labov, W., & Waletzky, J. (1997). Narrative analysis: Oral versions of personal experience. *Journal of Narrative and Life History, 7,* 39–44.

Lahey, M. (1988). *Language disorders and language development.* New York: Macmillan.

Lahey, M. (1990). Who shall be called language disordered? Some reflections and one perspective. *Journal of Speech and Hearing Disorders, 55,* 612–620.

Lahey, M. (1992). Linguistic and cultural diversity: Further problems for determining who shall be called language disordered. *Journal of Speech and Hearing Disorders, 56,* 638–639.

Laing, E., Hulme, C., Grant, J., & Karmiloff-Smith, A. (2001). Learning to read in Williams syndrome: Looking beneath the surface of atypical reading development. *Journal of Child Psychology and Psychiatry, 42*(6), 729–739.

Laing, S. P., & Espeland, W. (2005). Low intensity phonological awareness training in a preschool classroom for children with communication impairments. *Journal of Communication Disorders, 38*(1), 65–82.

Lamminmaki, T., Ahonen, T., Tolvanen, A., Michelsson, K., & Lyytinen, H. (1997). Two-year group treatment for children with learning difficulties: assessing effects of treatment duration and pretreatment characteristics. *Journal of Learning Disabilities, 30*(4), 354–364.

Langdon, H. W., & Cheng, L.-R. L. (2002). *Collaborating with interpreters and translators: A guide for communication disorders professionals.* Greenville, SC: Thinking Publications.

Larrivee, L. S., & Catts, H. W. (1999). Early reading achievement in children with expressive phonological disorders. *American Journal of Speech-Language Pathology, 8,* 118–128.

Larson, V. L., McKinley, N. L., & Boley, D. (1993). Service delivery models for adolescents with language disorders. *Language, Speech, and Hearing Services in Schools, 24,* 36–42.

Laski, K. E., Charlop, M. H., & Schreibman, L. (1988). Training parents to use the natural language paradigm to increase their autistic children's speech. *Journal of Applied Behavior Analysis, 21,* 391–400.

Law, J. (1999, November). Does speech and language therapy work? *Royal College of Speech Language Therapy Bulletin,* 14–15.

Law, J., Garrett, Z., & Nye, C. (2004). The efficacy of treatment for children with developmental speech and language delay/disorder: A meta-analysis. *Journal of Speech, Language, and Hearing Research, 47,* 924–943.

Leach, D., & Siddall, S. (1990). Parental involvement in the teaching of reading: A comparison of hearing reading, paired reading, pause, prompt, praise, and direct instruction methods. *British Journal of Educational Psychology, 60*(3), 349–355.

Leach, J. M., Scarborough, H. S., & Rescorla, L. (2003). Late-emerging reading disabilities. *Journal of Educational Psychology, 95*(2), 211–224.

Leahy, S. B., & Justice, L. M. (2006). Promoting reading fluency and motivation through readers theatre. In T. A. Ukrainetz (Ed.), *Contextualized language intervention: Scaffolding PreK–12 literacy achievement* (pp. 469–502). Eau Claire, WI: Thinking Publications.

Lederer, S. H. (2001). Efficacy of parent-child language group intervention for late-talking toddlers. *Infant-Toddler Intervention, 11*, 223–235.

Lee, L. L. (1974). *Developmental sentence analysis.* Evanston, IL: Northwestern University Press.

Lees, J. A. (2005). *Children with acquired aphasias* (2nd ed.). London: Whurr.

Leonard, L. B. (1981). Facilitating linguistic skills in children with specific language impairment: A review. *Applied Psycholinguistics, 2*, 89–118.

Leonard, L. B. (1989). Language learnability and specific language impairment in children. *Applied Psycholinguistics, 10*, 179–202.

Leonard, L. B. (1994). Some problems facing accounts of morphological deficits in children with specific language impairments. In R. V. Watkins & M. L. Rice (Eds.), *Specific language impairments in children* (pp. 91–105). Baltimore: Paul H. Brookes.

Leonard, L. B. (1998). *Children with specific language impairment.* Cambridge, MA: MIT Press.

Leonard, L. B., Ellis Weismer, S., Miller, C. A., Francis, D. J., Tomblin, J. B., & Kail, R. V. (2007). Speed of processing, working memory, and language impairment in children. *Journal of Speech Language Hearing Research, 50*, 408–428.

Leonard, L. B., & Fey, M. E. (1991). Facilitating grammatical development: The contribution of pragmatics. In T. M. Gallagher (Ed.), *Pragmatics of language: Clinical practice issues* (pp. 333–355). San Diego, CA: Singular.

Leonard, L. B., Schwartz, R. G., Chapman, K., Rowan, L. E., Prelock, P. A., Terrell, B., et al. (1982). Early lexical acquisition in children with specific language impairment. *Journal of Speech and Hearing Research, 25*, 554–564.

Levin, H. S., & Eisenberg, H. M. (1979). Neuropsychological impairment after closed head injury in children and adolescents. *Journal of Pediatric Psychology, 4*, 389–402.

Lewis, B. A., Freebairn, L. A., Hansen, A. J., Iyengar, S. K., & Taylor, H. G. (2004). School-age follow-up of children with childhood apraxia of speech. *Language, Speech, and Hearing Services in Schools, 35*, 122–140.

Lewis, B. A., Freebairn, L. A., Heeger, S., & Cassidy, S. B. (2002). Speech and language skills of individuals with Prader-Willi syndrome. *American Journal of Speech-Language Pathology, 11*, 285–294.

Lewis, B. A., O'Donnell, B., Freebairn, L. A., & Taylor, H. G. (1998). Spoken language and written expression—Interplay of delays. *American Journal of Speech-Language Pathology, 7*(3), 77–84.

Lidz, C. S., & Peña, E. D. (1996). Dynamic assessment: The model, its relevance as a nonbiased approach, and its ap- plication to Latino American preschool children. *Language, Speech, and Hearing Services in Schools, 27*, 367–372.

Lie, K. G. (1994). Sensitivity of perceptuomotor measures for very low birthweight (VLBW ≤ 1500 g) pre-schoolers. *Child: Care, Health and Development, 20*(4), 239–249.

Light, J., Binger, C., & Kelford Smith, A. (1994). Story reading interactions between preschoolers who use AAC and their mothers. *Augmentative and Alternative Communication, 10,* 255–268.

Light, J., & Kelford Smith, A. (1993). The home literacy experiences of preschoolers who use augmentative communicative systems and of their nondisabled peers. *Augmentative and Alternative Communication, 9,* 10–25.

Light, J., & McNaughton, D. (1993). Literacy and augmentative and alternative communication: The experiences and priorities of parents and teachers. *Topics in Language Disorders, 13*(2), 33–46.

Liles, B. Z. (1985). Narrative ability in normal and language disordered children. *Journal of Speech and Hearing Research, 28,* 123–133.

Liles, B. Z. (1987). Episode organization and cohesive conjunctives in narratives of children with and without language disorders. *Journal of Speech and Hearing Research, 30,* 185–196.

Liles, B. Z., Duffy, R. J., Merritt, D. D., & Purcell, S. L. (1995). Measurement of narrative discourse ability in children with language disorders. *Journal of Speech and Hearing Research, 38,* 415–425.

Lindamood, C. H., & Lindamood, P. C. (1979). *Lindamood Auditory Conceptualization Test (LACT).* Austin, TX: Pro-Ed.

Lindamood, C. H., & Lindamood, P. C. (1984). *Auditory Discrimination in Depth (ADD).* Austin, TX: Pro-Ed.

Lindamood, P., & Lindamood, P. (1998). *Lindamood Phonemic Sequencing Program for Reading, Spelling, and Speech (LiPS).* Austin, TX: Pro-Ed.

Lindfors, J. W. (1987). *Children's language and learning* (2nd ed.). Englewood Cliffs, NJ: Prentice-Hall.

Ling, D. (1989). *Foundations of spoken language in hearing impaired children.* Washington, DC: Alexander Graham Bell Association.

Loban, W. (1963). *The language of elementary school children* (NCTE Research Report No. 1). Urbana, IL: National Council of Teachers of English.

Loban, W. (1976). *Language development: Kindergarten through grade twelve.* Urbana, IL: National Council of Teachers of English.

Long, S. H., & Fey, M. E. (2002). Computerized profiling [Computer software]. Milwaukee, WI: Marquette University.

Lonigan, C. J., Burgess, S. R., & Anthony, J. L. (2000). Development of emergent literacy and early reading skills in preschool children: Evidence from a latent-variable longitudinal study. *Developmental Psychology, 36,* 596–613.

Lonigan, C. J., & Whitehurst, G. J. (1998). Relative efficacy of parent and teacher involvement in a shared-reading intervention for preschool children from low-income backgrounds. *Early Childhood Research Quarterly, 13,* 263–290.

Lord, C., Rutter, M., DiLavore, P. C., & Risi, S. (1989). *Autism Diagnostic Observation Schedule (ADOS).* Los Angeles: Western Psychological Services.

Lord, C., & Schopler, E. (1989). Stability of assessment results of autistic and nonautistic language impaired children from preschool years to early school age. *Journal of Child Psychology and Psychiatry, 30,* 575–590.

Lovaas, O. I. (1977). *The autistic child: Language development through behavior modification.* New York: Irvington.

Lovaas, O. I. (1981). *Teaching developmentally disabled children: The me book.* Austin, TX: Pro-Ed.

Lovaas, O. I. (1987). Behavioral treatment and normal educational and intellectual functioning in young autistic children. *Journal of Consultation in Clinical Psychology, 55*(1), 3–9.

Lovaas, O. I. (1993). The development of a treatment-research project for developmentally delayed and autistic children. *Journal of Applied Behavioral Analysis, 26,* 617–630.

Love, R. J. (2000). *Childhood motor speech disability.* Boston: Allyn & Bacon.

Lovett, M. W., Barron, R. W., Forbes, J. E., Cuksts, B., & Steinbach, K. A. (1994). Computer speech-based training of literacy skills in neurologically impaired children—A controlled evaluation. *Brain and Language, 47*(1), 117–154.

Lowe, M., & Costello, A. J. (1976). *The Symbolic Play Test.* Windsor, England: NFER.

Lucariello, J. (1990). Freeing talk from the here-and-now: The role of event knowledge and maternal scaffolds. *Topics in Language Disorders, 10*(3), 14–29.

Luthar, S. S., & Cicchetti, D. (2000). The construct of resilience: Implications for interventions and social policies. *Development and Psychopathology, 12,* 857–885.

Lyon, G. R., Shaywitz, S. E., & Shaywitz, B. A. (2003). A definition of dyslexia. *Annals of Dyslexia, 53,* 1–14.

MacDonald, J. (1989). *Becoming partners with children: From play to conversation.* Chicago: Riverside.

MacDonald, J., & Carroll, J. Y. (1992). Communicating with young children: An ecological model for clinicians, parents, and collaborative professionals. *American Journal of Speech-Language Pathology, 1,* 39–48.

MacWhinney, B. (1991). *The CHILDES project: Tools for analyzing talk.* Hillsdale, NJ: Lawrence Erlbaum.

MacWhinney, B. (1996). The CHILDES system. *American Journal of Speech-Language Pathology, 5*(1), 5–14.

Mahoney, G., & Snow, K. (1983). The relationship of sensorimotor functioning to children's response to early language training. *Mental Retardation, 21*(6), 248–254.

Mandler, J., Scribner, S., Cole, M., & DeForest, M. (1980). Remembrance of things parsed: Story structure and recall. *Cognitive Psychology, 9,* 111–151.

Manis, F. R., Seidenberg, M. S., & Doi, L. M. (1999). See Dick RAN: Rapid naming and the longitudinal prediction of reading subskills in first and second graders. *Scientific Studies of Reading, 3*(2), 129–157.

Manolson, A. (1992). *It takes two to talk: A parent's guide to helping children communicate* (rev. ed.). Toronto, Ontario, Canada: Hanen Centre.

Mar, R. A. (2004). The neuropsychological of narrative: Story comprehension, story production and their interrelation. *Neuropsychological, 42,* 1414–1434.

Mardell-Czudnowski, C., & Goldenberg, D. S. (1998). *Developmental Indicators for the Assessment of Learning* (3rd ed.) (DIAL-3). Circle Pines, MN: American Guidance Service.

Margolis, R. H., & Hunter, L. L. (2000). *Audiology: Diagnosis.* New York: Thieme.

Marino, M. T., Marino, E. C., & Shaw, S. F. (2006). Making informed assistive technology decisions for student with high incidence disabilities. *Teaching Exceptional Children, 38*(6), 18–25.

Marslen-Wilson, W., & Warren, P. (1994). Levels of perceptual representation and process in lexical access: Words, phonemes, and features. *Psychological Review, 101*(4), 653–675.

Martin, B., & Archambault, J. (1989). *Chicka chicka boom boom* (L. Ehlert, Illus.). New York: Simon & Schuster.

Martin, F. N., & Clark, J. G. (2006). *Introduction to audiology* (9th ed.). Boston: Allyn & Bacon.

Massie, R., & Dillon, H. (2006). The impact of sound-field amplification in mainstream cross-cultural classrooms: Part 1, Educational outcomes. *Australian Journal of Education, 50*(1), 62–77.

Mastergeorge, A. M. (2007). Maternal belief systems: The discourse of cultural practice as evidence. *Topics in Language Disorders, 27*(1), 62–73.

Masterson, J. J., Apel, K., & Wasowicz, J. (2002). *Spelling Performance Evaluation for Language and Literacy* (2nd ed.) (SPELL-2) [Computer software]. Evanston, IL: Learning By Design. Retrieved January 1, 2008, from www.learningbydesign.com

Mathes, P. G., Pollard-Durodola, S. D., Cárdenas-Hagan, E., Linan-Thompson, S., & Vaughn, S. (2007). Teaching struggling readers who are native Spanish speakers: What do we know? *Language, Speech, and Hearing Services in Schools, 38,* 260–271.

Mauer, D. M. (1999). Issues and application of sensory integration theory and treatment with children with language disorders. *Language, Speech, and Hearing Services in Schools, 30,* 383–392.

Mayer, M. (1969). *Frog, where are you?* New York: Puffin Books.

McCabe, A., & Bliss, L. (2003). *Patterns of narrative discourse: A multicultural, life span approach.* Boston: Allyn & Bacon.

McCabe, A., & Bliss, L. S. (2008). Comparison of personal versus fictional narratives of children with language impairment. *American Journal of Speech-Language Pathology, 17,* 1–13.

McCabe, A., & Peterson, C. (1991). Getting the story: Longitudinal study of parental styles in eliciting narratives and developing narrative skill. In A. McCabe & C. Peterson (Eds.), *Developing narrative structure* (pp. 217–253). Hillsdale, NJ: Lawrence Erlbaum.

McCabe, A., & Rollins, P. R. (1994). Assessment of preschool narrative skills. *American Journal of Speech-Language Pathology, 3,* 45–56.

McCalla, J. L. (1985). A multidisciplinary approach to identification and remedial intervention for adverse late effects of cancer therapy. *Nursing Clinics of North America, 20,* 117–129.

McCardle, P., & Chhabra, V. (Eds.). (2004). *The voice of evidence in reading research.* Baltimore: Paul H. Brookes.

McCardle, P., & Leung, C. Y. Y. (2006). English language learners: Development and intervention (An introduction). *Topics in Language Disorders, 26*(4), 302–304.

McCardle, P., Mele-McCarthy, J., & Leos, K. (2005). English language learners and learning disabilities: Research agenda and implications for practice. *Learning Disabilities Research and Practice, 20*(1), 68–78.

McCathren, R. B., Warren, S. F., & Yoder, P. J. (1996). Prelinguistic predictors of later language development. In S. F. Warren,

J. Reichle, K. N. Cole, P. S. Dale, & D. J. Thal (Eds.), *Communication and language intervention series: Vol. 6. Advances in assessment of communication and language* (pp. 57–76). Baltimore: Paul H. Brookes.

McCauley, R. J., & Swisher, L. (1984). Psychometric review of language and articulation tests for preschool children. *Journal of Speech and Hearing Disorders, 49,* 34–42.

McCauley, R. J., & Swisher, L. (1987). Are maltreated children at risk for speech or language impairment? An unanswered question. *Journal of Speech and Hearing Disorders, 52,* 301–303.

McClannahan, L. E., & Krantz, P. J. (2005). *Teaching conversation to children with autism: Scripts and script fading.* Bethesda, MD: Woodbine House.

McCune-Nicholich, L. (1981). Toward symbolic functioning: Structure of early pretend games and potential parallels with language. *Child Development, 52,* 785–797.

McDade, A., & McCartan, P. (1998). "Partnership with parents"—a pilot project. *International Journal of Disorders of Communication, 33*(Suppl.), 556–561.

McDermott, P. A., Goldberg, M. M., Watkins, M. W., Stanley, J. L., & Glutting, J. J. (2006). A nationwide epidemiologic modeling study of LD: Risk, protection, and unintended impact. *Journal of Learning Disabilities, 39,* 230–251.

McGee, J. J., & Menolaschino, F. J. (1991). *Beyond gentle teaching: A nonaversive approach to helping those in need.* New York: Plenum Press.

McGee, J. J., Menolaschino, F. J., Hobbs, D. C., & Menousek, P. E. (1987). *Gentle teaching: A non-aversive approach to helping persons with mental retardation.* New York: Human Sciences.

McGee, L. M., & Richgels, D. J. (1990). *Literacy's beginnings: Supporting young readers and writers.* Boston: Allyn & Bacon.

McGinnis, M. (1963). *Aphasic children.* Washington, DC: Alexander Graham Bell Association.

McGinty, A. S., & Justice, L. (2006). Classroom-based versus pull-out interventions: A review of the experimental evidence. *EBP Briefs, 1*(1), 1–25.

McGregor, K. K. (2000). Development and enhancement of narrative skills in a preschool classroom: Toward a solution to clinician–client mismatch. *American Journal of Speech-Language Pathology, 9,* 55–71.

McInnes, J. M., & Treffry, J. A. (1982). *Deaf-blind infants and children: A developmental guide.* Toronto, Ontario, Canada: University of Toronto Press.

McKay, S. (2006). Management of young children with unilateral hearing loss. *Volta Review, 106,* 299–319.

McKenna, M. C. (2004). Teaching vocabulary to struggling older readers. *Perspectives (Newsletter of the International Dyslexia Association), 30*(1), 13–16.

McKeown, M. G., & Beck, I. L. (2006). Encouraging young children's language interactions with stories. In D. K. Dickinson & S. B. Neuman (Eds.), *Handbook of early literacy research* (pp. 281–294). New York: Guilford Press.

McNaughton, S., & Lindsay, P. (1995). Approaching literacy with AAC graphics. *Augmentative and Alternative Communication, 11,* 212–228.

McSheehan, M., Sonnenmeier, R. M., Jorgensen, C. M., & Turner, K. (2006). Beyond communication access: Promoting learning of the general education curriculum by students with significant disabilities. *Topics in Language Disorders, 26*(3), 266–290.

Mehan, H. (1979). *Learning lessons: Social organization in the classroom.* Cambridge, MA: Harvard University Press.

Melzer, P., Morgan, V. L., Pickens, D. R., Price, R. R., Wall, R. S., & Ebner, F. F. (2001). Cortical activation during Braille reading is influenced by early visual experience in subjects with severe visual disability: A correlational fMRI study. *Human Brain Mapping, 14*(3), 186–195.

Meng, H., Smith, S. D., Hager, K., Held, M., Liu, J., Olson, R. K., Pennington, B. F., DeFries, J. C., Gelernter, J., O'Reilly-Pol, T., Somlo, S., Skudlarski, P., Shaywitz, S. E., Shaywitz, B. A., Marchione, K., Wang, Y., Paramasivam, M., LoTurco, J. J., Page, G. P., & Gruen, J. R. (2005). DCDC2 is associated with reading disability and modulates neuronal development in the brain. *PNAS, 102*(47), 17053–17058.

Mentis, M. (1994). Topic management in discourse: Assessment and intervention. *Topics in Language Disorders, 14*(3), 29–54.

Merritt, D., & Culatta, B. (1998). *Language intervention in the classroom.* San Diego, CA: Singular.

Merritt, D., & Liles, B. (1987). Story grammar ability in children with and without language disorder: Story generation, story retelling and story comprehension. *Journal of Speech and Hearing Research, 30,* 539–552.

Merritt, D., & Liles, B. (1989) Narrative analysis: Clinical applications of story generation and story retelling. *Journal of Speech and Hearing Disorders, 54,* 438–447.

Mervis, C. B. (2004). Cross-etiology comparisons of cognitive and language development. In M. L. Rice & S. F. Warren (Eds.), *Developmental language disorders: From phenotypes to etiologies* (pp. 153–185). Mahwah, NJ: Lawrence Erlbaum.

Meyer, B. J. F., Brandt, D. M., & Bluth, G. J. (1980). Use of top-level structure in text: Key for reading comprehension of ninth-grade students. *Reading Research Quarterly, 16,* 72–103.

Meyer, G., & Batshaw, M. (2002). Fragile X syndrome. In M. Batshaw (Ed.), *Children with disabilities* (5th ed., pp. 321–331). Baltimore: Paul H. Brookes.

Michaels, S. (1991). The dismantling of narrative. In A. McCabe & C. Peterson (Eds.), *Developing narrative structure* (pp. 303–352). Mahwah, NJ: Lawrence Erlbaum.

Michaud, L. J., Semel-Concepción, J., & Duhaime A-C., & Lazar, M. F. (2002). Traumatic brain injury. In M. L. Batshaw (Ed.), *Children with disabilities* (5th ed., pp. 525–545). Baltimore: Paul H. Brookes.

Miedzianik, D. (1990). I hope some lass will want me after reading all this. *Advocate (Newsletter of the Autism Society of America), 22*(1), 7.

Miller, G., & Gildea, P. (1987). How children learn words. *Scientific American, 257*(3), 94–99.

Miller, G. A. (1956). The magical number seven, plus or minus two: Some limits on our capacity for processing information. *Psychological Review, 63,* 81–97.

Miller, J., & Chapman, R. (2008). *Systematic Analysis of Language Transcripts* (SALT, Version 9) [Computer software]. Madison, WI: Waisman Center. Retrieved January 1, 2008, from www.saltsoftware.com

Miller, J., Heilmann, J., Iglesias, A., Fabiano, L., Nockerts, A., & Francis, D. (2006). Oral language and reading in bilingual children. *Learning Disabilities Research and Practice, 21,* 30–43.

Miller, J., & Iglesias, A. (2007). *Systematic Analysis of English and Spanish Language Transcripts* [Computer software]. Madison, WI: Language Analysis Lab.

Miller, J. F. (1981). *Assessing language production in children: Experimental procedures.* Austin, TX: Pro-Ed.

Miller, L. (1993). *What we call smart: A new narrative for intelligence and learning.* San Diego, CA: Singular.

Miller, L., Gillam, R., & Peña, E. (2001). *Dynamic assessment and intervention: Improving children's narrative abilities.* Austin, TX: Pro-Ed.

Miller, M. M., Menacker, S. J., & Batshaw, M. L. (2002). Vision: Our window to the world. In M. L. Batshaw (Ed.), *Children with disabilities* (5th ed., pp. 165–192). Baltimore: Paul H. Brookes.

Mills v. Board of Education, 348 F. Supp. 866 (D.D.C. 1972).

Milosky, L. M. (1987). Narratives in the classroom. *Seminars in Speech and Language, 8*(4), 329–343.

Minami, M. (2002). *Culture-specific language styles: The development of oral narrative and literacy.* Tonawanda, WA: Multilingual Matters.

Minshew, N. J., Goldstein, G., & Siegel, D. J. (1997). Neuropsychologic functioning in autism: Profile of a complex information processing disorder. *Journal of the International Neuropsychological Society, 3,* 303–316.

Mirenda, P. (2003). "He's not really a reader . . .": Perspectives on supporting literacy development in individuals with autism. *Topics in Language Disorders, 23*(4), 271–282.

Mirenda, P., & Erickson, K. A. (2000). Augmentative communication and literacy. In A. M. Wetherby & B. M. Prizant (Eds.), *Autism spectrum disorders: A transactional developmental perspective* (pp. 333–367). Baltimore: Paul H. Brookes.

Miyamoto, R. T., Houston, D. M., Kirk, K. J., Perdew, A. E., & Svirsky, M. A. (2003). Language development in deaf infants following cochlear implantation. *Acta Otolaryngologica, 123,* 241–244.

Miyamoto, R., Osberger, M., Robbins, A., Myres, W., & Kessler, K. (1993). Prelingually deafened children's performance with the nucleus multichannel cochlear implant. *American Journal of Otology, 14,* 437–445.

Moats, L. (2000). What is the role of the speech-language pathologist in assessing and facilitating spelling skills? *Topics in Language Disorders, 20*(3), 85–87.

Moeller, M. P., Schow, R. L., & Whitaker, M. M. (2007). Audiologic rehabilitation for children: Assessment and management. In R. L. Schow & M. A. Nerbonne (Eds.), *Introduction to audiologic rehabilitation* (pp. 303–366). Boston: Allyn & Bacon.

Moje, E. B. (2006). Motivating texts, motivating contexts, motivating adolescents: An examination of the role of motivation in adolescent literacy practices and development. *Perspectives (Newsletter of the International Dyslexia Association), 32*(3), 10–14.

Monsees, E. K. (1972). *Structured language for children with special language learning problems.* Washington, DC: Children's Hospital National Medical Center.

Monson, M. R., & Bowen, S. K. (2008). The development of phonological awareness by Braille users: A review of the research. *Journal of Visual Impairment and Blindness, 102,* 210–220.

Montague, M., Maddux, C., & Dereshiwsky, M. (1990). Story grammar and comprehension and production of narrative prose by students with learning disabilities. *Journal of Learning Disabilities, 23,* 190–197.

Montgomery, J. W. (1996). Sentence comprehension and working memory in children with specific language impairment. *Topics in Language Disorders, 17*(1), 19–32.

Moore-Brown, B. J., & Montgomery, J. K. (2005). *Making a difference: In the era of accountability.* Eau Claire, WI: Thinking Publications.

Moore-Brown, B. J., Montgomery, J. K., Bielinski, J., & Shubin, J. (2005). Responsiveness to intervention: Teaching before testing helps avoid labeling. *Topics in Language Disorders, 25,* 148–167.

Morris, N. T., & Crump, W. D. (1982). Syntactic and vocabulary development in the written language of learning disabled and nondisabled students at four age levels. *Learning Disability Quarterly, 5,* 163–172.

Mundy, P., Kasari, C., Sigman, M., & Ruskin, E. (1995). Nonverbal communication and early language acquisition in children with Down syndrome and in normal developing children. *Journal of Speech and Hearing Research, 38,* 157–167.

Munson, B., Edwards, J., & Beckman, M. E. (2005). Phonological knowledge in typical and atypical speech development. *Topics in Language Disorders, 25*(3), 190–206.

Murray-Seegert, C. (1989). *Nasty girls, thugs, and humans like us: Social relations between severely disabled and nondisabled students in high school.* Baltimore: Paul H. Brookes.

Musiek, F. E., Bellis, T. J., & Chermak, G. D. (2005). Nonmodularity of the central auditory nervous system: Implications for (central) auditory processing disorder. *American Journal of Audiology, 14,* 128–138.

Nathan, L., Stackhouse, J., Goulandris, N., & Snowling, M. J. (2004). Literacy skills and children with speech difficulties. *Journal of Speech, Language, and Hearing Research, 47,* 377–391.

Nation, K. (2005). Children's reading comprehension difficulties. In M. J. Snowling & C. Hulme (Eds.), *The science of reading: A handbook* (pp. 249–266). Oxford, England: Blackwell.

Nation, K., Clarke, P., Marshall, C. M., & Durand, M. (2004). Hidden language impairments in children: Parallels between poor reading comprehension and specific language impairment. *Journal of Speech, Language, and Hearing Research, 47,* 199–211.

Nation, K., & Snowling, M. J. (2004). Beyond phonological skills: Broader language skills contribute to the development of reading. *Journal of Research in Reading, 27*(4), 342–356.

National Association of State Directors of Special Education (NASDSE). (2005). *Response to intervention policy considerations and implementation.* Alexandria, VA: Author. Retrieved November 29, 2007, from www.nasdse.org/documents/RtIAnAdministratorsPerspective1–06.pdf

National Fragile X Foundation. (n.d.). Autism and fragile X. Retrieved August 4, 4007, from www.fragilex.org

National Institute of Child Health and Human Development (NICHD). (2000). *National Reading Panel—Teaching children to read: Reports of the subgroups* (NIH Publication No. 00–4754). Washington, DC: U.S. Department of Health and Human Services.

National Institute of Deafness and Other Communication Disorders (NIDCD). (2007). Landau-Kleffner syndrome. U.S. Department of Health and Human Services, National Institutes of Health. Retrieved August 5, 2007, from www.nidcd.nih.gov/health/voice/landklfs.htm

National Institute of Neurological Disorders and Stroke (NINDS). (2007). Rett syndrome fact sheet. U.S. Department of Health and Human Services, National Institutes of Health. Retrieved August 9, 2007, from www.ninds.nih.gov/disorders/rett/detail_rett.htm

National Joint Committee for the Communication Needs of Persons with Severe Disabilities. (2003). *Position statement on access to communication services and supports: Concerns regarding the application of restrictive "eligibility" policies* [Position statement]. Retrieved January 1, 2008, from www.asha.org/policy

National Joint Committee on Learning Disabilities (NJCLD). (1991). Learning disabilities: Issues on definition. *ASHA, 33*(Suppl. 5), 18–20.

National Joint Committee on Learning Disabilities (NJCLD). (2006). *Learning disabilities and young children: Identification and intervention.* Official document of the NJCLD. Accessed on December 1, 2008 from LD Online at www.ldonline.org/article/11511

National Research Council, Committee on Educational Interventions for Children with Autism. (2001). *Educating children with autism.* Washington, DC: National Academy Press.

National Research Council, Committee on the Prevention of Reading Difficulties of Young Children. (1998). *Preventing reading difficulties in young children.* Washington, DC: National Academy Press.

National Technical Assistance Consortium (NTAC) for Children and Young Adults Who Are Deaf-Blind. (2004). *Annual deaf-blind census.* Monmouth, OR: Teaching Research Division.

Nelson, K. (1973). Structure and strategy in learning to talk. *Monograph of the Society for Research in Child Development, 38*(Serial No. 149).

Nelson, K. A., & Dimitrova, E. (1993). Severe visual impairment in the United States and in each state, 1990. *Journal of Visual Impairment and Blindness, 87,* 80–85.

Nelson, K. E., & Camarata, S. M. (1996). Improving English literacy and speech-acquisition learning conditions for children with severe to profound hearing impairments. *Volta Review, 98*(2), 17–41.

Nelson, K. E., Camarata, S., Welsh, J., Butkovsky, L., & Camarata, M. (1996). Effects of imitative and conversational recasting treatment on the acquisition of grammar in children with specific language impairment and younger language-normal children. *Journal of Speech and Hearing Research, 39,* 850–859.

Nelson, N. W. (1981). An eclectic model of language intervention for disorders of listening, speaking, reading, and writing. *Topics in Language Disorders, 1*(2), 1–23.

Nelson, N. W. (1985). Teacher talk and child listening—Fostering a better match. In C. S. Simon (Ed.), *Communication skills and classroom success: Assessment of language-learning disabled students* (pp. 65–102). San Diego, CA: College-Hill.

Nelson, N. W. (1989). Curriculum-based language assessment and intervention. *Language, Speech, and Hearing Services in Schools, 20,* 170–184.

Nelson, N. W. (1992). Performance is the prize: Language competence and performance among AAC users. *Augmentative and Alternative Communication, 8,* 3–18.

Nelson, N. W. (1998). *Childhood language disorders in context: Infancy through adolescence* (2nd ed.). Boston: Allyn & Bacon.

Nelson, N. W., Bahr, C. M., & Van Meter, A. M. (2004). *The writing lab approach to language instruction and intervention.* Baltimore: Paul H. Brookes.

Nelson, N. W., Helm-Estabrooks, N., Hotz, G., & Plante, E. (2007). *Test of Integrated Language and Literacy Skills (TILLS)* (Beta research edition). Baltimore: Paul H. Brookes.

Nelson, N. W., & Hyter, Y. D. (1990). *How to use Black English Sentence Scoring.* Short course presented at the Annual Conference of the American Speech-Language-Hearing Association. Seattle, Washington.

Nelson, N. W., Plante, E., Brennan, A., Anderson, M., &. Johnson, B. (2005, November). *Anatomy of a test: Why knowing about test construction matters.* Miniseminar presentation at the Annual Conference of the American Speech-Language-Hearing Association, San Diego, CA, November 20, 2005.

Nelson, N. W., & Van Meter, A. M. (2002). Enhancing academic performance of students with LLD. *Topics in Language Disorders, 22*(2), 35–59.

Nelson, N. W., & Van Meter, A. M. (2006a). Finding the words: Vocabulary development for young authors. In T. A. Ukrainetz (Ed.), *Contextualized language intervention: Scaffolding PreK–12 literacy achievement* (pp. 95–144). Eau Claire, WI: Thinking Publications.

Nelson, N. W., & Van Meter, A. M. (2006b). The writing lab approach for building language: Literacy and communication abilities. In R. J. McCauley & M. E. Fey (Eds.), *Treatment of language disorders in children* (pp. 383–422). Baltimore: Paul H. Brookes.

Nelson, N. W., & Van Meter, A. M. (2007). Measuring written language ability in narrative samples. *Reading and Writing Quarterly, 23,* 287–309.

Nelson, N. W., Van Meter, A. M., Chamberlain, D., & Bahr, C. M. (2001). The speech-language pathologist's role in a writing lab approach. *Seminars in Speech and Language, 22,* 209–219.

Nelson, N. W., & Warner, C. (2007). Assessment of communication, language, and speech: Questions of "What to do next?" In B. A. Bracken & R. J. Nagle (Eds.), *Psychoeducational assessment of preschool children* (4th ed., pp. 361–395). Mahwah, NJ: Lawrence Erlbaum.

Nerbonne, M. A., & Schow, R. L. (2007). Auditory stimuli in communication. In R. L. Schow & M. A. Nerbonne (Eds.), *Introduction to audiologic rehabilitation* (5th ed., pp. 113–150). Boston: Pearson.

Nicholich, L. M. (1981). Toward symbolic functioning: Structure of early pretend games and potential parallels with language. *Child Development, 52,* 785–797.

Ninio, A., & Snow, C. (1996). *Pragmatic development.* Boulder, CO: Westview.

Nippold, M. A. (1994). Persuasive talk in social contexts: Development, assessment, and intervention. *Topics in Language Disorders, 14*(3), 1–12.

Nippold, M. A. (1998). *Later language development: The school-age years* (2nd ed.). Austin, TX: Pro-Ed.

Nippold, M. A., Hesketh, L. J., Duthie, J. K., & Mansfield, T. C. (2005). Conversational versus expository discourse: A study of syntactic development in children, adolescents, and adults. *Journal of Speech, Language, and Hearing Research, 47,* 1048–1064.

Nittrouer, S. (2002). From ear to cortex: A perspective on what clinicians need to understand about speech perception and language processing. *Language, Speech, and Hearing Services in Schools, 33,* 237–253.

No Child Left Behind Act (NCLB), P.L. 107-110, 115 Stat. 1425, 20 U.S.C. 6301 *et seq.* (2001).

Norris, J. A. (1995). Expanding language norms for school-age children and adolescents: Is it pragmatic? *Language, Speech, and Hearing Services in Schools, 26,* 342–352.

Norris, J. A., & Hoffman, P. R. (1990). Language intervention within naturalistic environments. *Language, Speech, and Hearing Services in Schools, 21,* 72–84.

Norris, J. A., & Hoffman, P. R. (2005). Goals and targets: Facilitating the self-organizing nature of a neuro-network. In A. Kamhi & K. Pollock (Eds.), *Phonological disorders in children: Clinical decision making in assessment and intervention* (pp. 77–87). Baltimore: Paul H. Brookes.

Northern, J. L., & Downs, M. P. (1991). *Hearing in children* (4th ed.). Baltimore: Williams & Wilkins.

Nye, C., Turner, H., & Schwartz, J. (2006). *Approaches to parent involvement for improving the academic performance of elementary school age children.* Retrieved March 29, 2008, from www.campbellcollaboration.org

O'Donnell, R. C., Griffin, W. J., & Norris, R. D. (1967). Syntax of kindergarten and elementary school children: A transformational analysis. (Research Report No. 8). Champaign, IL: National Council of Teachers of English.

Oetting, J. B., & MacDonald, J. L. (2001). Nonmainstream dialect use and specific language impairment. *Journal of Speech, Language, and Hearing Research, 44,* 207–223.

Oetting, J. B., & Newkirk, B. L. (2008). Subject relatives by children with and without SLI across different dialects of English. *Clinical Linguistics and Phonetics, 22,* 111–125.

Ogle, D. (1986). KWL: A teaching model that develops active reading of expository text. *Reading Teacher, 39,* 564–570.

Oliver, P. R., & Scott, T. L. (1981). Group versus individual training in establishing generalization of language skills with severely handicapped individuals. *Mental Retardation, 19*(6), 285–289.

Olswang, L. B., Coggins, T. E., & Svensson, L. (2007). Assessing social communication in the classroom: Observing manner and duration of performance. *Topics in Language Disorders, 27*(2), 111–127.

O'Neill, T. J. (1987). Foreword: The person comes first. In S. M. Pueschel, C. Tingey, J. E. Rynders, A. C. Crocker, & D. M. Crutcher (Eds.), *New perspectives on Down syndrome* (pp. xviii–xix). Baltimore: Paul H. Brookes.

Osofsky, J. D. (1990, Winter). Risk and protective factors for teenage mothers and their infants. *Newsletter of the Society for Research in Child Development,* 1–2.

Owen, A. J., & Leonard, L. B. (2006). The production of finite and nonfinite complement clauses by children with specific language impairment and their typically developing peers. *Journal of Speech, Language, and Hearing Research, 49,* 548–571.

Páez, M., & Renaldi, C. (2006). Predicting English word reading skills for Spanish-speaking children in first grade. *Topics in Language Disorders, 26*(4), 338–350.

Page, J. L., & Stewart, S. R. (1985). Story grammar skills in school-age children. *Topics in Language Disorders, 5*(2), 16–30.

Paley, V. (1990). *The boy who would be a helicopter.* Cambridge, MA: Harvard University Press.

Palincsar, A. S., & Brown, D. (1984). Reciprocal teaching of comprehension-fostering and comprehension-monitoring activities. *Cognition and Instruction, 1,* 117–175.

Palmer, C. V. (1998). Quantification of the ecobehavioral impact of a soundfield loudspeaker system in elementary classrooms. *Journal of Speech, Language, and Hearing Research, 41,* 819–833.

Pany, D., Jenkins, J. R., & Schreck, J. (1982). Vocabulary instruction: Effects on word knowledge and reading comprehension. *Learning Disability Quarterly, 5,* 202–215.

Papanicolaou, A. C., DiScenna, A., Gillespie, L., & Aram, D. M. (1990). Probe evoked potential findings following unilateral left hemisphere lesions in children. *Archives of Neurology, 47,* 562–566.

Papoušek, M. (2007). Communication in early infancy: An arena of intersubjective learning. *Infant Behavior and Development, 30,* 258–266.

Paradise, J. L., Feldman, H. M., Campbell, T. F., Dollaghan, C. A., Rockette, H. E., Pitcairn, D. L., Smith, C. G., Colborn, D. K., Bernard, B. S., Kurs-Lasky, M., Janosky, J. E., Sabo, D. L., O'Connor, R. E., & Pelham, W. E., Jr. (2007). Tympanostomy tubes and developmental outcomes at 9 to 11 years of age. *New England Journal of Medicine, 356*(3), 248–261.

Paris, A. H., & Paris, S. G. (2003). Assessing narrative comprehension in young children. *Reading Research Quarterly, 40,* 184–202.

Patterson, J. L. (1998). Expressive vocabulary development and word combinations of Spanish-English bilingual toddlers. *American Journal of Speech-Language Pathology, 7,* 46–56.

Patterson, J. L. (1999). What bilingual toddlers hear and say: Language input and word combinations. *Communication Disorders Quarterly, 21,* 32–38.

Patterson, J. L., & Westby, C. E. (1998). The development of play. In W. O. Haynes & B. B. Shulman (Eds.), *Communication development: Foundations, processes, and clinical applications* (2nd ed., pp. 135–163). Baltimore: Williams & Wilkins.

Paul, P. V. (1996). First- and second-language English literacy. *Volta Review, 98*(2), 5–16.

Paul, R. (2007). *Language disorders from infancy through adolescence: Assessment and intervention* (3rd ed.). St. Louis, MO: Mosby/Elsevier.

Paul, R., & Elwood, T. J. (1991). Maternal linguistic input to toddlers with slow expressive language development. *Journal of Speech and Hearing Research, 34,* 982–988.

Paul, R., & Smith, R. L. (1993). Narrative skills in 4-year-olds with normal, impaired, and late-developing language. *Journal of Speech and Hearing Research, 36,* 592–598.

Paulesu, E., Frith, U., Snowling, M., Gallagher, A., Morton, J., Frackowiak, R. S. J., & Frith, C. D. (1996). Is developmental dyslexia a disconnection syndrome? Evidence from PET scanning. *Brain, 119,* 143–157.

Pearson, B., Fernandez, S., & Oller, D. (1995). Cross-language synonyms in the lexicons of bilingual infants: One language or two? *Journal of Child Language, 7,* 337–352.

Pellegrini, A. D., Galda, L., Bartini, M., & Charak, D. (1998). Oral language and literacy naming in context: The role of social relationships. *Merrill-Palmer Quarterly, 44,* 38–54.

Pellegrino, L. (2002). Cerebral palsy. In M. L. Batshaw (Ed.), *Children with disabilities* (5th ed., pp. 443–466). Baltimore: Paul H. Brookes.

Peña, E. D., Spaulding, T. J., & Plante, E. (2006). The composition of normative groups and diagnostic decision making: Shooting ourselves in the foot. *American Journal of Speech Language Pathology, 15,* 247–254.

Pennington, L., Goldbart, J., & Marshall, J. (2005). Direct speech and language therapy for children with cerebral palsy: Findings from a systematic review. *Developmental Medicine and Child Neurology, 47*(1), 57–63.

Pennington, L., Smallman, C., & Farrier, F. (2006). Intensive dysarthria therapy for older children with cerebral palsy: Findings from six cases. *Child Language Teaching and Therapy, 22*(3), 255.

Pennsylvania Association for Retarded Children v. Commonwealth of Pennsylvania (PARC), 33H F. Supp. 1257 (E.D. Pa. 1971).

Perera, K. (1986). Language acquisition and writing. In P. Fletcher & M. Garman (Eds.), *Language acquisition* (2nd ed., pp. 494–518). Cambridge, England: Cambridge University Press.

Perry, B. D. (1997). Incubated in terror: Neurodevelopmental factors in the "cycle of violence." In J. Osofsky (Ed.), *Children, youth and violence: The search for solutions* (pp. 124–148). New York: Guilford Press.

Peter, B., & Stoel-Gammon, C. (2005). Timing errors in two children with suspected childhood apraxia of speech (sCAS) during speech and music-related tasks. *Clinical Linguistics and Phonetics, 19*(2), 67–87.

Petersen, D. B., Gillam, S. L., & Gillam, R. B. (2008). Emerging procedures in narrative assessment: The index of narrative complexity. *Topics in Language Disorders, 28,* 115–130.

Peterson, C., & McCabe, A. (1983). *Developmental psycholinguistics: Three ways of looking at a child's narrative.* New York: Plenum Press.

Philofsky, A., Hepburn, S. L., Hayes, A., Hagerman, R., & Rogers, S. J. (2004). Linguistic and cognitive functioning and autism symptoms in young children with Fragile X syndrome. *American Journal on Mental Retardation, 109*(3), 208–218.

Piaget, J. (1952). *The origins of intelligence in children.* New York: International Universities Press.

Piaget, J. (1959). *The language and thought of the child* (3rd ed.). London: Routledge & Kegan Paul. (Original work published 1926)

Pinker, S. (1994). *The language instinct.* New York: William Morrow.

Pinker, S. (2002). *The blank slate: The modern denial of human nature.* London: Allen Lane Science.

Plante, E. (1998). The Stark and Tallal legacy and beyond. *Journal of Speech, Language, and Hearing Research, 41,* 951–957.

Plante, E., & Vance, R. (1995). Diagnostic accuracy of two tests of preschool language. *American Journal of Speech-Language Pathology, 4,* 70–76.

Plaut, D. C. (2003). Connectionist modeling of language: Examples and implications. In M. T. Banich & M. Mack (Eds.), *Mind, brain, and language: Multidisciplinary perspectives* (pp. 143–167). Mahwah, NJ: Lawrence Erlbaum.

Polirstok, S. R., Dana, L., Buono, S., Mongelli, V., & Trubia, G. (2003). Improving functional communication skills in adolescents and young adults with severe autism using gentle teaching and positive approaches. *Topics in Language Disorders, 23,* 146–153.

Pollard-Durodola, S. D., Mathes, P. G., Vaughn, S., Cárdenas-Hagan, E., & Linan-Thompson, S. (2006). The role of oracy in developing comprehension in Spanish-speaking English language learners. *Topics in Language Disorders, 26*(4), 365–384.

Prelock, P. A. (2006). *Autism spectrum disorders: Issues in assessment and intervention.* Austin, TX: Pro-Ed.

Prelock, P. A., Beatson, J., Bitner, B., Broder, C., & Ducker, A. (2003). Clinical forum. Interdisciplinary assessment of young children with autism spectrum disorder. *Language, Speech, and Hearing Services in Schools, 34*(3), 194.

Premack, D., & Woodruff, G. (1978). Does the chimpanzee have a "theory of mind"? *Behavior and Brain Sciences, 4,* 515–526.

Pressley, M., Harris, K. R., & Marks, M. B. (1992). But good strategy instructors are constructivists! *Educational Psychology Review, 4,* 3–31.

Price, J. R., & Kent, R. D. (2008). Increasing speech intelligibility in Down syndrome and fragile X syndrome. In J. E. Roberts, R. S. Chapman, & S. F. Warren (Eds.), *Speech and language development and intervention in Down syndrome and Fragile X syndrome* (pp. 219–231). Baltimore: Paul H. Brookes.

Pring, L. (1994). Touch and go: Learning to read braille. *Reading Research Quarterly, 29,* 67–74.

Prizant, B. M. (1984). Assessment and intervention of communicative problems in children with autism. *Communication Disorders, 9,* 127–142.

Prizant, B. M. (1987). Theoretical and clinical implications of echolalic behavior in autism. In T. Layton (Ed.), *Language and treatment of autistic and developmentally disordered children* (pp. 65–88). Springfield, IL: Charles C Thomas.

Prizant, B. M., & Rydell, P. J. (1984). Analysis of functions of delayed echolalia in autistic children. *Journal of Speech and Hearing Research, 27,* 183–192.

Prizant, B. M., & Rydell, P. J. (1993). Assessment and intervention considerations for unconventional verbal behavior. In J. Reichle & D. P. Wacker (Eds.), *Communicative alternatives to challenging behavior* (pp. 263–297). Baltimore: Paul H. Brookes.

Prizant, B. M., Wetherby, A. M., Rubin, E., Laurent, A. C., & Rydell, P. J. (2006). *The SCERTS model: A comprehensive educational approach for children with autism spectrum disorders. Vol. I. Assessment; Vol. II. Program planning and intervention.* Baltimore: Paul H. Brookes.

Proctor, A. (1989). Stages of normal noncry vocal development: A protocol for assessment. *Topics in Language Disorders, 10*(1), 26–42.

Proctor-Williams, K., & Fey, M. E. (2007). Recast density and acquisition of novel irregular past tense verbs. *Journal of Speech, Language, and Hearing Research, 50*(4), 1029–1047.

Proctor-Williams, K., Fey, M., & Loeb, D. (2001). Parental recasts and production of copulas and articles by children with specific language impairment and typical development. *American Journal of Speech-Language Pathology, 10,* 155–168.

Prutting, C. A. (1982). Pragmatics as social competence. *Journal of Speech and Hearing Disorders, 47,* 123–134.

Prutting, C. A., & Kirchner, D. (1987). A clinical appraisal of the pragmatic aspects of language. *Journal of Speech and Hearing Disorders, 52,* 105–119.

Quill, K. A. (2000). *Do-Watch-Listen-Say: Social and communication intervention for children with autism.* Baltimore: Paul H. Brookes.

Ramer, A. (1976). Syntactic styles in emerging language. *Journal of Child Language, 3,* 49–62.

Rankin, J. L., Harwood, K., & Mirenda, P. (1994). Influence of graphic symbol use on reading comprehension. *Augmentative and Alternative Communication, 10,* 269–281.

Raphael, T. W., & Pearson, P. D. (1982). *The effects of metacognitive strategy awareness training on students' question answering behavior* (Tech. Report No. 238). Urbana: University of Illinois Center for the Study of Reading.

Rapin, I. (1998). Understanding childhood language disorders. *Current Opinion in Pediatrics, 10,* 561–566.

Rapin, I. (2007). Language and its development in the autism spectrum disorders. In J. M. Perez, P. M. Gonzales, M. L. Comi, & C. Nieto (Eds.), *New developments in autism: The future is today* (pp. 214–236). London: Jessica Kingsley.

Rapin, I., & Allen, D. (1983). Developmental language disorders: Nosologic considerations. In U. Kirk (Ed.), *Neuropsychology of language, reading, and spelling* (pp. 155–184). New York: Academic Press.

Ratey, J. J. (2001). *A user's guide to the brain.* New York: Pantheon Books.

Records, N. L., Tomblin, J. B., & Freese, P. R. (1992). The quality of life of young adults with histories of specific language impairments. *American Journal of Speech-Language Pathology, 1*(2), 44–53.

Redmond, S. M., & Johnston, S. S. (2001). Evaluating the morphological competence of children with severe speech and physical impairments. *Journal of Speech, Language, and Hearing Research, 44,* 1362–1375.

Rehabilitation Act, P.L. 93-112, 87 Stat. 355 (1973).

Reichle, J., & Wacker, D. P. (Eds.). (1993). *Communicative alternatives to challenging behavior: Integrating functional assessment and intervention strategies.* Baltimore: Paul H. Brookes.

Reid, D. K., Hresko, W. P., & Hammill, D. D. (1989). *Test of Early Reading Ability.* Austin, TX: Pro-Ed.

Renfrew, C. (1988). *Action Picture Test* (3rd ed.). Oxford, England: Author.

Renfrew, C. (1991). *The bus story: A test of continuous speech* (2nd ed.). Oxford, England: Author.

Rescorla, L. (1989). The Language Development Survey (LDS): A screening tool for delayed language in toddlers. *Journal of Speech and Hearing Disorders, 54,* 587–599.

Rescorla, L. (2002). Language and reading outcomes at age 9 in late-talking toddlers. *Journal of Speech, Language, and Hearing Research, 45,* 360–371.

Rescorla, L., & Fechnay, T. (1996). Mother-child synchrony and communicative reciprocity in late-talking toddlers. *Journal of Speech and Hearing Research, 39,* 200–208.

Rice, M. L. (2004). Growth models of developmental language disorders. In M. L. Rice & S. F. Warren (Eds.), *Developmental language disorders: From phenotypes to etiologies* (pp. 207–240). Mahwah, NJ: Lawrence Erlbaum.

Rice, M. L., Oetting, J. B., Marquis, J., Bode, J., & Pae, S. (1994). Frequency of input effects on word comprehension of children with specific language impairment. *Journal of Speech and Hearing Research, 37,* 106–122.

Rice, M. L., Sell, M. A., & Hadley, P. A. (1991). Social interactions of speech-and-language-impaired children. *Journal of Speech, Language, and Hearing Research, 34,* 1299–1307.

Rice, M. L., Tomblin, J. B., Hoffman, L., Richman, W.A., & Marquis, J. (2004). Grammatical tense deficits in children with SLI and nonspecific language impairment: Relationships with nonverbal IQ over time. *Journal of Speech Language and Hearing Research, 47,* 816–834.

Rice, M. L., & Warren, S. F. (2004). Introduction. In M. L. Rice & S. F. Warren (Eds.), *Developmental language disorders: From phenotypes to etiologies* (pp. 1–3). Mahwah, NJ: Lawrence Erlbaum.

Rice, M. L., & Wexler, K. (1996). A phenotype of specific language impairment: Entended optional infinitives. In M. L. Rice (Ed.), *Toward a genetics of language* (pp. 215–237). Mahwah, NJ: Lawrence Erlbaum.

Rice, M. L., & Wexler, K. (2001). *Test of Early Grammatical Impairment (TEGI).* San Antonio, TX: Harcourt Assessment.

Rice, M. L., Wexler, K., & Cleave, P. (1995). Specific language impairment as a period of extended optional infinitive. *Journal of Speech and Hearing Research, 38,* 850–863.

Rice, M., Wexler, K., & Hershberger, S. (1998). Tense over time: The longitudinal course of tense acquisition in children with specific language impairment. *Journal of Speech, Language, and Hearing Research, 41,* 1412–1431.

Richards, T. L., Aylward, E. H., Field, P. M., Grimme, A. C., Raskind, W., Richards, A. L., Nagy, W., Eckert, M., Leonard, C., Abbott, R. D., & Berninger, V. W. (2006). Converging evidence for triple word form theory in children with dyslexia. *Developmental Neuropsychology, 30*(1), 547–589.

Richardson, K., Calnan, M., Essen, J., & Lambert, L. (1976). The linguistic maturity of 11-year-olds: Some analysis of the written composition of children in the National Developmental Study. *Journal of Child Language, 3,* 99–115.

Ridley, M. (2003). *Nature via nurture: Genes, experiences, and what makes us human.* New York: HarperCollins.

Ritvo, E. R. (2006). *Understanding the nature of autism and Asperger's disorder: Forty years of clinical practice and pioneering research.* London: Jessica Kingsley.

Rizzolatti, G., Fadiga, L., Gallese, V., & Fogassi, L. (1996). Premotor cortex and the recognition of motor actions. *Cognitive Brain Research, 3,* 131–141.

Robbins, A., Koch, D., Osberger, M., Zimmerman-Phillips, S., & Kishon-Rabin, L. (2004). Effect of age of cochlear implantation on auditory skill development in infants and toddlers. *Archives of Otolaryngology–Head and Neck Surgery, 130,* 570–574.

Roberts, J., Jurgens, J., & Burchinal, M. (2005). The role of home literacy practices in preschool children's language and emergent literacy skills. *Journal of Speech, Language, and Hearing Research, 48,* 345–359.

Roberts, J. E., Prizant, B., & McWilliam, R. A. (1995). Out-of-class versus in-class service delivery in language intervention: Effects on communication interactions with young children. *American Journal of Speech-Language Pathology, 4,* 87–94.

Roberts, J. E., Wallace, I. F., & Henderson, F. W. (Eds.). (1997). *Otitis media in young children: Medical, developmental, and educational considerations.* Baltimore: Paul H. Brookes.

Roberts, T., & Meiring, A. (2006). Teaching phonics in the context of children's literature or spelling: Influences on first-grade reading, spelling, and writing and fifth-grade comprehension. *Journal of Educational Psychology, 98*(4), 690–713.

Robertson, S. B., & Ellis Weismer, S. (1999). Effects of treatment on linguistic and social skills in toddlers with delayed language development. *Journal of Speech, Language, and Hearing Research, 42,* 1234–1248.

Robinson, F. P. (1941). *Diagnostic and remedial techniques for effective study.* New York: Harper and Brothers. (Republished as *Effective study* in 1970)

Robinson, L. E., & Owens, R. E., Jr. (1995). Clinical notes: Functional augmentative communication and positive behavior change. *Augmentative and Alternative Communication, 11,* 207–211.

Robinson-Zañartu, C. (1996). Serving Native American children and families: Considering cultural values. *Language, Speech, and Hearing Services in Schools, 27,* 373–384.

Rocha, M. L., Schreibman, L., & Stahmer, A. C. (2007). Effectiveness of training parents to teach joint attention in children with autism. *Journal of Early Intervention, 29,* 154–172.

Rogers-Adkinson, D. L., & Stuart, S. K. (2007). Collaborative services: Children experiencing neglect and the side effects of prenatal alcohol exposure. *Language, Speech, and Hearing Services in Schools, 38,* 149–156.

Rogers-Warren, A., & Warren, S. F. (1980). Facilitating the display of newly trained language in children. *Behavior Modification, 4,* 361–382.

Rogoff, B. (1990). *Apprenticeship in thinking: Cognitive development in social context.* New York: Oxford University Press.

Roizen, N. J. (2002). Down syndrome. In M. L. Batshaw (Ed.), *Children with disabilities* (5th ed., pp. 307–320). Baltimore: Paul H. Brookes.

Romski, M. A., Sevcik, R. A., Cheslock, M., & Barton, A. (2006). The system for augmenting language: AAC and emerging language intervention. In R. J. McCauley & M. E. Fey (Eds.), *Treatment of language disorders in children* (pp. 123–147). Baltimore: Paul H. Brookes.

Roseberry-McKibbin, C. (2007). *Language disorders in children: A multicultural and case perspective.* Boston: Allyn & Bacon.

Rosen, C. D., & Gerring, J. P. (1986). *Head trauma: Educational reintegration.* Austin, TX: Pro-Ed.

Rosenthal, R., & Jacobson, L. (1992). *Pygmalion in the classroom* (Expanded ed.). New York: Irvington. (Original work published 1968)

Rosetti, L. (2005). *Rosetti infant-toddler language scale.* East Moline, IL: LinguiSystems, Inc.

Roskos, K. A., & Christie, J. F. (Eds.). (2000). *Play and literacy in early childhood: Research from multiple perspectives.* Mahwah, NJ: Lawrence Erlbaum.

Roth, F. P., & Clark, D. M. (1987). Symbolic play and social participation abilities of language-impaired and normally developing children. *Journal of Speech and Hearing Disorders, 52,* 17–29.

Roth, F. P., Speece, D. L., & Cooper, D. H. (2002). A longitudinal analysis of the connection between oral language and early reading. *Journal of Educational Research, 95,* 259–272.

Roth, F. P., & Spekman, N. J. (1984). Assessing the pragmatic abilities of children: Part I. Organizational framework and assessment parameters. *Journal of Speech and Hearing Disorders, 49,* 2–11.

Roth, F. P., & Spekman, N. J. (1986). Narrative discourse: Spontaneously generated stories of learning-disabled and normally achieving students. *Journal of Speech and Hearing Disorders, 51,* 8–23.

Rourke, B. P. (n.d.). Personal website. Retrieved March 24, 2007, from www.nld-bprourke.ca

Rourke, B. P. (1995). *Syndrome of nonverbal learning disabilities.* New York: Guilford Press.

Rumelhart, D. E. (1975). Notes on a schema for stories. In D. G. Bobrow & A. Collins (Eds.), *Representation and understanding: Studies in cognitive science* (pp. 211–236). New York: Academic Press.

Rumelhart, D. E., & McClelland, J. L. (1994). On learning the past tenses of English verbs. In P. Bloom (Ed.), *Language acquisition* (pp. 423–471). Cambridge, MA: MIT Press.

Russell, S. C., & Kaderavek, J. (1993). Alternative models for collaboration. *Language, Speech, and Hearing Services in Schools, 24,* 76–78.

Rutter, M. (2007). Proceeding from observed correlation to causal inference: The use of natural experiments. *Perspectives on Psychological Science, 2*(4), 377–395.

Rutter, M., Tizard, J., & Whitmore, K. (Eds.). (1970). *Education, health, and behaviour.* London: Longmans Green.

Rvachew, S. (2006). Longitudinal predictors of implicit phonological awareness skills. *American Journal of Speech-Language Pathology, 15,* 165–176.

Rvachew, S., Ohberg, A., Grawburg, M., & Heyding, J. (2003). Phonological awareness and phonemic perception in 4-year-old children with delayed expressive phonology skills. *American Journal of Speech-Language Pathology, 12,* 463–471.

Sackett, D. L., Straus, S. E., Richardson, W. S., Rosenberg, W., & Haynes, R. B. (2000). *Evidence-based medicine: How to practice and teach EBM* (2nd ed.). Edinburgh, Scotland: Churchill Livingstone.

Sadato, N., Pascual-Leone, A., Grafman, J., Deiber, M-P., Ibañez, V., & Hallett, M. (1998). Neural networks for Braille reading by the blind. *Brain, 121,* 1213–1229.

Sampson, G. (2005). *The "language instinct" debate.* London: Continuum International.

Saxton, M. (2005). "Recast" in a new light: Insights for practice from typical language studies. *Child Language Teaching and Therapy, 21,* 23–38.

Scarborough, H. S. (1990a). Index of productive syntax. *Applied Psycholinguistics, 11,* 1–22.

Scarborough, H. S. (1990b). Very early language deficits in dyslexic children. *Child Development, 61,* 1728–1743.

Scarborough, H. S. (1998). Predicting the future achievement of second graders with reading disabilities: Contributions of phonemic awareness, verbal memory, rapid serial naming, and IQ. *Annuals of Dyslexia, 48,* 115–136.

Scarborough, H. S. (2005). Developmental relationships between language and reading: Reconciling a beautiful hypothesis with some ugly facts. In H. W. Catts & A. G. Kamhi (Eds.), *The connections between language and reading disabilities* (pp. 3–24). Mahwah, NJ: Lawrence Erlbaum.

Scarborough, H. S., & Dobrich, W. (1990). Development of children with early language delays. *Journal of Speech and Hearing Research, 33,* 70–83.

Scarborough, H. S., & Dobrich, W. (1994). On the efficacy of reading to preschoolers. *Developmental Review, 14,* 245–302.

Scarola, D. (2007). Making progress with Usher syndrome. *Volta Voices, 14*(2), 34–36.

Schaffer, R. (1977). *Mothering.* Cambridge, MA: Harvard University Press.

Schairer, K. S., & Nelson, N. W. (1996). Communicative possibilities of written conversations with adolescents who have autism. *Child Language Teaching and Therapy, 12,* 164–180.

Scherer, N., & Olswang, L. (1984). Role of mothers' expansions in stimulating children's language production. *Journal of Speech and Hearing Research, 27,* 387–396.

Schery, T. K. (1985). Correlates of language development in language disordered children. *Journal of Speech and Hearing Disorders, 50,* 73–83.

Schery, T. K., & Peters, M. L. (2003). Developing auditory learning in children with cochlear implants. *Topics in Language Disorders, 23*(1), 4–15.

Schneider, C. B. (2007). *Acting antics: A theatrical approach to teaching social understanding to kids and teens with Asperger syndrome.* London: Jessica Kingsley.

Schopler, E., & Mesibov, G. B. (Eds.). (1985). *Communication problems in autism.* New York: Plenum Press.

Schopler, E., Reichler, R. J., & Renner, B. R. (2002). *The Childhood Autism Rating Scale (CARS).* San Antonio, TX: Pro-Ed.

Schow, R. L., & Nerbonne, M. A. (2007). Overview of audiology rehabilitation. In R. L. Schow & M. A. Nerbonne (Eds.), *Introduction to audiologic rehabilitation* (5th ed., pp. 3–30). Boston: Allyn & Bacon.

Schraeder, T., Quinn, M., Stockman, I. J., & Miller, J. (1999). Authentic assessment as an approach to preschool speech-language screening. *American Journal of Speech-Language Pathology, 8,* 195–200.

Schreibman, L. (1988). *Autism.* Newbury Park, CA: Sage.

Schuler, A. L., & Goetz, L. (1981). The assessment of severe language disabilities: Communicative and cognitive considerations. *Analysis and Intervention in Developmental Disabilities, 1,* 333–346.

Schumaker, J., Deshler, D., Alley, G., Warner, M., & Denton, P. (1984). Multipass: A learning strategy for improving reading comprehension. *Learning Disability Quarterly, 5,* 295–304.

Schwartz, J. B., & Wilson, S. J. (2006). The art (and science) of building an evidence portfolio. *Contemporary Issues in Communication Science and Disorders, 33,* 37–41.

Schwartz, R., Chapman, K., Terrell, B., Prelock, P., & Rowen, L. (1985). Facilitating word combination in language-impaired children through discourse structure. *Journal of Speech and Hearing Disorders, 50,* 31–39.

Scientific Learning Corporation. (1997). *Fast ForWord* (Version 1.5) [Computer software]. Berkeley, CA: Author.

Scientific Learning Corporation. (1998). *Fast ForWord–Language (FFW–L)* [Computer software]. Berkeley, CA: Author.

Scott, C. M. (1984). *What happened in that: Structured characteristics of school children's narratives.* Paper presented at the annual conference of the American Speech-Language-Hearing Association, San Francisco, CA.

Scott, C. M. (1988). Spoken and written syntax. In M. A. Nippold (Ed.), *Later language development* (pp. 49–96). Austin, TX: Pro-Ed.

Scott, C. M. (1994). A discourse continuum for school-age students: Impact of modality and genre. In G. P. Wallach & K. G. Butler (Eds.), *Language-learning disabilities in school-age children and adolescents.* Boston: Allyn & Bacon.

Scott, C. M. (2000). Principles and methods of spelling instruction: Applications for poor spellers. *Topics in Language Disorders, 20*(3), 66–82.

Scott, C. M., & Stokes, S. L. (1995). Measures of syntax in school-age children and adolescents. *Language, Speech, and Hearing Services in Schools, 26,* 309–319.

Scott, C. M., & Windsor, J. (2000). General language performance measures in spoken and written narrative and expository discourse of school-age children with language learning disabilities. *Journal of Speech, Language, and Hearing Research, 43,* 324–399.

Semel, E. (2000). *Following directions* [Computer software]. Winooski, VT: Laureate Learning Systems.

Semel, E., Wiig, E., & Secord, W. (2003). *Comprehensive Evaluation of Language Fundamentals* (4th ed.) (CELF–4). San Antonio, TX: Pearson Assessments.

Semrud-Clikeman, M. (2001). *Traumatic brain injury in children and adolescents.* New York: Guilford Press.

Seung, H. K., Ashwell, S., Elder, J. H., & Valcante, G. (2006). Verbal communication outcomes in children with autism after in-home father training. *Journal of Intellectual Disability Research, 50*(Part 2), 139–150.

Sevcik, R. A., Romski, M. A., Watkins, R. V., & Deffebach, K. P. (1995). Adult partner-augmented communication input to youth with mental retardation using the System for Augmenting Language (SAL). *Journal of Speech and Hearing Research, 38*(4), 902–912.

Seymour, H. N. (1992). The invisible children: A reply to Lahey's perspective. *Journal of Speech and Hearing Disorders, 56,* 640–641.

Seymour, H. N., Roeper, T. W., & de Villiers, J. (2003). *Diagnostic Evaluation of Language Variation (DELV).* San Antonio, TX: Psychological Corporation.

Shadish, W. R., Cook, T. D., & Campbell, D. T. (2002). *Experimental and quasi-experimental designs for generalized causal inference.* Boston: Houghton Mifflin.

Shaffer, D., Bijur, P., Chadwick, O. F. D., & Rutter, M. (1980). Head injury and later reading disability. *Journal of the American Academy of Child Psychiatry, 19,* 592–610.

Shah, A. P., Baum, S. R., & Dwivedi, V. D. (2006). Neural substrates of linguistic prosody: Evidence from syntactic disambiguation in the productions of brain damaged patients. *Brain and Language, 96,* 78–89.

Shane, H. (Ed.). (1994). *Facilitated communication: The clinical and social phenomenon.* San Diego, CA: Singular.

Shaywitz, B. A., Lyon, G. R., & Shaywitz, S. E. (2006). The role of functional magnetic resonance imaging in understanding reading and dyslexia. *Developmental Neuropsychology, 30*(1), 613–632.

Shaywitz, B. A., Shaywitz, S. E., Blachman, B. A., Pugh, K. R., Fulbright, R. K., Skudlarski, P., Mencl, W. E., Constable, R. T., Holahan, J. M., Marchione, K. E., Fletcher, J. M., Lyon, G. R., & Gore, J. C. (2004). Development of left occipitotemporal systems for skilled reading in children after a phonologically-based intervention. *Biological Psychiatry, 55,* 926–933.

Shaywitz, S. E., Shaywitz, B. A., Pugh, K. R., Fulbright, R. K., Constable, R. T., Mencl, W. E., Shankweiler, D. P., Liberman, A. M., Skudlarski, P., Fletcher, J. M., Katz, L., Marchione, K. E., Lacadie, C., Gatenby, C., & Gore, J. C. (1998). Functional disruption in the organization of the brain for reading in dyslexia. *Proceedings of the National Academy of Science, 95,* 2636–2641.

Shepard, N., Davis, J., Gorga, M., & Stelmachowicz, P. (1981). Characteristics of hearing impaired children in the public schools: Part I. Demographic data. *Journal of Speech and Hearing Disorders, 46,* 123–129.

Shriberg, L. D. (1997). Developmental phonological disorders: One or many? In B. W. Hodson & M. L. Edwards (Eds.), *Perspectives in applied phonology* (pp. 105–131). Gaithersburg, MD: Aspen.

Shriberg, L. D., Aram, D. M., & Kwiatkowski, J. (1997). Developmental apraxia of speech: I. Descriptive and theoretical perspectives. *Journal of Speech, Language, and Hearing Research, 40*(2), 273–285.

Shriberg, L. D., Friel-Patti, S., Flipsen, P., & Brown, R. L. (2000). Otitis media, fluctuant hearing loss, and speech-language outcomes: A preliminary structural equation model. *Journal of Speech-Language-Hearing Research, 43,* 100–120.

Shriberg, L. D., & Kwiatkowski, J. (1982). Phonological disorders II: A conceptual framework for management. *Journal of Speech and Hearing Disorders, 47,* 242–256.

Shriberg, L. D., & Kwiatkowski, J. (1994). Developmental phonological disorders I: A clinical profile. *Journal of Speech and Hearing Research, 37,* 1100–1126.

Shriberg, L. D., Tomblin, J. B., & McSweeny, J. L. (1999). Prevalence of speech delay in 6-year-old children and comorbidity with language impairment. *Journal of Speech, Language, and Hearing Research, 42,* 1461–1481.

Siegel-Causey, E., & Guess, D. (1989). *Enhancing nonsymbolic communication interactions among learners with severe disabilities.* Baltimore: Paul H. Brookes.

Silliman, E. R. (1987). Individual differences in the classroom performance of language-impaired students. *Seminars in Speech and Language, 8*(4), 357–375.

Silliman, E. R., Butler, K. G., & Wallach, G. P. (2002). The time has come to talk of many things. In K. G. Butler & E. R. Silliman (Eds.), *Speaking, reading, and writing in children with language learning disabilities* (pp. 3–25). Mahwah, NJ: Lawrence Erlbaum.

Silliman, E. R., & Lamanna, M. L. (1986). Interactional dynamics of turn disruption: Group and individual effects. *Topics in Language Disorders, 6*(2), 28–43.

Silliman, E. R., & Wilkinson, L. C. (1994). Discourse scaffolds for classroom intervention. In G. P. Wallach & K. G. Butler (Eds.), *Language-learning disabilities in school-age children and adolescents* (pp. 27–52). Boston: Allyn & Bacon.

Simons, C. S. (1987). *After the tears: Parents talk about raising a child with a disability.* San Diego, CA: Harcourt Brace Jovanovich.

Singer, B. D., & Bashir, A. S. (1999). What are executive functions and self-regulation and what do they have to do with language-learning disorders? *Language, Speech, and Hearing Services in Schools, 30,* 265–273.

Singer, B. D., & Bashir, A. S. (2004). EmPOWER: A strategy for teaching students with language learning disabilities how to write expository text. In E. R. Silliman & L. Wilkinson (Eds.), *Language and literacy learning* (pp. 239–272). New York: Guilford Press.

Skarakis-Doyle, E., & Dempsey, L. (2008). Assessing story comprehension in preschool children. *Topics in Language Disorders, 28*(2), 131–148.

Skinner, B. F. (1957). *Verbal behavior.* New York: Appleton-Century-Crofts.

Slobin, D., & Tomasello, M. (2005). Elizabeth Bates's aphorisms for the study of language, cognition, development, biology, and evolution. In M. Tomasello & D. I. Slobin (Eds.), *Beyond nature-nurture: Essays in honor of Elizabeth Bates* (pp. xxv–xxx). Mahwah, NJ: Lawrence Erlbaum.

Smaldino, J. J., & Crandell, C. C. (2001). Speech perception in the classroom. *Volta Review, 101*(5), 15–21.

Smith, A. E., & Camarata, S. (1999). Using teacher-implemented instruction to increase language intelligibility of children with autism. *Journal of Positive Behavior Interventions, 1,* 141–151.

Smith, F. (1975). *Comprehension and learning: A conceptual framework for teachers.* New York: Holt, Rinehart, & Winston.

Smith, M. W., Dickinson, D. K., Anasatopoulos, A., & Sangeorge, A. (2002). *Toolkit for assessing early literacy in classrooms.* Baltimore: Paul H. Brookes.

Smitherman, G. (2000a). *Talking that talk: Language, culture, and education in African America.* New York: Routledge.

Smitherman, G. (2000b). *Black talk: Words and phrases from the hood to the amen corner* (2nd ed.). Boston: Houghton Mifflin.

Snow, C. E. (1983). Literacy and language: Relationships during the preschool years. *Harvard Educational Review, 53,* 165–189.

Snow, C. E. (1991). Diverse conversational contexts for the acquisition of various language skills. In J. Miller (Ed.), *Research on child language disorders* (pp. 105–124). Austin, TX: Pro-Ed.

Snow, C. E., & Dickinson, D. K. (1990). Social sources of narrative skills at home and at school. *First Language, 10,* 87–103.

Snow, C. E., & Ninio, A. (1986). The contracts of literacy: What children learn from learning to read books. In W. Teale & E. Sulzby (Eds.), *Emergent literacy* (pp. 116–138). Norwood, NJ: Ablex.

Snowling, M. J. (1995). Phonological processing and developmental dyslexia. *Journal of Research in Reading, 18*(2), 132–138.

Snowling, M. J. (2000). *Dyslexia.* Oxford, England: Blackwell.

Snowling, M. J. (2005). Literacy outcomes for children with oral language impairments: Developmental interactions between language skills and learning to read. In H. W. Catts & A. G. Kamhi (Eds.), *The connections between language and reading disabilities* (pp. 55–75). Mahwah, NJ: Lawrence Erlbaum.

Snowling, M. J., Bishop, D. V. M., Stothard, S. E., Chipchase, B., & Kaplan, C. (2006). Psychosocial outcomes at 15 years of children with a preschool history of speech-language impairment. *Journal of Child Psychology and Psychiatry, 47,* 759–765.

Snowling, M. J., & Frith, U. (1986). Comprehension in "hyperlexic" readers. *Journal of Experimental Child Psychology, 42,* 392–415.

Snowling, M. J., Gallagher, A., & Frith, U. (2003). Family risk of dyslexia is continuous: Individual differences in the precursors of reading skill. *Child Development, 74*(2), 358–373.

Snowling, M. J., & Hayiou-Thomas, M. E. (2006). The dyslexia spectrum: Continuities between reading, speech, and language impairments. *Topics in Language Disorders, 26*(2), 110–126.

Sparks, S. N. (1989a). Speech and language in maltreated children. *Journal of Speech and Hearing Disorders, 54,* 124–126.

Sparks, S. N. (1989b). Assessment and intervention with at-risk infants and toddlers: Guidelines for the speech-language pathologist. *Topics in Language Disorders, 10*(1), 43–56.

Sparks, S. N. (1993). *Children of prenatal substance abuse.* San Diego, CA: Singular.

Sparrow, S. S., Balla, D. A., & Cichetti, D. V. (1984). *Vineland Adaptive Behavior Scales (VABS).* Circle Pines, MN: American Guidance Service.

Sparrow, S. S., Cicchetti, D. V., & Balla, D. A. (2005). *Vineland Adaptive Behavior Scale-II* (2nd ed.). Circle Pines, MN: Pearson Assessments.

Spaulding, T. J., Plante, E., & Farinella, K. A. (2006). Eligibility criteria for language impairment: Is the low end of normal always appropriate? *Language, Speech, and Hearing Services in Schools, 37,* 61–72.

Spencer, L., Tomblin, B., & Gantz, B. (1997). Reading skills in children with multi-channel cochlear implant experience. *Volta Review, 99,* 193–202.

Spivak, L. (2007). Exploring the pure tone audiogram. *Volta Voices, 14*(2), 10–14.

Spooner, A. L. R., Gathercole, S. E., & Baddeley, A. D. (2006). Does weak reading comprehension reflect an integration deficit? *Journal of Research in Reading, 29*(2), 173–193.

Spradley, J. P. (1979). *The ethnographic interview.* New York: Harcourt Brace Jovanovich.

Springer, S. P., & Deutsch, G. (1989). *Left brain, right brain.* New York: W. H. Freeman.

Sroufe, L. A. (1997). Psychopathology as an outcome of development. *Development and Psychopathology, 9,* 251–268.

Stackhouse, J. (1997). Phonological awareness: Connecting speech and literacy problems. In B. W. Hodson & M. L. Edwards (Eds.), *Perspectives in applied phonology* (pp. 157–196). Gaithersburg, MD: Aspen.

Stainback, S., & Stainback, W. (1988). *Understanding and conducting qualitative research.* Reston, VA: Council for Exceptional Children.

Stampe, D. (1979). *A dissertation on natural phonology.* New York: Garland.

Stanovich, K. E. (1986). Matthew effects in reading: Some consequences of individual differences in the acquisition of literacy. *Reading Research Quarterly, 30,* 894–906.

Stanovich, K. E. (1991). Cognitive science meets beginning reading. *Psychological Science, 2,* 70–81.

Stanovich, K. E., & Siegel, L. S. (1994). Phenotypic performance profile of children with reading disabilities: A regression-based test of the phonological-core variable-difference model. *Journal of Educational Psychology, 86,* 24–53.

Stark, R. E., Bernstein, L. E., Condino, R., Bender, M., Tallal, P., & Catts, H. (1984). Four-year follow-up study of language impaired children. *Annuals of Dyslexia, 34,* 49–68.

Stark, R., & Tallal, P. (1981). Selection of children with specific language deficits. *Journal of Speech and Hearing Disorders, 46,* 114–122.

Starr, A., Picton, T. W., Sininger, Y., Hood, L. J., & Berlin, C. I. (1996). Auditory neuropathy. *Brain, 119*(Part 3), 741–753.

Stein, M. A., Efron, L. A., Schiff, W. B., & Glanzmann, M. (2002). Attention deficits and hyperactivity. In M. L. Batshaw (Ed.), *Children with disabilities* (5th ed., pp. 389–416). Baltimore: Paul H. Brookes.

Stein, N., & Glenn, C. (1979). An analysis of story comprehension in elementary school children. In R. Freedle (Ed.), *The developmental psychology of time* (pp. 255–282). New York: Academic Press.

Stein, N., & Glenn, C. (1982). Children's concept of time: The development of a story schema. In W. Freeman (Ed.), *The developmental psychology of time* (pp. 255–282). Norwood, NJ: Ablex.

Steinman, B. A., LeJeune, B. J., & Kimbrough, B. T. (2006). Developmental stages of reading processes in children who are blind and sighted. *Journal of Visual Impairment and Blindness, 100*(1), 36–46.

Sternberg, L., Ritchey, H., Pegnatore, L., Wills, L., & Hill, C. (1986). *A curriculum for profoundly handicapped students.* Rockville, MD: Aspen.

Sterne, A., & Goswami, U. (2000). Phonological awareness of syllables, rhymes, and phonemes in deaf children. *Journal of Child Psychology and Psychiatry, 41,* 609–625.

Stevens, L. J., & Bliss, L. S. (1995). Conflict resolution abilities of children with specific language impairment and children with normal language. *Journal of Speech and Hearing Research, 38,* 599–611.

Stockman, I. J. (1996). The promises and pitfalls of language sample analysis as an assessment tool for linguistic minority children. *Language, Speech, and Hearing Services in Schools, 27,* 355–366.

Stone, C. A. (1998). The metaphor of scaffolding: Its utility for the field of learning disabilities. *Journal of Learning Disabilities, 31,* 344–364.

Stone-Goldman, J. R., & Olswang, L. B. (2003, January–March). Learning to look, learning to see: Using ethnography to develop cultural sensitivity. *ASHA Leader.* Retrieved November 11, 2006, from www.asha.org/about/publications/leader-online/archives/2003/q1/030318b.htm

Stothard, S. E., Snowling, M. J., Bishop, D. V. M., Chipchase, B. B., & Kaplan, C. A. (1998). Language-impaired preschoolers: A follow-up into adolescence. *Journal of Speech-Language-Hearing Research, 41,* 407–418.

Stout, G., & Windle, J. (1994). *Developmental Approach to Successful Listening (DASL II).* Englewood, CO: Resource Point.

Strand, E. A., Stoeckel, R., & Baas, B. (2006). Treatment of severe childhood apraxia of speech: A treatment efficacy study. *Journal of Medical Speech-Language Pathology, 14*(4), 297–307.

Straus, S. E., Richardson, W. S., Glasziou, P., & Haynes, R. B. (2005). *Evidence-based medicine: How to practice and teach EBM* (3rd ed.). Edinburgh, Scotland: Elsevier.

Stredler-Brown, A. (n.d.). *Developing a treatment program for children with auditory neuropathy.* Boulder, CO: Colorado Department of Education, Colorado School for the Deaf and the Blind. Retrieved June 24, 2008, from www.csdb.org/Early%20Education/resources/docs/aud_nueropathy.pdf

Streissguth, A. (1997). *Fetal alcohol syndrome: A guide for families and communities.* Baltimore: Paul H. Brookes.

Strickland, D. S., & Morrow, L. M. (1989). *Emerging literacy: Young children learn to read and write.* Newark, DE: International Reading Association.

Strong, C. J. (1998). *The Strong narrative assessment procedure.* Eau Claire, WI: Thinking Publications.

Strong, W. (1986). *Creative approaches to sentence combining.* Urbana, IL: ERIC Clearinghouse on Reading and Composition Skills and the National Conference on Research in English.

Stuart, M. (1995). Prediction and qualitative assessment of five and six-year old children's reading: A longitudinal study. *British Journal of Educational Psychology, 65,* 287–296.

Sturm, J. (2005). Literacy development of children who use AAC. In D. Beukelman & P. Mirenda (Eds.), *Augmentative and alternative communication: Supporting children and adults with complex communication needs* (3rd ed., pp. 351–389). Baltimore: Paul H. Brookes.

Sturm, J. M. (2008, March 15). *Providing high quality, multi-level writing instruction for students who use augmentative and alternative communication.* Paper presented at the annual conference of the Michigan Speech-Language-Hearing Association.

Sturm, J. M., & Koppenhaver, D. A. (2000). Supporting writing development in adolescents with developmental disabilities. *Topics in Language Disorders, 20*(2), 73–96.

Sturm, J. M., & Nelson, N. W. (1997). Formal classroom lessons: New perspectives on a familiar discourse event. *Language, Speech, and Hearing Services in Schools, 28,* 255–273.

Substance Abuse and Mental Health Services Administration (SAMHSA). (2007). *Fetal alcohol spectrum disorders by the numbers.* U.S. Department of Health and Human Services Publication No. (SMA) 06–4236. Retrieved August 6, 2007, from www.fascenter.samhsa.gov/documents/WYNK_Numbers.pdf

Sulzby, E., & Teale, W. (1991). Emergent literacy. In R. B. Barr, M. Kamil, P. B. Mosenthal, & D. B. Pearson (Eds.), *Handbook of reading research* (pp. 727–758). New York: Longman.

Sutherland, D., & Gillon, G. T. (2005). Assessment of phonological representations in children with speech impairment. *Language, Speech, and Hearing Services in Schools, 36*(4), 294–307.

Sutton-Smith, B. (1986). The development of fictional narrative performances. *Topics in Language Disorders, 7,* 1–10.

Swoger, P. A. (1989). Scott's gift. *English Journal, 78,* 61–65.

Szatmari, P. (1991). Asperger's syndrome: Diagnosis, treatment, and outcome. *Psychiatric Clinics of North America, 14*(1), 81–93.

Tabors, P. O. (1997). *One child, two languages: A guide for preschool educators of children learning English as a second language.* Baltimore: Paul H. Brookes.

Tabors, P. O., Snow, C. E., & Dickinson, D. K. (2001). Homes and schools together: Supporting language and literacy development. In K. K. Dickinson & P. O. Tabors (Eds.), *Beginning literacy with language: Young children learning at home and at school* (pp. 313–334). Baltimore: Paul H. Brooks.

Tagliamonte, S. (2005). *So* who? *Like* how? *Just* what? Discourse markers in the conversations of young Canadians. *Journal of Pragmatics, 37,* 1896–1915.

Tallal, P., Miller, S. I., Bedi, G., Byma, G., Wang, X., Nagarajan, S. S., Schreiner, C., Jenkins, W. M., & Merzenich, M. M. (1996). Language comprehension in language-learning impaired children improved with acoustically modified speech. *Science, 271,* 81–84.

Tallal, P., Stark, R., & Mellits, D. (1985). Identification of language-impaired children on the basis of rapid perception and production skills. *Brain and Language, 25,* 314–322.

Tannock, R., & Girolametto, L. (1992). Re-assessing parent-focused language intervention programmes. In S. Warren & J. Reichle (Eds.), *Causes and effects in communication and in normal and language impaired children* (pp. 49–80). Baltimore: Paul H. Brookes.

Tattershall, S. (2002). *Adolescents with language and learning needs: A shoulder-to-shoulder collaboration.* New York: Singular.

Teale, W. H., & Sulzby, E. (1986). Emergent literacy as a perspective for examining how young children become readers and writers. In W. H. Teale & E. Sulzby (Eds.), *Emergent literacy: Writing and reading* (pp. vii–xxv). Norwood, NJ: Ablex.

Telzrow, C. F., & Koch, L. C. (2003). Nonverbal learning disability: Vocational implications and rehabilitation treatment approaches. *Journal of Applied Rehabilitation Counseling, 34*(2), 9–16.

Templin, M. (1957). *Certain language skills in children.* Minneapolis: University of Minnesota Press.

Terrell, B., Schwartz, R., Prelock, P., & Messick, C. K. (1984). Symbolic play in normal and language-impaired children. *Journal of Speech and Hearing Research, 27,* 424–429.

Tétreault, S., Parrot, A., & Trahan, J. (2003). Home activity programs in families with children presenting with global developmental delays: Evaluation and parental perceptions. *International Journal of Rehabilitation Research, 26*(3), 165–173.

Thal, D., & Tobias, S. (1994). Relationships between language and gesture in normally developing and late-talking toddlers. *Journal of Speech and Hearing Research, 37,* 157–170.

Tharp, R. G., & Gallimore, R. (1988). *Rousing minds to life: Teaching, learning, and schooling in social context.* New York: Cambridge University Press.

Thibodeau, L. M. (2006, November 28). Five important questions about FM systems and cochlear implants. *ASHA Leader, 11*(16), 22–23.

Thiemann, K. S., & Goldstein, H. (2001). Social stories, written text cues, and video feedback: Effects on social communication of children with autism. *Journal of Applied Behavioral Analysis, 34,* 425–446.

Thomas, C., Englert, C. S., & Morsink, C. (1984). Modifying the classroom program in language. In C. V. Morsink (Ed.), *Teaching special needs students in regular classrooms* (pp. 239–276). Boston: Little, Brown.

Thordardottir, E. T., & Ellis Weismer, S. (2001). High-frequency verbs and verb diversity in the spontaneous speech of school-age children with specific language impairment. *International Journal of Language and Communication Disorders, 36,* 221–244.

Thorndike, R. L., Hagen, E. P., & Sattler, J. M. (1986). *Stanford-Binet Intelligence Test*—Revised. Chicago: Riverside Publishing.

Thorne, J. C., Coggins, T. E., Olson, H. C., & Astley, S. J. (2007). Exploring the utility of narrative analysis in diagnostic decision making: Picture bound reference, elaboration, and fetal alcohol spectrum disorders. *Journal of Speech, Language, and Hearing Research, 50,* 459–474.

Throneburg, R. N., Calvert, L. K., Sturm, J. J., Paramboukas, A. A., & Paul, P. J. (2000). A comparison of service delivery models: Effects on curricular vocabulary skills in the school setting. *American Journal of Speech-Language Pathology, 9*(1), 10–20.

Tierney, R. J. (1990). Redefining reading comprehension. *Educational Leadership, 47*(6), 37–42.

Tierney, R. J., & Cunningham, J. W. (1984). Research on teaching reading comprehension. In P. D. Pearson (Ed.),

Handbook of reading research (pp. 609–655). New York: Longman.

Timler, G. R., Olswang, L. B., & Coggins, T. E. (2005). "Do I know what I need to do?" A social communication intervention for children with complex clinical profiles. *Language, Speech, and Hearing Services in Schools, 36,* 73–85.

Timler, G. R., Vogler-Elias, D., & McGill, K. F. (2007). Strategies for promoting generalization of social communication skills in preschoolers and school-aged children. *Topics in Language Disorders, 27*(2), 167–181.

Tomasello, M. (1988). The role of joint attentional processes in early language development. *Language Sciences, 10,* 69–88.

Tomasello, M. (2003). Introduction: Some surprises for psychologists. In M. Tomasello (Ed.), *The new psychology of language: Cognitive and functional approaches to language structure* (pp. 1–14). Mahwah, NJ: Lawrence Erlbaum.

Tomasello, M., & Bates, E. (2001). General introduction. In M. Tomasello & E. Bates (Eds.), *Language development: The essential readings* (pp. 1–11). Malden, MA: Blackwell.

Tomasello, M., & Slobin, D. I. (Eds.). (2005). *Beyond nature–nurture: Essays in honor of Elizabeth Bates.* Mahwah, NJ: Lawrence Erlbaum.

Tomblin, J. B., Records, N. L., Buckwalter, P., Zhang, X., Smith, E., & O'Brien, M. (1997). Prevalence of specific language impairment in kindergarten children. *Journal of Speech, Language, and Hearing Research, 40,* 1245–1260.

Tomblin, J. B., Records, N. L., & Zhang, X. (1996). A system for the diagnosis of specific language impairment in kindergarten children. *Journal of Speech and Hearing Research, 39,* 1284–1294.

Tomblin, J. B., Spencer, L., Flock, S., Tyler, R., & Gantz, B. (1999). A comparison of language achievement in children with cochlear implants and children using hearing aids. *Journal of Speech, Language, and Hearing Research, 42,* 497–511.

Tomblin, J. B., & Zhang, X. (1999). Are children with SLI a unique group of language learners? In H. Tager-Flusberg (Ed.), *Neurodevelopmental disorders: Contributions to a new framework from the cognitive neurosciences* (pp. 361–382). Cambridge, MA: MIT Press.

Tomblin, J. B., & Zhang, X. (2006). The dimensionality of language ability in school-age children. *Journal of Speech-Language-Hearing Research, 49,* 1193–1208.

Tomblin, J. B., Zhang, X., Weiss, A., Catts, H., & Ellis Weismer, S. (2004). Dimensions of individual differences in communication skills among primary grade children. In M. L. Rice & S. F. Warren (Eds.), *Developmental language disorders: From phenotypes to etiologies* (pp. 53–76). Mahwah, NJ: Lawrence Erlbaum.

Torgesen, J. K. (1982). The learning disabled child as an inactive learner: Educational implications. *Topics in Learning and LD, 2,* 45–52.

Torgesen, J. K. (2000). Individual differences in response to early intervention in reading: The lingering problem of treatment resisters. *Learning Disabilities Research and Practice, 15,* 55–64.

Torgesen, J. K., Alexander, A., Wagner, R., Rashotte, C., Voeller, K., Conway, T., & Rose, E. (2001). Intensive remedial instruction for children with severe reading disabilities: Immediate and long-term outcomes from two instructional approaches. *Journal of Learning Disabilities, 34,* 33–58, 78.

Torgeson, J. K., Wagner, R. K., Rashotte, C. A., Burgess, S., & Hecht, S. (1997). Contributions of phonological awareness and automatic naming to the growth of word-reading skills in second- to fifth-grade children. *Scientific Studies of Reading, 1,* 161–185.

Torgesen, J. K., Wagner, R. K., Rashotte, C. A., Rose, E., Lindamood, P., Conway, T., et al. (1999). Preventing reading failure in young children with phonological processing disabilities: Group and individual responses to instruction. *Journal of Educational Psychology, 91*(4), 579–593.

Towbin, K. E., Mauk, J. E., & Batshaw, M. L. (2002). Pervasive developmental disorders. In M. L. Batshaw (Ed.), *Children with disabilities* (5th ed., pp. 365–387). Baltimore: Paul H. Brookes.

Trabasso, T., & Bouchard, E. (2002). Teaching readers how to comprehend text strategically. In C. C. Collins & M. Pressley (Eds.), *Comprehension instruction: Research-based best practices* (pp. 176–200). New York: Guilford Press.

Trapani, C. (1990). *Transition goals for adolescents with learning disabilities.* Boston: Little, Brown.

Treiman, R., & Bourassa, D. C. (2000). The development of spelling skills. *Topics in Language Disorders, 20*(3), 1–18.

Troia, G. A. (2004). Phonological processing and its influence on literacy learning. In C. A. Stone, E. R. Silliman, B. J. Ehren, & K. Apel (Eds.), *Handbook of language and literacy* (pp. 271–301). New York: Guilford Press.

Troia, G. A. (2005). Responsiveness to intervention: Roles for speech language pathologists in the prevention and identification of learning disabilities. *Topics in Language Disorders, 25,* 106–119.

Tyler, A. (2005a). Assessment for determining a communication profile. In A. G. Kamhi & K. E. Pollack (Eds.), *Phonological disorders in children: Clinical decision making in assessment and intervention* (pp. 43–50). Baltimore: Paul H. Brookes.

Tyler, A. (2005b). Planning and monitoring intervention programs. In A. G. Kamhi & K. E. Pollack (Eds.), *Phonological disorders in children: Clinical decision making in assessment and intervention* (pp. 123–137). Baltimore: Paul H. Brookes.

Tyler, A., Lewis, K. E., Haskill, A., & Tolbert, L. C. (2002). Efficacy and cross-domain effects of a morphosyntax and a phonology intervention. *Language, Speech, and Hearing Services in Schools, 33,* 52–66.

Tyler, A., Lewis, K., Haskill, A., & Tolbert, L. (2003). Outcomes of different speech and language goal attack strategies. *Journal of Speech, Language, and Hearing Research, 46,* 1077–1094.

Uchanski, R. M., Geers, A. E., & Protopapas, A. (2002). Intelligibility of modified speech for young listeners with normal and impaired hearing. *Journal of Speech, Language, and Hearing Research, 45,* 1027–1038.

Ukrainetz, T. A. (1998a). Beyond Vygotsky: What Soviet activity theory offers naturalistic language intervention. *Journal of Speech-Language Pathology and Audiology, 22,* 122–133.

Ukrainetz, T. A. (1998b). Stickwriting stories: A quick and easy narrative representation strategy. *Language, Speech, and Hearing Services in Schools, 29,* 197–206.

Ukrainetz, T. A. (2006a). Assessment and intervention within a contextualized skill framework. In T. A. Ukrainetz (Ed.), *Contextualized language intervention: Scaffolding PreK–12 literacy achievement* (pp. 7–58). Eau Claire, WI: Thinking Publications.

Ukrainetz, T. A. (2006b). Teaching narrative structure: Coherence, cohesion, and captivation. In T. A. Ukrainetz (Ed.), *Contextualized language intervention: Scaffolding PreK–12 literacy achievement* (pp. 195–246). Eau Claire, WI: Thinking Publications.

Ukrainetz, T. A. (2006c). The many ways of exposition: A focus on discourse structure. In T. A. Ukrainetz (Ed.), *Contextualized language intervention: Scaffolding PreK–12 literacy achievement* (pp. 247–288). Eau Claire, WI: Thinking Publications.

Ukrainetz, T. A. (2006d). Scaffolding young students into phonemic awareness. In T. A. Ukrainetz (Ed.), *Contextualized language intervention: Scaffolding PreK–12 literacy achievement* (pp. 429–468). Eau Claire, WI: Thinking Publications.

Ukrainetz, T. A., Cooney, M. H., & Dyer, S. K. (2000). An investigation into teaching phonemic awareness through shared reading and writing. *Early Childhood Research Quarterly, 15*(3), 331–355.

Ukrainetz, T. A., & Fresquez, E. F. (2003). What isn't language? A qualitative study of the role of the school speech-language pathologist. *Language, Speech, and Hearing Services in Schools, 34,* 284–298.

Ukrainetz, T. A., & Ross, C. L. (2006). Text comprehension: Facilitating active and strategic engagement. In T. A. Ukrainetz (Ed.), *Contextualized language intervention: Scaffolding PreK–12 literacy achievement* (pp. 503–564). Eau Claire, WI: Thinking Publications.

Ukrainetz McFadden, T. (1996). Creating language impairments in typically achieving children: The pitfalls of "normal" normative sampling. *Language, Speech, and Hearing Services in Schools, 27,* 3–9.

Underwood, N. (2006). A family's journey through due process. *Volta Voices, 13*(3), 40–44.

U.S. Census Bureau. (2006). 2005 American Community Survey. Retrieved December 13, 2007, from http://factfinder.census .gov/home/saff/aff_acs2005_quickguide.pdf

U.S. Department of Education. (n.d.). *Promoting educational excellence for all Americans.* Retrieved December 3, 2007, from www.ed.gov

U.S. Department of Education. (2005). Spellings announces new special education guidelines, details, workable "common-sense" policy to help states implement No Child Left Behind. Retrieved October 17, 2005, from www.ed.gov/news

U.S. Department of Health and Human Services. (n.d.). Definition of developmental disabilities. Retrieved March 11, 2007, from www.acf.hhs.gov/programs/add/addabout.html

U.S. Office of Education. (1977, August). Implementation of Part B of the Education of the Handicapped Act. *Federal Register,* p. 65083.

Valdez, F. M., & Montgomery, J. K. (1997). Outcomes from two treatment approaches for children with communication disorders in Head Start. *Journal of Children's Communication Development, 18*(2), 65–71.

Vallecorsa, A., & Gariss, E. (1990) Compositional skills of middle-grade students with learning disabilities. *Exceptional Children, 51,* 48–54.

van Dijk, J. (1965). The first steps of the deaf/blind child toward language. *Proceedings of the conference on the deaf/blind, Refnes, Denmark.* Boston: Perkins School for the Blind.

van Kleeck, A. (1990). Emergent literacy: Learning about print before learning to read. *Topics in Language Disorders, 10*(2), 25–45.

van Kleeck, A. (1994). Potential cultural bias in training parents as conversational partners with their children who have delays in language development. *American Journal of Speech-Language Pathology, 3*(1), 67–78.

van Kleeck, A., Gillam, R., Hamilton, L., & McGrath, C. (1997). The relationship between middle-class parents' book-sharing discussion and their preschoolers' abstract language development. *Journal of Speech-Language-Hearing Research, 40,* 1261–1271.

van Kleeck, A., Gillam, R. B., & McFadden, T. U. (1998). A study of classroom-based phonological awareness training for preschoolers with speech and/or language disorders. *American Journal of Speech-Language Pathology, 7,* 65–76.

van Kleeck, A., VanderWoude, J., & Hammett, L. A. (2006). Fostering literal and inferential language skills in Head Start preschoolers with language impairment using scripted book-sharing discussions. *American Journal of Speech-Language Pathology, 15,* 85–95.

Vandercook, T., York, J., & Forest, M. (1989). The McGill Action Planning System (MAPS): A strategy for building the vision. *Journal of the Association for Persons with Severe Handicaps, 14,* 205–215.

Vaughn, S., & Edmonds, M. (2006). Reading comprehension for older readers. *Intervention in School and Clinic, 41,* 131–137.

Vaughn, S., Mathes, P. G., Linan-Thompson, S., & Francis, D. J. (2005). Teaching English language learners at risk for reading disabilities to read: Putting research into practice. *Learning Disabilities Research and Practice, 20*(1), 58–67.

Vaughn, S., McIntosh, R., & Spencer-Rowe, J. (1991). Peer rejection is a stubborn thing: Increasing peer acceptance of rejected students with learning disabilities. *Learning Disabilities Research and Practice, 6,* 83–88.

Velleman, S. (2003). *Childhood apraxia of speech resource guide.* Clifton Park, NY: Thompson.

Velleman, S., & Strand, K. (1994). Developmental verbal apraxia. In J. E. Bernthal & N. W. Bankson (Eds.), *Child phonology: Characteristics, assessment, and intervention with special populations* (pp. 110–139). New York: Thieme.

Velleman, S., & Vihman, M. (2002). Whole-word phonology and templates: Trap, bootstrap, or some of each? *Language, Speech, and Hearing Services in Schools, 33,* 9–24.

Venter, A., Lord, C., & Schopler, E. (1992). A follow-up study of high functioning autistic children. *Journal of Child Psychology and Psychiatry, 33,* 489–507.

Verkerk, A., Pieretti, M., Sutcliffe, J. S., Fu, Y., Kuhl, D., Pizzuti, A., Reiner, O., Richards, S., Victoria, M., Zhang, F., Eussen, B., van Ommen, G., Blonden, L., Riggens, G., Chastain, J., Kunst, C., Galjaard, H., Caskey, C. T., Nelson, D., Oostra, B., & Warren, S. (1991). Identification of a gene (FMR-1) containing a CGG repeat coincident with a breakpoint cluster region exhibiting length variation in fragile X syndrome. *Cell, 65,* 905–914.

Verucci, L., Menghini, D., & Vicari, S. (2006). Reading skills and phonological awareness acquisition in Down syndrome. *Journal of Intellectual Disability Research, 50*(7), 477–491.

von Bertalanffy, L. (1968). *General system theory: Foundations, development, application.* New York: George Braziller.

Vygotsky, L. S. (1962). In E. Hanfmann & G. Vakar (Trans.), *Thought and language.* Cambridge, MA: MIT Press. (Work originally published 1934)

Vygotsky, L. S. (1978). In M. Cole (Trans.), *Mind in society: The development of higher psychological processes.* Cambridge, MA: Harvard University Press.

Waber, D. P., Silverman, L. B., Catania, L., Mautz, W., Rue, M., Gelber, R. D., Levy, D. E., Goldwasser, M. A., Adams, H., Dufresne, A., Metzger, V., Romero, I., Tarbell, N. J., Dalton, V. K., & Sallan, S. E. (2004). Outcomes of a randomized trial of hyperfractionated cranial radiation therapy for treatment of high-risk acute lymphoblastic leukemia: Therapeutic efficacy and neurotoxicity. *Journal of Clinical Oncology, 22,* 2701–2707.

Wagner, R. K., & Torgesen, J. K. (1987). The nature of phonological processing and its causal role in the acquisition of reading skills. *Psychological Bulletin, 101,* 192–212.

Wagner, R. K., Torgesen, J. K., & Rashotte, C. (1999). *Comprehensive Test of Phonological Processing (C-TOPP).* Minneapolis, MN: Pearson Assessments.

Wall, R., & Corn, A. (2004). Students with visual impairments in Texas: Description and extrapolation of data. *Journal of Visual Impairment and Blindness, 98,* 341–350.

Wallach, G. P. (2005). A conceptual framework in language learning disabilities: School-age language disorders. *Topics in Language Disorders, 25*(4), 292–301.

Waltzman, S. B., & Cohen, N. L. (1998). Cochlear implantation in children younger than 2 years old. *American Journal of Otology, 19,* 1083–1087.

Ward, F. R. (2005). Parents and professionals in the NICU: Communication within the context of ethical decision making—An integrative review. *Neonatal Network, 24*(3), 25–33.

Warren, S. F., & Bambara, L. M. (1989). An experimental analysis of milieu language intervention: Teaching the action-object form. *Journal of Speech and Hearing Disorders, 54,* 448–461.

Warren, S. F., Bredin-Oja, S. L., Fairchild, M., Finestack, L. H., Fey, M. E., & Brady, N. C. (2006). Responsivity education/ Prelinguistic milieu teaching. In R. McCauley & M. Fey (Eds.), *Treatment of language disorders in children* (pp. 47–75). Baltimore: Paul H. Brookes.

Warren, S. F., & Kaiser, A. P. (1986). Incidental language teaching: A critical review. *Journal of Speech and Hearing Disorders, 51,* 291–299.

Warren, S. F., & Kaiser, A. P. (1988). Research in early language intervention. In S. L. Odom & M. B. Karnes (Eds.), *Early intervention for infants and children with handicaps: An empirical base* (pp. 75–89). Baltimore: Paul H. Brookes.

Warren, S. F., McQuarter, R. J., & Rogers-Warren, A. K. (1984). The effects of mands and models on the speech of unresponsive socially isolate children. *Journal of Speech and Hearing Disorders, 47,* 42–52.

Washington, J., & Craig, H. (1992). Performances of low-income African American preschoolers with communication impairments. *Language, Speech, and Hearing Services in Schools, 23,* 203–207.

Washington, J. A., & Craig, H. K. (1994). Dialectal forms during discourse of poor, urban, African American preschoolers. *Journal of Speech and Hearing Research, 37,* 816–823.

Wasik, B. A., Bond, M. A., & Hindman, A. (2006). The effects of a language and literacy intervention on Head Start children and teachers. *Journal of Educational Psychology, 98,* 63–74.

Wasowicz, J., Apel, K., Masterson, J. J., & Whitney, A. (2004). *SPELL-Links to reading and writing.* Evanston, IL: Learning By Design. Retrieved January 1, 2008, from www.learningby design.com

Watkins, R. V. (1994). Specific language impairments in children: An introduction. In R. V. Watkins & M. L. Rice (Eds.), *Specific language impairment in children* (pp. 1–15). Baltimore: Paul H. Brookes.

Watkins, R. V., Kelly, D. J., Harbors, H. M., & Hollis, W. (1995). Measuring children's lexical diversity: Differentiating typical and impaired learners. *Journal of Speech and Hearing Research, 38,* 1349–1355.

Watkins, S. (2004). *SKI-HI curriculum: Family-centered programming for infants and young children with hearing loss.* Logan, UT: Hope.

Watson, L., Lord, C., Schaffer, B., & Schopler, E. (1989). *Teaching spontaneous communication to autistic and developmentally handicapped children.* Austin, TX: Pro-Ed.

Watzlawick, P., Beavin, J. H., & Jackson, D. D. (1967). *Pragmatics of human communication.* New York: W. W. Norton.

Way, I., Yelsma, P., Van Meter, A. M., & Black-Pond, C. (2007). Understanding alexithymia and language skills in children: Implications for assessment and intervention. *Language, Speech, and Hearing Services in Schools, 38,* 128–139.

Weaver, C. (1982). Welcoming errors as signs of growth. *Language Arts, 59,* 438–444.

Weaver, C. (1996). *Teaching grammar in context.* Portsmouth, NH: Boynton/Cook.

Webster, P. E., & Plante, A. S. (1992). Effects of phonological impairment on word, syllable, and phoneme segmentation and reading. *Language, Speech, and Hearing Services in Schools, 23,* 176–182.

Wechsler, D. (1989). *Wechsler Preschool and Primary Scale of Intelligence, Revised (WPPSI-R).* San Antonio, TX: Harcourt Brace Jovanovich.

Weiderhold, J. L., & Bryant, B. R. (2001). *Gray Oral Reading Test* (4th ed.) (GORT-4). Austin, TX: Pro-Ed.

Wells, G. (1986). *The meaning makers: Children learning language and using language to learn.* Portsmouth, NH: Heinemann.

Wertsch, J. C. (1981). *The concept of activity in Soviet psychology.* New York: M. F. Sharpe.

Westby, C. E. (1985). Learning to talk-talking to learn: Oral-literate language differences. In C. S. Simon (Ed.), *Communication skills and classroom success: Therapy methodologies for language-learning disabled students* (pp. 181–213). San Diego, CA: College-Hill.

Westby, C. E. (1988). Children's play: Reflections of social competence. *Seminars in Speech and Language, 9,* 1–14.

Westby, C. E. (1991). Understanding classroom texts. Presented as part of a teleconference on *Steps to Developing and Achieving Language Based Curriculum in the Classroom,* originating from the American Speech-Language-Hearing Association, Rockville, MD, October 4, 1991.

Westby, C. E. (1994a). The vision of full inclusion: Don't exclude kids by including them. *Journal of Childhood Communication Disorders, 16,* 13–22.

Westby, C. E. (1994b). The effects of culture on genre, structure, and style of oral and written texts. In G. P. Wallach & K. G.

Butler (Eds.), *Language-learning disabilities in school-age children and adolescents* (pp. 180–218). Boston: Allyn & Bacon.

Westby, C. E. (2006). There's more to passing than knowing the answers: Learning to do school. In T. A. Ukrainetz (Ed.), *Contextualized language intervention: Scaffolding PreK–12 literacy achievement* (pp. 319–388). Eau Claire, WI: Thinking Publications.

Westby, C. E., Burda, A., & Mehta, Z. (2003, April–June). Asking the right questions in the right ways: Strategies for ethnographic interviewing. *ASHA Leader.* Retrieved November 11, 2006, from www.asha.org/about/publications/leader-online/archives/2003/q2/f030429b.htm

Westby, C. E., StevensDominguez, M., & Oetter, P. (1996). A performance/competence model of observational assessment. *Language, Speech, and Hearing Services in Schools, 27,* 144–156.

Wetherby, A. M., & Prizant, B. (1993). *Communication and Symbolic Behavior Scales manual: Normed edition.* Baltimore: Paul H. Brookes.

Wetherby, A. M., & Prizant, B. M. (2000). Introduction to autism spectrum disorders. In A. M. Wetherby & B. M. Prizant (Eds.), *Autism spectrum disorders: A transactional developmental perspective* (pp. 1–7). Baltimore: Paul H. Brookes.

Wetherby, A. M., & Prizant, B. M. (2002). *Communication and Symbolic Behavior Scales (CSBS).* Baltimore: Paul H. Brookes.

Wetherby, A. M., Prizant, B. M., & Schuler, A. L. (2000). Understanding the nature of communication and language impairments. In A. M. Wetherby & B. M. Prizant (Eds.), *Autism spectrum disorders: A transactional developmental perspective* (pp. 109–141). Baltimore: Paul H. Brookes.

Wetherby, A. M., Yonclas, D. G., & Bryan, A. A. (1989). Communication profiles of preschool children with handicaps: Implications for early identification. *Journal of Speech and Hearing Disorders, 54,* 148–158.

White, K. R. (2006). Early intervention for children with permanent hearing loss: Finishing the EHDI revolution. *Volta Review, 106,* 237–258.

White, S. H. (1980). Cognitive competence and performance in everyday environments. *Bulletin of the Orton Society, 30,* 29–45.

Whitehurst, G. J., Arnold, D., Epstein, J. N., Angell, A. L., Smith, M., & Fischel, J. E. (1994). A picture book reading intervention in day care and home for children from low-income families. *Developmental Psychology, 30,* 679–689.

Whitehurst G. J., Falco, F. L., Lonigan, C. J., Fischel, J. E., DeFarshe, B. D., Valdez-Menchacha, M. C., & Caulfield, M. (1988). Accelerating language development through picture book reading. *Developmental Psychology, 24,* 552–558.

Whitehurst, G. J., & Lonigan, C. J. (1998). Child development and emergent literacy. *Child Development, 69*(3), 848–872.

Whiteman, N. J., & Roan-Yager, L. (2007). *Building a joyful life with your child who has special needs.* London: Jessica Kingsley.

Wiig, E., & Secord, W. (1989). *Test of language competence–Expanded edition (TLC–E).* San Antonio, TX: Psychological Corporation.

Wiig, E., Secord, W., & Semel, E. (1992). *Clinical evaluation of language fundamentals–Preschool* (2nd ed.) (CELF-P2). San Antonio, TX: Harcourt Assessment.

Wilcox, M. J. (2008). New ASHA documents on early intervention. *ASHA Leader, 13*(4), 16.

Wilcox, M., Kouri, T., & Caswell, S. (1991). Early language intervention: A comparison of classroom and individual treatment. *American Journal of Speech-Language Pathology, 1,* 49–62.

Wilde, M. E., & Sage, R. (2007). Developing the communicative competence and narrative thinking of four and five year olds in educational settings. *Early Child Development and Care, 177,* 679–693.

Wilkinson, K. M., & Hennig, S. (2007). The state of research and practice in augmentative and alternative communication for children with developmental/intellectual disabilities. *Mental Retardation ad Developmental Disabilities Research Reviews, 13,* 58–69.

Wilkinson, L. C., Milosky, L. M., & Genishi, C. (1986). Second language learners' use of requests and responses in elementary classrooms. *Topics in Language Disorders, 6*(2), 57–70.

Williams, J. P. (1993). Comprehension of students with and without learning disabilities: Identification of narrative themes and idiosyncratic text representations. *Journal of Educational Psychology, 85,* 631–641.

Williams Syndrome Association. (n.d.). Parents' roadmap to Williams syndrome. Retrieved March 11, 2007, from www.williams-syndrome.org

Wilson Reading System. (n.d.). Available online at www.wilsonlanguage.com/w_wrs.htm

Windsor, J., Scott, C. M., & Street, C. K. (2000). Verb and noun morphology in the spoken and written language of children with language learning disabilities. *Journal of Speech, Language, and Hearing Research, 43,* 1322–1336.

Wing, L. (1988). The continuum of autistic characteristics. In E. Schopler & G. B. Mesibov (Eds.), *Diagnosis and assessment in autism* (pp. 91–110). New York: Plenum Press.

Wing, L., & Potter, D. (2002). The epidemiology of autism spectrum disorders: Is the prevalence rising? *Mental Retardation and Developmental Disabilities: Research Reviews, 8,* 151–161.

Wolf, M., & Bowers, P. G. (1999). The double-deficit hypothesis for the developmental dyslexias. *Journal of Educational Psychology, 91,* 415–438.

Wolff Heller, K., & Kennedy, C. (1994). *Etiologies and characteristics of deaf-blindness.* Monmouth, OR: Teaching Research Publications.

Wolfram, W., Adger, C. T., & Christian, D. (1999). *Dialects in schools and communities.* Mahwah, NJ: Lawrence Erlbaum.

Wolgemuth, J. R., Cobb, R. B., & Alwell, M. (2008). The effects of mnemonic interventions on academic outcomes for youth with disabilities: A systematic review. *Learning Disabilities Research, 23*(1), 1–10.

Wong, B. Y. L. (1980). Activating the inactive learner: Use of questions/prompts to enhance comprehension and retention of implied information in learning disabled children. *Learning Disability Quarterly, 3,* 29–37.

Wood, D. (1998). *How children think and learn.* Oxford, England: Blackwell.

Wood, D. J., Bruner, J., & Ross, G. (1976). The role of tutoring in problem solving. *Journal of Child Psychiatry, 17,* 89–100.

Woodcock, R. W. (1998). *Woodcock Reading Mastery Test-Revised—Normative Update (WRMT-R/NU).* Minneapolis, MN: Pearson Assessments.

Woodcock, R. W., McGrew, K. S., & Mather, N. (2001). *Woodcock-Johnson III Tests of Achievement and Cognitive Ability* (Normative update) (WJ III NU). Chicago: Riverside.

Woodcock, R., McGrew, K., & Mather, N. (2005). *Woodcock-Johnson III NU Complete* (WJ III) (Includes the WJ-III Tests of Achievement and WJ-III Tests of Cognitive Ability). Chicago, IL: Riverside Publishing.

Woods, J. (2008). Providing early intervention services in natural environments. *ASHA Leader, 13*(4), 14–17, 23.

Woods, J. J., & Wetherby, A. M. (2003). Early identification of and intervention for infants and toddlers who are at risk for autism spectrum disorder. *Language, Speech, and Hearing Services in Schools, 34,* 180–193.

World Health Organization (WHO). (2001). *International Classification of Functioning, Disability and Health (WHO/ICF).* Geneva, Switzerland. Accessed March 24, 2007, at www.who.int/classification/icf

Wunsch, M. J., Conlon, C. J., & Scheidt, P. C. (2002). Substance abuse. In M. L. Batshaw (Ed.), *Children with disabilities* (5th ed., pp. 107–122). Baltimore: Paul H. Brookes.

Wyatt, T. A. (1996). Acquisition of the African American English copula. In A. G. Kamhi, K. E. Pollack, & J. L. Harris (Eds.), *Communication development and disorders in African American Children: Research, assessment, and intervention* (pp. 95–115). Baltimore: Paul H. Brookes.

Yoder, P., & Stone, W. L. (2006). A randomized comparison of the effect of two prelinguistic communication interventions on the acquisition of spoken communication in preschoolers with ASD. *Journal of Speech, Language, and Hearing Research, 49,* 698–711.

Yoder, P. J., & Warren, S. F. (2001). Relative treatment effects of two prelinguistic communication interventions on language development in toddlers with developmental delays vary by maternal characteristics. *Journal of Speech, Language, and Hearing Research, 44,* 224–237.

Yoder, P. J., & Warren, S. F. (2002). Effects of prelinguistic milieu teaching and parent responsivity education on dyads involving children with intellectual disabilities. *Journal of Speech, Language, and Hearing Research, 45,* 1158–1174.

Yoder, P. J., Warren, S. F., Kim, K., & Gazdag, G. E. (1994) Facilitating prelinguistic skills in young children with developmental delay II: Systematic replication and extension. *Journal of Speech and Hearing Research, 37,* 841–851.

Yoshinaga-Itano, C., & Downey, D. M. (1996). Development of school-aged deaf, hard-of-hearing, and normally hearing students' written language (Introduction to special section). *Volta Review, 98,* 3–7.

Yoshinaga-Itano, C., Sedey, A. L., Coulter, B. A., & Mehl, A. L. (1998). Language of early and later-identified children with hearing loss. *Pediatrics, 102,* 1168–1171.

Zeisel, S. A., & Roberts, J. K. (2003). Otitis media in young children with disabilities. *Infants and Young Children, 16*(2), 106–120.

Zeng, F.-G., & Liu, S. (2006). Speech perception in individuals with auditory neuropathy. *Journal of Speech, Language, and Hearing Research, 49,* 367–380.

Zimmerman, B. J., Bonner, S., & Kovach, R. (1996). *Developing self-regulated learners: Beyond achievement to self-efficacy.* Washington, DC: American Psychological Association.

Zimmerman, I., Steiner, V., & Pond, R. (2002). *Preschool Language Scale-Fourth Edition (PLS-4).* San Antonio, TX: Harcourt Assessment.

Zukowski, A. (2004). Investigating knowledge of complex syntax: Insights from experimental studies of Williams syndrome. In M. L. Rice & S. F. Warren (Eds.), *Developmental language disorders: From phenotypes to etiologies* (pp. 99–119). Mahwah, NJ: Lawrence Erlbaum.

Zwolan, T. A., Connor, C. M., & Kileny, P. R. (2000). Evaluation of the Foundations in Speech Perception software as a hearing rehabilitation tool for use at home. *Journal of the Academy of Rehabilitative Audiology, 33,* 39–51.

Index

Photo Credits: pp. i (left), vii (top), 3: Hisun Yun; pp. i (middle), viii (top), ix (top), x (top and bottom), xi
(top and bottom), xii (middle and bottom), 32 (bottom left), 55, 122, 177, 215, 239, 241 (top, middle, and
bottom), 246, 252, 264, 268, 316 (upper right), 333, 376: Nickola Wolf Nelson; pp. i (right), vii (bottom),
23, 316 (lower left): Janet Sturm; p. iii: John Massey; pp. viii (bottom), 87: Brynn Burns; pp. xiii, ix (bottom), 151, 442, 468: John Cosby; pp. xii (top), 282: Matthew C. Tattersall; pp. 27 (left and right), 28 (top,
middle, and bottom), 32 (bottom right), 171, 316 (lower right), 427: Chris Wolf Edmonds; p. 32 (top left, top
right): Machaela Edmonds; p. 77: courtesy of Albert M. Galaburda; p. 196: courtesy of Candyce Peterson;
pp. 316 (upper left): Elizabeth Savage Nelson.